# The Giant Panda

A
Morphological Study
of
Evolutionary Mechanisms

## D. Dwight Davis

# THE GIANT PANDA

## A Morphological Study
## of Evolutionary Mechanisms

## D. Dwight Davis
Curator, Division of Vertebrate Anatomy

CHICAGO
NATURAL HISTORY
MUSEUM
RESEARCH EDUCATION
FOUNDED
1893
BY MARSHALL FIELD

Fieldiana: Zoology Memoirs
Volume 3
*Originally published by*
Chicago Natural History Museum
December 7, 1964

"The field of macrotaxonomy... is not directly accessible to the geneticist... Here the paleontologist, the comparative anatomist, and the embryologist are supreme."

*Richard Goldschmidt*

THE GIANT PANDA MEI LAN

*Chicago Zoological Park, September 1952*

# PREFACE

This study of the anatomy of the giant panda was originally intended to determine the taxonomic position of this species. As the dissection progressed, other questions of rather broader interest developed, and the scope was widened to embrace them.

In studies of this kind the customary procedure is to compare structures with those of supposedly related organisms, and estimate relationships of organisms from these comparisons. In the background are the broader questions of the phylogeny and fundamental uniformity of vertebrate structures, which have long been the core problems of comparative anatomy. But superimposed on the underlying pattern of uniformity there is a bewildering array of differences, mostly adaptations to special ways of life. Phylogeny— continuity of ancestry—explains the uniformities in vertebrate structure. It cannot explain the differences, which represent the active creative aspect of evolution. Yet we cannot pretend to explain the history of vertebrate structure without rational theories to account for the differences as well as the uniformities.

The existence of an underlying uniformity in vertebrate structure is now so well documented that it is practically axiomatic, but comparative anatomists have scarcely begun to seek similarly adequate explanations for the differences in vertebrate structure. At this stage I believe it is of crucial importance to ask whether comparative anatomy can undertake to explain, in causal-analytical terms, the structural differences that characterize taxa among vertebrates. If it cannot, then I would agree with the statement once made by D. M. S. Watson, that comparative anatomy is a term "now obsolescent."

Such an extension of the goal of comparative anatomy assumes that the genetic backgrounds for the kind of morphological differences with which anatomists are concerned are so simple that they can be estimated with reasonable certainty by inferring causes from results, without resort to breeding experiments. For some of the primary differences at the generic level this appears to be true. Evidence is steadily accumulating that, in verte-

brates, a quite simple change in epigenetic mechanisms may have a profound and extensively different end result. Moreover, the result is an integrated organism. This suggests that in favorable cases, and at low taxonomic levels, the comparative anatomist may properly seek the mechanisms behind the differences he observes.

In many ways the giant panda seems to be almost ideally suited to a test of this thesis. I do not, of course, believe that I have explained completely how the morphology of the giant panda arose from the morphology of the bears, or that everyone will accept my interpretations. I ask only that this study be regarded as a first approximation, a first attempt to explain the structural differences between a derived and an ancestral organism in terms of causal mechanisms, an attempt to identify the raw materials on which natural selection acted.

I am indebted to several institutions and innumerable individuals for assistance in this study. On several occasions the United States National Museum allowed me to study skeletons housed there, and lent embalmed and osteological materials for detailed study in Chicago. The American Museum of Natural History and Carnegie Museum permitted me to study and measure skeletons in their collections. Much of the material on which the work was based, including all the embalmed giant panda material, originally came from the Chicago Zoological Park. Observations on living carnivores were made at both the Chicago Zoological Park and the Lincoln Park Zoo.

Over the years so many individuals have contributed to this study in various ways that it is impossible to thank them individually. I have profited particularly from numerous discussions with Dr. Harry Sicher, Dr. E. Lloyd DuBrul, Dr. Rainer Zangerl, Professor Bryan Patterson, and Dr. Carl Gans. Dr. Zangerl made many X-ray photographs for me. My late colleague, Dr. Karl P. Schmidt, repeatedly interrupted his own work to help me translate difficult German passages.

In a work of this kind the artist tends to become almost a collaborator. I have been particularly fortunate in the several artists who worked with

5

me from time to time: the late John C. Hansen, who made most of the bone drawings; John J. Janacek; Miss H. E. Story, who dissected out most of the finer blood vessels and nerves in addition to making most of the drawings of the soft anatomy; Miss Phyllis Wade; and Mrs. Edward Levin.

D. D. D.

# CONTENTS

## LIST OF NUMBERED TABLES

# INTRODUCTION

It is my intent to make this study a test, based on the anatomy of the giant panda, of whether the comparative method can yield information that goes beyond the customary goals of comparative anatomy. It is evident, to me at least, that more than fifty years ago comparative anatomy reached a stalemate that can be broken only by seeking answers to new and different questions. I believe it must shift its major emphasis from the conservative features of evolution to its radical features, from the features that organisms under comparison have in common to those they do not have in common. It must seek rational explanations for these differences, drawing on data from other fields where this is necessary and possible. In this study of the giant panda the structural differences between it and the bears, and the ways in which these differences arose, will be our primary concern.

The original problem that motivated the work—the proper taxonomic position of *Ailuropoda*—was soon settled; *Ailuropoda* is a bear and therefore belongs in the family Ursidae.[1] The further problem of attempting to infer the causal mechanisms involved in the origin of *Ailuropoda* from its ursid ancestors requires some discussion of goals and methods.

## GOALS AND METHODS OF COMPARATIVE ANATOMY

The classical goal of comparative anatomy was to demonstrate the existence of an essential and permeating uniformity or "ordering" in the structure of vertebrates. This goal has been reached. Details of the picture remain to be filled in, but the unifying concept itself is now so well documented that it is no longer open to serious debate. Phylogeny, the genetic relatedness of all vertebrates, provides an explanation for the uniformity. This aspect of the history of vertebrate structure cannot be expected to give rise to further concepts.

We may well ask where comparative anatomy is to go from here.

From the evolutionary standpoint the structural differences among vertebrates are just as important as the structural uniformities; these two are, in fact, the obverse and reverse of the phylogenetic picture of vertebrate structure. Years ago W. K. Gregory distinguished them as "habitus" and "heritage" characters. We cannot claim to have explained the particular structure of an organism if we explain only its heritage characters and offer no explanation for its habitus characters. An "explanation" must account for the differences in terms of evolutionary mechanisms, not merely relate them to the functional requirements of the organism— in other words, explain them in the same causal sense that common ancestry explains the heritage characters.

Classical comparative anatomy tended to concentrate on the major features of vertebrate structure—the differences that characterize orders and more often classes. Such, for example, are the homologies of the gill arch derivatives, of the elements of the mammalian middle ear, of the craniomandibular muscles. There was practically no interest in how and why such changes came about, and the morphogenetic and selective mechanisms involved in these massive alterations are probably irretrievably lost in the vast reaches of time anyway.

Structural differences at about the generic level are usually far less profound and more recently evolved, yet they often represent a level of morphological differentiation to which the methods of comparative anatomy can be applied. In this respect they differ from the characters with which the geneticist customarily deals. At about the generic level we may hope to decipher the mechanisms responsible for the observed differences in structure between two or more related forms. A procedure designed to yield such information is followed in this study. The procedure may be divided into a series of steps. These are:

(1) Identification of the structural differences between *Ailuropoda* and its structural ancestor, *Ursus*. At the outset nothing was known of pos-

---

[1] This conclusion is not based on one or a few characters, but on a host of similarities, many of them subtle, throughout the anatomy. I tried to present the data on the affinities of *Ailuropoda* before going on to other considerations, but this became so difficult that I gave it up. Therefore one of the primary conclusions is assumed throughout the text.

sible pleiotropic effects, allometric relationships, morphogenetic patterns, or obscure functional relationships. Therefore all differences were tabulated uncritically, without attempting to evaluate them. For the same reason the entire anatomy of the organism was covered so far as practicable.

(2) Correlation of the observed structural differences between *Ailuropoda* and *Ursus* with differences in habits or behavior. This is the first step in sorting out the adaptive features peculiar to the anatomy of *Ailuropoda*—features that presumably represent the modifications of the ursid morphology resulting from natural selection. This step results in two categories: (a) those differences that can be correlated with differences in habits or behavior, and (b) those that can not.

The differences in category b may be conspicuous, and their presence must be accounted for. They may be genetically related to an adaptive modification but not themselves adaptive. They may reflect the results of an inherited differential growth rate, whereby the proportions of a morphological unit may change with the absolute size of the unit. A classical example of this effect is the antlers of deer. They may merely reflect relaxed selection pressure on certain functions. The decision as to whether a condition is or is not adaptive is often very difficult, requiring considerable knowledge of mechanics and engineering, as well as intimate knowledge of the habits and behavior of the animal.

(3) Separation of the adaptive features that are genetically determined from those that are only indirectly related to the genetic substrate. Many conspicuous features in the skeleton depend only on the capacity of bone to respond to extrinsic forces. Many soft tissues have a considerable capacity to accommodate their form to the molding action of extrinsic forces. The caliber of blood vessels varies with the demands of the tissues they supply, even during the life of the individual; if one kidney is removed, the remaining one hypertrophies. Such conditions are adaptive, but they are not primary results of selection; they are the exogenous adaptations of Waddington (1953). They reflect the action of natural selection at second or third hand, so to speak. If we are seeking to isolate the structural features on which natural selection acted directly, these secondary and tertiary effects must be discounted.

These three steps have presumably isolated the morphological features in *Ailuropoda* that (1) differ from those in its structural ancestor, *Ursus*, (2) are functionally correlated with differences in habits and behavior, and (3) are genetically determined. They are the direct results of natural se-

lection in the step from bear to giant panda. As will appear in the sequel, these features seem to be surprisingly few; we are not interested here in minor polishing effects, but only in decisive differences. We do not yet know the *materials* on which natural selection acted to effect these changes. One final step remains:

(4) Determination of the morphogenetic mechanisms that were involved in effecting these changes. This should be an experimental problem, but obviously experimentation is impossible in the vast majority of cases, including this one. Fotunately, morphogenetic processes appear to be remarkably uniform among mammals. By a judicious combination of the comparative method with the known data of mammalian epigenetics I believe it is possible to infer, with varying degrees of confidence, the true mechanisms behind many of the major structural differences that distinguish *Ailuropoda* from the true bears. Many of the "unit characters" involved appear to be sizable morphological units, although it does not necessarily follow that the shift from bear condition to panda condition was made in one jump, or that such morphological units are controlled by simple genes. It is clear, however, that they are genetically controlled as units. It would be futile to attempt to reconstruct the history if major adaptive differences represent accumulations of numerous small mutation effects.

To the extent that these four steps are carried out successfully, the differences between the giant panda and the true bears will be explained rather than simply described.

Almost without exception, students of the higher taxonomic categories have been reluctant to believe that the kinds of morphological differences they observe represent accumulations of small mutation effects such as the geneticist customarily deals with. The once-popular solution—invoking unknown imminent forces to explain systemic differences—is no longer common. Modern students have sought genetic mechanisms capable of producing phenotypic differences of the magnitude they believed were involved. Goldschmidt (1940), for example, emphasized (among other things) the massive co-ordinated differences that can result from acceleration and retardation of gene-controlled developmental processes. Rensch (1960) listed pleiotropy, allometric growth rates, and compensatory correlations—among the agents accessible to natural selection—as capable of producing extensive generalized effects on the organism as a whole.

It is now generally recognized that growth is essentially a process of multiplication of cells. Multiplicative rates differ in different parts of the body, and in the same part at different times during its growth period. Regional growth rates may interfere with each other, resulting in negative interactions and in extreme cases even in deformation of the entire growth profile of the body. Correlation studies show clearly that both regional and general growth rates are genetically controlled as units. These insights stem chiefly from Huxley's *Problems of relative growth*, which in turn grew out of the earlier *On growth and form* of D'Arcy Thompson and Goldschmidt's *Physiologische Theorie der Vererbung*. They provide a mechanism capable of producing plastic deformation of a common pattern, which is what the comparative anatomist seems to see when he compares homeomorphic organisms. A bridge between genetics and comparative anatomy was sought in vain during the first third of this century; it now seems to have been found.

Partly because evolution is a cumulative and non-repetitive process, and partly because growth fields in vertebrates have proved refractory to experimental techniques, their role in the morphosis of animal form has been deciphered almost exclusively by morphological methods. The primary tool is demonstration of correlations; the method is comparative. Whether subtle correlations are sought by sophisticated statistical methods (as in recent studies of mammalian teeth), or more obvious correlations by means of coarser but no less rigorous comparative methods (as in the present study), the goal is the same. It is to identify and circumscribe the material bases for differences among homeomorphic organisms. This is a proper field for the comparative anatomist.

## MATERIALS AND METHODS

This study is based largely on the embalmed and injected body of a giant panda that lived in the Chicago Zoological Park from February, 1937, to April, 1938. The panda was popularly known as Su Lin. Unless otherwise stated, all statements relating to the soft anatomy are based on this specimen. Su Lin was a subadult male (teeth fully erupted). His age (estimated) was 16 months at death. He was in excellent condition and weighed 132 pounds. Preserved portions of the carcass (head, fore and hind limbs, heart, genitalia) and the skeleton of an adult male giant panda (known

as Mei Lan) were available. Mei Lan was estimated to be 15 years old at death. He was much emaciated, and weighed 205 pounds after autopsy.

The following skeletal material of *Ailuropoda* was available for detailed study:

CNHM 31128 ( ♂ ad.) Szechwan: Yehli. Complete skeleton.
CNHM 36758 ( ♀ ad.) Szechwan: Dun Shih Goh. Complete skeleton.
CNHM 34258 (− ad.) Szechwan: Mouping Dist. Skull, lower fore legs, fore and hind feet.
CNHM 74269 ( ♂ ad.) (zoo animal: Mei Lan). Complete skeleton.
CNHM 39514 (− ad.) Szechwan: Dun Shih Goh. Skull.
USNM 259076 ( ♀ jv.) Szechwan: Wen Chuan. Skull.
USNM 259027 ( ♂ ad.) Szechwan: Wen Chuan. Pelvis.
USNM 259403 ( ♀ ad.) Szechwan: Wen Chuan. Pelvis.

Most of the data on the soft anatomy of bears came from the following captive animals that died in the Chicago Zoological Park:

CNHM 48304 ( ♂ ad.) *Ursus thibetanus*, embalmed and injected body.
CNHM 49061 ( ♂ juv.) *Ursus americanus*, embalmed and injected body.
CNHM 57267 ( ♀ ad.) *Ursus americanus*, embalmed head, fore leg, and hind leg.
CNHM 57200 ( ♀ ad.) *Tremarctos ornatus*, embalmed head, fore leg, and hind leg.

The following bear skeletons were used for most of the detailed osteological data:

CNHM 43744 (− ad.) *Ursus arctos;* Iraq.
CNHM 47419 (− ad.) *Ursus arctos;* Iraq.
CNHM 44725 ( ♂ ad.) *Ursus americanus;* (zoo animal).

These three skeletons were supplemented with numerous skeletons and partial skeletons of bears, representing several genera and species, in the collections of Chicago Natural History Museum.

Partial dissections were made of several procyonids, all embalmed zoo animals, representing the genera *Procyon, Nasua, Bassariscus, Potos,* and *Ailurus.* Numerous skeletons of these genera, from both wild-killed and zoo animals, were available.

Linear measurements up to 150 millimeters were made with Vernier calipers graduated to 0.1 millimeter. Lengths beyond 150 millimeters were measured with large calipers and a meter stick. Weights up to 2 kilograms were determined with a small Ohaus triple beam balance. Larger objects were weighed on a large Ohaus beam balance with a capacity of 21 kilograms. In weighing preserved soft tissues the usual precautions of removing excess surface liquid by blotting were taken.

# HISTORY

The synonymy of *Ailuropoda melanoleuca* be summarized as follows:

## Ailuropoda melanoleuca (David)

*Ursus melanoleucus* David, 1869, Nouv. Arch. Mus. Hist. Nat., Paris, Bull. 5, p. 13.

*Ailuropoda melanoleuca* Milne-Edwards, 1870, Ann. Sci. Nat., Paris, (5), Zool., 13, art. 10.

*Pandarctos melanoleucus* Gervais, 1870, Nouv. Arch. Mus. Hist. Nat., Paris, 6, p. 161, footnote; 1875, Jour. Zool., Paris, 6, p. 87.

*Ailuropus melanoleucus* Milne-Edwards, 1871, Nouv. Arch. Mus. Hist. Nat., Paris, Bull. 7, p. 92.

*Aeluropus melanoleucus* Lydekker, 1891, *in* Flower and Lydekker, Mammals living and extinct, pp. 560-561, fig. 256.

During his stay in Mouping on the second of his three expeditions to China, the noted French explorer and naturalist Père Armand David learned of the existence of a curious black and white "bear." This animal, called *pei-hsuing* ("white bear") by the natives, aroused David's interest, and he employed hunters to capture specimens of it for him. After almost a month of unsuccessful hunting a young female was brought to him on March 19, 1869, and two weeks later he acquired an adult of the same sex. Although erroneously believing it to be a bear, David immediately recognized the animal as a novelty to science. He drew up a concise but adequate description under the name *Ursus melanoleucus* and despatched it to Alphonse Milne-Edwards at the Paris Museum with an explanatory note requesting its publication. David's letter, which was duly published in the *Nouvelles Archives* of the Paris Museum, introduced to science the animal now known as the giant panda. The subsequent history of the giant panda can best be presented in chronological form.

1870. Milne-Edwards, after examining David's material, noted that its osteological characters and dentition "clearly distinguish" the giant panda from the bears and approach those of the lesser panda and raccoons. He erected the genus *Ailuropoda* to receive it. Gervais, on the other hand, concluded from a study of an intracranial cast that its brain structure allies it to the bears. Gervais considered it worthy of generic distinction, however, and proposed the name *Pandarctos*.

1871. David published a few brief notes on the habits of the giant panda, and even today surprisingly little can be added to these original observations. David recorded that it is restricted to high altitudes, that it is herbivorous, and that it does not hibernate. Only one of his statements has not been substantiated: "It is said that it does not refuse meat when the occasion presents itself; and I even think that this is its principal nourishment in winter."

Milne-Edwards, believing that the generic name *Ailuropoda* was preoccupied by Gray's use of the name Aeluropoda for his "Section I. Cat-footed Carnivora" in the *Catalogue of Carnivorous, Pachydermatous and Edentate Mammalia in the British Museum* (1869, p. 3), proposed the name *Ailuropus* for the giant panda.

1868-74. Milne-Edwards, in the *Recherches des Mammifères*, gave a detailed description of the skin, skull, and dentition. His re-examination led him to the conclusion that *Ailuropus* should be placed between the bears and the [lesser] panda.

1875. Gervais, after an examination of the skeleton of David's panda, reasserted his former opinion that the giant panda is an aberrant bear.

1885. Mivart, in his careful review of the classification of the arctoid carnivores, concluded that *Ailurus* is a procyonid and that *Ailuropus* is allied to *Ailurus* and therefore is a procyonid, too. Mivart thus set the pattern that, with few exceptions, has been followed by British and American authors to the present day. His conclusion is based on the usual agreement of skull architecture and dental morphology that was to be stressed repeatedly by later authors.

1891. Flower and Lydekker, in their *Mammals Living and Extinct*, placed "*Aeluropus* sidae and "*Aelurus*" in the Procyonidae. Their emendation of Milne-Edwards' generic name *Ailuropus*, appearing in an authoritative work, resulted in considerable confusion in subsequent literature.

1895. Winge regarded the giant panda as a very close relative of the extinct *Hyaenarctos* [= *Agriotherium* of recent authors], these two genera forming a separate branch of the ursine stem.

14

*Ailurus*, on the other hand, he considered a procyonid. Winge's views have been adhered to without exception by continental European authors.

1901. Both Lankester and Lydekker, after independently studying the skull and limb bones, concluded that *Aeluropus* and *Aelurus* are closely allied, that they are procyonids, and that the Procyonidae should be subdivided into two subfamilies, the Procyoninae and the Ailurinae. This, of course, is merely a re-affirmation of the earlier views of Mivart. They emphasized the procyonid-like presence of both protocone and hypocone on the lingual border of $P^4$ (the protocone is absent in the Ursidae), the presence of an entepicondylar foramen, and numerous "minute coincidences" in the structure of the skull and long bones of the limbs.

Lankester and Lydekker deemed it desirable that *Aeluropus*, which hitherto had been called the "parti-coloured bear," should henceforth be called the "great panda." This appears to be the first published reference to *Ailuropoda* as a panda.[1]

1902. Beddard, in his *Mammalia*, followed Flower and Lydekker in placing "*Aeluropus*" in the Ursidae and "*Aelurus*" in the Procyonidae.

1904. Weber, in the first edition of *Die Säugetiere*, followed Winge in considering *Aeluropus* as an ursid closely related to *Hyaenarctos* and referring *Ailurus* to the Procyonidae.

1913. Bardenfleth made a detailed study of the dental and osteological characters of *Ailuropoda* and concluded that its resemblances to *Ailurus* are due to convergent development of the molar teeth based on herbivorous diet, and that its closest affinities are with the extinct ursids of the *Hyaenarctos* group.

1915. Woodward described the well-preserved skull of a Pleistocene giant panda, which he named *Aelureidopus baconi*, from Burma. This was the first proof that the giant panda once had a more extensive range than it has at present.

1921. Pocock, in a review of the classification of the Procyonidae, concluded that both *Ailuropoda* and *Ailurus* represent distinct and separate families. This view he re-affirmed in 1929 and also in his article "Carnivores" in the fourteenth edition of the *Encyclopaedia Britannica*, where no fewer than 13 families (compared with 7 of other authors) and 29 subfamilies (18 of other authors) of living fissiped carnivores are recognized. Pocock's "families" correspond roughly to the genera of other authors.

[1] The word "panda," which had been applied to the lesser panda (*Ailurus*) since the time of Cuvier, is "said to be a Nepal name." (Oxford Universal English Dictionary.)

1923. Matthew and Granger described giant panda material, under the name *Aeluropus forealis*, from Pliocene deposits in eastern Szechwan, thus farther extending the former range of the giant panda.

1928. Weber, in the second edition of *Die Säugetiere*, retained his views of 1904 as to the ursid affinities of *Ailuropoda*.

1929. Theodore and Kermit Roosevelt shot a giant panda at Yehli, Sikang Province. This individual, said to be the first giant panda shot by a white man, was mounted, together with a second skin purchased from natives, in a habitat group in Chicago Natural History Museum. The ensuing publicity started a cycle of "giant panda expeditions" that have greatly increased our knowledge of the distribution, habits, and morphology of this animal.

1936. Gregory examined the skull and dentition of *Ailuropoda*, *Ailurus*, and various fossil and recent procyonid and ursid carnivores. He concluded that Lankester and Lydekker were correct in referring *Ailuropoda* and *Ailurus* to the Procyonidae.

Raven, in the same year, studied the viscera of a giant panda, which had been preserved in the field by an American Museum expedition. He listed six points of agreement between *Ailuropoda* and *Ailurus*, and concluded that resemblances between the former and the bears "are an expression of convergence in size and food habits."

1937. Mrs. Ruth Harkness, of New York City, succeeded in bringing a living baby giant panda to the United States. This individual, named Su Lin, lived for 16 months in the Chicago Zoological Park. It formed the basis for the present monograph. The fanfare that surrounded the life and death of Su Lin started a new series of expeditions for living pandas. At least a dozen have since been exhibited in the United States and Europe.

1943. Segall made a study of the auditory region in the arctoid carnivores. The structure of the bony auditory region and auditory ossicles led him to associate the Ailuridae (*Ailurus* and *Ailuropoda*) with the Ursidae.

1945. Simpson, in his *Classification of Mammals*, adhered to the classical view of Mivart in grouping *Ailurus* and *Ailuropoda* in the subfamily Ailurinae of the family Procyonidae.

1946. Mettler and Goss, after studying the topography of the brain of an adult giant panda, concluded that "the configuration of the brain of *Ailuropoda melanoleuca* is identical with that of the bear."

1956. Leone and Wiens reported that comparisons of serum proteins by means of precipitin tests "clearly indicate that the giant panda belongs in the family Ursidae."

An examination of this history of research is instructive. There can be no doubt that the giant panda occupies a more or less isolated position among living carnivores, and that the features usually relied upon by mammalogists for determining affinities are masked by specializing adaptations in this form. Two conclusions may be drawn from these historical data.

1. Quite different conclusions have been reached by a succession of capable investigators on the basis of the same data. This indicates that the data employed are not sufficient to form a basis for an objective conclusion, and that opinion has been an important ingredient in arriving at conclusions.

2. Opinion as to the affinities of *Ailuropoda* is divided almost perfectly along geographic lines, which shows that authoritarianism rather than objective analysis has really been the determining factor in deciding the question. After the pioneering work of Milne-Edwards and Gervais, the first attempt at determining the affinities of *Ailuropoda* was made by Mivart in England. Mivart's conclusion—that both the giant and the lesser panda are procyonids—has been echoed by every British and American author down to 1943, except for the short-lived dissenting opinion of Flower and Lydekker.[1] In the meantime, on the continent, Winge in 1895 relegated *Ailuropoda* to the Ursidae and *Ailurus* to the Procyonidae, and every subsequent continental authority has followed in his footsteps. Such a cleavage of opinion along geographical and linguistic lines cannot be due to chance.

It is apparent that the relationships of *Ailuropoda* will never be decided on the basis of the data afforded by the skeleton and dentition. Thus the first task of this study was to examine data not previously available, with a view to determining the much-discussed affinities of this carnivore.

[1] Beddard (1902) merely copied Flower and Lydekker.

# DISTRIBUTION

The giant panda apparently has a very restricted distribution in the high mountains of western Szechwan and eastern Sikang in western China. This is the area of the extremely complex mountain escarpment that sharply separates the Min River Valley from the Tibetan highland to the west.

Localities where or near which specimens have been collected are shown on the accompanying map (fig. 1). The localities given on many museum specimens obviously represent the city where the skin was purchased (e.g., Mouping, Ya-chou) rather than the locality from which the specimen actually came. Localities given in the literature ("Moupin," David, 1869; "mountains of Mouping," Gervais, 1875; "Wassu mountains," "mountains east of Min valley," Jacobi, 1923a) are often very indefinite. Thus the localities that can be plotted with any certainty on a map are relatively few, although none of the unplottable localities extends the known range of this species. The distance between the southernmost record (Yehli) and the northernmost (25 miles west of Wenchuan) is only about 175 miles. All records, except Yehli are on the slopes of the Chuing-lai mountains surrounding the valley of the Min River. Yehli, where the Roosevelt brothers shot their panda, is on the slopes of the Ta-liang Mountains south of the Tung River.

Pen (1943) reported *Ailuropoda* from "the upper source of the Yellow [Yangtze] River where it connects the two lakes, the Tsaring Nor and the Oring Nor, near the central part of Chinghai province" at 34° 7′ N. Lat. Pen refers, without citation, to a record by Berozovski at 34° N. Lat., but I have been unable to find such a reference. Pen collected no specimens, but there seems to be no reason for doubting his identification of the animals he saw. Even allowing this provisional extension of range, the north-south distribution amounts to only about 470 miles.

Sowerby (1932) has suggested even greater extensions of the range of *Ailuropoda*. He writes: "The range of the giant panda is now admitted to be much more extensive than formerly supposed. . . . We came across indisputable evidence of the

giant panda in the Tai-pei Shan region of Southwestern Shensi, where the local takin hunters described its appearance to us accurately and also showed us its droppings and the places where it had torn up the culms of bamboos for food. From this region it ranges southward throughout all the wilder mountainous areas at least to the Yunnan border, everywhere being known to the native hunters by its native name, *pei-hsiung*." Sowerby (1937a) later defined the range as "more or less restricted localities from the Tsing Ling range of mountains in southern Shensi and eastern Tibet to northern Yunnan." Others have emphasized the unreliability of reports by native hunters, however, even after being shown pictures of the animal, and it seems best to await more positive evidence before accepting Sowerby's broad extensions of range.

*Ailuropoda* had a much more extensive distribution in comparatively recent geological times, as is shown by the two fossil records. Smith-Woodward (1915) described a Pleistocene panda under the name *Aelureidopus baconi*, from Mogok, Northern Shan States, Burma. This is in the Irrawaddy River drainage and is more than 500 miles southwest of the southern limit of the panda's range as now known. Granger (*in* Matthew and Granger, 1923) found giant panda material, which was named *Aeluropus fovealis*, in Pliocene deposits near Wan-hsien in eastern Szechwan. Wan-hsien is situated on the Yangtze River (of which the Min is a tributary), about 250 miles due east of Chengtu.

## VERTICAL DISTRIBUTION

The vertical distribution of *Ailuropoda* is as limited as its geographic distribution. All who have studied its habits agree that this animal is sharply limited to the bamboo zone, which lies between about 5,000 and 10,000 feet.

Limited to the Si-fan region at altitudes of 1600 to 3300 m., consequently to the region of almost impenetrable bamboo jungle on the steep slopes. Here it forces tunnels through the thickets, which are 1½ to 5 m. high and are often matted by snow pressure. (Jacobi, 1923b, p. 72.)

. . . in the bamboo jungles in altitudes varying between six and fourteen thousand feet. We came to the conclusion that it could safely be assumed that where there were no

FIG. 1. Western Szechwan and eastern Sikang provinces, showing locality records for *Ailuropoda melanoleuca*.

bamboo jungles, there were no beishung. (Theodore and Kermit Roosevelt, 1929, p. 261.)

The limits of the giant panda's altitudinal range is determined largely by the extent of the bamboo growth. Two exceptions to this statement were observed, however. In one case we found unmistakable panda droppings high on the Chen Lliang Shan range, 1000 feet above the rhododendron forest, and probably 1500 feet above the nearest bamboo. It was interesting to find that on occasion the panda must travel above its regular habitat to the bare grasslands of the blue sheep country. In another instance I saw where a giant panda had climbed a small pine tree just above the village of Tsapei on Chengou River. It was located 300 feet above the river bottom on an open slope, with the nearest bamboo across the valley. (Sheldon, 1937.)

The vertical distribution of the bamboo bear, which avoids the hot arid canyons as well as the high alpine zones, extends on the high levels between 1500 and about 4000 m., where it is closely confined to the moist, subtropical bamboo zone. (Schäfer, 1938.)

Pen's sight record of a giant panda at the upper source of the Yangtze River was on the open steppe of the Tibetan plateau. He speculates that these animals may have reached the plateau country by migrating north and west along the bamboo zone of the mountains, and that there is here an annual summer migration onto the plateau, with a winter retreat into the less rigorous environment of the mountains.

# HABITS AND BEHAVIOR

Because of the inaccessible and rugged nature of its habitat, there has been little field observation of the giant panda. Various authors have recorded information, beginning with the original notes of David, and the observations are in close agreement. Details of behavior are known only from observations on captive individuals (Schneider, 1939; Haas, 1963).

## HABITAT

The giant panda appears to be closely confined to the moist bamboo zone on the slope of the high mountains. The bamboo culms, which are slender (up to an inch and a half in diameter) and grow to a height of 10 to 12 feet, form dense impenetrable thickets that are often matted by snow pressure. The bamboo jungle is associated with forests of fir trees, and at higher altitudes the bamboo gives way to rhododendron, into which the panda does not wander. The mountain slopes "under the influence of the summer-like monsoon rains, exhibit a comparatively mild subtropical climate." (Schäfer, 1938.)

The panda shares this habitat with such other large mammals as the golden monkey (*Rhinopithecus*), leopard (*Panthera pardus*), red dog (*Cuon alpinus*), black bear (*Ursus thibetanus*), wild pig (*Sus cristatus*), barking deer (*Muntiacus*), serow (*Capricornis*), and takin (*Budorcas*). Only the leopard and the red dog would be likely to attack the giant panda, and such encounters would be uncommon.[1] Thus the giant panda is practically without natural enemies—an important point in estimating the selection pressures to which this species is subjected.

Wilson (1913) described the vegetation on the mountain Wa Shan as follows:

At one time a dense forest of Silver Fir covered the mountain. . . . Some of these Firs could not have been less than 150 feet in height and 20 feet in girth. . . . Besides the Silver Fir (*Abies Delavayi*), the only other conifers are *Tsuga yunnanensis, Juniperus formosana*, and *Picea complanata*. Rhododendrons constitute the conspicuous feature of the vege-

[1] Seton (Lives of game animals, 2, 1929) lists the grizzly bear and the mountain lion as enemies of the American black bear, an animal about the same size as the giant panda.

tation. . . . They begin at 7500 feet, but are most abundant at 10,000 feet and upwards. In the ascent I collected 16 species. They vary from diminutive plants 4 to 6 inches high, to giants 30 feet or more tall. . . . One of the commonest species is *R. yanthinum*. . . . Above this [7200 feet], for 500 feet, comes a wellnigh impenetrable thicket of Bamboo scrub. The species (*Arundinaria nitida*) is of remarkably dense growth, with thin culms, averaging 6 feet in height. Next above this, till the plateau is reached, is a belt of mixed shrubs and herbs, conspicuous amongst which are *Syringa Sargentiana, Hydrangea anomala, H. villosa, Neillia affinis, Dipelta ventricosa, Ribes longeracemosum,* var. *Davidii, Enkianthus deflexus, Styrax roseus, Deutzia* (2 spp.), *Rubus* (5 spp.), *Viburnum* (4 spp.), *Spirea* (4 spp.), *Acer* spp., *Malus* spp., *Sorbus* spp., *Meconopsis chelidonifolia, Fragaria filipendulus, Lilium giganteum,* and the herbs of the lower belt. A few Rhododendrons occur chiefly on the cliffs. The plateau (8500 feet) is about half a mile across, marshy in places, and densely clad with shrubby vegetation and Bamboo scrub. . . . From 10,000 feet to the summit of the mountain Rhododendron accounts for fully 99 per cent of the ligneous vegetation.

## FOOD

All observers (except Pen, see below) agree that in its native state the giant panda subsists exclusively on bamboo. McClure (1943) identified the bamboo native to the haunts of the giant panda as *Sinarundinaria* sp.

"Its food seems to consist exclusively of bamboo shoots, but by no means merely the young shoots, which even man himself eats with relish, but also those as thick as a finger. In winter, in fact, only strongly woody and silicified stalks are available. All this can be ascertained from fresh droppings, which consist almost exclusively of chewed-up stalks, often as long as a finger joint, whether in the middle of July or in the beginning of January." (Jacobi, 1923a.)

Not only is the giant panda entirely herbivorous, but it is known to live on the dwarf bamboo of the northeastern spur of the Himalayas to the exclusion of *all* other vegetable matter. . . . The food supply in the mountains of west Szechuan is inexhaustible. . . . We found giant panda eating not only the bamboo shoots, but the stalks and leaves of fully mature sprouts, often an inch and one-half in diameter." The author followed a fresh morning trail and found "that at an average of every hundred yards there were from one to three large droppings (4 to 6 inches long and 2 inches thick, tapering at each end). At a conservative estimate there were 40 droppings. . . . Below the resting place was a pile of at least 30 more droppings, making a total of 70 excreted between early morning and 9 A.M. . . . These droppings

20

FIG. 2. Sitting posture and use of fore paws in *Ailuropoda*. A–C, "Happy" eating bamboo in Leipzig Zoo (from Schneider, 1939). D, Mei Lan eating green cornstalks in Chicago Zoological Park.

emerge almost totally undigested. It seems logical to assume that an animal of such large proportions must have to eat tremendous quantities to secure the nourishment that it requires. . . . I estimate that they would have to spend from 10 to 12 hours a day feeding. (Sheldon, 1937.)

The bear [*Ailuropoda*] prefers the young and succulent bamboo shoots to the woody stems. For this reason, in the main district of bamboo-bears I found no bamboo shoots in the spring, since they had been systematically 'browsed' by bears. The bulk of its nourishment consists, however, of stone-hard bamboo stems thicker than a finger. With its powerful molar teeth the bear bites off the 3 to 6 m. long stems about 20 to 40 cm. above the ground, lays them down and eats the middle part up to the beginning of the leaves, while it regularly rejects the lower, hard part and

lets it lie. Such chewed places are not particularly hard to find, although they are always concealed in the middle of the jungle. Usually they are not larger than one to two square meters. In these places perhaps 15 to 20 stems are bitten off, and the rejected parts cover the ground. (Schäfer, 1938.)

McClure (1943) listed nine species of bamboo that are palatable to the giant panda, expressing astonishment at the range of its tastes. Sowerby (1937a) stated that a half-grown pet giant panda that wandered at will on a Chinese farmer's land "ate grass and other plants."

Pen (1943) stated that a giant panda he observed at a distance of 2000–3000 meters on the

FIG. 3. Use of fore paws in pandas. A, *Ailuropoda* (Mei Lan) using both fore paws to manipulate food; Chicago Zoological Park, September, 1952. B-D, Lesser panda (*Ailurus fulgens*) using fore paws to manipulate bamboo; Lincoln Park Zoo.

Tibetan plateau was eating plants of various kinds, "principally gentians, irises, crocus, *Lycium chinense* and tufted grasses." Unfortunately it is not clear from his description how careful his observation was, and this is the only reported field observation of the giant panda's eating anything other than bamboo.

Captive specimens of *Ailuropoda* have eaten—in addition to various bamboos—porridge, green corn stalks and ears, stalks of celery, carrots, and other vegetables. They refuse meat in captivity.

Thus in nature the giant panda lives immersed in its food supply. It has practically no natural enemies, does not pursue prey, and does not need to wander in search of food. Demands on locomotor efficiency are absolutely minimal.

## FEEDING AND MANIPULATION OF FOOD

The manner of eating bamboo was well described by Schneider (1939), who carefully observed a 200-pound female temporarily exhibited in the Leipzig Zoo. The animal always sat or lay when eating bamboo, thus freeing the fore feet (fig. 2). Only the stalks were eaten; the leaves were rejected. The bamboo stalks were held in the fore foot and carried to the mouth. The tough outer layer was quickly and skillfully stripped off with the incisors, in which case the stalk was inserted transversely into the mouth, or with the canines and anterior premolars, in which case it was shoved lengthwise between the upper and lower tooth-rows. The stripped outer layer was torn off with a twisting movement of the forefoot coupled with a lateral turning of the head. The peeled stalk was then placed crosswise in a corner of the mouth, at the level of the large cheek teeth, where it was bitten off and chewed up.

The giant pandas in the Chicago Zoological Park manipulated green corn stalks, celery stalks, and carrots in a similar manner. The animals invariably sat down, or stood on their hind legs with one fore leg braced against the bars of the cage, when eating such food. They often sat with a piece of corn stalk or a carrot in each fore paw. Items were carried to the mouth in the fore paw, inserted transversely between the large cheek teeth, and bitten off. Chewing was a succession of vertical chopping movements.

Field observers (Weigold *in* Jacobi, 1923a; Sheldon, 1937) have emphasized the poorly chewed and undigested condition of pieces of bamboo in the droppings of the giant panda.

The skill and precision with which objects are grasped and manipulated by the fore feet is astonishing. I have observed animals in the Chicago Zoological Park pick up small items like single straws and handle them with the greatest precision. Small disks of candy less than an inch in diameter were handled deftly and placed in the mouth. Objects are grasped between the radial pad and the palmar pad and are held in the shallow furrow that separates these two pads. The actions of the fore paw suggest a human hand grasping through a thumbless mitten but are less clumsy than this comparison would indicate.

Bears and raccoons, of course, can grasp objects with their fore paws. In this action the digits, aligned side by side, are closed over the object, which is thus held between the digital pads and the transverse palmar pad. This is a quite different mechanism from the grasp of the giant panda. The lesser panda (*Ailurus*) grasps objects almost as skillfully as the giant panda, and apparently in a similar way (fig. 3).

### DIETS OF OTHER CARNIVORES

It is remarkable that the food habits of none of the bears have ever been adequately studied. Cottam, Nelson, and Clarke (1939) analyzed the contents of 14 stomachs of black bears (*Ursus americanus*) killed in early winter, and found that fruits and berries, mast, and foliage accounted for 93 per cent of the bulk and vertebrates for 4

per cent. Brehm (1915, Tierleben, Säugetiere, **3**, p. 394) states that "more than the rest of the carnivores, the bears appear to be omnivorous in the fullest sense of the word, to be able to nourish themselves for a long time from the plant kingdom alone." Seton (Lives of Game Animals, **2**, (1), 1929) emphasizes the omnivorous nature of the diet of each of the species of North American bears.

No quantitative study of the diet of *Bassariscus* has been made. Grinnell, Dixon, and Linsdale (Fur-bearing Mammals of California, **1**, p. 179) state that "mice and other small rodents constitute the largest part of the food eaten by the ringtailed cat. Small birds and berries are the other two most important items found in the stomachs examined.... Their jaws and teeth were so strong that they could chew up the leg bones of chicken without any trouble."

The seasonal or annual diets of several other American arctoid carnivores have been determined quantitatively through large-scale analysis of stomach contents and scats. These, of course, provide the only reliable data on the diet, as opposed to what may be eaten under exceptional circumstances, of any animal that is not positively restricted to a single food item. The diet of *Procyon* is more than 50 per cent (by bulk) vegetable (fruits, berries, nuts, and grains). Among the Canidae, the fall and winter diet of the red fox (*Vulpes*) is about 20 per cent herbivorous (fruits, grains, grasses), the winter diet of the gray fox (*Urocyon*) about 20 per cent herbivorous, and the annual diet of the coyote (*Canis latrans*) only 2 per cent herbivorous. Many mustelids (*Mustela vison, Taxidea, Lutra*) are exclusively carnivorous or nearly so, but the skunks (*Mephitis, Spilogale*) may include up to 50 per cent of plant material in their diets.

From these data it is evident that the closest living relatives of the giant panda (the Ursidae) are, next to *Ailuropoda* itself, the most herbivorous of living carnivores.[1] If the diet of *Procyon* is typical, the Procyonidae are likewise heavily herbivorous, though less so than the bears. The dogs and foxes are true carnivores, including only relatively small amounts of plant material in their diets. Thus *Ailuropoda* is a member of a group of carnivores (the procyonid-bear branch) that is already heavily herbivorous, and it is most closely related to the most herbivorous element of this group. The exclusively herbivorous diet of the

[1] Unfortunately, no information, beyond vague general statements, is available on the diet of the lesser panda (*Ailurus*). Sowerby (1936a) says it feeds largely on bamboo leaves, and specimens in the Lincoln Park Zoo in Chicago ate green bamboo ravenously.

FIG. 4.  Postures of *Ailuropoda:* standing (Mei Lan, Chicago Zoological Park) and climbing ("Happy," Leipzig Zoo).

giant panda is merely an extension, via an intermediate stage (the Ursidae), of a non-carnivorous dietary trend already present in the group from which this species was derived.

## POSTURE

The postures of *Ailuropoda* are similar to, but by no means identical with, the corresponding postures of *Ursus*.

The normal standing posture is similar to that of bears.  Both fore and hind feet are fully plantigrade but are toed in more sharply than in *Ursus*. The prominent shoulder hump of bears is much less conspicuous in *Ailuropoda*, and the hind quarters are somewhat higher.  As in bears, there is relatively little angulation at elbow and knee.  The head is carried low, and the tail is clamped tightly against the body.  The panda has a stocky appearance, less dog-like than that of bears.

The animal often sits on the hind quarters with the fore feet free of the ground.  This posture is almost invariably assumed during eating, since it frees the fore feet for manipulating food (fig. 2).

The panda does not normally sit erect, as bears often do, with the weight resting on the ischial surfaces.  Instead, the back is curved like the letter C, and the weight appears to rest on the posterodorsal surface of the pelvis.  In this posture the hind legs are thrust forward, their lateral surfaces resting on the ground, with the knees slightly bent and the soles of the hind feet turned inward. Bears sometimes sit with their hind legs similarly extended, although more frequently the legs are drawn up in dog fashion.

*Ailuropoda* often rests, half sitting and half reclining, in the crotch of a tree.  The back is then arched sharply, the weight resting on the lower part of the back rather than on the ischia.

Like bears, *Ailuropoda* readily stands erect on its hind legs (fig. 4).  This posture is assumed both in the open without any support for the fore feet and, more frequently, with the fore feet resting against the bars of the cage.  The hind feet are nearly fully plantigrade, the femur and tibia in a straight vertical line.  The zoo animals show no

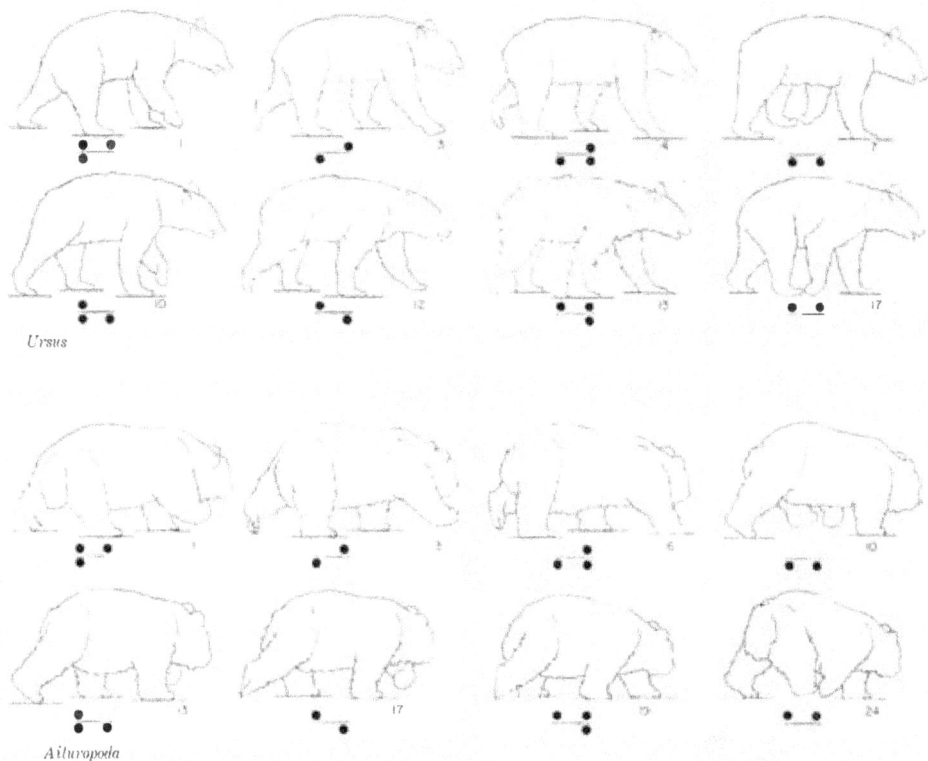

FIG. 5. The eight phases of the slow diagonal walk, with its footfall formula, of *Ailuropoda* and *Ursus americanus*. Tracings from motion picture film taken at 16 f.p.s. Numerals are frame numbers in the sequences.

more tendency to stand erect than bears do. I have never observed a panda walking in the erect position. "Bears are able to stand erect on their hind legs, and to walk a short distance in an unsteady but not particularly awkward movement." (Brehm.)

## LOCOMOTION

The normal gait of the giant panda is a "fast diagonal walk" (figs. 5, 6) in A. B. Howell's terminology. Howell (1944) states that this gait is regularly employed by nearly all mammals. It is used by bears and raccoons. When moving more rapidly the panda breaks into a clumsy trot. Whether it is capable of galloping at still higher speeds is not known.

The walk of *Ailuropoda* is bear-like, but less smooth and graceful. The head is carried well below the shoulder line, and the tail is closely appressed against the body. The stride is considerably longer than in bears, and as a result the gait

is more rolling, with much more lateral rotation of the shoulders and hips than in *Ursus*. This gives a pronounced waddling character to the locomotion. The heavy head is swayed from side to side.

The sole of the fore foot is fully apposed to the ground, but the heel of the hind foot does not touch the ground. Indeed, the panda appears to be incapable of flexing the ankle joint enough to permit plantigrady (p. 144). In this respect *Ailuropoda* contrasts with *Ursus*, in which the sole is naked to the heel and the foot is fully plantigrade.

During the recovery phase of the stride the fore feet are directed inward much more than in *Ursus*, and this "pigeon-toed" position of the foot is maintained during the support phase. During the recovery phase the hind feet are rotated medially so that the soles are directed medially. During the support phase, when the hind foot is resting on the ground, the toes point inward. At the end of the support phase the feet roll off the ground with the lateral toes receiving the major thrust.

FIG. 6. Two types of walking locomotion in the giant panda Mei Mei. The
top figure is the fast diagonal walk, corresponding approximately to no. 19 in
figure 5. The bottom figure is a slow
walk.

In captivity the giant panda is a persistent
climber when young (fig. 4). The movements are
often astonishingly clumsy but successful. In
climbing vertical or near vertical tree trunks the
movements are bear-like. The animal embraces
the tree, with the soles of all four feet pressed
against the bark, and progresses by a series of
"caterpillar" movements. The animal takes advantage of branches or other projections to hoist
itself up. It descends tail first, unless the slope is
gentle enough to allow it to walk down head first.

The claws appear to be of less importance in
climbing than the friction of the soles against the
bark, although the claws are used, especially if the
animal slips unexpectedly. In this type of climbing, called "bracing" or "prop" climbing (Stemm-
klettern) by Böker (1935), the portion of the body
not supported by the hind legs is suspended from
the fore legs.

## DISPOSITION

Young individuals are active and playful, and
thousands of zoo visitors have been entertained
by their clownish antics. As they grow older they

become much less active. Some individuals, at
least, become surly and dangerous in captivity. The
giant panda "Mei-Lan," while in captivity in the
Chicago Zoological Park, mauled one of his keepers
so severely that an arm had to be amputated.

Sheldon (1937), who hunted Ailuropoda, wrote:
"My experience convinced me that the panda is
an extremely stupid beast. On one occasion at a
distance of 350 yards I observed two individuals
on the edge of a bamboo jungle. Driven out by
four dogs and warned by several high-powered
bullets whistling about them, neither animal even
broke into a run. The gait was a determined and
leisurely walk. Again, Dean Sage and I observed
another panda pursued by four dogs. In this instance he *walked* to within eight feet of Dean and
was stopped only by bullets. He gave absolutely
no evidence that he saw either of us, and seemed
completely to disregard both the shots and the
loud talking and shouts of a few minutes previous."

## SUMMARY

The giant panda is confined to the moist bamboo zone on high mountain slopes, where the leop-

ard and the red wolf are its only potential natural enemies. Its natural diet consists exclusively of bamboo, with which it is always surrounded. Selection pressure for locomotor efficiency is absolutely minimal. Bamboo stalks are consumed in enormous quantities, but are poorly chewed and poorly digested. The fore feet are constantly used to manipulate the food. Objects grasped in the fore paws are held between the radial pad and the palmar pad. This grasping mechanism differs from that used by bears and raccoons but is similar to that of the lesser panda (*Ailurus*).

*Ailuropoda* is a member of a group (the bear-raccoon line) of carnivores whose diet is more than 50 per cent herbivorous. Its closest living relatives (the bears) appear to be more than 90 per cent herbivorous.

Posture and locomotion are similar to those of bears. Locomotion is less efficient. *Ailuropoda* climbs clumsily but persistently when young.

# EXTERNAL CHARACTERS

The general habitus of *Ailuropoda* is ursine. The head and fore quarters are heavy and powerful, the hind quarters relatively weak. The build is much stockier than that of bears of comparable size.

## I. DESCRIPTION

The pelage is thick and woolly, as befits an animal frequenting high altitudes. The characteristic parti-colored pattern is shown in figure 9. This pattern is unique among carnivores, although it is approached by the ratels (*Mellivora*), and by the lesser panda (*Ailurus*) except that the areas that are white in *Ailuropoda* are for the most part reddish-brown in *Ailurus*. The coloration of *Ailuropoda* is certainly a "constitutional" pattern rather than a "biological" pattern conditioned by natural selection.

The most unusual feature of the hair arrangement is found in the nasal region. The short hair on the top of the rostrum, from a point just in front of the eyes down to the muzzle (a distance of about 55 mm.), is directed straight forward. Two whorls are formed, 35 mm. apart, in front and mesad of the eyes, from which the hair radiates. Attention was first drawn to this character, which is unique among arctoid carnivores, by Kidd (1904). Kidd's later suggestion (1920), that this reversal of hair stream resulted from rubbing the hair toward the muzzle in cleaning it, cannot be taken seriously. It is noteworthy that a similar reversal occurs in other short-nosed carnivores (e.g., *Felis*).

The facial *vibrissae* (fig. 7) are rather feebly developed, although not so poorly as Pocock (1929) concluded from an examination of prepared skins. The superciliary tuft is represented by about three moderately long hairs over the eye. There is a relatively heavy growth of mystacial bristles along the upper lip, extending back almost to the angle of the mouth. On the lower lip they extend as far as the angle of the mouth. These bristles are much worn and broken on the specimen at hand, so that their length cannot be determined. They certainly do not reach any great length, however. Inter-ramal and genal tufts are absent.

The *rhinarium*, as pointed out by Pocock, is hairy above, with a well-haired infranarial area on

either side of the midline below. The naked area roughly resembles an inverted triangle and is continued ventrally into a short, grooved philtrum. There is also a V-shaped notch between the nostrils dorsally. The transverse groove below the nostrils referred to by Pocock is not evident on the fresh animal. The nostrils are transverse.

The *external ear* is erect, relatively larger than in bears, arising from a curiously constricted base. The margin is rounded, as in bears. The ear is well haired internally far down into the meatus. There is no bursa. The height of the pinna in Su Lin is about 85 mm., its breadth about 80 mm. The ears are set higher on the head and closer together than in bears—a consequence of the enormously developed masticatory musculature.

The *fore foot* (fig. 8) is short and powerful. The digits are enclosed in the common skin of the foot up to the base of the digital pads. Examination of the fresh animal corrects several errors made by Pocock. All the pads are thick and cornified. The digital pads are elliptical in outline, those of the second, third, and fourth toes approximately equal in size. That of the fifth toe is slightly smaller, and the pad of the pollex is the smallest of all and is joined to the palmar pad by a narrow isthmus of naked skin. The palmar pad extends as a narrow strip across the entire foot. There is no evidence of its breaking up into interdigital pads. The outer end of the pad is expanded slightly, and its inner end curves proximally to join the prominent radial lobe, from which it is separated by a transverse furrow.

The radial lobe is smaller than the outer carpal lobe. This lobe is wanting in bears. It is elliptical in outline, the long axis running anteroposteriorly, and is hemispherical in cross section. It is associated with the prominent radial sesamoid bone, which lies directly beneath it; Pocock was not sure that it represents the missing inner carpal lobe. Objects held in the hand lie in the furrow between the radial lobe and the inner end of the palmar pad and are grasped between these two pads.

The outer carpal lobe is large and roughly circular in outline and is situated somewhat farther

FIG. 7. Side view of head of *Ailuropoda*, showing pattern of vibrissae and hair-slope.

29

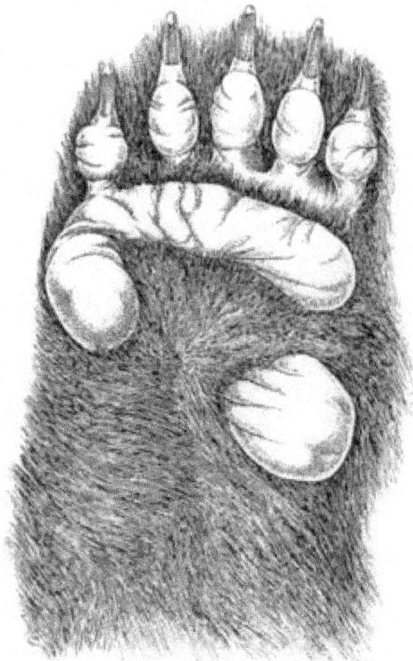
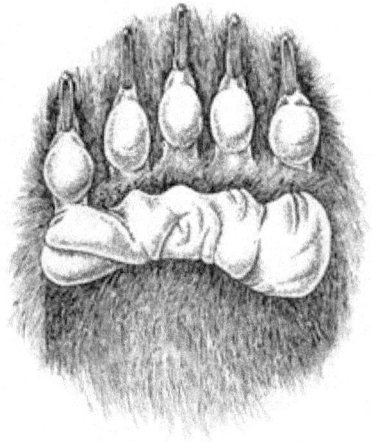
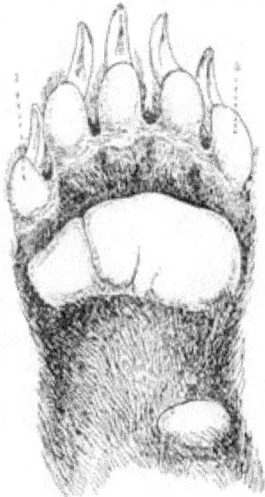
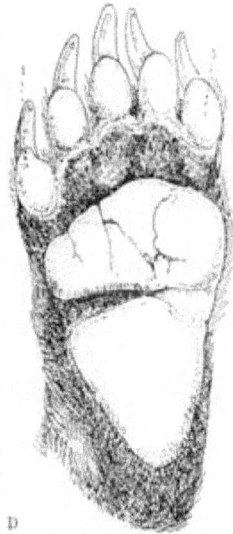

FIG. 8. Ventral surfaces of left fore and hind feet of *Ailuropoda melanoleuca* (A, B) and *Ursus americanus* (C, D). *Ursus* after Pocock reversed.

proximally than the radial lobe, lying about a third of its own width behind the palmar pad, much closer than in *Ursus*.

The remainder of the palmar surface is densely covered with long hair.

The *hind foot* (fig. 8) is slightly narrower than the fore foot and is remarkable for the limited extent of the cornified hairless areas. The absence of the posterior lobe of the plantar pad is associated with the inability of *Ailuropoda* to flex the foot beyond 45° from the vertical (fig. 80). The digits are enclosed in the common skin of the foot nearly to the bases of the digital pads. The digital pads are elliptical in outline, and all are approximately the same size. The pad of the hallux is joined to the plantar pad by a narrow isthmus of naked skin similar to that on the pollex. The plantar pad is a narrow transverse cushion, feebly convex anteriorly and very faintly divided into five lobes (not four as Pocock stated). The pad lies beneath the metatarso-phalangeal articulation. It is somewhat wider at the outer end than at the inner, and the lobe under the hallux is more clearly indicated than the others are. Metatarsal pads are absent; the remainder of the sole is densely covered with long woolly hair.

The *claws* on all the digits are strongly compressed and taper from a wide base to a sharp tip. The upper edge of the claw describes almost a perfect quadrant of a circle; the lower edge is sinuous.

The *tail* is relatively small but longer and considerably heavier than that of any of the bears. It measures 115 mm. in length in Su Lin (the caudal vertebrae measure 203 mm. in the skeleton of an adult) and tapers abruptly from a heavy base. The base of the tail is flattened dorsoventrally; its width is about 35 mm. while its depth is only about 25 mm. (see p. 83). The entire organ is densely clothed in long, coarse hairs.

There are two pairs of *nipples*, one pair pectoral and the other abdominal. The pectoral pair lies over the seventh rib, the abdominal pair 200 mm. behind the posterior end of the sternum. The bears have three pairs of mammae.

The external structures in the perineal region are described on page 221.

## II. MEASUREMENTS

No flesh measurements of an adult giant panda are available. The following measurements were made on the mounted skeleton of the adult male killed by the Roosevelt brothers. Flesh measurements of an adult female black bear, quoted from Seton (1929, Lives of Game Animals, 2 (1), p. 119) are given for comparison.

| | *Ailuropoda* | | *Ursus americanus* | |
|---|---|---|---|---|
| | mm. | inches | mm. | inches |
| Snout to tail tip...... | 1422 | 56 | 1613 | 63.5 |
| (along curve) | | | | |
| Tail................. | 203 | 8.5 | 127 | 5 |
| Height at shoulder.... | 635 | 25 | 648 | 25.5 |
| Approximate mean weight of adult..... | pounds 275 | | pounds 250 | |

The female "Happy" (weight 223 pounds), measured by Schneider (1939), had a shoulder height of about 660 mm.

No actual weight figures for adult giant pandas exist. Schäfer estimated that an adult male would weigh 275 pounds; *Ailuropoda* is fully grown at 4–5 years. The adult male Mei Mei weighed 205 pounds at death but weighed 296 pounds some months earlier. The weight of the male Mei Lan was estimated by zoo officials at 300 pounds when he was six years old. Skeletal measurements (Table 6, p. 45) show that Mei Lan was much the largest panda on record. A male at the St. Louis Zoo weighed about 280 pounds at eight years of age, and a female 240 pounds at five years. Thus it appears that the adult weight of the giant panda is 250–300 pounds, which is close to the average for the American black bear. The giant panda Su Lin weighed 132 pounds at death. The snout-vent length of this individual was 1195 mm.

## III. GROWTH

Weight increments for about the first 18 months of life are available for three individuals. These figures are, of course, for captive animals and do not include the first month or two after birth. Figures for "Pandah" and "Pandee" were kindly supplied by Dr. Leonard J. Goss of the New York Zoological Society. Weight figures are shown in the accompanying graph (fig. 9). The average monthly gain was 9 pounds.

## IV. PROPORTIONS

Measurements of the linear dimensions of anatomical structures serve two different purposes. The simpler of these is as a means of expressing relative sizes of homologous parts in two or more organisms. Thus, if femur length is 75 mm. in A and 60 mm. in B, we say that the femur is longer in A, or is 15 mm. longer, or we may express the difference as a percentage and say that femur length in B is 80 per cent of femur length in A. Such simple manipulations are much used in taxonomy and comparative anatomy. They rarely present serious difficulties as long as the organisms being compared are fairly closely related.

On the other hand, attempts to compare proportions between two or more species or genera often present serious difficulties. If A and B represent different species, the fact that the femur of A is longer than that of B may reflect the fact

they are not). This difficulty has plagued comparative anatomists from the beginning and has never been satisfactorily resolved.

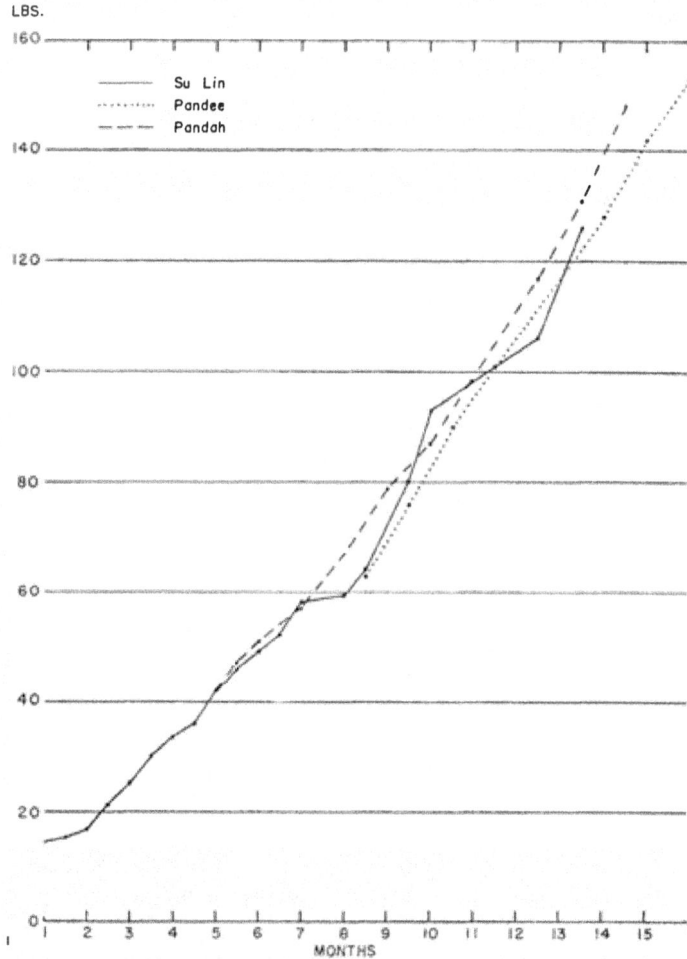

FIG. 9.　Growth curves of *Ailuropoda*.

that A is a larger organism than B, or that the femur is relatively longer in A or is relatively shorter in B, or a combination of all of these factors. The difficulty in determining what is involved arises from the fact that there is no common standard to which the variable (in this case femur length) can be related; for practical purposes all measurements on an organism must be treated as independent variables (although in fact

Many structures in mammals function as lever systems. Interpretation of the mechanical advantage of one lever system over another does not depend on knowing how the differences in proportions were achieved, but a true understanding of the morphology of the organism obviously does. Index figures, obtained by dividing one dimension (e.g., tibia length) by another larger dimension from the same individual (e.g., femur length) and multi-

FIG. 10. Body outlines of representative arctoid carnivores to show posture and proportions. All drawn from photographs of living animals (not to scale). TOP: Wolverine (*Gulo luscus*), a generalized mustelid; cacomistl (*Bassariscus astutus*), a generalized procyonid. MIDDLE: Raccoon (*Procyon lotor*) and lesser panda (*Ailurus fulgens*). BOTTOM: Black bear (*Ursus americanus*) and giant panda (*Ailuropoda melanoleuca*).

plying by a constant (commonly 100), are widely used because they are independent of the absolute size of the original figures and therefore directly comparable between individuals of the most disparate sizes. Uncritical comparisons of such index figures may, however, lead to grossly erroneous conclusions. In the present study the femorotibial index $\left( \frac{\text{length tibia}}{\text{length femur}} \times 100 \right)$ for a group of badgers happened to be identical with the corresponding index for a series of giant pandas, 76 in both cases. Analysis of the figures for femur and tibia length, using a third dimension (length of 3 vertebrae) as a common standard, revealed that the tibia is abnormally short and the femur about normal in the badgers, whereas in the panda the reverse is true: the femur is abnormally long and

the tibia about normal. These relationships may be of no importance in comparing the limbs as lever systems, but they are of the utmost importance in interpreting the morphology, and particularly the phylogeny, of the limbs. They could not have been detected from the dimensions of femur and tibia alone, but required the use of a third dimension as a common standard.

BODY PROPORTIONS

Comparative proportions of the body in a series of animals may be expressed by equating spine length to 100 and expressing the dimensions of other body parts as percentages of spine length (Hildebrand, 1952). These proportions are shown pictorially (fig. 10) and graphically (fig. 11) for a series of carnivores.

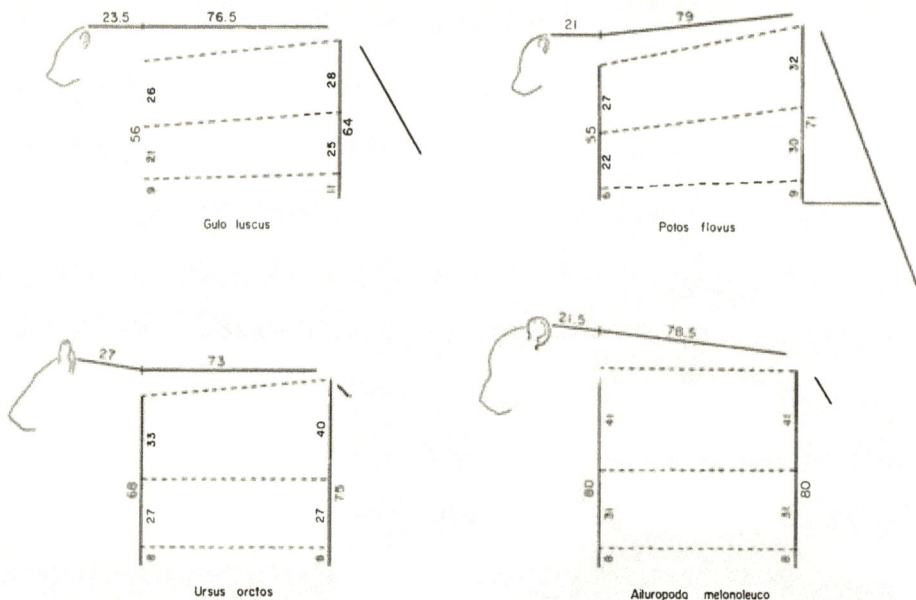

FIG. 11. Body proportions in representative carnivores (based on one specimen of each). In each case pre-sacral vertebral length was equated to 100, and lengths of other parts were indicated as percentages of vertebral length. Limb length is the "functional limb length" of Howell (lengths of propodium + epipodium + metapodium).

The wolverine (*Gulo*) represents a generalized terrestrial carnivore, in which length of hind limbs exceeds that of fore limbs by about 10 per cent, the epipodial segments (radius and tibia) are slightly shorter than the propodials (humerus and femur), and the metapodials (metacarpals and metatarsals) are long. In an arboreal carnivore (*Potos*) the hind limbs are elongated and the metapodials slightly shortened. In canids, which are typically cursorial runners, the legs are relatively long, especially the epipodial and metapodial segments.

These all represent rather obvious adaptations for locomotor efficiency. Adaptation is less obvious in certain other carnivores. The bears, which are mediportal ambulatory walkers (p. 38), have legs relatively as long as the cursorial canids and the proportion between length of front and hind limb is about normal for carnivores. The bears and the giant panda are remarkable among carnivores in having a long femur associated with a short tibia, without corresponding reduction in radius length; this condition is characteristic of heavy graviportal mammals (A. B. Howell, 1944). In *Ailuropoda* the spine has been shortened by elimination of lumbar vertebrae, a condition otherwise unknown among carnivores. The trunk in *Ailuropoda* is relatively shorter than in any other

known carnivore; the index "length thoracics 10–12/length thoracolumbar vertebrae × 100" is 18 and 22 for two pandas, whereas it is 14 (13–15) for all other carnivores examined except a specimen of *Mellivora*, for which it is 16. This exaggerates apparent leg length, but the legs actually are relatively long (Table 2). Length of fore and hind legs is subequal in *Ailuropoda*; this condition is otherwise encountered among carnivores only in the hyenas, although the proportions of the limb segments in hyenas are quite different from those of *Ailuropoda*.

## LIMB PROPORTIONS

In studies on small rodents, body length (measured on the freshly killed animal) is often used as the independent variable. This is impractical in work on skeletons of large mammals, for which measurements of body length are rarely recorded. Hildebrand (1952) used length of the vertebral column in his work on body proportions of the Canidae. Length of vertebrae probably varies as little as any convenient linear dimension, but for material as heterogeneous as the whole Order Carnivora it is desirable to eliminate the lumbar region, which, like the limbs, is intimately involved in the mechanics of locomotion and would there-

TABLE I.  LIMB SEGMENT RATIOS IN CARNIVORES

|  | No. | Humero-radial index | Femoro-humeral index | Femoro-tibial index | Tibio-radial index | Inter-membral index |
|---|---|---|---|---|---|---|
| Canis lupus | 4 | 100.6 | 89.8 | 98.4 | 90.7 | 98.5 |
| Canis latrans | 3 | 104.4 | 87.8 | 99.6 | 92.0 | 89.9 |
| Chrysocyon brachyurus | 2 | 108.1 | 91.0 | 107.8 | 91.4 | 91.2 |
| Bassariscus astutus | 4 | 79.0 | 89.8 | 97.2 | 72.8 | 81.4 |
| Bassaricyon | 3 | 74.8 | 88.5 | 101.7 | 65.4 | 76.9 |
| Nasua | 3 | 85.1 | 82.4 | 91.0 | 76.9 | 79.8 |
| Procyon lotor | 4 | 100.9 | 85.3 | 100.8 | 83.6 | 83.5 |
| Potos flavus | 3 | 80.6 | 89.2 | 94.9 | 74.9 | 84.2 |
| Ailurus fulgens | 3 | 74.7 | 94.9 | 94.2 | 75.3 | 85.5 |
| Ursus americanus | 2 | 81.1 | 86.4 | 72.2 | 96.9 | 90.8 |
| Ursus arctos | 2 | 81.5 | 84.2 | 68.5 | 100.2 | 90.6 |
| Ailuropoda | 7 | 77.1 | 98.4 | 76.1 | 98.5 | 99.3 |
| Gulo luscus | 3 | 78.9 | 94.3 | 90.2 | 82.5 | 88.8 |
| Martes pennanti | 2 | 76.0 | 90.4 | 99.0 | 69.4 | 79.9 |
| Taxidea taxus | 3 | 76.2 | 98.2 | 76.1 | 98.1 | 98.1 |
| Mellivora | 1 | 79.9 | 90.2 | 75.5 | 95.5 | 92.5 |
| Lutra canadensis | 3 | 71.5 | 98.9 | 111.4 | 63.5 | 80.2 |
| Enhydra | 2 | 75.7 | 95.9 | 112.4 | 64.6 | 79.7 |
| Viverra tangalunga | 5 | 90.1 | 81.3 | 96.2 | 76.1 | 78.8 |
| Paradoxurus | 4 | 77.0 | 91.7 | 90.9 | 77.5 | 84.9 |
| Herpestes | 1 | 76.5 | 82.9 | 90.3 | 70.3 | 76.9 |
| Felis onca | 2 | 77.6 | 87.0 | 80.9 | 85.4 | 86.0 |
| Felis leo | 4 | 90.3 | 86.5 | 84.6 | 92.3 | 89.2 |
| Felis tigris | 1 | 81.3 | 83.6 | 82.2 | 82.7 | 83.2 |
| Total | 71 | | | | | |

fore be expected to bias the results. A group of three thoracic vertebrae is convenient to measure and yields a linear dimension of convenient size. The combined length of thoracics 10-12 has therefore been used as the independent variable in the present study. An obvious disadvantage of using this measure as the independent variate is that it is the least accurate of all the measures in the set, and errors of measurement in the independent variate will bias the results, even though the errors are random.

Furthermore, length of centrum is itself a variable; simple inspection shows that vertebrae are relatively longer in Mustela than in Ursus, for example. Therefore, index figures derived from this common standard have no absolute value for purposes of comparison. They are only approximations, their reliability depending upon the range of variation in relative vertebral length within the sample. Reliability is certainly great enough to demonstrate gross deviations from the norm.

A further problem in interpreting these data is the selection of a norm against which the index figure can be evaluated. Femur length cannot be judged "short" or "long" unless it is shorter or longer than some standard femur length for the Carnivora. Probably the best that can be done is to use the index figure for the least specialized representative of the Carnivora as a norm. In Table 2 the figures for the wolverine (Gulo), whose locomotor habits are as generalized as those of any

living carnivore, are used as a norm, the figures being rounded off to the nearest multiple of 5.

From the table it appears that arm length is the most conservative among the four limb segments and forearm length the most variable.

These indexes correlate quite well with what is known of the locomotor habits of the animals. There are puzzling non-conformities (e.g., long proximal segments in Ailurus, short arm in Viverra, long fore arm associated with long thigh in Felis leo, etc.) that cannot be explained on the basis of existing knowledge. Disregarding these exceptions, limb proportions appear to correlate with locomotor types as follows in the Carnivora:

Ambulatory walking.....norm
Running ...............all segments long,
                        especially forearm
Arboreal climbing
   Type A.............hind legs long
   Type B.............forearm short,
                      other segments norm
Digging.............distal segments short
Swimming ...........all segments very short,
                     especially forearm

The bears and the giant panda, in which a short tibia is associated with length in the other three segments, do not fit any of these categories, and this combination is difficult to justify on a mechanical basis. Elongated limbs are generally associated with running, where a long stride is advantageous. The limbs are also long in graviportal animals (e.g., elephants, titanotheres), although the mechanical factors involved are unknown. The bears

TABLE 2. –LIMB PROPORTIONS IN CARNIVORES[1]

| | N | V L. humerus (norm=40) | V L. radius (norm=50) | V L. femur (norm=40) | V L. tibia (norm=40) | |
|---|---|---|---|---|---|---|
| Canis lupus | 4 | 35 | 35 | 31 | 32 | |
| Canis latrans | 3 | 36 long | 34 very long | 32 long | 32 long | all long; forearm very long |
| Chrysocyon | 1 | 27 very long | 25 extremely long | 25 very long | 22 very long | all very long; forearm extremely long |
| Bassariscus | 4 | 43 norm | 54 sl. short | 38 norm | 40 norm | forearm slightly short |
| Nasua | 1 | 37 norm | 43 long | 31 long | 24 very long | hind legs long; all distal segments long to very long |
| Procyon | 3 | 34 long | 34 very long | 29 very long | 28 very long | all very long, except humerus long |
| Potos | 3 | 39 norm | 48 norm | 34 long | 36 long | hind legs long |
| Ailurus | 2 | 36 slightly long | 48 norm | 34 long | 37 norm | proximal segments long |
| Ursus | 4 | 32 long | 39 very long | 27 very long | 39 norm | all long-very long, except tibia norm |
| Ailuropoda | 2 | 34 long | 44 long | 34 long | 45 short | all long, except tibia short |
| Gulo | 2 | 40 norm | 50 norm | 38 norm | 42 norm | all norm |
| Martes pennanti | 1 | 41 norm | 73 extremely short | 37 norm | 37 norm | forearm extremely short |
| Martes flavigularis | 1 | 45 short | 60 short | 40 norm | 41 norm | forelegs short |
| Taxidea and Mellivora | 4 | 42 norm | 55 short | 40 norm | 53 very short | distal segments short; tibia very short |
| Lutra canadensis | 3 | 68 very short | 95 extremely short | 67 extremely short | 60 very short | all very short, forearm extremely so |
| Enhydra | 2 | 77 extremely short | 102 extremely short | 74 extremely short | 66 extremely short | all extremely short, especially forearm |
| Viverra tangalunga | 5 | 47 short | 51 norm | 37 norm | 39 norm | arm short |
| Paradoxurus | 3 | 42 norm | 54 slightly short | 39 norm | 42 norm | forearm slightly short |
| Herpestes | 1 | 50 short | 65 very short | 41 norm | 46 short | all short-very short, except femur |
| Crocuta | 1 | 33 long | 32 very long | 27 very long | 36 long | all long; forearm and thigh very long |
| Hyaena | 1 | 33 long | 30 very long | 30 long | 34 long | all long; forearm very long |
| Felis onca | 2 | 40 norm | 51 norm | 35 long | 43 norm | long thigh |
| Felis leo | 4 | 38 norm | 42 long | 33 long | 39 norm | long forearm and thigh |
| Felis tigris | 1 | 43 norm | 52 long | 36 long | 43 norm | long thigh |

[1] V=length of thoracics 10–12. Norm=±3 from norm. Long=−4 to −10. Short=+4 to −10. Very long or short= ±11 to 20. Extremely long or short= ±21 or more.

## SUMMARY OF LIMB SEGMENT RATIOS IN CARNIVORES

| | Humeroradial | Femorohumeral | Femorotibial | Tibioradial | Intermembral |
|---|---|---|---|---|---|
| Ambulatory walking | 80<br>radius short | 95<br>subequal | 90+<br>tibia short | 75+<br>radius shorter | 90+<br>hind legs long |
| Running | 100+<br>equal | 90−<br>femur longer | 98+<br>equal | 90+<br>radius short | 90+<br>hind legs long |
| Half-bound (cats) | 80–90<br>radius short | 85+<br>femur longest | 85−<br>tibia shorter | 85+<br>radius shorter | 85+<br>hind legs longer |
| Climbing | 80−<br>radius shorter | 90−<br>femur longer | 95+<br>subequal | 75+<br>radius shorter | 85−<br>hind legs longer |
| Digging | 80−<br>radius shorter | 90+<br>femur long | 75±<br>tibia shortest | 95+<br>subequal | 92+<br>hind legs long |
| Swimming | 75<br>radius shortest | 95+<br>subequal | 110+<br>tibia longest | 65−<br>radius shortest | 80<br>hind legs longest |
| **Mediportal types** | | | | | |
| *Ursus* | 80+<br>radius shorter | 85<br>femur much<br>longer | 70<br>tibia very much<br>shorter | 96+<br>subequal | 90<br>hind legs long |
| *Ailuropoda* | 77<br>radius much<br>shorter | 98<br>equal | 76<br>tibia much<br>shorter | 99<br>equal | 99<br>equal |

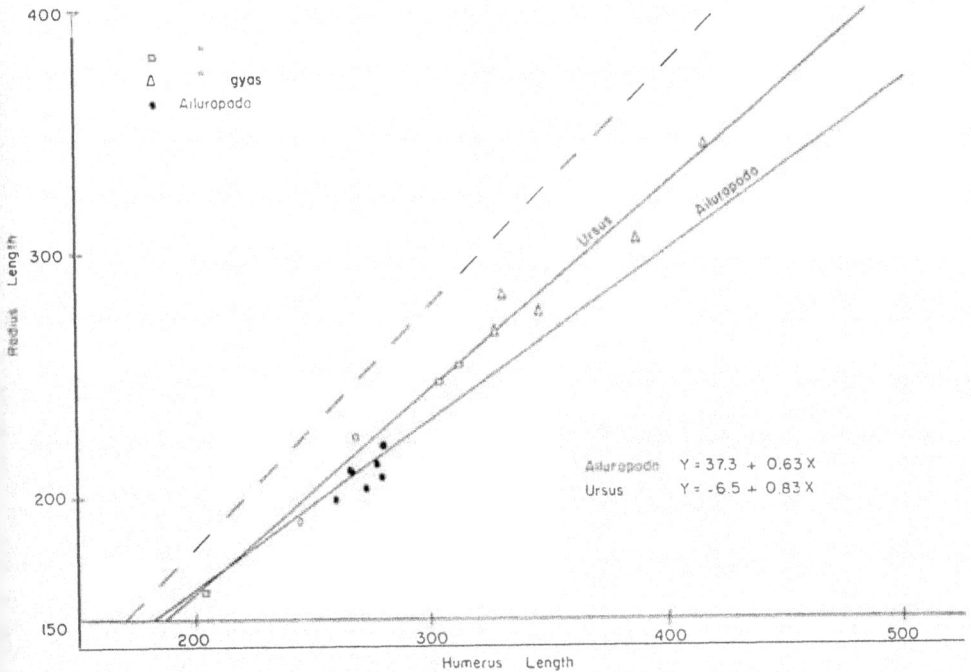

FIG. 12. Scatter diagram, with fitted regression lines, showing length of radius and length of humerus in panda and bears. (Dashed line = slope of 1.)

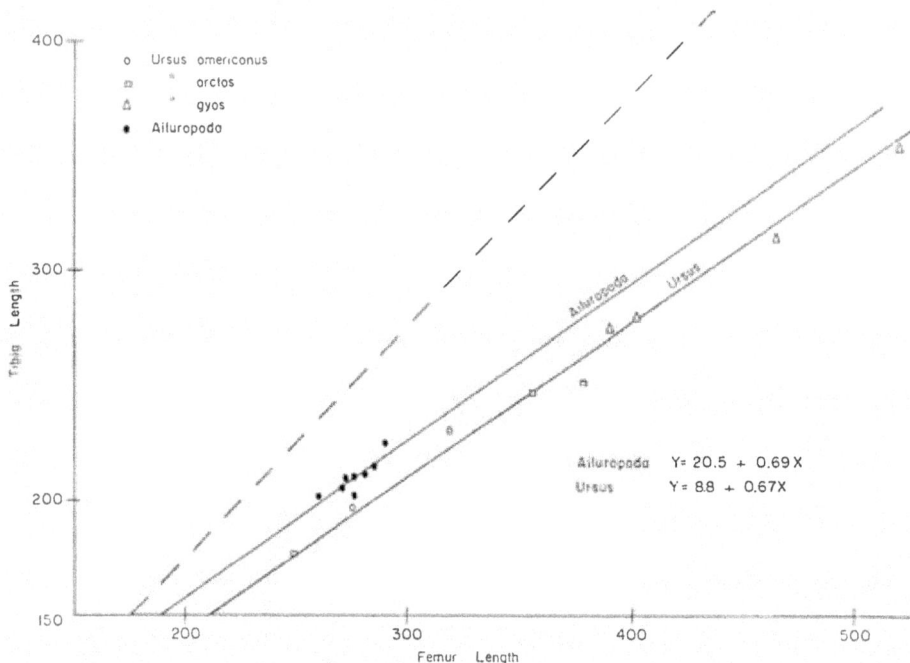

FIG. 13. Scatter diagram, with fitted regression lines, showing length of tibia and length of femur in panda and bears. (Dashed line=slope of 1.)

and the panda are relatively slow-moving ambulatory walkers and lack the elongation of the metapodials that characterizes runners. Shortening of the distal segments characterizes digging animals, in which the mechanical advantage of increasing effective power at the distal ends of the limbs is obvious. Gregory (*in* Osborn, 1929) noted that among ungulates the tibia shortens with graviportal specialization, whereas relative radius length either remains stationary or shortens to a less degree than tibia length. This is exactly the situation in the bears and the giant panda, whose limb proportions are those of mediportal or graviportal animals.

INTRAMEMBRAL INDEXES

Ratios of limb segments with respect to each other reflect the same pattern as ratios derived from an independent variable. They have the advantage over the preceding ratios of greater mathematical reliability and of widespread usage (see A. B. Howell, 1944). Limb segment ratios of representative carnivores are given in Table 2.

These figures are associated with locomotor types as shown in the following summary. Several

forms (e.g., *Procyon, Ailurus, Viverra, Herpestes*) do not fit well into any of the categories, and again it must be assumed that unknown factors are involved in determining the limb proportions of such forms.

Ratios for the bears agree with those of mediportal or graviportal ungulates. Furthermore, this agreement is associated with other mediportal adaptations, such as flaring ilia and relatively slight angulation of the limbs at elbow and knee.

The peculiar ratios in *Ailuropoda* do not occur in any other known mammal, and they often differ from the corresponding ratios in *Ursus*. They are most closely approached by those of the burrowing mustelids. Functional lengths of humerus and femur are equal in a very few scattered forms (*Tamandua, Icticyon, Dolichotis;* A. B. Howell, 1944). Equality in length of radius and tibia is more common but follows no pattern. Equality in the intermembral index occurs elsewhere among terrestrial mammals only in a few aberrant forms (giraffe, hyenas, the extinct forest horse *Hippidium;* A. B. Howell, 1944). I conclude that limb proportions in *Ailuropoda* are attributable to factors other than mechanical requirements—that

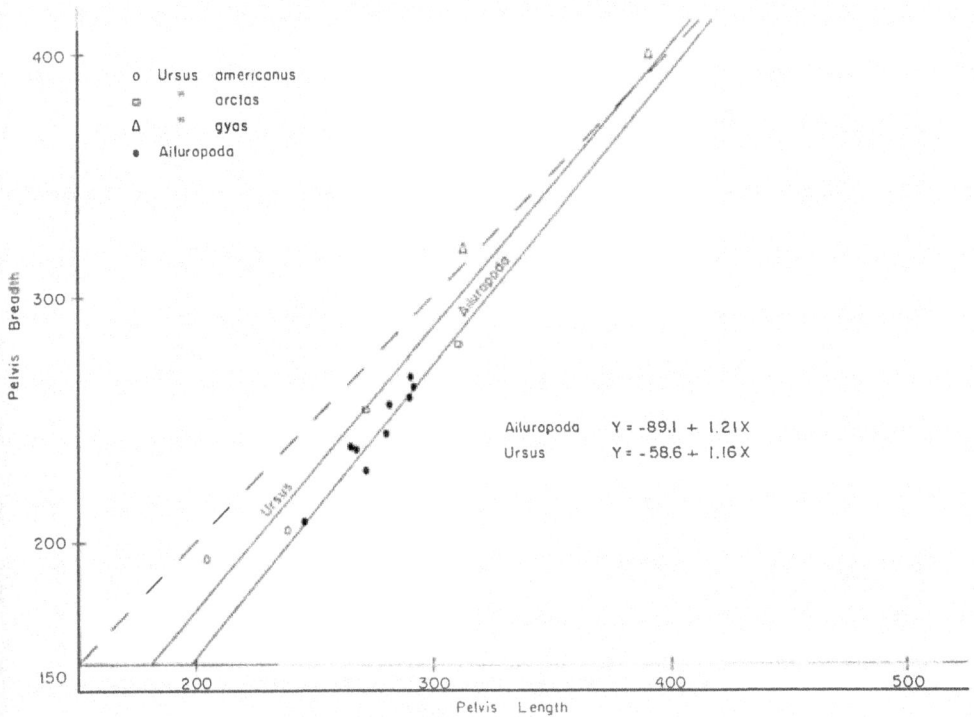

FIG. 14. Scatter diagram, with fitted regression lines, showing breadth and length of pelvis in panda and bears. (Dashed line=slope of 1.)

selection for mechanical efficiency has been over-ridden by some other factor or factors.

### ALLOMETRY

Examination of linear measurements of the limb bones of *Ailuropoda* (Table 6, p. 45) shows that proportions vary with the absolute size of the bones. When pairs of measurements for all individuals are plotted on scatter diagrams, clustering of observations along a line that deviates from a 45° angle is evident for nearly all limb proportions. This indicates that limb proportions conform to the well-known allometric equation $y = a + bx$, where $x$ and $y$ are the two measurements being compared, and $a$ and $b$ are constants. Regression lines were fitted to the data by the method of least squares (Simpson and Roe, 1939).

For the limb bones of *Ailuropoda* the plotted points are somewhat scattered (figs. 12, 13), indicating considerable individual variation in proportions. The slopes of the regression lines diverge from unity, indicating an allometric relationship

between proximal and distal segments of the legs; radius and tibia become increasingly short relative to the proximal segments as total organism size increases.

Conditions in *Ursus* are similar, although allometry is considerably less for the radius than in *Ailuropoda*. The plotted observations for all proportions cluster much more closely around a straight line, indicating relatively little individual variation.

The deviations of the regression lines from unity are not statistically significant for either *Ailuropoda* or *Ursus*. The close clustering of the values, especially for *Ursus*, suggests that they would be significant in a larger sample.

Similar analyses of data on limb proportions in other carnivores are available only for the domestic dog. Lumer (1940) found a close correlation, but only a very slight deviation from unity in the slopes of regression lines, in both humeroradial ($b = 1.098$) and femorotibial ($b = 1.090$) proportions in an analysis of data from a wide variety of breeds of dogs.

The limb girdles in the panda and bears are less consistent than the limb segments. In the scapula of the panda there is little correlation between height and breadth (r=0.45, N=9). In *Ursus*, on the contrary, there is a very close correlation between height and breadth of scapula (r=0.98, N=9), but only a slight indication of allometry (b=0.94). The pelvis shows a high correlation in total length/breadth across ilia in both *Ailuropoda* and *Ursus*. There is also a strong allometric relationship (b=0.75 in *Ailuropoda*, b=0.57 in *Ursus*), the iliac breadth becoming increasingly great as size of pelvis increases (fig. 14).

The "law of allometry' has been tested by many workers in a wide variety of cases, and found to be a valid empirical representation of ontogenetic growth relations. We may therefore postulate that the allometric relations demonstrable in *Ailuropoda* and *Ursus* reflect genetically determined processes that are as characteristic of the species or genus as are any morphological feature, representing what Lumer has called "evolutionary allometry." The intensity of expression of such size-dependent relationships is a function of organism size. Therefore the proportions at any particular phylogenetic stage (strictly, at any particular organism size) may not be, and in extreme cases certainly are not, directly related to the requirements of the organism. If selection has favored increased organism size, then proportions may become increasingly grotesque until a point is reached where the disadvantages of mechanically unfavorable proportions balance the advantages of further increase in organism size.

## V. CONCLUSIONS

1. The external characters of the giant panda are basically similar to those of *Ursus*. Differences from the bears are for the most part conditioned by more fundamental differences in underlying structures.

2. The absolute size of the giant panda is almost identical with that of the American black bear.

3. Body proportions of the bears and the giant panda differ from those of all other living carnivores. They resemble the proportions of mediportal or graviportal animals, although the mass of the smaller bears and of the giant panda is less than that of mediportal ungulates. It is also less than that of the larger cats, which show no mediportal specializations.

4. The trunk in the giant panda is relatively shorter than in any other known carnivore.

5. Limb proportions in the giant panda resemble those of bears, but differ in some important respects. In neither the panda nor the bears can they be explained on the basis of functional requirements.

6. Limb proportions in the panda and the bears show indications of allometry, the distal segments being relatively shorter in larger individuals. Pelvic proportions are also allometric, but scapular proportions are not.

7. Body proportions in the pandas and bears are not the result of selection for mechanical efficiency. Rather they reflect pleiotropic correlations with other features that have been altered through natural selection.

# SKELETON

Most of the literature on the mammalian skeleton is purely descriptive, with no real consideration of the soft parts to which the bones are intimately related in form and function, of the functions of the bones themselves, or of the factors responsible for observed differences between species. Comparisons are often unreal, for bones are compared as if they were inanimate geometrical forms rather than artificially segregated parts of living organisms. As a result there has been little attempt to evaluate differences in other than purely quantitative terms. Even the descriptions are often inadequate because the observer described only what he saw. The primary objectives have been to find "characters" on which a classification of mammals can be based, or to reconstruct the phylogenies of organisms or of structures. These are important but severely limited goals.

The gross features of the skeleton are determined by heredity, conditioned by events in the remote past; mammals have one bone in the thigh and two in the leg because they inherit this pattern from their remote ancestors—not because it is particularly suited to the needs of mammals. Within the limits set by this inherited framework, the primary function of the skeleton is support, and the form and architecture of bones reflect primarily the stresses and strains associated with this function. Each bone is also subjected to an assortment of constantly varying localized stresses and strains resulting from the action of muscles and ligaments. Besides these mechanical factors, the skeleton also serves as a store for calcium salts. Consequently the architecture of a bone is far more complex than is generally assumed, and attempts to analyze bones from the engineering standpoint have not been entirely successful (see Wyss, 1948).

In the individual the basic features of the skeleton, including accumulated adaptive features acquired during phylogeny, are determined genetically. We cannot go far beyond this obvious general statement, although Stockard (1941) and Klatt (1941–43) made a beginning at discovering the nature of this genetic control, and Sawin (1945, 1946) and his co-workers demonstrated gene control of morphogenetic fields in the skeleton. Scott (1957) concluded that growth and differentiation of the skeleton depend on two distinct processes: (a) a length-regulating process controlled by conversion of cartilage into bone (interstitial growth), and (b) a robustness-regulating process that determines the thickness of the limb bones, the size of the vertebrae, etc., and involves the activity of the subperiosteal cellular tissue (appositional growth).

It is likewise obvious that the inherited features of the skeleton are modified, within limits, by the activities of the individual. This is seen, if proof is needed, in the vertebral column of Slijper's bipedal goat (Slijper, 1946), in the adaptations to pathological conditions described by Weidenreich (1926, 1940), and in the experiments of J. A. Howell (1917), Washburn (1947), Wolffson (1950), Moss (1958), and others. This non-hereditary[1] factor is of unknown, but probably considerable, importance in determining the morphology of the bones. Howell, for example, found that in the bones of the fore leg of the dog most or all growth in diameter (appositional growth) is dependent on extrinsic mechanical factors, whereas growth in length (interstitial growth) is largely independent of mechanical factors.

Finally, it is reasonable to assume that the capacity of the individual skeleton to respond adaptively to specific functional demands is inherited, and that this capacity varies with the age of the individual.

The description of the skeleton of the giant panda here presented is somewhat unorthodox. The customary detailed description of each bone has been largely omitted; the illustrations should supply such information. The relations between bones and muscles, blood vessels, and nerves has been emphasized; and mechanical factors, which seem to have been of more than usual importance in molding the morphology of the giant panda, have been treated to the best of my ability. I have aimed not merely to describe and compare, but so far as possible to interpret.

[1] The muscles and other soft parts that act on the bones, as well as the psychology that directs the basic activities of the animal, are presumably gene-controlled. Thus even this factor is hereditary, at second hand, so to speak.

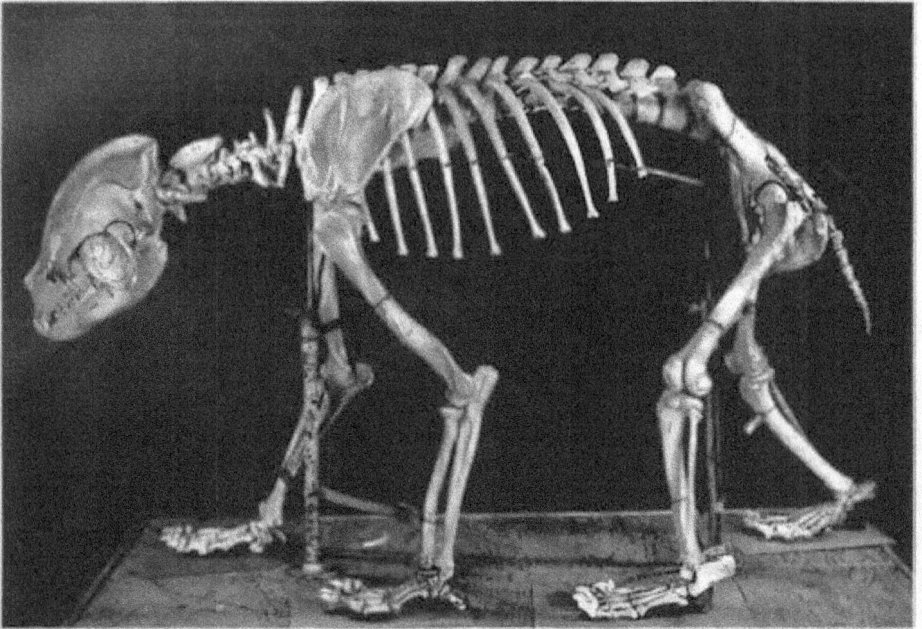

FIG. 15. Skeleton of *Ailuropoda melanoleuca* (CNHM no. 31128, adult male).

## I. THE SKELETON AS A WHOLE

The skeleton (fig. 15) resembles in general appearance that of a bear of similar size. The massive skull and short vertebral column give a somewhat non-ursid aspect to the skeleton. As in *Ursus*, surface modeling on the limb bones is prominent.

The mass of the skeleton is greater than that of a black bear of similar size. This is largely but not entirely due to the much heavier skull (Table 3).

TABLE 3. —WEIGHT IN GRAMS OF DRY SKELETON

| CNHM | | Sex | Total | Skull | Skull as percentage of total |
|---|---|---|---|---|---|
| 36758 | *Ailuropoda* | — | 5550 | 1581 | 29 |
| 31128 | *Ailuropoda* | ♂ | 6055 | 1383 | 26 |
| 44725 | *Ursus americanus* | ♂ | 5029 | 818 | 16 |
| 18864 | *Ursus americanus* | — | 3690 | 694 | 19 |
| 47419 | *Ursus arctos* | — | 11018 | 1923 | 18 |
| 65803 | *Ailurus fulgens* | ♀ | 269.6 | 67.5 | 25 |
| 49895 | *Procyon lotor* | ♂ | 384.5 | 67.8 | 18 |
| 54015 | *Canis lupus* | ♀ | 2013 | 377.5 | 19 |
| 46078 | *Hyaena striata* | — | 2083 | 465 | 22 |
| 18855 | *Crocuta crocuta* | — | 3947 | 864 | 22 |

For the giant panda and black bear these figures represent about 4 per cent of total body weight.

Further analysis of weight figures shows (Table 4) that percentages of total postcranial skeleton weight formed by the trunk, fore limbs, and hind limbs are very similar in giant panda and bears. These ratios vary considerably among the other carnivores.

It is evident that, except for the skull, the relative proportions of total skeleton weight formed by each of the major regions of the skeleton in *Ailuropoda* do not differ significantly from those of *Ursus*. This is not true of the skull, which is extraordinarily dense in the giant panda. The skull-postcranial ratio is quite constant at 16–19 per cent in other carnivores examined, except *Ailurus* and the hyenas, in which the masticatory apparatus is likewise exceptionally powerful.

The weight of the bones of the fore limbs is relatively greater in *Ailuropoda*, *Ursus arctos*, and the hyenas than in the other carnivores (Table 4). Klatt and Oboussier (1951) found this likewise true of bulldogs compared with greyhounds, although the disproportion (bulldog 69 : 31, greyhound 61 : 39, on fresh bones) was greater than in any of our material. Klatt and Oboussier found a comparable disproportion in total weight (i.e., including soft parts) of the limbs, and an even greater disproportion for the head. They concluded that the bulldog proportions result from a

TABLE 4.—WEIGHT RATIOS IN DRY POSTCRANIAL SKELETON

| CNHM | | Percentage of Total Postcranial Skeleton | | | Fore limbs : Hind limbs | | |
|---|---|---|---|---|---|---|---|
| | | Trunk (incl. pelvis) | Fore limbs | Hind limbs | | | |
| 36758 | Ailuropoda | 44 | 31 | 25 | 55 | : | 45 |
| 31128 | Ailuropoda | 46 | 31 | 23 | 57 | : | 43 |
| 44725 | Ursus americanus | 46 | 29 | 25 | 54 | : | 46 |
| 18864 | Ursus americanus | 42 | 30 | 28 | 52 | : | 48 |
| 47419 | Ursus arctos | 46 | 32 | 22 | 59 | : | 41 |
| 65803 | Ailurus fulgens | 47 | 27 | 26 | 50 | : | 50 |
| 49895 | Procyon lotor | 47 | 23 | 30 | 43 | : | 57 |
| 54015 | Canis lupus | 40 | 32 | 28 | 53 | : | 47 |
| 46078 | Hyaena striata | 43 | 34 | 23 | 59 | : | 41 |
| 18855 | Crocuta crocuta | 45 | 32 | 23 | 59 | : | 41 |

generalized regional effect, centered in the head but affecting the whole forequarters.

Taylor (1935) has shown that the relative mass of the skeleton increases, whereas relative bone area decreases, with increasing body size in a series of mammals. He presented data for a series of forms ranging in size from the albino rat to the domestic cow. Surface areas of a humerus and a femur of an adult male giant panda and an adult male black bear were measured according to Taylor's method. Each bone was carefully covered with adhesive tape. The tape was then removed and weighed (the number of square centimeters per gram of tape having been determined). This method yielded highly consistent results on our material. The data are given in Table 5.

In the giant panda the surface area of the humerus exceeds that of the femur by 6 per cent, whereas in the bear the reverse is true and the area of the femur is 6 per cent greater than that of the humerus. The surface area per gram of bone in the bear is exactly the same as the figure for man, as computed by Taylor; in the panda it is slightly less, because of the greater thickness of the walls. Taylor found that this ratio decreases with increasing organism size from 10.6 square centimeters per gram of bone in the rat to 0.69 in the domestic cow. The bear falls in about its

proper place in his table; in the giant panda the long bones are heavier than would be expected in a mammal of its size.

Thickness of the walls of long bones was measured at the center of the shaft on X-ray photographs. The walls are notably thicker in Ailuropoda than in a bear of comparable size; the walls of the humerus are about 30 per cent thicker, those of the femur about 60 per cent thicker (Table 5). The diameter of the medullary cavity is correspondingly decreased in the panda, showing that the abnormal cortical thickness results from a slowing down of resorption rather than from increased osteoblastic activity. The ulna is about 20 per cent thicker in Ailuropoda, and the tibia about 27 per cent thicker. Such increased cortical thickness cannot be attributed to mechanical requirements; it must instead reflect a pleiotropic effect or important differences in mineral metabolism. Indeed, it is well known that thickening the walls of a tube internally adds very little to the strength of the tube, whereas adding the same quantity of material to the outer surface does increase its strength significantly. Increase in muscle mass leads only to increase in the surface area of bone, not to an increase in thickness (Weidenreich, 1922).

TABLE 5.—SURFACE AREAS OF LIMB BONES

| | Bone weight gms. | Bone length cm. | Surface area cm.² | Area per gm. of bone cm.² | Thickness of wall at center of shaft mm. |
|---|---|---|---|---|---|
| Ailuropoda | | | | | |
| Humerus | 268.9 | 27.8 | 368.1 | | 6.5 |
| Femur | 251.3 | 28.2 | 344.6 | | 8 |
| Total | 520.2 | | 712.7 | 1.36 | |
| Ursus | | | | | |
| Humerus | 214.6 | 26.3 | 344.6 | | 5.5 |
| Femur | 239.8 | 31.6 | 364.9 | | 5 |
| Total | 454.4 | | 709.5 | 1.56 | |

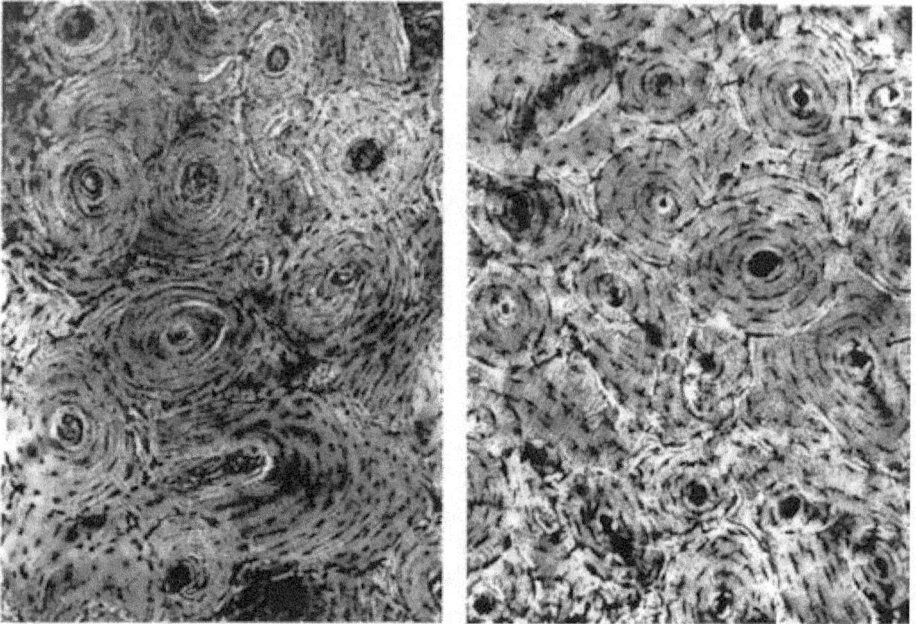

FIG. 16. Ground sections of compacta from middle of shaft of femur of *Ailuropoda* (left) and *Ursus gyas* (× 100).

These measurements also indicate the existence of regional differences in rate of bone deposition or resorption. The walls are significantly thicker in the hind leg than in corresponding bones of the fore leg, and the proximal segments are relatively thicker than the distal.

The histological structure of the compacta of the long bones shows no differences between *Ailuropoda* and *Ursus* (fig. 16). The bone is typically lamellar, with well-developed Haversian systems. Partly destroyed Haversian systems are numerous, and osteocytes are present in normal numbers. There is no evidence of retarded internal reorganization of the bone.

Mineral metabolism involves the skeleton. The normal diet of *Ailuropoda* contains quantities of certain minerals (especially silicon) that are abnormal for a carnivore. It therefore seemed desirable to determine the relative amounts of minerals in the bone. The following semi-quantitative spectrochemical analysis of bone samples from wild-killed animals was made by the Spectrochemical Laboratory of the University of Chicago. Obviously there is no significant difference between them.

In summary, the skeleton of *Ailuropoda* is more dense throughout than that of *Ursus*, due to

|  | *Ursus americanus* | *Ailuropoda* |
|---|---|---|
| CaO | ~48$^c_c$ | ~45$^c_c$ |
| MgO | 0.9$^c_c$ | 0.95$^c_c$ |
| SiO₂ | x¹ | .6 × x¹ |
| Sr | ~1200 ppm | ~1200 ppm |
| Ba | ~300 ppm | ~300 ppm |

¹ Working curve not available, but $SiO_2$ is less than 1$^c_c$, probably about 0.1–0.4$^c_c$. *Ailuropoda* has less $SiO_2$ than *Ursus* by a factor of 0.6.

greater thickness of the compacta. This is particularly true of the skull. The increase in quantity of compacta cannot be attributed to mechanical requirements. Regional differences in relative thickness of compacta indicate that rate of bone deposition or resorption is not uniform throughout the skeleton. There appears to be a gradient in which relative thickness of compacta decreases distally.

## II. MEASUREMENTS

Most of the bone measurements used in this study, except for those of the pelvis, are given in Table 6. These include all measurements used in calculating ratios and proportions for the most important of the species used in this study.

Lengths of the leg bones are not greatest overall length, but the much more meaningful "functional length" recommended by Howell. Functional length is the distance between the termina

TABLE 6.—MEASUREMENTS OF CARNIVORE SKELETONS[1]

AMNH=American Museum of Natural History;  CM=Carnegie Museum;  CNHM=Chicago Natural History Museum; USNM=United States National Museum

| | Sex | Skull — Greatest length | Condylobasal length | Palatal length | Zygomatic breadth | Mastoid breadth | Spine — Total length | Length thoracics 10-12 | Fore Leg — Scapula height | Scapula breadth | Humerus length | Radius length | Longest metacarpal | Hind Leg — Femur length | Tibia length | Longest metatarsal |
|---|---|---|---|---|---|---|---|---|---|---|---|---|---|---|---|---|
| *Ailuropoda melanoleuca* CNHM | | | | | | | | | | | | | | | | |
| 31128 | ♂ | 278 | 252 | 131 | 206 | 152 | 685 | 96 | 164 | 184 | 279 | 209 | 50.5 | 282 | 212 | 53 |
| 34258 | | 285 | | | | 168 | | | | | | 224 | 51.2 | | 216 | 55.9 |
| 36758 | ♀ | 267 | 250 | 132 | 206 | 149 | 665 | 92 | 164 | 160 | 277 | 214 | 53.0 | 273 | 210 | 57 |
| 39514 | | 277 | 257 | 129 | 207 | 153 | | | | | | | | | | |
| 47432[2] | ♂j | 264 | 246 | 130 | 180 | 132 | | | | | | | | | | |
| 74269[2] | ♂ | 308 | 289 | 144 | | | 826 | 105 | 197 | 217 | 282 | 222 | 58 | 314 | | |
| CM | | | | | | | | | | | | | | | | |
| 18390 | | 284 | 254 | 131 | 210 | 154 | | | | | | | | | | |
| AMNH | | | | | | | | | | | | | | | | |
| 110451 | ♀ | 275 | 251 | 133 | 202 | 143 | | | | | | | | 276 | 211 | |
| 110452 | ♀ | 265 | 245 | 126 | 207 | 145 | | | 170 | 184 | 266 | 212 | | 276 | 211 | |
| 110454 | | 280 | 254 | 130 | 193 | 141 | | | 173 | 180 | 267 | 211 | | 271 | 206 | |
| USNM | | | | | | | | | | | | | | | | |
| 258423 | | 274 | 253 | 134 | 199 | 142 | | | 160 | 157 | 260 | 199 | | 260 | 202 | |
| 259027 | ♂ | 295 | 267 | 135 | 213 | 164 | 737 | | 192 | 186 | 280 | 222 | 53 | 290 | 225 | 57 |
| 259074 | ♂ | 282 | 256 | 130 | 206 | 167 | 680 | | 164 | 164 | 272 | | 57.5 | 280 | | |
| 259401 | ♂ | 266 | 247 | 122 | 200 | 150 | | | | | | | | | | |
| 259402 | ♂ | 290 | 261 | 142 | 213 | 159 | 794 | | 162 | 185 | 256 | | 52.5 | 285 | 215 | 58 |
| 259403 | ♀ | 268 | 240 | 125 | 202 | 159 | | | | | | | | | | |
| 259076 | ♀ | 238 | 229 | 123 | 172 | 120 | | | | | | | | | | |
| 258984 | | 213 | 203 | 106 | 142 | 100 | | | | | | 128 | | | 129 | |
| 259400 | ♀ | 243 | 239 | 124 | 181 | 124 | | | | | | | | | | |
| 132095 | | 234 | 224 | 120 | 167 | 113 | | | | | | | | | | |
| 259075 | ♂ | 273 | 255 | 138 | 206 | 145 | | | | | | | | | | |
| 258834 | ♂ | 273 | 253 | 133 | 202 | 145 | | | | | | | | | | |
| 259029 | ♂ | 304 | | 142 | 215 | 165 | | | | | | | | | | |
| 258836 | ♂ | 276 | 255 | 136 | | 149 | | | | | | | | | | |
| 258425 | ♂ | | | 131 | | | | | 171 | 163 | 273 | 204 | | 276 | 203 | |
| CNHM *Ursus arctos* | | | | | | | | | | | | | | | | |
| 43744 | | 321 | 320 | 152 | 190 | 155 | 922 | 93 | 209 | 192 | 304 | 247 | 73.5 | 355 | 248 | 78 |
| 47419 | | 360 | 330 | 172 | 227 | 172 | 950 | 101 | 236 | 220 | 312 | 255 | 73.5 | 377 | 253 | 78 |
| 84467 | ♀j | 241 | 234 | 128 | 132 | 95 | | | 136 | 117 | 204 | 162 | | 249 | 179 | |
| *Ursus ggas* | | | | | | | | | | | | | | | | |
| 49882[2] | ♀ | 358 | 332 | 180 | | | | | 263 | 222 | 330 | 283 | 90 | 402 | 280 | 93 |
| 63802 | ♂ | 450 | 433 | 225 | 267 | 232 | | | 352 | 336 | 415 | 345 | 109 | 519 | 355 | 116 |
| 27268 | | 440 | 390 | 208 | 267 | 221 | | | 311 | 301 | 386 | 305 | 105 | 464 | 315 | 107 |
| 27270 | | 293 | 285 | 153 | 158 | 125 | | | 253 | 230 | 346 | 276 | | | | |
| 63803 | ♀ | | | | | | | | 247 | 221 | 327 | 268 | 91 | 390 | 275 | 96 |
| *Ursus americanus* | | | | | | | | | | | | | | | | |
| 18864 | | 256 | 242 | 130 | 139 | 106 | 761 | 81 | 150 | 151 | 244 | 191 | 65.4 | 276 | 197 | 67 |
| 44725[2] | ♂ | 273 | 270 | 133 | 155 | 124 | 818 | 86 | 172 | 157 | 268 | 225 | 70.5 | 318 | 232 | 73 |
| *Ailurus fulgens* | | | | | | | | | | | | | | | | |
| 65803[2] | ♀ | 112 | 102 | 53 | 76.5 | 38.5 | 375 | 40.5 | 61 | 57 | 107 | 83.2 | | 115.5 | 107 | |
| 57193[2] | ♂ | | | | | | 366 | 40 | 64 | 58 | 105.2 | 83 | 30 | 115.5 | 104 | 38 |
| 57211[2] | ♂ | | | | | | | 40.5 | 65 | 59 | 111 | 80 | 30.5 | 116.5 | 104.5 | 38.5 |
| *Procyon lotor* | | | | | | | | | | | | | | | | |
| 49895 | ♂ | 116 | 115 | 70.5 | 75.5 | | 360 | 38.0 | 75 | 70 | 110.8 | 110.3 | | 134.7 | 136.4 | |
| 49227 | ♂ | 115 | 113 | 70 | 76 | | 342 | 36.5 | 72 | 65 | 109 | 112 | | 130.5 | 127.5 | |
| 49057 | ♂ | 120 | 116 | 72 | 76 | | 303 | 33 | 62.5 | 59 | 96 | 95.5 | | 113.5 | 116 | |
| 47386 | ♂ | 114 | 113 | 71 | 79.5 | 61 | 327 | 35 | 69 | 59.5 | 99 | 101 | 30 | 118.5 | 121 | 37.5 |
| *Gulo luscus* | | | | | | | | | | | | | | | | |
| 57196 | ♀ | 158 | 149 | 82 | | | | 53.5 | 86 | 80 | 139 | 107.5 | | 145 | 131.5 | |
| 74056 | ♂ | | 145 | 79 | 104 | 90 | 530 | 57 | 88 | 84 | 139 | 112 | 47 | 148 | 134 | 56 |
| 79409 | ♂ | 167 | 154 | 83.5 | 110 | 95 | | | 92.5 | 90 | 141 | 111 | 47.5 | 151 | 135 | 56 |
| *Canis lupus* | | | | | | | | | | | | | | | | |
| 21207 | ♀ | 246 | 234 | 122 | 129 | 77 | | 74 | 157 | 107 | 209 | 213 | 94 | 234 | 233 | 107 |
| 51772 | ♂ | 263 | 248 | 135 | 139 | 81.6 | 795 | 80 | 164 | 108 | 228 | 227 | | 255 | 246 | 109 |
| 51773 | ♀ | 253 | 241 | 130 | 133 | 80.5 | 763 | 76 | 157 | 110 | 216 | 210 | 96 | 241 | 233 | 104 |
| 54015 | ♀ | 238 | 225 | 120 | 133 | 76 | | 69 | 154 | 100 | 209 | 207 | 95.5 | 230 | 232 | 108 |

[1] Pelvic measurements on p. 103.
[2] Zoo specimen.

45

articular surfaces of the bone. In most instances the appropriate point on the articular surface is either the same as that used for greatest over-all length or can be fixed with equal precision. In a few instances—both ends of the radius, and the distal end of the tibia—the shape of the articular surface makes it impractical to fix exactly the proper point from which to measure, and consequently the corresponding measurements are less precise. I have measured from the approximate center of such oblique articular surfaces. In a study of the present kind the advantages of comparing functional lengths outweigh any disadvantages resulting from slightly lessened precision.

For metacarpal and metatarsal length the longest bone was measured, regardless of which one it happened to be. For *Ailuropoda* this is metacarpal 4 and metatarsal 5; for all other species in the table it is metacarpal 4 and metatarsal 4.

In measuring the scapula, height was measured along the spine, from the glenoid cavity to the vertebral border. Breadth is the distance between two lines that are parallel to the spine and intersect the anterior and posterior borders of the scapula.

Length of the vertebral column was measured from the anterior border of the ventral arch of the atlas to the posterior border of the centrum of the last lumbar. The column of the smaller species was still articulated by the natural ligaments, and length was measured along the curves of the articulated spine. For the larger species, in which the bones were disarticulated, the vertebrae were laid out in proper sequence on a flat surface, following the natural curves of the backbone. Length was then measured along the curves.

All measurements are in millimeters.

## CRANIAL CAPACITY

Cranial capacity was measured by filling the cranial cavity with dry millet seed and then measuring the volume of the millet seed in a graduated cylinder. Ten trials were made for each skull, and the trial that gave the highest reading was regarded as the closest approximation to the true cranial capacity. The difference between the lowest and highest reading averaged less than 4 per cent for all skulls, and in no case was it greater than 6 per cent.

In cranial capacity, as in other basic size characteristics, the giant panda resembles the American black bear very closely.

## III. THE SKULL

The skull of *Ailuropoda* is characterized by its great density and by extreme development of the sagittal crest and expansion of the zygomatic

TABLE 7.—CRANIAL CAPACITY OF CARNIVORES

*Ailuropoda melanoleuca*

| CNHM | | C.C. | |
|---|---|---|---|
| 31128 | ♂ | 320 | |
| 36758 | ♀ | 288 | |
| 39514 | — | 282 | |
| Mean | | | 297 |

*Ursus americanus*

| CNHM | | | |
|---|---|---|---|
| 16027 | — | 280 | |
| 18146 | — | 261 | |
| 18151 | — | 310 | |
| 18152 | ♂ | 313 | |
| 51641 | ♂ | 312 | |
| 68178 | ♂ | 327 | |
| Mean | | | 300 |

*Ursus arctos*

| CNHM | | |
|---|---|---|
| 25713 | — | 412 |
| 81509 | — | 335 |

arches in comparison with other arctoid carnivores. These features are associated with very powerful dentition and masticatory musculature. The cranial skeleton and to a lesser extent the facial skeleton are profoundly modified by the demands of mastication. The cranium gives the impression of having been subjected to plastic deformation by the temporal muscle, which has attempted, so to speak, to achieve maximal volume. Expanding to the limit in all directions, the temporal muscle has displaced and compressed surrounding structures to the mechanical limit on the one hand, and to the limits of functional tolerance on the other. The face, on the contrary, is relatively unmodified except where it is hafted to the cranium, and in the expansion of the alveolar area in association with the enlarged cheek teeth.

The sutures between bones are almost completely obliterated in adult skulls. The bones of the cranium are much thickened. In the parietal region total thickness is 5 mm. (two individuals), whereas in a skull of *Ursus arctos* the bone in the same region measures 2.3 mm. and in a skull of *Ursus americanus* only 1.7. The increased thickness in the panda involves only the outer lamina of the bone; the inner lamina is no thicker than in the bears. This is likewise true of the basicranial region: in a sectioned skull of *Ailuropoda* the outer lamina of the sphenoid is 2.6 mm. thick below the sella, whereas in a skull of *Ursus americanus* it is only 0.9 mm. The difference is similar in the mandible; at the level of the posterior border of $M_2$ the body is 12.2 mm. thick from the mandibular canal to the external surface of the bone in *Ailuropoda* (3.6 mm. in *Ursus americanus*), and 5 mm. from the mandibular canal to the inner surface (3.4 mm. in *Ursus americanus*).

The bones of the face, on the contrary, are little if any thicker in *Ailuropoda* than in *Ursus*.

*Ailurus* agrees more or less closely with the giant panda in skull proportions. As was pointed out by the earliest investigators, there is also a superficial resemblance to the hyenas, associated with similar masticatory requirements.

In the following description the skull of the European brown bear (*Ursus arctos*) is used as a basis for comparison. Four adult skulls of *Ailuropoda* in the collection of Chicago Natural History Museum were available for detailed examination. One of these (no. 36758) was bisected in the sagittal plane and cut frontally through the right auditory region. None of these skulls shows the sutures; these were determined on a young female skull borrowed from the U. S. National Museum (USNM No. 259076).

## A. THE SKULL AS A WHOLE

### (1) Dorsal View

In dorsal view (*norma verticalis*) the skull of *Ailuropoda* is dominated by the tremendously expanded zygomatic arches. These form nearly a perfect circle, compared with the triangular outline in *Ursus* and other carnivores. The primary result of this expansion is to increase the volume of the anterior third of the temporal fossa.

The muzzle appears to be shortened and has often been so described. This is not true, however; the pre-optic length is nearly identical in *Ailuropoda* and *Ursus*. The muzzle is no wider anteriorly than in *Ursus;* its borders diverge posteriorly instead of being nearly parallel as in *Ursus*, but this merely reflects the broader cheek teeth of the panda. The postorbital process on the frontal is scarcely indicated, and in one skull it is absent. The alveolar pocket of the tremendous second upper molar is conspicuous immediately behind the floor of the orbit; this is invisible from above in *Ursus* but is equally prominent in *Ailurus* and *Procyon*. The interorbital diameter is not greater in the bears than in the giant panda, but the postorbital constriction is more pronounced in the panda, and this increases the volume of the anterior part of the temporal fossa. This constriction is reflected in the form of the brain, which in *Ailuropoda* is much narrower anteriorly, in both transverse and vertical diameters, than in *Ursus*. The maximal cranial diameter is about 10 per cent greater in *Ailuropoda*, and this, together with the greater postorbital constriction, gives a characteristic hourglass outline to the skull in dorsal view.

Thus the volume of the *anterior* part of the temporal fossa has been increased by expansion both laterally and medially, whereas the volume of the posterior part of this fossa has been far less affected. The skull of *Ailurus* exhibits a similar increase in the volume of the anterior part of the temporal fossa. In the hyenas, in which the volume of the temporal fossa is also notably increased, it is the *posterior* part of the fossa that is expanded by posterior extension. The reasons for this difference between herbivorous and carnivorous forms are discussed later (see p. 155).

The horizontal shelf formed by the posterior root of the zygoma is not wider in *Ailuropoda* than in *Ursus*, but it is carried farther forward along the ventral border of the arch, thus increasing the articular surface of the glenoid cavity on its inferior surface and the area of origin of the zygomaticomandibular muscle on its superior surface. There are conspicuous muscle rugae, barely indicated in *Ursus*, on the inner face of the posterior half of the zygoma.

The sagittal crest appears to have a conspicuous sagittal suture, but the juvenile skull shows that this is actually the first suture to close, and that the "suture" in the adult results from secondary upgrowth of the frontals and parietals. The smoothly curved outline of the lambdoidal crest contrasts with the sinuous crest seen in *Ursus, Ailurus*, and *Procyon;* it reflects the posterior expansion of the temporal fossa.

### (2) Lateral View

In *norma lateralis* (fig. 17) the skull of the panda contrasts sharply with the bears in the facial angle as measured from the Frankfort horizontal. In *Ursus* the toothrow is depressed from the Frankfort horizontal at an angle of about 22°, whereas in *Ailuropoda* these two lines are nearly parallel. Reference to the ventral axis of the braincase reveals, however, that the angle formed by the toothrow is nearly identical in *Ailuropoda* and *Ursus*. Actually the position of the orbit is depressed in *Ailuropoda*, as a part of the over-all expansion of the temporal fossa, and therefore the Frankfort horizontal is misleading in this animal.

The strongly convex dorsal contour of the skull increases the area of the temporal fossa dorsally. At the same time the vertical diameter of the masseteric fossa of the mandible is much greater than in *Ursus*. Thus the whole postorbital part of the skull appears expanded, and the skull has a trapezoidal outline when viewed from the side.

The margin of the nasal aperture in the panda curves sharply dorsally, its dorsal third lying at a right angle to the long axis of the skull. Behind

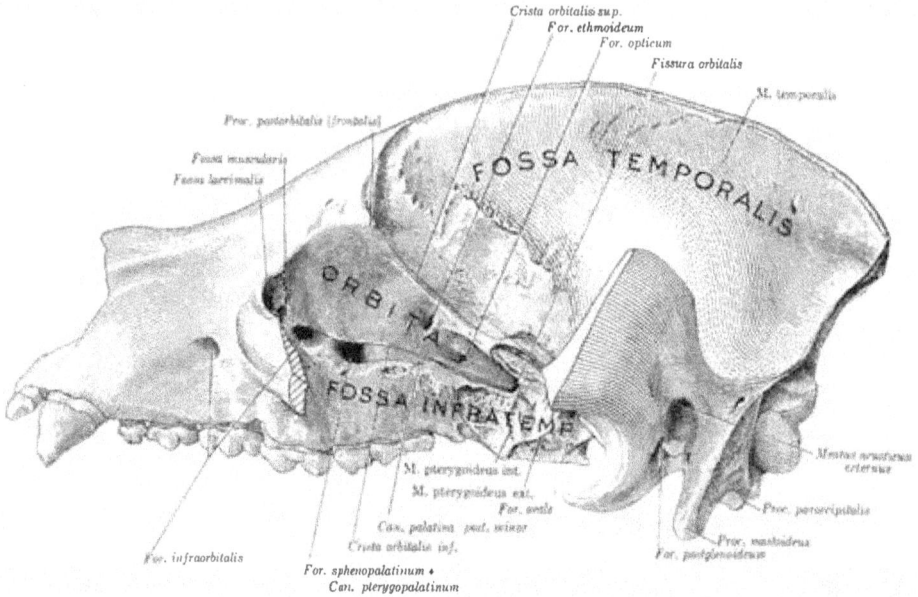

FIG. 17.  Skull of *Ailuropoda* seen from left side (*norma lateralis*).

the nasal aperture the surface of the nasal and premaxillary bones shows a pattern of shallow grooves, in which lie the terminal ramifications of the infraorbital and external nasal vessels, and small foramina through which nutrient twigs from these vessels entered the bone. The infraorbital foramen is small and less elliptical in cross section than in *Ursus*. Below and in front of the orbit the anterior root of the zygomatic arch bulges forward conspicuously. The postorbital process of the jugal is less prominent than in the bears, in which it reaches its maximal development among the Arctoidea.

The temporal fossa in *Ailuropoda* is relatively enormous, in keeping with the size of the temporal muscle. Its anteroventral boundary, separating it from the orbit, is well marked by the superior orbital ridge. Anteroventrally the fossa is provided with about three well-developed muscle ridges, paralleling the superior orbital ridge; in *Ursus* corresponding muscle ridges are present, but scarcely more than indicated; in *Ailurus* there is a single ridge in old adults. In the upper posterior part of the fossa, near the juncture of the sagittal and lambdoidal crests, is a conspicuous nutrient foramen; a similar foramen is present in the bears but is lacking in other arctoids.

In *Ailuropoda* the infratemporal fossa is separated from the orbit above by the well-marked inferior orbital ridge throughout most of its length. Behind the orbital fissure it is separated from the temporal fossa by an indistinct elevation extending from the superior orbital ridge in front of the orbital fissure to the anterior lip of the glenoid fossa. The infratemporal fossa is relatively small. The anterior half of the infratemporal fossa contains the entrance to the infraorbital foramen, the common foramen for the sphenopalatine (sphenopalatine artery and nerve; nasal branches of sphenopalatine ganglion) and pterygopalatine (descending palatine artery and nerve) canals. These exit by separate foramina in *Ursus* and other carnivores, but are combined in *Ailurus;* they have undoubtedly been crowded together in the two pandas by the enlarged maxillary tuberosity. The posterior half of the fossa, from which the pterygoid muscles arise, exhibits muscle rugosities. The areas of origin of the pterygoid muscles are sharply marked on the bone. The area of pterygoid origin is much reduced, both vertically and horizontally, as compared with *Ursus*.

In *Ailuropoda* the foramen rotundum (maxillary branch of trigeminus) is confluent with the orbital fissure, although the identity of the two openings is usually indicated by a low ridge and on one side of one skull there is a paper-thin partition separating them. This is a feature in which *Ailuropoda* differs from all other canoids; it is associated with the general crowding together of non-masticatory structures in the skull. *Ailuropoda* also lacks an alisphenoid canal, which is present in *Ursus*. In forms having an alisphenoid canal (Canidae, Ursidae, *Ailurus*) the foramen rotundum is situated within the canal; in *Ailurus* it is separated from the orbital fissure only by a thin septum, but the two are some distance apart in the dogs and bears. In forms lacking an alisphenoid canal (Procyonidae, Mustelidae), the foramen and the orbital fissure are separated by a thin septum.

In *Ursus* the vertical diameter of the infratemporal fossa is much greater than in *Ailuropoda*. This is also true in *Canis* but not in the procyonids, in which the relatively much larger orbit encroaches on it. Reduction of the infratemporal fossa in *Ailuropoda* is correlated with the more ventral position of the eye, and thus secondarily with the ventral expansion of the temporal fossa. The tremendously enlarged maxillary tuberosity, associated with the enlargement of the molar teeth, further reduces the volume of the fossa.

THE ORBIT.—The orbit in *Ailuropoda*, as in other arctoids, is poorly defined on the skull; only the medial wall is entire. The orbit is an elongate cone with the base formed by the incomplete bony ring of the eye socket (completed by the orbital ligament), and the apex by the orbital fissure. On its medial wall the dorsal and ventral boundaries, separating the orbit from the temporal fossa above and the infratemporal fossa below, are well marked by the superior and inferior orbital ridges. These ridges are less prominent in other arctoids. Elsewhere the boundaries of the orbit are poorly marked on the skull; because of the feebly developed postorbital processes on both frontal and jugal, even the anterior limits are poorly indicated in *Ailuropoda* as compared with those of other arctoids.

The orbit is rotated slightly ventrad as compared with that of *Ursus*. Its long axis (from the orbital fissure to the center of the eye socket) forms an angle of about 10° with the long axis of the skull in *Ursus*, whereas in *Ailuropoda* the axes are parallel. At the ventral boundary of the orbital opening there is a prominent crescent-shaped depression, which in life lodges a cushion of extraocular fat.

The lacrimal fossa, which lodges the lacrimal sac, is a large funnel-shaped pit at the anteromedial corner of the orbit. The nasolacrimal canal opens into the bottom of the fossa. The canal is only a millimeter or two long, opening almost at once into the nasal cavity, immediately beneath the posterior end of the maxilloturbinal crest. *Ursus* is unique in having the nasolacrimal canal open into the maxillary sinus. Immediately behind the lacrimal fossa is a shallow pit, the **fossa muscularis**, in which the inferior oblique muscle of the eye arises; the thin floor of this pit is usually broken through on dry skulls, and then resembles a foramen. In *Ursus* and other arctoids the lacrimal fossa is much smaller than in *Ailuropoda*, but otherwise similar. The fossa muscularis in *Ailurus* is very similar to that of *Ailuropoda;* in *Ursus* it is relatively enormous—as large as the lacrimal fossa and several millimeters deep. The fossa muscularis is completely wanting in the Canidae and Procyonidae.

Three foramina in a row, about equidistant from each other, pierce the medial wall of the posterior half of the orbit. Each leads into the cranial fossa via a short canal directed posteriorly, medially, and ventrally. The most anterior is the **ethmoidal foramen**, which conducts the external ethmoidal nerves and vessels into the anterior cranial fossa. Behind this is the **optic foramen** (optic nerve, ophthalmic vessels), and most posteriorly and much the largest is the combined **orbital fissure** and **foramen rotundum** (oculomotor, trigeminal, trochlear, and abducens nerves; anastomotic and accessory meningeal arteries; orbital vein). Except for the confluence of the orbital fissure and foramen rotundum, which is peculiar to *Ailuropoda*, the pattern of these three foramina is similar in all arctoids. Most variable is the ethmoidal foramen, which differs in size among the genera and may be characteristically multiple (e.g., in *Canis*). The foramen ovale, in forms in which it is separate from the orbital fissure, transmits the third (mandibular) branch of the trigeminus and the middle meningeal artery.

The **zygomatic arch** functions in the origin of the temporal fascia from its superior border, the temporal and zygomaticomandibular muscles from its internal surface, and the masseter from its inferior surface. Its anterior root lies over the first upper molar (over the second molar in *Ursus*), its posterior root over the glenoid fossa; the arch is therefore important in resolving the forces generated during mastication. As pointed out above, the anterior part of the arch is expanded laterally, which increases the volume of the anterior third of the temporal fossa. In lateral view the arch is straighter than in *Ursus* and other arctoids. Its posterior half is much extended dorsally, which increases the available area of origin for the zygomaticomandibularis muscle. The whole structure

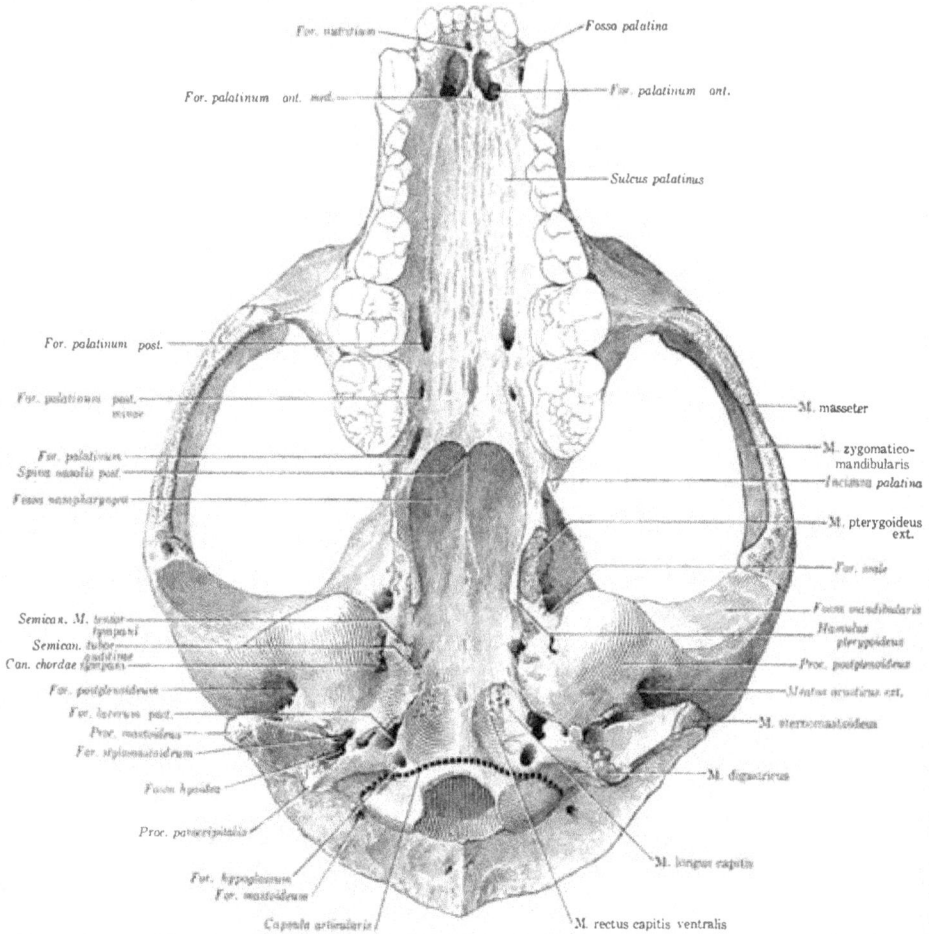

FIG. 10. Skull of *Ailuropoda* seen from below (*norma ventralis*).

is extraordinarily massive. The anterior root is bulky but relatively thin-walled, since it is extensively excavated internally by the maxillary sinus. It bulges forward anteriorly, and posteriorly forms the floor of the orbit for a short distance before passing into the alveolar pocket of the second molar; the infraorbital canal is thus considerably lengthened posteriorly. The posterior root of the arch is expanded posteriorly to accommodate the large mandibular (glenoid) fossa; it has encroached considerably on the space between the postglenoid and mastoid processes, in which the external auditory meatus lies, and the meatus is consequently much compressed.

(3) *Ventral View*

In ventral view (*norma ventralis*, fig. 18) the facial region is dominated by the massive dentition, the cranial region by the immense mandibular fossae.

It has often been stated that the palate extends farther posteriorly in *Ursus* than in *Ailuropoda*, but this is an illusion created by the enlarged teeth of the latter. In relation to the anterior end of the braincase, the palate actually extends farther posteriorly in the panda. The lateral borders of the palate are parallel, as in *Ursus*; in other arctoids they diverge posteriorly. The anterior palatine foramina, which transmit nerves, vessels, and the incisive duct, are situated in the posterior part of the large palatine fossa as in other arctoids. There is a median nutrient foramen between the fossae anteriorly, and a small **median anterior palatine foramen** (large in *Ursus* and procyonids) opening into a minute canal that arches back through the anterior part of the bony septum, lies between the fossae posteriorly. A shallow groove, the **sulcus palatinus** in which the anterior palatine artery lay, connects each anterior palatine foramen with the **posterior palatine foramen**, which is situated at the level of the first molar and represents the outlet of the pterygopalatine canal. Immediately behind the posterior palatine foramen, at the level of the second molar, is a much smaller opening, the **foramen palatina posterior minor**. In other arctoid carnivores this foramen (often several) connects directly with the pterygopalatine canal, but in *Ailuropoda*, because of the immense development of the second molar, its canal comes to the surface briefly as a groove on the lateral wall of the choana (fig. 20), then re-enters the bone and finally emerges several millimeters behind the entrance to the pterygopalatine canal (fig. 18). A shallow groove, not seen in other arctoids, passes posteriorly from the posterior palatine foramen to the **palatine notch** (occasionally closed to form a foramen). As in other arctoids, the posterior border of the palate bears a prominent median spine.

The **choanae** (posterior nasal apertures) are separate, the bony septum formed by the vomer extending to (dorsally beyond) the posterior border of the palate. There is much variation in the posterior extent of this septum in arctoids. In *Ursus*, representing the opposite extreme from *Ailuropoda*, the septum ends far anteriorly at about the juncture of the middle and posterior thirds of the palate, and the posterior third of the nasopharyngeal meatus is accordingly undivided. Other genera are intermediate between *Ailuropoda* and *Ursus* in the posterior extent of the septum.

The **nasopharyngeal fossa**, situated behind the choanae and between the pterygoid processes, is absolutely and relatively wider than in *Ursus*. The anterior half of the roof of the fossa bears a prominent median keel, the presence and degree of development of which varies with the posterior extent of the septum. The pterygoid processes present nothing unusual.

The **mandibular (glenoid) fossa** is the key to other modifications of the skull in *Ailuropoda*. The transverse cylindrical mandibular articulation, limiting jaw action to a simple hinge movement vertically and a very restricted lateral movement horizontally, is a carnivore heritage that is ill-adapted to the feeding habits of this animal.

In *Ailuropoda* the transverse diameter of the fossa is much greater than in other arctoids. This dimension amounts to 30 per cent of the basal length of the skull, while in other arctoids it ranges between 15 and 20 per cent, only slightly exceeding 20 per cent even in *Ailurus*. The increase in the length of the fossa in *Ailuropoda* has taken place wholly in the lateral direction; the medial ends of the two mandibular fossae are no closer together than in *Ursus*.

The articular surfaces of the medial and lateral halves of the fossa in *Ailuropoda* are in quite different planes. In the medial half the articular surface is almost wholly posterior (against the anterior face of the **postglenoid process**), while laterally the articulation is wholly dorsal (against the root of the zygomatic arch). Transition between these two planes is gradual, producing a spiral fossa twisted through 90°. The form of the fossa is similar, though less extreme, in *Ursus* and other arctoids. The mechanical significance of this arrangement is discussed below.

THE BASIOCCIPITAL REGION.—The basioccipital region in *Ailuropoda*, like other parts of the skull not directly associated with mastication, is compressed. It is somewhat shorter (about 5 per cent) anteroposteriorly than in *Ursus*, and since in addition the postglenoid process is expanded posteriorly and medially, the structures in this region (foramina, auditory bulla) are considerably crowded together. It is noteworthy that the areas of attachment of the rectus capitis and longus capitis muscles have maintained their size, partly at the expense of surrounding structures.

The **foramen ovale** (mandibular branch of trigeminus; middle meningeal artery) occupies its usual position opposite the anterointernal corner of the mandibular fossa. There is no **foramen spinosum**, since as in carnivores in general the middle meningeal artery passes through the foramen ovale; the foramen spinosum is sometimes present in *Canis* (Ellenberger and Baum, 1943). A small foramen situated dorsomedially at the mouth of the foramen ovale opens into a canal that runs medially and anteriorly through the cancellous bone of the basicranium to a point beneath the hypophyseal fossa, where it meets its mate from the opposite side. This canal apparently contained a nutrient vessel; its counterpart was found in *Ursus*, but not in other arctoids.

A single large opening, the entrance to the **canalis musculotubarius**, is situated at the anteromedial corner of the bulla. The canal is partly divided by a prominent ventral ridge into a lateral **semicanalis M. tensoris tympani** and a medial semicanalis tubae auditivae. The foramen lacerum medium, which normally lies just medial to the musculotubular canal, is usually wanting in *Ailuropoda*.[1]

Laterad of the musculotubular canal, at the medial border of the postglenoid process, is an irregular longitudinal slit, the **canalis chordae tympani** (canal of Hugier), which transmits the chorda tympani nerve. The position of this opening is the same as in *Ursus* (and arctoids in general), but in *Ailuropoda* it is somewhat deformed by the enlarged postglenoid process.

The **foramen lacerum posterior**, which in *Ailuropoda* includes the carotid foramen, is situated at the posteromedial corner of the bulla. It transmits the ninth, tenth, and eleventh cranial nerves, the internal carotid artery, and veins from the transverse and inferior petrosal sinuses. The **posterior carotid foramen**, through which the internal carotid enters the skull, is situated in the anterior part of the lacerated foramen; this is true also of the Ursidae and *Ailurus*. In other carnivores (Procyonidae, Mustelidae) the carotid foramen is removed from the lacerated foramen, lying anterior to the latter along the medial wall of the bulla. Segall (1943) found the positional relations of the posterior carotid foramen to be consistently correlated with recognized family groupings among the Arctoidea.

The **postglenoid foramen**, in the posterior wall of the postglenoid process near the external auditory meatus, connects the temporal sinus (intracranial) with the internal facial vein (extracranial). The foramen is smaller and more laterally situated than in *Ursus*.

Laterad of the posterior lacerated foramen, and bounded by the bulla anteriorly and medially, the mastoid process laterally, and the paroccipital process posteriorly, is a pit. This pit, a conspicuous element of the basicranium, is not present in man and does not seem to have been named. I propose to call it the **hyojugular fossa** (fossa hyojugularis). The **stylomastoid foramen** (facial nerve, auricular branch of vagus nerve, stylomastoid artery) lies at the anterolateral corner of the fossa; a conspicuous groove, which lodges the

facial nerve, runs laterad and ventrad from the foramen to pass between the postglenoid and mastoid processes. The **hyoid fossa**, at the bottom of which the hyoid articulates with the skull, lies in the fossa immediately behind and mesad of the stylomastoid foramen, from which it is separated by a thin wall. Farther posteriorly (sometimes on the crest connecting the paroccipital process with the bulla) is a foramen that transmits a branch of the internal jugular vein that passes to the inferior petrosal sinus.

The hyojugular fossa is almost identical in *Ursus*, except that it is deeper and more extensive posteriorly. In *Ailurus* it is widely open posteriorly, between the mastoid and paroccipital processes. The fossa tends to disappear when the bulla is greatly inflated (in procyonids, except *Nasua*), but it is present in *Canis*.

The **hypoglossal (condyloid) foramen** (hypoglossal nerve, posterior meningeal artery) lies behind and slightly mesad of the foramen lacerum posterior. In *Ursus* it is usually connected with the foramen lacerum posterior by a deep groove. A similar groove is present in *Ailurus* but not in other arctoids.

The **mastoid process** functions in the insertion of the lateral flexors of the head on its posterior surface, and in the origin of the digastric muscle on its medial surface. The process closely resembles the corresponding structure in *Ursus* but projects much farther ventrally than in the latter. It is a powerful tongue-like projection, directed ventrally and anteriorly, extending far below the auditory meatus. The process is strikingly similar in *Procyon* but is much smaller in other procyonids. It is also small in *Ailurus* and *Canis*.

The **paroccipital process**, which functions in the origin of the digastric muscle, is much smaller than the mastoid. As in *Ursus*, it is a peg-like projection connected by prominent ridges with the mastoid process laterally and the bulla anteromedially. In forms with inflated bullae (e.g., *Procyon*, *Canis*) the bulla rests against the anterior face of the paroccipital process.

The bulla is described in connection with the auditory region (p. 318).

### (4) *Posterior View*

In posterior view (fig. 19) the outline of the skull has the form of a smooth arch; the constriction above the mastoid process seen in *Ursus* and other arctoids is not evident. To this extent the nuchal area is increased in *Ailuropoda*. The posterior surface of the skull serves for the insertion of the elevators and lateral flexors of the head and bears the occipital condyles.

---

[1] In carnivores the foramen lacerum medium (anterior of some authors) transmits chiefly a venous communication between the pharyngeal veins extracranially and the cavernous sinus intracranially. It also carries an anastomotic twig between the ascending pharyngeal artery (extracranial) and the internal carotid; this anastomotic artery is of considerable size in the cats, but in the pandas, bears, and procyonids it is minute or absent. In *Ursus* the foramen lacerum medium is larger than the canalis musculotubarius, and two openings, the outlet of the carotid canal posteriorly and the entrance to the cavernous sinus anteriorly, are visible within it.

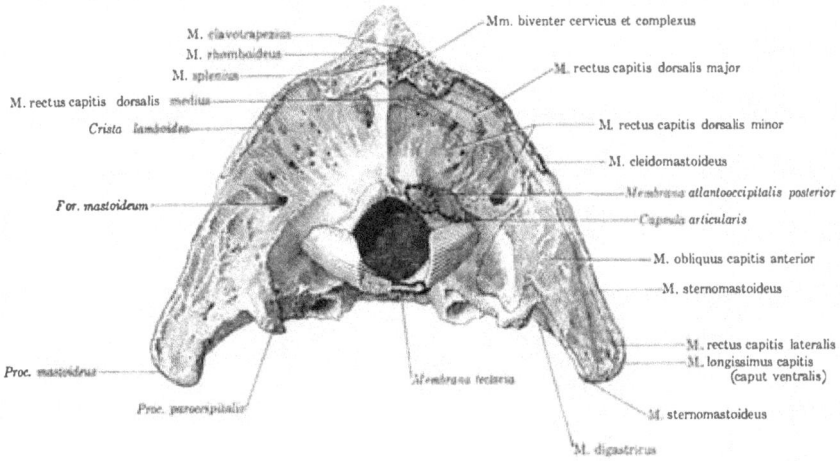

FIG. 19. Skull of *Ailuropoda* seen from rear.

M. clavotrapezius
M. rhomboideus
M. splenius
M. rectus capitis dorsalis medius
Crista lamboidea
For. mastoideum
Proc. mastoideus
Proc. paroccipitalis
Membrana tectoria
Mm. biventer cervicus et complexus
M. rectus capitis dorsalis major
M. rectus capitis dorsalis minor
M. cleidomastoideus
Membrana atlantooccipitalis posterior
Capsula articularis
M. obliquus capitis anterior
M. sternomastoideus
M. rectus capitis lateralis
M. longissimus capitis (caput ventralis)
M. sternomastoideus
M. digastricus

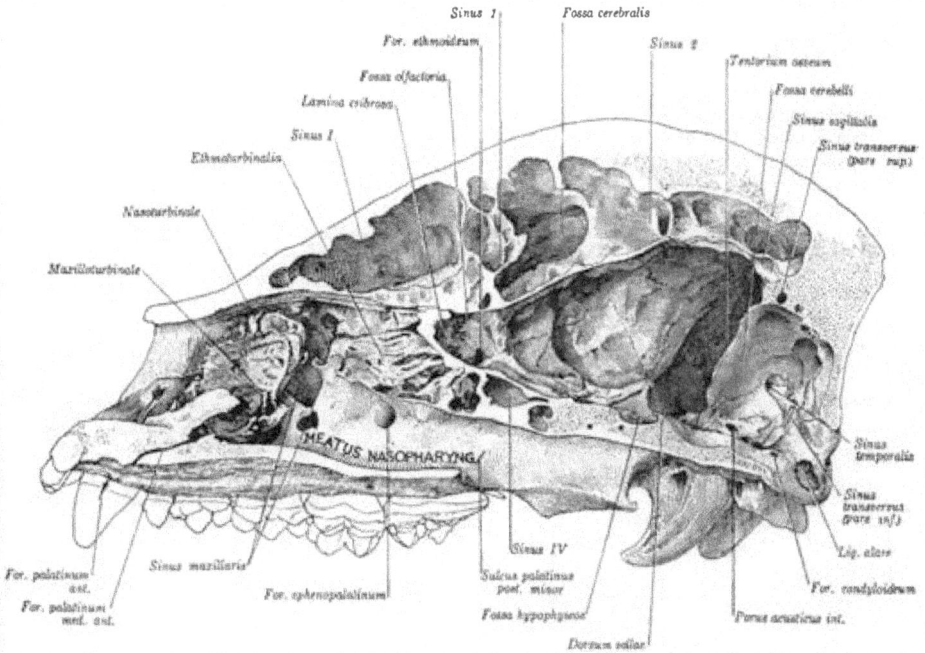

FIG. 20. Sagittal section of skull of *Ailuropoda* slightly to left of midline.

Sinus 1
Fossa cerebralis
For. ethmoideum
Sinus 2
Fossa olfactoria
Tentorium osseum
Lamina cribrosa
Fossa cerebelli
Sinus I
Sinus sagittalis
Ethmoturbinalis
Sinus transversus (pars sup.)
Nasoturbinale
Maxilloturbinale
HEATUS NASOPHARYNG.
Sinus temporalis
Sinus transversus (pars inf.)
For. palatinum ant.
Sinus maxillaris
For. palatinum med. ant.
For. sphenopalatinum
Sinus IV
Sulcus palatinus post. minor
Fossa hypophyseos
Dorsum sellae
Lig. alare
For. condyloideum
Porus acusticus int.

53

In *Ailuropoda* the peripheral area of muscular attachment is sharply set off from the central condylar area by a ridge that runs dorsad from the medial border of the paroccipital process and then curves mesad above the condyle. This ridge marks the attachment of the atlanto-occipital articular membrane; it is not so well marked in other arctoids. A median nuchal line, prominent in most arctoids, runs vertically from the foramen magnum to the junction of the lambdoidal and sagittal crests, separating the nuchal area into right and left halves.

The area of muscular attachment is rugose, and is punctured with numerous nutrient foramina. A conspicuous scar near the dorsal midline, seen in all except the smallest arctoids, marks the insertion of the biventer cervicis and complexus muscles. The **mastoid foramen** (meningeal branch of posterior auricular artery; vein from transverse sinus) lies directly above the paroccipital process.

The condylar area is relatively smooth, and the condyloid fossae present an excavated appearance because of the posterior position of the paroccipital and mastoid processes. The **occipital condyles** are more obliquely placed than in *Ursus*, their long axis forming an angle of about 45° with the vertical compared with about 25° in *Ursus*. The condylar area is interrupted at the ventral border of the foramen magnum, as it is in *Ailurus*. This condition is usual, but not invariable, in *Ursus*. In procyonids and canids the condylar area is always carried across as a narrow isthmus below the foramen magnum. In *Ailuropoda* the form of the **foramen magnum** varies from a transverse oval to almost square.

### (5) *Internal View*

A sagittal section through the skull of *Ailuropoda* (fig. 20) reveals the nasal cavity, the sinuses, and the cranial cavity.

NASAL CAVITY.—The nasal cavity is high, narrow, and elongate in the arctoid Carnivora. This is especially evident in the Ursidae. In *Ailuropoda* the nasal cavity is slightly higher (index .14) than in *Ursus* (index .10–.12), and slightly shorter (index .41 vs. .45–.51). In *Ailurus* the relative height is the same as in *Ailuropoda*, but the cavity is shorter (index .37).

The structures of chief interest in the nasal cavity are the turbinates, consisting of three elements: the maxilloturbinals, the nasoturbinals, and the ethmoturbinals. These complex structures were described in detail for various Carnivora by Paulli (1900), and again by Anthony and Iliesco (1926). In some respects, particularly with reference to the ethmoturbinals, it is difficult to reconcile these

two studies. Paulli worked chiefly from frontal sections of the skull, made immediately anterior to the cribriform plate, while Anthony and Iliesco apparently worked from sagittal sections of the skull.

The **maxilloturbinal** (fig. 20) is situated in the anterior part of the nasal cavity, which it nearly fills. It is kidney-shaped, much higher (45 mm.) than long (30 mm.), and its vertical axis is inclined posteriorly at an angle of 20°. It lies entirely anterior to the ethmoturbinals. The maxilloturbinal is attached to the lateral wall of the nasal cavity by a single long basal lamella, which runs anteroposteriorly in a slightly sinuous line about parallel to the long axis of the skull. The line of attachment extends on the premaxilla and maxilla from near the anterior nasal aperture to a point several millimeters caudad of the anterior border of the maxillary sinus. The basal lamella promptly breaks up into an extremely complex mass of ramifying branches that make up the body of the maxilloturbinal.

In the Ursidae, according to Anthony and Iliesco, the maxilloturbinal is characterized by its great dorsoventral diameter and its extremely rich ramification; *Ailuropoda* exceeds *Ursus* in both. According to these authors the Mustelidae resemble the bears in the height of the maxilloturbinal and its degree of ramification, although it may be added that in these the upper ethmoturbinals overhang the maxilloturbinal. In the Canidae and Procyonidae this element is much longer than high, is less complex, and is overhung by the upper ethmoturbinals. In *Ailurus* it is high (height/length ratio 1) as in *Ailuropoda* and the Ursidae but is overhung by the ethmoturbinals; its lamina of origin differs from that of all other arctoids in curving ventrad at a right angle to the axis of the skull, reaching the floor of the nasal cavity at the level of PM[2].

The **nasoturbinal** in *Ailuropoda* (fig. 20) is, as in other arctoids, an elongate structure situated in the dorsal part of the nasal cavity. It arises from the upper part of the anterior face of the cribriform plate and extends forward, above the maxilloturbinal, to within a few millimeters of the anterior nasal aperture.

The **ethmoturbinal** (figs. 20, 21) is very similar to that of *Ursus*. As in other carnivores it is composed of a medial series of plate-like outgrowths (endoturbinals, internal ethmoturbinals) from the anterior face of the cribriform plate, and a similar more lateral series (ectoturbinals, external ethmoturbinals), that together fill the posterior part of the nasal cavity. The whole structure constitutes the ethmoidal labyrinth. The rela-

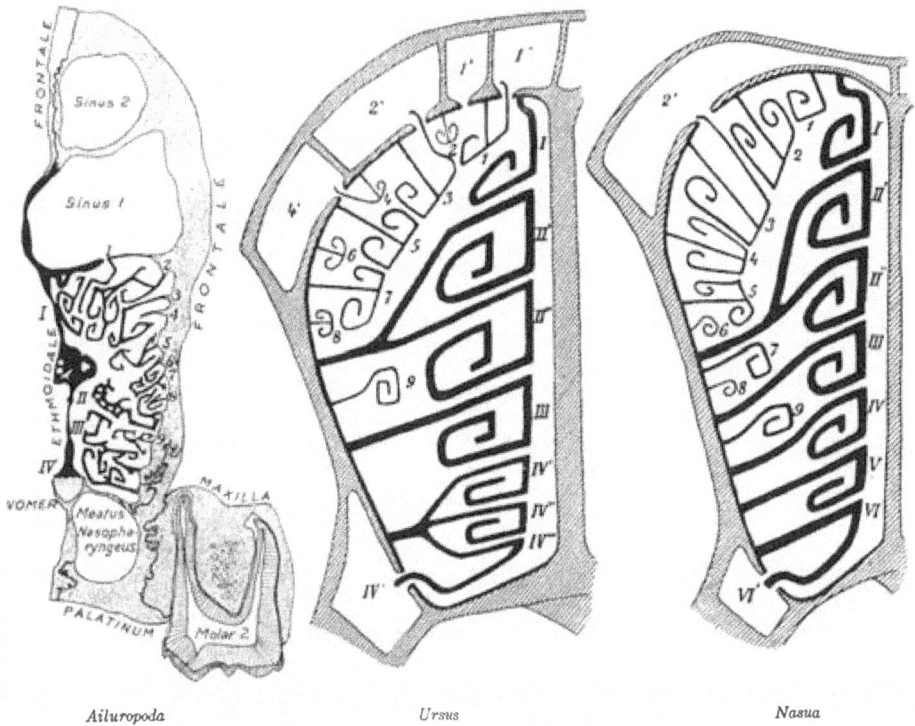

*Ailuropoda*          *Ursus*          *Nasua*

FIG. 21. Frontal section through turbinates, just anterior to cribriform plate. Roman numerals refer to endoturbinals, Arabic numerals to ectoturbinals. (Diagrams for *Ursus* and *Nasua* from Paulli.)

tions of these elements are best seen on a frontal section made immediately in front of the cribriform plate (fig. 21).

The endoturbinals number four, the typical number for all Carnivora except the Procyonidae. In the latter, according to Paulli, the fourth endoturbinal has split into three to produce a total of six. It is impossible to decide, on the basis of the section available to me, how many olfactory scrolls the endoturbinals divide into in *Ailuropoda*. It is apparent, however, that the complexity is greater than in the Ursidae, in which there are seven.

The ectoturbinals number nine, as in the Ursidae and Procyonidae. Except for *Meles*, in which there are 10 (Paulli), this is the largest number known for any carnivore. *Ailuropoda* further resembles the Ursidae and differs from the Procyonidae in having the first eight ectoturbinals situated between endoturbinals I and II, and in having the ectoturbinals arranged in a median and an external series, a long one alternating with a short one to produce the two series.

Anthony and Iliesco state that there are seven or eight endoturbinals and that "on peut estimer que les Ours possèdent plus de 40 ethmoturbinaux externes." These figures are obviously based on a quite different, and I believe less careful, interpretation than Paulli's.

PARANASAL SINUSES.—The paranasal sinuses are evaginations of the nasal cavity that invade and pneumatize the surrounding bones of the skull, remaining in communication with the nasal cavity through the relatively narrow ostia. The cavities lying on either side of the dorsal midline are separated by a vertical median septum. The occurrence, extent, and relations of the individual sinus cavities vary greatly among mammals, often even among individuals, and hence topography is an unsafe guide to homologies. The cavity in the frontal bone of many mammals, for example, is not always homologous, and therefore cannot be indiscriminately referred to as a "frontal sinus." Paulli found that the relations of the ostia to the ethmoidal elements are constant, as would be expected from the ontogenetic history, and he there-fore based his homologies on these. He rejected the descriptive terminology of human anatomy as unusable in comparative studies, and substituted a system of numbers for all except the maxillary sinus. His terminology has been followed here.

The dorsal sinuses are enormous in *Ailuropoda* (fig. 20), far exceeding those of any other carnivore. At the dorsal midline they separate the relatively thin true roof (inner lamina) of the cranial cavity from a much heavier false roof (outer lamina) situated above it. Intrusion of the sinuses into the supracranial area greatly increases the area of the temporal fossa.

The relations of the ostia to the ethmoidal elements cannot be determined without cutting the latter away. The single bisected skull available to me could not be mutilated in this way, but similarity between the sinuses of *Ailuropoda* and *Ursus* is so close that there can be no doubt as to nomenclature. As in *Ursus*, there is no communication between the sinuses.

**Sinus I**, which occupies the frontal region, is much longer, higher, and wider than in *Ursus*. It is responsible for the characteristic convex forehead of the giant panda. The posterior wall of the cavity lies at the level of the postorbital process, as in *Ursus*, and from here the sinus extends forward into the base of the nasals. Its lateral wall is formed by the outer wall of the skull. The large oval ostium in the floor of the cavity opens into the nasal cavity just anterior to the first endoturbinal. None of the ectoturbinals extends into this cavity. In *Ursus* the corresponding cavity is narrower, the maxillary sinus lying laterad of it, and a leaf of the first ectoturbinal projects through the ostium into the cavity.

**Sinus 1** is a small cavity, measuring only about 15 mm. in length by 20 mm. in height, lying above the olfactory fossa some distance behind sinus I. It is surrounded by sinus 2 on all sides except ventrally. The small round ostium is situated in the floor. In the skull that was dissected this cavity is asymmetrical; it was present on the right side only.

**Sinus 2** is by far the largest of the sinuses. It begins at the level of the postorbital process and extends back through the frontal and parietal bones nearly to the occiput. It is very irregular, with numerous out-pocketings and partial septa. The long slit-like ostium lies in the extreme anterior part of the cavity, and as in *Ursus* a leaf of one of the ectoturbinals projects through the ostium into the sinus.

**Sinus IV** (sphenoidal sinus of authors) is a large, irregular cavity in the presphenoid. The ostium is situated in its anterior wall, and as in *Ursus* the

posterior end of the last ectoturbinal projects through the ostium into the cavity.

The **maxillary sinus** lies almost entirely in the maxillary root of the zygomatic arch, a condition that is unique among carnivores. It is situated farther laterad than in *Ursus* and other arctoids. This hollowing out of the zygomatic root makes possible a considerable increase in bulk without adding appreciably to its weight. The sinus is an irregular cavity lying directly above the posterior end of the fourth premolar, the first molar, and the anterior end of the second molar. It opens into the nasal cavity, immediately behind and below the crest of the maxilloturbinal, by a much smaller ostium than in *Ursus*.

Thus there are five pairs of pneumatic cavities in the skull of the giant panda. Although these greatly exceed the corresponding cavities of *Ursus* in size, the arrangement and relations are very similar. *Ursus* has an additional small cavity in the roof of the skull; in *Ailuropoda* the area it occupies has been taken over by sinus 2, and this enormous sinus has almost absorbed sinus 1.

In other arctoids pneumatization of the skull is much less extensive in number of sinuses and in the extent of the individual sinuses. In the Mustelidae only the maxillary sinus is present, but other arctoids also exhibit at least some pneumatization in the frontal region. *Ailurus* has the same cavities as *Ailuropoda*, but sinus 2 is much less extensive, extending back only to the level of the optic foramen.

Paulli generalized that the extent of pneumaticity is dependent on the size of the skull, and pointed out that this is borne out in large vs. small breeds of dogs. Another over-riding factor obviously has operated in the pandas. In *Ailurus* the absolute size of the skull compares with that of *Procyon*, but the sinuses are more extensive. In *Ailuropoda* the skull is about a third smaller than that of *Ursus arctos*, but the dorsal and lateral sinuses are much larger. The secondary factor in pandas is a mechanical one.

It is well known that the sinuses develop as evaginations of the walls of the nasal cavity, and that with increasing age these out-pocketings gradually invade the surrounding bone. The process is called "pneumatic osteolysis," but the nature of pneumatic osteolysis is unknown. In Su Lin (age 16± months, all permanent teeth in place) sinus 2 had not yet invaded the parietal; it terminated at about the fronto-parietal suture. In this animal, sinus I in the nasofrontal region also falls short, by about 20 mm., of its adult anterior extension. The vertical height of both these cavities, on the other hand, is as great as in the adult.

Thus considerable peripheral growth takes place in the larger sinuses after essentially adult skull size has been attained.

CRANIAL CAVITY.—The cranial cavity (fig. 20) is a mold of the brain, and in the panda it differs far less from the typical arctoid condition than do other parts of the skull. The cavity is divided into the usual three fossae: olfactory, cerebral, and cerebellar (anterior, middle, and posterior of human anatomy).

The olfactory fossa is much reduced in diameter as compared with that of *Ursus*, but is otherwise very similar. It houses the olfactory bulbs. The floor of this fossa is on a higher level than the remaining cranial floor. In the midline of the floor a prominent ridge, the crista galli of human anatomy, extends nearly the entire length of the fossa. The cribriform plate, forming the anterior wall, is perforated by numerous foramina for filaments of the olfactory nerve. These foramina are larger and more numerous at the periphery of the plate. In the lateral wall of the fossa is a larger opening, the ethmoidal foramen.

The cerebral fossa, much the largest of the cranial fossae, houses the cerebrum. As in the bears, a vertical ridge (the site of the sylvian fissure of the brain) separates a larger anterior fronto-parietal region from a smaller posterior temporal-occipital region. This ridge is less obvious in the smaller arctoids. The walls of the fossa bear numerous ridges and furrows that conform to the gyri and sulci of the cerebral cortex of the brain. A conspicuous groove immediately in front of the sylvian ridge lodges the middle meningeal artery; a smaller groove, which houses a branch of this artery, lies in the posterior region of the fossa (fig. 22). In *Ursus* and other arctoids the groove for the middle meningeal artery lies in the posterior region of the fossa.

The cerebellar fossa is largely separated from the cerebral fossa by the tentorium osseum, which forms most of its anterior wall. The tentorium is exceptionally well developed in the bears and pandas. The cerebellar fossa communicates with the cerebral fossa via the tentorial notch, a large opening that in *Ailuropoda* is much higher than wide; in *Ursus* it is more nearly square. The tentorium slopes backward at an angle of only about 10° in *Ailuropoda*, while in *Ursus* this angle is about 25°. The slope is much greater in other arctoids (about 45°).

The walls of the cerebellar fossa are grooved and perforated by various venous sinuses (see p. 281); otherwise they conform to the shape of the cerebellum. The medial face of the petrosal is visible in the wall of this fossa. As in *Ursus* and *Ailurus*, the tentorium is in contact with the petrosal along the entire petrosal crest, and covers the part of the petrosal anterior to this line. In *Canis* and the procyonids, in which the tentorium is not so well developed, an anterior face of the petrosal is also exposed in the cerebral fossa. The enlarged tentorium in the bears and pandas has also crowded out the trigeminal foramen—the large opening in the petrosal near the apex that is so conspicuous in canids and procyonids. In the ursids the root of the trigeminal nerve passes over, instead of through, the apex to enter the trigeminal fossa. In *Ailuropoda* the most conspicuous feature on the medial face of the petrosal is the internal acoustic opening, leading into the internal acoustic meatus. Immediately behind this opening is a smaller foramen, the aquaeductus vestibuli, overhung by a prominent scale of bone. Just above and behind the acoustic opening is a bulge in the surface of the petrosal, the eminentia arcuata, caused by the superior semicircular canal. In all other arctoids examined (except *Procyon*) there is a deep pit, larger than the acoustic meatus and situated directly above it, that houses the petrosal lobule or "appendicular lobe" of the cerebellum; this pit is wanting in *Ailuropoda* and *Procyon*. The inferior border of the petrosal is grooved for the inferior petrosal sinus, and the superior angle is crossed by the groove for the transverse sinus.

The floor of the cerebral and cerebellar fossae exhibits several features of interest (fig. 22). The dorsum sellae marks the boundary between the cerebral and cerebellar spaces. Most anteriorly, near the middle of the cerebral fossa, is the opening for the optic nerve. It leads into a canal, nearly 25 mm. long, that opens in the orbit as the optic foramen. This canal is of comparable length in *Ursus* but is short in other arctoids. Behind the optic opening is a prominent sulcus for the optic chiasma, of which the canal itself is a continuation. The sella turcica lies in the midline at the posterior end of the cerebral fossa. Of the components of the sella, the tuberculum sellae is wanting anteriorly, but the anterior clinoid processes at the anterior corners are well developed; these processes, to which the dura is attached, are often wanting in arctoids. The posterior clinoid processes are plate-like lateral extensions of the dorsum sellae, overhanging the cavernous sinuses laterally. These processes, to which the dura also attaches, are well developed in all arctoids examined except *Canis*, where they are wanting. The hypophyseal fossa is a well-bounded pit in all arctoids except *Canis*, in which there is no anterior boundary.

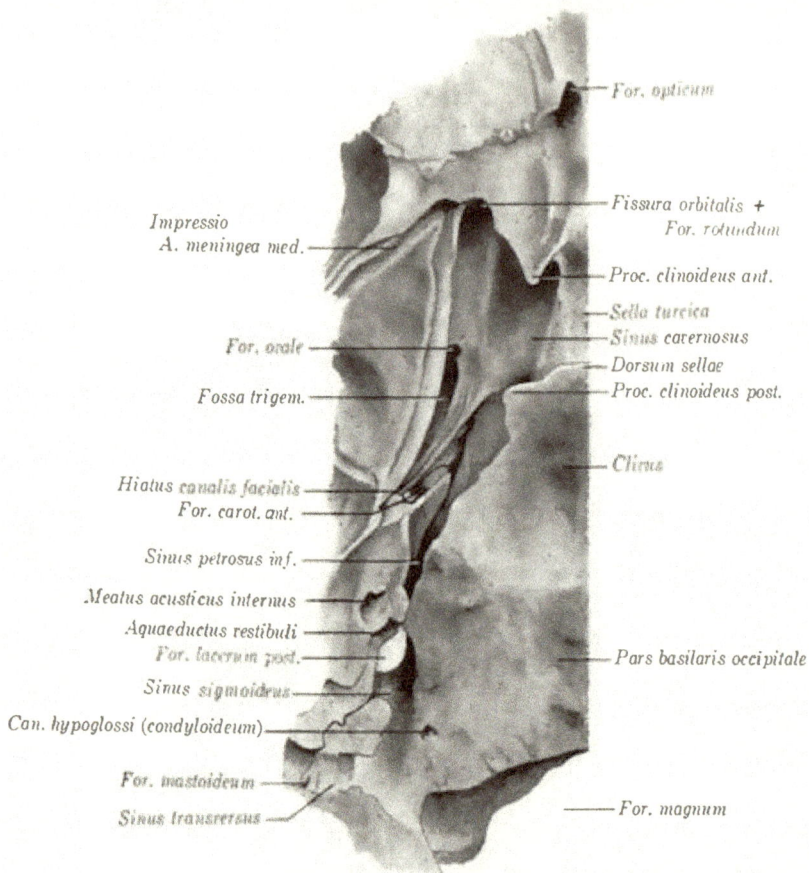

FIG. 22.  Left half of basicranium of *Ailuropoda*, internal view.

On either side of the sella turcica is a wide longitudinal sulcus, extending from the orbital fissure anteriorly to the petrosal bone posteriorly, in which the **cavernous sinus** lies. Anteriorly the sulcus opens into the orbit through the large opening formed by the combined orbital fissure and foramen rotundum; fusion of these two foramina is peculiar to *Ailuropoda*. A ridge on the floor of the sulcus marks the boundary between the orbital fissure (medial) and foramen rotundum (lateral) of other arctoids. In the posterior part of the sulcus, just in front of the apex of the petrosal, is a deep narrow niche, the **trigeminal fossa**, which lodges the semilunar ganglion of the trigeminal nerve. The foramen ovale (third and fourth branches of trigeminus) opens into the floor of the niche anteriorly; in *Ursus*, in which the trigeminal fossa

extends farther anteriorly, both the foramen rotundum (second branch of trigeminus) and the foramen ovale open directly into it. A small round opening at the posterior end of the trigeminal fossa is the outlet of the **hiatus canalis facialis,** through which the great superficial and deep petrosal nerves enter the cranial cavity. Immediately above this is a smaller opening (more conspicuous in *Ursus*), the **foramen petrosum superior,** the anterior outlet of the superior petrosal sinus.

The **anterior carotid foramen** lies at the anterior corner of the petrosal, directed anteriorly and medially. In *Ailuropoda*, in which there is no foramen lacerum medium, the internal carotid artery passes from the carotid canal directly into the cavernous sinus, and the anterior carotid foramen is thus intracranial. In *Ursus*, the artery, after leaving the carotid canal, passes ventrad into the foramen lacerum medium, where it immediately doubles back upon itself to pass nearly ver-

sinus runs nearly vertically, connecting the sagittal sinus above with the vertebral vein below. It is sharply divided into inferior and superior parts. The inferior section, much larger in caliber, lies

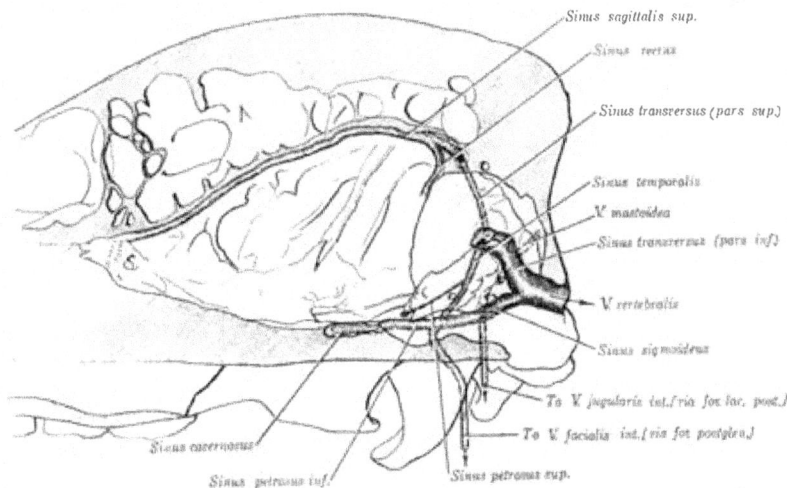

FIG. 23. Sinuses and diploic veins. Right half of skull of *Ailuropoda*, internal view (semi-diagrammatic).

tically into the cavernous sinus. Thus in *Ursus* the foramen in the floor of the cavernous sinus is the internal opening of the foramen lacerum medium, and the anterior carotid foramen is visible only externally within the foramen lacerum medium. The situation in *Ailurus* and *Procyon* is similar to that in *Ursus*. Obliteration of the foramen lacerum medium and of the associated flexure in the internal carotid artery in *Ailuropoda* is undoubtedly correlated with the general crowding of non-masticatory structures in this region and is therefore without functional or taxonomic significance. *Canis*, as usual, is quite different from either the Ursidae or Procyonidae.

The inferior petrosal sinus lies just mesad of the petrosal, largely roofed over by a lateral wing of the clivus. The sinus is continuous anteriorly with the cavernous sinus and posteriorly with the sigmoid sinus, which name it assumes at the foramen lacerum posterior, at the posterior corner of the petrosal. The superior petrosal sinus is reduced to thread-like caliber in *Ailuropoda* and *Ursus* as a result of the great development of the tentorium. It opens into the trigeminal fossa via the superior petrosal foramen, at the apex of the petrosal. From here the sinus arches posteriorly around the petrosal, enclosed in the temporal bone, and enters the temporal sinus. The transverse

in an open groove behind the petrosal, the upper part of the groove crossing the petrosal. The mastoid foramen and several diploic veins open into this part of the sinus. At the dorsal border of the petrosal the sinus gives off the large temporal sinus, which descends as a closed canal to open extracranially via the postglenoid foramen. The superior section of the transverse sinus continues dorsad as a closed canal, much reduced in caliber, to open into the sagittal sinus at the dorsal midline. The sagittal sinus is visible for a variable distance as a shallow groove along the midline of the roof of the cerebral fossa. The short sigmoid sinus runs posteriorly from the foramen lacerum posterior, meeting the transverse sinus at a right angle about 5 mm. behind the posterior border of the petrosal. Beyond the confluence of the inferior petrosal and transverse sinuses a groove, which houses the vertebral vein, continues caudad through the lateral corner of the foramen magnum. The vertebral vein lies in a similar groove in *Ursus*, while in all other arctoids examined (including *Ailurus*) the groove is roofed over to form a canal.

From the dorum sellae the floor of the basicranium slopes backward and downward as the clivus. This region is basin-shaped to conform to the shape of the pons, and is separated by a transverse ridge from the basilar portion of the

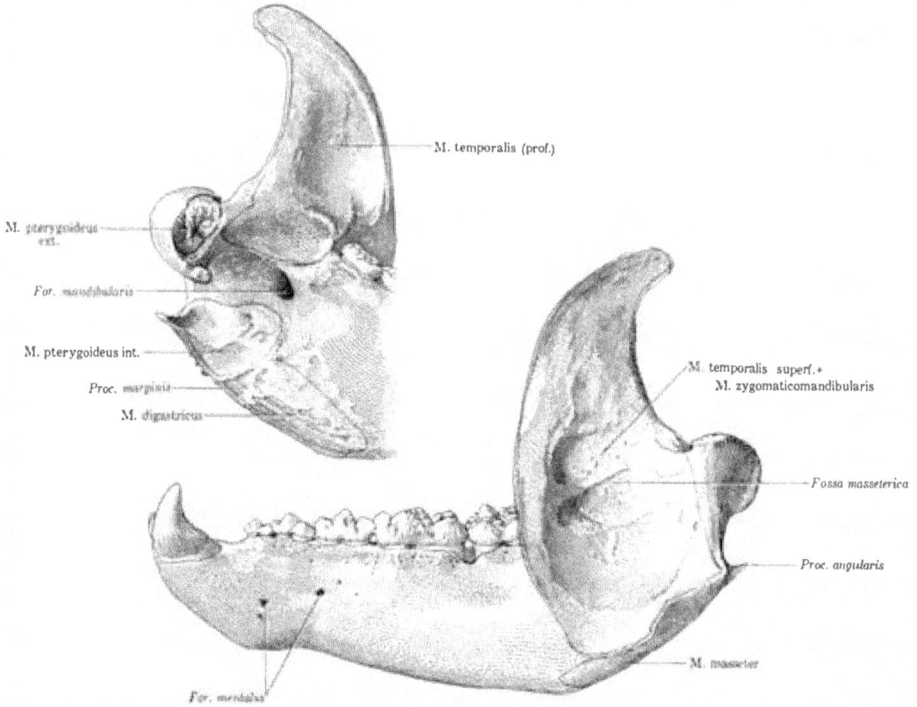

FIG. 24. Left mandible of *Ailuropoda:* external surface lower right, internal surface upper left.

basioccipital bone lying behind it, which supports the medulla. The whole plate-like floor of the basicranium lying behind the dorsum sellae is shorter and wider in *Ailuropoda* than in *Ursus*. The **hypoglossal (condyloid) foramen** pierces the floor of the basilar portion in a lateral and slightly anterior direction, just anterior to the foramen magnum.

MANDIBLE.—The mandible of *Ailuropoda* is notable for its extreme density. Its weight is more than twice that of the mandible of a much larger bear. The two halves of the mandible are firmly fused at the symphysis, with no trace of a suture, in all adults examined. This is contrary to the condition in *Ursus* and other arctoids. Fusion is nearly complete in a young adult *Ailuropoda*, in which most skull sutures are still open. The length of the symphysis is also remarkable. It is relatively nearly as long as in *Ursus*, and extends to the anterior border of the first molar instead of the third premolar. In *Ailurus*, by contrast, the symphysis is short (barely reaching the first premolar), and the two halves of the mandible do not fuse.

The **body** of the mandible, viewed from the side, tapers from the ramus forward, whereas in *Ursus* (but not in other arctoids) the height of the body is quite uniform. Among several mandibles of *Ailuropoda* the inferior border is curved in varying degrees, reaching its nadir below the second molar; in one mandible this border is nearly as straight as in *Ursus*. The body is less high anteriorly than in *Ursus*, and higher posteriorly, and this is probably correlated with the relatively feebly developed canines and the large molars. The upper or alveolar border of the body lies about 30 mm. below the level of the articular condyle, whereas in *Ursus* these are at very nearly the same level (fig. 25). There are typically two **mental foramina**, as in arctoids in general. These are subequal in size. The more anterior foramen is often broken up into several smaller foramina.

Throughout its length the body is more than twice as thick as in *Ursus*, and viewed from below the body arches abruptly laterad at the posterior end of the symphysis, giving a Y-shape to the ventral outline of the jaw.

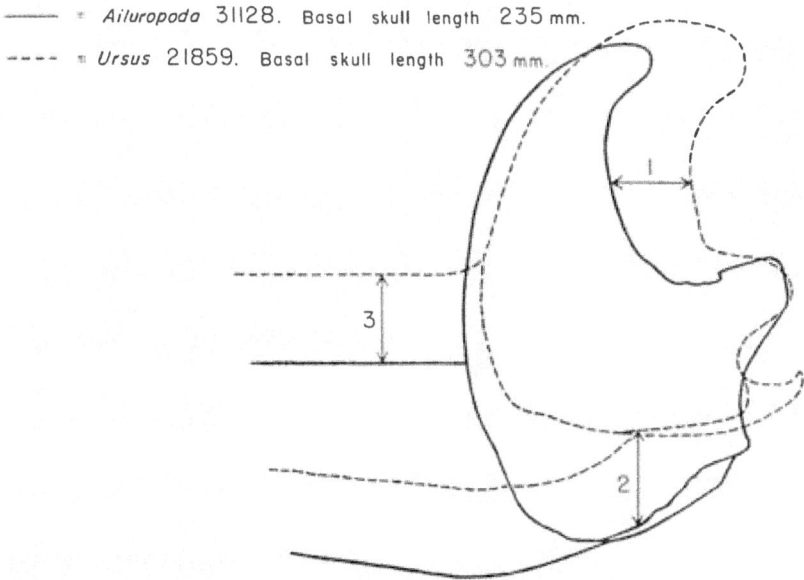

——— = *Ailuropoda* 31128. Basal skull length 235 mm.

– – – – = *Ursus* 21859. Basal skull length 303 mm.

FIG. 25. Outlines of posterior ends of mandible of *Ailuropoda* (solid line) and *Ursus horribilis* (broken line) superimposed. Note (1) the excavation of the posterior border of the coronoid process, (2) the much deeper masseteric fossa, and (3) the depressed occlusal plane in *Ailuropoda*.

The **ramus**, which is that part of the mandible lying posterolaterad of the last molar, differs from that of *Ursus* in several important respects. Besides bearing the mandibular condyle, the ramus functions chiefly for the insertion of the muscles of mastication. The areas where these muscles attach are large, well marked, and rugose in *Ailuropoda*.

The **masseteric fossa**, in which the zygomaticomandibular muscle inserts, is larger than in *Ursus* in both vertical and transverse diameters. The vertical diameter in particular has been increased relative to *Ursus* (and other arctoids) by extension ventrad. It is also deeper, for the edges have been built out. The surface of the fossa is extremely rugose, and is marked by several prominent transverse ridges (cristae massetericae) for the attachment of tendinous sheets in the muscle. The **coronoid process**, into which the masseteric fossa grades imperceptibly, functions in the insertion of the temporal muscle on both its lateral and medial surfaces. This process is similar to that of *Ursus*, except that its posterior border is eroded away, giving it a scimitar-like form and greatly reducing the area available for temporal insertion (fig. 25). The **angular process** is a small but conspicuous prominence on the posteromedial

border of the ramus, below the condyle. It projects medially and posteriorly, instead of posteriorly as in other arctoids. This process characteristically provides insertion for part of the masseter on its outer surface and part of the internal pterygoid on its inner surface; none of the masseter fibers reach it in *Ailuropoda*. In *Ursus* and other arctoids (including *Ailurus*) the angular process is large and tongue-like, with well-marked muscle scars for both the masseter and the internal pterygoid. In *Ursus* a conspicuous **marginal process** (Toldt's terminology) on the inferior border of the ramus, anterior to the angular process, provides the main insertion for the digastric muscle. This process is wanting in other arctoids. In *Ailuropoda* the insertion of the digastric is more diffuse than in *Ursus*, and the marginal process, while present, is less clearly marked and is situated on the medial surface of the mandible immediately in front of the internal pterygoid scar.

Hypertrophy of the jaw-closing muscles in the giant panda is reflected in the relatively larger areas of attachment on the skull. The total area of insertion of the masseter and temporal on the lateral surface of the mandible was calculated roughly by plotting on millimeter paper. In *Ailuropoda* (basal skull length 252 mm.) this area amounted to 5368 mm.[2], while in a much larger

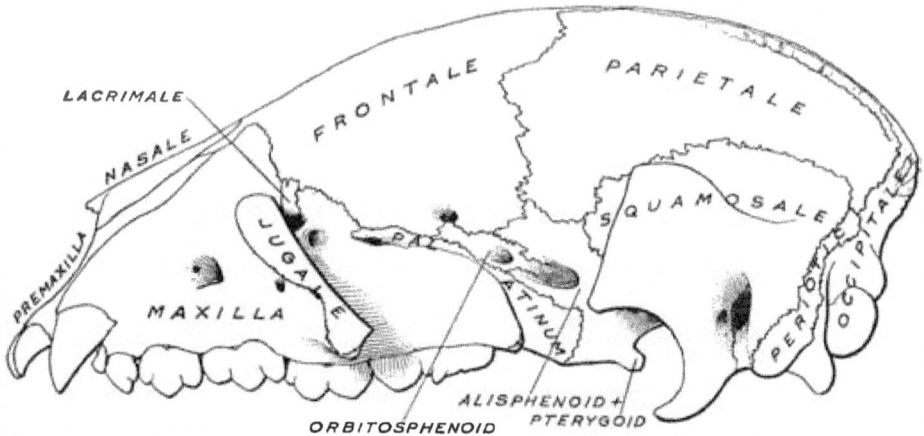

FIG. 26. Lateral view of juvenile skull of *Ailuropoda* (USNM 259076), showing sutures.

*Ursus horribilis* (basal skull length 303 mm.) it was only 4774 mm.[2]

The medial surface of the ramus exhibits conspicuous scars marking the attachment of several muscles. A rugose area occupying most of the medial surface of the coronoid process marks the insertion of the deep layer of the temporal muscle. The anterior border of this area sweeps back behind the last molar, leaving a triangular space (about one-fourth of the total medial coronoid surface) free of muscle attachment. The ventral border of the temporal area is a prominent horizontal crest at the level of the alveolar border, extending back immediately above the mandibular foramen; this is the level to which the temporal insertion extends in other arctoids. Immediately behind this crest, on the dorsal surface of the condyle, is the extraordinarily conspicuous, pock-like pterygoid depression that marks the insertion of the external pterygoid muscle. A much larger scar, below the condyle and extending back onto the angular process, marks the insertion of the internal pterygoid. A triangular rugose area in front of this, beginning posteriorly at the marginal process, marks the insertion of the digastric. The mandibular foramen, for the inferior alveolar vessels and nerve, is circular instead of oval in cross section. It lies immediately above the marginal process.

The condyloid process has the transverse semicylindrical form characteristic of the Carnivora, but in *Ailuropoda* this region is an exaggeration of the usual arctoid condition. The neck supporting the capitulum is short, flattened, and twisted through 90°—the typical carnivore arrangement.

As a result, the medial half of the capitulum is buttressed anteriorly but unsupported below, while the lateral half is buttressed below but unsupported anteriorly. In all arctoids the articular surface tends to conform to this support pattern, the medial half facing posteriorly and the lateral half more or less dorsally. In *Ailuropoda* this tendency reaches full expression, and the articular surface is a spiral track rotated through more than 90°, "like a riband wound obliquely on a cylinder," as Lydekker stated. To some extent at least, this spiral form is correlated with the large size and dorsal position of the pterygoid depression, which in *Ailuropoda* occupies a part of the area of the articular surface of other carnivores.

The width of the capitulum much exceeds that of any other carnivore. The index *basal skull length/width capitulum* is .27 to .31 for *Ailuropoda*, while for *Ursus* it is only .15 to .17. *Ailurus* is intermediate, with an index of .22 to .23, while all other carnivores examined were below .18 except an old male zoo specimen of *Tremarctos ornatus*, in which it was .21. The long axis of the capitulum is oriented at nearly a right angle to the axis of the skull in both horizontal and vertical planes. As in carnivores in general, however, the medial end of the axis is tilted slightly caudad and ventrad of 90°.

B. CRANIAL SUTURES AND BONES OF THE SKULL

As was mentioned above, the sutures disappear early in *Ailuropoda*, and nearly all are completely obliterated on fully adult skulls. The following account of the bones of the skull is based on a young female skull, with a basal length of 213 mm.,

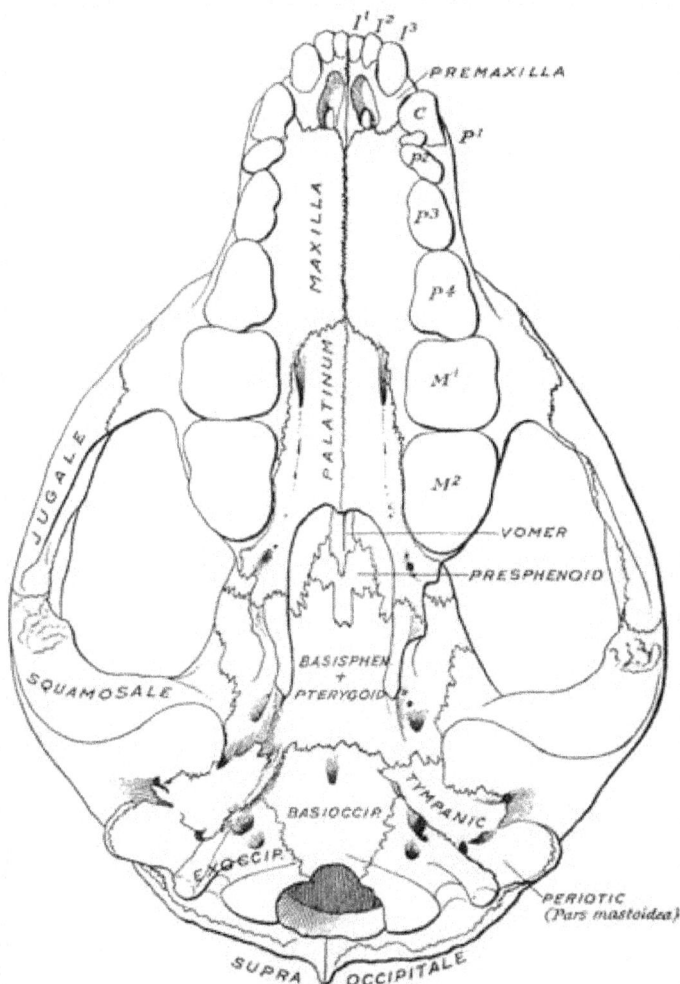

FIG. 27. Ventral view of juvenile skull of *Ailuropoda* (USNM 259076), showing sutures.

on which all but a few of the sutures are still open (figs. 26, 27). This skull is intact, so that only surface features could be examined.

For the most part, the relations of the bones differ so little from those of *Ursus* that there is no point in a detailed description. The exact positions of the sutures are shown in the accompanying drawings.

The **premaxilla** is essentially similar to that of *Ursus*.

The **maxilla** is modified to accommodate the enlarged cheek teeth. The posterior part of the

bone forms an enormous maxillary tuberosity that supports the second molar. The tuberosity carries the maxilla back to the level of the optic foramen, whereas in *Ursus* it extends only to the pterygopalatine foramen. In the juvenile skull this posterior extension of the maxilla has a remarkably plastic appearance, as if the bone had flowed back over the vertical plate of the palatine, squeezing the pterygopalatine and sphenopalatine foramina upward against the inferior orbital crest. A section through this region (fig. 21) shows that the maxilla lies outside the palatine—that the latter is not displaced backward.

As in *Ursus*, at the anteromedial corner of the orbit the maxilla is wedged in between the lacrimal and jugal, forming a part of the anterior, all the lateral, and a part of the medial boundaries of the lacrimal fossa.

The anterior zygomatic root contains a lateral extension of the maxillary sinus, not seen in any other carnivore.

The nasals, as in *Ursus*, are short and their lateral borders are not prolonged forward as in other arctoids.

The lacrimal closely resembles the corresponding bone in *Ursus*, which Gregory characterized as "much reduced, sometimes almost vestigial." It is a minute plate, about 5 mm. wide and 12 mm. high, withdrawn entirely from the anterior rim of the orbit, and forming only a small part of the medial surface of the lacrimal fossa. The lacrimal of *Ailurus* is essentially similar. It is slightly better developed in the procyonids.

The jugal (malar) does not depart in any essential respect from the typical arctoid pattern.

The palatine, except for the superficial modification produced by the posterior prolongation of the maxilla over the pars perpendicularis, is similar to that of other arctoids. The pars horizontalis extends forward on the palate slightly anterior to the first molar.

The vomer differs from that of *Ursus* and most other arctoids in the great posterior extent of its pars sagittalis. Otherwise its relations are similar to those of *Ursus*.

The frontal, parietal, squamosal, and occipital have all suffered more or less change in form with the remodeling of the skull to accommodate the enormous masticatory musculature. Except for the morphologically insignificant differences resulting from this remodeling, the relations of these bones are typical.

The frontoparietal suture, which is relatively straight and about at a right angle to the axis of the skull in *Ursus* and other arctoids, here arches forward to the level of the optic foramen. At the dorsal midline a narrow tongue of the frontal projects posteriorly between the parietals for about 15 mm., i.e., to about the level of the whole frontoparietal suture in *Ursus*. This suggests that in *Ailuropoda* the parietal has increased anteriorly at the expense of the frontal.

The interparietal suture is obliterated, and a secondary upgrowth of bone is approaching the site of the future sagittal crest.

On the skull examined, the basioccipital-supraoccipital suture was still open, but the exoccipital-supraoccipital suture was closed.

The mastoid portion of the periotic is exposed, as is usual in arctoids, on the posterior side of the mastoid process, where it is wedged in between the squamosal and the occipital. The suture between the periotic and the tympanic disappears early in all arctoids, and was gone in the skull of *Ailuropoda* studied.

The tympanic, in so far as it is visible externally, differs considerably in shape from the corresponding bone in *Ursus*. It is obvious, however, that this bone has merely been crowded by the surrounding structures, particularly the postglenoid process. The relations of the tympanic are almost exactly as in *Ursus*, and posterior expansion of the postglenoid process as seen in *Ailuropoda* might be expected to alter the form of the tympanic precisely as it has. (This region is described in detail on p. 319).

The sphenoidal complex has been affected relatively little by the remodeling of the skull and is very similar to the corresponding region in *Ursus*. In the skull examined, the four elements constituting the complex (basisphenoid, presphenoid, alisphenoid, orbitosphenoid) are still distinct. They differ only in the most trivial respects from the corresponding elements in a young *Ursus* skull.

The pterygoid is completely fused with the sphenoid, and this is one of the very few sutures of the skull that have been obliterated at this age. This condition contrasts sharply with *Ursus* at a comparable age, in which the pterygoid is still entirely separate.

The ethmoid is not visible on the surface of the skull.

The following sutures are closed in the young skull examined: tympanic–periotic, exoccipital–supraoccipital, pterygoid–sphenoid, interparietal. The first two fusions are characteristic of carnivores at this stage of development. The last two are not, and represent departures from the carnivore pattern.

### C. HYOID

The hyoid (fig. 28) differs little from that of bears and other arctoid carnivores. It is composed of the usual nine rodlike bony elements, suspended from the basicranium by a pair of cartilaginous elements, the thyrohyals. The hyoid fossa, at the bottom of which the thyrohyal articulates with the skull, lies in the hyojugular fossa.

The hyoid consists of a transverse body and two horns (cornua), an anterior composed of three pairs of bones plus the cartilaginous thyrohyals, and a posterior composed of a single pair of bones.

Like all other bones of the skeleton, the hyoid bones of *Ailuropoda* exhibit more pronounced scars

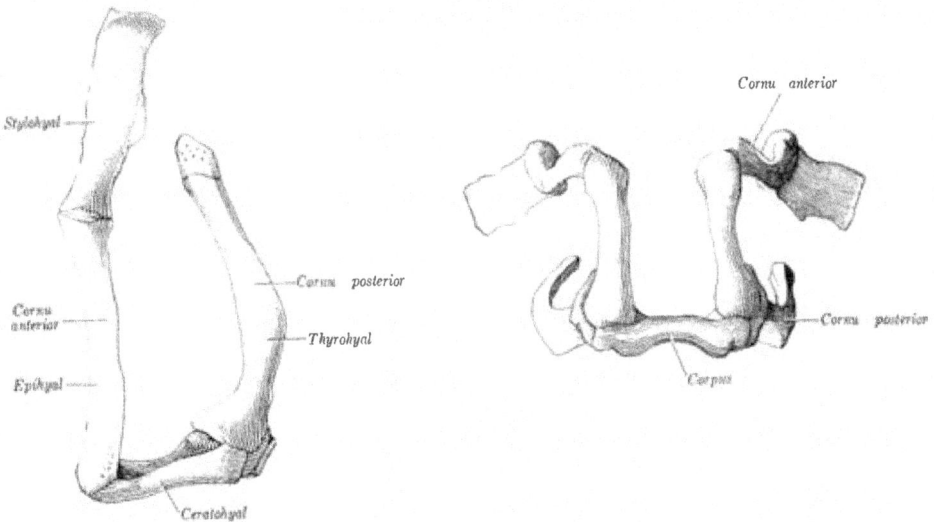

Fig. 28. Hyoid of *Ailuropoda*, lateral and ventral views.

for muscle attachments than they do in *Ursus*, although the bones themselves are no more robust. In both the giant panda and the bears the body is a transverse rod, less plate-like than in other arctoids. The ceratohyal is also less expanded than in other arctoids, and in *Ailuropoda* it has a distinct longitudinal furrow on the dorsal surface. The epihyal presents nothing noteworthy. The stylohyal is flattened and plate-like, with an irregular outline, in *Ailuropoda*. The thyrohyal is slightly curved and rodlike.

## D. REVIEW OF THE SKULL

The skull and teeth of *Ailuropoda* were described in some detail by A. Milne-Edwards (1868-1874), Lydekker (1901), Bardenfleth (1913) and Gregory (1936). Each of these made point by point comparisons with the Ursidae on the one hand and with *Ailurus* and the Procyonidae on the other, in an attempt to determine the affinities of *Ailuropoda*. Conclusions were conflicting; the only legitimate conclusion is that the skull and dentition of the giant panda are so modified that the affinities of this animal cannot be determined from these structures alone. I have therefore used other characters in deciding the affinities of *Ailuropoda*, which are unquestionably with the Ursidae. Here the only important consideration is that no skull or dental character shall point unequivocally to relationship with any other group of carnivores.

The demands of the masticatory apparatus in *Ailuropoda* have resulted in such extensive and permeating modifications in the skull that many elements have been modified beyond the limits of inter-generic or even inter-family differences within the Carnivora. Among those not so affected are the pattern (but not the extent) of the paranasal sinuses, the turbinates, and the middle ear – all intimately associated with primary sense organs and not affected by muscle action. *Each of these structures is very similar to the corresponding structure in Ursus.* Klatt (1912) has shown that the extent of the frontal sinus is determined by the mass of the temporal muscle, as would be expected, because the sinus lies between the outer and inner lamina of the cranium. The temporal attaches to the outer lamina, whereas the inner lamina encapsulates the brain.

Aside from its function of encapsulating the brain and sense organs, the generalized carnivore skull is designed primarily for seizing and cutting up prey. Skulls of omnivorous or herbivorous carnivores are secondary modifications of this primary predatory type. Consider the skull of a generalized carnivore, such as *Canis* or *Viverra*, as a construction. How does such a construction compare with those of other generalized mammals in architecturally or mechanically significant ways?

1. The skull is elongate and relatively slender (see Table 8). Elongation of the head is a primitive mammalian feature that has been retained in

TABLE 8.—SKULL PROPORTIONS IN GENERALIZED AND SPECIALIZED CARNIVORES

| | Generalized Flesh-eating Carnivores | | Predominantly Herbivorous Carnivores | | | Extremely Powerful Jawed Carnivores | |
|---|---|---|---|---|---|---|---|
| | Canis lupus | Viverra tangalunga | Procyon lotor | Ailurus fulgens | Ursus | Ailuropoda | Hyaena |
| N = | 3 | 5 | 3 | 3 | 5 | 3 | 4 |
| **SKULL LENGTH:** | | | | | | | |
| Condylobasal length | 3.2 | 2.9 | 3.1 | 2.9 | 3.2 | 2.7 | 3.5 |
| Length thor. vert. 10–12* | (3.08–3.23) | (2.75–2.95) | (3.04–3.24) | (2.53–3.21) | (2.99–3.44) | (2.63–2.72) | |
| **FACE LENGTH:** | | | | | | | |
| Gnathion–ant. end braincase | 51 | 42 | 38 | 36 | 50 | 49 | 49 |
| Condylobasal length | (50–51) | (40–43) | (37–39) | (34–38) | (46–52) | (47–53) | (48–50) |
| Preoptic length | 45 | 33 | 30 | 23 | 33 | 31 | 32 |
| Condylobasal length | (42.1–46.6) | (31.8–33.6) | (29.1–30.1) | (22.4–24.1) | (31.4–35.5) | (29.2–32.0) | (30.5–33) |
| **SKULL DEPTH:** | | | | | | | |
| Vertex–inf. border mandible | 49 | 43 | 59 | 68 | 52 | 71 | 71 |
| Condylobasal length | (48–51) | (40–47) | (56–62) | (67–69) | (47–57) | (70–72) | |
| **SKULL BREADTH:** | | | | | | | |
| Zygomatic breadth | 57 | 50 | 68 | 75 | 63 | 82 | 71 |
| Condylobasal length | (55–60) | (49–52) | (65–70) | (71–79) | (57–69) | (81–82) | (66.5–75) |
| Least diam. braincase | 18 | 15 | 21 | 22 | 24 | 18 | 18 |
| Condylobasal length | (17–19) | (14–16) | (20–22) | (22–23) | (22–26) | (15–20) | (16–20) |

* See page 35.

the Carnivora; the skull was elongate in the creodont ancestors of the carnivores and is characteristic of generalized mammals.

As a tool for seizing and cutting up prey an elongate skull (particularly an elongate face) has certain inherent mechanical advantages and disadvantages. Speed of jaw closure at the level of the canines is achieved, though at the cost of power. But production of useful force at the sectorial teeth is mechanically very unfavorable, since more than twice as much disadvantageous force is developed at the mandibular articulation (see p. 69).

Preoptic length is a useful measure of face length for our purpose, since it approximately divides the tooth-bearing anterior part of the skull from the posterior muscle-attachment part. Calculated in this way, the face is long in Canis, moderately long in Viverra. Both fall within the known range of the Paleocene Arctocyonidae, the oldest and most primitive of all carnivores: Deltatherium 31 per cent, Eoconodon 38 per cent, Loxolophodon 45 per cent.[1]

Depth and breadth of skull, both intimately associated with mechanics of the jaw, are moderate in both Canis and Viverra. The civet is more slender in both dimensions.

2. Two areas dominate the dental battery: the enlarged dagger-like canines anteriorly, and the en-

[1] Calculated from illustrations in Matthew (1937).

larged scissor-like carnassials ($P^4$ and $M_1$) posteriorly. The remainder of the dentition is more or less degenerate. These two specialized areas of the dentition are the key adaptation of the Carnivora. All other modifications of the skull away from the generalized mammalian condition are effectors of these seizing and cutting tools. These modifications are as follows:

3. The mandibular articulation is a transverse cylinder rotating in a trough-like fossa that is strongly buttressed above and behind. This arrangement permits only a hinge movement of the mandible, plus limited lateral shifting of the mandible; the two may be (and probably normally are) combined in a spiral screw movement. The two halves of the mandible are not fused at the symphysis, which indicates that they are capable of at least some independent movement.

4. The mandibular articulation is at the level of the occlusal plane, and therefore upper and lower toothrows operate against each other like the blades of a pair of shears.

5. The canines interlock and act as a guide for the anterior part of the mandible as the jaws approach closure (and the carnassials begin to function). This is very evident from the wear areas on the canines. The interlocking restricts lateral movement and guides the two blades of the shear very precisely past each other. No such arrangement exists in such generalized marsupials as the opossum or in generalized insectivores.

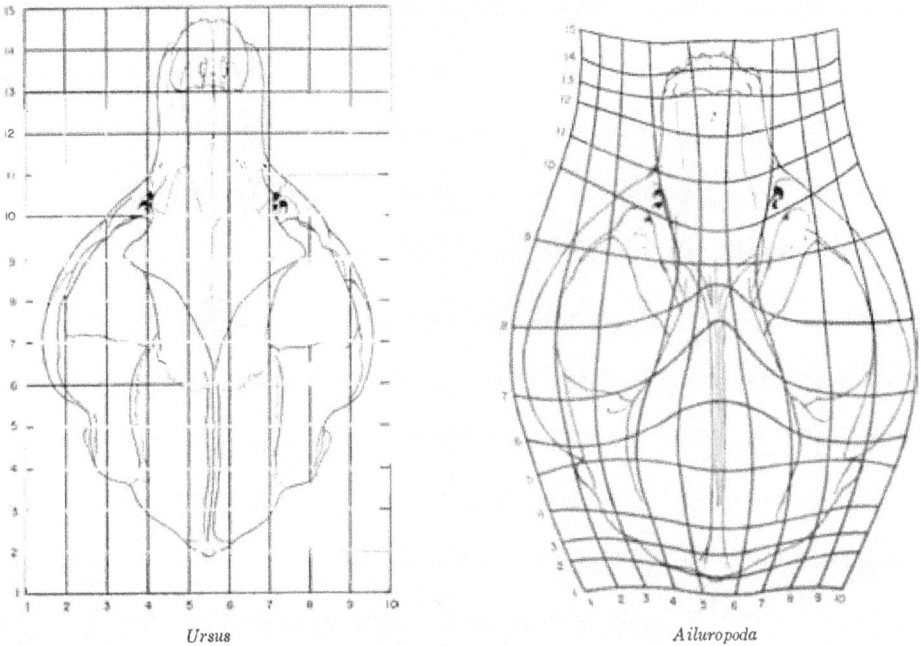

*Ursus*

*Ailuropoda*

FIG. 29. Differences of skull proportions in *Ursus horribilis* and *Ailuropoda melanoleuca* shown by deformed coordinates.

6. The temporal fossa is large, providing space, and particularly attachment surface, for the large temporal muscle (see p. 150). This fossa is similarly large in generalized primitive mammals. The masseteric fossa does not differ significantly from that of primitive mammals. The pterygoid fossa is small or wanting. This fossa is well developed in primitive mammals; its reduction in the Carnivora is associated with the reduced size and importance of the pterygoid muscles.

7. The zygomatic arch is strong and forms a smooth uninterrupted curve in both the sagittal and frontal planes. The anterior buttress of this arch system lies directly over the primary cheek teeth, the posterior buttress over the mandibular fossa— the two sites where pressure is applied during mastication. The zygomatic arch represents the "main zygomatic trajectory" of Starck (1935); it is the principal structure within which are resolved the disintegrating forces generated by the powerful jaw muscles. The arch is well constructed and extremely powerful in *Didelphis*. In generalized insectivores, by contrast, the arch is structurally weak: the curvature is interrupted (*Erinaceus*), parts of the arch are almost threadlike (*Echinosorex*, Talpidae), or the central part of the arch is missing (Soricidae).

Support for the canines, by contrast, is relatively weak in generalized Carnivora. The main element of this support system is the "vertex trajectory," which in generalized carnivores is weak and often interrupted at the glabella.

What, now, has happened to this basic carnivore construction in herbivorous carnivores, and particularly in the purely herbivorous giant panda?

The skull is still elongate, but slightly less so than in *Canis* or *Viverra* (Table 8). In *Ursus* the skull is even slightly longer than in *Canis* or *Viverra*. There is, in fact, little variation in relative skull length among all arctoids examined.

Face length in the giant panda is only slightly less than in *Viverra*, and in the bears it is practically identical with *Viverra*. Proportions vary among other herbivorous carnivores: the face is very short in *Ailurus*, of normal length in *Procyon*. Face length is extremely variable among the Carnivora in general, and the significance of this variability has not been explored. The face varies independently of the cranium in mammals (p. 72).

*We may conclude that* Ailuropoda *and* Ursus *show no significant differences from the generalized carnivore condition in longitudinal proportions of the skull.*

*Canis*

*Ailuropoda*

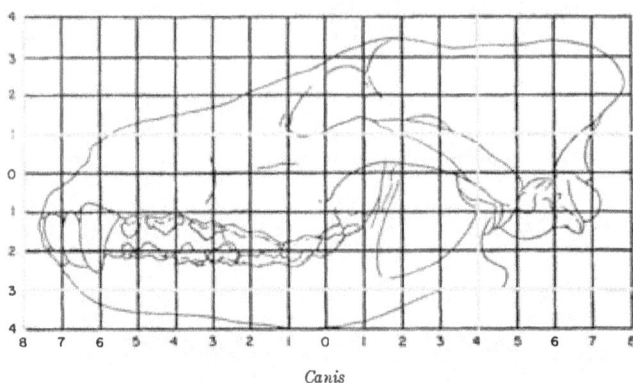

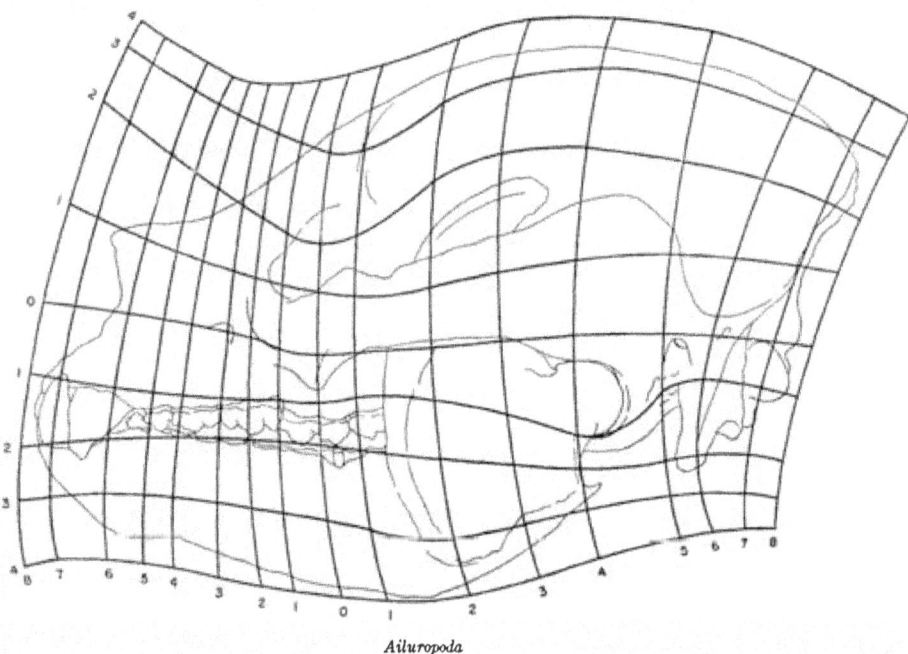

FIG. 30.  Differences of skull proportions in *Canis lupus* and *Ailuropoda melanoleuca* shown by deformed coordinates.

Depth and breadth of skull, on the contrary, in all herbivorous carnivores depart significantly from the generalized condition (see figs. 29 and 30, and Table 8). Among these, depth is least in *Ursus,* in which it scarcely exceeds that of the wolf. Depth of skull in *Ailuropoda* is equaled among carnivores only in *Hyaena;* in both the panda and the hyena, depth is achieved largely by development of a high sagittal crest, the inner lamina of the skull roof remaining unaffected. The skull is typically deep in all arctoids that have forsaken a purely carnivorous diet. Increase in depth involves only the external lamina of the cranium and adjoining parts of the mandible—not the face or the direct housing of the brain. The vertical height of the posterior half of the zygomatic arch, the area from which the zygomaticomandibularis takes origin, is also greatly increased in *Ailuropoda.*

Zygomatic breadth is consistently greater than in generalized flesh-eaters, and once again this is maximal in *Ailuropoda* and least in *Ursus*. Breadth in the powerful-jawed *Hyaena* is equal to that in most herbivorous carnivores, but is considerably less than in *Ailuropoda*.

*We may conclude that breadth and depth of skull are increased in all herbivorous carnivores, and that these reach a maximum in Ailuropoda.*

Increased breadth and depth of the cranium produce increased volume of the temporal fossa. In *Ailuropoda* the volume of this fossa has been further increased, especially anteriorly, by crowding the orbit downward from its normal position, by carrying the temporal fossa anteriorly at the expense of the postorbital process and the posterior part of the frontal table, and by decreasing the anterior breadth of the braincase. The volume of this fossa probably approaches the maximum that is compatible with normal functioning of surrounding structures.

Besides providing space for a greater volume of craniomandibular musculature, increased depth of skull greatly improves efficiency for production of pressure at the level of the cheek teeth. Worthmann (1922) uses a simplified system of vector analysis to compare relative masticatory efficiency in man and several carnivores. He represents the action of the masseter and temporal muscles by straight lines connecting the midpoints of origin and insertion areas. The axis of the masticatory system is represented by a straight line connecting the center of rotation of the mandibular articulation with the last molar tooth.

From the structural standpoint, greater depth of skull increases the magnitude of vertical forces that the skull is capable of withstanding.

Comparison of masticatory efficiency in a generalized carnivore (*Canis*) and in the purely herbivorous *Ailuropoda* by Worthmann's method reveals a striking improvement in the panda (fig. 31). In the wolf the axis of the masseter ($m$) intersects the masticatory axis GK at a point about 30 per cent of the distance from G to K. Thus force at the joint (G) would be to force at the cheek teeth (K) as 7 : 3; in other words joint force is about 2.5 times as great as useful chewing force. In the panda, by contrast, $k : g = 55 : 45$ approximately. Similarly for the temporalis $k : g = 28 : 72$ for *Canis*, whereas $k : g = 47 : 53$ for *Ailuropoda*.

In the cheek-tooth battery emphasis has shifted from the sectorial teeth to the molars (p. 128), and the anterior buttress of the zygomatic arch now lies over the first (*Ailuropoda*) or second (*Ursus*) upper molar. This shift, by shortening the resist-

ance arm of the jaw lever, increases the mechanical efficiency of the system for production of pressure.

The form of the mandibular articulation has not changed—*it is still a transverse cylinder rotating in a trough*. The extensive horizontal movements of upper molars against lower that characterize other herbivorous mammals are therefore limited to a slight lateral displacement in herbivorous carnivores. Because of the interlocking canines at the anterior end of the system, no lateral shifting is possible with the teeth in full occlusion.[1]

In *Ursus* the mandibular articulation is at the level of the occlusal plane as in generalized flesh-eating carnivores. In *Ailuropoda* the articulation lies considerably *above* the occlusal plane. Lebedinsky (1938) demonstrated that elevating the articulation above the occlusal plane imparts an anteroposterior grinding movement at the occlusal plane, even when the mandible is swinging around a fixed transverse axis.

Lebedinsky's interpretation may be analyzed further. Figure 32, A, represents a mandible with the mandibular articulation (O) at the level of the toothrow. A point $x$ on the lower dentition travels through the arc $x$–$x'$ when the mouth is opened. The tangent to this arc at point $x$ is perpendicular to the occlusal plane, and therefore there is no anteroposterior component in the movement of $x$ with respect to the axis AO, and an object placed between the upper and lower dentitions would be crushed or sheared. This would likewise be true at any other point on the axis AO.

Figure 32, B, represents a mandible with the mandibular articulation (O) elevated above the level of the toothrow. A point $x$ travels through the arc $x$–$x'$ when the mouth is opened, but in this case the tangent to the arc at $x$ forms an acute angle with the occlusal plane, A–B, and there is a very definite anteroposterior component in the movement of $x$ with respect to the axis AB. The angles formed by successive tangents along AB become increasingly acute as B is approached, until at B there is no longer any vertical component at all. Thus, as Lebedinsky pointed out, any object placed between the upper and lower dentitions would be subjected to anteroposterior forces even with pure hinge movement of the jaw. Moreover, the anteroposterior force becomes increasingly great as a point (B) directly beneath the articulation is approached. In *Ailuropoda*, therefore, an anteroposterior grinding action is achieved by elevating the articulation, and its effectiveness is increased by extending the toothrow posteriorly.

[1] In *Ailurus fulgens* a lateroventral shifting of more than 2 mm., *with the cheek teeth in complete occlusion*, is possible. This is true grinding, otherwise unknown in the Carnivora.

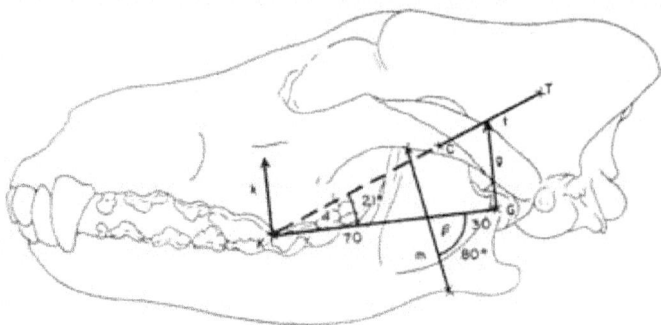

Canis

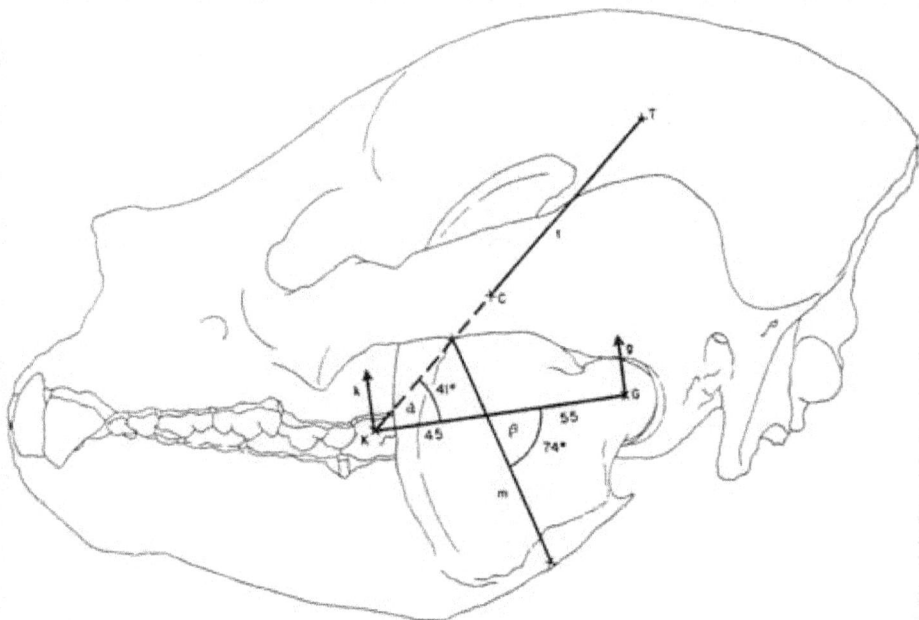

Ailuropoda

FIG. 31. Relative masticatory efficiency in a generalized carnivore (*Canis*) and the giant panda (*Ailuropoda*). The line KG, representing the masticatory axis, connects the center of rotation of the mandibular joint (G) with the midpoint of the functional cheektooth area (K) (boundary between P⁴ and M₁ in *Canis*, anterior quarter of M² in *Ailuropoda*). The line *m* represents the axis of the masseter. The line *t*, the axis of the temporalis, connects the approximate center of origin (T) of the temporalis with the approximate center of insertion (C). The line *t* may be projected beyond C to K, since a force acting on an immovable system may be displaced in its own direction without altering the result. True masticatory force is represented by *k*, articular pressure by *g*.

A          B

C

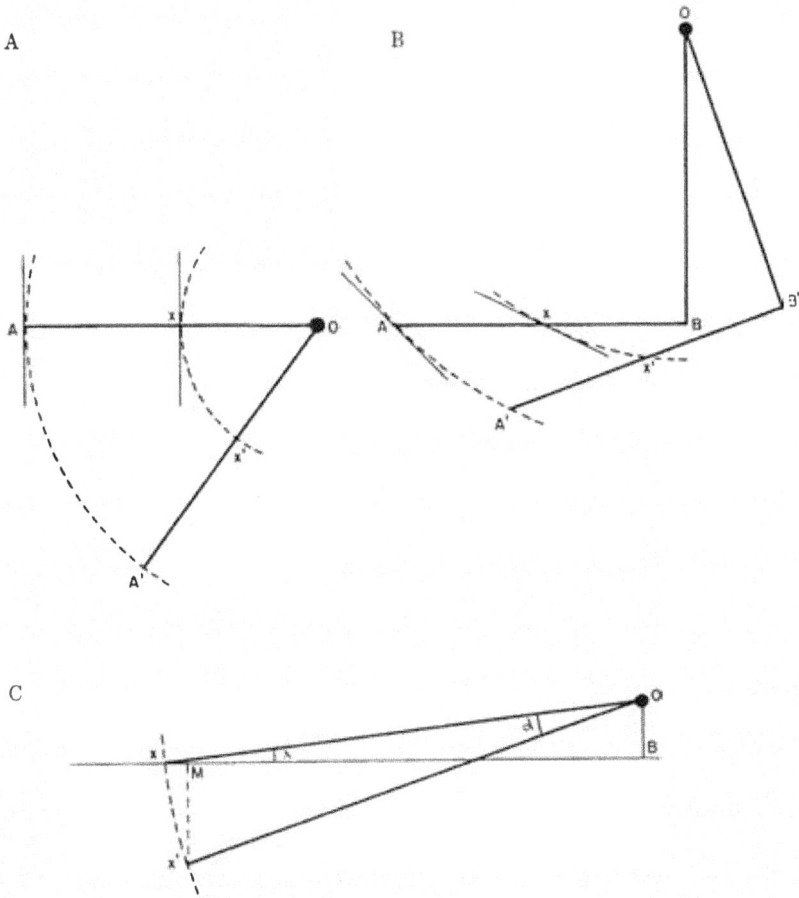

FIG. 32. Occlusal relations in a mandible with mandibular articulation at level of toothrow (A), and elevated above level of toothrow (B). The lines AO and ABO represent the mandible in occlusion, A'O and A'B'O its position when the mouth is opened. The points $x$ and $x'$ represent the positions of a cusp on one of the lower cheekteeth. (C) Occlusal relations in *Ailuropoda* in biting down at point $x$ on an object 25 mm. in diameter (see text).

Stöcker (1957) has calculated for the elephant the anteroposterior displacement of a point on the occlusal surface of a lower molar when the jaw is lowered. A similar calculation may be made on a panda skull (fig. 32, C). A point $x$ at the anterior end of the first lower molar is 125 mm. from the center of rotation of the mandible, O. The line $xO$ was found to form an angle, $\lambda$, of 7° with the occlusal plane, $x$ B. The panda is known to chew up bamboo stalks up to 38 mm. in diameter (p. 20); to be conservative let us assume a bamboo stalk 25 mm. in diameter.

An object 25 mm. in diameter placed between the upper and lower teeth at the level $x$ displaces

point $x$ on the lower molar to position $x'$. The two lines $x$ O and $x'$ O form an angle, $a$, of 11° 30'. The horizontal displacement, $x$ M, of $x$ with respect to the occlusal plane may be calculated as

$$xM = x O \cos \lambda - x O \cos (\lambda + a)$$
$$= x O [\cos \lambda - \cos (\lambda + a)]$$

Substituting the values given above, this equation gives a value for $x$ M of 5.4 mm., which is the horizontal distance through which a point $x$ on the lower molar travels as the teeth are brought into occlusion. This represents the anteroposterior grinding component that would be brought to bear on the bamboo stalk.

The mandibular symphysis remains unfused in *Ursus* and other herbivorous carnivores, although the two halves interlock so intimately that no movement is possible. Its fusion in *Ailuropoda* reflects the general increase in bone tissue that characterizes the skull as a whole.

We may conclude that the skull of *Ailuropoda* represents an attempt to adapt the carnivore type of skull—already highly adapted for seizing and cutting—to the radically different requirements of grinding siliceous plant fibers. Efficient grinding requires horizontal movements, but these are almost completely inhibited by the cylindrical mandibular articulation and the interlocking of teeth during occlusion, although *Ailurus* shows that effective horizontal grinding can be achieved in a carnivore. A compromise solution was to replace the unattainable mechanical efficiency seen in true herbivores with more power. This attempt to achieve maximal power in the masticatory equipment is the key to the architecture of the panda skull.

The skulls of other more or less herbivorous carnivores except *Ailurus* exhibit most of the modifications seen in *Ailuropoda*, but to a much less extreme degree. Thus the skull of *Ailuropoda* may be considered an ultimate expression of adaptation for herbivory within the Carnivora.

What can be deduced of the morphogenetic mechanisms whereby these results were achieved —in other words, the mechanism through which natural selection had to operate? To what extent does the skull of *Ailuropoda* as compared with that of *Ursus* merely reflect extrinsic mechanical factors arising from the massive musculature, and to what extent intrinsic factors, other than the ability of the bone to respond to mechanical stress?

Some anatomists have recently attempted to re-examine the mammalian skull from an analytical rather than a purely descriptive standpoint (see Biegert, 1957, for a review). In these studies the skull is regarded as merely the bony framework of a major functional unit, the head. During ontogeny and phylogeny there is a complex interplay among the various organs making up the head, and the skull adapts itself to the changing spatial, mechanical, and static demands. In a given phylogenetic sequence one of the head organs (e.g., brain, feeding apparatus, eyes) typically comes to dominate the whole and sets the pattern, so to speak, for further evolution within the group. Changes in the skull are thus not simply additive, but are a function of changes in other head organs, which in turn may be functionally irreversible and therefore in effect "fix" the pattern of further evolution within the group. The causal factors that

determine changes in skull form are interpreted as an interplay between the inherited basic plan of the skull and the demands of other head structures extrinsic to the skull itself. This approach isolates some of the forces modeling the skull, but in the end it does little more than describe structural correlations. It fails to come to grips with the problem of the mechanics of evolution.

Correlation studies have shown that the facial part of the skull varies as if it were genetically distinct from the cranium, as it is in fact phylogenetically (Cobb, 1943; and especially Starck, 1953, for a review). This genetic independence, and the further independence of the mandible, have been proved in breeding experiments on dogs (Stockard, 1941; Klatt, 1941-43). Such independence means that a genetic factor affecting the ontogenetic growth rate of the cranium (or a component of the cranium) need not affect the face, and vice versa. The union between face and cranium, however disparate these structures may be, is maintained by mutual accommodation during growth. Genetic control of growth rates in dental fields is well known to be distinct from that of any other part of the skull. Numerous observations (e.g., Cobb, 1943) indicate that the alveolar areas of the skull accommodate directly to the space requirements of the teeth during the growth process.

The mammalian skull, in short, is a mosaic of independent morphogenetic units that are fitted into a functional unit partly by natural selection acting on their several time-tables of growth and differentiation, and partly by accommodation to extrinsic forces. The extent of the morphogenetic units may vary with time during ontogeny: the earlier in ontogeny a genetic effect is manifested, the more extensive its target is likely to be. A beginning has been made at identifying and isolating these morphogenetic units (Starck, 1953; Landauer, 1962), but they are still inadequately known.

Thus, in considering the morphosis of the skull, two sets of factors must be kept in mind. These are the location and extent at any moment during ontogeny of the morphogenetic units of which the skull is composed (intrinsic to the skull), and the modeling effects on the skull of other head structures (extrinsic to the skull as such).

In the skull of *Ailuropoda* the increase in quantity of compacta is clearly limited to two major morphogenetic units, the cranium and the mandible, and absent in a third, the face. The hypertrophy of bone substance affects not only the skull, but all compacta in the body in a gradient falling off from the dorsal body axis, and including structures such as the tail and the proximal ends of the ribs where hypertrophy can scarcely represent structural adaptation. We do not know the time-table of mammalian ontogeny in enough detail to know whether these effects could have been predicted and delimited *a priori*. The additional bone substance certainly strengthens the skull, although it is not distributed along trajectory lines of the skull as it should be if it were primarily functional. We cannot say whether increased bone substance in the skull of *Ailuropoda* was a primary target of natural selection, whether it is genetically linked with increase in the mass of the masticatory muscles, or whether it simply reflects disturbed metabolic or endocrine relations.

Cephalization in bulldogs is in some respects similar to but less extreme than in *Ailuropoda*. Klatt and Oboussier (1951) found that all structures of the head (skull, masticatory musculature, brain, eyeballs, hypophysis) are heavier in bulldogs than in "normal" dogs. These authors conclude that the bulldog condition results from an increase in the growth rate of the anterior end of the embryo. More likely it represents a temporary intensification of the general growth rate of the embryo during the period when the head region is undergoing its most rapid growth. The effects are less generalized in *Ailuropoda;* here the brain and eyeballs (and the internal ear) are of "normal" size, a condition that would result if the ontogenetic growth rate were increased *after* the central nervous system and its sensory adnexa had experienced their period of most rapid growth. The condition in the panda is, in fact, the reverse of the condition in man, where the brain is enlarged while all other cranial (but not facial) structures are of "normal" size. As interpreted by Weidenreich (1941), in man the ontogenetic growth rate is temporarily intensified during the period when the brain is undergoing its most rapid growth, and returns to normal *before* the rapid growth period of other cranial structures is reached.

It is known from comparative studies that surface relief of the mammalian cranium is determined chiefly by the craniomandibular muscles (Weidenreich, 1922). The developing cranium is, as Anthony (1903) put it, molded between the brain and the masticatory musculature. Direct evidence of the role of the cranial muscles in determining skull form in mammals is limited to the effects of unilateral paralysis or removal of muscles in young rats, rabbits, guinea pigs, and dogs. Unilateral paralysis of the facial muscles (Washburn, 1946a), removal of one masseter (Horowitz and Shapiro, 1955, and earlier workers), of one temporal (Washburn, 1947, and earlier workers), or of neck muscles (Neubauer, 1925), all resulted

in asymmetrical development of the skull, with failure of associated bony crests and ridges to form. Removal of the temporal was followed by resorption of the coronoid process but did not alter the internal form of the braincase. No one has removed simultaneously the temporal, zygomatico-mandibularis, and masseter from one side to determine the part played by these major muscles in determining the form of the zygomatic arch; it is very probable that bizygomatic breadth is intimately related to these muscles.

These experiments were performed far too late in ontogeny to provide the intimate knowledge of the factors of embryogenesis we have for the limb bones of the chick (Murray, 1936). So far as they go, the experiments strongly reinforce the observational data of comparative anatomy. Practically nothing is known of the development of the form of the skull, but from what is known of developing limb bones in vertebrates (Murray, 1936; Lacroix, 1951) the primary form of both dermal and cartilage bones of the skull is probably determined by intrinsic growth patterns, whereas modeling is determined by pressures and tensions extrinsic to the bones, created by musculature, brain, sense organs, vessels and nerves, and mechanical interaction between the developing bones themselves. We may assume that, except for differences resulting from increase in volume of bone tissue, the considerable differences in form between the skull of the panda and that of the bears are largely, perhaps almost entirely, dependent on such extrinsic factors—that of the cranium on the musculature, and that of the face on the dentition.

The only features for which intrinsic factors must be postulated appear to be the tremendous increase in the bone substance making up the skull (by proliferation of connective tissue) and the elevation of the mandibular articulation (by proliferation of cartilage). Elevation of the articulation enhances horizontal movements of the mandible. It occurs in some degree in all herbivorous mammals and surely is a direct result of natural selection operating on the skull. The morphogenetic mechanism whereby it is achieved is unknown, but the fundamental similarity to the acromegalic mandible suggests that it is simple.

We may conclude that no more than four, and perhaps only three, factors were involved in the transformation of the ursid type of skull into that of *Ailuropoda*. Two of these—hypertrophy of jaw musculature and dentition—are extrinsic to the skull and therefore involve only the ability of the bone to respond to mechanical stress. Two —general hypertrophy of bone substance and elevation of the mandibular articulation—are intrinsic to the skeleton but involve different growth mechanisms. Thus only two factors acting directly on the skull itself may distinguish the skull of *Ailuropoda* from that of other ursids. Natural selection has no doubt had additional minor polishing effects, although the whole morphology of the giant panda indicates that the morphological integration produced by such refined selection is at a relatively low level.

## E. SUMMARY OF SKULL

1. The skull of *Ailuropoda* is basically similar to that of *Ursus*. Agreement is particularly close in structures relatively unaffected by masticatory requirements: the turbinates, the paranasal sinuses, the middle ear, and the inner lamina of the cranial cavity.

2. The outer lamina of the cranium and the mandible are remarkable for the thickness and density of the bone. This greatly exceeds mechanical requirements, and therefore is not directly adaptive.

3. All parts of the skull associated with the masticatory apparatus are greatly expanded. The volume of the temporal fossa in particular, especially its anterior third, has been increased at the expense of surrounding structures. Similar adaptive changes appear convergently in *Ailurus* and, in slightly altered form, in hyenas.

4. From the genetic standpoint these adaptive changes are probably extrinsic to the bone itself, involving only the ability of the bone to respond to mechanical forces during ontogeny.

5. The only obvious intrinsic factors are the great increase in bone tissue in the cranium and mandible, and the elevation of the mandibular articulation above the occlusal plane.

6. Thus only two major factors acting directly on the skull itself may distinguish the skull of *Ailuropoda* from that of *Ursus*.

7 Certain features usually regarded as diagnostic of the Ursidae (e.g., by Flower, 1869) have been obliterated in *Ailuropoda* by the expansion of the masticatory apparatus. Among these are postorbital processes on frontal bones, presence of alisphenoid canal, non-confluence of foramen rotundum and orbital fissure, and presence of foramen lacerum medium. Such secondary differences cannot be used as evidence of non-relationship between the panda and the bears.

## II. THE VERTEBRAL COLUMN

### A. THE VERTEBRAL COLUMN AS A WHOLE

The vertebral column of the giant panda is in many respects the most remarkable among living carnivores. Slijper (1946) showed that the archi-

tecture of the developing column is responsive to the mechanical demands of posture and locomotion. Morphogenetically the mammalian column behaves like other homiotic structures (Kühne, 1936; Sawin, 1945, 1946). Therefore it is preferable to consider the column as a whole, rather than as a chain of independent units. The analytical study of the vertebrae of the Carnivora made by Stromer von Reichenbach (1902) showed that the morphological details of individual vertebae exhibit no important features consistently correlated with the major categories, and are therefore of little systematic importance. For this reason no detailed description and comparison of individual vertebrae of *Ailuropoda* is presented here.

The number of presacral vertebrae is extremely constant in carnivores. The normal number of thoraco-lumbars in all living Carnivora is twenty, and individual variations rarely exceed one above or below this figure. The giant panda is consequently remarkable in having only eighteen trunk vertebrae; in one of nine skeletons this number was further reduced to seventeen, and in one there were nineteen (Table 9).

The number of lumbar vertebrae in *Ailuropoda* is five in 50 per cent of the cases, and four in the remaining 50 per cent; in *Ursus* it is six in 79 per cent, and five in the remaining 21 per cent. (Other genera of the Ursidae appear to differ from *Ursus*, but the samples are too small to permit conclusions.) The modal number of lumbars is either four or five in *Ailuropoda*, and six in *Ursus;* the mean is 4.5 and 5.8, respectively, indicating that the lumbar region has been reduced by more than one vertebra in *Ailuropoda*. The thoracics show a similar but somewhat more limited tendency toward reduction: the mean is 13.5 in *Ailuropoda*, 14.2 in *Ursus*. There was evidence of disturbance at the cervico-thoracic boundary in one individual (p. 85). Thus in the column as a whole there is an anterior displacement of the boundaries of the several regions in *Ailuropoda*, and this displacement shows a gradient decreasing in intensity from the sacrum toward the head.

A remarkable feature of the column in *Ailuropoda* is its variability. Of nine skeletons examined, the thoraco-lumbar juncture was asymmetrical on the two sides of the body in three, and four different vertebral formulae are represented among the remaining six individuals (Table 9). This variability is greater than was found in any of the numerous arctoid and ailuroid carnivores examined.

The proportions of the three main divisions of the column in *Ailuropoda* differ from those in other carnivores, as shown below. These proportions also show a far greater range of variation than in

TABLE 9.—VERTEBRAL COUNTS IN CARNIVORES

| | Number of individuals | Thoracics | Lumbars | Thoracics + lumbars |
|---|---|---|---|---|
| Canis latrans............ | 15 | 13 | 7 | 20 |
| Canis lupus............ | 9 | 13 | 7 | 20 |
| | 1 | 14 | 7 | 21 |
| Vulpes fulva.......... | 9 | 13 | 7 | 20 |
| | 1 | 13/14 | 7/6 | 20 |
| Urocyon cinereoargenteus | 4 | 13 | 7 | 20 |
| | 1 | 13 | 6 | 19 |
| Bassariscus astutus..... | 5 | 13 | 7 | 20 |
| | 1 | 13 | 6 | 19 |
| | 1 | 13 | 5 | 18 |
| Nasua narica.......... | 1 | 15 | 5 | 20 |
| Nasua nasua.......... | 5 | 15 | 5 | 20 |
| Procyon lotor.......... | 11 | 14 | 6 | 20 |
| | 2 | 15 | 5 | 20 |
| | 1 | 14 | 5 | 19 |
| | 1 | 13 | 6 | 19 |
| Bassaricyon alleni..... | 5 | 13 | 7 | 20 |
| | 1 | 14 | 7 | 21 |
| | 1 | 14 | 6 | 20 |
| | 1 | 14/13 | 6/7 | 20 |
| Ailurus fulgens[1]........ | 5 | 14 | 6 | 20 |
| Ursus (various species)[2] | 7 | 14 | 6 | 20 |
| Ursus[1]................ | 2 | 15 | 5 | 20 |
| Ursus[1]................ | 1 | 14/15 | 6/5 | 20 |
| Ailuropoda melanoleuca. | 1 | 14 | 5 | 19 |
| | 2 | 14 | 4 | 18 |
| | 3 | 14/13 | 4/5 | 18 |
| | 2 | 13 | 5 | 18 |
| | 1 | 13 | 4 | 17 |

[1] One record from Flower (1885).

[2] Three records from Flower (1885).

any other carnivore examined. The cervical region is shorter in *Ailuropoda* than in *Ursus* but is only slightly shorter than in *Ailurus* and *Nasua* and no shorter than in *Procyon*. The thoracic region is relatively longer than in any other arctoid carnivore, resembling that of burrowing mustelids. The lumbar region is short in both *Ailuropoda* and *Ursus*. The proportions of the vertebral column

of the giant panda are similar to those of the anthropoid apes and man, and to those of such burrowing carnivores as *Taxidea*, *Meles*, and *Mellivora* —columns designed to withstand anteroposterior thrust.

The vertebrae of *Ailuropoda* are heavier than in *Ursus;* the weight of thoraco-lumbar vertebrae is about 16 per cent greater in a specimen of the panda than in a black bear of comparable size.

## The Mechanics of the Vertebral Column

The vertebral column of mammals, with its associated muscles and ligaments, is an extremely complex mechanism that has never been satisfactorily analyzed. Yet it is only on the basis of its functioning that the differences, often extremely subtle, exhibited in this region from animal to animal can be intelligently considered. Slijper (1946) made a painstaking comparative study of the column in mammals in an effort to correlate morphology and function. Many of his findings are relevant in the present connection.

Slijper rejects former comparisons of the vertebral column with an arched roof, a bridge with parallel girders, or a cantilever bridge, and compares it with a bow flexed by a bow-string (the sternum, abdominal muscles, and linea alba).

VERTEBRAL BODIES.—Slijper points out that the principal static function of the column is to resist bending, chiefly in the sagittal plane, and that differences in the size and shape of the vertebral bodies reflect the forces acting on them. He used as a criterion of the stress to which any part of the column is subjected the *moment of resistance* to bending, which he computed for each vertebral body by using the formula: breadth of articular face of body $\times$ square of height of body $(bh^2)$. Plotting these data for the entire column in a series of mammals yields characteristic curves of the moments of resistance at successive points along

TABLE 10.—RELATIVE PROPORTIONS OF DIVISIONS OF THE VERTEBRAL COLUMN IN CARNIVORES[1]

| | N | Cervical (%) | Thoracic (%) | Lumbar (%) |
|---|---|---|---|---|
| Canis........................ | 2 | 30 | 39.5 (39–40) | 30.5 (30–31) |
| Vulpes....................... | 2 | 28.8 (28–29.5) | 39.8 (39.5–40) | 31.5 |
| Bassariscus.................. | 1 | 24 | 42 | 34 |
| Nasua....................... | 1 | 22 | 45 | 33 |
| Procyon..................... | 4 | 21.4 (21–22) | 47.7 (47–48) | 30.9 (30–31.5) |
| Ailurus...................... | 3 | 22 (21.3–22) | 47 (47–47.5) | 31 (31.0–31.2) |
| Ursus....................... | 3 | 26.2 (25.5–27.4) | 45.9 (45.6–46.3) | 27.9 (26.3–28.9) |
| Ailuropoda.................. | 6 | 22 (21–23.2) | 55 (51.7–59) | 23 (20–26) |
| Taxidea..................... | 2 | 23 | 50.5 (50–51) | 26.5 (26–27) |
| Meles....................... | 1 | 25 | 53 | 22 |
| Mellivora.................... | 1 | 25 | 56 | 19 |

[1] *Ursus* and *Ailuropoda* determined on disarticulated skeletons.

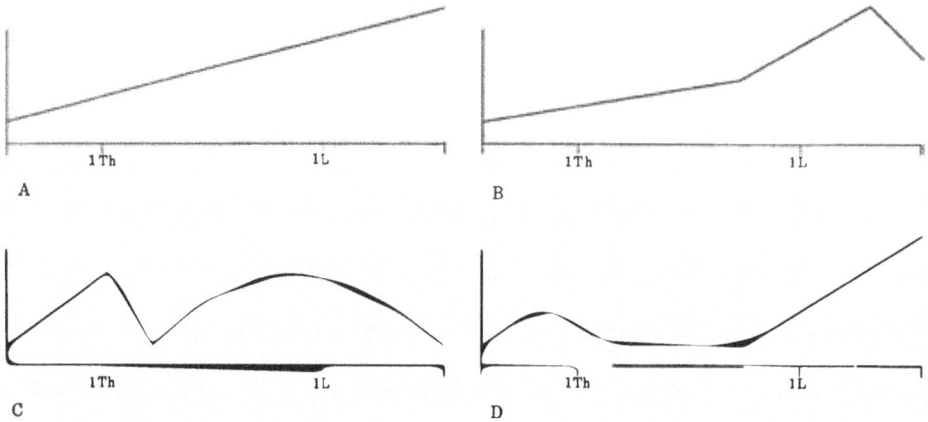

FIG. 33.   Diagrams of moments of resistance in the vertebral columns of various mammals:

A.   Moments of resistance in a beam supported at one end.

B.   Slijper's Type I*b* curve of moments of resistance in the vertebral column of mammals with an erect or semi-erect posture (compare with A and fig. 34).

C.   Theoretical moments of resistance in quadrupedal mammals, in which the vertebral column is compared to a bow, with a beam supported at one end attached to the cranial (left) end of the bow.

D.   Slijper's Type II curve of moments of resistance in the vertebral column, characteristic of carnivores other than bears and *Ailuropoda* (compare with C).

the column.   Slijper divides these curves into three major types, each with several subtypes.

Of the few carnivores examined by Slijper (*Canis, Vulpes, Ursus, Felis, Panthera*), all except *Ursus* yielded curves of Type II, characterized by a hump in the posterior cervical region, and a flat anterior thoracic region, followed by a rise in the posterior thoracic and lumbar regions (fig. 33, D).[1] For *Ursus* the curve slopes upward gradually from the anterior cervical region to about the tenth thoracic, then abruptly breaks more steeply upward, sloping downward again in the posterior lumbar region.   This is Slijper's Type I*b* curve, characteristic of bipedal animals, including man (fig. 33, B).   The curve for Slijper's bipedal goat was also modified in this direction.   This type of curve agrees closely with the diagram of the theoretical moments of resistance if the column is regarded as an erect or semi-erect beam supported at one end (fig. 33, A).

The curve of the moments of resistance for *Ailuropoda* was plotted for two individuals, which showed only minor differences (fig. 34).   This curve is very similar to that for *Ursus*, differing chiefly

[1] Slijper lists the domestic cat (along with the bear and the anthropoid apes and man) as having a Type I*b* curve. This is obviously a mistake.   I have measured and plotted a disarticulated cat column, and find that it has a typical Type II curve.

in its more even slope without the sharp upward break at the level of the diaphragmatic vertebra (eleventh thoracic in *Ursus*, eleventh or twelfth in *Ailuropoda*).   In this respect *Ailuropoda* resembles the anthropoid apes and man more closely than *Ursus* does.

It is evident that the vertebral axis in the bears, and especially in the giant panda, is constructed to withstand anteroposterior thrust.

NEURAL SPINES.—The length and angle of inclination of the neural spines do not depend upon the static demands made upon the column, but upon the structure and development of the epaxial muscles that attach to them (Slijper).   Thus the structure of the spines is ultimately determined by posture and locomotion, plus such secondary factors as absolute body size, length of neck, and weight of head.   Both length and inclination of a spine are resultants of the several forces exerted by the muscles attaching to it, the spine acting as a lever transmitting the muscle force to the vertebral body.

Plotting the lengths of neural spines as percentages of trunk length permits comparison of the resulting curves for various animals.   These curves apparently follow a common pattern in all mammals, although the relative lengths of the spines

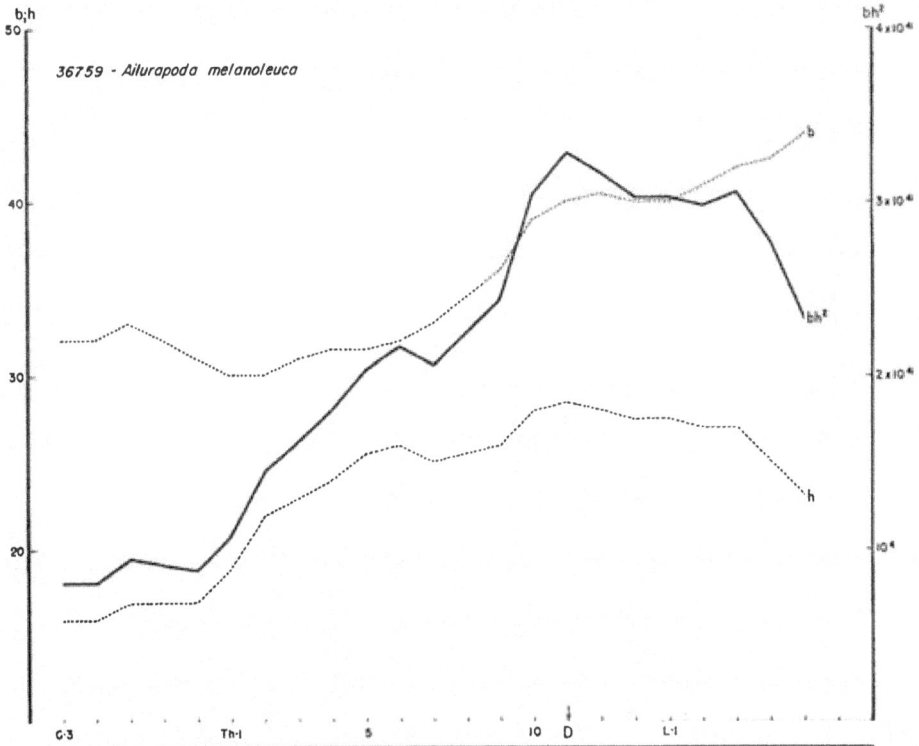

FIG. 34. Curve showing height ($h$), breadth ($b$), and moments of resistance ($bh^2$) in the vertebral column of *Ailuropoda*. D = diaphragmatic vertebra.

vary greatly from species to species. The spines are longest on the anterior thoracic vertebrae (attachment of cervical muscles and ligaments), decrease in length back to the anticlinal or diaphragmatic vertebra, and are slightly longer again on the posterior thoracic and lumbar vertebrae (attachment of longissimus and spinalis muscles). Both *Ursus* and *Ailuropoda* exhibit this type of curve, although in both forms the spines are relatively short along the whole length of the column (fig. 35).

The inclination of the spines conforms less closely to a common pattern than does the height. According to Slijper the direction of a given spine tends, for mechanical reasons, to be perpendicular to the most important muscle inserting into it. The spines of the pre-anticlinal (or pre-diaphragmatic) vertebrae are inclined posteriorly in all carnivores, as they are in all mammals. Among the arctoid Carnivora the post-diaphragmatic spines are inclined anteriorly in the Canidae and Procy-

onidae, are variable among the Mustelidae (from an anterior inclination of 45° in the martens to a slight posterior inclination in the skunks and badgers), and are posteriorly inclined or at most vertical in the Ursidae. In *Ailuropoda* all the post-diaphragmatic vertebrae are posteriorly inclined, the minimum inclination in two skeletons being 20° (fig. 36). According to Slijper the direction of the post-diaphragmatic spines in Carnivora and Primates is determined chiefly by the length of the vertebral bodies, because the angle of attachment of the multifidus muscle depends upon this length. The bodies of the lumbar vertebrae are short in both giant panda and bears, but they are not notably shorter in *Ailuropoda* than in *Ursus*, although the posterior inclination of the spines is much greater. Thus, other factors must be involved in *Ailuropoda*. It is at least suggestive that among the primates and burrowing mustelids a posterior inclination of the post-diaphragmatic spines is associated with anteroposterior thrust along the column.

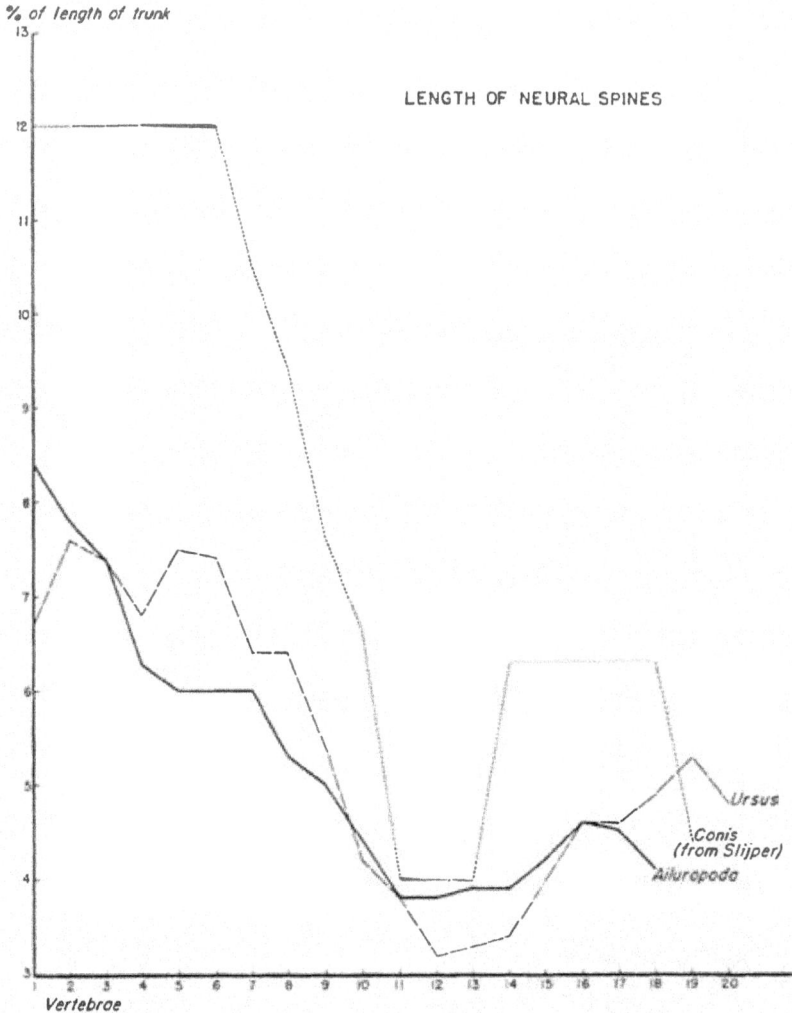

FIG. 35. Curves showing lengths of neural spines in *Ailuropoda*, *Ursus arctos*, and *Canis familiaris*.

## B. DESCRIPTIONS OF VERTEBRAE

### 1. *Cervical Vertebrae*

The cervical vertebrae in *Ailuropoda* are remarkable for their breadth, which gives the cervical region a compressed appearance, especially when viewed from below. Transverse broadening is evident on all vertebrae including the atlas and epistropheus, and greatly exceeds that in any other land carnivore. The vertebrae are shorter anteroposteriorly than in the long-necked *Ursus*, but are

no shorter than in *Procyon* and *Ailurus*. There are seven cervicals in each of the eight skeletons examined.

Except for the distortion resulting from broadening, the cervicals differ little from those of other carnivores. The atlas is similar to that of *Ursus* in the arrangement of foramina; in both there is an alar foramen (vertebral artery and vein), instead of a mere notch as in other arctoids, into which open the atlantal foramen (intervertebral of authors; transmits first spinal nerve and verte-

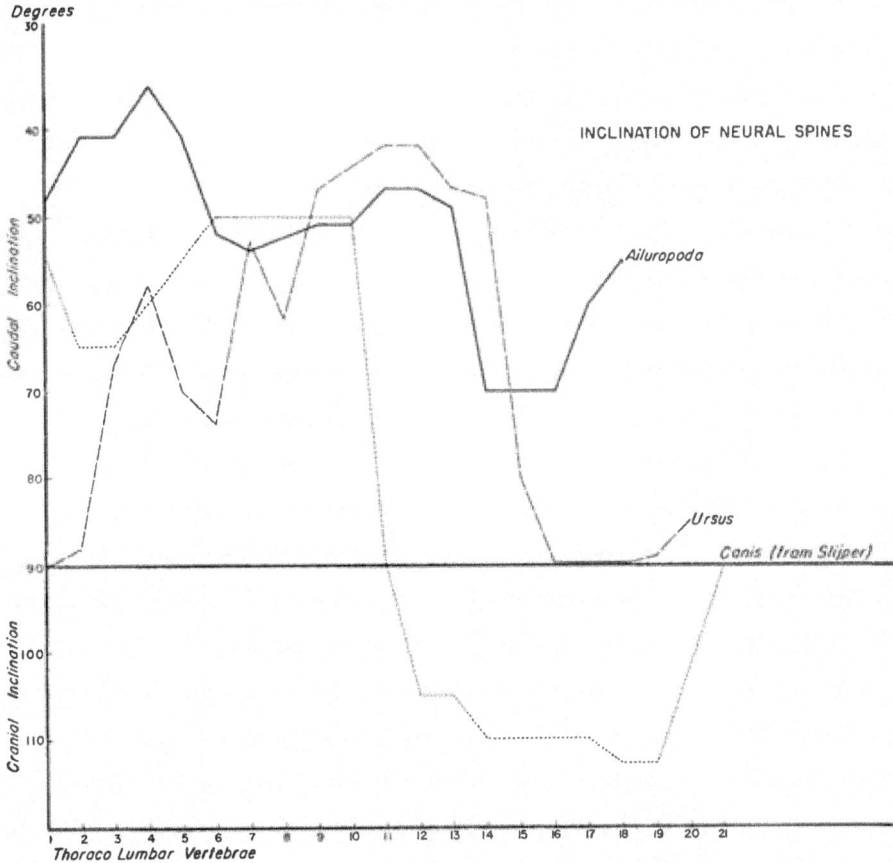

FIG. 36. Curves showing inclination of neural spines in *Ailuropoda*, *Ursus arctos*, and *Canis familiaris*.

bral artery) and transverse foramen (vertebral artery and vein). The foramina on the atlas are crowded together as compared with *Ursus* (fig. 37). The transverse diameter across the wings is greater than in *Ursus*, but the wings are narrower anteroposteriorly.

The third to sixth cervicals are notable chiefly for the conspicuous, backwardly directed hyperapophysis (Mivart) atop each postzygopophysis; these are barely indicated in *Ursus*, and are wanting in other arctoids. The spines are nearly obsolete on the third, fourth, and fifth cervicals, but are of normal length on the sixth and seventh.

## 2. Thoracic Vertebrae

The thoracic region in *Ailuropoda* is notable for its length. Since the number of thoracic vertebrae averages about one less than in *Ursus*, the greater thoracic[1] length must be attributed to longer centra on individual vertebrae, but I have been unable to demonstrate this satisfactorily.

There is, of course, no anticlinal vertebra in *Ailuropoda*, since the neural spines all slope in the same direction. A true anticlinal is also wanting in *Ursus* for the same reason. The *diaphragmatic vertebra* is that transitional vertebra on which the prezygapophyseal facets look upward (horizontal), while the postzygapophyseal facets look outward (vertical or oblique). The diaphragmatic vertebra is the eleventh thoracic in one specimen of *Ailu-*

[1] This length of thorax is approached or even exceeded in some burrowing mustelids, e.g., *Taxidea*, *Mephitis*, *Mellivora*. In these forms, however, the thoracic region has taken over the anterior lumbars, and the thoracic count is 16 or 17.

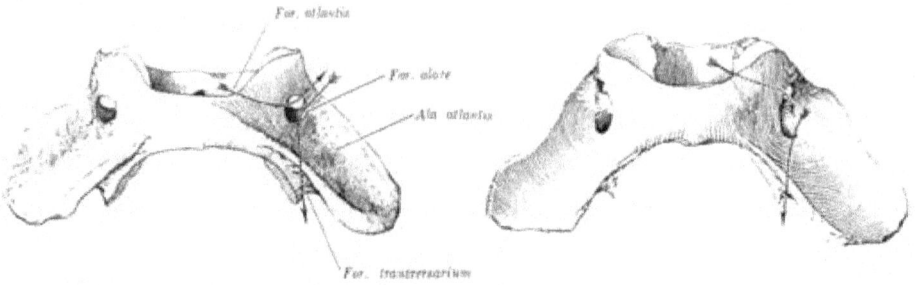

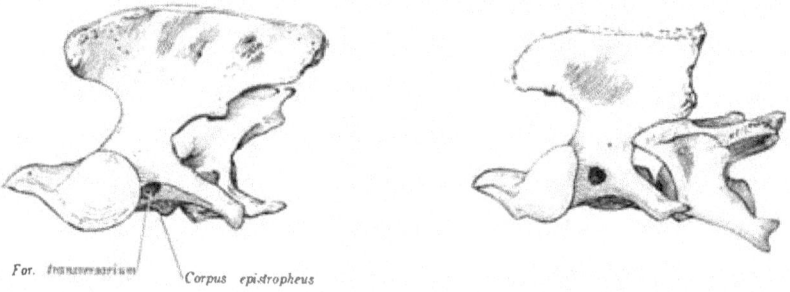

*Ailuropoda*                                        *Ursus americanus*

FIG. 37.   Cervical vertebrae of *Ailuropoda* and *Ursus*.   A, atlas from below; B, epistropheus and third cervical from left side.

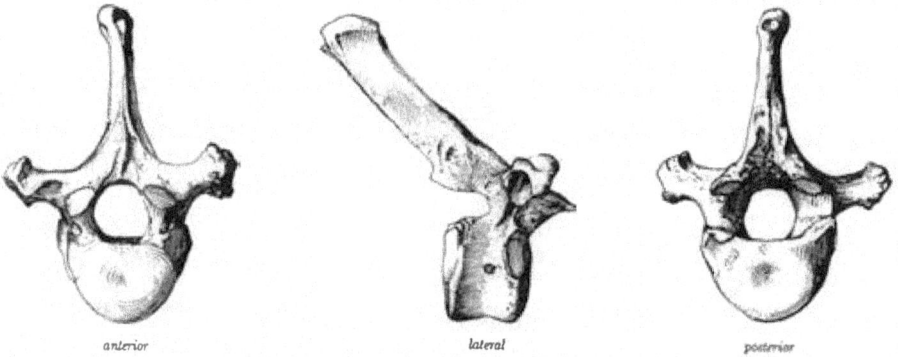

anterior                          lateral                          posterior

FIG. 38.   Fifth thoracic vertebra of *Ailuropoda*.

ropoda, the twelfth in another. It is the eleventh in *Ursus*. It is uniformly Th. 10 in the Canidae. The Procyonidae vary: *Bassariscus*, Th. 10; *Bassaricyon*, Th. 10; *Ailurus*, Th. 11; *Procyon* and *Nasua*, Th. 12.

There are fewer lumbar vertebrae (an average of 4.5 in the eight skeletons examined) than in any other arctoid carnivore.[1] The lumbar spines all slope posteriorly; this is not encountered in any other arctoid, but is approached in *Ursus*.

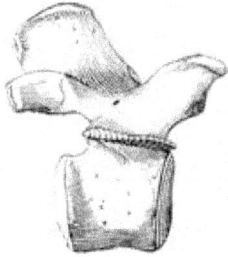

Ailuropoda

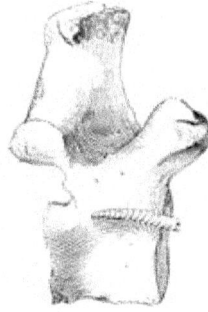

Ursus americanus

FIG. 39. Third lumbar vertebra of *Ailuropoda* and fourth lumbar of *Ursus*, seen from the left.

There are few significant differences in morphological details. The intervertebral foramina (spinal nerves and vessels) are conspicuously larger than in *Ursus*, owing chiefly to the larger size of the posterior vertebral notch. The width across prezygapophyses and postzygapophyses is much greater in *Ailuropoda* than in *Ursus* and other arctoids, which should contribute to the stability of this region. The spines are capitate, especially on the anterior vertebrae. Their posterior borders are less produced than in *Ursus*, and their lateral surfaces present prominent muscle rugosities that are lacking in other arctoids.

3. *Lumbar Vertebrae*

The lumbar region is shorter than in any other arctoid carnivore examined. It is short in burrowing mustelids (*Meles* 22 per cent, *Mellivora* 19 per cent, but *Taxidea* 26–27 per cent) and hyenas (18–20 per cent). The length relative to the total column is not much greater in *Ursus* than in *Ailuropoda* (see Table 10), but because of the long neck in bears this does not properly reflect the true shortness of the lumbar region in *Ailuropoda*. The *absolute* length of the lumbar region in *Ailuropoda* is only 165–180 mm. (32–33 per cent of thoraco-lumbar length), while in a bear of comparable size (*Ursus americanus*) it measures 233 mm. (38 per cent of thoraco-lumbar length).

The form of the vertebrae is similar to that in *Ursus*. The centra are very short in both. As with the thoracics, the intervertebral foramina are larger, and the pre- and postzygapophyses are wider than in *Ursus*.

The lumbar spines in both the giant panda and the bears are short and stumpy, and are either vertical (*Ursus*) or posteriorly inclined (*Ailuropoda*). Slijper believes that the vertical position of the spines in *Ursus* is correlated with the shortness of the lumbar centra, which results in greater mechanical efficiency in the longissimus and multifidus muscles attaching to them.

The transverse processes are not well developed in either *Ailuropoda* or *Ursus*. In both they are relatively short, and directed transversely instead of anteriorly as in other arctoids. These processes provide attachment for the ilio-costal and quadratus lumborum muscles, which function in extension and flexion of the column and hence are important in movements of the back during running.

Anapophyses (accessory process of Reighard and Jennings and Baum and Zietzschmann) are pres-

[1] In some of the burrowing mustelids (*Arctonyx, Conepatus, Mellivora*) four is apparently the normal number of lumbars. In these, however, the number of thoracics is correspondingly increased, and the thoraco-lumbar count is 20 or 21, the typical carnivore formula. The curve of the moments of resistance is also altogether different.

ent on the first two lumbars, are barely indicated on the third, and are obsolete on succeeding vertebrae. *Ursus* is practically identical. These processes are present on all lumbars except the last in *Procyon* and *Nasua*, and on all but the last two in

Four pelves of *Ailuropoda* were available for detailed examination. Three full vertebrae are involved in the sacro-iliac joint in two, and two and a part of the third are involved in two individuals. In one sacrum articulating by three full vertebrae,

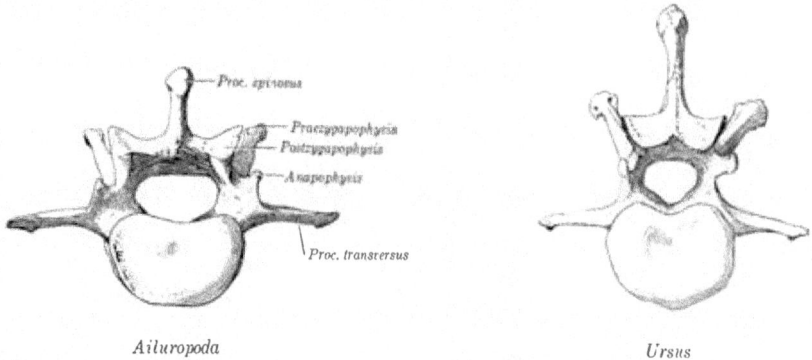

Ailuropoda

Ursus

FIG. 40. Second lumbar vertebra of *Ailuropoda* and *Ursus americanus*, seen from the rear.

other procyonids and *Canis*. They provide insertion for the tendons of the longissimus muscle, which functions in extension and flexion movements of the vertebral column.

### 4. Sacral Vertebrae

The sacrum is composed of five fused vertebrae in all eight skeletons of *Ailuropoda* examined. As will be seen from the accompanying table, *Ursus* is remarkably varied in this respect, although the most frequent number is likewise five. In all other arctoid carnivores the normal number of sacrals is three. (Sacrals are reckoned, according to the definition of Schultz and Straus, as "the vertebrae composing the sacrum and possessing intervertebral and sacral foramina ringed completely by bone in the adult.")

Number of Sacral Vertebrae

| | 2 | 3 | 4 | 5 | 6 |
|---|---|---|---|---|---|
| Canis latrans.... ......... | 1 | 14 | | .. | .. |
| Canis lupus.......... | | 10 | .. | .. | .. |
| Vulpes fulva ... | | 10 | .. | .. | .. |
| Urocyon cinereoargenteus.. | | 5 | | .. | ... |
| Bassariscus astutus. | | 7 | | | |
| Nasua narica........ | | 1 | | .. | .. |
| Nasua nasua... | | 5 | .. | .. | .. |
| Procyon lotor... | | 13 | 3 | | .. |
| Bassaricyon alleni... | 2 | 6 | .. | .. | .. |
| Ailurus fulgens* | | 5 | | .. | |
| Ursus sp.**.... | | 1 | 3 | 6 | 2 |
| Ailuropoda melanoleuca.... | | | | 8 | |

\* One record from Flower.   \*\* Six records from Flower.

the first sacral has the appearance of a transformed lumbar—well-formed pre- and postzygapophyses, enormous sacral foramina, incomplete fusion of the centra ventrally—although on the basis of the total column it is numerically equivalent to the first sacral of the second individual. This is of interest in connection with the reduced number of thoracolumbars in *Ailuropoda*, and the extraordinary instability of the thoraco-lumbar boundary. It is further evidence of the genetic instability of the posterior part of the vertebral column in this species.

In the primary condition in arctoids, as seen in *Canis, Bassariscus*, and *Nasua*, the sacro-iliac articulation is restricted almost entirely to a single vertebra, the first sacral. In *Procyon* and *Ursus* the articulation is more extensive, including the first two sacrals, while in *Ailuropoda* it reaches its maximum among the arctoid carnivores with the third vertebra participating more or less completely.

It is interesting and suggestive that the increase in length of sacrum and extent of sacro-iliac articulation among the Carnivora is paralleled among the Primates. The figures given by Schultz and Straus (1945) show that the number of sacrals increases abruptly in the anthropoid apes and man over the number found in other Primates (except the aberrant Lorisinae). Examination of a series of primate skeletons shows that the extent of the sacro-iliac articulation is likewise increased in the bipedal apes and man.

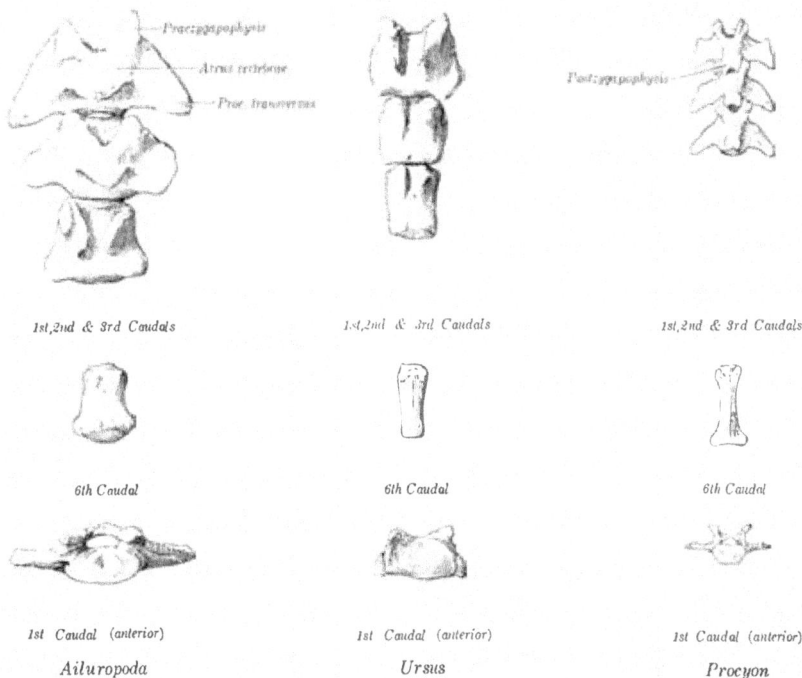

1st,2nd & 3rd Caudals       1st,2nd & 3rd Caudals       1st,2nd & 3rd Caudals

6th Caudal       6th Caudal       6th Caudal

1st Caudal (anterior)       1st Caudal (anterior)       1st Caudal (anterior)

*Ailuropoda*       *Ursus*       *Procyon*

FIG. 41. Caudal vertebrae of *Ailuropoda, Ursus americanus*, and *Procyon lotor*. First three caudals, dorsal view; sixth caudal, dorsal view.

The morphology of the sacrum in *Ailuropoda* is similar to that of *Ursus* but differs in a number of respects. The long axis of the bone is nearly straight in the panda, while in the bears it is slightly curved ventrad. In the panda the sacrum, like the remainder of the vertebral column, appears to be expanded laterally and depressed dorso-ventrally. The spines are fused to form a continuous median sacral crest, which forms a peak on the first sacral and becomes nearly or quite obsolete on the fifth. The intervertebral foramina are minute, irregular, and nearly obliterated. There are four pairs of dorsal sacral foramina (dorsal divisions of sacral nerves, branches of lateral sacral arteries). The first two pairs are irregular, often small and almost obliterated as a result of bone growth in connection with the sacro-iliac ankylosis. The last two pairs are larger and more regular. The four pairs of ventral sacral foramina (ventral divisions of sacral nerves, branches of lateral sacral arteries) are much larger and more regular than the dorsal foramina.

### 5. Caudal Vertebrae

The tail is short and almost vestigial, but neither as short nor as degenerate as in the bears.

Nowhere is the shortening and dorso-ventral flattening of all the vertebrae of *Ailuropoda* more apparent than in the tail. All the caudals are heavy and stocky; even those toward the tip of the tail lack the slender rod-like form characteristic of other carnivores. This is undoubtedly to be interpreted as a gratuitous extension of the factors influencing the remainder of the column, since in *Ailuropoda*, as in the bears, the tail is functionless.

The tail is composed of eleven vertebrae in the one specimen in which it is complete. This is within the range of variation of *Ursus*, in which there are eight to eleven or more vertebrae. Other arctoids have much longer tails, with from eighteen to twenty or more vertebrae, each of which is relatively much longer than in *Ailuropoda* or *Ursus*.

The first two caudals are well formed in *Ailuropoda*, with complete neural arch but no neural spine, wide transverse processes, and prezyga-pophyses; postzygapophyses, which are present in other arctoids except *Ursus*, are wanting. On the first vertebra the transverse processes extend the entire length of the centrum, and even anteriorly beyond the centrum onto the prezygapophysis. There are no chevron bones. In *Ursus*, in contrast, the neural arches are wanting on all caudals (*L. americanus*) or are present on only the first vertebra, and the transverse processes are almost completely obsolete even on the first caudal. Chevron bones are wanting in the bears.

Viewed from the front, the first caudal exhibits to a striking degree the dorso-ventral flattening of the vertebrae (fig. 41).

The remaining caudals are short and stocky, exhibiting less of the typical rod-like form than is seen even in *Ursus*. The broadening effect is evident at least back to the seventh vertebra, the transverse processes becoming entirely obsolete on the eighth.

### C. Review of the Vertebral Column

The contrast between Gadow's explanation of the evolution of the vertebral column (1933) and that of Slijper (1946) is a measure of the altered point of view with respect to this complex structure. To Gadow the column is a series of discrete entities, each with its own almost independent phylogenetic history. A lumbar vertebra is fundamentally a lumbar, regardless of whether it has been "transformed" into a thoracic in one instance or a sacral in another. The functioning of the column, as well as mechanisms by which observed differences could have been achieved, are ignored. The goal is to discover the "true homologies" of elements—a goal that, with respect to the vertebrae, we now know is largely a will-o'-the-wisp. This is the classical outlook of many of the older comparative anatomists.

Slijper, on the other hand, has regarded the column, along with its muscles and ligaments, as an architectural construction responsive to the mechanical demands of posture and locomotion. He has tried to determine correlations between structure and function under varying conditions. Homologies are not considered. His work is essentially an engineering study.

Neither Gadow nor Slijper considered the question of how, from the standpoint of evolutionary mechanisms, the differences they observed could have been brought about. Studies by Kühne (1936) and others on the inheritance of variations in the human vertebral column showed that differentiation of the column, like that of other homiotic structures, is genetically controlled as a series of fields or gradients of differentiation and growth. These fields correspond to the thoracic, lumbar, and sacral regions of the column. The anlage of a vertebra is indifferent; its differentiated form depends on its position in a particular field. There is also a general cranio-caudal gradient of differen-

tiation; so increasing the tempo of development would shift the boundaries of all regions cranially, and vice versa. Kühne emphasized that all displacements were always in the same direction in a given individual. Moreover, "besides the trunk skeleton, the field of action embraces the peripheral nervous system (limb plexuses), musculature, blood vessels, and a large part of the organs of the thoracic and abdominal cavities" (Kühne). Kühne concluded that all the variations he observed could be explained by assuming a single pair of alleles, "craniad" and "caudad." These deductions were verified experimentally by Sawin (1945, 1946), who concluded from breeding experiments on rabbits that displacements of the boundaries of vertebral regions are determined primarily by a single pair of genes.

Among the arctoid carnivores the thoracolumbar boundary is shifted caudad in the Procyonidae (except the primitive *Bassariscus*) and Ursidae. The functional significance, if any, of this shift is unknown. It did not affect the number of thoracolumbar segments, which remain at the typical 20. In *Ailuropoda* the thoracolumbar boundary is variable, but obviously has been shifted cranially from its position in the Ursidae. The lumbosacral boundary has likewise been shifted cranially two to three vertebrae from its typical position in arctoid carnivores. Thus in *Ailuropoda*, as in the higher primates, there is a general cranial displacement in the regional boundaries of the column. In both the panda and the higher primates this cranial shift is associated with intense differentiation in the anteriormost part of the body axis— the head. In both cases this "cephalization" represents an increase in the tempo of differentiation or growth, although very different tissues are involved. Because of the axial gradient, the cephalization is accompanied by a cranial shift in the boundaries of the regions of the column. Consequently, shortening of the column and displacement of its regional boundaries in *Ailuropoda* (and probably also in the higher primates) are not themselves adaptive, but are *consequential results of a process of cephalization*. In bulldogs, which are likewise characterized by cephalization, Klatt and Oboussier (1951) reported malformations of the vertebral column (but no reduction in number of vertebrae) in about 80 per cent of their specimens.

The vertebrae are also broadened and depressed in *Ailuropoda* in comparison with *Ursus* and other carnivores. There is no way of determining how much this is due to secondary postnatal factors extrinsic to the bone itself, although there is no evidence that the condition is adaptive. The facts that it is markedly evident in the tail, where the static influences of posture and locomotion do not exist, and that the same effect is evident on the proximal ends of the ribs, strongly suggest that this is a part of the field effect involving the entire axial region of the body.

Homiotic variability in the column of *Ailuropoda* is greater than in any other carnivore examined. This indicates that the mechanism regulating differentiation of the column is not yet stabilized around a new norm, which in turn suggests an absence of strong selection pressure on this region.

Thus the vertebral column of *Ailuropoda* differs from that of *Ursus* in several respects. The differences are not random, but rather form some kind of pattern. We must assume as a working hypothesis that the differences are adaptive—that they are a product of natural selection. We then seek answers to two questions: (1) what is their functional significance, and (2) what morphogenetic mechanism, intrinsic to the bone tissue, lies behind them?

It has been noted repeatedly throughout the description that the column of *Ailuropoda* resembles columns designed to withstand strong thrust forces acting anteroposteriorly in the direction of the sacrum. Among terrestrial mammals such forces, and correlated modifications of the column, occur only in fossorial and bipedal forms. The work of Slijper shows that the mammalian column responds adaptively to such forces, even nongenetically. *Ailuropoda* is, of course, in no way fossorial; and it is no more bipedal than the bears, in which the column shows slight—almost trivial compared with that in *Ailuropoda*—convergence toward the column of truly bipedal forms. The column of *Ailuropoda* cannot be explained on the basis of mechanical requirements, and therefore the differences from *Ursus* cannot be attributed to natural selection acting on the column. The seemingly adaptive modifications must be "pseudo-adaptations."

The data of Sawin and Hull suggest an alternative explanation. All those areas of a tissue that are in a state of competence at a given moment during ontogeny are known to be affected by a genetic factor operating at that moment. Thus the lumbosacral peculiarities of *Ailuropoda* may reflect an accident of ontogenetic timing rather than the action of selection on the lumbar region. If the differentiating lumbar region were competent at the same moment as some other region on which selection was acting strongly (e.g., the skull), then in the absence of strong selection *against* the induced lumbar modifications, such modifications would be carried as a pleiotropic effect. If they

were strongly selected against they would presumably be buffered out. The extraordinary homiotic variability of the lumbosacral region in *Ailuropoda* supports this interpretation, as does the otherwise unintelligible modification of the pelvis (p. 113).

On the basis of the available evidence it must be concluded that primary differences between the column of *Ailuropoda* and that of *Ursus* are not adaptive, but represent a pleiotropic effect resulting from an accident of ontogenetic timing. The genetic basis for such an effect is probably very simple.

D. CONCLUSIONS

1. The vertebral column of *Ailuropoda* differs from that of *Ursus* (and other arctoid carnivores) in several important respects.

   (a) The regional boundaries are shifted cranially in a gradient that decreases in intensity from the lumbosacral boundary (greatest) to the thoracocervical (least).

   (b) All vertebrae are broadened and depressed.

   (c) Homiotic variability exceeds that known in any other carnivore.

2. The differences are not adaptive.

3. The differences are associated with intensified growth at the anterior end of the body axis—the head. Similar correlations are evident in primates and in bulldogs.

4. The characteristic basic features of the vertebral column in *Ailuropoda* are a pleiotropic effect resulting from an accident of ontogenetic timing.

V. THE THORAX

The thoracic region, as pointed out above, is relatively longer in *Ailuropoda* than in any other arctoid carnivore. This is true when the extent of the thorax is measured dorsally, along the vertebral column. On the other hand the ventral length of the thorax, measured along the sternum, is notably less than in any other arctoid carnivore.

A. RIBS

The number of ribs varies between 13 and 14 pairs in the eight skeletons examined, with a high proportion of asymmetries on the two sides of the same animal (see Table 9, p. 75). On the basis of the available material it is impossible to determine which is the typical number.

In one skeleton (31128), which shows other gross abnormalities, the first rib on the left side is short, not reaching the manubrium, and the tubercular head is pathological. The second rib resembles the first of the opposite side, but its sternal end is bifurcate and attaches to the manubrium by a wide bifurcate costal cartilage.

of the sternum in this animal. In Su Lin two pairs of the false ribs are floating.

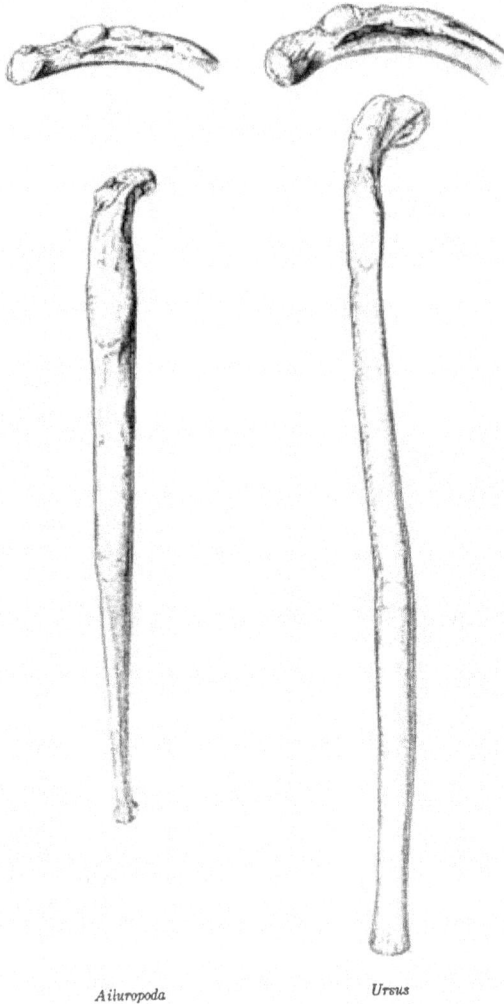

*Ailuropoda*                    *Ursus*

FIG. 42. Tenth rib, lateral view. Above, posterior views of heads of same ribs.

In two skeletons there are nine pairs of true ribs, which is the normal number for arctoid carnivores. The eighth and ninth pairs are not attached to sternebrae in *Ailuropoda*, however; instead, the ends of the sternal cartilages of each pair meet at the ventral midline, ventral of the xiphoid cartilage. This is obviously a result of the shortening

The first costal cartilage is about 20 mm. long, the ninth about 230 mm., in Su Lin. In an adult the costal cartilages are very heavily calcified, with coarse granular deposits appearing on the surface.

The ribs are very similar in length and curvature to those of bears of comparable size ( *Ursus americanus*). All the ribs are remarkable, however, for

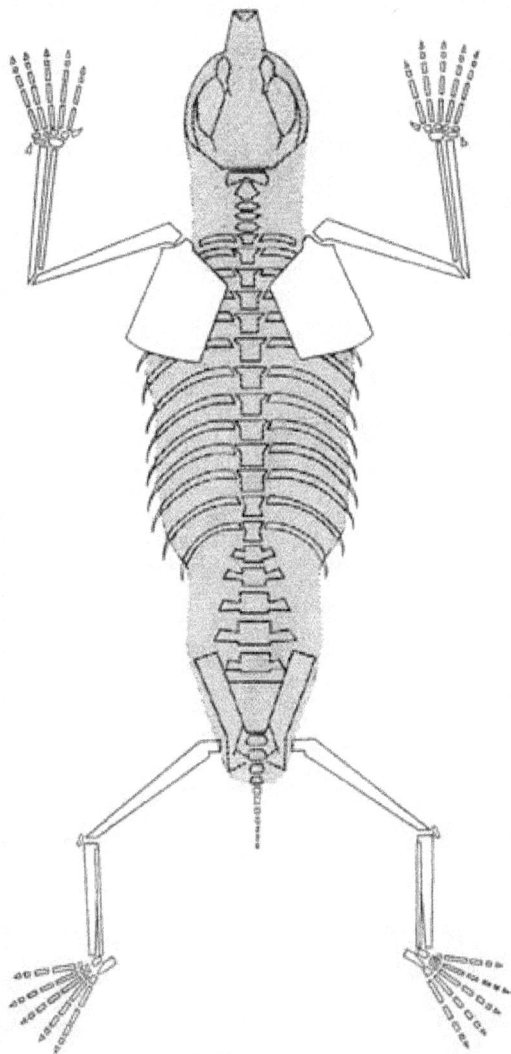

FIG. 43.  Approximate area of maximal increase in thickness of cortical bone in *Ailuropoda*.

the immense bulk of their vertebral ends (fig. 42). The transverse diameter of the neck of a given rib in *Ailuropoda* is at least twice the diameter in *Ursus americanus*.  The disparity becomes increasingly less toward the sternal end of the rib, until the sternal third is no larger in the panda than in the bear.  It is at least suggestive that the maximum broadening is in that part of the rib closest to the vertebra, where, as we have seen, a pronounced broadening effect is apparent, and that the width gradually decreases to normal as we move along the rib away from the vertebra.

B. STERNUM

The sternum is composed of a short body and an extremely long xiphoid cartilage.  The body is about 55 per cent of the length of the thorax in

*Ailuropoda*, while in other arctoids it is from 75 to 100 per cent.

There are six sternebrae (including the manubrium) in each of three skeletons of *Ailuropoda* examined. In other arctoids there are nine, except in the Canidae, which usually have only eight. All the sternebrae are short.

The **manubrium** is short, compared with that of *Ursus* and other arctoids, and is relatively wider transversely. In other arctoids this bone is produced anteriorly into a point, so that the outline is similar to a spear head. This point is much less evident in *Ailuropoda*, and in one of three specimens is totally lacking so that the anterior border of the manubrium is truncated. A single pair of costal cartilages articulates with the manubrium.

The remaining sternebrae, five in number, are short and spool-shaped, rectangular in cross section. The first four measure about 25 mm. in length, the fifth about 20 mm.

The **xiphisternum** is a remarkably long (120 mm.) cartilaginous rod, tapering gradually to a point. It provides attachment for the sternal part of the diaphragm and the posterior elements of the transverse thoracic muscle. Elongation of the xiphisternum appears to be a compensation for the shortness of the body of the sternum, since the origin of the sternal part of the diaphragm is thus brought into line with the origin of the costal part of this muscle.

In the Canidae and Procyonidae the xiphisternum is composed of an ossified rod ending in an expanded flattened cartilage. In the Ursidae it is a cartilaginous rod, with an ossicle of variable size embedded in the anterior end.

In the Procyonidae the last sternebra is only about half the thickness of those preceding it, producing a "step" in the sternum. The last costal cartilages meet their fellows beneath this bone, instead of inserting into its lateral edges as they normally do. A similar condition is often seen in bears, in which this sternebra may be entirely unossified. The posterior end of the sternum seems to be undergoing regression in this group.

### C. REVIEW OF THE THORAX

Two points are of interest in the bones of the thorax: the extraordinary expansion of the proximal ends of the ribs, and the shortening of the sternum.

No mechanical advantage can be assigned to the rib condition. It is most easily explained as an extension of the morphogenetic field effect that is operating on the adjoining vertebrae, and hence without functional significance as far as the ribs

are concerned. Thus a region of increased bone deposition extends the entire length of the head and body and extends laterally over the proximal two-thirds of the rib cage (fig. 43). Since the cortex of the long bones is also thickened, the effect is general over the entire skeleton though reduced peripherally. An astonishingly similar condition is seen in the ribs of the Triassic marine nothosaur *Pachypleurosaurus* (1931, Peyer, Abh. Schweiz. Paleont. Ges., 51, pl. 25; 1935, Zangerl, op. cit., 56, fig. 23). In the reptile, enlargement of the proximal ends of the ribs is associated with pachyostosis; there is no evidence of this in *Ailuropoda*.

The extreme shortening of the sternum seen in *Ailuropoda* is foreshadowed in the related procyonids and bears, in which a tendency toward reduction from the rear forward is evident. There is no obvious mechanical advantage to this shift, which is inversely correlated with elongation of the thorax in these animals. The sternum has been shortened repeatedly in various mammalian lines, but to my knowledge this has never been studied from the standpoint of animal mechanics.

We may conclude, provisionally, that (1) *the broadening of the vertebral column has extended morphogenetically to the proximal ends of the ribs in Ailuropoda*, and (2) *the shortening of the sternum is the final expression of a trend, of unknown significance, seen in related forms.*

## VI. THE FORE LEG

In the giant panda, the bears, and the procyonids the fore legs are used for manipulating objects, especially during feeding, to a far greater extent than in other carnivores. This requires a wider range of movement, particularly of abduction of the humerus and rotation of the fore arm, than in typical carnivores. All these forms are also more or less arboreal, and in the heavier forms at least this has profoundly altered the architecture of the shoulder and fore leg (Davis, 1949). Such uses of the fore limb are secondary; in the primary carnivore condition the fore leg is modified for cursorial locomotion, and the structure of the limb in all carnivores has been conditioned by this fact.

### A. BONES OF THE FORE LEG

The **clavicle** is vestigial or absent in all Carnivora, never reaching either the acromion or the sternum when a clavicle is present. Among the Arctoidea it is normally absent in *Canis*, exceptionally being represented by a small nodule of cartilage or bone (Ellenberger and Baum). It is present as a small spicule of bone embedded in the cephalohumeral muscle in *Bassariscus*, *Procyon*, and *Ailurus*. It is completely wanting in the Ursidae, and

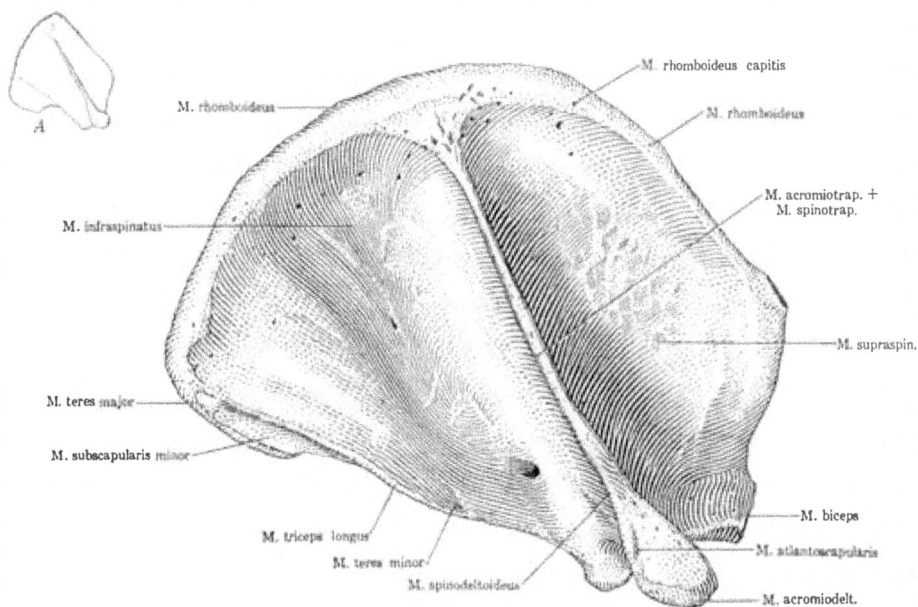

FIG. 44. Right scapula of *Ailuropoda*, lateral view. A, right scapula of *Ursus arctos*.

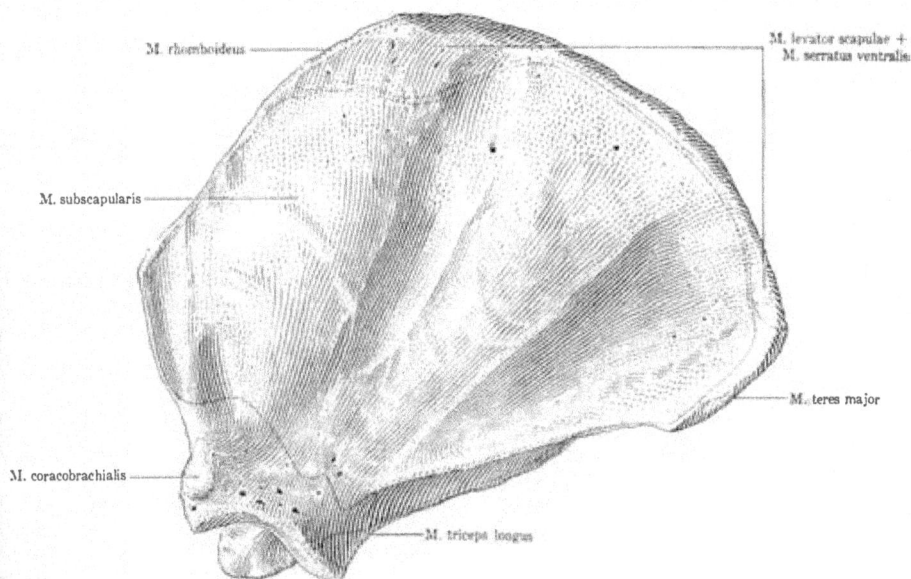

FIG. 45. Right scapula of *Ailuropoda*, medial view.

89

there is no indication of a clavicle in *Ailuropoda*. The clavicle is less degenerate in the Feloidea.

## 1. *Scapula*

It has been stated repeatedly that the scapula is influenced by muscular action probably to a greater degree than any other bone in the body. Dependence of scapula shape on muscle function has been demonstrated experimentally for rats (Wolffson, 1950). The forces involved in molding the scapula are extremely complex, no fewer than 17 muscles arising or inserting on the scapula in carnivores, and interpretation of differences in scapular form is difficult. No adequate study of the relation between form and function of the mammalian scapula exists, although such a study was attempted by Reinhardt (1929).

The scapula of the giant panda appears at first glance to be quite strikingly different from that of any other arctoid. This is due to the unorthodox outline of the bone (fig. 44). Actually, all the features that distinguish the scapula of *Ursus* from other arctoids are also present in *Ailuropoda*, although the large postscapular fossa of the bears is reduced in the panda. These ursid features are: prominent postscapular fossa, large table-like acromion with poorly differentiated metacromion, breadth of neck exceeding long diameter of glenoid fossa, well-defined spiral groove on axillary border, and narrow glenoid cavity. There can be no doubt that the scapula of the giant panda is basically a bear scapula.

I have tried to show (Davis, 1949) that the shoulder architecture of bears, and hence the form of the scapula, is adapted to resist pulling forces (the opposite of the thrust associated with normal locomotion) developed in connection with climbing, the morphological effects of which are exaggerated because of the size of the animal. The tremendous postscapular fossa, from which the subscapularis minor muscle arises, is the most conspicuous feature associated with this reversed force direction; it is even larger in such powerful diggers as the anteaters and armadillos, in which similar pulling forces are involved.

The posterior angle (and thus the scapular index) is influenced chiefly by the posterior part of the serratus ventralis muscle. This part of the serratus is a posterior rotator of the scapula, and is used in protraction of the arm (A. B. Howell, 1926). The posterior part of the serratus is well developed in *Ailuropoda*, and this may account, at least in part, for the pulling out of the posterior angle.

MORPHOLOGY.—The scapula of *Ailuropoda* is more fan-shaped than the almost rectangular scap-

ula of *Ursus*. Of the three borders, the coracoid border is produced anteriorly in some individuals (fig. 44) to form a sharp angle that marks the anterior limit of the insertion of the rhomboideus, which is remarkable for the length of its insertion line. In other individuals this angulation is missing. The scapular notch, which is at best poorly developed in nearly all carnivores, is almost obliterated in *Ailuropoda* and *Ursus*. The vertebral border forms a smooth, gentle curve, with no clear indication of the juncture of the coracoid and vertebral borders (the anterior angle; median angle of human anatomy). This blurring of the anterior angle is characteristic of Carnivora. The posterior extent of the vertebral border is determined by the serratus ventralis; the rhomboids apparently have no influence in determining the position of the posterior angle. The axillary border, from which the long triceps arises, is relatively straight and clearly defined. Its juncture with the vertebral border (the posterior angle; inferior angle of human anatomy) marks the juncture of the serratus ventralis and teres major muscles, and is clearly defined.

*In the Carnivora the outline, and hence the major indices, of the scapula are determined by two muscle groups related to the vertebral border: the rhomboids, and the levator scapulae + serratus ventralis.*

The lateral surface is slightly concave, and is divided by the spine into the supraspinous and infraspinous fossae. The infraspinous fossa considerably exceeds the supraspinous in area, and is relatively much larger than in the bears. This increased size is due to an extension posteriorly of the axillary border, as is shown by the angle formed by the axillary border with the spine; this is 38–40° in *Ailuropoda*, 20–30° in *Ursus*. The floors of both fossae are marked by vermiculate rugosities similar to those seen in the giant anteater, and there is a nutrient foramen in each above the glenoid cavity. The coracoid border of the supraspinous fossa is sometimes raised and sometimes not, a variation also found in bears. In some individuals of *Ailuropoda* it is raised, so that the fossa is concave in cross section, while in others it is depressed, producing a prominent convexity in the fossa. The axillary border of the infraspinous fossa is influenced by the triceps longus, whose origin in the bears and giant panda extends nearly or quite to the posterior angle. This border is sinuous in *Ailuropoda*, straight in the bears. The teres major process lies behind the axillary border at the posterior angle. The teres major muscle arises from its posterior border. The lateral surface of this process is excavated into the postscapular fossa, from which the subscapularis minor muscle arises.

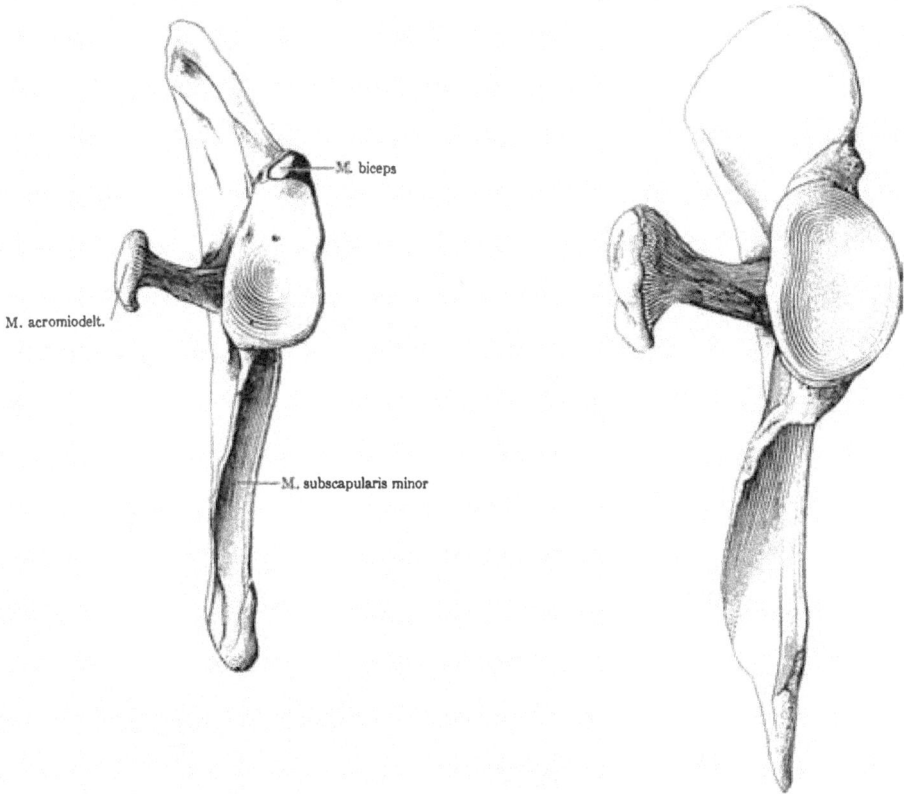

FIG. 46. Ventral view of right scapula of *Ailuropoda* (left) and *Ursus arctos* (right).

In *Ailuropoda* the postscapular fossa is well marked, but has been much reduced by the posterior extension of the infraspinous fossa so that it is much less conspicuous than in *Ursus*. The postscapular fossa is continued toward the glenoid cavity as a wide trough that extends the entire length of the axillary border, separated from the medial surface of the blade by a prominent ridge, and from the lateral surface by the inferior scapular spine. This trough (fig. 46), which lodges the subscapularis minor muscle, is twisted through 180°.

The glenoid cavity is pear-shaped, with the apex anteriorly, as it is in other carnivores and in mammals generally. The notch that appears in the margin opposite the spine in certain carnivores (*Canis*, *Felis*) is wanting in *Ailuropoda* and most other carnivores. In *Ailuropoda* the cavity is narrower (index $\dfrac{\text{length} \times 100}{\text{breadth}} = 645$, mean of two specimens)

than in any other carnivore. It is also narrow in bears (index 670, mean of 6 specimens), and generally narrower in arctoids than in aeluroids. The cavity is shallow in both *Ailuropoda* and *Ursus*.

The neck is notable for its great anteroposterior diameter, although this is slightly less than in *Ursus*. The supraglenoid tuberosity, for the origin of the tendon of the biceps, is a prominent scar immediately above the anterior border of the glenoid cavity. Above and mesad of it is a slight elevation, the coracoid process, bearing on its medial surface a scar from which the tendon of the coracobrachialis arises. The infraglenoid tuberosity, from which the anteriormost fibers of the long triceps take tendinous origin, is much less prominent than in *Ursus*. It is merely a roughened triangular area above the lip of the glenoid cavity that continues without interruption into the axillary border.

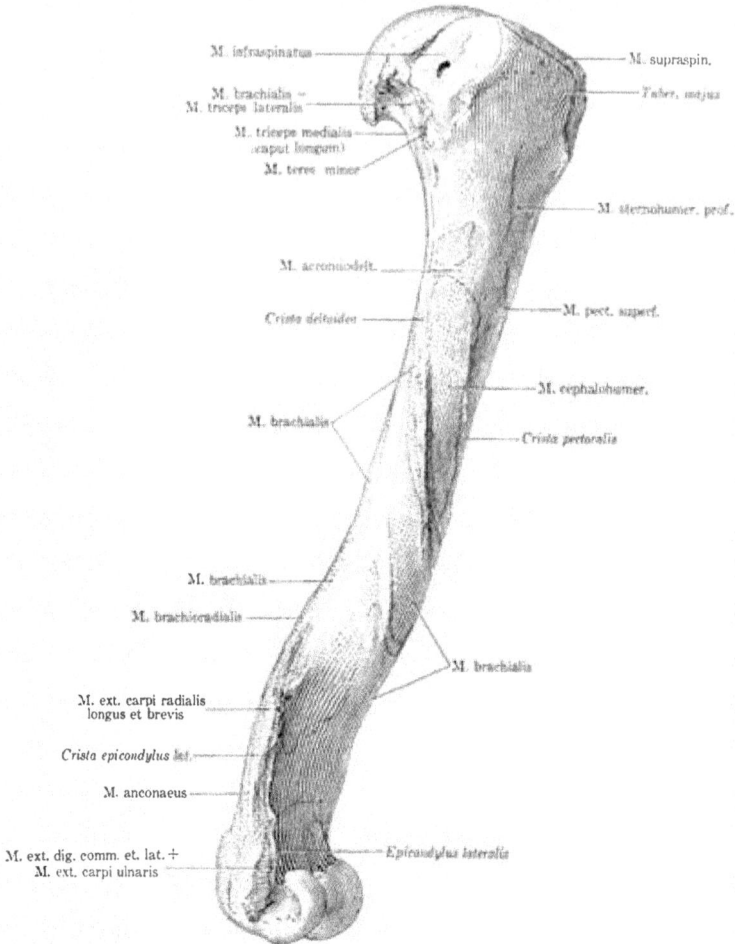

FIG. 47. Lateral view of right humerus of *Ailuropoda*.

The spine is slightly twisted, as it is also in bears, reflecting the action of the deltoid and trapezius muscles. The line formed by the crest of the spine is convex posteriorly, in some individuals markedly so (reflecting the pull of the acromiotrapezius?). The inferior part of the spine, just above the acromion, is inclined slightly anteriorly, while the posterior part is vertical or inclined slightly posteriorly. The lateral (free) border, again as in bears, is squared in cross section. The spine is continued ventrally into a heavy acromion process, which functions in the origin of the acromiodeltoid and levator scapulae ventralis muscles. The metacromion, the process on the posterior border from which the levator scapulae ventralis arises in most carnivores, is not indicated in *Ailuropoda* and is scarcely more prominent in *Ursus*. The lateral surface of the acromion is flat and table-like in both bears and panda.

In summary, the scapula of *Ailuropoda* agrees with *Ursus* in all features that distinguish the bear scapula from that of other carnivores. The most notable difference between the panda and the bears is the posterior expansion of the infraspinous fossa in *Ailuropoda*, which seriously encroaches on but does not obliterate the typically ursid postscapular fossa. The infraspinous fossa is associated with the infraspinous and long triceps muscles, which

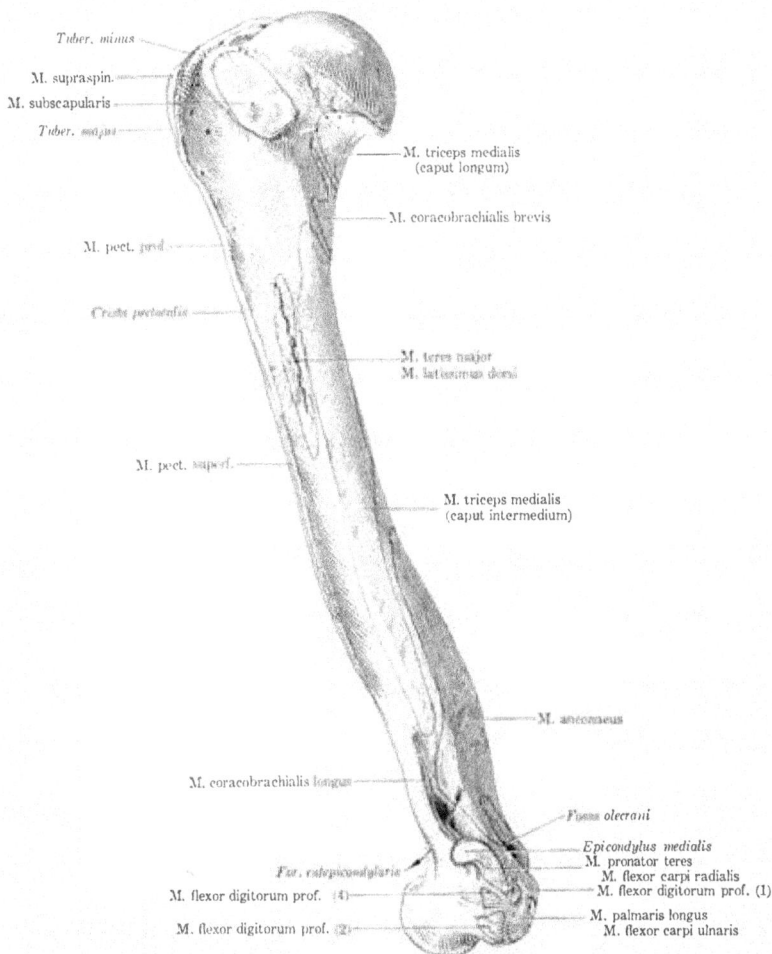

FIG. 48. Medial view of right humerus of *Ailuropoda*.

are involved in fixation and flexion of the shoulder joint.

## 2. *Humerus*

The humerus in the Carnivora serves for the origin or insertion of 28 muscles. Of these, 12 belong to the shoulder joint and 16 to the elbow joint or lower arm and manus. The form of the humerus is determined largely by these muscles.

In *Ailuropoda* the humerus is longer than the radius, as it is in all arctoid carnivores except *Procyon* and most dogs. The mean ratios (length of radius × 100/length of humerus) for various genera are as follows:

| | N | Humeroradial index* |
|---|---|---|
| *Bassaricyon* | 1 | 72.7 |
| *Ailurus* | 3 | 74.7 (72.1–77.8) |
| *Ailuropoda* | 7 | 77.1 (74.7–79.7) |
| *Bassariscus* | 4 | 79.0 (77.9–79.5) |
| *Ursus* (various species) | 6 | 82.3 (78.3–85.8) |
| *Nasua* | 2 | 85.5 (82.7–88.2) |
| *Canis lupus* | 4 | 100.6 (98.1–102.9) |
| *Procyon* | 4 | 100.9 (99.5–102.5) |

* In generalized mammals the radius length is about 85 per cent of the humerus; this is true in such generalized terrestrial insectivores as *Echinosorex*, *Erinaceus*, and *Solenodon*. A. B. Howell (1944) states that in the generalized condition the humerus and radius are about the same length, but this is obviously not true for mammals at least. For simple mechanical reasons the radius tends to lengthen with cursorial locomotion, but reasons for shortening this bone are not so clear. In man (European) the index is about 74.

The humerus of *Ailuropoda* (figs. 47, 48) does not differ notably from that of other arctoid carnivores. It is slightly convex anteriorly. Muscle scars are extremely prominent, and the area above the olecranon fossa, where the anconeus muscle arises, is marked by vermiculate rugosities similar to those on the scapula. The angulation in the profile at the inferior end of the deltoid ridge, characteristic of bears, is wanting in the giant panda.

The head is offset posteriorly from the shaft; a line drawn through the center of the shaft just touches the anterior edge of the head. This is similar to other arctoids, except *Ursus* in which the head lies almost on top of the shaft.[1] The articular surface greatly exceeds the opposing surface on the scapula in area. The head in transverse section forms a perfect arc of about 170°, thus nearly a semicircle. In frontal section it forms a much smaller sector (about 65°) of a circle nearly twice the diameter, so that the head appears flattened when viewed from the rear. In *Ursus* the transverse section of the head is nearly identical with that of *Ailuropoda*, but the frontal section forms a slightly larger sector (78°–93°) of a circle only slightly larger than that formed by the transverse section. In other words, in the bears the humeral head represents a part of a nearly perfect hemisphere, while in *Ailuropoda* it tends toward the almost cylindrical structure seen in such highly cursorial forms as the horse.

The anatomical neck is scarcely indicated, except posteriorly. The tubercles are low and very bear-like. The **greater tubercle** scarcely rises above the level of the head. It is sharply defined anteriorly, where it continues into the pectoral ridge; its posterior boundary is almost obliterated by the infraspinatus impression. The supraspinatus impression extends almost the entire length of the dorsal lip of the greater tubercle. There are several large nutrient foramina between the greater tubercle and the head. The **lesser tubercle is** prominent; the well-marked subscapularis impression covers practically its entire medial surface. The **intertubercular** (bicipital) **groove** between the two tubercles is wide and deep. In life it is bridged over by the transverse humeral ligament to form a canal. The groove lodges the tendon of the biceps and transmits a branch of the internal circumflex artery. There are a number of nutrient foramina in the floor of the groove.

The shaft is triangular in cross section, because of the several prominent crests. The single nutrient canal that is prominent on the posterior surface of the shaft in other arctoids is represented by sev-

eral minute foramina in *Ailuropoda*. The pectoral ridge (crista tuberculi majoris, BNA), on the anteromedial surface, extends from the greater tubercle nearly down to the distal end of the shaft. It is a very prominent crest that provides insertion for the superficial and deep pectoral muscles. The **deltoid ridge** begins immediately below the posterior end of the greater tubercle, on the posterolateral surface of the shaft; near the middle of the shaft it arches across the anterior surface of the shaft and joins the pectoral ridge just below the middle of the humerus. The deltoid ridge provides origin for the long head of the brachial muscle and insertion for the cephalohumeral. Midway between the pectoral and deltoid ridges there is a third ridge, which marks the medial boundary of the insertion of the cephalohumeral. Mesad of the pectoral ridge, on the flat medial surface of the shaft, is a prominent elongate scar 40–50 mm. long that marks the insertion of the latissimus dorsi and teres major.

Distally the shaft bears the tremendous wing-like expansion of the **lateral epicondylar ridge** on its posterolateral surface. This ridge extends proximad nearly to the middle of the shaft. It provides origin for the short head of the brachialis, the brachioradialis, and the extensor carpi radialis longus and brevis. These are all forearm flexors, although the extensor carpi radialis is chiefly an extensor of the hand. The lateral part of the anconeus arises from its posterior face. This ridge is well developed in all procyonids, in some of which (e.g., *Nasua*) it is as prominent as in *Ailuropoda*. It is about as well developed in bears as in the giant panda. It is likewise present in mustelids, and is extremely well developed in burrowers such as *Taxidea* and *Meles*. It is scarcely indicated in the cursorial dogs.

The distal end of the shaft is thinner anteroposteriorly but wider than it is farther proximally; it is relatively slightly wider and much thinner than in bears. The **trochlea** (= capitulum + trochlea of human anatomy) is almost identical with that of *Ursus*, except that it is somewhat wider. The trochlea is divided into lateral and medial parts by a faint ridge that runs spirally posterolaterally to terminate in the ridge bordering the olecranon fossa. The lateral part of the trochlea, with which the radius and a small part of the ulna articulate, forms a semi-cylinder with only a very faint anteroposterior groove. The medial part of the trochlea, which forms the major ulnar articulation, forms a trough-shaped spiral path extending posteriorly well into the olecranon fossa. This spiral trough forces the ulna to shift medially 5 mm. or more as the elbow is flexed. The poste-

---

[1] In other ursids (*Thalarctos*, *Melursus*, *Helarctos*) the head is offset. *Tremarctos* is similar to *Ursus*.

rior part of this trough has an extremely prominent external lip on which the articular surface faces medially. The **coronoid fossa**, above the trochlea anteriorly, is entirely wanting, as it is also in bears. The **olecranon fossa**, above the trochlea posteriorly, is deep and relatively wider than in *Ursus*.

ratio, length pelvis/length radius is 130.3 (126.8–132.7) in *Ailuropoda*, 110.3 (107.3–118.4) in *Ursus*, 100.9 (95.5–103.3) in *Procyon*, 108.2–108.8 in *Ailurus*, 110.9 (105.3–113.9) in *Bassariscus*, and 78.4 (76.3–80.1) in *Canis*. The significance of the reduced radius length in *Ailuropoda* is discussed below (p. 102). In both panda and bears the radius

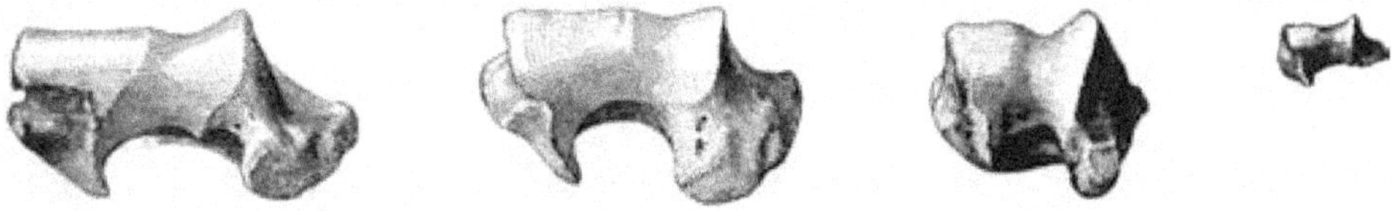

Ailuropoda                    Ursus                         Canis              Procyon

FIG. 49.   Distal ends of humeri of *Ailuropoda, Ursus americanus, Canis lupus,* and *Procyon lotor.*

The **medial epicondyle** is more prominent and more vertically compressed than in *Ursus*. It provides origin for the pronator teres, flexor carpi radialis, flexor digitorum profundus, palmaris longus, and flexor carpi ulnaris. These are all flexors of the hand, except the pronator teres, which pronates the forearm.    The **entepicondylar foramen**, which transmits the median nerve and median artery, was present in all specimens of *Ailuropoda* examined. This foramen is absent in the Ursidae (except *Tremarctos ornatus*) and Canidae, present in the Procyonidae, in *Ailurus*, and in most Mustelidae. Its presence in *Ailuropoda* and *Tremarctos* is probably a secondary condition correlated with the large size of the epicondyle in these two genera.

The **lateral epicondyle** is less prominent than in *Ursus*, and is considerably narrower. It provides origin for the extensor digitorum communis and lateralis and the extensor carpi ulnaris. These are all extensors of the manus, although the extensor carpi ulnaris chiefly abducts the hand ulnarward. It has no direct genetic basis, and in this instance cannot be used as a "character."

The humerus of *Ailuropoda* is so similar to that of the bears, especially to such forms as *Tremarctos* and *Melursus*, that Lydekker's statement (1901) to the contrary is almost incomprehensible.

### 3.   Ulna and Radius

The ulna is slightly heavier than in a bear of comparable size, while the radius is slightly more slender. The radius is shorter in relation to pelvic length than in any other carnivore measured. The

lies almost entirely laterad of the ulna at the elbow joint. The radius is slightly more dorsal in *Procyon* and *Ailurus*, and in the narrow elbow joint of the cursorial dogs it lies almost in front of the ulna.

The form of the ulna is very similar to that of *Ursus*. The olecranon, measured from the center of the semilunar notch, averages 14 per cent of the length of the humerus;[1] this is likewise true for *Ursus, Procyon,* and *Ailurus*, while in *Canis* it is longer (19 per cent). The olecranon, which provides insertion for the triceps complex and the flexor carpi ulnaris, is a heavy knob-like extension of the ulna, bent slightly medially. The medial surface is concave and is devoid of muscle attachments; the lateral surface provides attachment for parts of the triceps and anconeus. Anteriorly the olecranon forms the prominent **anconeal process**, which interlocks with the olecranon fossa of the humerus and forms the posterior part of the semilunar notch.

The **semilunar notch**, bounded anteriorly by the coronoid process and posteriorly by the anconeal process, is almost a perfect semicircle in profile. It is arched in cross section, lacking the median guiding ridge seen in dogs. The anconeal process has an extensive external face that rides against the external lip on the posterior part of the trochlea, and the coronoid process an internal face that rides against the inner wall of the trochlear groove. This arrangement effectively locks the elbow joint and prevents any medial shifting

[1] Calculation as percentage of ulna length gives misleading values in forms with elongated fore arm, such as *Procyon* and *Canis*.

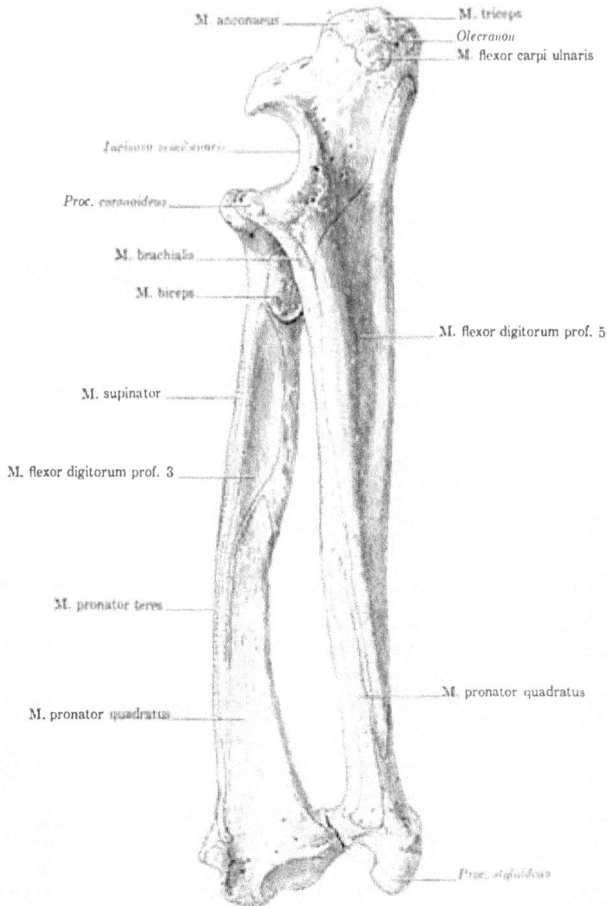

FIG. 50.  Right ulna and radius of *Ailuropoda*, posteromedial view.

of the distal end of the ulna; there is no such protection against lateral shifting.

The **radial notch** is a shallow depression on the lateral side of and immediately below the coronoid process, in which the head of the radius rotates.

The shaft tapers gradually toward the distal end.  It is slightly bowed, with the convexity outward.  The bone is wider anteroposteriorly than it is from side to side.  Immediately below the coronoid process, on the anterior surface of the bone, there is a prominent ovoid depression that marks the insertion of the brachialis tendon.  In most specimens a wide rugose ridge along the middle third of the lateral surface of the shaft marks the attachment of the interosseous ligament.

The distal end of the ulna is slightly expanded. Dorsally it bears a circular, much-rounded articular facet for the radius.  Beyond this the shaft is continued into the short peg-like **styliform process**, which bears a rounded facet for the cuboid and pisiform on its anteromedial surface.

The **radius** is curved in both planes; it is slightly convex anteriorly, and forms a long S-curve in the lateral plane.  This complex curvature of the radius is seen to some degree in all Carnivora except the cursorial dogs.

The **capitulum** of the radius is set off by a very distinct neck.  It is an elliptical disk, the long diameter running from anterolateral to posteromedial.  The ratio of long to short diameter is about 10 : 7, and this ratio is about the same as in *Ursus*. In burrowing forms (*Taxidea, Meles*) the capitulum is even more ovate, whereas in ar- cumference of the head; the medial one-fourth, where the capitular eminence is situated, has no articular surface.

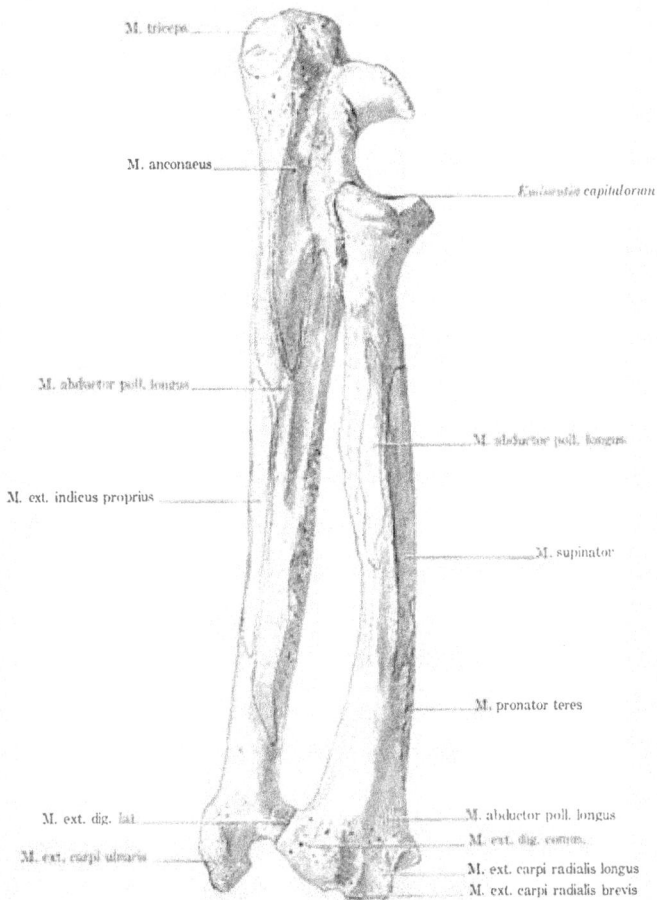

FIG. 51.  Right ulna and radius of *Ailuropoda*, anterolateral view.

boreal forms (*Procyon, Nasua, Potos*) it is more nearly circular.

The capitular depression, which articulates with the lateral part of the trochlea of the humerus, is very shallow.  On its anteromedial circumference it bears a low elevation, the capitular eminence, that forms the anterior lip of the radiohumeral articulation in all positions of the radius, and acts as a stop that limits the excursion of rotatory movements of the radius.  The articular circumference, which articulates with the radial notch of the ulna, is not continuous around the entire cir-

The shaft of the radius is triangular in cross section, the base of the triangle forming the flat ventral surface of the bone.  The radial tuberosity, for the insertion of the biceps tendon, is on the ventromedial surface immediately below the neck.  Opposite this, on the anterior aspect, is a scar marking the attachment of the lateral collateral ligament.  The interosseous crest, for the attachment of the interosseous ligament, begins below the radial tuberosity as a wide, roughened scar for the heavy proximal part of the ligament.  A little above the middle of the bone it changes abruptly into a ridge-like crest.

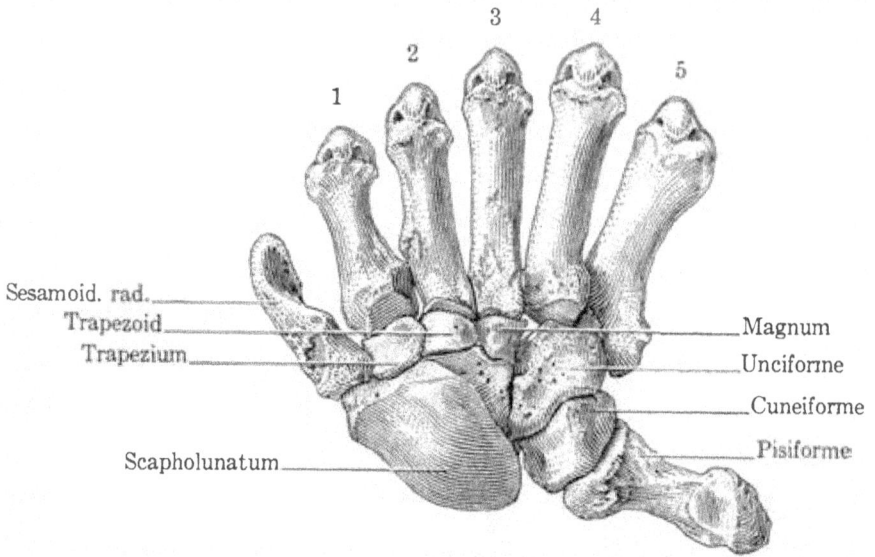

Sesamoid. rad.
Trapezoid
Trapezium

Magnum
Unciforme
Cuneiforme
Pisiforme

Scapholunatum

1   2   3   4   5

Fig. 52. Right carpus and metacarpus of *Ailuropoda*, dorsal view.

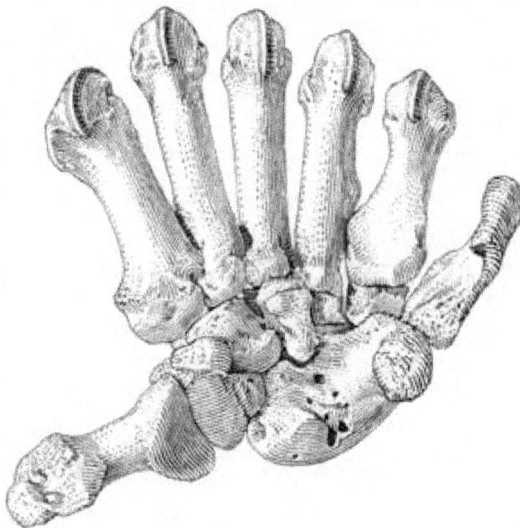

Fig. 53. Right carpus and metacarpus of *Ailuropoda*, ventral view.

The distal end of the radius is expanded and bears two articular surfaces, the large concave carpal surface for articulation with the scapholunar, and laterally the small flat ulnar notch for articulation with the ulna. The carpal surface is narrower from side to side but wider anteroposteriorly than in *Ursus*, thus providing a less trough-like articulation for the carpus. The prominent saddle shape of the articular area on the styloid process that is seen in *Ursus* is scarcely indicated in *Ailuropoda*. Also the medial end of the articular surface is in *Ailuropoda* deflected proximally toward the ulnar notch. The styloid process is a blunt projection on the medial side; a deep furrow on its dorsolateral surface lodges the tendon of the abductor pollicis longus. Just laterad of this, on the dorsal surface of the styloid process, is a shallow furrow for the tendon of the extensor carpi radialis longus, separated by a ridge from the furrow for the extensor carpi radialis brevis. Another shallow furrow near the lateral border lodges the tendon of the extensor digitorum communis.

## 4. Carpus

The carpus (figs. 52, 53) is very similar to that of bears, except for the tremendous development of the radial sesamoid and the modifications of the scapholunar associated therewith. The carpus-forearm articulation is largely between the scapholunar and the radius, which form an almost ball-and-socket joint permitting very extensive excursion. The styloid process of the ulna, as in bears and procyonids, is lodged in a widely open notch formed by the cuneiform and pisiform.

The carpus is dominated by the **scapholunar.** This bone greatly exceeds any of the other carpals in size, and articulates with all the other carpal bones except the pisiform, and with the radius and the radial sesamoid. The articular surface for the radius occupies almost the entire dorsal and posterior surfaces of the bone, forming an ovate articulation that in some individuals is in contact anteriorly with the articular surface for the trapezium. This is more extensive than in any other carnivore, although in *Ailurus* and *Potos* it is closely approached. In *Ursus* the lateral part of this surface has a dimple-like depression, to receive the saddle on the distal end of the radius; this depression is completely wanting in *Ailuropoda* and in *Ailurus* and *Potos*. The anteromedial end of the bone is produced into a stout hook-like process, directed ventrally, that bears a prominent articular surface for the radial sesamoid on its anteromedial surface. This articular surface is an elongate oval, its long axis vertical, and is convex in both planes. The anterior surface of the scapholunar bears three irregular shallow excavations for the trapezium,

trapezoid, and magnum, and the lateral surface bears articular facets for the magnum and unciform.

The **cuneiform** is very similar to the corresponding bone in *Ursus*, but relatively slightly larger. It articulates with the scapholunar, the pisiform, and the unciform.

The **pisiform** is, next to the scapholunar, the largest bone in the carpus, and is very similar to the corresponding bone in *Ursus*. It articulates with the cuneiform, forming with it a shallow V-shaped notch dorsolaterally, in which the styliform process of the ulna articulates. The bone extends posteriorly, ventrally, and slightly laterally from the carpus, its expanded tip embedded in a large fibro-fatty pad that underlies the lateral carpal pad. Five muscles and five ligaments attach to the bone. The tendon of the flexor carpi ulnaris attaches to the posterior surface, the opponens and abductor digiti quinti and palmaris brevis to the anterior surface, and the flexor digiti quinti to the inner border. A prominent scar near the tip on the anteromedial surface marks the attachment of the transverse carpal ligament, and another scar on this surface proximally marks the attachment of the pisometacarpal ligament.

In the distal row the **trapezium** and **trapezoid** are very small, articulating distally with metacarpals 1 and 2 respectively. The **magnum** is larger, and articulates with metacarpal 3. The **unciform** bears metacarpals 4 and 5.

The **radial sesamoid** (fig. 54) is the most extraordinary bone in the fore foot. It is about 35 mm. in length, and lies in line with the metacarpals, closely resembling a sixth metacarpal on the medial border of the hand. It underlies the accessory lobe of the carpal pad. The bone is compressed from side to side, measuring about 15 mm. in height by only 6 or 7 mm. in thickness. The distal end hooks sharply inward toward the first metacarpal. The radial sesamoid articulates extensively with the enlarged medial process of the scapholunar, and is in contact with the medial border of the first metacarpal. The articular surface for the scapholunar is ovate with the long axis dorsoventral, and is concave both laterally and dorsoventrally. The contact surface with the first metacarpal is dorsomedial, and is not cartilage covered. A large depression on the outer surface of the radial sesamoid near the base marks the attachment of the tendon of the abductor pollicis longus. The abductor pollicis brevis and opponens pollicis arise from its medial surface.

A sizable radial sesamoid articulating with the scapholunar is present in all the other arctoid carnivores, and a corresponding bone exists in many

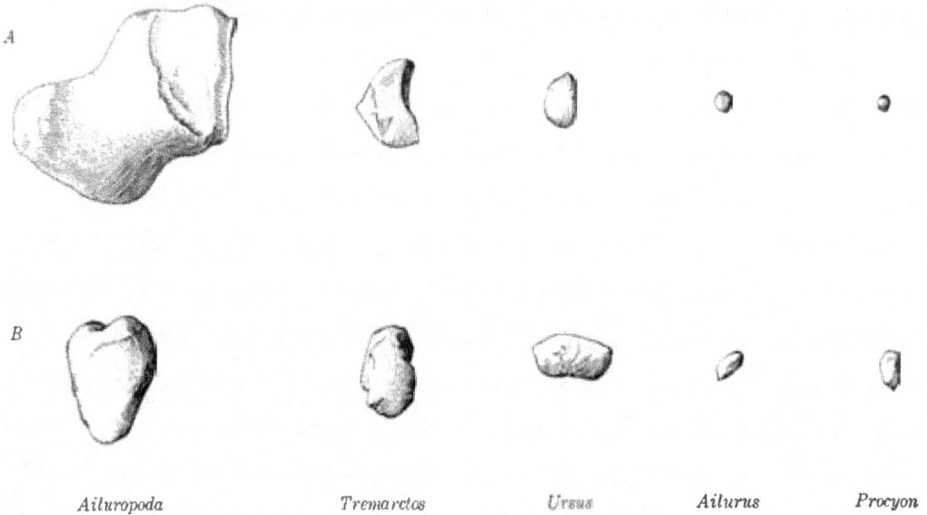

FIG. 54. Relative sizes of (A) right radial sesamoid, and (B) right tibial sesamoid in representative carnivores.

other mammals. In no other arctoid does it approach the proportions seen in *Ailuropoda*, however. In *Bassariscus, Procyon,* and *Nasua* it is a small bony nodule, and in *Procyon* at least it lies beneath the tendon of the long abductor. The radial sesamoid is also relatively small in *Ursus* but provides attachment for a part of the long abductor and opponens (fig. 54). The bone is relatively larger in *Ailurus*, and the tendon of the long abductor inserts into it exclusively, as in *Ailuropoda* (see also p. 180).

Comparison of the relative sizes of the radial sesamoid and the tibial sesamoid, the corresponding bone in the hind foot, is very suggestive (fig. 54). The tibial sesamoid has no function corresponding to that of the radial sesamoid, yet as is evident from the figure it undergoes a corresponding increase in size. This indicates a genuine serial homology between these two bones, with a common genetic control of the size factor at least, i.e. that the radial and tibial sesamoids represent a morphogenetic field despite their physical remoteness from one another.

5. *Manus*

The **metacarpals** are short and stout, relatively considerably shorter than in a bear of comparable size. As in other arctoids (except *Canis*), the fifth is heavier than the other four. Length relations are the same as in *Ursus*, although the differences are more exaggerated; the fourth is the longest, followed in order by the fifth, third, second, and

first. *Ailurus* is similar, while in *Procyon, Nasua,* and *Bassariscus* the third metacarpal is longest.

The distal articular surface of the metacarpals is narrower than in *Ursus*, especially dorsally, and the median ridge is more prominent. A conspicuous scar on the radial side of the second metacarpal, just proximad of the middle, marks the insertion on the tendon of the extensor carpi radialis longus, and a similar scar, situated farther proximad on the third metacarpal, the insertion of the extensor carpi radialis brevis.

The **phalanges** are similar to those of *Ursus*, except that they are somewhat stouter. Those of the proximal row are all slightly convex dorsally, more so than in *Ursus*. The bones of the middle row are very similar to the corresponding bones in bears. On the distal articular surface the median furrow is slightly deeper than in *Ursus*, corresponding with the more prominent median ridge on the terminal phalanges. In the terminal phalanges the core of the claw is higher vertically than in *Ursus;* the dorsal margin is more curved than in bears, the ventral margin less so.

A pair of **sesamoid bones** is present beneath the metacarpophalangeal articulation of each digit There are 10 in all. This is typical for all arctoid carnivores except the Canidae, in which the first digit has only one.

B. REVIEW OF THE FORE LEG

The bones of the fore leg of *Ailuropoda* agree closely with those of *Ursus* in all essential respects.

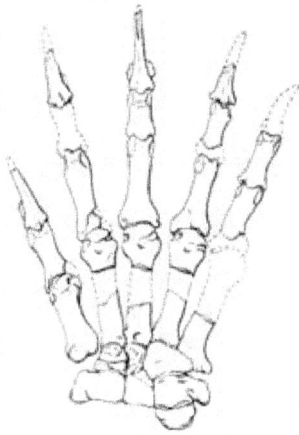

Claenodon corrugatus

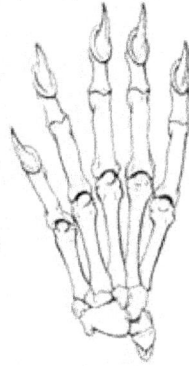

Potos flavus

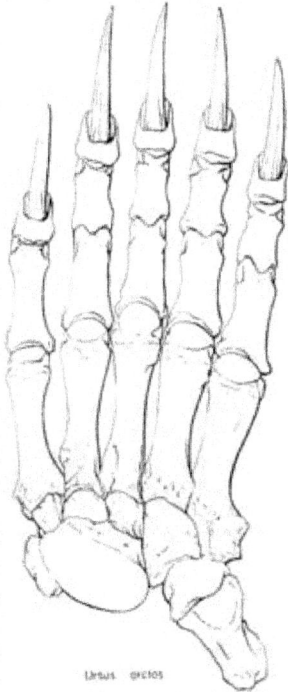

Ursus arctos

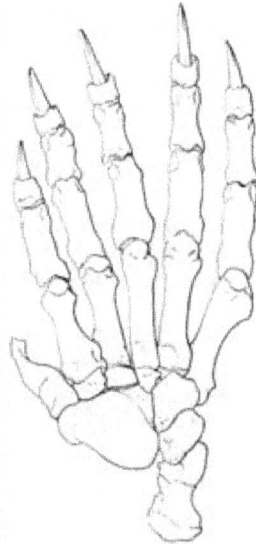

Ailuropoda melanoleuca

FIG. 55. Right manus of representative carnivores, dorsal view. (*Claenodon* from AMNH 16543.)

101

The differences may be examined briefly for evidence of their significance in interpreting the morphology of the giant panda.

All the large bones in the panda exhibit more prominent modeling, and this is broadly adaptive. Details of modeling, however, are determined by surrounding muscles rather than genetically (p. 147), and this difference therefore merely reflects the more powerful musculature of this animal.

The presence of an entepicondylar foramen in *Ailuropoda* contrasts with its absence in all bears except *Tremarctos*. This likewise appears to be merely a secondary result of enlarged muscles and their bony attachments (see Stromer, 1902). The presence or absence of this variable structure, which has aroused so much discussion in the literature, probably has no direct genetic basis.

There are considerable differences between the giant panda and bears in the form of several articular surfaces. The shoulder articulation allows a greater range of lateral movement in bears, which cannot be correlated with any known difference in habits or behavior. There is no appreciable difference in the elbow. The articulation between forearm and wrist permits notably greater dorsoventral excursion in the giant panda than in bears, and this is very obviously correlated with the greater maneuverability of the hand in the giant panda. Articulations reflect, rather than determine, range of movement in a joint (p. 145), however, and here again no genetic control can be postulated for adaptive differences in the skeleton.

As shown by the radiohumeral index, the forearm is significantly shorter than the upper arm in the giant panda, relatively shorter than in *Ursus* where it is near the norm for generalized mammals. Little is known of the functional significance of shortened forearm, and even less of mechanisms controlling the lengths of long bones. It has been concluded (p. 38) that the limb proportions in *Ailuropoda* do not reflect mechanical requirements.

The enlarged, maneuverable radial sesamoid in the giant panda is the most notable departure from the ursid pattern. This remarkable mechanism is unquestionably a direct product of natural selection. The correlated enlargement of the tibial sesamoid, together with a consideration of the muscles and ligaments functionally associated with the radial sesamoid (p. 183), clearly indicate that simple hypertrophy of the bone was all that was required to produce the whole mechanism. The genetic mechanism underlying such hypertrophy may be, and indeed probably is, quite simple. A further, but relatively minor, polishing effect of natural selection is evident in the detailed modeling of the bone.

Thus of the appreciable morphological differences in the bones of the fore leg of the giant panda and the bears, most are seen to be physiological adjustments to primary differences in the musculature. Such adjustments are not intrinsic to the bones, and therefore not gene controlled. Minor details, such as slight differences in individual carpal bones and the shape of the terminal phalanges, reflect at most minor polishing effects of natural selection. *Only two adaptive features, the relative shortness of the forearm and the remodeling of the radial sesamoid, appear to result directly from natural selection on the bones themselves.*

## VII. THE HIND LEG

In quadrupeds the hind leg during locomotion is more important than the fore leg as an organ of propulsion. The mass of the musculature of the hind quarters accordingly exceeds that of the fore quarters. In most mammals the hind leg has far less varied functions than the fore leg; it is primarily an organ of *support* and *propulsion*. The forces acting on the pelvis and hind limb are therefore usually less varied and less complex than those on the fore leg. In the giant panda the fore leg has diverged far more from the normal quadrupedal function than the hind leg, and this is only slightly less true of the bears and procyonids.

Like the fore leg, the hind leg of carnivores is basically designed for cursorial locomotion.

### A. BONES OF THE HIND LEG

#### 1. *Pelvis*

The pelvis, like the scapula, is molded primarily by muscular action. Thrust from the ground is transmitted from the femur to the sacrum through the body of the ilium, and this, together with the acetabulum and the iliosacral union, reflects chiefly non-muscular forces.

The pelvis of the giant panda differs remarkably from that of any other arctoid. The ilia lie in the frontal, rather than the sagittal plane, the pubis is shortened, and the length of the sacroiliac union is increased (see p. 82). The pelvis most closely resembles that of burrowing forms such as *Taxidea* and especially *Mellivora;* actually it is most similar to the pelvis of the burrowing marsupial *Vombatus.* This extraordinary convergence in animals with dissimilar habits is understandable when the forces operating on the pelvis are analyzed (p. 109).

Table 11 gives measurements and proportions of the pelvis of a number of arctoid carnivores. From these figures it is evident that certain proportions remain relatively constant, regardless of the habits of the animal, while others vary con-

Table 11.—MEASUREMENTS AND INDEXES OF PELVIS IN CARNIVORES

| | A | B | C | D | E | F | G | INDEXES | | | | | |
| | Length pelvis | Preace- tabular length | Iliac breadth | Width iliac crest | Length sym- physis | Width across dorsal acetab. | Width across ischia | B×100/A | C×100/A | D×100/A | E×100/A | F×100/A | G×100/A |
|---|---|---|---|---|---|---|---|---|---|---|---|---|---|
| *Ailuropoda* | | | | | | | | | | | | | |
| 31128 | 272 | 168 | 230 | 75 | 51 | 133 | 145 | 62 | 85 | 28 | 18.4 | 49 | 53 |
| 110452 | 290 | 179 | 268 | | 54 | 148 | 160 | 62 | 93 | | 18.6 | 51 | 55 |
| 110454 | 280 | 168 | 245 | | 54 | 135 | 156 | 60 | 88 | | 18.2 | 48 | 56 |
| 259027 | 292 | 193 | 265 | 88 | 54 | 150 | 166 | 66 | 91 | 30 | 19.0 | 51 | 57 |
| 259401 | 268 | 166 | 239 | | 50 | 129 | 148 | 62 | 89 | | 17.9 | 48 | 55 |
| 259403 | 282 | 176 | 257 | 82 | 51 | 145 | 177 | 62 | 91 | 29 | 18.7 | 51 | 63 |
| 259402 | 290 | 180 | 260 | | 52 | 140 | 166 | 62 | 90 | | 19.2 | 48 | 57 |
| 258425 | 266 | 170 | 240 | | 45 | 135 | 155 | 64 | 90 | | 18.4 | 53 | 58 |
| MEANS: | | | | | | | | 62.5 | 89.6 | 29 | 18.6 | 49.9 | 56.7 |
| *Ursus amer.* | | | | | | | | | | | | | |
| 18864 | 205 | 130 | 194 | 86 | 78 | 118 | 133 | 64 | 95 | 42 | 38 | 53 | 65 |
| 44725 | 238 | 148 | 206 | 95 | 93 | 130 | 133 | 62 | 87 | 40 | 39 | 55 | 56 |
| *Ursus arctos* | | | | | | | | | | | | | |
| 43744 | 271 | 175 | 255 | 90 | 95 | 140 | 171 | 65 | 94 | 33 | 35 | 52 | 63 |
| 47419 | 302 | 196 | 282 | 114 | 115 | 146 | 168 | 65 | 93 | 38 | 38 | 48 | 56 |
| *Ursus gyas* | | | | | | | | | | | | | |
| 27268 | 390 | 215 | 401 | 167 | 155 | 199 | 237 | 55 | 103 | 43 | 39 | 51 | 61 |
| 63803 | 312 | 181 | 320 | 131 | 113 | 155 | 186 | 58 | 103 | 42 | 36 | 50 | 60 |
| MEANS: | | | | | | | | 61.5 | 95.8 | 39.7 | 37.5 | 51.5 | 60.2 |
| *Ailurus fulgens* | | | | | | | | | | | | | |
| 65803 | 90 | 57 | 50 | 23 | 21 | 46.5 | 45 | 63 | 56 | 25 | 23 | 52 | 50 |
| 44875 | 74 | 47 | 41 | 18 | 16 | 38.5 | 36.5 | 64 | 55 | 24 | 22 | 52 | 52 |
| *Procyon lotor* | | | | | | | | | | | | | |
| 49895 | 114 | 69.5 | 72 | 29 | 26 | 58 | 61 | 61 | 63 | 25 | 23 | 51 | 54 |
| 49227 | 107 | 64 | 72 | 26 | 26.5 | 56.5 | 62 | 60 | 67 | 24 | 25 | 53 | 58 |
| 49057 | 98 | 57 | 68.5 | 26 | 26 | 50 | 53 | 58 | 70 | 27 | 27 | 51 | 54 |
| 47386 | 103 | 60 | 77 | 29 | 28.5 | 59 | 59 | 58 | 75 | 28 | 28 | 57 | 57 |
| *Canis lupus* | | | | | | | | | | | | | |
| 51772 | 197 | 114 | 108 | 65 | 65 | 91 | 141 | 58 | 55 | 33 | 33 | 46 | 72 |
| 54015 | 177 | 112 | 117 | 57 | 58 | 85.5 | 123 | 63 | 66 | 32 | 33 | 48 | 70 |
| 21207 | 184 | 112 | 107 | 63 | 59 | 88 | 133 | 61 | 58 | 34 | 32 | 48 | 72 |
| *Mellivora* | | | | | | | | | | | | | |
| 43298 | 89 | 53 | 80 | 22 | 18 | 45 | 50 | 59 | 90 | 25 | 20 | 51 | 56 |
| *Vombatus* | | | | | | | | | | | | | |
| 49085 | 185 | 119 | 168 | 55 | 31 | 100 | 121 | 65 | 91 | 30 | 17 | 54 | 65 |

siderably. Using total length of pelvis as a base, the position of the acetabulum (indicated by pre-acetabular length, B) varies little. This is also true of the distance between acetabula (F), which is the functional diameter of the pelvis. On the other hand, breadth across the ilia (C), breadth across the ischia (G), and length of symphysis (E) vary greatly with habits. This is also true of the slope of the wings of the ilia and of the descending ramus of the ischium with respect to the frontal plane.

The pelvis is very short in *Ailuropoda;* length pelvis/length Th 10–12[1] = 33 and 35 in two individuals. The pelvis is also short in *Ursus* and the badgers.

MORPHOLOGY.—The pelvis is rectangular in dorsal outline (fig. 56), depressed in lateral view (fig. 57). In posterior view it is U-shaped rather than

[1] See page 35.

V-shaped as in *Ursus.* In *Ailuropoda* the greatest length of pelvis is about 40 per cent of the length of the vertebral column, compared with about 29 per cent in *Ursus americanus* and 31 per cent in *Procyon lotor.* This merely reflects the shortened column in the panda, however; measured against three thoracic vertebrae the pelvic length is comparable to that of *Ursus.*

In all specimens examined the sacro-iliac union is more or less fused dorsally but open ventrally. This is likewise true in *Ursus,* and contrasts with the open articulation in other arctoids.

The ilium is composed of a remarkably narrow, almost parallel-sided ala, and a short heavy corpus. The ala is widest across the iliac crest, which is of normal width; behind the anterior superior iliac spine the inferior border is deeply excised and the diameter of the ilium correspondingly narrowed.

The anterior superior iliac spine, which gives origin to the sartorius and tensor fasciae latae

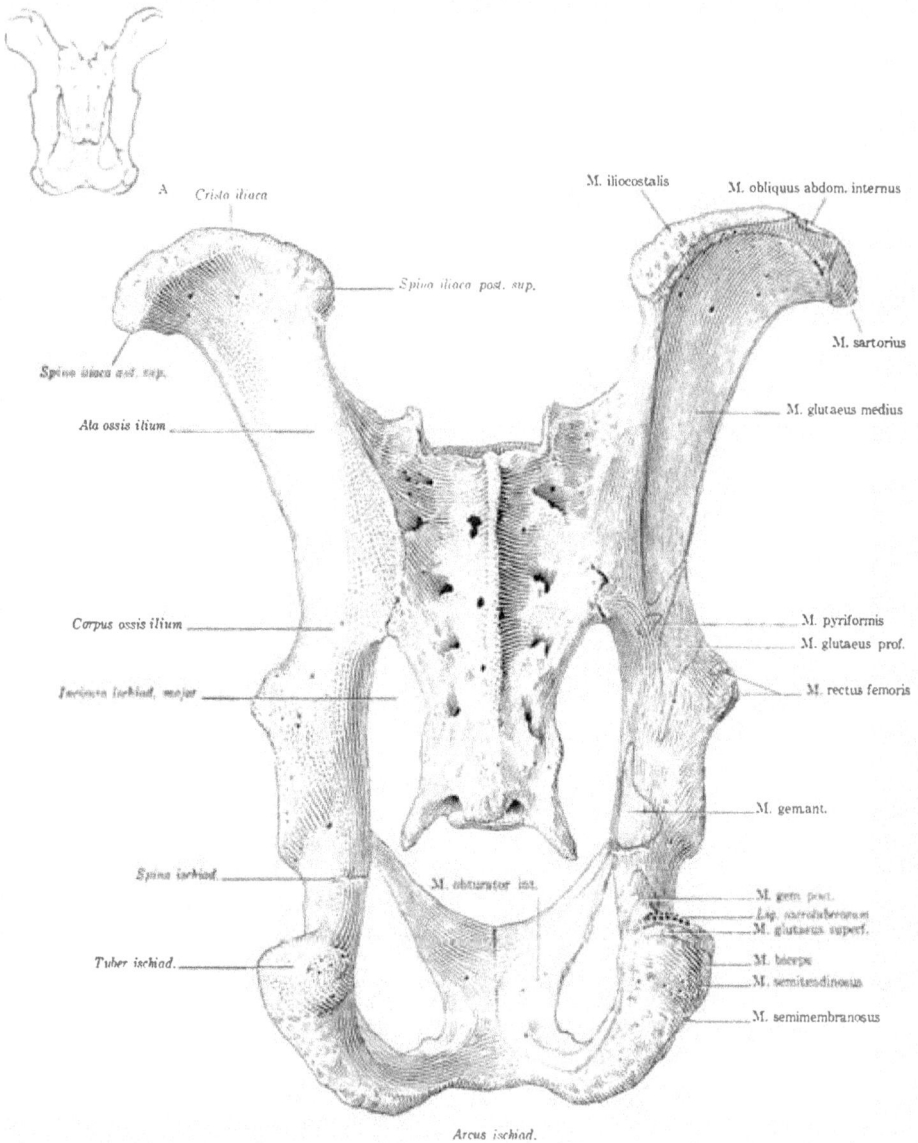

Crista iliaca

M. iliocostalis

M. obliquus abdom. internus

Spina iliaca post. sup.

M. sartorius

Spina iliaca ant. sup.

M. glutaeus medius

Ala ossis ilium

Corpus ossis ilium

M. pyriformis

M. glutaeus prof.

Incisura ischiad. major

M. rectus femoris

M. gem.ant.

Spina ischiad.

M. obturator int.

M. gem. post.

Lig. sacrotuberosum

M. glutaeus superf.

Tuber ischiad.

M. biceps

M. semitendinosus

M. semimembranosus

Arcus ischiad.

FIG. 56.  Male pelvis of *Ailuropoda*, dorsal view.  (Inset, A, pelvis of *Ursus arctos*.)

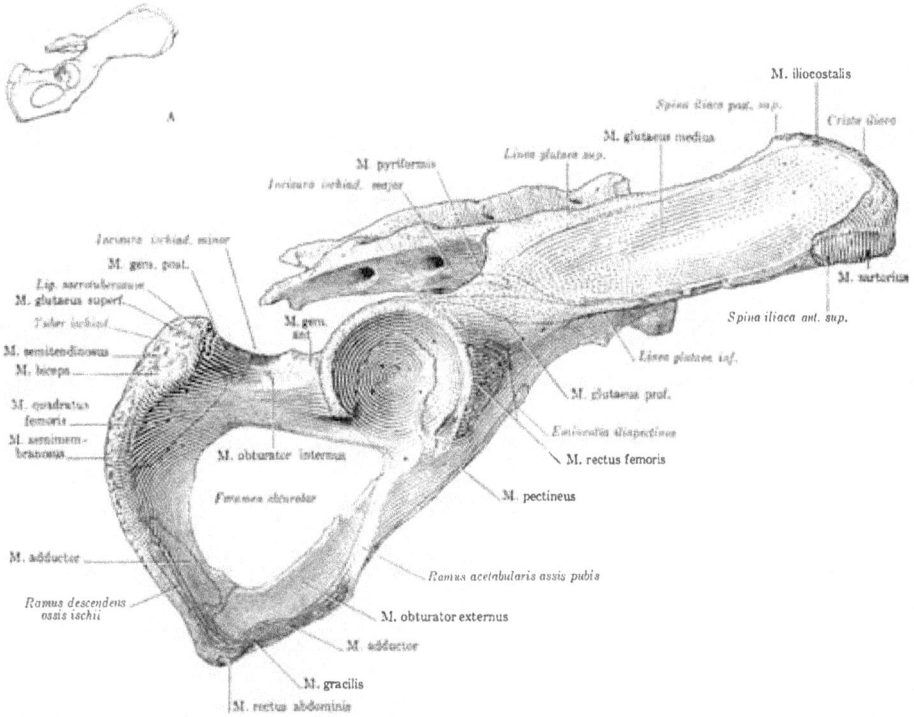

FIG. 57. Male pelvis of *Ailuropoda*, lateral view. (Inset, A, pelvis of *Ursus arctos*.)

muscles and the anterior end of the inguinal ligament, is thick and heavy. It lies farther anterior than in *Ursus*, and the iliac crest is correspondingly shorter and less curved. The posterior superior iliac spine is also relatively heavy. The anterior and posterior inferior iliac spines are not even indicated. The dorsolateral surface of the ilium, which provides origin for the middle and deep gluteals, is a shallow elongated trough, the gluteal fossa. It is devoid of surface modeling except for a faint vermiculation near the iliac crest. The area of the gluteal fossa is about 5700 and 7500 mm.² in two specimens of *Ailuropoda*, 7200 mm.² in a specimen of *Ursus americanus*, and 11,900 mm.² in a specimen of *Ursus arctos*.[1] The ventro-medial surface of the ilium (fig. 58), which provides origin for the iliacus, quadratus lumborum, and sacrospinalis muscles, is slightly convex along both its axes. A faint longitudinal ridge, not always evident, divides the surface into a lateral iliac area and a medial sacrospinal area; this is called the pubic border by Flower, Straus, and

[1] See p. 43 for method used in measuring areas on bones.

other anatomists. A low but prominent elevation near the middle of the ridge is associated with the origin of the sacrospinalis. A large foramen-like opening at the posterior end of the ridge, and lying in the sacroiliac articulation, is filled with fat and connective tissue in life; it is present but is usually less foramen-like in *Ursus*, and apparently represents the separation between the dorsal and ventral elements of the embryonic transverse processes of the first sacral.

The corpus is short and heavy, only slightly laterally compressed as in *Ursus*. Its superior border bounds the greater sciatic notch, which has been crowded posteriorly by the posterior extension of the sacroiliac union. The inferior surface is rounded, without crests or ridges. The iliopectineal eminence is a low elevation, much less prominent than in *Ursus*, on the inferior surface just anterior to the acetabulum. The inferior gluteal line, separating the gluteal and iliac surfaces of the ilium, is scarcely indicated on the corpus. Immediately in front of the acetabulum it passes into the iliopubic eminence, which is likewise much less

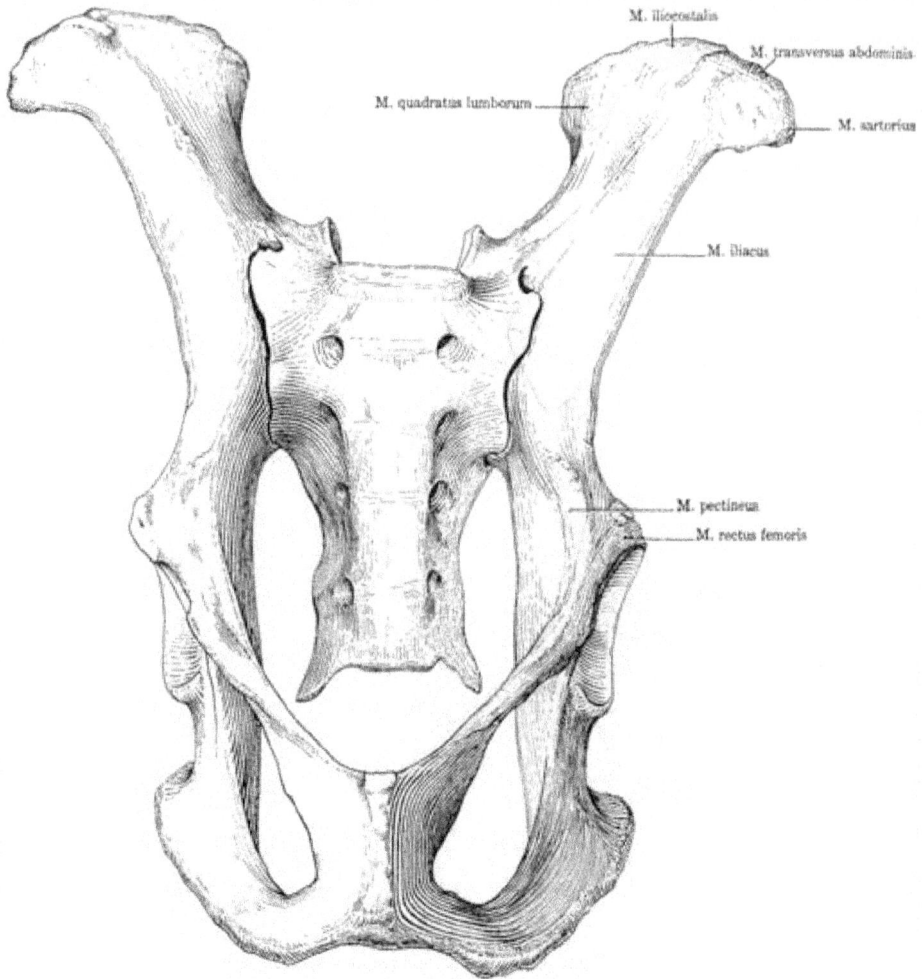

FIG. 58.  Male pelvis of *Ailuropoda*, ventral view.

prominent than in *Ursus;* it marks the attachment of the rectus femoris.

The articular surface of the ilium (fig. 59), which articulates with the auricular surface of the sacrum, resembles that of *Ursus* but is relatively longer and narrower.  It is an elongate horseshoe, open anteriorly, with a very irregular surface, the irregularities interlocking closely with corresponding irregularities on the sacrum.  The narrow space enclosed by the horseshoe is filled with fibrocartilage.  The extensive articulation, intimate dovetailing, and partial fusion of the sacroiliac joint

contrast sharply with the relatively smooth and much smaller auricular surface of other arctoids.

The **pubis** is the most delicate bone in the pelvis.  It is more lightly built than in *Ursus*, and much more so than in the cursorial dogs.  The corpus, which forms the ventral part of the acetabulum, is the heaviest part of the bone.  The acetabular ramus is very slender and elongate; it had been fractured bilaterally in one specimen examined.  The reduction in the length of the symphysis has taken place anteriorly, and the angle formed by the acetabular ramus with the symphy-

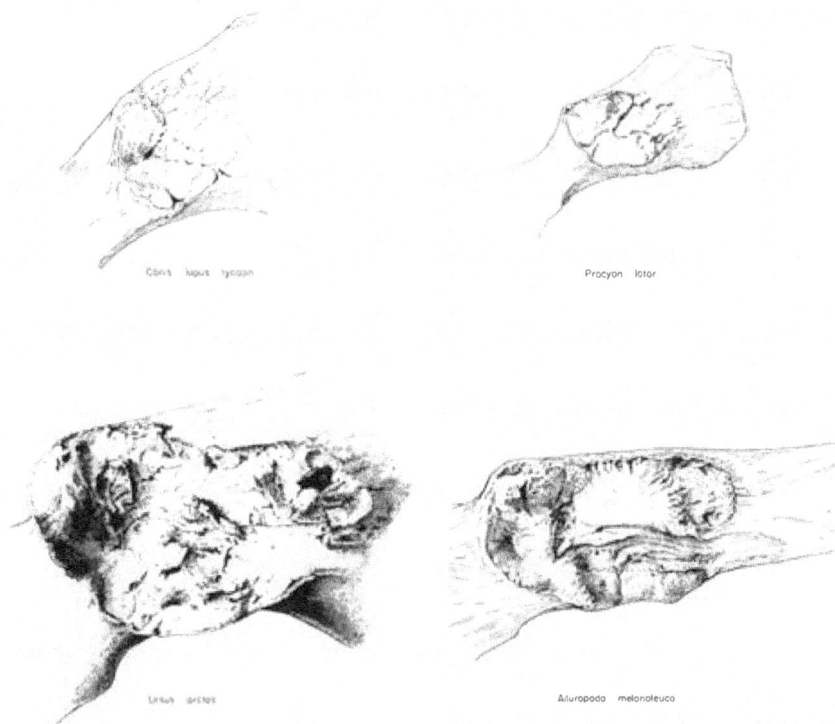

Canis lupus lycaon

Procyon lotor

Ursus arctos

Ailuropoda melanoleuca

FIG. 59. Articular surface of left ilium in representative arctoid carnivores.

sis in the sagittal plane is about 45° instead of 25–35° as in *Ursus*, and the acetabular ramus is correspondingly longer. The length of the symphyseal ramus cannot be determined, since no available specimen is young enough to show the suture between the pubis and the ischium. It is obviously very short, however, and is relatively much wider than in *Ursus*. The external surface of the symphyseal ramus provides origin for the anterior parts of the gracilis, adductor, and external obturator muscles; the internal surface provides origin for the anterior part of the internal obturator.

The ischium is not directly involved in the support function of the pelvis, except during sitting; it functions chiefly as anchorage for the posterior thigh muscles. The ischium does not differ much from that of *Ursus* or *Procyon*. It is composed of a stout acetabular ramus and a more slender descending ramus (tabula ischiadica of veterinary anatomy), and a heavy symphyseal ramus. The acetabular ramus is relatively shorter than in *Ursus*, and is ovate in cross section. Its shaft is almost free of muscle attachments; only the tiny gemelli

arise from it. The sciatic spine, which separates the greater and lesser sciatic notches, is a short prominent transverse ridge as in *Ursus*. A small scar immediately anterior to the spine marks the attachment of the anterior gemellus, and immediately behind the spine there is a smooth area, covered with cartilage in life, over which the internal obturator rides. The saddle-shaped area between the sciatic spine and the ischial tuberosity is the lesser sciatic notch. It is converted into a foramen by the sacrotuberous ligament, and transmits the distal end of the internal obturator muscle and various vessels and nerves.

The ischial tuberosity is by far the most prominent feature of the ischium, and most of the muscles attaching to the ischium are inserted on or near it. The tuberosity is knob-like, about 35 mm. in diameter, with a much roughened posterior surface It has no inferior boundary, but continues directly into the roughened swollen posterior edge of the descending ramus, which narrows gradually as it descends and terminates abruptly about 40 mm. above the symphysis. The muscle attachments are around the periphery of the tuberosity; the major part of its roughened posterior face lies directly beneath the skin. The tuberosity is similar, but more sharply bounded inferiorly, in *Ursus*.

The lower third of the descending ramus, below the swollen area just described, is much the slenderest part of the ischium; it is no heavier than the acetabular ramus of the pubis. It provides attachment for the posterior ends of the adductor and gracilis externally, and for the internal obturator internally. The descending ramus forms an angle of about 55° with the sagittal plane. This angle is similar in other arctoids examined except in *Canis*, in which it is only about 20° (fig. 61).

The symphyseal ramus, forming the posterior part of the symphysis pelvis, is broad and thick; the minimum transverse diameter of the entire symphysis (from obturator foramen to obturator foramen) is 40–50 mm. in *Ailuropoda*, whereas in a bear of comparable size it is 20–30 mm. In dorsal view the sciatic arch, which is often non-existent in bears, is relatively deep.

The **acetabulum**, composed of a horseshoe-shaped articular portion embracing a non-articular fossa, differs little from that of *Ursus* and other arctoids. It looks slightly more laterally, forming an angle with the vertical of 11° and 14°, respectively, in two individuals, 15° in three specimens of *Ursus*. The acetabulum looks more ventrally in the cursorial wolf, forming an angle of 29° (26–31) in three specimens of *Canis lupus*.

The acetabulum is situated farther dorsad in *Ailuropoda* than in *Ursus*, its dorsal border lying well above the margin of the greater sciatic notch. The entire rim of the acetabulum is extremely heavy. The acetabular notch is almost twice as wide as in a bear of comparable size; the anterior boundary of the notch has been shifted forward to produce this increased width. The acetabular fossa is also relatively wider, and has increased its diameter by encroaching on the anterior arm of the articular portion, which accordingly is narrower than in *Ursus*.

The **obturator foramen** is triangular in outline, rather than ovate as in *Ursus*.

ARCHITECTURE AND MECHANICS.—The mammalian pelvis is an extraordinarily complex structure, subject to varied and often subtle forces. Moreover, it has had a long history, and treating the mammalian pelvis as if it were engineered *de novo* leads to difficulties and often even to absurdities. Mijsberg's work (1920) was one of the first attempts to analyze the architecture and mechanics of the non-human mammalian pelvis. Other such studies have been made by Elftman (1929), Rey-

nolds (1931), Kleinschmidt (1948), and Maynard Smith and Savage (1956).

The mammalian pelvis serves three dissimilar purposes: (1) to provide support; to transmit thrust from the legs to the vertebral column, and from the column to the legs; (2) to provide attachment surfaces and lever arms for hip and thigh muscles; and (3) to transmit the terminal parts of the digestive and urogenital canals, especially important being the birth canal. Each of these has participated in molding the pelvis, but the basic architecture was largely determined by the support function. Elftman believed that the pelvis is "roughly modeled so as to fit the viscera and with finer detail so developed as to provide optimum support against gravity and leverage for locomotion."

As a supporting structure the pelvis is a complex system of arches and levers designed to provide strength and elasticity. Absorption of shock resulting from impact between the feet and the ground seems to have been a major factor in the design of limbs and girdles in mammals. The architecture of the mammalian pelvis, which is far less rigid than that of their reptilian ancestors, is otherwise unintelligible.

In the frontal plane (fig. 60, B) the pelvis is composed of two round arches meeting at the acetabula: a heavy dorsal arch composed of the two ilia and the sacrum, and a much lighter ventral iliopubic arch. Only the dorsal arch is directly involved in the support function of the pelvis; the ventral arch is concerned with the structural stability of the pelvis. The dorsal arch is loaded both from above (weight of body, $W$) and from below (upward thrust of legs, $T$). In addition to bending and shearing stresses, the loaded arch develops horizontal thrust which reaches a maximum at the base (the acetabula, $A$, $A$) whether loading is from above or below. The sole function of the iliopubic arch, aside from providing a base for muscle attachment, appears to be as a bottom tie for the dorsal arch, to counteract this horizontal thrust.

Viewed from the side (fig. 60, D) the pelvis is not a simple arch as it is in reptiles. The acetabulum lies well behind the sacroiliac articulation, and upward thrust through the acetabulum is translated into a vertical rotational force around the sacroiliac articulation as a center; the coxa is cantilevered to the sacrum. The sacroiliac articulation is not normally fused in quadrupeds, but it is practically immovably fixed by the sacroiliac ligaments, often augmented by interlocking denticulations on the two articular surfaces. Thus, under loading, shearing forces are developed along the neck of the ilium—the axis connecting acetab-

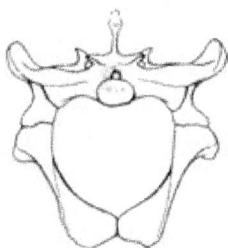

A.  Transverse iliosacral arch is similar to arch
    of quadrupedal mammals (B).

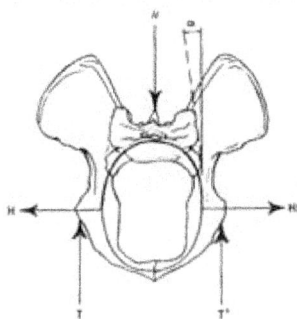

B.  Canis  Upward thrust T, T' through acetabula is resolved
    in transverse iliosacral arch. This arch is also loaded
    from above by the weight of the body, W. Horizontal
    thrust, H, H, developed in the transverse arch by both T
    and W, is counteracted by the ventral iliopubic arch act-
    ing as a tie.

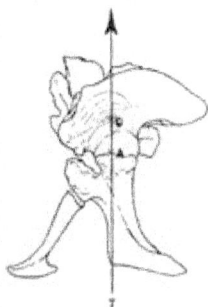

C.  Alligator  Thrust T through acetabulum is transmitted
    directly to sacroiliac joint O. The iliosacral arch
    functions as simple arch.

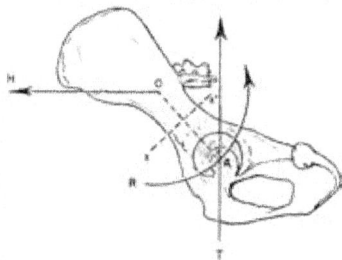

D.  Canis.  Thrust T through acetabulum is translated into
    rotational force R around sacroiliac joint O as a cen-
    ter. This produces a shear along the axis O-A, as
    indicated by x-x'. Horizonal thrust H is developed dur-
    ing locomation.

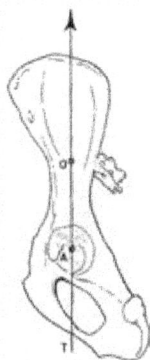

E.  Canis  Upward thrust T is transmitted
    directly to vertebral column through ilium
    and sacroiliac joint. A shear is pro-
    duced at the sacroiliac joint and com-
    pression in the neck of the ilium. The
    sacroiliac arch functions as a simple
    arch.

FIG. 60.  Forces acting on the pelvis in quadrupeds.  A, transverse arch in a reptile, anterior view;  B, transverse arch in
a mammal, anterior view;  C, transverse arch in a reptile, lateral view;  D, cantilevered transverse arch of a mammal, lateral
view;  E, forces acting on mammalian pelvis in erect posture, lateral view.

ulum and sacroiliac articulation—and this is by far the most destructive force to which this part of the arch is subjected.

The rotational force acting on the sacroacetabular axis produces a powerful rotational shear or torque on the sacroiliac articulation, similar to that on a bolt being tightened by a wrench. This force would tend to displace the anterior part of the articulation downward, the posterior part upward. The posterior upward force of the couple is counteracted by the firm union of the auricular surfaces of the sacrum and ilium. The anterior downward force is met by the shape of the sacrum, which is wedged between the ilia like an inverted keystone (fig. 60, B, a). This angle is about 15° in *Canis*, and rises to 40° or more in the Bovidae. In the bears and *Ailuropoda*, in which the articulation is synostotic, the angle approaches zero, and this is also true in the giant anteater (*Myrmecophaga*), where the joint is fused.

During locomotion the sacro-iliac articulation is also subjected to momentary horizontal thrust (fig. 60, D, *H*) that tends to displace the ilium anteriorly on the sacrum. This force results from the anterior thrust of the hind legs, and is especially evident during galloping or leaping, when the femur is nearly or quite in line with the sacroacetabular axis, as is evident in Muybridge's (1957) photographs of horses and dogs. This force is counteracted by the wedge shape of the sacrum in the frontal plane: the bone is wider anteriorly than posteriorly. The plane of the auricular surface forms an angle with the mid-sagittal plane of 11–14° in *Canis*, *Ursus*, and *Ailuropoda*, and in a specimen of *Bison* this angle amounts to 34°.

*Forces on the Pelvis in the Erect Posture*

If a quadruped stands erect on its hind legs the forces acting on the pelvis are approximately doubled, since the pelvis then bears the entire weight of the animal. They are also significantly altered in direction. The transverse arch still functions as before, but the ilia are no longer cantilevered to the sacrum. The thrust is now along the sacroacetabular axis (fig. 60, E, *T*). Instead of shearing forces along the sacroacetabular axis there is now compression. The rotational shear at the sacroiliac articulation is converted into a simple shear, which is largely or entirely counteracted by the wedge shape of the sacrum. This is a stronger construction than in the quadrupedal posture, but most of the elasticity is gone; if the sacroiliac articulation fuses there is virtually no elasticity in the pelvis.

Horizontal forces, i.e., forces approximately parallel to the sacro-acetabular axis, predominate in

burrowing animals that use their hind legs for bracing while digging. Thus the dominant forces acting on the pelvis in such forms are very similar to those in the erect posture, and this is reflected in a striking similarity in pelvic architecture.

Examination shows that seven features characterize the pelvis in mammals in which forces parallel to the long axis of the pelvis predominate, i.e., those that stand erect and those that use their hind legs for bracing while digging. These are:

1. The wings of the ilia tend to shift into the frontal plane.

2. The pelvis is short anteroposteriorly.

3. The sacroiliac articulation is strengthened by including additional sacral vertebrae (increased area) and/or by strengthening the joint through interlocking bony processes, synostoses, etc.

4. The lateral diameter of the corpus of the ilium is increased, and it tends to become circular in cross section.

5. The pubo-ischiadic symphysis is greatly shortened. This reduction is in the anterior part of the symphysis.

6. The total number of sacral vertebrae is increased.

7. The tail is usually, but not always, shortened.

In marsupials Elftman (1929) attributed the shape of the wing of the ilium anterior to the sacroiliac joint chiefly to the "sizes of the three muscle masses whose areas of origin form its three borders —the erector spinae mesially, the gluteus medius and gluteus minimus dorso-laterally, and the iliacus ventro-laterally." Waterman (1929) concluded that the form of the ilium in primates is largely determined by muscles. Elftman believed that in *Vombatus*, however, the width of the trunk is partly responsible for the lateral flare of the anterior part of the ilium.

In the bears and *Ailuropoda* the mass of the middle and deep gluteals is relatively no greater than in the cursorial dogs and cats (see Table 15). Even in man the relative mass of these muscles is no greater than in cursorial carnivores. The iliopsoas in *Ailuropoda* is slightly heavier than in bears and dogs but it is smaller than in the lion, which has a notably narrow pelvis. In the lion the great size of the iliopsoas (almost identical with man) is associated with leaping.

If the relative masses of the large muscles attaching to the wing of the ilium are nearly constant, then differences in size, shape, and slope of the iliac wing must be attributable to other causes.[1] The most consistent character of the iliac wing in

[1] The long iliac crest (=broad iliac wing) characteristic of bears must be attributable to peculiarities, still unknown, in the abdominal wall muscles and iliocostalis that attach to this crest. Elsewhere among carnivores the crest tends to be short in climbing and aquatic forms, "normal" in terrestrial forms.

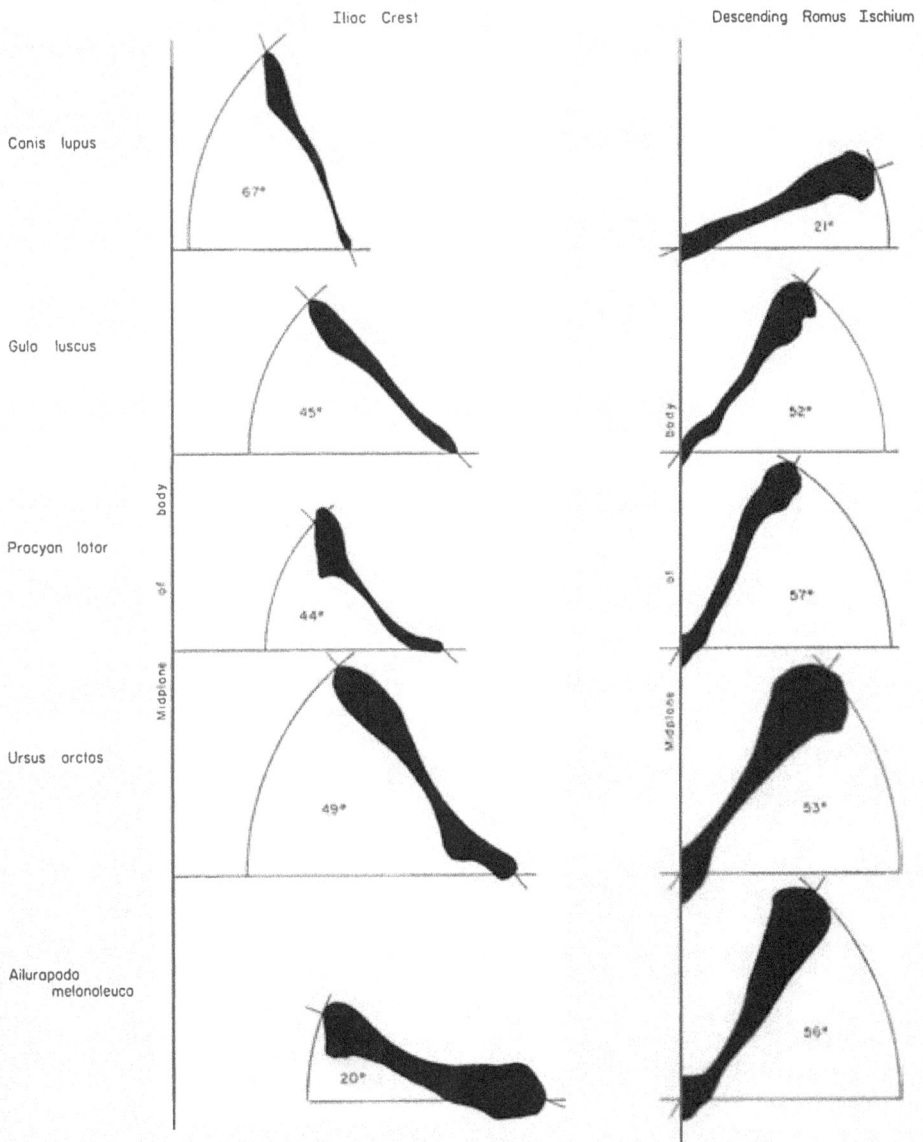

FIG. 61. Anterior views of pelves of carnivores, to show angle of inclination of iliac and ischiadic planes.

111

mammals in which forces parallel to the long axis of the pelvis predominate is that the wing tends to shift into the frontal plane (fig. 61). The iliac crest forms an angle with the frontal plane of 20–21° in *Ailuropoda*, 22° in a *Mellivora*, 28° in a *Meles*, and only 12° in a *Vombatus*. In the bears and American badgers the slope of the crest is about normal for terrestrial carnivores, 45–50°. In the cursorial wolf the slope approaches the vertical, 70–80° (fig. 61).

The main advantage of a frontal position of the wing of the ilium is leverage; in both the erect and the burrowing posture the gluteals and iliacus are in an increasingly favorable position to stabilize the pelvis and vertebral column as these muscles approach the frontal plane. Waterman (1929) has discussed the relation between erect posture and the muscles attaching to the iliac crest in primates. The muscles attaching to this crest in *Ailuropoda* are shown in figs. 56–58; the corresponding relations in other carnivores are unknown.

Shortening of the pelvis is symmetrical, affecting the preacetabular and postacetabular regions about equally. The pelvis is almost as short in bears (index 36) as in the panda, and is only slightly longer in *Meles* (41) and *Taxidea* (41). *Mellivora* is a striking exception (index 50). The norm for terrestrial carnivores is about 46. The advantage of reduction in pelvis length with increased horizontal forces on the pelvis is not clear to me.

Strengthening of the sacroiliac articulation with increase in horizontal forces on the pelvis is so obviously functional that it requires no comment. It reaches a maximum in the Myrmecophagidae, in which the sacroiliac articulation is supplemented by a strong sacroischiadic articulation occupying the normal site of the sacrotuberous ligament. Increased diameter of the body of the ilium is likewise associated directly with increased horizontal thrust; relative diameter of the body reaches a maximum in the Old World badgers.

Shortening of the symphysis is invariably correlated with increased horizontal thrust on the pelvis. It is seen in the wombat (Marsupialia), the extinct ground sloths and the anteaters (Edentata), the anthropoids (Primates), and in badgers and *Ailuropoda* among the carnivores. The symphysis is also short in aquatic forms: in the otters and particularly so in the seals.

Various attempts, all more or less speculative, have been made to explain reduction in length of symphysis. All explicitly or implicitly regard symphysis length as proportional to the forces the symphysis must withstand. Weidenreich (1913) attributed shortening of the symphysis in primates to the weight of the viscera and the pull of the

sacrotuberous and sacrospinous ligaments drawing the pubic rami apart. Mijsberg (1920) suggested that vertical forces acting on the pelvis in quadrupeds produce exorotation of the coxa around the sacrum, and that this exorotation is resisted by the symphysis, whose length is proportional to the exorotatory force. Mijsberg's interpretation is supported by the fact that the seals (Phocidae), in which vertical forces acting on the pelvis are negligible or absent, have no true symphysis. Elftman (1929) accepted Mijsberg's explanation, but suggested further that in *Vombatus* shortening of the symphysis posteriorly is necessary to provide a proper outlet for the pelvis. Nauck (1938) believed he could detect a correlation between dorsal shifting of the acetabulum—which he maintains would reduce the exorotatory forces on the pelvis—and reduction in symphysis length. Nauck's correlation exists only in selected cases, and obviously is not a general explanation.

All investigators[1] agree that the iliopubic arch functions primarily as a tie to counteract horizontal thrust ("exorotatory forces") developed in the dorsal iliosacral arch. All agree further that reduced symphysis length is somehow associated with reduced tensile stresses in the iliopubic arch. The resolution of vertical vs. horizontal forces within the pelvis has not been demonstrated experimentally, however, and consequently all explanations are conjectural. A correlation between increased force parallel to the long axis of the pelvis and reduced symphysis length remains as an empirical fact.

Increased sacral length *behind* the sacroiliac articulation is associated with increased horizontal thrust on the pelvis both in forms that stand erect and in those that use their hind legs for bracing while digging. Extending the sacrum posteriorly increases the attachment area for the multifidus and sacrospinalis muscles. The main action of both of these muscles is to extend the vertebral column when acting on the vertebrae, or to extend the pelvis when acting on the sacrum. These actions are obviously important for spinal fixation both in the erect posture and in burrowing.

It seems likely that reduction in tail length is a consequence of increased sacral length, although critical data are lacking. If sacral length is increased to provide additional area for the spinal erectors, this area could be provided only at the expense of the basal tail muscles. The special cases of long sacrum associated with long tail in the anteaters and aardvark suggest a fundamental difference in either the spinal erectors or the caudal

[1] Braus (1929, p. 456) interprets the human pelvis as a ring under spring-like internal tension.

muscles in these forms, but pertinent data are lacking.

THE PELVIS OF AILUROPODA.—The pelvis of the giant panda is notably different from that of the bears, which it resembles no more closely than it does the pelvis of several other arctoid carnivores. The bear pelvis, in turn, is unique among arctoids in its combination of long iliac crest, very broad iliac wing with normal slope in the transverse plane, and extremely long symphysis.

The pelvis of *Ailuropoda* exhibits, to a far greater degree than any other carnivore, the seven features that characterize the mammalian pelvis when forces parallel to the body axis predominate (p. 110). These forces predominate during burrowing, and when the animal stands erect on its hind legs. *Ailuropoda* is not a burrower, nor does it stand erect to any greater extent than do the bears. There is, in fact, no reason for believing that horizontal forces on the pelvis in *Ailuropoda* are greater or more sustained than in *Ursus* or other carnivores. This indicates that some other (non-adaptive) factor is responsible for the form of the pelvis in *Ailuropoda*.

The pelvis adjoins the lumbosacral region of the body axis. In this region in *Ailuropoda* the axial skeleton, the urogenital system, and the circulatory system all show non-adaptive deviations from the norm. The most plausible explanation for the pelvic form in *Ailuropoda* is that it reflects the serious disturbance in the axial gradient that is associated with cephalization (p. 84).

2. *Femur*

The femur in the Carnivora serves for the origin or insertion of 22 muscles. Of these, 15 belong to the hip joint and 7 to the knee joint or lower leg and foot. In the Carnivora the form and architecture of the femur are determined largely by the static requirements of support, to a far greater degree than for the humerus. Except for the trochanters, the external form of the femur is scarcely modified by the muscles that attach to it.

It was found (Table 2) that if femur length is calculated against the length of three thoracic vertebrae, the femur in *Ailuropoda* is longer than the norm for carnivores but not so long as in *Ursus*. Relative femur length of the panda is similar to that of the cats, whereas the bear femur is among the longest known for the Carnivora, equal to *Crocuta* and exceeded only by *Chrysocyon*.

If the position of the acetabulum remains relatively constant (as it does among arctoid carnivores; see Table 11), then a long femur would result in fast but weak movements of the femur

around the acetabulum, as compared with a short femur.[1] From the standpoint of locomotor efficiency, the ratio between femur length and tibia length is much more significant than is femur length relative to pelvis length.

The femur of *Ailuropoda* (fig. 62) is similar in form to that of *Ursus* and the Procyonidae, with a low greater trochanter and a straight shaft. As in most arctoid carnivores, the bone shows little torsion.[2] In two wild-killed pandas the torsion angle is —1° and —3°; in a third, reared in captivity, it is —13°. The mean of twelve wild-killed arctoids is about 1°, extremes —3 to +14. Four wild-killed *Ursus* range from —2 to +14, mean +2°. The greatest torsion among arctoids is in the Procyonidae: 10 and 14 in two individuals of *Procyon*, 6 in a *Nasua*. Torsion in two cage-reared *Ailurus* is 3 and 12.

In *Ailuropoda* the head of the femur is hemispherical, about 38 mm. in diameter, slightly larger than in a bear of comparable size. The fovea, for the ligamentum teres, occupies the same position as in *Ursus*, but is wider and deeper. The neck is distinct, and forms an angle of about 130° with the shaft; it is slightly more angulated than in *Ursus* (134–138°) or *Procyon* (135°). Angulation of the neck is 125–140° in arctoid carnivores in general. The neck is narrower anteroposteriorly but slightly wider dorsoventrally than it is in *Ursus*.

The **greater trochanter**, which provides attachment for the middle and deep gluteals and the piriformis, does not differ significantly from that of *Ursus*. It is a broad knoblike structure scarcely rising above the level of the neck. Its anterior border is continued distally as a low crest that terminates at the level of the lesser trochanter in a prominent scar, the gluteal tuberosity, marking the insertion of the superficial gluteal muscle. The **trochanteric fossa**, which receives the tendons of the obturator muscles, is deep and well defined. The **lesser trochanter**, on which the iliacus and psoas major muscles attach, is a low conical eminence projecting posteromedially, as in other arctoid carnivores. A crescent-shaped transverse scar extending across the posterior surface of the bone, from the lesser trochanter nearly to the gluteal tuberosity, marks the attachment of the quadratus femoris.

---

[1] Disregarding differences in tension and velocity of contraction of muscles. See Maynard Smith and Savage (1956) for methods of calculating relative mechanical advantages in limbs.

[2] Torsion was measured by the method given by Schmid (1873). My figures do not always agree with his, and I suspect this is because many of his skeletons were from zoo animals.

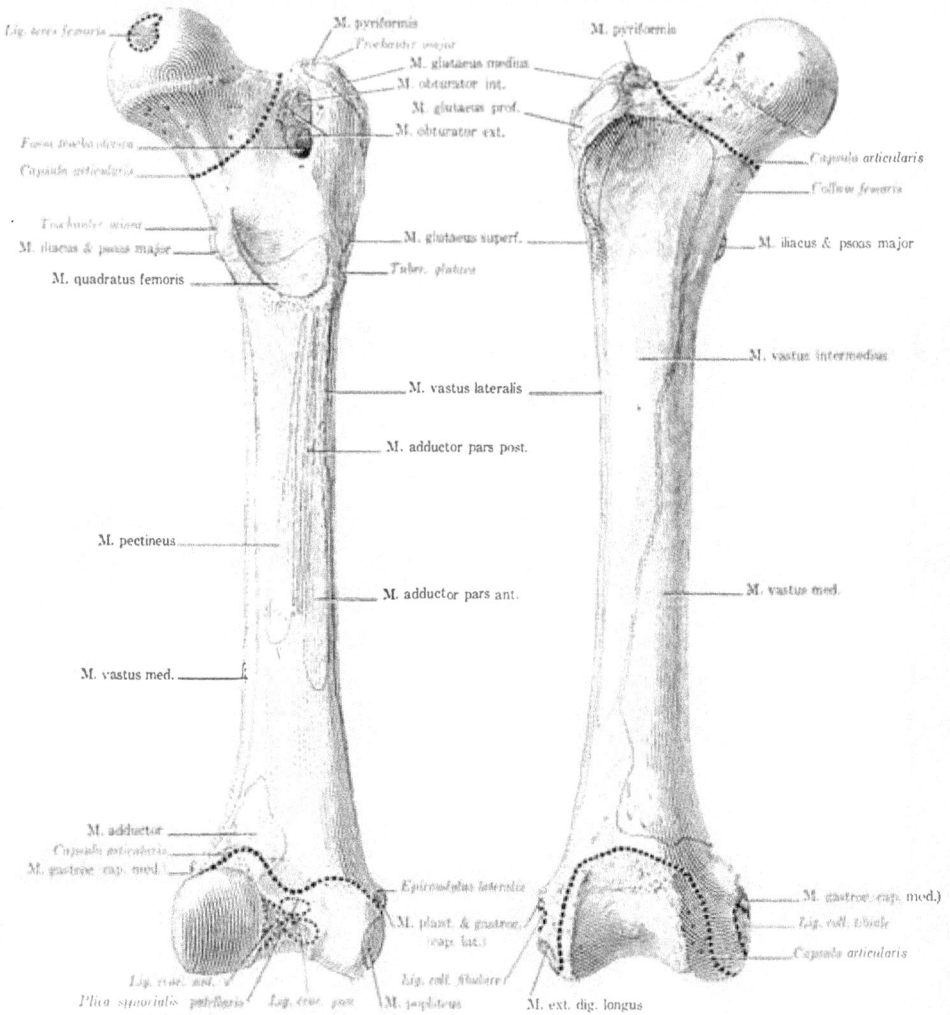

FIG. 62.  Right femur of *Ailuropoda*, posterior and anterior view.

The shaft of the femur is nearly or quite straight; it is convex anteriorly to a greater or lesser degree in *Ursus* and other arctoids. The anterior surface is faintly reticulated. As in other arctoids the shaft is wider transversely than anteroposteriorly: the ratio is about 80. The linea aspera on the posterior surface of the shaft is scarcely indicated, even less so than in *Ursus*. Slight roughenings on the proximal two thirds of the shaft mark the attachments of the pectineus and adductor muscles; these are wanting in the distal third of the bone

where the femoral vessels are in contact with the bone. The anterior, medial, and lateral surfaces of the shaft are overlain by the vastus muscles, and are devoid of any modeling.

The inferior end of the femur differs in details from that of *Ursus*. The condyles are roller-like, rather than ball-like as in *Ursus* and other arctoids, and the intercondyloid fossa (in which the cruciate ligaments attach) is relatively broader. The **lateral condyle** is wider and longer than its fellow and its articular surface is more oblique.

The lateral epicondyle contains a large crater-like depression in which the lateral collateral ligament attaches; the plantaris and the lateral head of the gastrocnemius arise from the prominent superior rim of the crater. A dimple-like depression immediately below the crater marks the attachment of the popliteus. The **median condyle** is much narrower than the corresponding condyle in *Ursus*, as a result of encroachment by the intercondylar fossa. The medial epicondyle contains a large depression for the medial collateral ligament; its anterodorsal rim is elevated into a prominent tubercle on which the medial head of the gastrocnemius arises. The patellar surface does not differ from the corresponding area in *Ursus* and other arctoids.

The femur of *Ailuropoda* thus differs from that of *Ursus* chiefly in details of modeling, torsion, and angulation—features that certainly represent post-natal adaptive adjustments. The only feature that cannot be so interpreted is the relative length of the femur in *Ailuropoda*, which probably demands a genetic basis. I can find no mechanical explanation for the shortening of this bone in *Ailuropoda* relative to *Ursus*; the matter is discussed further on p. 38.

### 3. Patella

The patella (fig. 63) is ovate, about 37 mm. long by 32 mm. wide. It is relatively wider and more disk-shaped than the corresponding bone in *Ursus*, but is otherwise very similar. The anterior surface bears longitudinal striae. The articular surface is broader than high, and the lateral and medial articular facets are not clearly marked. The scar for the attachment of the quadratus femoris tendon is prominent on the superior and lateral surfaces, as is the attachment area for the patellar ligament on the anterior surface at the apex.

### 4. Tibia and Fibula

The tibia and fibula are very short. These bones are also short relative to other limb segments in *Ursus*, and are very short in badgers (Table 2). Short distal segments result in relatively powerful but slow movements in the distal part of the limb. Hence the advantage of a low femorotibial index in graviportal animals and in digging forms that use the hind legs for bracing.

The tibia (fig. 63) is basically similar to that of *Ursus*. It differs chiefly in being shorter and more compact, and in the greater torsion of the distal end. The head, which measures 65–70 mm. in transverse diameter, is relatively broader than in *Ursus*. The **lateral condyle** is about the same size as the medial, as in the bears. A crater-like

depression on its lateral side, for the attachment of the lateral collateral ligament, is larger but shallower than in *Ursus*. The lateral articular surface is ovate, its anteroposterior diameter greatest; it encroaches on the anterior intercondyloid fossa more than in *Ursus*. The **medial condyle** projects medially some distance beyond the border of the shaft. The articular facet for the head of the fibula lies farther posterior than in *Ursus*, but is otherwise similar. The medial articular surface is almost circular in outline. Both the anterior and the posterior condyloid fossae are wider than in the bear. The tibial tuberosity, on which the patellar ligament attaches, is prominent in *Ursus* but is scarcely indicated in *Ailuropoda*.

The shaft of the tibia is almost straight. It is bowed very slightly medially, as in *Ursus*, and this bowing appears to be (but is not) exaggerated by the medial extension of the proximal and distal ends of the bone. This latter circumstance greatly increases the interosseous space between tibia and fibula, and the total width across the leg (from medial border of tibia to lateral border of fibula). The shaft is most slender near the middle, flaring somewhat both proximally and distally. The **anterior crest**, which is associated with the insertions of the gracilis, sartorius, biceps, and semitendinosus, is well marked, especially proximally; it continues distally into the medial malleolus. The **interosseous crest** on the lateral surface of the shaft, on which the interosseous membrane attaches, is a prominent ridge beginning below the lateral condyle and extending down to the distal fibular articulation. On the posterior surface of the shaft several ridges mark the boundaries between the flexor hallucis longus, the tibialis posterior, and the popliteus (fig. 63).

The distal end of the tibia is very similar to that of *Ursus*, except that it is rotated farther on the shaft; the torsion angle of the transverse axis of the distal end against the bicondylar axis of the proximal end is 35°–48° in *Ailuropoda*, whereas in *Ursus* it is only about 20°. The transverse axis also is inclined more obliquely with respect to the long axis of the bone: about 120° in *Ailuropoda*, about 105° in *Ursus*. The **medial malleolus** is short and wide anteroposteriorly. A deep groove, the sulcus malleolaris, on its posterolateral surface lodges the tendon of the posterior tibial muscle; a similar groove is present in *Ursus*. The inferior articular surface, which articulates with the astragalus, is ovate, wider medially and narrower laterally than in *Ursus*. It bears a median ridge, bounded on either side by a depression, that fits a corresponding surface on the astragalus. At the lateral end of the articular surface is a small

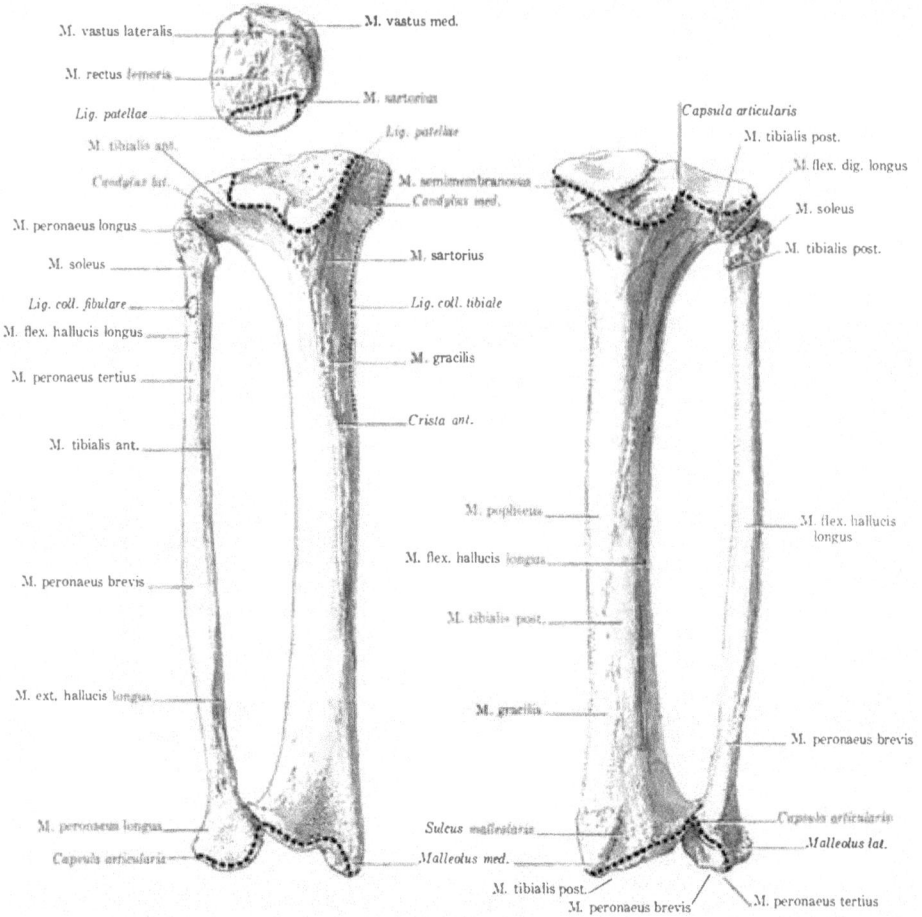

FIG. 63. Right patella, tibia, and fibula of *Ailuropoda*; anterior and posterior views.

obliquely situated articular facet for the distal end of the fibula.

The fibula (fig. 63) is slightly heavier than the fibula of *Ursus*, and is bowed slightly laterally, which further exaggerates the transverse diameter of the leg. It articulates with the tibia by a synovial joint at each end and therefore, as in *Ursus*, represents the mobile type of fibula.

The head is an expansion of the proximal end differing from that of *Ursus* only in minor details. The articular facet is a flat ovate surface, set obliquely and directed medially and posteriorly. No scar marks the attachment of the lateral collateral ligament on the lateral surface immediately below the head. The shaft is triangular in cross

section throughout most of its length, but is considerably flattened distally. Almost its entire surface provides attachment for muscles, of which seven arise from the shaft, and roughened longitudinal elevations on the shaft mark the attachments of aponeuroses and intermuscular septa separating many of these muscles. The most conspicuous crest, on the medial surface, is the interosseous crest to which the interosseous membrane attaches.

The distal end of the fibula is an irregular expansion, larger than the proximal expansion, that forms the lateral malleolus. It is relatively larger and heavier than the lateral malleolus of *Ursus*, but is otherwise comparable. The lateral malle-

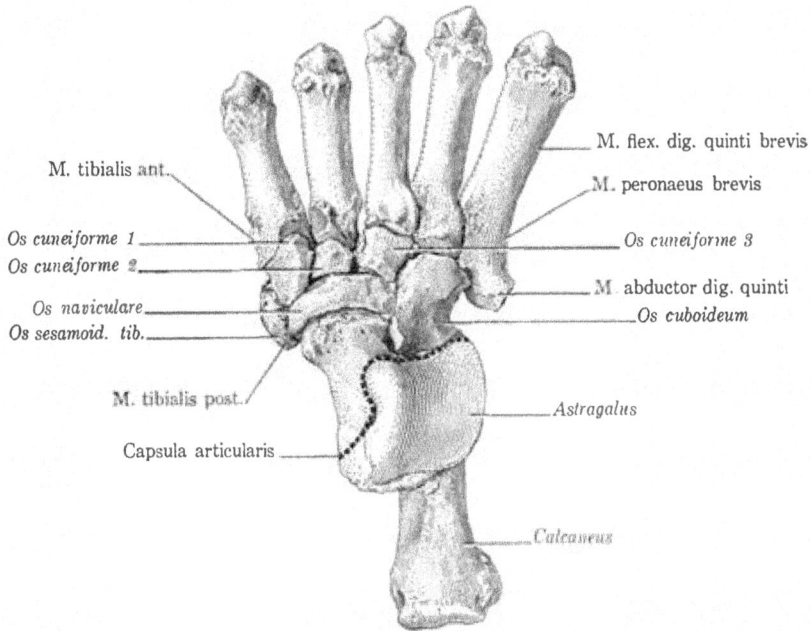

M. tibialis ant.

Os cuneiforme 1
Os cuneiforme 2

Os naviculare
Os sesamoid. tib.

M. tibialis post.

Capsula articularis

M. flex. dig. quinti brevis
M. peronaeus brevis

Os cuneiforme 3

M. abductor dig. quinti
Os cuboideum

Astragalus

Calcaneus

FIG. 64. Right tarsus and metatarsus of *Ailuropoda*, dorsal view.

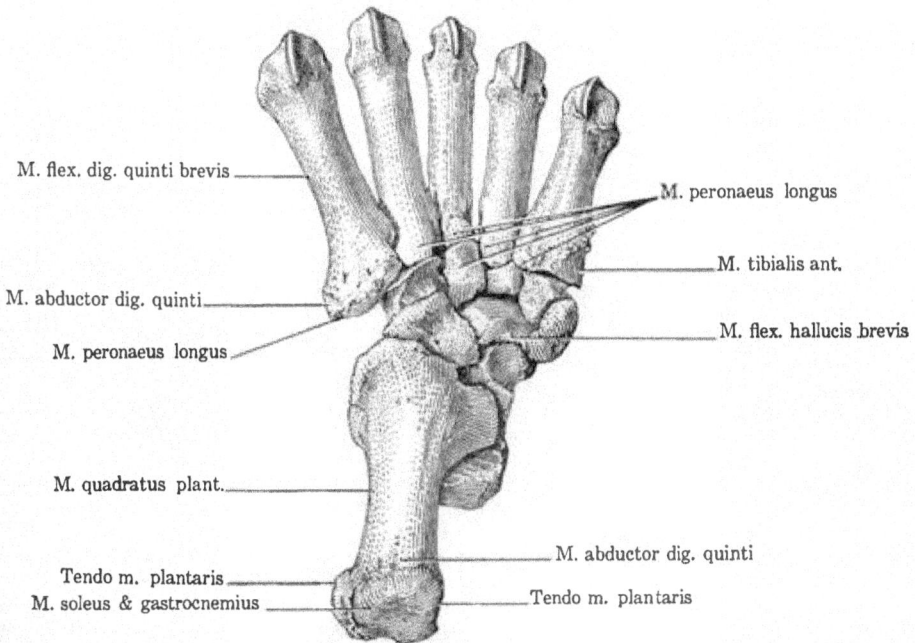

M. flex. dig. quinti brevis

M. abductor dig. quinti

M. peronaeus longus

M. quadratus plant.

Tendo m. plantaris
M. soleus & gastrocnemius

M. peronaeus longus

M. tibialis ant.

M. flex. hallucis brevis

M. abductor dig. quinti

Tendo m. plantaris

FIG. 65. Right tarsus and metatarsus of *Ailuropoda*, plantar view.

117

olus does not project so far distad as the medial malleolus, and its articular surface is less extensive anteroposteriorly. The lateral surface bears a prominent elevation, the processus lateralis fibulae (new name), that separates the peroneal tendons into two groups: the long peroneal tendon lies immediately anterior to the process, while the tendons of the brevis and tertius lie immediately behind it. In *Ursus* this process is a sharply projecting knob-like structure, and in other carnivores (except the Canidae) it forms a hook that arches backward over the tendons of the peronaeus brevis and tertius. The medial surface of the malleolus bears two articular surfaces: a smaller proximal one facing proximally and medially that articulates with the tibia, and a larger distal one facing distally and medially that articulates with the astragalus.

5. *Tarsus*

The tarsus (figs. 64, 65) is in general more conservative than the carpus. The tarsus of living procyonids actually differs little from that of the more generalized Paleocene creodonts, in which it is adapted to arboreal life (Matthew, 1937, p. 317); and the tarsus of modern bears is strikingly similar to that of the Middle Paleocene creodont *Claenodon*. In the bears the ankle shows a characteristic shortening and broadening of all the tarsal bones; this is also evident, though less pronounced, in *Ailuropoda*.

The tarsus of *Ailuropoda* is, in fact, morphologically more "primitive" than that of *Ursus*. This is seen in the less pronounced broadening of all the tarsal bones, in the presence of a large astragalar foramen, and particularly in the form of the two transverse ankle joints—the transverse tarsal and tarsometatarsal joints (fig. 65). In *Ursus* both of these joints are essentially continuous across the ankle (as in man), whereas in *Ailuropoda* and generalized carnivores both joints consist of two or more transverse segments offset from each other. The ursid-human form of these joints is a secondary adaptation to plantigrade walking, whereas the interrupted joints seen in more generalized carnivores increase the lateral stability of the tarsus.

A unique feature of the tarsus of *Ailuropoda* is the extraordinarily loose fit between the astragalus and calcaneus. The lateral and medial articular surfaces of the two bones cannot be brought into congruence at the same time, but only alternatively by sliding the astragalus sideways over the calcaneus. In association with this, the diameter across the two articular surfaces on the astragalus greatly exceeds the diameter across the corresponding surfaces on the calcaneus.

The astragalus (BNA: talus) (fig. 66) is relatively larger than in *Ursus*, but differs chiefly in its longer neck and narrower head, and in the presence of a large astragalar foramen. The trochlea is broader than long, and is characterized by a very shallow groove and relatively small malleolar surfaces; the upper tarsal joint is less secure and permits greater lateral rotation than in *Ursus*. The superior articular surface is not continued posteriorly over the posterior process as in procyonids. The arc of the trochlea is thereby reduced by about 35°; it measures about 165° in *Ailuropoda* and *Ursus*, and about 200° in procyonids.

The medial malleolar surface, which in *Ursus* extends over the neck nearly to the margin of the head, reaching as far distad as does the lateral malleolar surface, is much shorter in *Ailuropoda*, ending at the base of the neck. The lateral malleolar surface is similar to that of *Ursus* except that it is flatter. Immediately posterior to the trochlear groove there is a large astragalar foramen in all specimens examined. This foramen, characteristic of creodonts, occurs sporadically among generalized modern procyonids (Bassariscus) and mustelids (Gulo, Taxidea); I also find a small astragalar foramen in one specimen of *Ursus americanus*. Behind the trochlea a deep groove for the flexor hallucis longus tendon is present in *Ursus* and other carnivores; this groove is wanting in *Ailuropoda*.

On the inferior surface the lateral (posterior in human anatomy) and medial articular surfaces, articulating with corresponding articular surfaces on the calcaneus, resemble those of *Ursus*. They are oblong, relatively shallowly concave areas separated by a deep astragalar groove. The lateral is more extensive than the medial, and in *Ailuropoda* their axes diverge slightly distally. As in other carnivores, the medial articular surface lies mostly beneath the neck of the astragalus. Of the accessory facets (Davis, 1958) only the anterior marginal facet of the medial articular surface is represented. It is a narrow extension of the medial surface, continuous anteriorly with the navicular articular surface, and it rests on the cuboid.

The head and neck, on the contrary, resemble those of procyonids and generalized mustelids and viverrids more closely than they do those of *Ursus*. The neck is relatively long, narrower than in *Ursus*, and deflected toward the medial border of the foot, forming an angle of about 98° with the transverse axis of the trochlea. The head bears two articular surfaces, as in other carnivores: an oval convex area anteriorly and medially for the navicular, and a small triangular area inferiorly

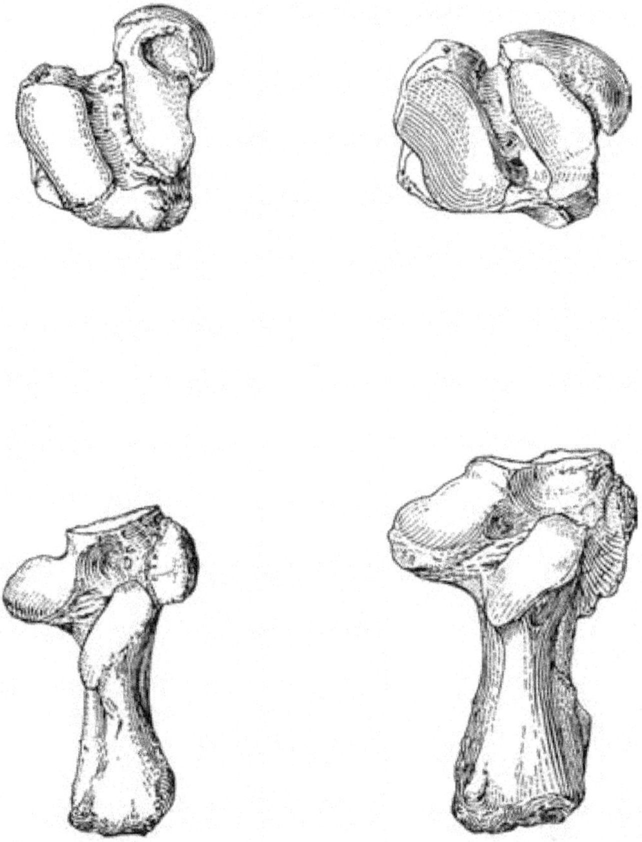

*Ailuropoda*          *Ursus*

FIG. 66. Opposing surfaces of right astragalus and calcaneus of *Ailuropoda* and *Ursus arctos*.

and laterally for the cuboid. On the inferior surface, immediately behind the navicular articular surface, a deep pit marks the attachment of the talocalcaneal interosseous ligament.

The **calcaneus** (fig. 66) is longer and more slender than in *Ursus*. On the superior surface the lateral articular surface is an elongate oval, extending farther posteriorly than in *Ursus*. As in bears, it describes a continuous spiral track: anteriorly it faces slightly laterally, while its posterior end is almost vertical, facing medially. This articular surface is scarcely curved in cross section, and the curvature along the long axis is relatively slight; in this flatness the bears and panda differ sharply from other carnivores. The medial artic-

ular surface is a flat discoidal area on the superior surface of the sustentaculum. As in *Ursus*, the posterior end of this articular surface is deflected sharply downward, forming an angle of almost 90° with the main articular surface. This arrangement, which is present in *Nasua* and indicated in *Gulo* but is wanting in other carnivores, increases stability of the lower tarsal joint at the expense of mobility.

The medial articular surface is continued anteriorly into a narrow accessory facet that extends forward to the anterior border of the calcaneus, articulating with the anterior marginal facet of the astragalus. This accessory facet, which increases the stability of the lower tarsal joint, is present in most, but not all, carnivores.

Opposite the sustentaculum the lateral surface of the calcaneus is produced into a prominent projection, the coracoid process (Baum and Zietzschmann, 1936), from which arise the extensor digitorum brevis and quadratus plantae muscles. In *Ursus* the coracoid process is a long shelf-like structure extending posteriorly to the posterior border of the lateral articular surface, while in other carnivores it is less extensive.

The cuboid articular surface is more oblique than the corresponding surface in *Ursus* but is otherwise similar. The posterior end of the calcaneus is expanded into a knob-like structure. Almost the entire posterior face is occupied by a large depressed scar that marks the attachment of the tendo Achillis and its associated bursa.

The **navicular** articulates with the astragalus, the cuboid, and the three cuneiforms, as in *Ursus* and other carnivores. The posterior surface is composed almost entirely of a large ovate concave articular facet that receives the head of the astragalus (fig. 64). The anterior surface is convex, its superior part indistinctly divided into three facets for the three cuneiform bones; inferiorly it is roughened at the attachment site of the plantar naviculari-cuneiform ligaments. On the medial surface a smooth prominence marks the articulation site of the tibial sesamoid. A narrow articular facet on the inferolateral surface articulates with the cuboid, and immediately mesad of this on the inferior surface is a rounded prominence, the navicular tuberosity.

The **cuboid** resembles that of *Ursus* in shape, but is relatively longer and narrower.[1] Its posterior surface presents a rectangular convex articular surface for the calcaneus (fig. 64); its anterior surface bears a slightly concave surface for the fourth and fifth metatarsals, a faint ridge dividing the two areas. Its medial surface presents two articular surfaces, a vertical surface posteriorly that articulates with the head of the astragalus, and an irregularly shaped surface that articulates with the navicular and the third cuneiform. The inferior surface bears a prominent transverse ridge for the attachment of the long plantar ligament.

The **cuneiform bones** articulate with the navicular posteriorly and the first three metatarsals anteriorly. The first is the largest; the tibial sesamoid articulates partly with its posteromedial cor-

ner. The third cuneiform articulates laterally with the cuboid.

The **tibial sesamoid** is relatively much larger than in *Ursus* (fig. 54); it measures 20 mm. in length by 13 in breadth. As in other carnivores, it articulates with the navicular and first cuneiform. The bone is flattened from side to side. The tendon of the posterior tibial muscle inserts on its posterior border, and a part of the flexor hallucis brevis muscle arises from its medial face (fig. 102).

### 6. Pes

The **metatarsals** decrease in length from the fifth to the first; in *Ursus* the fourth is the longest, and in procyonids the third and fourth are subequal. As in *Ursus*, the metatarsals are short. The fifth is relatively heavier than in *Ursus*, but the others are of comparable size. As in other carnivores, the proximal end of the fifth metatarsal bears a prominent lateral process to which the tendon of the peroneus longus and brevis and the abductor digiti quinti attach.

As in the manus, the distal articular surfaces of the metatarsals are narrower than in *Ursus*, and the median ridge is more prominent.

The **phalanges** are similar to those of *Ursus*, relatively shorter than those of the procyonids. In the proximal row a pair of elevations on the inferior surface of each bone, near the distal end, marks the attachment of the interosseous muscles. A conspicuous pit-like excavation on the inferior surface of each bone of the middle row, immediately behind the trochlea, receives the large plantar process of the terminal phalanx.

A pair of **sesamoid bones** is present beneath the metatarsophalangeal articulation of each digit. There are ten in all.

### B. REVIEW OF THE HIND LEG

The bones of the hind leg of *Ailuropoda*, like those of the fore leg, agree with the corresponding bones of *Ursus* in all essential respects. As in the fore leg, differences in details of modeling, torsion, and angulation probably represent postnatal responses to stresses extrinsic to the bone tissue itself.

Relative lengths of limb segments agree with the proportions in graviportal animals. This suggests that limb proportions in *Ailuropoda* are broadly adaptive, although the animal is much too small to be truly graviportal and the adaptive significance, if any, of the limb proportions is not clear. Short distal segments result in relatively powerful but slow movements in the distal part of the limb. Hence the advantage of a low femorotibial index to heavy graviportal animals and to digging forms that use the hind limbs for bracing. Length of

---

[1] The tarsus and pes are relatively broader in bears than in other carnivores. It is interesting and suggestive that the relative breadth of the cuboid increases with absolute size in the genus *Ursus*. The ratio breadth length × 100 in a series of bears is: *Ursus americanus* 81, *U. arctos* 92, *U. gyas* 95. The only available specimen of *U. spelaeus* is a shade smaller than my very large *U. gyas* and has a ratio of 94. The corresponding ratio for *Ailuropoda* is 64.

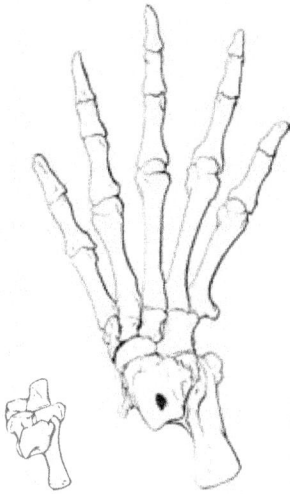

Claenodon corrugatus

Potos flavus

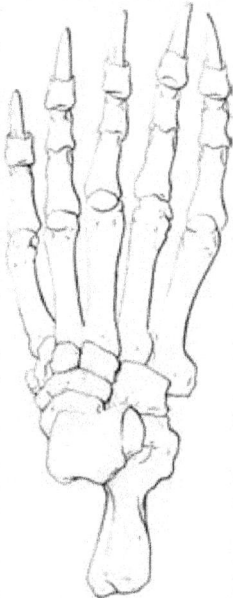

Ursus arctos

Ailuropoda melanoleuca

FIG. 67.  Right tarsus and pes of representative carnivores.  The small inset to the left of *Claenodon corrugatus* is *Claenodon montanensis* (Bull. U.S. Nat. Mus., 169).

121

long bones is certainly gene-controlled, but the mechanism of such control is unknown.

Fuld (1901) demonstrated a slight but significant increase in tibia length in dogs that had been bipedal since puppyhood. Colton (1929) found that in the rat, on the contrary, bipedalism results in a slight increase in femur length. In neither the dogs nor the rats was the difference anywhere near as great as the difference between the relative lengths of these bones in *Ailuropoda* and *Ursus*.

The hypertrophied tibial sesamoid is a product of natural selection, *but of selection acting on the radial sesamoid*. The fact that the tibial sesamoid has hypertrophied along with the radial sesamoid shows that these two bones are homeotic from the genetic standpoint as well as serially homologous from the morphological standpoint.

Thus only one (presumably) adaptive feature in the bones of the hind leg—the relative lengths of the long bones—appears to result directly from natural selection acting on the bones themselves. Even this does not appear to be adaptive and may be a pleiotropic effect.

## VII. DISCUSSION OF OSTEOLOGICAL CHARACTERS

It is evident from the foregoing description that the skeleton supplies abundant and convincing evidence that *Ailuropoda* is much closer to the Ursidae than to any other group of living carnivores. Missing "ursid characters" have been partly responsible for disagreement among mammalogists as to the affinities of *Ailuropoda* (e.g., Mivart, 1885a; Weber, 1928). It is now obvious that these missing characters have been obliterated by phylogenetically recent factors that for the most part are extrinsic to the skeleton. The most important of these extrinsic factors is hypertrophy of the skeletal musculature. Yet, despite close similarity in all essential respects, the panda skeleton differs from the bear skeleton in a number of very puzzling ways. It is the interpretation of these differences that is pertinent to our central problem. *The panda skeleton resembles the bear skeleton in all essential respects.*

The bear skeleton itself differs from the generalized carnivore condition in a number of features that cannot be interpreted as adaptive, and I am certain that many ursid characters represent what Grüneberg (1948) has called "subordinated gene effects" effects that are genetically, physiologically, or even mechanically connected with a primary gene effect on which natural selection has operated, without themselves being adaptive. Such non-adaptive characters might persist indefinitely

if selection against them is less intense than selection for the primary effect. Among the most conspicuous of these in the bears are limb proportions, curve of moments of resistance in the vertebral column, shortness of lumbar region, shortness of tail, length of sacrum, form of pelvis. *Ailuropoda* shares most of these characters with *Ursus*, and has superimposed additional features, likewise mostly non-adaptive, on the ursid pattern.

Many of the differences between panda and bear skeletons are adaptive, but their cause is extrinsic to the bone itself; that is, they merely reflect the response of the bone tissue to external pressures, stresses and strains, and other purely mechanical factors. In the absence of the appropriate stimulus such characters fail to appear. Among such features are the surface modeling of bones, torsions, form and extent of articular areas, and size and position of foramina. These are characteristic features of the skeleton of *Ailuropoda*, and they may be clearly adaptive in the sense of promoting the efficiency of the organism, but they are epigenetic to the bone and therefore are not the result of natural selection *on the skeleton*.

The most conspicuous way in which the skeleton of *Ailuropoda* differs from that of *Ursus* is in a general increase in the quantity of compact bone throughout the entire skeleton. Except for masticatory requirements, no differences from the habits of bears would demand such increased thickness of compacta for mechanical reasons. A generalized effect of this kind, involving an entire tissue and with sharply localized advantage to the organism, would almost surely have a single cause. Comparable generalized effects, involving the whole skeleton and localized in a single genetic factor, are well known in laboratory and domestic animals (Stockard, 1941; Grüneberg, 1952; Klatt and Oboussier, 1951). Wherever they have been analyzed, it has been found that such effects are mediated through the endocrine system. We may postulate that in the panda, because of masticatory requirements, selection strongly favored increased thickness of compacta *in the skull*. This increase was actually achieved via a process that results in generalized thickening of the compacta throughout the skeleton. The functionally unnecessary increase of bone tissue in the postcranial skeleton is no great disadvantage because of the non-predatory habits of this species, which places no premium on speed and agility.

*The most significant feature in the panda skeleton is a generalized increase in the quantity of compact bone. This probably has an extremely simple genetic base. The increased thickness of compacta is advantageous only in the skull.*

Many proportions in the skeleton of the panda —and to a lesser extent in the skeleton of bears— are a mixture of those seen in bipedal, in burrowing, and in graviportal forms. In part these proportions are mutually contradictory—adaptations associated with bipedalism are not the same as those associated with graviportalism—and in part they are not contradictory, since adaptations for withstanding anteroposterior thrust are similar in bipedal and burrowing forms. Still other proportions in the panda, particularly in the limbs, cannot be reconciled with any mechanical requirements, and appear to represent disharmonious relations of the "subordinated gene effect" variety. The fact is that the panda does not burrow, it is bipedal only to the extent that, like many other mammals, it occasionally stands erect for short periods, and it is not heavy enough to qualify as graviportal. These facts show that the ill-assorted features distinguishing the postcranial skeleton of the panda from that of *Ursus* are not truly adaptive, and that where they agree with conditions that presumably are adaptive in other specialized forms (bipedal, fossorial, graviportal) such agreements are either fortuitous or based on something other than functional demands.

Thus we are confronted with a highly modified and strongly adaptive skull associated with a considerably modified postcranial skeleton in which the departures from the "ursid norm" appear to be completely non-adaptive, even inadaptive to the extent of producing a disharmonious organism. From what is known of the genetics of acromegaly, achondroplasia, and other pathological conditions of the skeleton in dogs and mice (Stockard, 1941; Grüneberg, 1948) the most economical interpretation, consistent with all known facts, of the syndrome of non-adaptive features in the skeleton of *Ailuropoda* is that they are associated pleiotropically with the one definitely adaptive feature. It is even highly probable that the whole complex has a very simple genetic base.

The persistence of such morphological disharmonies in a natural population is unusual but not unique, and might in fact be anticipated in highly specialized forms whose adaptive niche places a low premium on all-around mechanical efficiency. Similar disharmonies are clearly evident in the hyenas, which like *Ailuropoda* are highly specialized for masticatory power but do not need speed or agility either to escape from enemies or to capture prey.

It is suggestive that bipedal, fossorial, and graviportal mammals are all characterized by local strengthening of the skeleton (i.e., by increase in quantity of compacta). The changes in form and proportions associated with such local strengthening are presumptively adaptive, and in some instances it can be shown unequivocally that they are—the moments of resistance in the vertebral column of bipedal forms, for example. In other instances attempts at a functional explanation have been unsuccessful; for example, pelvic architecture in bipedal and burrowing forms. In many instances no functional explanation has even been attempted; for example, limb proportions in graviportal forms. If it can be demonstrated that certain features in the skeleton are correlated with increased quantity of compacta rather than with other functional requirements, then an association between such features and a particular functional requirement is merely a chance association. Attempts to read adaptive significance into such associations are, of course, based on a false assumption and can only lead to false conclusions. The existence in the panda skeleton of numerous ill-assorted conditions convergent with conditions in bipedal, fossorial, and graviportal forms suggests that such spurious correlations with functional requirements may be more common than has been assumed. Much more data are required to prove this suggestion.

*Numerous ill-assorted disharmonies in the postcranial skeleton of the panda are connected pleiotropically, as subordinated gene effects, with the increase in quantity of compacta.*

One other feature in the skeleton demands attention: the specialized and obviously functional radial sesamoid. It was concluded (p. 183) that all that would be required to derive this mechanism from the radial sesamoid of *Ursus* is simple hypertrophy of the bone. This symmetrical increase in the dimensions of a single bone is quite a different thing from the hypertrophy of the compacta seen elsewhere in the skeleton. The localized remodeling seen in the sesamoid surely has a specific genetic base, as is strongly indicated by the "sympathetic" hypertrophy of the tibial sesamoid. The parallel and non-functional hypertrophy of the tibial sesamoid also indicates that the genetic mechanism is a very simple one, perhaps involving no more than a single gene.

*The highly specialized and obviously functional radial sesamoid has a specific, but probably very simple, genetic base.*

Disregarding any minor polishing effects of natural selection, aimed at reducing disharmonious relations, it appears that the differences between the skeleton of *Ailuropoda* and that of *Ursus* could be based on no more than two gene effects. There is, of course, no way of proving that the situation actually was so simple, but mechanisms capable of producing comparable effects on the skeleton have been demonstrated experimentally in other mammals. The alternative explanation—numerous small gene effects screened by natural selection —postulates a vastly more complex process, and leaves unexplained the many clearly inadaptive features in the skeleton. We could, of course, assume that these several inadaptive features appeared one by one during the evolution of *Ailuropoda*, and persisted simply because there was little or no selection against them. But if each of these is unconnected with any of the other gene effects, then *any* selection pressure would have eliminated them. Obviously there is some selection against any inadaptive feature; no feature is truly adaptively neutral. Therefore it seems to me that probability strongly favors a single gene effect as the causal agent for all the hereditary differences between the skeleton of *Ailuropoda* and *Ursus*, except in the radial sesamoid.

*The major features distinguishing the skeleton of* Ailuropoda *from that of* Ursus *may depend on as few as two gene effects. These are:*

(a) *Generalized hypertrophy of compacta.*

(b) *Specific hypertrophy of the radial sesamoid.*

## VIII. CONCLUSIONS

1. The skeleton of *Ailuropoda* resembles the skeleton of *Ursus* in all essential respects.

2. Many skeletal differences between *Ailuropoda* and *Ursus* are epigenetic to the bone tissue, and therefore do not result from natural selection on the skeleton.

3. The most significant feature in the panda skeleton is a generalized increase in the quantity of compact bone. This probably has an extremely simple genetic base.

4. The increased thickness of compacta is advantageous only in the skull.

5. Numerous ill-assorted disharmonies in the postcranial skeleton are connected pleiotropically, as subordinated gene effects, with the increase in quantity of compacta.

6. The highly specialized and obviously functional radial sesamoid has a specific, but probably very simple, genetic base.

7. Thus, the major features distinguishing the skeleton of *Ailuropoda* from that of *Ursus* may depend on as few as two genetic factors. These are: (a) generalized hypertrophy of compacta; (b) specific hypertrophy of the radial sesamoid.

# DENTITION

## I. DESCRIPTION

The classification of mammals has depended more on the dentition than on any other single feature of morphology. The teeth of the giant panda have repeatedly been studied and discussed in great detail (Gervais, 1875; Lydekker, 1901; Bardenfleth, 1913; Gregory, 1936; McGrew, 1938). These studies have led to the most divergent views as to the homologies of the various cusps, and inferences as to the affinities of *Ailuropoda* based on such homologies. I conclude that the cheek teeth of *Ailuropoda* are so modified from those of any other known carnivore that interpretations based on them have been largely subjective.

The dental formula of *Ailuropoda* is

$$I\tfrac{3}{3} \ C\tfrac{1}{1} \ P\tfrac{4}{4} \ M\tfrac{2}{3}=42,$$

which is the primitive form for the recent Carnivora. The formula is the same in small species of *Ursus*, but various additional teeth have been lost in large species of *Ursus* and in other genera of the Ursidae. In the Procyonidae and *Ailurus* the third lower molar has disappeared, giving the formula

$$I\tfrac{3}{3} \ C\tfrac{1}{1} \ P\tfrac{4}{4} \ M\tfrac{2}{2}=40.$$

The **incisors** are in no way remarkable in *Ailuropoda*. As in carnivores in general, in both jaws they increase in size from the first to the third. As in *Ursus* (much less so, if at all, in other arctoids), the third incisor in both jaws is abruptly larger than the second, and in the upper jaw is less chisel-shaped and more caniniform than the two more medial incisors. The third incisor is relatively larger in *Ailuropoda* than in *Ursus*, and is separated from the canines by a very short diastema. The shortness of the diastema is the only evidence of crowding in the anterior dentition. The incisors are, of course, single rooted.

The six incisors in each jaw are closely crowded, their combined occlusal surfaces forming an essentially continuous, slightly arched, scraper or chisel edge. The resulting tool, lying between and often slightly in front of the canines, is one of the most characteristic features of the dentition of the Carnivora.

The **canines** are more robust than in *Ursus*, in both long and transverse diameters. Their relative length is almost identical in bear and panda, however, and this gives the canines of *Ailuropoda* a relatively stumpy appearance. In the unworn dentition there is a vertical ridge on both anterior and posterior surfaces of the upper canine, and on the posterior surface only of the lower. Similar ridges are seen in other arctoids (e.g., *Procyon*), but not in *Ursus*. *Ailurus*, along with the procyonids *Bassaricyon* and *Potos*, has vertical grooves on its canines. The phylogenetic and functional significance, if any, of these surface sculpturings is unknown.

The upper canine in *Ailuropoda* projects forward at an angle of about 30°. The same tooth forms an angle of about 15° in *Ursus*, while in other arctoids examined it does not deviate more than a couple of degrees from the vertical.

The **premolars** increase in size from the first to the fourth, as in all arctoids. The first premolar is degenerate and peg-like in both jaws, and is often missing. In size and structure it contrasts sharply with the remaining premolars. The remaining three teeth are crowded, and in both upper and lower jaws P2 is rotated at an angle of about 30° from the axis of the tooth row.

In the upper series, $P^2$ is tri-lobed, two-rooted, and with no indication of internal (lingual) cusps. $P^3$ is very similar to $P^4$, except in size. The fourth upper premolar, the **upper carnassial** of the Carnivora, has been the chief object of discussion and speculation in the dentition of the giant panda. It is the largest of the premolars, but is nevertheless considerably smaller than the two upper molars. The tooth exhibits five prominent cusps arranged in two longitudinal rows. The three on the labial side are considerably higher than those on the lingual, with the central one the highest of all. These have been homologized, from front to rear, with the parastyle, paracone, and metacone. The two cusps on the lingual side are regarded as the protocone (anteriorly) and the hypocone (posteriorly). There are no cingula. The tooth has three powerful roots, arranged in the form of a triangle. The anteriormost root supports the para-

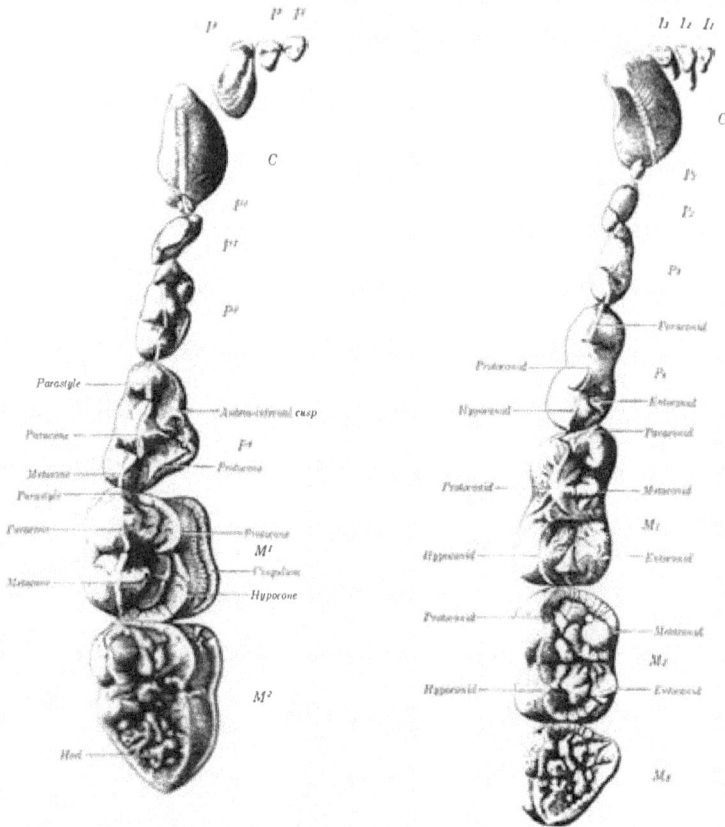

FIG. 68.   Occlusal views of unworn right upper and left lower dentitions of *Ailuropoda* (×1).

style, the protocone, and the anterior half of the paracone. The posteroexternal root supports the metacone and the posterior half of the paracone. The posterointernal root supports the hypocone.

Five cusps, occupying similar positions, are found on the upper carnassial of *Procyon* and *Ailurus*. The mode of origin of the *Procyon* crown pattern from the primitive three-cusped shearing carnassial is well known and documented by fossil material (McGrew, 1938). Morphologically the crown pattern of *Ailuropoda* is very similar to that of *Procyon*, but the relation of the cusps to the roots is quite different and essentially nothing is known of the history of this tooth in the panda. The form of the crown in *Ailurus* is like that of *Procyon* and *Ailuropoda*, and the relation of cusps to roots is like that of *Procyon*, not like that of *Ailuropoda*. It has been assumed by Lydekker, Gregory, and McGrew that the morphological similarity in

cusp arrangement between the raccoon and the giant panda denotes homology and hence common ancestry. Winge and Bardenfleth, on the contrary, argued that the different cusp root relations show that the similarity in crown pattern is the result of convergence.

In the Ursidae, by contrast, $P^4$ is degenerate by normal carnivore standards. It is relatively and absolutely small, abruptly smaller than the molars, and its crown usually bears only three cusps: the paracone, metacone, and protocone; in small individuals of *Ursus* (e.g., *U. americanus*) there may be a minute parastyle. The relation of cusps to roots is identical with *Ailuropoda*.

The lower premolars are simpler and more uniform than the upper, but otherwise follow the trend of the latter closely. As in the upper jaw, the first premolar is small and peg-like and contrasts sharply with the following teeth. It is often missing. $P_2$, like its antagonist, is rotated at an angle of about 30° from the axis of the tooth row.

$P_{2-4}$ increase in size from front to rear, but $P_4$ is much smaller than the following $M_1$. All are trilobed, with three conical cusps in series along the axis of the tooth. $P_4$ has a small postero-internal cusp, sometimes subdivided into several small tubercles. Thus the posteriormost part of the lower premolar series is slightly broadened. All the lower premolars, except $P_1$, are two-rooted.

The **upper molars** are enormous and richly cuspidate, dominating the entire upper tooth row. They are abruptly and conspicuously larger than the upper premolars, and are closely crowded. $M^1$ is almost square, slightly broader than long. It bears two prominent conical cusps, the para-cone and the metacone, on the labial side. Lingually and directly opposite these there is a second pair of smaller and lower cusps, the protocone and hypocone. A third pair of poorly defined cusps is situated in the valley between the outer and inner rows of cusps; the homology, if any, of these cusps is unknown. The internal border of the tooth forms a broad shelf-like cingulum whose occlusal surface is very regularly serrate. $M^2$ is divided into two subequal parts, a trigonid anteriorly and a large talonid posteriorly. The anterior part of the tooth is very similar to $M^1$ in form and arrangement of cusps and cingulum. The occlusal surface of the talonid is richly tuberculate, with a long blade-like cusp medially (immediately behind the protocone, and perhaps representing an elongate hypocone) and a narrow cingulum. There are three roots on $M^1$, two lateral and one medial, as is typical of the Carnivora. The medial root is greatly expanded anteroposteriorly, and is partly divided by a groove into two pillars that lie beneath the two medial cusps. $M^2$, in addition to the usual three roots, has a fourth large root supporting the talon.

The upper molars of *Ailuropoda* are fundamentally similar to those of *Ursus*, but they differ in two seemingly important respects: their relatively larger size, especially their greater breadth; and the rich development of secondary tubercle-like elevations. The extinct European cave bear, *Ursus spelaeus*, reached a larger size than any other known member of the genus *Ursus*, and hence had the largest molars. It is therefore extremely suggestive that the molars of the cave bear, while retaining their ursid outlines, exhibit the same rich development of secondary cusps and tubercles as is seen in the giant panda. The similarity of the molars in these two forms, except for the broadening of the crown in *Ailuropoda*, is quite astonishing.

The lower molars are simpler and less broadened than the upper. $M_1$, the **lower carnassial**, has lost its sectorial character and is quite similar to the corresponding tooth in both *Ursus* and *Procyon*. There are five cusps, which retain the primitive arrangement (fig. 68). The facing slopes of the entoconid and hypoconid exhibit low tubercle-like elevations similar to the medial row of cusps on $M^1$, but these are lacking between the proto-conid and metaconid. There is a poorly defined cingulum externally. $M_2$ is more tuberculate than $M_1$, and the cusps are less sharply defined. The paraconid, which is prominent on $M_1$, cannot be identified with certainty on $M_2$. This cusp is often almost completely coalesced with the protoconid in *Ursus*. It is also associated with the protoconid in *Ailurus*, but there is no indication of it in *Procyon*. $M_3$ has a rounded triangular outline in *Ailuropoda*, and the cusps are almost completely obliterated on its flattened crown. The occlusal surface, which opposes the talon of $M^2$, is thrown up into a complex pattern of low tubercles. The outline and crown pattern of $M_3$ in *Ailuropoda* are quite different from the more typically molariform $M_3$ of *Ursus*. It is noteworthy, however, that Rode (1935, pl. 7) illustrates, as "abnormal" examples, several lower third molars of the gigantic *Ursus spelaeus* and these are almost exactly like $M_3$ of *Ailuropoda*.

## II. DISCUSSION OF DENTITION

It has long been the custom of systematists to regard individual teeth, and even individual cusps, as the basic units of the dentition. Thus, by implication, these units are construed as individually gene-controlled and therefore subject to individual selection. The tooth as a whole, to say nothing of the dentition as a whole, would then be a mosaic of individually derived elements, each of which survives or perishes according to the way in which it functions in the dental activities of the animal. Similarities between adjacent teeth are ascribed to convergence resulting from selection. Such a view naturally places great emphasis on "homologies" between cusps and similar elements as indicating affinities between animals. Furthermore, the minute structure of each tooth is perforce directly correlated with function.

In practice, the teeth are minutely scrutinized and compared, element by element, for similarities in structure. Identity or near identity in architecture is construed as an infallible indicator of relationship, and vice versa. Certain teeth ($P^4$ in the Carnivora) are often assumed to be better indicators of affinities than others. This method has worked in the majority of cases because in closely related forms the dentitions, like other morphological features, usually are closely similar. There is a considerable residue of forms with specialized dentition, however, whose relationships cannot be resolved by any amount of peering at the teeth as discrete entities. As Bateson remarked more than half a century ago, "the attribution of strict individuality to each member of a repeated series of repeated parts leads to absurdity." No better example of the limitations of this method could be asked than the giant panda.

On the basis of a mechanical point-by-point comparison, the teeth of *Ailuropoda* are in some respects more similar to the teeth of the Procyonidae than to those of the Ursidae. The whole premolar series is strikingly degenerate in the bears. P1-3 are peg-like vestiges, often missing in part. Even P⁴ (the carnassial), normally the largest tooth in the upper battery in carnivores, is greatly reduced in all bears. In *Ailuropoda*, in striking contrast, only P1 is degenerate and the remaining premolars are robust functional teeth. P⁴ is large, with five well-formed cusps occupying the same relative positions on the crown as they do in *Procyon* and *Ailurus* (though they are differently related to the roots). On the other hand, the molars of *Ailuropoda* are far more bear-like than procyonid-like, especially in the presence of a large talon on M² and in the retention of M₃, which is lacking in the Procyonidae. It was the opinion of Lydekker, Gregory, and McGrew, however, that the premolar features are "more important" than the molar.

Two recent concepts have greatly changed our ideas of the evolution of dentitions. Structures such as teeth or vertebrae are serially repeated (homeotic) elements. It has been found that such structures are at least partly controlled by genes exerting a generalized effect over a region comprising several adjacent elements, rather than on each isolated element. This is the *field control concept*. Sawin (1945, 1946) and Sawin and Hull (1946) have so interpreted hereditary variations in vertebral formula in rabbits. Butler (1939, 1946) has applied the field concept to the teeth of mammals, arguing that they are homeotic structures that have evolved as parts of a continuous morphogenetic field rather than as isolated units, and that a common morphogenetic cause must have acted on more than one tooth germ to account for the close similarity between adjacent teeth. The second concept is that of *differential growth*, which was developed chiefly by Huxley (1932). According to this theory, now voluminously documented, various structures may have a different growth rate from that of the organism as a whole. Thus, with increase in the size of the organism during phylogeny, structures may attain a relative size or degree of differentiation that is not directly determined by the action of selection on the structure itself. The classic examples of the mandibles of lucanid beetles and the antlers of deer are well known, but it is not so well understood that this principle may apply also to the teeth of mammals.

How do these concepts relate to the dentition of *Ailuropoda*? In the primitive carnivore dentition, as represented by *Canis*, the dental gradient of the upper cheek teeth centers in P⁴ and M¹, falling off steeply on either side of this center. More specialized carnivore dentitions exhibit a shifting of this center anteriorly or posteriorly along the tooth row, and expansion or contraction of the center to embrace one or several teeth (fig. 69). The Ursidae differ from other Carnivora in that the center lies wholly in the molar region, falling off abruptly at the boundary between molars and premolars. The molar emphasis is further reflected in the conspicuous posterior extension of M² in the form of a large talon. In *Ailuropoda* the whole premolar-molar battery has been secondarily enlarged, but there is still the same molar emphasis as in the bears. The dental gradient is quite distinctive and different from that of the Procyonidae.

Enlargement in *Ailuropoda* begins abruptly at the boundary between the first and second premolars; the teeth anterior to this line (first premolar, canine, and incisors) are no larger than in *Ursus*, whereas teeth posterior to the line are all enlarged to approximately the same degree. These correspond almost exactly to the canine and incisor fields and the molarization field, respectively, of Butler. An astonishingly close parallel to this condition is seen in the fossil anthropoid *Paranthropus robustus* (Broom and Robinson, 1949), in which the premolar-molar series is so much and so abruptly larger than the canine-incisor series that it is difficult to believe they belong to the same individual.

The data of Rode (1935) on the dentition of fossil and recent bears present a clear picture of changes directly correlated with skull size in the genus *Ursus*. Such changes are the result of differential growth rather than of direct selection on the dentition, and are only secondarily (if at all) related to the functioning of the teeth. The premolar dentition is reduced in all members of the genus, no doubt as a result of selection, but deterioration becomes progressively more pronounced with increased skull size. In small forms ( *Ursus americanus*) the formula is typically P⅔; among the medium-sized species it is ½ in *U. arctos* and

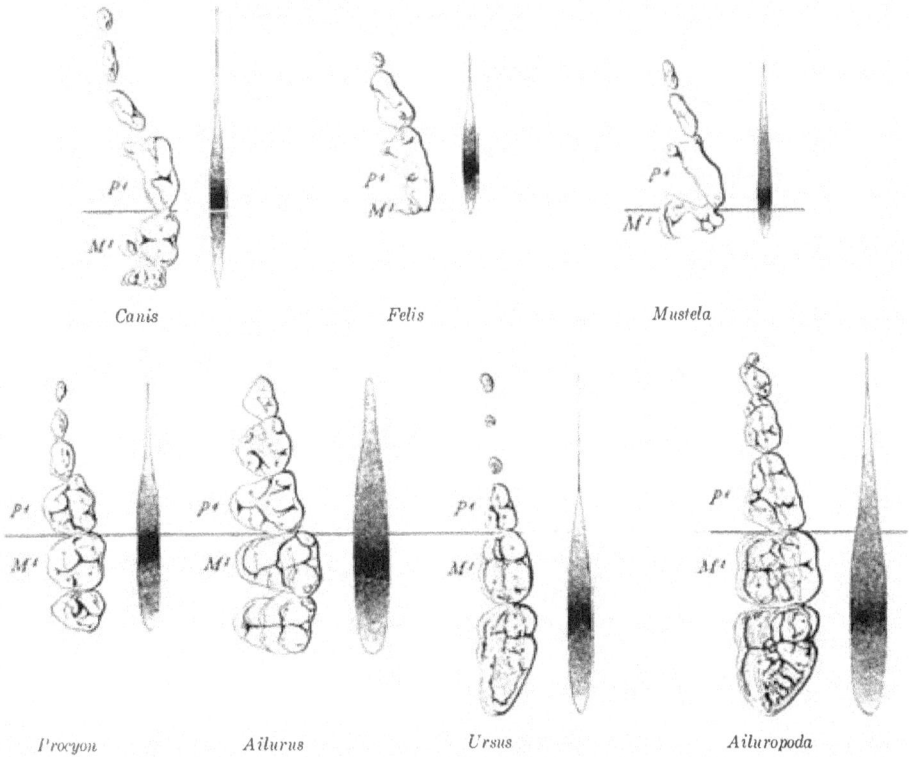

FIG. 69.  Upper cheek teeth of representative carnivores to show varying gradients in the premolar-molar field.

$\frac{2}{3}$ in *U. horribilis*, but in the huge *U. spelaeus* it is $\frac{1}{4}$ or even $\frac{1}{6}$.[1]  Thus there is an inverse correlation between skull size and premolar development in *Ursus*, and reduction of the premolars is a feature of the growth pattern of this genus, its expression becoming increasingly pronounced with increased skull size.  It is probable, furthermore, that the growth pattern was established early in bear phylogeny, in animals of relatively small size, in adapting the primitive carnivore dentition to the requirements of the bear stock.  The almost total suppression of the premolars in large species would then be merely an expression of the growth pattern of the bear stock, a direct result of selection for larger size, *not* of selection on the dentition itself.  If an individual American black bear grew

[1] The Alaskan brown bear (*Ursus gyas*), with a basal skull length up to 405 mm., may rival *U. spelaeus* in size.  The cheek teeth of *gyas* are the same absolute size as in the grizzly, however, showing that a new and different factor (probably resulting from direct selection on the dentition) has affected the teeth in *gyas*.  The premolar formula is typically $\frac{3}{4}$.

to the size of a cave bear, we should expect its premolars to resemble those of a cave bear.

With respect to the molars, Rode's data show a direct correlation between tooth size and elaboration of the crown sculpture in the form of secondary wrinkles and tubercles.  The cingula also become wider and better defined with increased tooth size.  Both reach a peak in *Ursus spelaeus*.  Thus, elaboration of the molar crown pattern is directly correlated with tooth size, and is an expression of the growth pattern of the bear stock.  The condition seen in *U. spelaeus* results from the absolutely larger teeth, *not* from selection on the teeth themselves.

The consequences of differential growth thus reveal two significant features of the dentition of bears.  These probably could not have been detected, and certainly could not have been verified, at the stage when they were under the active influence of natural selection.  The later effects seen on larger individuals, by exhibiting the results of the pattern in exaggerated form, leave little doubt.

The two ursid features are: (1) almost total shift of emphasis to the molar region of the cheek-tooth field, with the great talon suggesting a tendency to carry the center as far posteriorly as possible, and (2) elaboration of the crown sculpturing of the molars.

The basal skull length of *Ailuropoda* is slightly less than that of the American black bear. The molar teeth are disproportionately large, their absolute *length* agreeing with the much larger gizzly. But the whole tooth row of *Ailuropoda* is also enormously *broadened*, and the molars equal ($M^2$) or exceed ($M^1$) those of the cave bear in width. The broadening affects the premolars as well as the molars (i.e., it extends over the whole cheek-tooth field), and the disparity between premolar and molar size is not as obvious as in the bears. Nevertheless the molar dominance is still evident in *Ailuropoda*.

Broadening of the premolars in *Ailuropoda* is associated with the development of an internal row of cusps, as it is in *Procyon* and *Ailurus*, the other two arctoids in which the cheek teeth are broadened. These cusps are, of course, conspicuously wanting in the reduced premolars of *Ursus*. Now, their presence in *Ailuropoda* may (1) indicate affinities with the procyonids, or (2) be an expression of the common genetic background of the arctoid carnivores. As will appear in the sequel, there can be no doubt of the ursid affinities of the giant panda, and therefore the second of these alternatives is correct. The internal row of cusps in *Ailuropoda* is the result of broadening of the premolars.

The surface sculpturing of the molars is much more elaborate in *Ailuropoda* than in the small and medium-sized bears, *but it is almost identical with that of the gigantic Ursus spelaeus*. If, as pointed out above, elaboration of sculpturing is a function of absolute tooth size in the bear stock, then this is exactly what we should expect in the huge molars of *Ailuropoda*. Any relation between the "bunodont" character of the molars of *Ailuropoda* and its diet is fortuitous. It is only the enlargement and broadening of the teeth that are so correlated.

Thus, given the morphogenetic pattern of the bear stock, only two (perhaps only one) important new factors have appeared in *Ailuropoda*. In the ursid stock the morphogenetic field is concentrated in the molar region, with the premolar field essentially vestigial. In *Ailuropoda* the ursid pattern has been further altered by two[1] simple morphogenetic factors: (1) secondary enlargement of the whole cheek-tooth field, and (2) secondary broadening of the whole field. Note that both of these factors affect the cheek-tooth field as a whole (except P1, which is vestigial), with no indication of a gradient that did not already exist in the bears. It is these two factors that represent adaptation in the dentition of *Ailuropoda*, and not the detailed architecture of each individual tooth.

## III. CONCLUSIONS

1. In *Ursus* the expression of the dentition is a function of skull and or tooth size. Elements in the premolar field degenerate progressively with increasing skull size among the species of *Ursus*, whereas the molar crown pattern becomes increasingly elaborate as absolute tooth size increases.

2. The dentition of *Ailuropoda* is an ursid dentition in which all elements in the premolar-molar field (except P1) have become uniformly much enlarged and broadened. The result is a disharmonious relation between skull and dentition, which is reflected in the displacement of P2.

3. The molar crown pattern of *Ailuropoda* closely resembles that of the gigantic *Ursus spelaeus*. The molar crown pattern of *Ailuropoda* is therefore a function of tooth size, not of selection for a particular pattern.

4. Successive disappearance of premolars, which accompanied increased skull and or tooth size in *Ursus*, is not evident in *Ailuropoda*, although the ursid proportions between premolar and molar size are retained.

5. In *Ailuropoda*, selection was for increased cheek-tooth size. Selection operated on the morphogenetic field of the cheek-tooth battery as a whole rather than on individual units. The result is that all units in this field are enlarged to the same relative degree.

6. The genetic mechanism behind this transformation is probably very simple and may involve a single factor.

[1] Increased tooth length may, of course, be merely a secondary result of broadening, in which case only a single new factor would be involved.

# ARTICULATIONS

Descriptions of the joints of mammals other than man are very few, and are incomplete for even the common domestic mammals. This is unfortunate, since no mechanism—the masticatory apparatus or the hand, for example—can be understood unless the structure and functioning of the joints are known. Comparative arthrology, the comparative anatomy of the joints, cannot be said to exist as an organized body of knowledge.

No attempt is made here to describe all the joints of the giant panda. Those forming parts of mechanisms that are much modified in *Ailuropoda*—the mandibular, wrist, and ankle joints—were studied in detail and compared with the corresponding joints in the bears. A few other joints, chiefly those important in locomotion, are also described.

## I. ARTICULATIONS OF THE HEAD

### MANDIBULAR JOINT

The mandibular joint is a sliding hinge joint, as in all carnivores. The two joint surfaces are very closely congruent, as they are also in *Ursus;* they are less so in some other carnivores. The joint in *Ailuropoda* is not quite transverse, its axis in the frontal plane forming an angle of 5–10° with the transverse axis of the skull. This compares with a range of 5–20° in a series of *Ursus*. In the transverse plane the axis is depressed toward the midline at an angle of about 10°, compared with about 2° in *Ursus*. These deviations from the transverse axis represent sectors of two circles, one in the transverse and one in the frontal plane, whose common center lies some distance in front of the canines. They reflect the fact that the canines interlock as they come into occlusion, checking transverse movement at this point and causing the canines to act as a point of rotation. Since the canines are conical rather than cylindrical, the actual point of rotation lies in front of the canines.

The mandibular joint is remarkable for its massiveness, its relative size exceeding that of any other carnivore. It is also displaced dorsally and posteriorly relative to its position in *Ursus*. This displacement increases the mechanical efficiency

of the jaw apparatus for crushing and grinding (p. 69).

The articular capsule is a close-fitting sac, heavy posteriorly but much thinner anteriorly, where it is intimately associated with fibers of the temporal muscle. The capsule is attached to the margin of the mandibular fossa all around, and to the margin of the articular surface on the capitulum of the mandible. There is no thickening at the lateral end corresponding to the temporomandibular ligament of human anatomy.

The articular disk is almost paper-thin and is imperforate. It increases slightly in thickness from anterior to posterior and is not notably thinner at the center than at the periphery. The disk is firmly attached to the capsule throughout its entire periphery, and is more tightly attached to the fossa than to the condyle. None of the external pterygoid fibers insert into it.

A single ligament is associated with the mandibular joint (fig. 70). This apparently represents the stylomandibular ligament combined with the posterior end of the sphenomandibular ligament; in *Ursus* these two are separate and distinct and attach at the normal sites. The ligament is a band about 5 mm. wide, attached anteriorly to the angular process of the mandible. From this attachment it runs posteriorly, dorsally, and medially beneath the outer end of the postglenoid process. Here it bifurcates, one branch going to the inferior surface of the bony auditory meatus (the normal attachment of the sphenomandibular ligament) and the other to the inferior surface of the cartilaginous auditory meatus (the normal attachment of the stylomandibular ligament). The absence of the anterior part of the sphenomandibular ligament, which normally attaches at the entrance to the mandibular foramen, is probably associated with the great size of the postglenoid process.

Movement in the mandibular joint consists, as in all carnivores, of two components: hinge movement around an approximately transverse axis, in which the cylindrical head rotates in the trough-like fossa; and sliding movement, in which the head shifts transversely in the fossa. These two movements are combined into a spiral screw move-

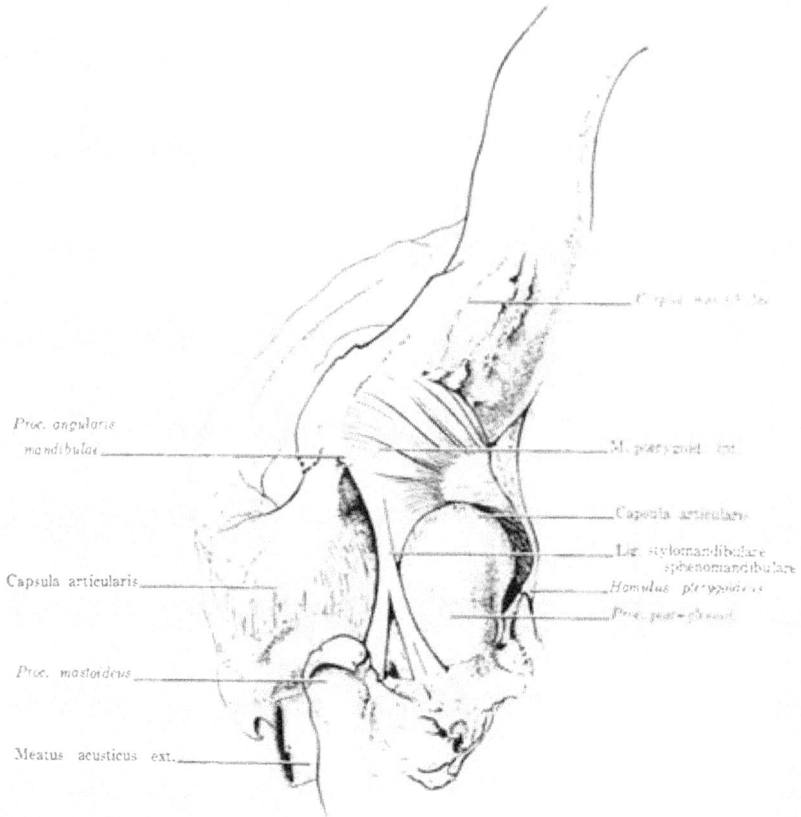

Proc. angularis
mandibulae

Capsula articularis

Proc. mastoideus

Meatus acusticus ext.

Capsula articularis

M. pterygoid. int.

Capsula articularis

Lig. stylomandibulare
sphenomandibulare
Hamulus pterygoideus
Proc. post-glenoid.

FIG. 70. Right mandibular joint of *Ailuropoda*, external view.

ment, as is evident from the wear surfaces on the
teeth. Measured on the dry skull, the lateral component amounts to about 6 mm. after the cheek
teeth first begin to come into occlusion. The corresponding lateral component is about 3 mm. in
a specimen of *Ursus arctos*.

In summary, the mandibular joint of *Ailuropoda* differs from that of *Ursus* chiefly in being
larger and more robust, and in being displaced
dorsally and posteriorly. These are all directly
adaptive modifications. They can scarcely be
attributed to extrinsic factors, but probably represent the results of selection operating on intrinsic
hereditary factors. It is even plausible that the
increase in quantity of bone tissue in the skull as
a whole reflects the generalized working of the
morphogenetic machinery whereby increased size
of the bony elements of the mandibular joint was
effected.

## II. ARTICULATIONS OF THE FORE LEG

### A. SHOULDER JOINT

The shoulder joint is an extremely simple joint,
as it is in all mammals that lack a clavicle. The
only ligament is the loose articular capsule, and
consequently the joint is held in position solely by
muscles. As pointed out by Baum and Zietzschmann for the dog, the powerful tendon of the infraspinatus laterally, and that of the subscapularis
medially, functionally represent collateral ligaments of the shoulder joint. In addition to their
function of retaining the joint in position, these
tendons must also tend to limit adduction and
abduction of the humerus, and thus to restrict
movement to a pendulum-like flexion and extension.

The glenoid cavity of the scapula is remarkable
for its narrowness in comparison with other carnivores. The articular surface of the head of the

humerus, in contrast, is broader than in other carnivores. The fibrous glenoid lip is inconspicuous except along the posterior border of the glenoid cavity, where it projects a couple of millimeters beyond the edge of the bone.

The articular capsule is a loose sac enclosing the shoulder joint on all sides. It extends from the prominent rough surface around the margin of the glenoid cavity of the scapula, to the head of the humerus. On the humerus the capsule is attached to the roughened area at the periphery of the head. In the intertubercular area it is prolonged distad into the intertubercular sheath that encloses the tendon of the biceps.

The posterior (superficial) fibers of the triceps medialis separate from the anterior (deep) fibers at their origin, and arise from the inferior surface of the capsule instead of from bone. Contraction of this muscle would consequently exert traction on the capsule. A very few of the posteriormost tendon fibers of the triceps lateralis are also attached to the joint capsule.

## B. Elbow Joint

The elbow joint (figs. 71, 72) depends for its strength and security on bony structures rather than on the number, strength, or arrangement of its ligaments, as is the case with the knee. In the giant panda and bears the elbow joint is a screw joint rather than a simple hinge joint as in other carnivores. The spiral trough formed by the medial half of the trochlea (fig. 49) forces the ulna to travel medially 5 mm. or more as the elbow is flexed. With the foot in the normal position of pronation, this would throw the foot medially as the elbow is flexed, and would account, at least in part, for the rolling motion characteristic of the fore feet in bears and the giant panda.

The capsule is a large and capacious sac to which the collateral ligaments are inseparably united. The supinator and a small part of the abductor pollicis longus muscles arise directly from the capsule. The bony attachments of the capsule are as follows: (1) on the humerus it encloses the vestigial coronoid fossa anteriorly and the olecranal fossa posteriorly; laterally and medially it attaches to the sides of the trochlea and the distal ends of the epicondyles; (2) on the ulna it attaches to the edges of the semilunar notches; (3) on the radius it attaches just distad of the articular facet.

The lateral collateral ligament arises from the lateral epicondyle and runs distad across the radiohumeral articulation. At the annular ligament it is interrupted by the origin of the supinator muscle, beyond which it continues distad to its attachment on the anterolateral surface of the radius about 30 mm. below the head. A prominent scar marks its radial attachment. There are two lateral ligaments in the dog (Baum and Zietzschmann) and cat (Reighard and Jennings), one going to the ulna and the other to the radius.

The medial collateral ligament is stronger and better marked than the lateral ligament. On the humerus it is attached to the area in front of the medial epicondyle. The nearly parallel fibers pass across the joint and attach on the ulna in the conspicuously roughened area immediately distad of the semilunar notch. In both the dog and the cat the medial ligament is double, consisting of radial and ulnar heads.

The oblique ligament is a slender band running diagonally across the anterior (flexor) surface of the lateral epicondyle. Distally it attaches to the distal lip of the semilunar notch. In the dog the oblique ligament divides distally to embrace the tendons of the biceps and brachialis (Baum and Zietzschmann). Parsons (1900) says it is absent in *Ursus*, and Reighard and Jennings do not mention it in the cat.

## C. Union of the Radius with the Ulna

The radius and ulna are united at three places: a proximal and a distal radioulnar articulation, and a mid-radioulnar union via the interosseous ligament.

The proximal articulation is composed of the radial notch of the ulna and the smooth circumference of the head of the radius that rotates in it. Two ligaments are special to the joint. The lateral transverse ligament (fig. 71) is a short diagonal band extending from the annular ligament just below the lateral collateral ligament to the border of the semilunar notch immediately behind the radial notch. This ligament is absent in the dog (Ellenberger and Baum, 1943) but is present in the bears. The annular ligament of the radius is a well-defined band of strong fibers about 15 mm. wide, encircling the head of the radius. It forms about 60 per cent of a ring, which is completed by the radial notch of the ulna. The annular ligament is thickest over the notch in the head of the radius. It is strongly attached at either end to the margins of the radial notch, and is much more feebly attached by loose fibers to the neck of the radius below the epiphyseal line.

Since the head of the radius is elliptical in outline, it acts as a cam and imparts an eccentric motion to the radius during movements of pronation and supination. The cam action can easily be felt through the annular ligament when the radius is rotated on a ligamentary preparation. This eccentric motion has the effect of permitting

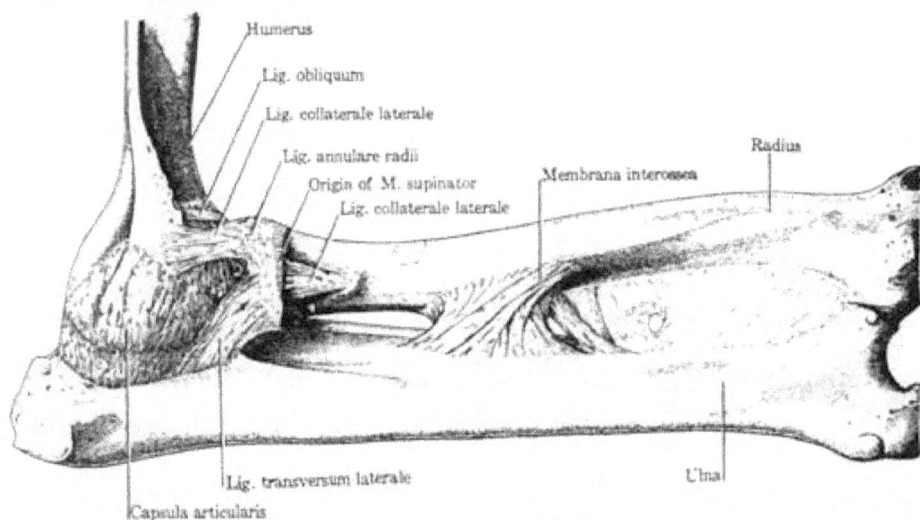

FIG. 71. Right elbow joint of *Ailuropoda*, bent at right angle, lateral view. Forearm halfway between pronation and supination.

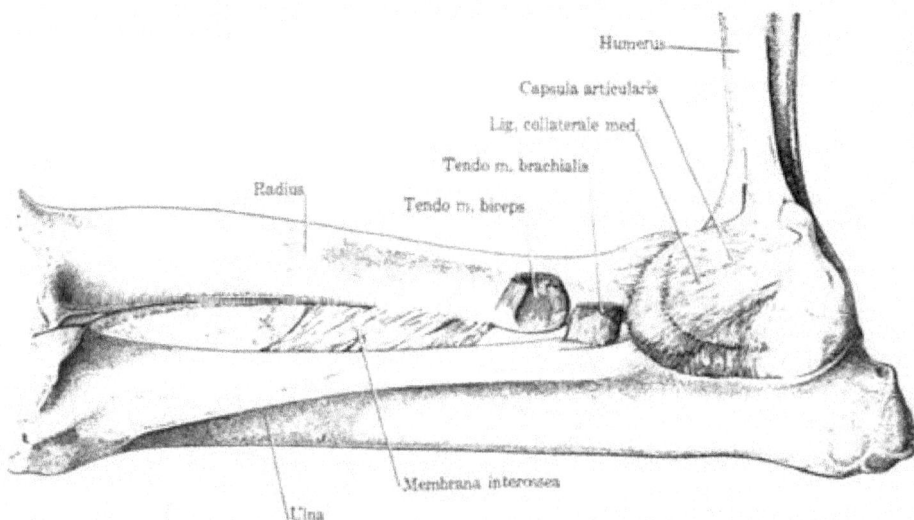

FIG. 72. Right elbow joint of *Ailuropoda*, bent at right angle, medial view. Forearm halfway between pronation and supination.

a certain amount of rotation of the radius without stretching the interosseous ligament.

The range of movement in the proximal radioulnar articulation appears to be severely limited in *Ailuropoda*. The pronation-supination range was about 40° (compared with 120 140° in man) on a ligamentary preparation when the radius was

ments lying just distad of the radioulnar articulation. The **dorsal radioulnar ligament** (fig. 73) is a rope-like band attached at one end to a pit-like depression on the neck of the styloid process of the ulna, between the radioulnar articulation and the head. The other end attaches to the radius immediately below and in front of the radio-

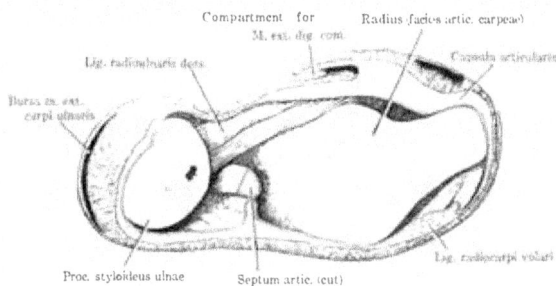

FIG. 73. Proximal articular surfaces of right antebrachiocarpal joint of *Ailuropoda*.

rotated by grasping its distal end and manipulating it by hand. Further rotatory movement was checked by the capsule of the proximal radioulnar articulation, by the interosseous ligament, and by the distal radioulnar ligaments.

The **interosseous ligament** (figs. 71, 72) is a thick tract of glistening fibers extending between the ulna and the radius except for the proximal quarter of the interosseous space. The ligament is heaviest in the middle third of the interosseous space, becoming thin and almost membranous in the distal third. Most of the fibers run diagonally distally from the radius to the ulna, but on the anterior surface a large group of proximal fibers runs in the opposite direction. The interosseous ligament is so heavy that it binds the ulna and radius firmly together, permitting very little movement between them.

Nothing comparable to the **oblique chord** of human anatomy is present in *Ailuropoda*.

The distal radioulnar articulation (fig. 73) opposes a flat, almost circular surface on the radius to a slightly convex, almost circular surface of the ulna. The surface on the radius is parallel to the midline of the radius (which curves toward the ulna in its distal quarter), whereas the surface on the ulna lies at an angle of about 45° to the long axis of the ulna. The articulation is enclosed in a capsule. This articulation, which closely resembles that of *Ursus*, permits the distal end of the radius to roll around the ulna in a limited arc.

In *Ailuropoda* the distal ends of ulna and radius are held together by two strong transverse liga-

ulnar articulation. The **volar radioulnar ligament** attaches at one end to the neck of the styloid process and at the other to the border of the distal articular surface of the radius, near the radioulnar articulation. It lies mostly deep to the volar radiocarpal ligament.

### D. HAND AND INTERCARPAL JOINTS

The range of movement of the hand as a whole is very great in primitive carnivores. All the possible angular movements— rotation, flexion and extension, and abduction and adduction, together with combinations of these— can be carried out. One of the most important and extensive of these movements, rotation (inversion and eversion), is scarcely a function of the hand joint, but results almost entirely from movements of pronation and supination of the forearm and rotation in the shoulder joint.

The essential hand joint for movement of the hand as a whole is the antebrachiocarpal joint (the radiocarpal joint of human anatomy). In all the other joints movement is extremely restricted, consisting only of a slight gliding of one bone upon another, which serves to give elasticity to the carpus. In a ligamentary preparation of *Ailuropoda*, movement in the intercarpal and carpometacarpal joints is almost non-existent, whereas in a similar preparation of the bear *Tremarctos* there is considerable movement in these joints, particularly in the direction of adduction and extension.

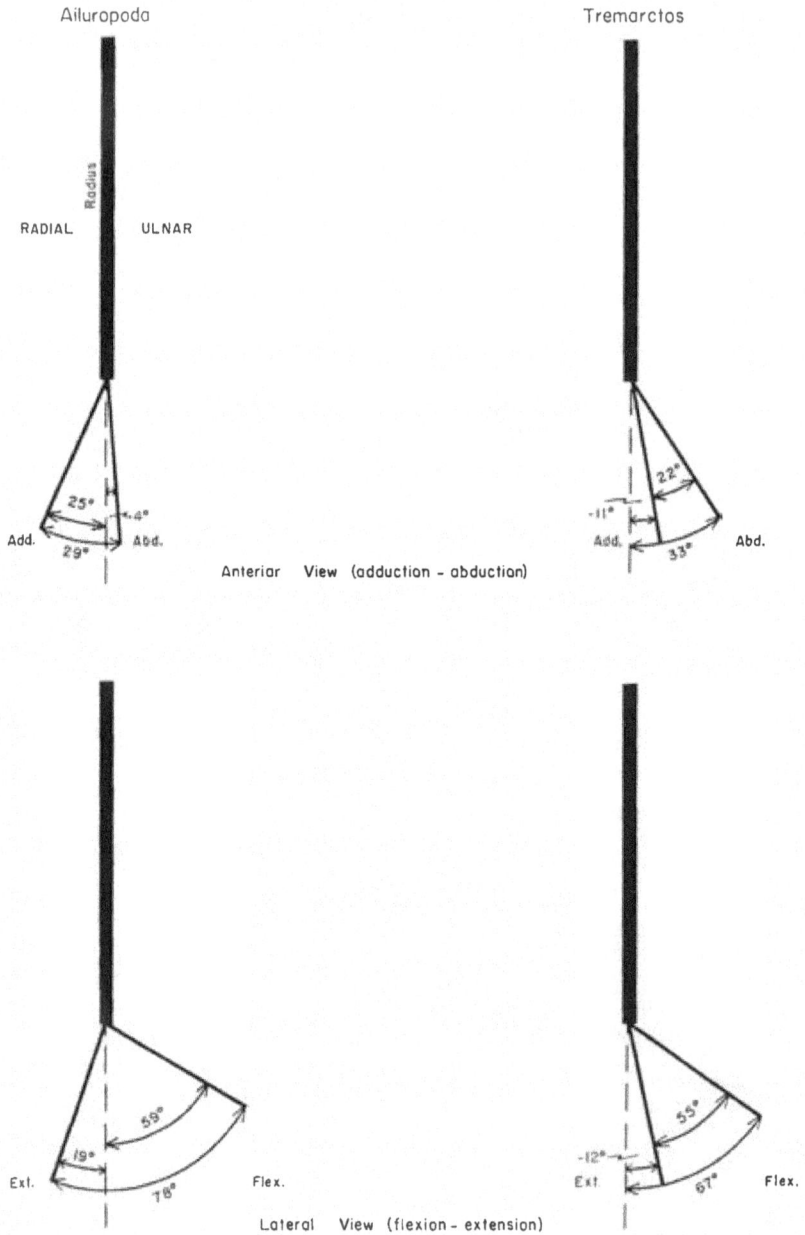

Ailuropoda Tremarctos

RADIAL    ULNAR

Radius

Add.  25°  ◄–4°  Abd.
      29°

Anterior    View    (adduction – abduction)

-11°  22°
Add.  ◄  33°  Abd.

Ext.  19°  59°  Flex.
      78°

Lateral    View    (flexion – extension)

-12°  55°
Ext.  ◄  67°  Flex.

FIG. 74. Diagrams showing ranges of movement in the left antebrachiocarpal joint in ligamentary preparations of a giant panda and a spectacled bear. See text.

136

*Antebrachiocarpal Joint*

A double joint, consisting of the radius scapholunar articulation medially, and the ulna cuneiform and pisiform articulation laterally. The joint cavity is partly divided into radial and ulnar compartments by an incomplete septum of fibrocartilage (fig. 73). This septum, the "triangular fibro-cartilage" of Parsons, is attached proximally to the radial side of the neck of the styloid process of the ulna; distally it passes into the notch between the scapholunar and cuneiform and attaches to the scapholunar. Along its volar edge the septum is continuous with the joint capsule, thus closing off the radial and ulnar compartments, but dorsally it stops abruptly at the level of the dorsal radioulnar ligament, leaving the radial and ulnar compartments in communication with each other.

The distal articular surface on the radius is broader anteroposteriorly than in *Ursus*, and lacks the conspicuous saddle over the styloid process. The opposing articular surface on the scapholunar is smoothly ovate, lacking the depression into which the saddle fits in *Ursus*, and is about a third more extensive than the radial articular surface. Thus this part of the joint is an almost perfect ellipsoid articulation, capable of extensive movements of flexion, extension, abduction, and adduction. Of these, only abduction is seriously restricted by the styloid process of the ulna and the ulnar collateral ligament, which also inhibits rotation almost completely. Range of the other movements is greatly facilitated by the disposition of the antebrachiocarpal ligaments.

The ulnar-carpal part of the antebrachiocarpal joint is notable for the extent and flatness of the articular surface on the cuneiform-pisiform complex. Instead of forming a socket into which the styloid process of the ulna fits, as in *Ursus*, in *Ailuropoda* there is an extensive articular area over which the styloid process can wander. This articular area faces laterally, and therefore cannot transmit thrust from the carpus to the fore arm as it does in *Ursus*. Thus this part of the antebrachiocarpal joint in *Ailuropoda* has the function of steadying the radio-scapholunar part of the joint.

The following measurements of ranges of movement in the antebrachiocarpal joint were made on an embalmed adult panda and an adult spectacled bear. All muscles and tendons crossing the carpus were removed, but all ligaments were left intact. The fore leg was immobilized and the manus manipulated from the distal end, the operator taking care not to force the manus beyond its normal limits or to induce movements in intercarpal or carpometacarpal joints. Angulation was read off

directly on a protractor, two or more readings being made for each position. The long axis of metacarpal 3 was used as the axis of the manus (see fig. 74).

|  | *Ailuropoda* | *Tremarctos* |
|---|---|---|
| Abduction—adduction | 29° | 22° |
|   Abduction (from radial axis=0) | 4° | 9° |
|   Adduction (from radial axis=0) | 25° | 13° |
| Flexion-extension | 78° | 55° |
|   Flexion (from radial axis=0) | 59° | 67° |
|   Extension (from radial axis=0) | 19° | −12° |

These figures indicate that the position of the manus in relation to the fore arm in the panda is quite different, in both planes, from its position in the bear. The axis of the radius is not the true axis of the fore arm, but it is close enough to show that in the "rest" position the hand of *Ailuropoda* is adducted whereas that of *Tremarctos* is abducted, and that the metacarpus is more strongly flexed in *Ailuropoda* than in *Tremarctos*. The figures also indicate that the range of movement in the antebrachiocarpal joint is greater in the panda than in the bear, particularly movements of extension. The figures confirm the statement of Lips that the bears are incapable of extending the metacarpus beyond the long axis of the fore arm.

*Ligaments of the Carpus*

The carpal ligaments have not been described for any generalized carnivore. In the present study the ligaments of an adult spectacled bear (*Tremarctos ornatus*) were dissected, for comparison, at the same time as those of *Ailuropoda*. The only significant differences were the presence in *Tremarctos* of stout dorsal radiocarpal and radial collateral ligaments. The absence of these ligaments in *Ailuropoda* contributes greatly to the mobility of the antebrachiocarpal articulation, particularly to the range of dorsal flexion.

*Antebrachiocarpal Ligaments*

The *volar radiocarpal ligament* (figs. 73, 76) is a thick flat band of fibers with a predominantly transverse direction. It is attached medially to the radius above the styloid process, and laterally to the neck and base of the pisiform; its deep surface presumably attaches to the scapholunar and cuneiform. The proximal border of this ligament is thick and sharply defined; distally it continues into the transverse carpal ligament.

The *dorsal radiocarpal* and *radial collateral ligaments* of human anatomy are absent in the panda. Instead there is a roomy, tough-walled articular capsule enclosing the radiocarpal articulation dorsally and laterally (fig. 73). The capsule attaches to radius and scapholunar near the margins of their articular surfaces.

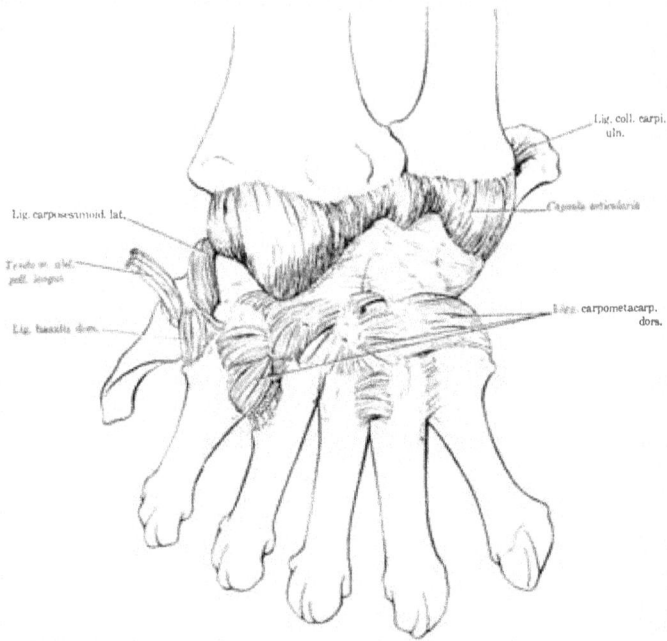

FIG. 75.  Dorsal carpal ligaments of *Ailuropoda*.

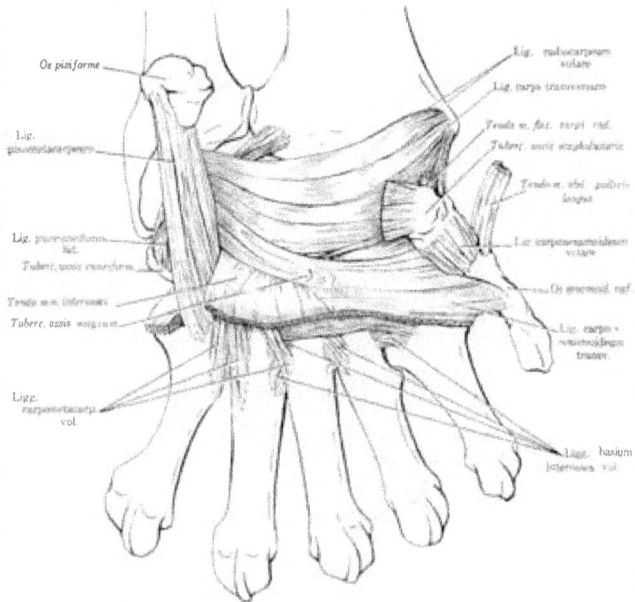

FIG. 76.  Volar carpal ligaments of *Ailuropoda*.

138

The *ulnar collateral ligament* of the wrist (fig. 75) is a heavy band of fibers extending from the latero-dorsal surface of the styloid process of the ulna to the distal end of the pisiform, where it attaches to a prominent scar on the posterior surface of the bone.

### Intercarpal Ligaments

The *transverse carpal ligament* (fig. 76) is an extensive tract of transverse fibers, continuous proximally with the volar radiocarpal ligament. The band is cupped to form a trough for the tendon of the deep digital flexors. Attachment medially is to the ventral process of the scapholunar, laterally to the base of the pisiform. Its deep surface presumably attaches to the ventral processes of the magnum, unciform, and cuneiform.

The *pisohamate ligament* is a short band on the lateral aspect of the carpus. It attaches to the pisiform near the margin of the articular surface of the cuneiform, and to the lateral surface of the ventral process of the cuneiform.

A system of short *dorsal intercarpal ligaments* (fig. 75) ties the carpal bones together. These are all short bands passing across from one bone to its neighbor.

### Ligaments of the Pisiform Bone

Two ligaments connect the pisiform with the cuneiform. A *volar pisocuneiform ligament* passes from the volar surface of the pisiform to the volar surface of the cuneiform, median to the tubercle. It is inseparable from the pisometacarpal ligament throughout most of its length. A short *lateral pisocuneiform ligament* passes from the lateral surface of the pisiform, directly beneath the articular surface, to the tubercle of the cuneiform (fig. 76).

A strong *pisometacarpal ligament* (fig. 76) extends from the volar surface of the pisiform to the base of the fifth metacarpal.

### Carpometacarpal Joints

The distal surfaces of the distal row of carpals present a composite articular surface for the four lateral metacarpals. In *Ursus* and most other carnivores the otherwise smooth contour of this composite articulation is broken by a wedge-shaped projection of metacarpal 2 that thrusts back between the trapezium and trapezoid. This wedge is absent in *Ailuropoda*, and the transverse contour of the composite joint is therefore uninterrupted. Otherwise the joint is similar to that of *Ursus*. The proximal articular surfaces on the metacarpals are convex dorso-ventrally, with a very slight transverse concavity on metacarpals 2-4 that produces a modified saddle joint. The

saddle joint is most pronounced on metacarpal 4, and is wanting on metacarpal 5.

The first metacarpal articulates with the trapezium by a saddle joint. The transverse curvature of the saddle is shallow, as in the lateral metacarpals. It is relatively deeper in *Ursus*, indicating a greater range of adduction-abduction movement.

### Carpometacarpal Ligaments

*Volar carpometacarpal ligaments* are associated with digits 3, 4, and 5 but are wanting on digits 1 and 2 (fig. 76). These are short stout bands arising from the deep surface of the tendinous plate by which the digital adductors take origin—thus eventually attaching to the magnum and unciform—and inserting asymmetrically into the metacarpals near their bases. The ligament to digit 5 attaches to the radial side of the bone, those to digits 3 and 4 to the ulnar side.

A short *dorsal carpometacarpal ligament* extends between the base of each metacarpal and the dorsal surface of the adjoining carpal bone (fig. 75).

### Carposesamoid Joint

The articulation between the radial sesamoid and the scapholunar is a true diarthrosis, capable of quite extensive movements of abduction and adduction, but probably incapable of dorsal and volar flexion. On a ligamentary preparation this bone could be manipulated through a range of about 20° of abduction-adduction, but was practically immobile in the direction of flexion-extension.

The radial sesamoid in *Ursus* has no such diarthrodial articulation, but the bone occupies the same positions relative to the scapholunar.

### Ligaments of the Radial Sesamoid

Four strong and well-marked ligaments are associated with the radial sesamoid bone. A short *volar carposesamoid ligament* (fig. 76) passes from the volar surface of the tubercle of the scapholunar to the volar surface of the sesamoid bone. A broad *lateral carposesamoid ligament* (fig. 75) passes from the lateral surface of the scapholunar tubercle to the lateral surface of the sesamoid, where it attaches proximad of the insertion of the tendon of the adductor pollicis longus. A *transverse carposesamoid ligament* (fig. 76) passes from the lateral (ulnar) surface of the sesamoid into the transverse carpal ligament. On the dorsal side a *dorsal basal ligament* (fig. 75) connects the base of the sesamoid with the adjacent base of the first metacarpal.

In *Tremarctos* the ligaments of the radial sesamoid are similar to, but smaller than, those in *Ailuropoda*.

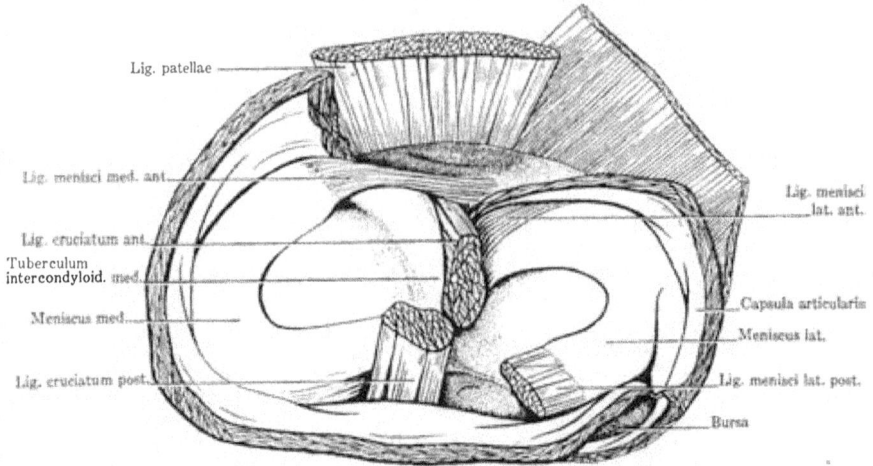

FIG. 77.  Joint structures on head of right tibia of *Ailuropoda*.

### Review of Hand Joint

Parsons (1900) reviewed very briefly the major carpal ligaments of the Carnivora in relation to those of other mammals, and concluded that the wrist joint in carnivores is modified to permit a "moderate amount" of supination. Lips (1930) described in great detail the structure and functioning of the hand joint in *Ursus arctos* in comparison with other arctoid carnivores, unfortunately without considering the ligaments. Lips concluded that the hand joint of *Ursus* represents a "universal" (we would say *unspecialized*) type among the arctoid carnivores, capable of many-sided movements.

The hand joint of *Ailuropoda* is very similar to that of *Ursus*, but the panda has gone beyond the bear in the range of movement possible in the antebrachiocarpal joint, particularly extension. This is accomplished by extending and reshaping articular surfaces, and by eliminating or reducing ligaments that would restrict dorsal flexion. Such minor remodeling reflects the action of the muscles that operate these joints (largely the carpal extensors and flexors), and demands little or no morphogenetic action on the bones and ligaments themselves. Even the diarthrodial joint of the radial sesamoid requires only the well-known capacity of bone to produce true joints wherever movement occurs.

### III. ARTICULATIONS OF THE HIND LEG

#### A. KNEE JOINT

The knee joint (fig. 77) is an incongruent compound joint involving the femur, the patella, and the tibia. The incongruence between the roller-like condyles of the femur and the relatively flat superior articular surface of the tibia is compensated by the menisci. The internal ligaments of the knee joint of the horse, cow, pig, and dog were described by Zimmerman (1933). The structure of this joint in bears and procyonids is unknown.

The **menisci** are unequal in size; the medial meniscus is larger than the lateral and its structure is typical. The lateral meniscus has a prominent ridge on the femoral side that separates a medial articular area from a lateral non-articular area. The non-articular part of the meniscus terminates posteriorly at the entrance to a large bursa, which is situated above and immediately behind the fibular articulation. Each meniscus is attached to the capsule throughout its entire circumference, and each is also held in place by its own system of ligaments. Each meniscus is tightly attached to the head of the tibia at one end and more loosely attached at the other, which gives to both a certain freedom of movement on the tibial head.

The lateral meniscus is continued into a ligament at each end. The anterior ligament passes mesad beneath the anterior cruciate ligament, to attach to the medial wall of the anterior intercondyloid fossa; the posterior one runs mesad and dorsad, to attach to the intercondyloid fossa of the femur. The medial meniscus is continued into a ligament only at its anterior end; the posterior end is tightly attached to the medial lip of the posterior intercondyloid fossa. The anterior end of the medial meniscus has no direct attachment to the tibial head; it is continued into a powerful ligament that passes across immediately in front of the anterior cruciate ligament to attach to the anterior intercondyloid fossa in the area in front of the *lateral* condyle, laterad of the attachment of the anterior cruciate ligament. There is no transverse tract uniting the menisci anteriorly, corresponding to the transverse ligament of human anatomy; Zimmermann states that this tract was demonstrable in 94 per cent of the dogs that he studied.

The **cruciate ligaments** are strong and rope-like. The anterior cruciate ligament is attached to the medial half of the anterior intercondyloid fossa of the tibia, near the medial intercondyloid tubercle. It runs upward, backward, and slightly laterad to the medial surface of the lateral condyle of the femur, where it attaches. The posterior cruciate ligament is considerably longer than the anterior. It attaches to the tibia on a prominence at the extreme posterior end of the posterior intercondyloid fossa. From here it passes upward and nearly straight forward, crossing the posterior horn of the medial meniscus, and attaches to the femur in the medial half of the intercondyloid fossa.

The only significant difference in the internal ligaments of the knee joint between *Ailuropoda* and the mammals described by Zimmermann is the less tight fixation of the menisci, especially the medial meniscus, in the panda. The resulting greater freedom permits more extensive pronation and supination in *Ailuropoda*.

## B. ANKLE JOINT

The essential joints for movements of the foot as a whole in the primitive carnivore are the upper ankle joint, the transverse tarsal joint, and the lower tarsal joint. Each of these joints is primarily involved in a particular movement. In the upper ankle joint, movement is a hinge movement in the sagittal plane (flexion and extension of the foot). In the transverse tarsal joint, movement is rotation around the longitudinal axis of the foot (inversion and eversion of the foot). In the lower ankle joint, movement is an oblique gliding between the astragalus and calcaneus (largely abduction and adduction of the foot). None of these joints acts entirely independently of the others, and only the upper tarsal joint is confined to a single fixed axis. The resulting combined movements are extremely subtle and complex.

The small bones of the distal tarsal row are probably mechanically unimportant. They function chiefly to break shocks and to increase the general flexibility of the foot.

### *Upper Ankle Joint* (talo-crural)

A perfect hinge joint between tibia and fibula proximally and astragalus distally. Axis runs transversely through trochlea of astragalus. Movement is restricted to dorsiflexion and plantar flexion of the foot.

### *Lower Ankle Joint* (subtalar)

An incongruent gliding joint between astragalus and calcaneus. No definite axis can be fixed; Fick called the movement in this joint in man a "compromise" movement consisting of the summation of successive rotations around a great number of momentary axes. In the bears and giant panda the congruence is less than in man, and it seems impossible to determine even a "compromise" axis. In procyonids the congruence is close and the movement is a screw movement. Movement is in general oblique: abduction coupled with eversion and dorsal flexion of the foot, or adduction coupled with inversion and plantar flexion (Sivers, 1931). X-ray photographs (fig. 79) show that movement in this joint is relatively slight in *Ailuropoda* and *Ursus*.

### *Transverse Tarsal Joint* (Chopart's articulation)

A combination of rotatory and sliding joints, between the head of the astragalus and the navicular (rotatory) and the calcaneus and cuboid (gliding). The axis of rotation runs longitudinally through the head and neck of the astragalus and the approximate center of the navicular; the calcaneus glides over the cuboid in an arc. Movement, which involves compensatory adjustments between the astragalus and calcaneus, is inversion and eversion and/or abduction and adduction of the foot. Dorsiflexion and plantar flexion of the foot, which is the main movement of this joint in man, is very slight. X-ray photographs (fig. 79) show that in *Ailuropoda* and *Ursus* rotatory movements in this joint are extensive, though less extensive than between the navicular and the distal tarsal row.

Most students of the comparative anatomy of the tarsus in quadrupeds (Tornier, 1888; Sivers, 1931; Schaeffer, 1947) have emphasized the transverse tarsal and lower ankle joints, dismissing the upper ankle joint as a simple hinge. In the tarsus of the generalized carnivores the most conspicuous difference is the relation of the axis of the upper ankle joint to the remainder of the ankle and foot. This difference is not apparent unless the astragalus is examined *in situ*, with the foot lying flat on the ground (fig. 78, A). Then the position of the axis with relation to the surrounding structures shows that the relation of the foot to the lower leg differs significantly from species to species. Angles

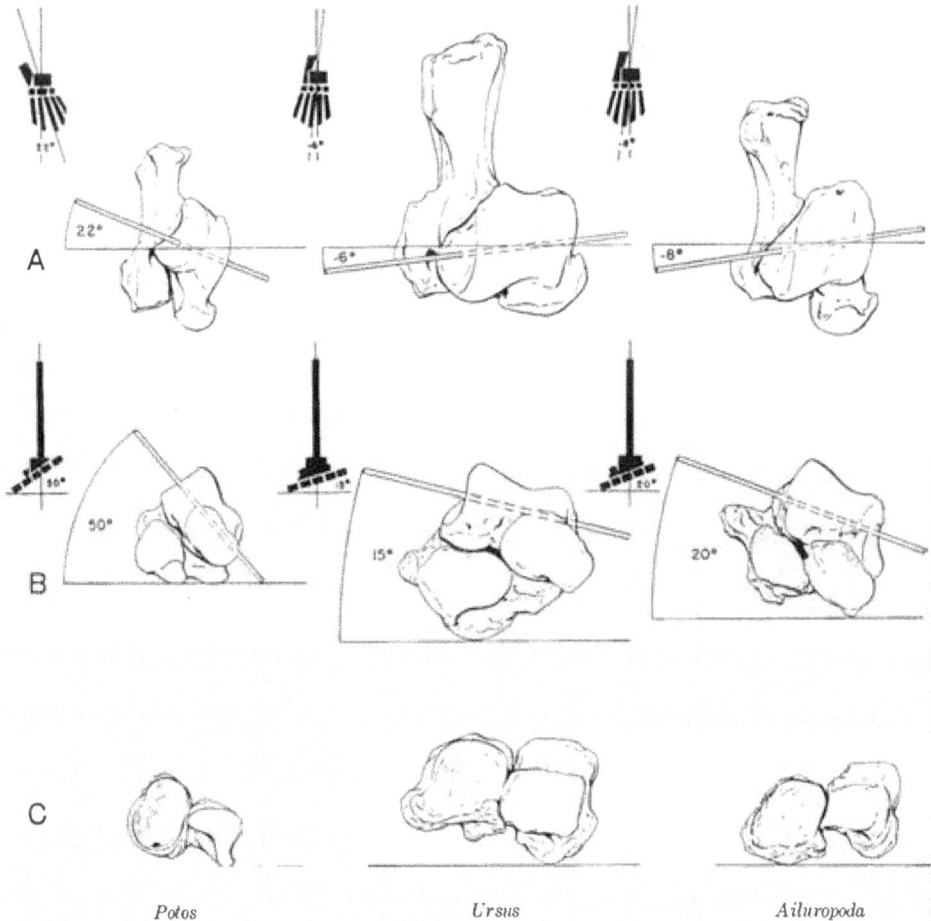

FIG. 78. Dorsal (A) and anterior (B) views of right astragalus and calcaneus of *Potos flavus* (an arboreal form) and *Ursus arctos* and *Ailuropoda* (terrestrial forms), to show differences in the angulation of the axis of the upper tarsal joint. In the dorsal views the horizontal line is drawn at right angles to the long axis of the foot. The anterior views are drawn with the foot flat on the ground, the horizontal line representing the horizon. The diagram associated with each drawing does not show the normal position of the foot, but the indicated position of the foot if the tibia were oriented (A) with the transverse axis of the inferior articular surface of the tibia parallel to the transverse axis of the body, and (B) with the long axis of the tibia vertical. C, proximal articular surfaces of navicular and cuboid in the same positions as B.

were measured with a protractor on dried ligamentary preparations with the foot in normal unstrained position. In dorsal view the axis is nearly transverse to the long axis of the foot in *Ursus* and *Ailuropoda*; actually it is rotated slightly counterclockwise (−6° to −8°), so that the foot would have a slight tendency to toe out. In *Claenodon*, a primitive Paleocene creodont, the axis is rotated counterclockwise about 22°. In *Potos* and other procyonids, on the contrary, the axis is rotated

clockwise (22° in *Potos*, 15° in *Procyon*, 15° in *Ailurus*), so that the foot would tend to toe in.

In anterior view (looking at the distal faces of astragalus and calcaneus (fig. 78, B), there are similar though less extreme differences. In *Ursus* and *Ailuropoda* the axis is tilted clockwise 15-20°, which would tend to produce moderate inversion of the foot. This tilting is greater in procyonids (50° in *Potos*) and would tend to produce strong

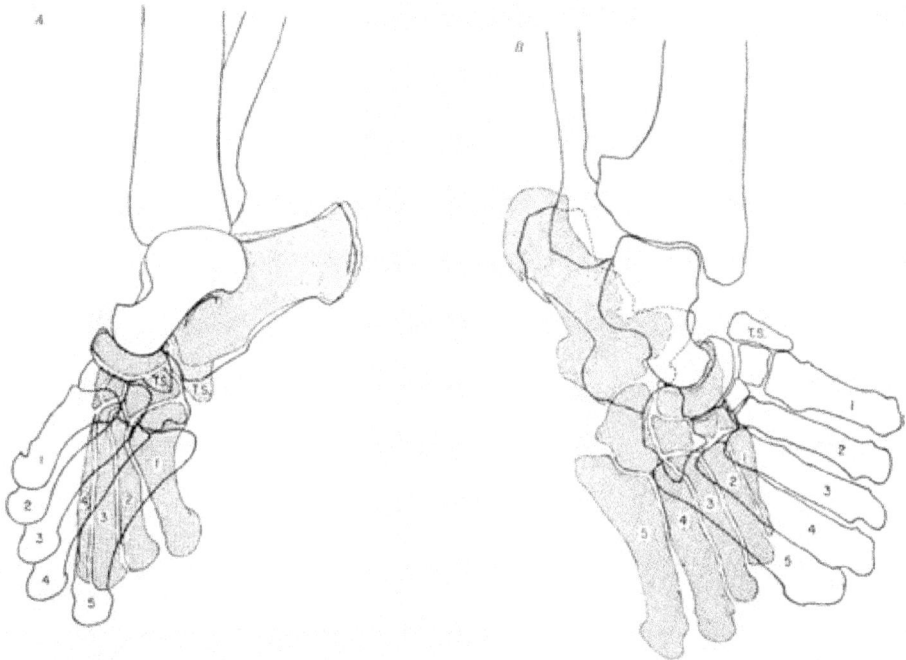

FIG. 79. Tracings from X-ray photographs of the right foot of the panda Mei Lan, to show areas in which joint movement takes place. A, medial view, foot abducted and inverted (solid line), superimposed on tracing of foot adducted and everted (shaded); the tibia, fibula, and calcaneus were superimposed in tracing. In abduction-eversion the calcaneus is rotated mesad on its long axis (note decreased width across sustentacular process—trochlear process), in addition to sliding laterad and proximad. Note, however, that the major movements of eversion-inversion and abduction-adduction take place in the transverse tarsal joint and the more distal parts of the ankle. B, dorsal view, the foot adducted and inverted (solid line), superimposed on tracing of foot abducted and everted (shaded). The calcaneus has rotated mesad on its long axis (note position of sustentacular process and decreased width across sustentacular process—trochlear process), in addition to sliding laterad and proximad. Note that the major movements of eversion-inversion and abduction-adduction take place in the transverse tarsal joint and the more distal parts of the ankle.

inversion of the foot. The angle is about 45° in *Claenodon*.

Sivers pointed out that the lateral and medial facets on the astragalus and calcaneus are more convex (or concave) in *Mustela* and *Gulo*, and that the facets are inclined toward one another. It may be added that the articular surface of the astragalar head is very extensive, and only part of it contacts the concavity of the navicular at any one time. This is likewise true of *Procyon* and *Potos*. These conditions permit a considerable range of inversion-eversion movement, wherein the astragalus rotates in a screw movement on the calcaneus, which remains relatively stationary with respect to the cuboid (movement in the intertarsal joint), while the astragalar head rotates extensively in the concavity of the cuboid (movement in the medial half of the transverse tarsal joint). Extensive inversion and eversion are obviously associated with the arboreal habits of these animals. It

is functional *eversion* that permits these animals to apply the sole to a flat surface, as in standing on the ground.

In *Ursus* and *Ailuropoda*, on the contrary, the lateral and medial facets are flatter and are less inclined toward one another, and the area of the astragalar head exceeds the area of the concavity of the navicular only slightly. This signifies a less extensive range of movement (particularly of eversion and inversion) in the ankle. Moreover, as Sivers pointed out for *Ursus*, movement between the astragalus and calcaneus (the lower ankle joint) is largely horizontal—rotation around a vertical axis running through astragalus and calcaneus; this is affirmed by our x-ray photos (fig. 79). This would increase the stability of the ankle, and would favor abduction and adduction rather than inversion and eversion. It also explains the fact that in the bears and panda the combined diameter across the lateral and medial facets on the astragalus exceeds the diameter of those on the calcaneus.

The following measurements of ranges of movement were made on the fresh unskinned hind leg (except *Ailuropoda*, which was skinned). The *Ursus americanus* was about a quarter grown, the other two fully adult. The tibia was placed in a vise and the foot manipulated by hand by grasping the base of the metatarsals, the operator taking care not to force the foot beyond its normal limits. Angulation was read off directly on a protractor, two or more readings being made for each position.

|  | *Procyon* | *Ailuropoda* | *Ursus* |
|---|---|---|---|
| Abduction-adduction... | 32° | 28–29° | 38° |
| Flexion-extension....... | 130–135° | 45° | 67–69 |
| Flexion (from right∠0) . | −40−−43° | +45° | −32 |
| Extension |  |  |  |
| (from right∠0)...... | +90−+92° | +90° | +35° |
| Eversion-inversion...... | 87–89° | 48–50 | 42–50° |
| Eversion.... | 58–62° | 0° | 17° |
| Inversion........... | 27–29° | 48–50 | 25° |

Differences in abduction-adduction are negligible among these three animals. Otherwise the total range of movement is notably greater in *Procyon* than in the bear or panda, and this presumably reflects the arboreal habits of *Procyon*.

In *Ailuropoda* and *Ursus* not only is the range of flexion-extension more restricted than in *Pro-*

*cyon*, but the pattern is different both from *Procyon* and from each other (fig. 80). In *Ursus* flexion and extension, measured from a line at right angles to the tibial axis, are about equal. In *Ailuropoda* the whole range of flexion-extension lies completely outside the range in *Ursus*, and well below the 90° axis; i.e., the foot in *Ailuropoda* is permanently extended on the tibia.

The situation is comparable, although less extreme, for eversion-inversion (fig. 80). In *Procyon* eversion exceeds inversion. The reverse is true of *Ursus*, which also has a much more restricted range of movement. In *Ailuropoda* the range of movement is similar to that of *Ursus*, but is all in the direction of inversion; the foot cannot be everted on the tibia at all. I can find no differences in the transverse tarsal joint of these two forms that would account for the differences in eversion-inversion. The difference probably lies in the torsion angle of the tibia (p. 115) and inclination of the upper ankle joint.

No detailed dissection of the tarsal ligaments of *Ailuropoda* was made.

In summary, the ankle joint in the bears is a relatively unspecialized structure, combining moderate flexibility with adequate support (Davis, 1958); it is neither as flexible as the ankle of arboreal forms, nor as stable as the ankle of cursorial forms. The ankle joint of *Ailuropoda*, so far as

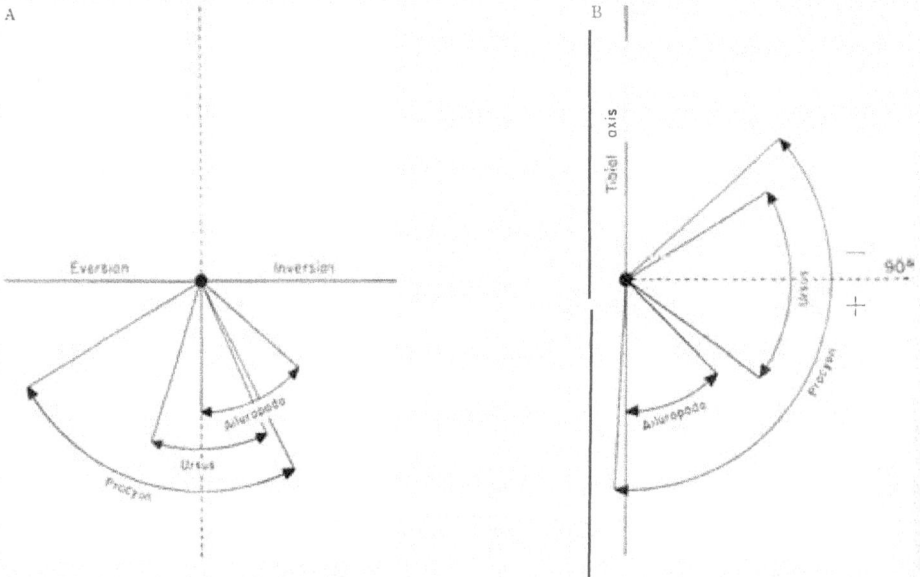

FIG. 80. Diagrams of ranges of movement in the ankle joint of carnivores. A, eversion-inversion. B, flexion-extension. (See figures in adjoining table).

known, is very similar to that of the bears. Certainly the resemblance is closer than in the hand joint.

## IV. REVIEW OF JOINTS

In the developing individual the primary gross model of a joint is determined by intrinsic (hereditary) factors, but the further shaping of the joint depends almost wholly on extrinsic (non-hereditary) mechanical factors (Murray, 1936). The importance of mechanical factors in determining joint form is heavily underscored by the pseudarthroses (joint-like structures in places where normally there should be no joint) that have been described in the literature. Failure of a fracture to heal may, even in the fully mature adult, lead to the formation of a "a structure so exactly mimicking a normal joint that the first half of the word 'pseudarthrosis' does it less than justice" (Murray, 1936). Such pseudarthroses may involve joint-like expansions of the apposed ends of the bones, cartilage-covered articular surfaces, a capsule, ligaments, and synovial fluid.

If only the gross model of an articulation is inherited, then natural selection can act *directly* only on the gross model. The articulation is, of course, a part of a total functional mechanism that is subjected to selection. The articulation's response to such extrinsic factors as posture and movement may therefore, by limiting the range of possible functional mechanisms, limit or channel the gene-controlled changes in other elements of the total mechanism and thus *indirectly* play an active role in natural selection. In seeking a causal explanation for the differences between two closely related organisms, however, we must assign a passive role to differences in the articulations. This will not be true if we are comparing distantly related organisms (perhaps above the family level), where differences in the gross model, attributable to intrinsic factors, are likely to be involved. Nor will it be true for grossly adaptive differences, such as those in the mandibular articulation of the panda, if these involve differences in the gross model. The chief value of the joints in comparisons between closely related forms is, then, as extremely sensitive indicators of differences in other elements that are related mechanically to the joints.

Except for the mandibular joint, the joints of *Ailuropoda*, so far as they have been studied, differ little from those of *Ursus*. Such differences as there are tend to increase the range of movement in the joints. None of these differences seems to depend on intrinsic factors other than the capacity of the joint to respond to extrinsic factors.

# THE MUSCULAR SYSTEM

The muscles of the Carnivora are comparatively well known, but even for this order our knowledge is at a primitive level. Descriptions are incomplete and inaccurate, often doing little more than establish the fact that a given muscle is present in species dissected. Even for the domestic carnivores—the dog and the cat—the standard reference works are full of inaccuracies and are inadequately illustrated. Most of the genera of Carnivora have never been dissected at all.

Within an order as compact as the Carnivora there are few differences of the "present" versus "absent" variety (see Table 16, p. 197), and questions of muscle homology are of no importance. There has, however, been a good deal of adaptive radiation within the Carnivora, as is obvious if the agile predaceous cats are compared with the lumbering semi-herbivorous bears, or the cursorial cheetah with the burrowing badgers. Such differences in habit are reflected in differences in the muscular system. These muscular differences—their nature, their directions, their limitations—are important elements of the over-all problem of evolutionary mechanisms. They show what has happened (and what has *not* happened) to the muscle pattern inherited by the Carnivora from creodont ancestors. Such empirical data form the basis on which the nature of mammalian evolution at the sub-ordinal level must be judged.

How can such differences be detected and evaluated? Certainly not on the basis of existing descriptions and illustrations.

## DATA OF COMPARATIVE MYOLOGY

Observation indicates that within a group of related organisms a muscle is responsive, within limits, to mechanical demands in (1) relative size, and (2) position most favorable for the required lever action. Limits are set, on the one hand, by the heritage of the group; the cephalohumeral of the Carnivora, for example, has never reverted to the original deltoid and trapezial elements from which it arose, no matter how mechanically advantageous such a course might be. On the other hand, the structures surrounding a muscle definitely limit the range of adaptive change of a muscle. No alteration can continue to a point

where it interferes with the vital activities of other structures. A remarkable instance of this type of limitation is seen in the temporal muscle of the giant panda (see p. 69).

A few generalizations as to the mode of phylogenetic alterations of muscles at the sub-ordinal level may be listed. These have been derived empirically from direct observation.

1. The bony attachments of a muscle may wander almost at random (within the limits of its area of embryonic origin), provided they do not encroach on some other vital structure. This is seen throughout the muscular system. It is particularly apparent, for example, in the origin of the triceps in carnivores (fig. 81).

2. Phylogenetic *decrease* in the volume of a muscle presents no problem, since surrounding structures simply move in and occupy the vacated space (e.g., loss of the short head of the biceps in carnivores). The power of a given muscle is usually *increased* phylogenetically by increasing its area of cross section (i.e., increasing the number and or diameter of fibers). In muscles with diffuse origin this involves increasing the area of origin, and this is accomplished in various ways:

(a) The bone surface may be increased, as in the temporal fossa of the giant panda, or the postscapular fossa on the scapula of bears.

(b) Flat muscles may be reflected, like folding a sheet of paper, to increase the total length of origin without increasing the over-all linear extent on the bone. This is seen in the deep pectoral of the bears and giant panda compared with those of more primitive carnivores.

(c) Accessory origin may be gained from superficial aponeuroses or from a tendon sheet embedded in the muscle, as in the temporal muscle of carnivores.

(d) Surrounding muscles may be displaced from their bony attachment, and arise or insert instead on the fascia of other muscles. This is seen in the deltoids of the giant panda.

3. It has long been known that muscles may become more or less completely transformed into

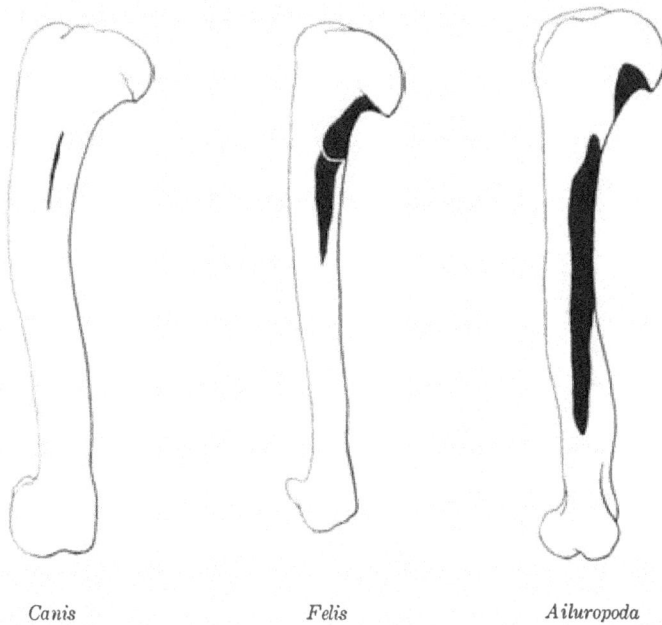

Canis             Felis             Ailuropoda

FIG. 81. Medial view of humerus of *Canis* (after Bradley), *Felis* (after Reighard and Jennings), and *Ailuropoda* to show variation in the origin of the medial head of the triceps.

tendons during phylogeny, and Haines (1932) has demonstrated that tendons increase at the expense of muscle substance during ontogeny in man. He suggests that "tendon is lengthened by metamorphosis of muscle tissue in response to a limitation of the range of possible contraction determined by the nature of the attachment of the muscle."

Confirmation of this thesis is seen in the zygomaticomandibularis of the dog, where two layers cross at an angle and the deeper layer is devoid of muscle fibers exactly to the boundary of the more superficial layer that partly overlies it. A similar situation exists in the trapezius muscles of the giant panda; muscle fibers are wanting exactly as far as the border of the scapula (fig. 88). In both of these examples pressure has limited the range of contraction of part of a muscle, and in the areas subjected to pressure, muscle tissue is replaced by tendon.

Haines' further suggestion, that "it is no longer necessary to postulate complex co-ordinating mechanisms to govern the sizes of the muscles, nor a vast series of genes to suit muscles to their work," is an over-simplification. In cursorial mammals, for example, the limb muscles are concentrated near the center of limb rotation, resulting in long terminal tendons. This is for the obvious mechan-

ical reason that such an arrangement reduces the moment of inertia of the limb, not because of any limitation of the range of possible contraction. The tendons are already greatly lengthened in a fetal horse.

Degree of tendinization may be (1) an active mechanical adaptation, or (2) a reflection of limitation of range of contraction resulting from (a) pressure from surrounding tissues or (b) simple degeneration, as in the short head of the biceps. Tendinization of type (2) is probably an individual response to local conditions, not dependent upon gene action.

4. The relation between muscle attachment and bone relief at the site of attachment was reviewed by Weidenreich (1922, 1926) and Dolgo-Saburoff (1929, 1935). It is well known that the surface relief of bone is attributable almost entirely to the muscles and their adnexa, and the ligaments. The nature of this relationship is not well understood. Weidenreich emphasized that ridges and tuberosities represent portions of tendons or ligaments that have ossified under tension and are then incorporated into the underlying bone. The extent of this ossification tends to be directly proportional to the mass of the musculature, and thus to the force to which the connective tissue is subjected.

Where a muscle mass is enlarged beyond the available attachment surface on the bone, attachment is extended onto the adjacent fascia; consequently the size of a muscle cannot always be judged from its mark on the bone (Weidenreich, 1922). Beautiful examples of this phenomenon are seen in the limb musculature of *Ailuropoda*. Transgression onto the fascia may lead to ossification of the fascia and its incorporation into the skeleton, as is easily seen in the development of the sagittal crest in many mammals.

## DATA OF MORPHOGENESIS

We know almost nothing of the genetic basis for the differentiation and development of muscles, of the relative roles of intrinsic (genetic) vs. extrinsic (non-genetic) factors, or of the parts played by generalized and localized gene effects. The extensive catalog of genes in the laboratory mouse compiled by Grüneberg (1952) does not contain a single reference to the muscular system. This almost total ignorance contrasts sharply with the considerable body of such knowledge for the skeleton and joints, and makes it almost impossible to postulate the nature of the machinery involved in producing adaptive differences in the muscular system.

The differentiation and growth of muscle in the individual were reviewed by Scott (1957). There is an intimate relation between differentiation and growth of a skeletal muscle and the nerve supplying it, and the nerve seems to be the determining agent in this relationship. Initial differentiation of muscle fibers and their grouping into individual muscles can take place in the absence of any nerve connection; that is, muscles have a certain capacity for self-differentiation. But without nerve-muscle connections the muscle fibers do not develop beyond a certain stage and later undergo degeneration. Yet Pogogeff and Murray (1946) and others have maintained adult mammalian skeletal muscle in vitro for months, without innervation of any kind, and during this time the tissue regenerated and multiplied. The developing muscles in the individual are at first independent of the skeletal elements, to which they gain attachment only later; a muscle develops normally even in the absence of the skeletal elements to which it normally gains attachment. Independence of the musculature from a factor affecting the skeleton was demonstrated in achondroplastic rabbits by Crary and Sawin (1952), who found the muscles of normal size whereas the bones with which they are associated were shorter. The muscles had to "readjust their bulk and area of attachment to the new bone shapes." During early ontogeny, skeletal muscles grow by division of developing fibers

or by differentiation of additional muscle-forming cells, but during later ontogeny, growth is believed to be exclusively by hypertrophy of individual fibers.

Growth of muscles in bulk, even in the adult, seems to be controlled at least in part by the nervous system. In man, disease of peripheral nerves (such as polyneuritis) may be followed by abnormal nerve regeneration and associated hypertrophy of the related muscles, and hypertrophy of the masseters is often associated with evidence of disorder of the central nervous system (Scott, 1957). Such growth is by hypertrophy of individual muscle fibers.

Muscular hypertrophy as a hereditary condition has appeared in various breeds of domestic cattle (Kidwell et al., 1952). In this condition the muscles are enlarged, and most authors (but not Kidwell et al.) describe duplication of muscles. The effect is typically localized in the hind quarters and loin (Kidwell et al. state that in their stock the muscles of the withers and brisket were also somewhat hypertrophied). All authors describe the muscles as coarse-grained, and mention a general reduction in the quantity of fat, both subcutaneous and intra-abdominal. Kidwell et al. concluded from breeding experiments that the condition "appears to be inherited as an incomplete recessive with variable expressivity." In other words, a simple genetic mechanism capable of producing a generalized effect on the musculature has been demonstrated.

The data of Fuld (1901) reveal differences from his control animals in the relative mass of certain muscles of the hind limb in dogs that were bipedal from puppyhood. Most of the limb muscles were unaffected, but four showed differences of more than 5 per cent in their mass relative to the total mass of hip and thigh muscles. These were the gluteus medius (7.6 per cent heavier), quadriceps extensor (6.4 per cent lighter), biceps femoris (8.2 per cent lighter), and adductors (9.4 per cent heavier). Two of these differences (middle gluteal and biceps) are in the direction of the weight relations found in man, whereas the other two are in the opposite direction. The dogs were said to hop rather than to walk on their hind legs, however, and the differences from the control animals may well have been adaptive, or at least reflected differences in the demands made on the muscles. Under any circumstances they certainly were not hereditary.

These scanty data provide few significant clues to the nature of the morphogenetic machinery involved in the evolution of adaptive differences in the musculature.

## ABSOLUTE VS. RELATIVE
## MUSCLE MECHANICS

Attempts to study muscle mechanics have dealt almost wholly with absolute values—absolute contractile force per unit of muscle cross section, lever actions of individual muscles or groups of muscles, or direct measurements of the power of an organ, such as a limb. This approach has yielded indifferent results because of the complexity of even the simplest bodily movement, and the still obscure relation between nerve impulse and the intensity of muscle reaction.

A. B. Howell attempted to determine the relations between various locomotor specializations (cursorial, saltatorial, aquatic) and musculature by comparing various representatives of such locomotor types regardless of their taxonomic affinities. This approach to muscle mechanics is indirect, and involves no mechanical analysis or estimate of forces. The intent is simply to discover a consistent correlation between a particular function and a particular modification of the muscle pattern. It may be confidently assumed that any such correlation is mechanically significant, even though no engineering analysis is made. Howell himself repeatedly expressed his disappointment at the meager results of this method. It is apparent that because of the diversity of genetic background in so heterogeneous an assemblage of more or less remotely related forms, only the crassest morphological convergences would be evident.

The lower the taxonomic level the more homogeneous the genetic background that lies behind the muscle pattern. Among representatives of a superfamily or family we may focus more sharply on *divergences* from the basic muscle pattern of the group, for differences at this taxonomic level are not likely to represent the accumulated load of innumerable earlier specializations in different ancestral lines. Here *any* departure from the norm may be assumed to be adaptive, even though the mechanics are too complex or too subtle to analyze. For example, in a series of carnivores ranging from most carnivorous to most herbivorous the relative masses of the external masseter and zygomaticomandibularis vary reciprocally, whereas all other elements of the masticatory musculature remain constant (Davis, 1955). Even without analyzing the complex and subtle functioning of the masticatory complex we may be sure that in this instance the mechanically significant alterations are localized in these two muscles. Bringing representatives of other orders, with their different heritage, into this comparison would have obscured this relation, which is valid *only within the*

*masticatory pattern of the Carnivora.* Besides mass or area of cross section, the relative values of force diagrams and leverage systems may be compared among closely related forms in the same way. Thus an insight into the functioning of a muscle or a group of muscles may be had at second hand, without the actual direct mechanical analysis, or determination of absolute forces, that has so far proved impossible to achieve.

The possibilities of this method of assessing relative muscle mechanics have not been explored. It will be used here, so far as existing data permit.

## NOMENCLATURE AND
## ARRANGEMENT

The nomenclature used here is the BNA, with such obvious modifications as are necessary because of differences from human anatomy.

There is, of course, no "proper" sequence in which muscles can be arranged, and various systems have been advocated. The arrangement adopted here is that of Howell's *Anatomy of the Wood Rat*, which is largely topographical. It may be suggested that the index is a more satisfactory means of locating a given description than attempting to find it via some system of arrangement.

Innervation of muscles is given only in special cases, since the nerve supply of carnivore muscles is given in any standard anatomy of the dog or cat.

Perhaps the most important consideration in evaluating muscle (and skeletal) differences within an order or family is an accurate picture of the bony attachments. This cannot be obtained from verbal descriptions alone; only carefully drawn maps will do. The exact areas of attachment of all muscles (except axial and a few others) in *Ailuropoda* have therefore been carefully plotted on the bones, and appear in the section on the skeleton. Unfortunately, comparable data for other carnivores exist only for the dog (later editions of Bradley) and cat (Reighard and Jennings).

## I. MUSCLES OF THE HEAD
### A. SUPERFICIAL FACIAL MUSCULATURE

M. platysma is much reduced. It extends as a band of rather uniform width from a point above and behind the auditory meatus to the corner of the mouth. A few of the dorsal fibers swing upward in front of the ear, to lose themselves in the superficial fascia. Anteriorly a few of the most dorsal fibers are separated from the main mass, arising over the zygoma.

M. buccinator (figs. 82, 84) is a heavy flat muscle sheet that forms the foundation of the cheek. It is not divisible into buccal and molar parts as it is in most mammals. Instead, the muscle forms a uniform sheet of fibers that converges partly into the mucosa of the lips near the angle of the mouth, and partly into a horizontal raphe running back from the angle of the mouth.

The dorsal fibers arise from the alveolar surface of the maxilla just outside the last upper molar, beginning at about the level of the middle of this tooth. The line of origin runs caudad onto the rugose triangular area immediately behind the tooth. Ventrad of this area, fibers arise from the pterygomandibular ligament, which extends caudad across the inner face of the internal pterygoid muscle. The ventral fibers arise from the alveolar surface of the mandible, just outside the molar teeth, beginning behind the last lower molar and extending as far forward as the middle of the first lower molar.

The remaining superficial facial muscles were damaged in removing the skin and were not dissected.

## B. MUSCLES OF THE EAR

**M. levator auris longus** (cervico-auricularis-occipitalis of Huber) is a fan-shaped sheet arising from the dorsal midline just behind the posterior end of the sagittal crest. There is no division into two parts. The posterior half of the muscle inserts on the pinna. The anterior half is continued forward over the top of the head.

**M. auriculus superior** is a narrow band lying behind, and partly covered by, the levator auris longus. Arising from the midline beneath the levator auris longus, it inserts on the pinna just caudad of that muscle, and separated from it by the insertion of the abductor auris longus.

**M. abductor auris longus** lies immediately anterior to, and partly above, the auriculus superior, and has approximately the same width. Distally it emerges from beneath the levator auris longus, and inserts on the pinna just behind it.

**M. auriculus inferior** lies wholly beneath the levator auris longus, and has the same general relations. It is more powerfully developed than the auriculus superior or the abductor auris longus, and is more than twice as wide.

**M. abductor auris brevis** is the most caudal of the auricular muscles. Its origin is beneath that of the levator auris longus, but the belly of the muscle emerges and inserts low on the posterior face of the pinna.

**M. adductor auris superior** (auricularis anterior inferior of Huber) is a narrow band arising from the posterior end of the scutiform cartilage. It inserts on the anteromesal face of the pinna.

**M. adductor auris medius** arises from the extreme posterior end of the scutiform cartilage, beneath the origin of the superior. It extends as a narrow band back to the posterior surface of the pinna, where it inserts proximad of the abductors.

## C. MASTICATORY MUSCULATURE

The masticatory muscles, which are chiefly responsible for the characteristic skull form of *Ailuropoda*, are remarkable for their enormous development. Otherwise they do not differ much from the typical carnivore pattern. In all Carnivora the temporal is the dominant element of the masticatory complex, forming at least half of the total mass of the masticatory muscles. The insertion tendon of the temporal extends into the substance of the muscle as a tendinous plate, into which most of the muscle fibers insert. Thus the temporal is a bipennate (or if several such tendinous plates are present, a *multipennate*) muscle, in which the functional cross section per unit of volume is much greater than in a parallel muscle such as the masseter (Pfuhl, 1936). In carnivores, because of the form of the mandibular articulation, fast snapping movements of the jaws depend largely on the masseter, whereas slower and more powerful cutting and crushing movements depend largely on the temporal.

The masticatory muscles arise ontogenetically from the mandibular arch, by condensation about the peripheral end of the mandibular nerve. Other muscles arising from the mandibular arch, and likewise supplied by the third branch of the trigeminal nerve, are the anterior belly of the digastric, mylohyoid, tensor tympani, and tensor veli palatini.

**M. temporalis** (figs. 82, 83) is enormously developed, filling the greatly expanded temporal fossa except for a small area behind the orbit that is occupied by fat. In an old, badly emaciated male (Mei Lan) this muscle weighed more than twice as much as in a black bear of comparable size, and the temporal and zygomaticomandibularis together nearly three times as much. The muscle is covered externally by a tough deep temporal fascia, more than half a millimeter thick, that arises from the sagittal and lambdoidal crests and postorbital ligament and extends to the superior border of the zygomatic arch. A few superficial fibers of the temporal muscle attach to the zygomatic arch immediately behind the temporal fascia and insert into its inferior edge, thus forming a tensor of the temporal fascia.

The external face of the temporal muscle is covered with an extremely heavy tendinous aponeurosis, the deep temporal fascia, from which the

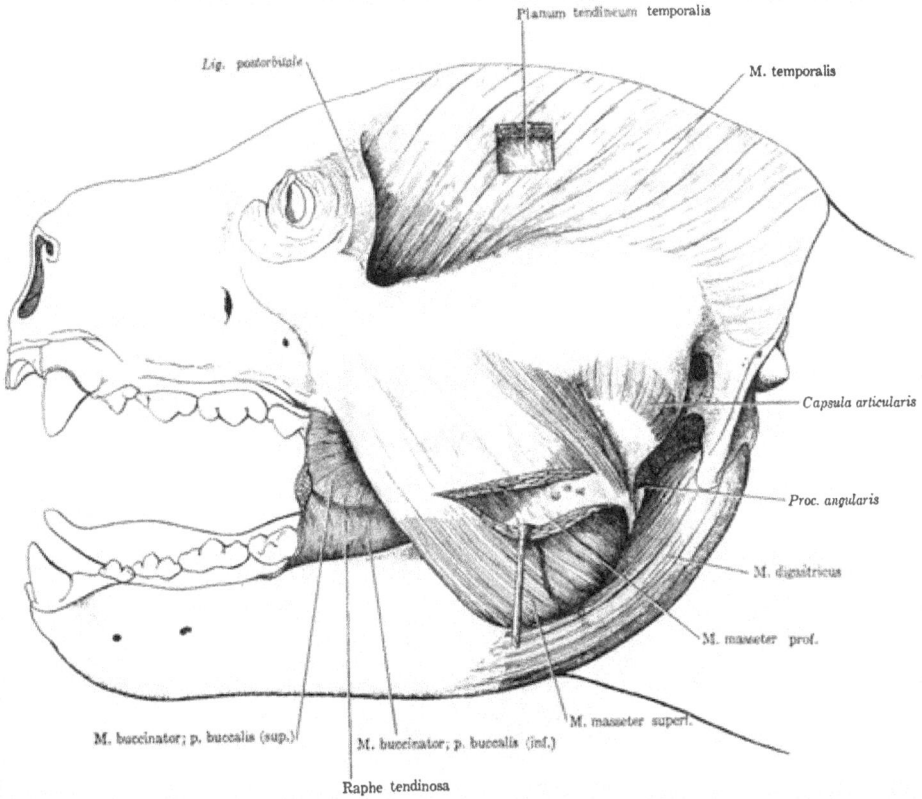

FIG. 82. Masticatory muscles of *Ailuropoda*, seen from the left side. The temporal and masseteric fasciae have been removed, and a window cut in the temporal muscle to expose the tendinous plane that separates the superficial and deep layers of the temporal muscle. The superficial and deep layers of the masseter are inseparable anteriorly. Note that the insertion of the superficial masseter does not extend posteriorly onto the angular process of the mandible.

superficial fibers of the muscle take origin. As is usual in carnivores, the muscle is divided into superficial and deep parts, separated by a heavy tendinous plate, the insertion tendon of the muscle, that extends between the sagittal crest and the superior and posterior borders of the coronoid process. Muscle fibers attach to both surfaces of this tendinous plate. Additional tendon sheets embedded in the substance of the muscle insert into the coronoid process (fig. 83), making this complex a truly multipennate muscle composed of innumerable short fibers. These additional tendon sheets do not occur in *Ursus* (Sicher, 1944, fig. 13; Schumacher, 1961a), and the temporal is therefore a simpler and less powerful muscle in the bear.

The superficial part arises from the whole deep surface of the tendinous aponeurosis except for a small area near the orbit, and, at the periphery of the muscle, from the edges of the temporal fossa. The fibers converge to insert on the external face of the coronoid process of the mandible and into the external surface of the tendinous plate. Along its inferior border this muscle is incompletely separable from the zygomaticomandibularis.

The deep part of the temporal is much thicker than the superficial part and its structure is more complex. A tendinous sheet extends between the prominent crest running obliquely upward on the floor of the temporal fossa, some distance above the superior orbital crest, and a crest on the coronoid process above the mandibular foramen. This sheet separates the anterior part of the deep temporal into superficial and deep parts. Additional smaller tendon sheets, embedded in the substance of the muscle, eventually attach to the inner face

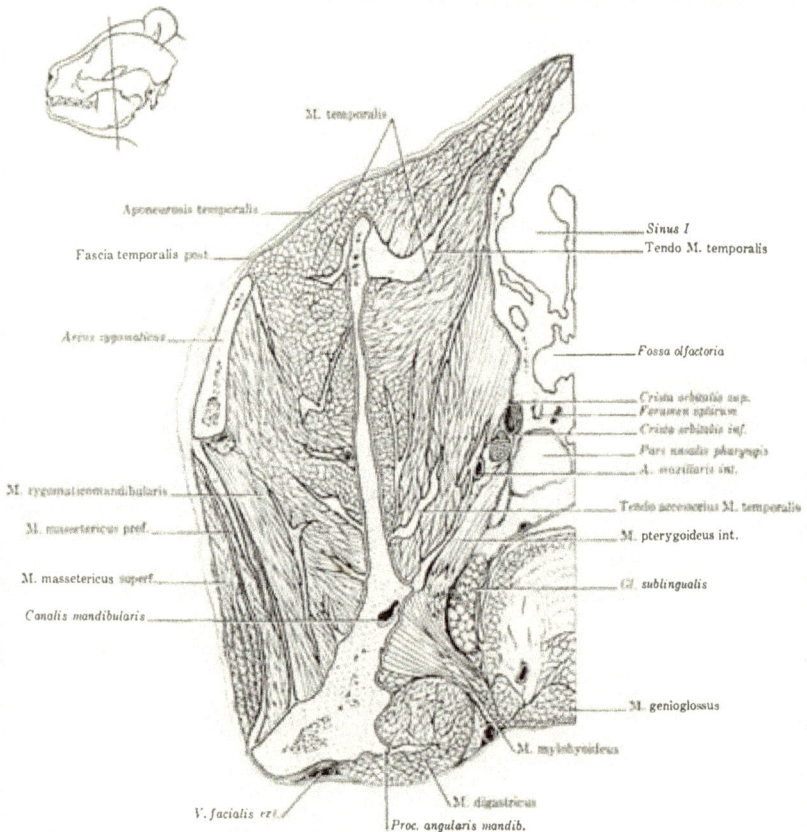

FIG. 83. Frontal section through head of an old emaciated male *Ailuropoda* (Mei Lan). The section passes through the coronoid process of the mandible (see inset).

of the coronoid process. Muscle fibers arise from the whole floor of the temporal fossa, and from the deep surfaces of the several tendon sheets. Some of the fibers insert into the surface of the coronoid process, the insertion area extending ventrad as far as the mandibular foramen. Other fibers insert into the superficial surfaces of the several tendon sheets.

The temporal is an elevator of the mandible. Because of its multipennate structure it produces slow but very powerful movements.

**M. zygomaticomandibularis** (fig. 83) is relatively larger than in any other carnivore examined. It is completely hidden beneath the masseter and zygomatic arch, and fills the masseteric fossa. Origin is from the whole internal face of the zygomatic arch. The fibers converge toward the masseteric fossa, into which they insert by both muscle and tendon fibers. Tendon sheets embedded in the muscle near its insertion attach to crests on the floor of the masseteric fossa, and these tendons increase the available insertion area. The fiber direction of the zygomaticomandibularis is downward, mesad, and slightly backward. In the sagittal plane the fibers are almost vertical, forming an angle of about 80° with the occlusal plane. In the frontal plane the angle is about 75° with the transverse axis of the head. In both planes the angles become increasingly vertical as the jaw is opened.

The zygomaticomandibularis is primarily an elevator of the mandible. The muscle of one side of the head, in conjunction with the pterygoids of the opposite side, shifts the mandible transversely toward the side of the contracting zygomaticomandibularis. This motion is the grinding component of the jaw movements in *Ailuropoda* and other carnivores.

**M. masseter** (figs. 82, 83) is powerfully developed. It is more or less divisible into the usual two layers, although these are fused and inseparable anteriorly.

The pars superficialis is a thin sheet covering all but the posterior part of the profunda. More than the proximal half of the external face of the superficialis is covered with a heavy tendinous aponeurosis (aponeurosis 1 of Schumacher, 1961a), which is continuous posteriorly with the aponeurosis of the profunda. The muscle arises by this aponeurosis and by underlying muscle fibers from the anterior half of the inferior border of the zygomatic arch. The fibers run backward and downward at an angle of about 45° with the occlusal plane, to insert non-tendinously into the inferior edge of the mandible, immediately below the coronoid fossa, the insertion extending back as far as the angular process. At its insertion the muscle forms a tendinous intersection with the internal pterygoid. The posteriormost fibers do not extend beyond the angular process at the posterior end of the mandible to insert into the stylomandibular ligament, as they do in *Ursus* and other carnivores.

The internal face of the superficialis is in very intimate contact with the underlying profunda, the two layers being inseparable anteriorly.

The pars profunda is covered by the superficialis, except for a narrow area along its posterior edge. It arises by fleshy and tendon fibers from the entire inferior border of the zygomatic arch, back to within 10 mm. of the mandibular fossa. The fibers have a slightly more vertical direction than do those of the superficialis. A tendon sheet embedded in the posterior part of the profunda, attaching to the zygomatic arch, partly divides the muscle into superficial and deep layers. The external face of the mandibular half of the profunda is covered with a heavy glistening aponeurosis (aponeurosis 2 of Schumacher, 1961a). Insertion is made by means of this aponeurosis into the mandible along the inferior border of the coronoid fossa. The fibers run backward and downward at an angle of about 55° with the occlusal plane.

The masseter is an elevator of the mandible. Because it is composed of long parallel fibers it produces quick snapping movements, relatively less powerful than those of the temporal muscle.

**M. pterygoideus internus** (figs. 70, 83, 84; lateralis of authors) is a rectangular group of parallel fibers arising from the ventral edge and outer side of the perpendicular plate of the palatine, pterygoid, and sphenoid bones. The muscle is thin and delicate posteriorly, and is relatively smaller than in any other known carnivore. It shows a tendency to break up into three or more subequal elements. Insertion is into the prominent fossa on the inner side of the lower border of the ramus of the mandible, extending onto the angular process. A few of the delicate posterior fibers insert into the anterior end of the stylomandibular ligament.

The internal pterygoids acting together elevate the mandible. Unilateral contraction simultaneously elevates the mandible and shifts it toward the contralateral side.

**M. pterygoideus externus** (figs. 83, 84; medialis of authors) is much shorter, but considerably thicker, than the internal pterygoid muscle. Its lateral end lies dorsad of the internal pterygoid, and its medial end posterior to it. Origin is by two heads, which are separated by the buccinator nerve. The more ventral head arises from the outer side of the pterygoid plate at its posterior end, extending as far back as the combined foramina ovale and rotundum. The other head continues this origin up onto the skull, behind the optic foramen. The two heads fuse, and the resulting muscle extends straight laterad to its insertion, which is into the prominent pit on the anteromedial end of the condyle of the mandible.

The two external pterygoids are antagonistic. Unilateral contraction shifts the mandible toward the contralateral side.

*Discussion of Masticatory Muscles*

We have seen (p. 72) that the skull in *Ailuropoda*, and in herbivorous carnivores in general, is designed to promote the production of maximum forces at the level of the cheek teeth by (a) improving lever advantages, (b) increasing the space available to muscle tissue, and (c) resisting disintegrating forces.

The active forces themselves are of course supplied by the craniomandibular muscles. These may further enhance the efficiency of the masticatory apparatus in three purely morphological ways: (a) generalized increase in mass of contractile tissue, (b) selective increase in mass, involving only those elements that produce the forces involved in pressure and grinding movements, and (c) increase in functional[1] cross section. Each of these is evident in the masticatory musculature of the giant panda.

[1] The functional cross section is a section at right angles to the fibers. The anatomical cross section is a section at right angles to the long axis of the muscle. In a parallel-fibered muscle these two sections may coincide; in a pennate muscle they never do.

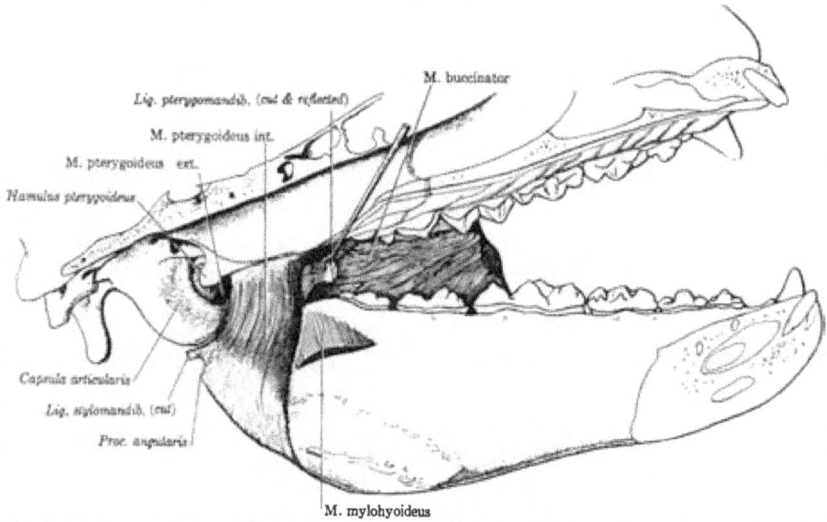

Fig. 84. Masticatory muscles of *Ailuropoda*, medial view.

GENERALIZED INCREASE IN MASS.—I have used brain weight as a standard for computing an index of the relative mass of the total masticatory musculature of one side of the head. The data are given in the accompanying Table 12. The weights are all from zoo animals, and consequently the values for the musculature are undoubtedly low, although all except the panda were in good flesh at time of death. The panda (Mei Lan), in addition to his years in captivity, was much emaciated at the time of his death. Nevertheless these figures show that the relative mass of the masticatory musculature in *Ailuropoda* is at least twice as great as in bears of comparable body size.

That this increase is truly generalized is shown by the fact that the mass of the digastric, a muscle not involved in jaw closure, equaled 30 per cent of brain weight in *Ailuropoda*, whereas in the bears it was less than 10 per cent of brain weight. It is impossible to determine whether both bellies of the digastric are equally hypertrophied; certainly the anterior belly is involved.

The masticatory musculature, except for the posterior belly of the digastric, is derived from the mandibular arch of the embryo. Also derived from this arch are the mylohyoid, tensor tympani, and tensor veli palatini. The mylohyoid is in no way involved in jaw closure, yet in *Ailuropoda* it is hypertrophied like the craniomandibular muscles (p. 157). I was unable to decide from inspection whether the tiny tensors were relatively larger than in the bears. It is evident, however, that what is enlarged in the panda is not a functional unit, but a morphological unit—*the muscular derivatives of the mandibular arch.* The fact that all are hypertrophied shows that, in this instance at least, *the morphological unit is also a genetic unit.* Indeed, hypertrophy extends in a decreasing gradient, beyond the derivatives of the mandibular arch, to the entire musculature of the anterior part of the body (p. 182). The morphogenetic mechanism involved in the hypertrophy is probably very simple. Selection undoubtedly favored an increase in the mass of the jaw-closing muscles

TABLE 12.—RELATIVE MASS OF MASTICATORY MUSCULATURE

| | Masticatory Musculature (gms.) | Digastric (gms.) | Brain (gms.) | Index: Masticatory Musculature / Brain |
|---|---|---|---|---|
| *Ailuropoda melanoleuca* (♂ ad.) | 890 | 92 | 277 | 3.2 |
| *Ursus americanus* (♀ ad.) | 322 | 26 | 238 | 1.4 |
| *Thalarctos maritimus* (♂ ad.) | 910 | 86 | 498* | 1.8 |

* Mean of two brain weights (489 gms., 507 gms.) given by Crile and Quiring (1940). The brain of the polar bear from which I dissected the muscles was not weighed.

in the panda, but the results extend far beyond the functional unit.

SELECTIVE INCREASE IN MASS.—Relative masses of individual components of the masticatory complex may be compared by reducing each to a percentage of the mass of the total masticatory complex (Davis, 1955). Data are given in the accompanying table.

other mammals, including man) the insertion tendon of the temporal muscle continues into the muscle substance as a broad tendon sheet. Fibers of the temporal muscle insert obliquely into both sides of this tendon sheet, and the temporal is therefore a *pennate* muscle. In *Ailuropoda* the temporal has been converted into a *multipennate* muscle by tendinization of numerous fascial planes

TABLE 13.—RELATIVE WEIGHTS OF MASTICATORY MUSCLES IN CARNIVORES
(Including data from Davis, 1955)

| | Ailuropoda [Mei Lan] Wt. in gms. | Ailuropoda [Mei Lan] % | Tremarctos ornatus % | Ursus americanus* % | Procyon lotor % | Thalarctos maritimus % | Canis familiaris % | Felis onca % |
|---|---|---|---|---|---|---|---|---|
| Masseter superf............... | 44 | 5 | 7.5 | 10 | 5 | } 12 { | 15 | 21 |
| Masseter prof................ | 60 | 7 | 2.5 | 2 | 3 | | 3 | 2.5 |
| Zygomaticomand............ | 188 | 21 | 14 | 11 | 13 | 7 | 6 | 2.5 |
| Temporalis.................. | 477 | 54 | 58 | 62 | 63 | 66 | 58 | 59 |
| Pterygoideus internus....... | 18 | 2 | 7 | 5 | 6 | 4 | 7.5 | 6.5 |
| Pterygoideus externus...... | 11 | 1 | 1 | 1 | 1 | 1 | 0.5 | 0.5 |
| Digastric................... | 92 | 10 | 10 | 9 | 9 | 10 | 9.5 | 8 |
| Totals.................... | 890 | 100 | 100 | 100 | 100 | 100 | 99.5 | 100 |

*Means of two specimens; data for one individual from Starck (1935). All other figures from one individual each.

I have pointed out elsewhere (Davis, 1955) that in the Carnivora the masses of only two muscles, the superficial masseter and the zygomaticomandibularis, appear to vary significantly with differences in food habits, and that these two muscles vary reciprocally. A large superficial masseter appeared to be associated with carnivorous habits, a large zygomaticomandibularis with herbivorous habits. The additional data presented here confirm this relation. Moreover, in *Ailuropoda* the superficial masseter is relatively smaller (except in *Procyon*, where it is equally small) and the zygomaticomandibularis larger, than in any other carnivore examined.

The masseter, because it is composed of long parallel fibers, is particularly effective in producing quick snapping movements of the mandible—a movement obviously important to predaceous carnivores. There is an important horizontal component in the action of the zygomaticomandibularis. This muscle, which in bulk far exceeds the more horizontally situated but tiny external pterygoid, is primarily responsible for lateral shifting of the mandible—a movement important to herbivorous carnivores. Thus, in addition to the generalized increase, there is a *selective* increase in mass among the masticatory muscles, and the results conform to the requirements of differing dietary habits.

INCREASE IN FUNCTIONAL CROSS SECTION.—In the temporal muscle of all carnivores (and of many

in the substance of the muscle, with muscle fibers attaching to both surfaces of these tendon sheets.

What are the mechanical advantages of pennation in a muscle? A pennate fiber is the diagonal of a parallelogram of which one component represents force along the axis of the insertion tendon while the other component tends to pull the insertion tendon toward the origin. Only the first of these two components represents useful work. The second is waste effort, whose magnitude varies with the angle of pennation but in all cases represents an important fraction of the total energy of the contracting fiber. There is no such waste of energy in a parallel-fibered muscle, which is therefore more efficient than a pennate muscle. Some advantage must offset the inefficiency of the pennate structure.

Eisler (1912) suggested maximum utilization of attachment area as a factor in the pennation of muscles. He pointed out that powerful muscles are pennate in situations where available attachment area is limited, whereas other powerful muscles remain parallel-fibered in situations where the attachment area can be expanded. Eisler compared the multipennate human deltoid, with its anatomically restricted areas of attachment, with the parallel-fibered gluteus maximus, which has been able to expand its areas of attachment unhindered. Available attachment area is obviously a limiting factor in the temporalis of *Ailuropoda*.

The temporal fossa has been expanded in all directions, apparently to the limits that are compatible with other vital functions of the head (p. 46). The mass of the muscle, particularly its area of origin, cannot be increased further to achieve additional power.

Pfuhl (1936) attempted to work out the mechanics of pennate muscles. The work ($a$) of a muscle is expressed in two terms: force ($F$), and the distance ($d$) through which the force is exerted:

$$a = F \cdot d \qquad (1)$$

The force of a muscle may be expressed by the equation

$$F = k \cdot q \qquad (2)$$

where $q$ is the functional cross section and $k$ is a constant representing the unit of muscle power.[1] Thus for any value of $a$ in equation (1) the proportion of $F$ can be increased by increasing the functional cross section of the muscle, that of $d$ by increasing its length. For a given mass of muscle tissue, maximum force would therefore be achieved by arranging the muscle as a series of minimally short parallel fibers, which would give maximum functional cross section. Such an arrangement would usually produce architectural difficulties, since areas of origin and insertion would become unduly large. An alternative is the arrangement of the fibers in pennate fashion between more or less parallel sheets of bone or tendon. This loses a portion of the total energy of the muscle, as shown above, but enormously increases the functional cross section and therefore the power per unit of mass. Thus pennation is a device permitting maximum production of force in a minimum of space, and utilizing limited attachment area on the skeleton. This effect is multiplied by multipennation.

The craniomandibular musculature of *Ailuropoda* represents an extension of conditions in the bears, which in turn are a modification of conditions in more generalized carnivores. Indeed, in *Tremarctos*, the most herbivorous of the bears, the craniomandibular musculature appears to be about intermediate between *Ursus* and *Ailuropoda*.

As will appear in the sequel, the generalized increase in the mass of the craniomandibular muscles of *Ailuropoda* is associated with a generalized hypertrophy of the skeletal muscles of the shoulder region, and probably has a very simple genetic basis. The morphogenetic basis underlying the other two adaptive modifications—increase in relative mass of individual muscles, and increase in functional cross section—is unknown.

## D. INTERRAMAL MUSCULATURE

These three muscles form a topographic, but not a morphological, unit. Ontogenetically they are derived from two different sources: the anterior belly of the digastric and the mylohyoid (from the mandibular arch) are supplied by the trigeminal nerve; the posterior belly of the digastric and the stylohyoid (from the hyoid arch) are supplied by the facial nerve. At least the elements derived from the mandibular arch are hypertrophied like the craniomandibular muscles derived from this arch. Of the elements derived from the hyoid arch, the stylohyoid is absent in *Ailuropoda* and there is no way of determining whether hypertrophy of the digastric involves the fibers of its posterior belly.

M. digastricus (figs. 82, 83, 85) is a powerfully developed muscle, triangular in cross section, with the base of the triangle ventrad. The muscle has a thickness of 22 mm. The mass of the muscle is shot through with powerful longitudinal tendon fibers. Origin is from the paroccipital process and the ridge connecting this process with the mastoid process. The muscle is covered with a tendinous aponeurosis at its origin; there is also a small accessory tendinous origin from the mastoid process. Insertion is into the inner surface of the mandible, from a point opposite the second molar tooth back as far as the mandibular foramen.

A fine tendinous inscription runs across the belly of the muscle near its middle, marking the juncture of the anterior and posterior bellies.

The digastric is relatively much larger than in the bears (Table 12), but there is no way of determining whether both bellies share in this hypertrophy. Certainly the anterior belly is enlarged.

M. stylohyoideus is absent. This muscle is typically composed of two parts in carnivores, a superficial slip external to the digastric and a deeper part internal to the digastric. Either may be absent, although there seems to be no previous record of both being absent simultaneously. Nothing corresponding to either part could be found in the specimens of *Ailuropoda* dissected.

M. mylohyoideus (figs. 83, 84, 85) is a thick sheet that fills, with its fellow, most of the space between the rami of the mandible. Anteriorly a small space exposes the end of the genioglossus. The muscle arises from the medial surface of the mandible just below the alveoli of the teeth, from a point opposite the first molar to the angular process. The general direction of the fibers is transverse, although anteriorly and posteriorly

[1] The unit of muscle power is the tension produced by a muscle with a functional cross section of 1 cm². For purposes of calculation it is assumed to be 10 kg.

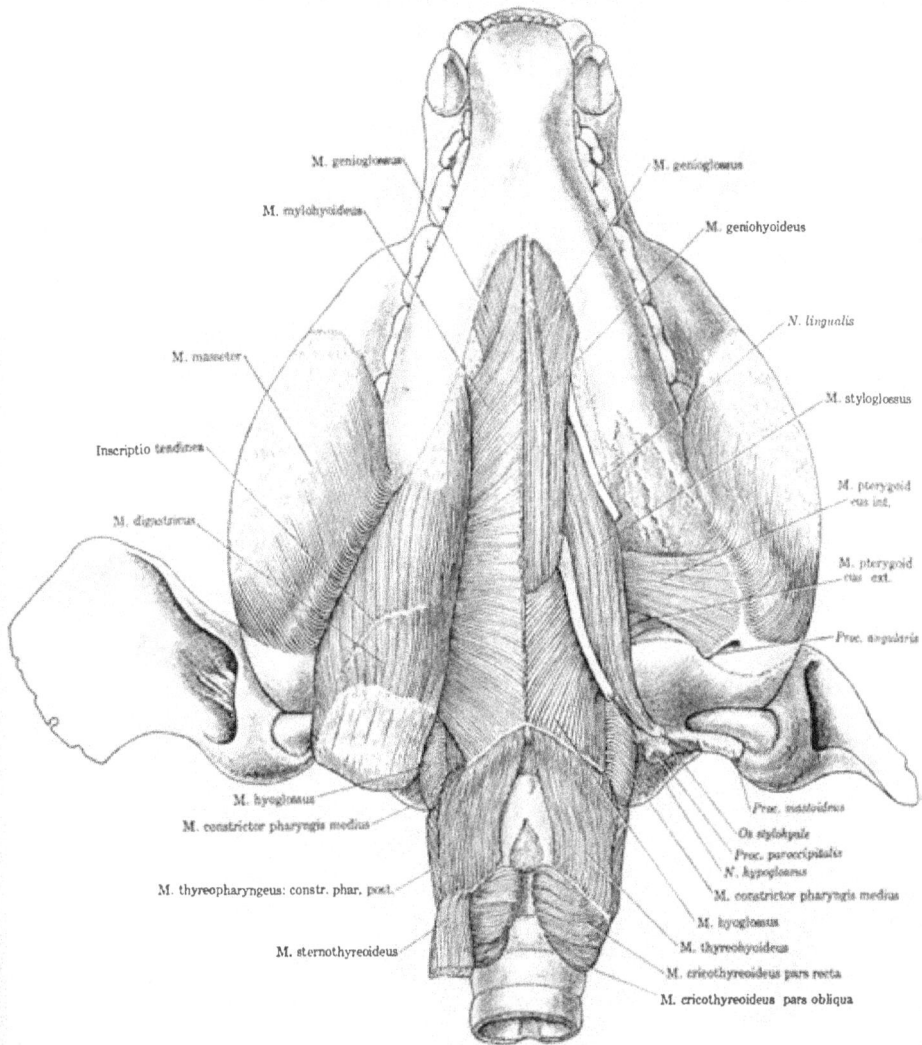

M. genioglossus

M. mylohyoideus

M. genioglossus

M. geniohyoideus

N. lingualis

M. masseter

M. styloglossus

Inscriptio tendinea

M. pterygoid eus int.

M. digastricus

M. pterygoid eus ext.

Proc. angularis

M. hyoglossus

M. constrictor pharyngis medius

Proc. mastoideus

Os stylohyale

Proc. paroccipitalis

N. hypoglossus

M. thyreopharyngeus: constr. phar. post.

M. constrictor pharyngis medius

M. hyoglossus

M. sternothyreoideus

M. thyreohyoideus

M. cricothyreoideus pars recta

M. cricothyreoideus pars obliqua

FIG. 85. Muscles of the head of *Ailuropoda*, ventral view.

they diverge to the mandibular symphysis and the hyoid, respectively. Insertion is made in the usual way into a median raphe with the opposite muscle, and posteriorly into the hyoid bone. Medially the inner surface of the mylohyoid is almost inseparably united to the geniohyoid.

The mylohyoid is much thicker, particularly near its origin (fig. 83), than is the mylohyoid of bears.

### E. MUSCLES OF THE TONGUE

The extrinsic muscles of the tongue show none of the hypertrophy that characterizes the craniomandibular muscles. Ontogenetically these tongue muscles arise from the ventral portion of the occipital myotomes. They are innervated by the hypoglossal nerve.

**M. styloglossus** (fig. 85) takes extensive origin from the stylohyal segment of the hyoid apparatus. The fibers diverge over the ventrolateral surface of the tongue before they disappear into the substance of the tongue itself.

**M. hyoglossus** fig. 85) arises from the inferior surface of the body of the hyoid, except for the area occupied medially by the origin of the geniohyoideus, and the proximal part of the posterior horn. The fibers run straight anteriorly for a short distance before they penetrate the tongue, behind and laterad of the genioglossus and mesad of the styloglossus.

**M. genioglossus** (figs. 83, 85) is a narrow band arising from the symphysis just laterad of the midline. The origin of this muscle is ventral and lateral to the origin of the geniohyoideus. The muscle runs posteriorly, separated from the ventral midline by the geniohyoideus, and enters the tongue partly anterior to and partly medial to the hyoglossus.

## II. MUSCLES OF THE BODY

### A. MUSCLES OF THE NECK

#### 1. *Superficial Group*

**M. sternomastoideus** (fig. 86) is a heavy flat band about 40 mm. wide at its widest part (near its insertion). It arises, partly tendinously and partly fleshily, from the anterior border of the manubrium and the proximal end of the first costal cartilage. The muscle widens somewhat at its insertion, which is made on the lateral and ventral borders of the mastoid process. There is no indication that the sternomastoideus fuses with its mate at the midline.

**M. cleidomastoideus** fig. 86) arises from the dorsal edge of the sternomastoid, at a point about 70 mm. anterior to the origin of the latter muscle. With a maximum width of only 25 mm., it is considerably narrower than the sternomastoideus. The two muscles run forward side by side, the cleidomastoideus inserting on the lower part of the lambdoidal crest as a direct continuation of the insertion of the sternomastoideus, although the two muscles remain completely separate.

#### 2. *Supra- and Infrahyoid Group*

**M. omohyoideus** (figs. 86, 89) is a narrow ribbon, about 16 mm. wide, arising from the coracovertebral angle of the scapula. It runs forward and downward, passing between the scalenus and the sternohyoideus. Near its insertion it divides into two bellies. The larger of these inserts on the hyoid, deep to the insertion of the sternohyoideus. The other belly inserts aponeurotically on the ventral face of the digastric, near its medial border.

**M. sternohyoideus** figs. 86, 87, 89, 90 arises from the anterodorsal surface of the manubrium, a few of the most lateral fibers reaching the costal cartilages. It runs craniad as a narrow, flat band, in contact with its mate of the opposite side near its origin, but diverging from it farther anteriorly. Insertion is made on the thyrohyal element of the hyoid.

**M. sternothyroideus** (figs. 85, 87, 89, 90) is inseparable from the sternohyoid at its origin and as far forward as a tendinous intersection which crosses the common mass of these two muscles about 40 mm. in front of the manubrium. Anterior to this point the sternothyroid lies partly above (dorsal) and partly lateral to the sternohyoid. It inserts on the thyroid cartilage, just above the insertion of the sternohyoid.

**M. thyrohyoideus** (figs. 85, 87, 89) is a wide, flat band on the ventrolateral surface of the thyroid cartilage. Arising from the posterior border of the thyroid cartilage, just laterad of the midline, the fibers run anteriorly to their insertion on the posterior border of the thyrohyal and the body of the hyoid.

**M. geniohyoideus** fig. 85) is a narrow band running from the symphysis mandibuli to the body of the hyoid, closely applied to its fellow of the opposite side. Arising from the symphysis deep to and laterad of the genioglossus, it inserts on the anteroventral surface of the body of the hyoid, just laterad of the midline.

#### 3. *Deep Lateral and Subvertebral Group*

**M. scalenus** (figs. 86, 89) is divisible into the usual *longus* and *brevis*. The short division lies mostly beneath the much more powerful long division. The scalenus longus arises by short, stout tendons from the third to seventh ribs, its origins interdigitating with the serratus anticus. The longus is subdivided into a dorsal part, which arises from the second to the fifth ribs, and a medial part from the sixth and seventh ribs. The brevis arises fleshily from the first rib near its junction with the costal cartilage. The two divisions unite in the cervical region, and the resulting common mass inserts on the transverse processes of the last five cervical vertebrae.

**M. longus colli** arises from the ventral surfaces of the bodies of the first six thoracic vertebrae and from the ventral sides of the transverse processes of the sixth to third cervical vertebrae. The usual simple distinction of the thoracic and cervical parts of the muscle because of difference in their fiber directions is scarcely possible on the present specimen. The fibers arising from the thoracic vertebrae are gathered into a tendinous band that in-

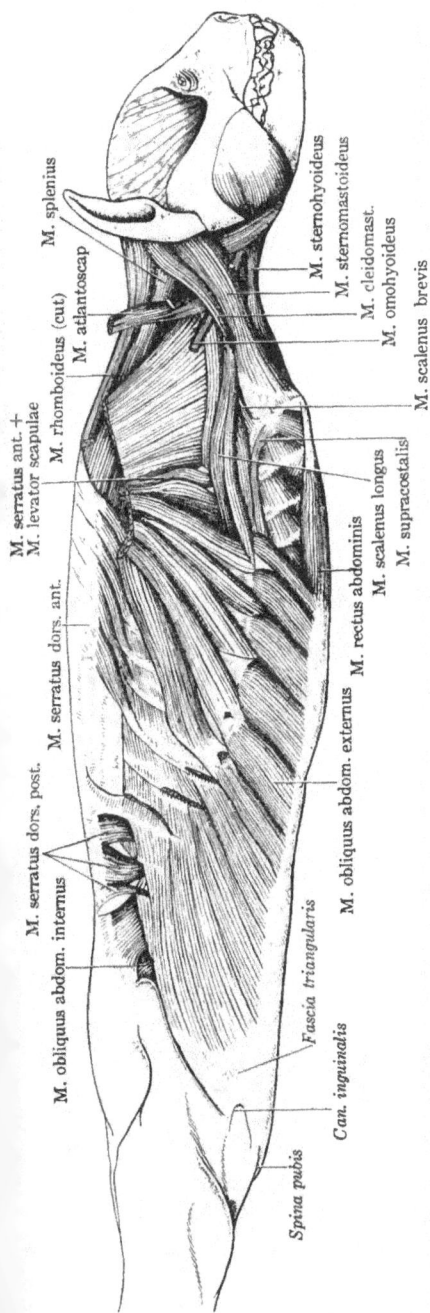

M. serratus ant. +
M. levator scapulae

M. splenius

M. rhomboideus (cut)

M. atlantoscap

M. serratus dors. ant.

M. serratus dors. post.

M. obliquus abdom. internus

Spina pubis

Can. inguinalis

Fascia triangularis

M. obliquus abdom. externus

M. sternohyoideus
M. sternomastoideus
M. cleidomast.
M. omohyoideus
M. scalenus brevis

M. scalenus longus
M. supracostalis

M. rectus abdominis

Fig. 86.  Lateral view of body musculature of *Ailuropoda*, superficial layer.

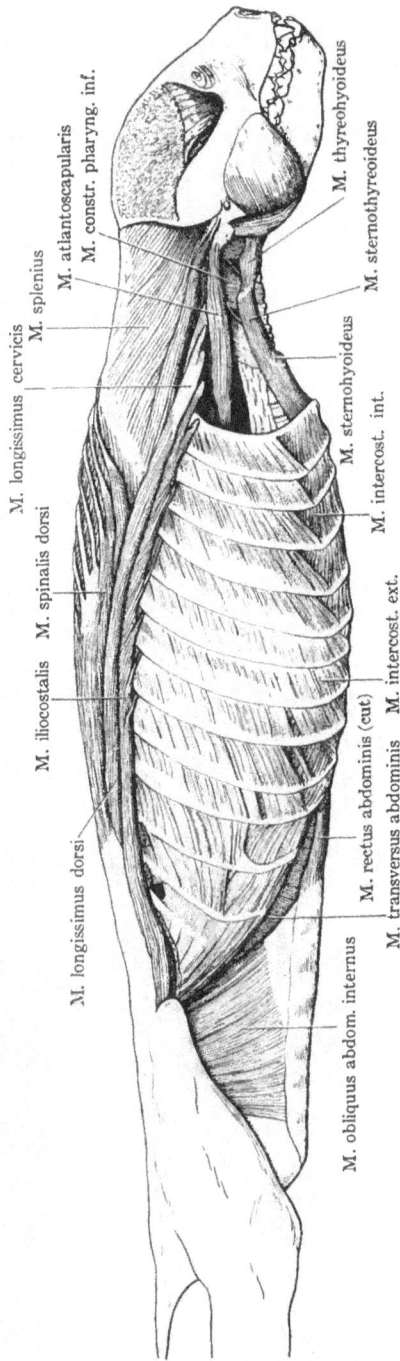

M. longissimus cervicis

M. splenius

M. atlantoscapularis
M. constr. pharyng. inf.

M. thyreohyoideus

M. sternothyreoideus

M. sternohyoideus

M. intercost. int.

M. spinalis dorsi

M. iliocostalis

M. longissimus dorsi

M. obliquus abdom. internus

M. transversus abdominis

M. rectus abdominis (cut)

M. intercost. ext.

Fig. 87.  Lateral view of body musculature of *Ailuropoda*, deep layer.

159

serts into the transverse process of the sixth cervical. The fibers from the cervical vertebrae have the customary insertion into the next vertebra craniad of the one from which they arise, and into the ventral surface of the arch of the atlas.

M. longus capitis is a prominent subcylindrical muscle, somewhat flattened dorsoventrally. It arises by fleshy fasciculi from the tips of the transverse processes of the sixth to the second cervical vertebrae. Insertion is into the prominent scar on the ventral side of the basioccipital.

M. rectus capitis ventralis is a very slender muscle lying mesad of the longus capitis, and in contact with its mate of the opposite side at the midline. It has the customary origin from the ventral surface of the body of the atlas, and insertion into the basioccipital mesad and caudad of the longus capitis.

## B. MUSCLES OF THE TRUNK

### 1. *Muscles of the Thorax*

M. panniculus carnosus is rather feebly developed; the dorsal division is represented only by an almost insignificant vestige. The borders of the ventral division do not reach the midline either dorsally or ventrally. A few fibers arise on the inner surface of the thigh, and the sheet then broadens as it passes anteriorly, reaching its greatest width over the posterior ribs. At this point it is approximately 170 mm. from the dorsal midline and 80 mm. from the ventral. The sheet then gradually decreases in width as it passes craniad. At the point where it passes under the pectoralis it is only about 50 mm. wide. The ventral fibers insert on the bicipital arch, the dorsal ones on the inner face of the pectoralis profundus.

The dorsal division is represented only by two narrow ribbons, lying immediately dorsad of the ventral division, that run up onto the shoulder for about 50 mm. and insert into the epitrochlearis immediately below the latissimus.

M. pectoralis superficialis (fig. 89). As in the bears, the superficial pectoral sheet is a compound muscle composed of the pectoralis superficialis anteriorly and the reflected posterior edge of the profundus posteriorly. Fusion is so intimate that the boundary between superficialis and profundus cannot be determined, but as in the bears the posterior part of the superficial layer is innervated by the medial anterior thoracic nerve.

Along its posterior border the superficial sheet is folded sharply under and continued forward as a deeper layer (the profundus) immediately beneath the superficial one. Thus a very deep and well-marked pectoral pocket, open anteriorly and closed posteriorly, is formed.

The superficial sheet arises from the entire manubrium and from the corpus sterni back to the level of the eighth sternal rib. The fibers converge toward the humerus, and insert into the pectoral ridge in a narrow line along the middle half of the bone. In other carnivores (including the bears) insertion is into the deltoid ridge. In *Ailuropoda* the proximal end of the insertion line deviates slightly from the pectoral ridge toward the deltoid ridge, but by no means reaches the latter. Probably the tremendous development of the deltoid and lateral triceps in the panda has crowded the superficial pectoral off the deltoid ridge and forward onto the pectoral ridge.

M. sternohumeralis profundus is a narrow band anterior to the superficial sheet. It arises from the anterior end of the manubrium, increases in width as it passes toward the shoulder along the anterior border of the superficial sheet, and inserts on the lateral surface of the humerus immediately below the greater tuberosity, in a line that continues proximad from the insertion of the superficial sheet. The lateral anterior thoracic nerve and its accompanying blood vessels pass through the split between this muscle and the superficialis.

M. pectoralis profundus (figs. 89, 133) lies mostly beneath the superficialis, although as stated above its posterior edge is folded forward and fused with the posterior border of the superficialis. It is by far the widest element of the pectoral complex. It is not divisible into anterior and posterior parts. Origin is from the corpus sterni posteriorly, deeper fibers arising from the sternal cartilages, from the eighth forward to the third. At the anterior level of the third and fourth sternal cartilages the muscle arises wholly from the cartilages, none of the fibers reaching the sternebrae. The most posterior fibers are joined on their under side by the panniculus. Insertion extends almost the entire length of the humerus, beginning proximally on the greater tuberosity at the edge of the bicipital groove, and continuing distad on the pectoral ridge to within 60 mm. of the distal end of the humerus.

M. pectoralis abdominalis (fig. 89) is a narrow thin band lying posterior to the profundus. It arises from the rectus sheath at the level of the costal arch, passes beneath the posterior edge of the profundus, and inserts with the panniculus on the deep surface of the profundus, not reaching the bicipital arch. The abdominalis is degenerate.

M. subclavius is entirely wanting.

M. serratus ventralis (magnus or anterior of some authors) and M. levator scapulae (fig. 86) form a perfectly continuous sheet, so that the boundary between them cannot be determined. The common muscle arises from the atlas and all succeeding cervical vertebrae, and by fleshy fibers from the first nine ribs. The slip arising from the fifth rib lies over the scalenus; those farther forward lie beneath it. Insertion is made along the inner surface of the whole vertebral border of the scapula.

**Mm. intercostales externi** (figs. 87, 89). The fibers of these muscles run craniodorsad as far back as the eleventh rib. Between the eleventh and fourteenth ribs they run nearly horizontally. The muscles reach the costal cartilages of all but the first two ribs, although the intercostales interni are exposed medially as far back as the seventh rib. The part of the muscle between the ribs is fleshy anteriorly, becoming quite tendinous posteriorly. Between the costal cartilages this arrangement is reversed, the muscles being tendinous anteriorly and fleshy posteriorly.

A small group of fibers arises from the first costal cartilage near the manibrium and inserts on the inner face of the tendon of the rectus. The dorsal edge of the muscle forms a raphe with the intercostal fibers lying dorsad of it, and the fiber direction is more vertical than that of the intercostales. It is not known whether this represents a part of the intercostalis internus or not.

**Mm. intercostales interni** (figs. 87, 90) are, as usual, more extensive than the external intercostals. They occupy all the space between the ribs and the costal cartilages. The fibers take the usual forward and downward direction.

**M. supracostalis** (fig. 86) is a narrow band arising from the fourth rib. Running anteriorly closely applied to the ventral edge of the scalenus, it swings ventrad to insert on the costal cartilage of the first rib.

**M. transversus thoracis** (fig. 90) is a thin sheet, more or less divisible into separate bands, that occupies the space between the third and eighth sternal cartilages on the inner side of the thoracic wall. Origin is from all the sternal segments except the first two and from the anterior third of the xiphoid cartilage, and insertion is made on the sternal cartilages and aponeurotically on the fascia covering the inner surface of the internal intercostals.

A narrow ribbon of muscle arises from the third sternal segment and passes forward to insert aponeurotically into the fascia of the intercostals. It is not known whether this represents a part of the transversus thoracis or not.

**M. diaphragma** (fig. 90). Pars lumbalis is divided into three crura. *Crus laterale*, which is the largest of the three, has a double origin. The lateral fibers arise by means of a stout tendon from

the ventrolateral surface of the third lumbar vertebra. Medial fibers arise, at the level of the second lumbar vertebra, from the lateral edge of a long tendon that runs cephalad from the ventral surface of the fourth lumbar vertebra. This tendon runs forward along the medial border of the pars lumbalis as far as the aortic notch, and gives rise to all the remaining fibers of this part of the diaphragm. On the deep surface of the lateral crus some of the fibers also arise directly from the second lumbar. *Crus intermedium* is very narrow. It is separated from the lateral crus throughout almost its entire length by a branch of the phrenic nerve, while its medial border slightly overlaps the lateral border of the medial crus. It arises from the medial tendon mentioned above, at the level of the anterior border of the second lumbar vertebra, its origin being continuous with that of the lateral crus. *Crus mediale* arises from the medial tendon at the level of the posterior border of the first lumbar vertebra, its origin being continuous with that of the intermediate crus. The medial crus fuses with its fellow of the opposite side cephalad of the hiatus aorticus, which is situated below the thirteenth thoracic vertebra.

Pars costalis arises from the ninth to the eleventh costal cartilages by a series of interdigitations with the transversus abdominis. These interdigitations do not correspond perfectly in number with the ribs, some costal cartilages receiving more than one digitation each; nor do the digitations correspond exactly on either side of the sternum.

Pars sternalis arises from the lateral border of the posterior part of the elongate xiphoid process. It is a narrow band that promptly joins the adjacent medial border of the pars costalis.

### 2. *Muscles of the Abdomen*

**M. rectus abdominis** (figs. 86, 87, 89, 91) extends as a thin, rather narrow, band from the pelvic symphysis to the first costal cartilage. It reaches its greatest width of 100 mm. at about the level of the sixth sternal cartilage. Tendinous inscriptions are absent. The muscle arises by fleshy fibers, covered by a heavy aponeurosis, from the posterior part of the pelvic symphysis, the origin extending anteriorly along the ventral midline. A few of the fibers nearest the midline insert into the linea alba just behind the xiphoid cartilage. Successive slips farther laterad insert on the fifth, sixth and seventh costal cartilages, and slightly less than the lateral half of the muscle is continued forward, to insert by a wide tendon on the first costal cartilage. This tendon begins at the level of the third costal cartilage. The rectus does not participate in the formation of the inguinal canal.

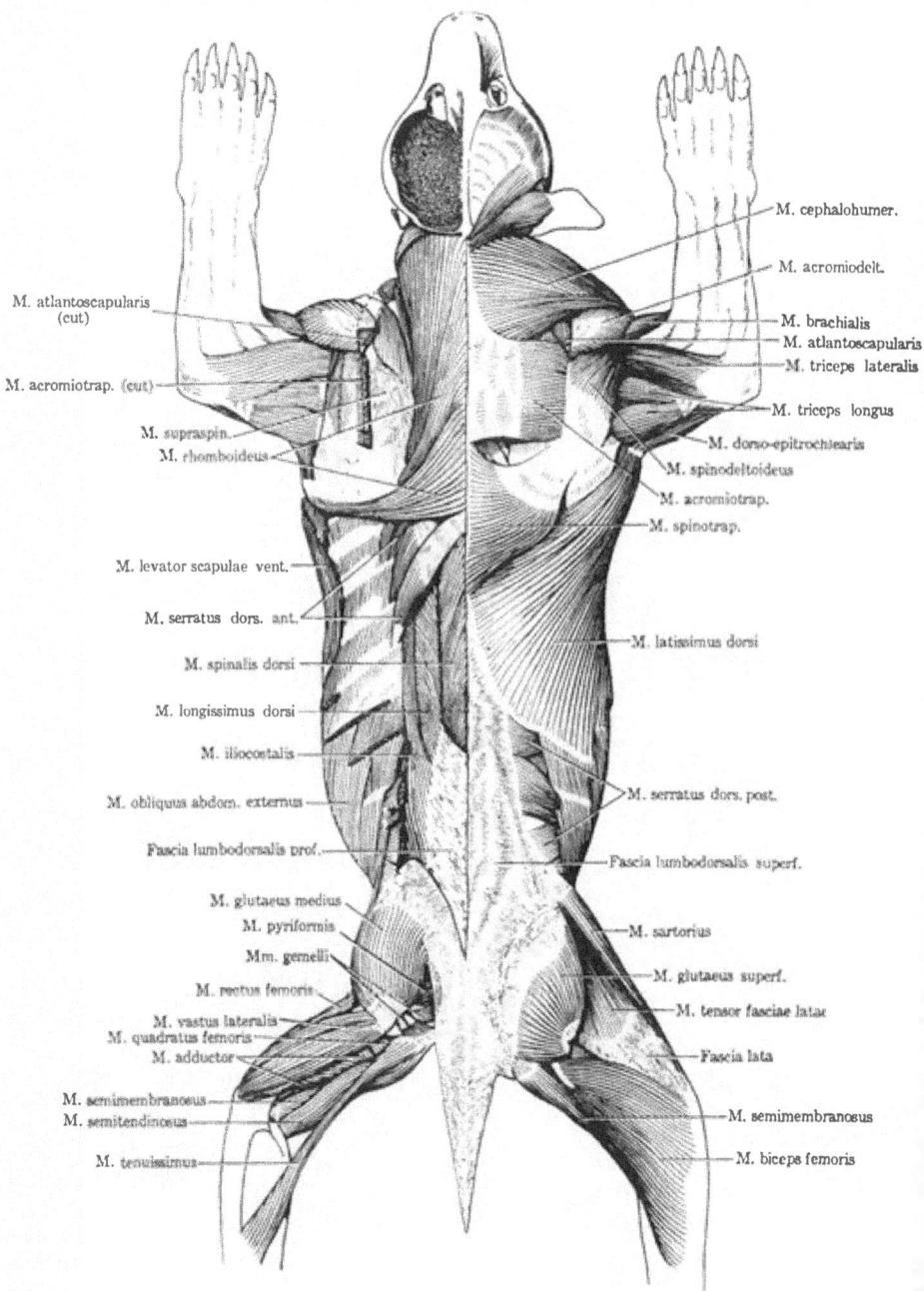

M. cephalohumer.

M. acromiodelt.

M. atlantoscapularis (cut)

M. acromiotrap. (cut)

M. brachialis
M. atlantoscapularis
M. triceps lateralis

M. triceps longus

M. supraspin.
M. rhomboideus

M. dorso-epitrochlearis
M. spinodeltoideus
M. acromiotrap.
M. spinotrap.

M. levator scapulae vent.

M. serratus dors. ant.

M. spinalis dorsi

M. longissimus dorsi

M. iliocostalis

M. obliquus abdom. externus

Fascia lumbodorsalis prof.

M. latissimus dorsi

M. serratus dors. post.

Fascia lumbodorsalis superf.

M. glutaeus medius
M. pyriformis
Mm. gemelli
M. rectus femoris

M. sartorius

M. glutaeus superf.

M. tensor fasciae latae

M. vastus lateralis
M. quadratus femoris
M. adductor

Fascia lata

M. semimembranosus
M. semitendinosus

M. semimembranosus

M. tenuissimus

M. biceps femoris

FIG. 88. Dorsal view of body musculature of *Ailuropoda*, superficial layer on right, deeper layer on left.

162

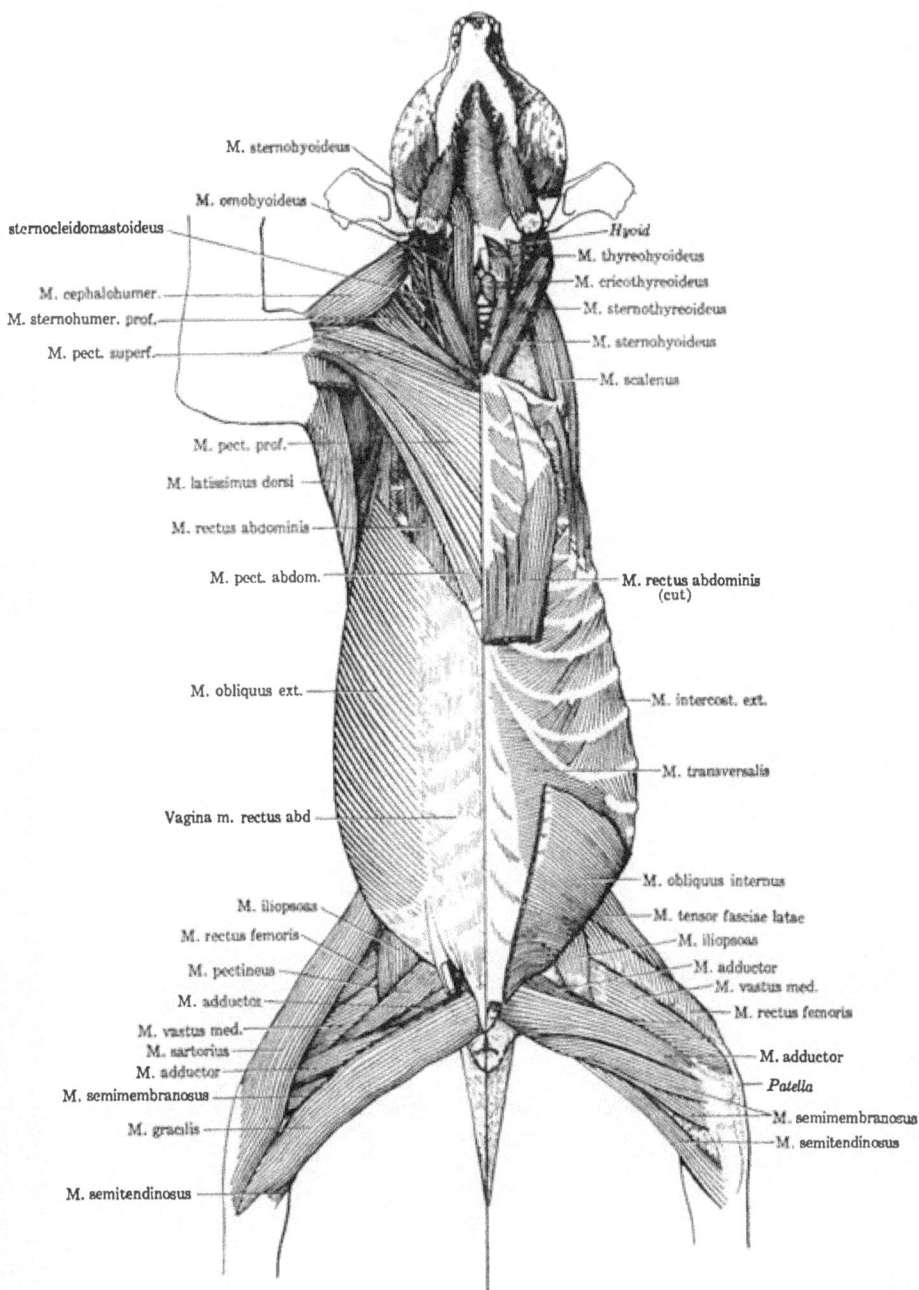

M. sternohyoideus

M. omohyoideus

sternocleidomastoideus

M. cephalohumer.

M. sternohumer. prof.

M. pect. superf.

M. pect. prof.

M. latissimus dorsi

M. rectus abdominis

M. pect. abdom.

M. obliquus ext.

Vagina m. rectus abd

M. iliopsoas

M. rectus femoris

M. pectineus

M. adductor

M. vastus med.
M. sartorius
M. adductor
M. semimembranosus

M. gracilis

M. semitendinosus

Hyoid

M. thyreohyoideus

M. cricothyreoideus

M. sternothyreoideus

M. sternohyoideus

M. scalenus

M. rectus abdominis
(cut)

M. intercost. ext.

M. transversalis

M. obliquus internus

M. tensor fasciae latae

M. iliopsoas

M. adductor
M. vastus med.

M. rectus femoris

M. adductor

Patella

M. semimembranosus

M. semitendinosus

FIG. 89. Ventral view of body musculature of *Ailuropoda*, superficial layer on right, deeper layer on left.

M. sternohyoideus +
M. sternothyreoideus

M. sternomastoideus

A. & V. mammaria int.

M. transv. thoracis

M. intercost. int.

M. diaphragma,
pars sternalis

Proc. xiphoideus

M. diaphragma,
pars costalis

M. transversus
abdominis

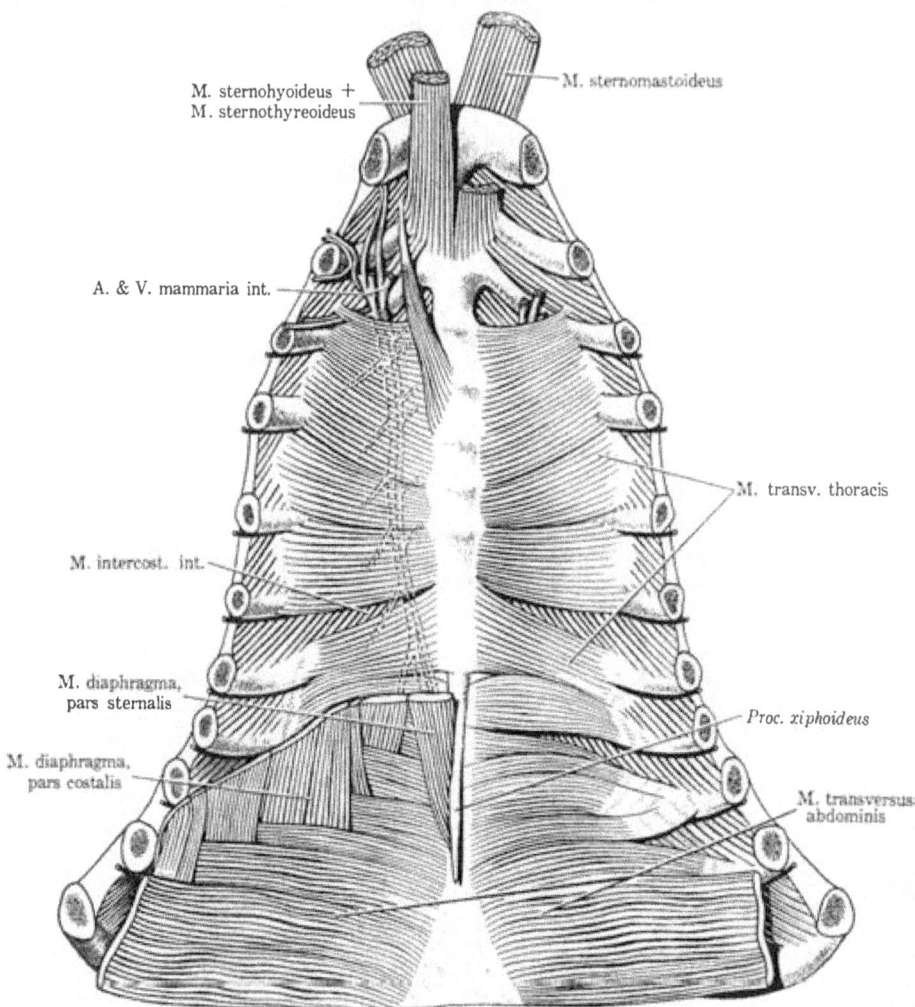

FIG. 90.   Ventral wall of thorax of *Ailuropoda*, internal view.

**M. obliquus abdominis externus** (figs. 86, 88, 89, 91) arises by short tendons from the fourth to the ninth ribs, and by fleshy fibers from the tenth to the thirteenth. Apparently none of the fibers reach the dorsal fascia. Posterior to the serratus ventralis the obliquus attaches to the ribs (10 13) immediately behind the origins of the latissimus dorsi. It is difficult to determine whether the fibers dorsal to the origins of the latissimus represent continuations of the obliquus or whether they are external intercostals, as the fiber direc-

tion is exactly the same. When the dorsal border of the obliquus is lifted, however, the muscle sheet dorsal to it is found to be perfectly continuous with the intercostals lying beneath the obliquus. Insertion: the muscle fibers slightly overlap the lateral edge of the rectus before giving way to the tendinous aponeurosis that extends over the rectus to the linea alba at the ventral midline (the rectus sheath). In the inguinal region the aponeurosis expands into a large triangular sheet, the abdominal tendon (see below), which inserts into the posterior third of the inguinal ligament.

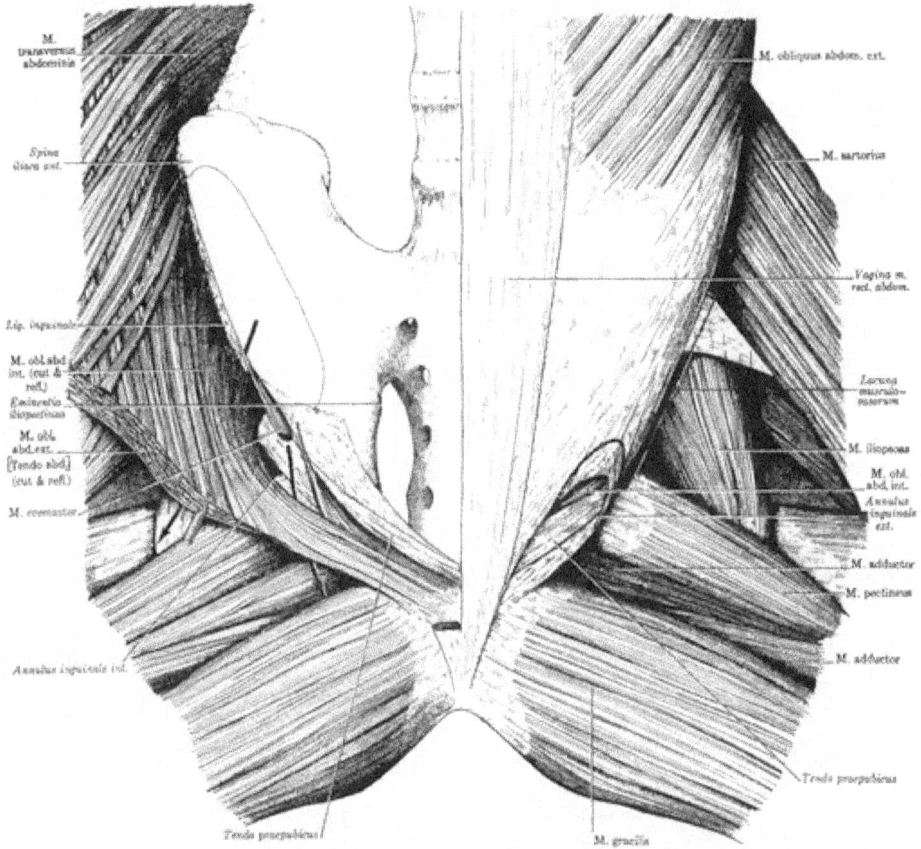

FIG. 91. The inguinal region of *Ailuropoda*. The dotted line shows the position of the internal inguinal ring. The arrows pass through the lacuan musculo-vasorum (lateral) and inguinal canal (medial).

**M. obliquus abdominis internus** (fig. 87, 89, 91) is much less extensive than the externus. It is rather sharply divided into two parts: an anterior division (pars costalis) that inserts on the last ribs, and a more extensive posterior part (pars abdominalis+pars inguinalis) that inserts aponeurotically into the ventral belly wall. These two divisions are separated by a considerable gap ventrally. The anterior division arises from the crest of the ilium from the anterior superior iliac spine mesad nearly to the middle of the crest, and from the iliac end of the inguinal ligament, and inserts on the last three ribs. The posterior division arises exclusively from the inguinal ligament. Posteriorly the fibers run almost vertically downward, or may even run slightly ventrocaudad; anteriorly they run diagonally forward and downward. The

muscle terminates in a tendinous aponeurosis that participates in the formation of the rectus sheath (see below). This aponeurosis is more extensive anteriorly, where the muscle fibers fail by 40 mm. to reach the edge of the rectus. Posteriorly the muscle fibers extend to the edge of the rectus. In the inguinal region the internal oblique is perforated by the inguinal canal.

**M. transversus abdominis** (figs. 87, 89, 90, 91) arises from the cartilages of the last six ribs, interdigitating with the origins of the diaphragm. Additional origin is taken from the lumbodorsal fascia, from the tip of the ilium, and from the anterior end of the inguinal ligament. The muscle terminates in a tendinous aponeurosis that fuses with the inner layer of the aponeurosis of the internal oblique to form the inner sheath of the rectus. The posteriormost fibers insert into the lateral third of the iliac crest.

**M. cremaster** (fig. 91) arises as a fine tendon from the inguinal ligament 25 mm. anterior to the internal inguinal ring. The tendon takes accessory origin from the transverse fascia on its way to the inguinal canal. As it enters the canal the tendon fans out into a band of muscle fibers that passes through the canal dorsad of the spermatic cord, and expands to form the cremasteric fascia around the tunica vaginalis of the testis.

**M. quadratus lumborum** (fig. 100) is a complex muscle arising from the last three thoracic vertebrae and ribs and the transverse processes of all the lumbar vertebrae. Insertion is into the transverse processes of the lumbars and the internal lip of the iliac crest for about its middle third and the adjacent inferior surface of the ilium.

3. *The Inguinal Region.* Figure 91.

The structures in the inguinal region are somewhat modified in *Ailuropoda*, in comparison with related carnivores, because of the extremely short pelvic symphysis.

The **abdominal tendon** [Bauchsehne + Beckensehne of German veterinary anatomists] is the insertion aponeurosis of the external oblique muscle. Anteriorly the aponeurosis of this muscle passes into the outer rectus sheath, while in the inguinal region it forms a large triangular sheet that fills the angle between the linea alba and the inguinal ligament. The aponeurosis is perforated by the inguinal canal; the part anterior to this perforation is the "abdominal tendon," the part posterior to it the "pelvic tendon" of the German anatomists.

The aponeurosis inserts into the posterior third of the inguinal ligament, from the level where the femoral vessels emerge back to the symphysis. The *lamina femoralis*, which in the dog and other domestic quadrupeds splits off from the abdominal aponeurosis at the lateral border of the inguinal ring and runs onto the medial surface of the thigh, appears to be wanting in *Ailuropoda*.

The **prepubic tendon** is a heavy, compact ligament extending from the iliopectineal eminence back to the anterior border of the pelvic symphysis, where it meets its mate of the opposite side. The tendon is more or less continuous with the inguinal ligament anteriorly. It lies superficial to the pectineus muscle, and arises chiefly from the origin tendon of that muscle. Where it passes over the origin tendon of the gracilis near the symphysis, the prepubic tendon is inseparably fused with the tendon of that muscle. The tendon provides attachment for the linea alba and the posteriormost fibers of the internal oblique.

The **inguinal ligament** lies at the juncture of the medial surface of the thigh and the wall of the abdomen. It extends from the anterior iliac spine to the iliopectineal eminence. Beyond the eminence it is continued posteriorly as the prepubic tendon. As in other quadrupeds, the inguinal ligament is poorly defined in *Ailuropoda*. Anteriorly it is little more than a fiber tract from which the posterior fibers of the internal oblique take origin. Posteriorly, where it bridges over the lacuna musculovasorum, it is a heavier and more sharply defined ligament.

Between the inguinal ligament and the ventral border of the pelvis there is a large gap, the **lacuna musculovasorum** (lacuna musculorum + lacuna vasorum of human anatomy; the iliopectineal ligament, which separates these in man, is wanting in quadrupeds). Through this opening the iliopsoas muscles and the femoral vessels and nerve pass from the abdominal cavity onto the thigh. In *Ailuropoda* (as in the dog) the femoral vessels lie *ventrad* of the iliopsoas, rather than posterior to it, and no true femoral ring can be distinguished. The lacuna is about 50 mm. long.

The **inguinal canal** is very short, its length being little more than the thickness of the abdominal wall. It is about 12 mm. long, and is directed posteriorly and slightly medially. It is situated about 30 mm. in front of the pelvic symphysis. The inlet to the canal, the *internal inguinal ring*, is formed by a hiatus in the internal oblique muscle; the anterodorsal border, between the limbs of the opening in the muscle, is formed by the inguinal ligament. The rectus abdominis does not participate in forming the medial border of the ring, as it does in the dog. The internal ring measures about 30 mm. in long diameter. The outlet, the *external inguinal ring*, is associated with the abdominal tendon of the external oblique. In the inguinal region this sheet splits to form the lateral and medial limbs of the ring. The fibers of the lateral limb radiate into the origin tendon of the pectineus and the prepubic tendon, while the fibers of the medial limb pass into the rectus sheath. The ring is completed posterodorsally by the prepubic tendon; i.e., the two limbs do not re-unite posteriorly, but merely form a ventral arch around the spermatic cord.

The **sheath** of the rectus abdominis is formed externally by the aponeurosis of the external oblique fused with the ventral layer of the aponeurosis of the internal oblique. Internally the sheath is formed by the dorsal layer of the aponeurosis of the internal oblique fused with the aponeurosis of the transversus abdominis. Thus the rectus muscle is embraced between the dorsal and ventral layers of the internal oblique aponeurosis. In the dog the inner layer of the rectus sheath ". . . is formed for the most part by the terminal aponeurosis of the transversus abdominis . . . and in the anterior portion in addition by an inner layer of the terminal aponeurosis of the obliquus abdominis internus." (Baum and Zietzschmann.)

The inguinal region of *Ailuropoda* differs from that of the dog (Baum and Zietzschmann; the only other carnivore in which this region is known) in several respects. The following peculiarities of the giant panda may be mentioned:

(1) The rectus does not participate in the formation of the inguinal canal.

(2) The rectus inserts into the posterior part of the symphysis.

(3) The cremaster does not arise from the posterior border of the internal oblique.

(4) The abdominal tendon of the external oblique does not form the entire circumference of the external inguinal ring.

### 4. Muscles of the Back

SUPERFICIAL SECONDARY BACK MUSCLES.—**M. cephalohumeralis** (= clavodeltoideus + clavotrapezius) (figs. 88, 134) is powerfully developed. Near its insertion it has a thickness of about 20 mm. Its origin, which is continuous with that of the acromiotrapezius, extends on the lambdoidal crest from the level of the dorsal border of the zygoma to the dorsal midline, then by aponeurosis from the ligamentum nuchae for 90 mm. along the midline of the neck. The anterior border is slightly overlapped by the temporalis. The fibers converge over the anterior border of the shoulder, and insert fleshily into the lower half of the deltoid ridge and the area between this ridge and a second ridge midway between the deltoid and pectoral ridges. At its insertion the muscle forms a partial raphe with the acromiodeltoid laterally and with the pectoralis superficialis and profundus medially.

The clavotrapezial part of the cephalohumeral is innervated by the spinal accessory, and the clavodeltoid part by the axillary nerve.

ACTION: Chief extensor of the fore leg.

**M. acromiotrapezius** (figs. 88, 134) is a thin, rectangular sheet arising from the dorsal midline by a long, broad aponeurotic sheet; fleshy fibers appear as the muscle crosses the scapular border. The muscle is thus sharply divided into two parts, a fleshy part lying over the scapula and an aponeurotic part between the vertebral border of the scapula and the dorsal midline. Its origin is continuous with the aponeurotic origin of the cephalohumeral anteriorly, and extends a distance of

110 mm. along the dorsal midline. The fleshy part of the muscle has a length of only 70 mm. Insertion is made for a distance of 105 mm. into the humeral half of the scapular spine.

**M. spinotrapezius** (figs. 88, 134) is triangular in outline. The anterior border is sharply concave, so that a portion of the underlying rhomboids and supraspinous fascia is exposed between this muscle and the acromiotrapezius. The posterior edge is concave and thin, but the muscle becomes quite heavy anteriorly. Origin is from the spinous processes of the thoracic vertebrae for a distance of 160 mm. The anterior border is overlapped slightly by the acromiotrapezius near the midline. The fleshy part of the muscle stops abruptly at the posterior border of the scapula, and the muscle continues forward and downward across the scapula as a wide, heavy aponeurosis that inserts into the superficial fascia of the infraspinatus. Thus the condition in the spinotrapezius is the reverse of that in the acromiotrapezius, where the part of the muscle lying over the scapula is fleshy and the part beyond the scapula is aponeurotic.

The relations of fleshy and aponeurotic parts of the acromio- and spinotrapezius to the underlying scapula in *Ailuropoda* appear to be pressure phenomena. Similar conditions are known from human anatomy, e.g., the digastric. It is noteworthy, however, that the trapezius is almost exactly the same in the Ursidae (verified in our specimens of *Selenarctos* and *Tremarctos*), and is surprisingly similar, considering the difference in body size and proportions, in *Ailurus*. The development of these extensive aponeurotic sheets is even indicated in *Bassariscus* and *Procyon*. The dogs, on the other hand, show nothing comparable to it, nor do other carnivores, including such large forms as the hyenas and lion.

ACTION: The trapezius muscles elevate the scapula and rotate it counterclockwise.

**M. latissimus dorsi** (figs. 88, 134) is very powerfully developed. It has the customary triangular form. The anterior border is overlapped by the spinotrapezius. It arises mostly by aponeurosis from the mid-dorsal line, fleshy fibers reaching the midline only at a point just behind the spinotrapezius. Ventrally and ventro-posteriorly the muscle takes origin from the seventh to eleventh ribs. Origin from the seventh rib is limited to a very few fibers, but the origin from each successive rib increases in length until on the eleventh it extends over 95 mm. The fibers converge toward the axilla, and insertion is made by two heads. The smaller head inserts chiefly into the inner face of the panniculus carnosus, a few of the most posterior fibers reaching the epitrochlearis. The main mass of the muscle forms a powerful raphe with the epitrochlearis, and these two muscles make a common insertion into the tendon of the teres major.

ACTION: Chief flexor of the arm.

M. rhomboideus (figs. 86, 88, 92, 134) is more or less divisible into two parts. The muscle is elongate triangular in outline, and arises in a continuous line from the lambdoidal crest at about the level of the dorsal border of the zygoma up to the dorsal midline, then back for 270 mm. along the midline of the neck. The muscle may be separated, particularly near its insertion, into anterior and posterior masses, of which the posterior is much the more extensive. Insertion is made into the dorsal half of the coracoid border and entire vertebral border of the scapula. The anterior edge of the posterior part lies partly over that of the anterior.

ACTION: Draws the scapula toward the vertebral column.

M. occipitoscapularis (rhomboideus anterior or capitis of authors) (fig. 134) is a narrow band arising from the lambdoidal crest. The muscle runs backward, separated from the rhomboideus by the dorsal branch of the A. and V. transversa colli, to insert on the coracovertebral border of the scapula, beneath the insertion of the anterior part of the rhomboideus.

ACTION: Draws the scapula forward.

M. atlantoscapularis (levator scapulae ventralis of authors; omo-cleido-transversarius of Carlsson) (figs. 86, 134) is a narrow, heavy band arising from the transverse process of the atlas. For a short distance it is inseparable from the first digitation of the levator scapulae, with which it has a common origin. Immediately distad of its origin it is easily separable into two subequal parts, which embrace a branch of the fourth cervical nerve between them. This separation loses its identity near the insertion, which is made, by means of a short fine tendon, into the metacromion of the scapula, at the juncture of the acromiodeltoideus, the spinodeltoideus, and the acromiotrapezius.

M. serratus dorsalis anterior (fig. 86) arises by fleshy slips from the posterior borders of the fifth to tenth ribs. The fibers from these six origins more or less unite to form a continuous sheet that inserts aponeurotically into the dorsal fascia.

M. serratus dorsalis posterior (fig. 86) is limited to two slips. The more anterior of these arises from the twelfth rib; the posterior from the

thirteenth, with a few fibers coming from the fourteenth. The fibers run straight dorsad, to insert independently of one another into the dorsolumbar fascia by means of aponeuroses.

DEEP INTRINSIC BACK MUSCLES.—M. splenius (figs. 86, 87, 92) is very powerfully developed, particularly along its lateral border, where it attains a thickness of 15 mm. Posteriorly the muscle arises by a wide tendinous aponeurosis from the dorsolumbar fascia at about the level of the fifth thoracic vertebra; this aponeurosis lies beneath the origin of the serratus posterior superior. Origin, by a similar aponeurosis, is taken along the midline as far forward as the lambdoidal crest of the skull. This medial aponeurosis has a width of 15-20 mm. Insertion is made on the lambdoidal crest, just beneath the insertion of the rhomboideus, and from the mastoid process down to its tip. Tendinous intersections are absent.

The usual undifferentiated muscle mass occupies the trough formed by the spines and transverse processes of the lumbar vertebrae. At the level of the last rib it divides to form three muscles: the iliocostalis, the longissimus, and the spinalis. The medial part of the muscle mass is covered with a heavy aponeurosis, which gives rise to many of the superficial fibers of all three muscles.

M. iliocostalis (figs. 87, 88, 92) is the most lateral of the superficial back muscles. It gives off a tendinous slip to each of the ribs near its angle and to the transverse process of the last cervical vertebra. The more posterior tendons pass over one rib before inserting, those farther forward over two. Slips from all the ribs except the first four join the muscle as it runs craniad.

M. longissimus (figs. 87, 88, 92) is the middle one of the three superficial back muscles. There is no demarcation between the pars dorsi and pars cervicis of human anatomy. On the other hand, the muscle is sharply divided into a lumbar part (M. ilio-lumbalis [Virchow], Pars lumborum m. longissimus dorsi [Winckler], M. longissimus lumborum [Eisler]), arising from the ilium and covered by the heavy deep layer of the lumbar fascia; and a thoracic part. The thoracic part arises from the lumbar fascia, and farther anteriorly from the fascia between itself and the spinalis. There is the usual double insertion: medially by fasciculi into the anapophyses of the lumbar and thoracic vertebrae, and laterally by long tendons into all but the last four ribs and into the transverse processes of the last six cervical vertebrae.

M. longissimus capitis (fig. 92) arises from the transverse processes of the last three cervical ver-

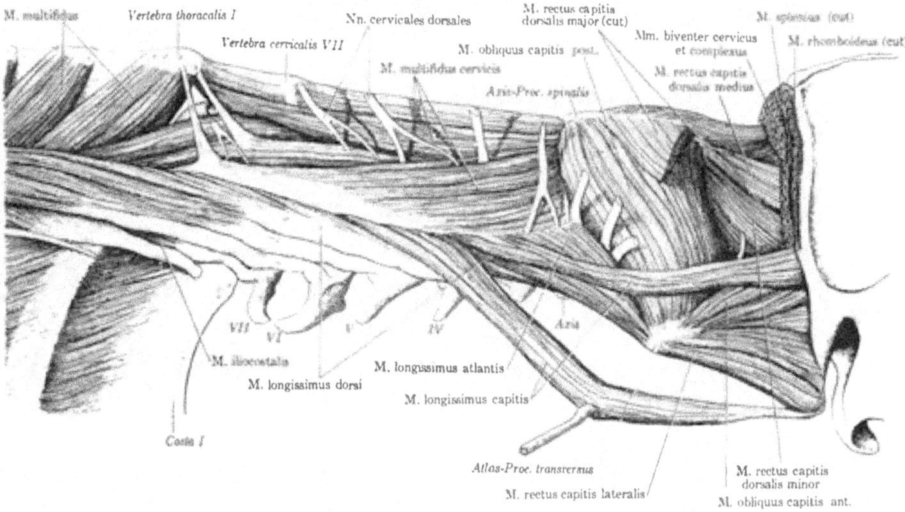

FIG. 92. Deep muscles of neck and anterior thorax of *Ailuropoda*, right side.

tebrae. It is composed of two very slender heads. One of these joins the ventral border of the splenius in the usual way, and thus inserts into the mastoid process. The other head, which comes from the anterior fibers of the common origin, lies deep to the splenius along the ventral border of the complexus, inserting with it into the occipital bone.

**M. longissimus atlantis** (fig. 92) is slightly larger than the combined heads of the longissimus capitis. It arises from the articular processes of the third, fourth, and fifth cervicals, and inserts into the tip of the wing of the atlas.

**M. spinalis dorsi** (figs. 87, 88) is the most medial and most extensive of the superficial back muscles. It is present only in the thoracic region. Origin is from the anterior edge of the deep lumbar fascia, and farther anteriorly from the fascia between itself and the longissimus. The fibers run diagonally craniad and mesad, and insert, by tendons that become progressively longer, anteriorly into the tips of the spinous processes of all the thoracic and the first cervical vertebrae.

**M. semispinalis** is represented only by the capitis, which is separable into a dorsal biventer cervicis and a ventral complexus. **M. biventer cervicis** (fig. 92) has three diagonal tendinous intersections. The muscle begins at the level of the fifth thoracic vertebra, arising posteriorly from a wide aponeurotic fascia that covers the underlying muscles. Additional origin is taken by means of tendinous fasciculi from the tips of the spines

of the fourth, third, and second thoracics, and anterior to this from the ligamentum nuchae, as well as from the transverse processes of the second to fifth thoracics. Insertion is fleshily into the occipital crest near the dorsal midline. **M. complexus** lies beneath the biventer cervicis posteriorly. It begins at the level of the second thoracic vertebra, arising posteriorly from an aponeurotic fascia similar to that of the biventer. Additional origin is taken from the transverse processes of the first two thoracic and last four cervical vertebrae. Insertion is made, by mingled fleshy and tendon fibers, into the medial half of the occipital bone. The muscle lies partly deep to the biventer cervicis at its insertion.

**M. multifidus** (fig. 92) is continued craniad from the extensor caudae medialis. In the lumbar region it is deep to the spinalis. The muscle is, as usual, best developed in the lumbar region, where it is not separable into individual fasciculi; at the anterior end of the deep lumbar fascia it is fused with the spinalis. In the thoracic region the multifidus is more or less separable into fasciculi, which arise by mingled tendon and muscle fibers from the transverse processes of the vertebrae and pass forward over one vertebra to insert on the spinous process of the next. *M. multifidus cervicis* is well developed, consisting of three bundles of longitudinal fibers extending between the articular processes and the spines of the cervical vertebrae.

**M. rectus capitis dorsalis major** (fig. 92) is a rather thin triangular muscle arising from the anterior two-thirds of the crest of the spine of the axis, and inserting into the occipital bone below the lambdoidal crest. The muscles from either side diverge as they leave the axis, so that a triangular cavity, bounded ventrally by the atlas and filled with fat, remains between their medial borders.

M. rectus capitis dorsalis medius (fig. 92) is apparently represented by a few fibers, superficial to the medial fibers of the rectus minor and with a less oblique fiber direction, that arise from the anterior tip of the spine of the atlas and follow the border of the triangular cavity described above, to insert with the rest of the rectus on the skull.

M. rectus capitis dorsalis minor (fig. 92) lies partly beneath and partly laterad of the medius. It is a large muscle with the usual origin from the anterior border of the dorsal arch of the axis, and inserts into the occipital bone beneath the major and medius.

M. rectus capitis lateralis (fig. 92) is a relatively small muscle lying along the ventral border of the obliquus capitis anterior. Origin is from the ventral surface of the tip of the wing of the atlas, deep to the origin of the rectus capitis ventralis. The muscle expands somewhat toward its insertion, which is made into the posterior surface of the mastoid process near its outer edge.

M. obliquus capitis anterior (fig. 92) is also relatively small. It is triangular in outline, arising from the tip of the wing of the atlas and inserting into the back of the skull just above the mastoid process. The dorsal edge of the muscle is overlain by the second head of the longissimus capitis.

M. obliquus capitis posterior (fig. 92) greatly exceeds the anterior in size. Origin is from the entire spinous process of the atlas. The fiber direction is nearly vertical. Insertion is into the wing of the atlas.

5. *Muscles of the Tail* Figure 93.

M. extensor caudae medialis is the posterior continuation of the multifidus, and is in contact with its mate along the dorsal midline. Origin is from the spinous processes of the last two lumbar vertebrae and from the spine of the sacrum. Insertion is into the prezygapophyses (on the anterior vertebrae) and dorsal surfaces (posterior vertebrae) of the caudals from the second on, by tendons that unite with the tendons of the extensor caudae lateralis.

M. extensor caudae lateralis arises from the deep surface of the deep lumbar fascia, from the fused transverse processes of the sacral vertebrae, and from the transverse processes (or bodies, where these are absent) of the caudal vertebrae. Long

tendons extend posteromesad over three vertebrae, uniting with the tendons of the extensor caudae medialis.

M. abductor caudae externus arises from the dorsal surface of the fused transverse processes of the sacrum, from the fascia surrounding the base of the tail, and from the transverse processes of the first four caudals; there is no attachment to the ilium. Insertion is into the transverse processes (or the sides) of the three following vertebrae.

M. abductor caudae internus is a relatively small fusiform muscle lying ventrad of the external abductor. Origin is by a rather wide, flat tendon that splits off from the tendon of the iliocaudalis, thus coming from the medial surface of the ilium. Insertion is into the transverse processes of the first six caudals, in common with the insertions of the external abductor.

M. iliocaudalis is a thin triangular sheet. Origin, by means of a wide tendinous sheet externally and fleshy fibers internally, is from the medial surface of the ilium caudad of the sacro-iliac articulation. A long terminal tendon from the fusiform part of the muscle joins a tendon of the medial division of the flexor caudae longus, to insert into the ventral side of the sixth caudal. The remainder of the muscle inserts fleshily into the transverse processes of the posterior sacral and first two caudal vertebrae.

M. pubocaudalis is a very wide, thin sheet lying immediately external to the levator ani. The dorsal fibers arise from the tendon of the iliocaudalis, the ventral fibers from the dorsal (inner) surface of the symphysis pelvis. Insertion is into the ventral surfaces of the fourth and fifth caudals.

M. flexor caudae longus is composed of two sets of fasciculi, which are separated proximally by the iliolumbalis. The *lateral* division consists of successive fasciculi arising from the posterior end of the sacrum and from the transverse processes (or sides) of the caudal vertebrae. The strong terminal tendons pass over three vertebrae before inserting into the transverse process (or side) of the fourth succeeding vertebra. The *medial* division arises just mesad of the lateral division. It extends from the anterior end of the sacrum to the third caudal vertebra, and its ventral edge is partly united to the adjacent edge of the iliocaudalis. It is composed of three successive fasciculi, each of which terminates in a tendon. The tendon of the most anterior fasciculus joins the much stouter tendon of the middle fasciculus; together they insert with the pubocaudalis into the ventral surface of the fifth caudal. The tendon of the most posterior fasciculus joins a tendon of the long flexor, and inserts into the ventral side of the sixth caudal.

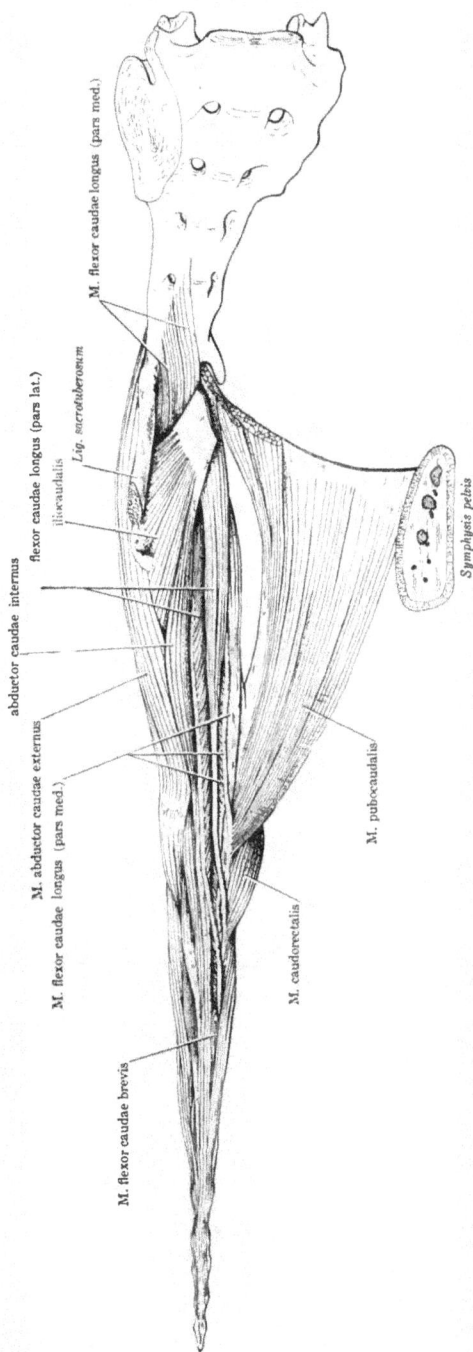

M. flexor caudae longus (pars med.)

flexor caudae longus (pars lat.)

Lig. sacrotuberosum

iliocaudalis

abductor caudae internus

M. abductor caudae externus

M. flexor caudae longus (pars med.)

Symphysis pelvis

M. pubocaudalis

M. caudorectalis

M. flexor caudae brevis

FIG. 93. Muscles of the tail of *Ailuropoda*, oblique ventral view.

171

M. flexor caudae brevis consists of short fasciculi lying along the ventral midline from the fifth caudal on. Origin is from the ventral surface of the vertebra, and the fibers pass over one vertebra to insert into the next.

### 6. Muscles of the Perineum

M. levator ani is a thin triangular sheet of muscle lying deep to the coccygeus, and over the lateral surfaces of the rectum and urethra. Its fiber direction is at right angles to that of the coccygeus. Origin is chiefly by means of a thin aponeurosis from the medial surface of the ascending ramus of the pubis; some of the posterior fibers are continued from the retractor penis, and some are blended with the sphincter ani externus. Insertion is into the centra of the anterior caudal vertebrae.

M. sphincter ani externus is a narrow ring of muscle fibers surrounding the anus. The two halves of the muscle meet below the anus and immediately behind the bulbus urethrae; some of the fibers are continued into the suspensory ligament of the penis, which attaches to the posterior end of the symphysis; others attach to the bulbus urethrae and ischiocavernosus.

M. ischiocavernosus is a very short muscle arising from the posterior border of the ischium, 25 mm. above the symphysis. It is closely applied to the posterior wall of the corpus cavernosum penis, and terminates by spreading out over this structure.

M. bulbocavernosus is a thin layer of diagonal muscle fibers surrounding the bulbus urethrae. The two muscles arise from a median raphe on the ventral side, and insert into the posterior part of the root of the penis.

M. sphincter urethrae membranaceae is a delicate layer of transverse muscle fibers surrounding the urethra proximad of the bulb. It encases the urethra for a distance of 30 mm.

M. retractor penis is a pale muscle arising as a continuation of fibers from the levator ani. It meets its mate from the opposite side just below the rectum, and the two muscles run side by side to the base of the glans penis, where they insert. A few fibers split off and insert into the side of the radix penis.

M. caudorectalis is a prominent unpaired muscle lying along the midline in the anal region. It is distinctly lighter in color than the surrounding musculature. Origin is from the dorsal side of the rectum in the midline. The fibers pass backward and upward as a fusiform mass, to insert on the ventral surface of the sixth caudal vertebra.

### III. MUSCLES OF THE FORE LEG
#### A. MUSCLES OF THE SHOULDER GIRDLE

M. supraspinatus (figs. 88, 95, 96, 133) is covered externally by the usual heavy tendon-like fascia, which cannot be detached without cutting into the muscle substance. This tendinous fascia is continued diagonally downward to insert on the acromion process, immediately behind the origin of the acromiodeltoideus; the fascia over the distal end of the muscle is normal. The muscle occupies the whole of the supraspinous fossa, overlapping the cephalic border. It is powerfully developed, having a maximum thickness of 50 mm. Insertion is by fleshy fibers into the greater tuberosity of the humerus.

ACTION: Extends the arm on the scapula.

M. infraspinatus (fig. 95) arises from the entire infraspinatus fossa. It is covered with a tendinous aponeurosis down to the origin of the spinodeltoideus. The muscle is divisible into two parts, the one nearest the glenoid border of the scapula being slightly the smaller. The insertion tendons of the two parts are more or less distinct, but are fused where they are in contact. Insertion is into the prominent infraspinatus fossa on the greater tuberosity of the humerus.

ACTION: Chief lateral rotator of the arm. Its tendon acts as a lateral collateral ligament of the shoulder joint.

M. acromiodeltoideus (figs. 88, 95, 134) is powerfully developed, having a thickness of 23 mm. at its posterior edge. It is covered with tendinous fascia superficially. The muscle arises, partly fleshily and partly tendinously, from the whole tip of the acromion. It is bipennate, to two halves of approximately equal width. Insertion is by two heads, which correspond to the halves of the bipennate muscle. The anterior half inserts on the shaft of the humerus immediately above the insertion of the cephalohumeral, anterior to the deltoid ridge. The posterior part inserts partly on the lateral head of the triceps, posteriorly forming a strong raphe with the spinodeltoid.

ACTION: Chief abductor of the arm.

M. spinodeltoideus (fig. 88) arises almost wholly from the fascia of the infraspinatus; only its anterior tip reaches the scapular spine. Most of its fibers meet the acromiodeltoideus in a tendinous raphe, although a few insert on the triceps lateralis.

ACTION: Flexes the arm.

M. teres minor (fig. 95) is a small muscle, closely applied to the inferior border of the infraspinatus, from which it is inseparable at its origin; it is not attached to the long head of the triceps. It arises by heavy aponeurotic fibers that are firmly attached to the underlying infraspinatus on the deep surface, from a small area on the axillary

M. subscapularis (figs. 96, 133) is composed of three main divisions. The two anterior subdivisions are composed of numerous bipennate units, whereas the posterior one is made up of units with parallel fibers. Insertion is into the proximal end

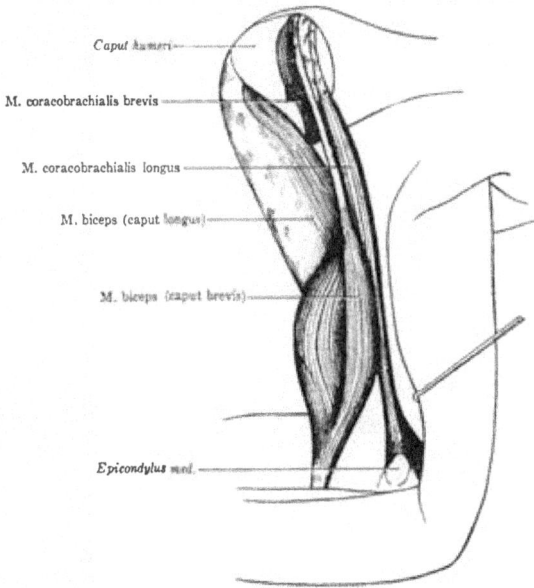

FIG. 94. Right arm of bear (*Ursus americanus*) to show short head of biceps. Medial view.

border of the scapula just proximad of the middle. Insertion is made by a short stout tendon into the head of the humerus, immediately distad of the insertion of the infraspinatus.

ACTION: Flexes the arm and rotates it laterally.

M. teres major (figs. 95, 96) is powerfully developed. It arises from the usual fossa at the distal end of the glenoid border of the scapula, and from a raphe that it forms with the subscapularis on one side and the infraspinatus on the other. Insertion is made, by means of a powerful flat tendon 30 mm. in width, common to it and the latissimus dorsi, on the roughened area on the medial surface of the shaft of the humerus, distad of the bicipital groove and immediately mesad of the pectoral ridge. An extensive bursa (Bursa m. teretis major of human anatomy) is inserted between the tendon and the shaft of the humerus.

ACTION: Assists the latissimus dorsi in flexing the arm, and the subscapularis in medial rotation of the arm.

of the humerus, immediately below and behind the lesser tuberosity. The insertion tendon of the first (crania) unit is superficial to those of the other two units.

ACTION: Chief medial rotator of the arm. The upper part of the muscle acts as an extensor of the arm.

B. MUSCLES OF THE UPPER ARM

M. biceps brachii (figs. 96, 97, 133) is a fusiform muscle that, in the position in which the arm was fixed, is rather sharply flexed at the site of the bicipital arch. The muscle displays a rather curious structure. It arises by a single (glenoid) head, but in the proximal two-thirds of the muscle a narrow anterior group of fibers is more or less separable from the main mass of the muscle. These fibers, which are particularly conspicuous because they lack the glistening tendinous covering of the rest of the muscle, arise from the origin tendon of the biceps as it passes through the bicipital groove and insert extensively into the anterior surface of

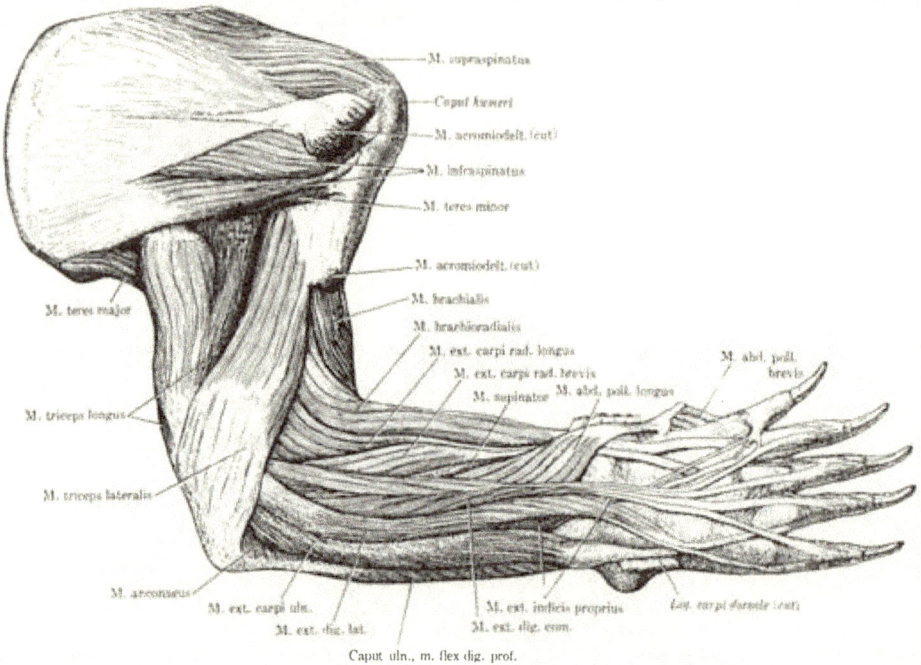

FIG. 95.  Muscles of the right fore leg of *Ailuropoda*, lateral aspect.

the main mass of the biceps, as far distad as the bicipital arch.  There was no indication of a short head in two specimens dissected.

The biceps arises from the bicipital tubercle at the glenoid border of the scapula, by a long, flattened tendon that runs through the bicipital groove, enclosed in the joint capsule, onto the anterior surface of the humerus.  The tendon is continued into an extensive area of tendinous aponeurosis on the external surface of the belly of the muscle, and a more limited area of similar tissue on the internal surface.  The most medial (superficial) fibers of the biceps terminate in a well-defined lacertus fibrosus, which is continued into the fascia over the pronator teres.  The tendon of insertion begins midway on the deep surface of the muscle and continues distad as a distinct tendinous band on the deep surface of the muscle; this band does not form a longitudinal furrow as it does in the dog.  The muscle fibers insert into it along its length at a very oblique angle, so that the biceps is a pennate muscle rather than a parallel-fibered one as in man.  This tendinous band is continued into a short, very stout, flattened tendon, 12 mm. in width, that passes between the brachioradialis and pronator

teres to insert into the prominent bicipital tubercle of the radius.

ACTION: Flexes the forearm.

The biceps is normally, but not invariably, two-headed in the bears, a degenerate short head usually arising from the coracoid process with the brachioradialis (Windle and Parsons, 1897, p. 391).  I have dissected the biceps in a young black bear, with the following results (fig. 94).  The long head is similar to that of *Ailuropoda* except that the small group of accessory fibers coming from the origin tendon lies along the posterior border of the muscle, and the tendon of insertion does not begin far proximad on the deep surface of the muscle.  The short head begins as a slender flattened tendon arising from the fascia of the coracobrachialis just below the head of the humerus.  At about the middle of the humerus the tendon begins to form a slender muscle belly that lies against the posterior surface of the long head.  A few of the most superficial fibers insert via a lacertus fibrosus into the fascia over the pronator teres, but most of this belly inserts with the long head.  The biceps was similar in an adult *Tremarctos ornatus* dissected by me.  Windle and Parsons found a "very feebly

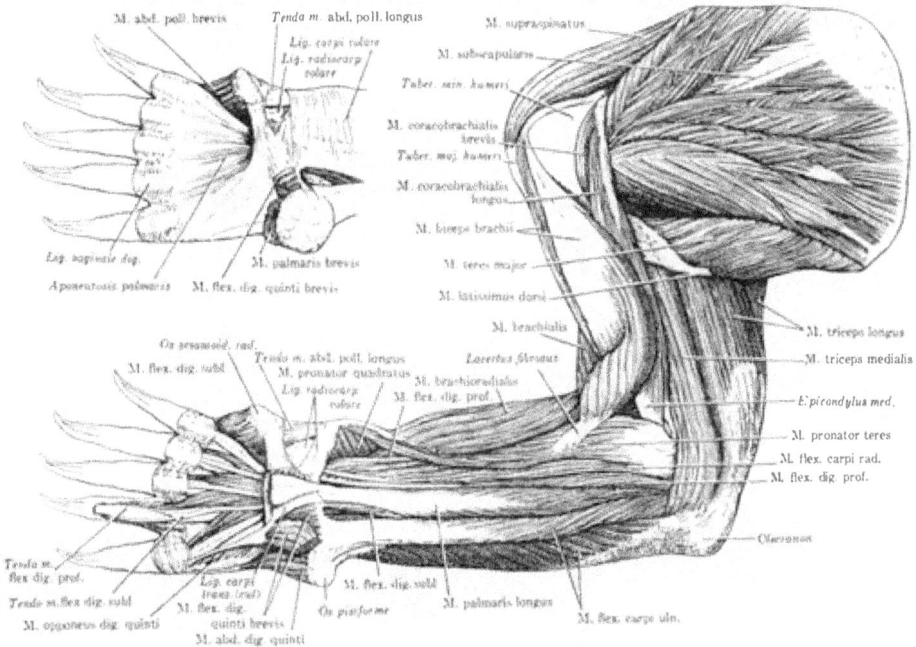

FIG. 96.   Muscles of the right fore leg of *Ailuropoda*, medial aspect.

marked" short head in *Procyon*, and it was also present in *Potos*. According to Carlsson (verified by me) there are two heads in *Ailurus*.

**M. coracobrachialis** (fig. 96) is composed of two heads, a brevis and a longus. The two heads arise, by a common flattened tendon, from the coracoid process of the scapula. The short head arises from the tendon deep to the long head; the tendon itself bifurcates and is continued along the posterior border of each head. The branch of the musculocutaneous nerve that supplies the biceps passes between the two heads.

The short head passes around the end of M. sub-scapularis and inserts into the posterior angle of the shaft of the humerus immediately proximad of the tendon of the latissimus dorsi.

The long head runs to the elbow behind the biceps. Near its insertion it bifurcates, the anterior fibers inserting on the bony bridge over the entepicondylar foramen, while the posterior fibers insert on the humerus immediately behind the foramen. The median nerve and branches of the profunda vein pass between these two parts of the muscle.

ACTION: Assists the supraspinatus in extending the arm on the scapula, and helps return the arm

to the intermediate position from either medial or lateral rotation.

**M. brachialis** (figs. 88, 95, 96, 133, 134) is composed of two heads, a long head arising along the deltoid ridge, and a short head arising from the lateral condylar ridge of the humerus. The two heads unite to make a common insertion. The *long head* is intimately fused with the lateral head of the triceps proximally, where the two muscles are attached by a common tendon to the surgical neck of the humerus immediately behind the deltoid ridge. From here the origin of the brachialis continues distad in a U-shaped line, one limb following the deltoid ridge, then the pectoral ridge below the juncture of these two ridges, to within 50 mm. of the distal end of the shaft; the other limb extends down the posterior side of the shaft to the beginning of the lateral epicondylar ridge at about the middle of the humerus. The *short head* arises in a narrow line from the anterior border of the lateral epicondylar ridge down to within 20 mm. of the distal articulation, then across the anterior face of the humerus to meet the distal end of the origin line of the long head.

The two heads make a common insertion. Some of the fibers insert into the distal two-thirds of a tendinous arch that extends from the coronoid process of the ulna upward (ectad) and forward (distad) to the intermuscular septum between the pronator teres and the brachioradialis. The main insertion is by a stout tendon into the prominent depression on the anterior surface of the ulna, immediately below the coronoid process.

INNERVATION: The long head is supplied by the radial nerve, the short head by the musculocutaneous nerve.

ACTION: Flexes the forearm.

Windle and Parsons (1897, p. 393), in their review of the musculature of the Carnivora, state that they did not find the short head in any carnivore, and that they encountered only radial innervation, although "further observation is necessary before a definite statement can be made." They regarded two heads, with radial and musculocutaneous innervation, respectively, as the "typical arrangement" for the Mammalia. Carlsson (1925) describes a single muscle, with both radial and musculocutaneous innervation, in *Ailurus*.

M. epitrochlearis (fig. 88) is an extremely powerful muscle embracing the whole posterior part of the upper arm. The internal border is carried well around onto the medial border of the arm. The main mass of the muscle arises, by means of a stout tendinous raphe, from the latissimus dorsi. A few of the fibers on the medial border, representing the medial head of the muscle, arise from a raphe that is formed with the ventral fibers of the panniculus carnosus. Insertion is by means of a tendinous aponeurosis into the posterior and medial parts of the olecranon.

ACTION: Extends the forearm.

M. triceps longus (figs. 88, 95, 96, 133, 134) is a complex and extremely powerful muscle, composed of incompletely separable lateral and medial heads. The lateral head is triangular in form, and proximally shows an incipient division into a superficial posterior part and a slightly deeper anterior part. It arises, by muscle fibers covered externally by tendon fibers, from the proximal two-thirds of the axillary border of the scapula. The medial head takes a short tendinous origin, deep to that of the lateral head, from the axillary border of the scapula near the neck.

The two heads fuse distally, the external fibers of the lateral head forming a powerful tendon that receives fibers from the triceps lateralis. Insertion is into the tip of the olecranon.

M. triceps lateralis (figs. 88, 95, 134) is a powerful prismatic muscle running diagonally across the external surface of the upper arm and extending medially behind the humerus. It has a maximum width (near the humero-ulnar articulation) of 45 mm.; medially it is continuous with the long head of the triceps medialis, except near its origin. The muscle arises chiefly from the surface of the brachialis lying immediately beneath it. These two muscles are covered by a heavy common tendon layer proximally. The common origin begins on the surgical neck of the humerus in the area immediately behind the deltoid ridge, a few of the fibers coming from the articular capsule. The lateral triceps immediately becomes superficial to the brachialis, and takes further extensive origin from the surface of the latter, until the two are separated by the brachioradialis. Insertion of the lateral triceps is made chiefly into the posterolateral border of the olecranon, although the distal part of the anterior edge of the muscle makes a powerful insertion into the fascia of the forearm and posteriorly there is some insertion into the lateral head of the triceps longus.

M. triceps medialis (figs. 96, 133, 134) is the smallest of the three heads of the triceps. It is composed of two very poorly defined heads, the posterior of which is separable from the triceps lateralis only for a short distance after its origin. The muscle is visible only on the medial surface of the arm, where the posterior head appears as a narrow muscle lying between the triceps longus and the coracobrachialis longus.

The posterior (long) head arises from a triangular area on the posterior surface of the neck of the humerus, the base of the triangle lying against the lip of the articular surface. The most superficial fibers arise from the joint capsule. It is independent of the intermediate head only for about its proximal third, the main branch of the radial nerve and branches of the profunda brachialis artery and vein passing through the interval between them. Immediately distad of its origin the lateral (deep) edge of this head fuses with the adjacent edge of the triceps lateralis, and from this point on, the two muscles are completely inseparable.

The intermediate head of the triceps medialis takes an extensive tendinous origin along the posteromedial side of the shaft of the humerus. Its origin extends from a point above the scar for the teres major distad almost as far as the end of the pectoral ridge. This head has little independence from the other head of the triceps medialis.

Insertion of the fibers coming from the triceps medialis is made, without intervention of a tendon, into the medial and dorsomedial surface of the olecranon.

ACTION: The triceps is the chief extensor of the forearm; it also acts (especially the lateralis) as a tensor of the forearm fascia.

M. anconaeus (figs. 95, 134) is a powerful triangular muscle extending more than one-third the distance up the shaft of the humerus. Medially it is inseparable from the triceps. It arises from the well-marked triangular area on the posterior side of the distal end of the shaft of the humerus, the origin extending down over the posterior side of the lateral epicondyle. Insertion is on the posterior side of the olecranon, immediately above the insertion of the triceps.

ACTION: Assists the triceps in extending the forearm.

M. epitrochleo-anconaeus (anconaeus internus) is not present as an independent muscle. The most medial fibers of the distal part of the triceps medialis partly overlie the ulnar nerve and are innervated by a branch of it, however, and apparently represent the epitrochleo-anconaeus. These fibers insert on the inner side of the olecranon, but they arise from the shaft of the humerus some distance above the epicondyle.

### C. MUSCLES OF THE FOREARM

M. palmaris longus (fig. 96) is single. It is square in cross section, and fusiform when viewed from the medial side of the forearm. The muscle takes a very restricted origin from the medial epicondyle immediately proximad of the origin of the humeral part of the flexor carpi ulnaris, from which its fibers are incompletely separable near the origin. Near the carpus the muscle separates into a stout superficial tendon and an entirely separate deeper fleshy part. The tendon expands into the palmar aponeurosis, while the fleshy part inserts into the proximal edge of the transverse fibers of the palmar aponeurosis (see below), which here form a sheath for the tendon. The fleshy part does not represent the "palmaris longus internus" of Windle and Parsons.

ACTION: Flexes the manus and tenses the palmar aponeurosis.

The Aponeurosis palmaris (fig. 96) consists chiefly of fibers that arise from the tendon of the long palmar muscle and radiate toward the digits. The fibers extend about equally to all five digits, lying on the palmar surface as far distad as the metacarpophalangeal joint. Here the palmar aponeurosis gives way to the vaginal ligaments on the volar surface of the digit, although fibers of the aponeurosis are continued distad for some distance along the sides of the digit. A powerful group of fibers arises from the palmar aponeurosis over metacarpal 5 and sweeps transversely across the palm, to insert on the distal end of the radial sesamoid. The *fasciculi transversi* of human anatomy could not be demonstrated.

Transverse fibers in the antebrachial fascia corresponding to the Lig. carpi volare are present chiefly on the radial side, where they form a wide band running across the wrist as far as the tendon of the long palmar muscle.

M. pronator teres (figs. 96, 97, 133) is a flat muscle lying partly beneath the brachioradialis. It arises from the anterior side of the proximal end of the medial epicondyle of the humerus. It is inseparable from the adjacent border of the flexor carpi radialis for about half the length of the forearm. The fibers run distad and radialward, partly beneath the brachialis. Insertion is made, mostly beneath the insertion of the brachialis, by means of a wide aponeurotic tendon into the radial side of the distal two-thirds of the radius.

ACTION: Pronates the forearm, turning the palm upward; flexes the forearm.

M. flexor carpi radialis (figs. 96, 133) is so intimately united to the pronator teres at its origin that the two appear as a single muscle. It arises from about the center of the anterior side of the medial epicondyle, its origin being continuous with that of the pronator teres. The muscle tapers gradually toward its insertion, becoming tendinous on its ulnar side at about the middle of the forearm but remaining fleshy down to the carpus on its radial side. The stout terminal tendon enters the hand through an osteofibrous canal lying partly beneath the tubercle of the scapholunar, and inserts into the base of the second metacarpal (fig. 99; Wood-Jones says the second and third metacarpals).

ACTION: Flexes the wrist.

M. flexor carpi ulnaris (figs. 96, 133) consists of two completely independent parts, which are separated by the ulnar nerve. The pars ulnaris is the more superficial, and forms the ulnar contour of the forearm. It arises, chiefly by fleshy fibers, from the posteromedial part of the olecranon. Additional origin is taken medially from the fascia of the upper arm; and the lateral border, which is tendinous, is continued with the antebrachial fascia for about 70 mm. distad of the elbow. The fibers converge to a narrow terminal tendon, which inserts on the proximal side of the pisiform dorsad of the insertion of the pars humeralis. The pars humeralis lies mostly internal to the pars ulnaris. It arises from the distal side of the medial epicondyle, where it is inseparable from the palmaris longus for a short distance, and terminates in a wide, flat tendon that inserts on the proximal side of the pisiform (fig. 98).

ACTION: Flexes the wrist and abducts the hand ulnaward.

M. flexor digitorum sublimis (figs. 97, 98) is represented by three small fleshy heads arising from the volar surface of the flexor digitorum profundus. Proximally their fibers interdigitate inextricably with the most superficial head (1) of the profundus. The sublimis extends only about the distal third

quadratus, so that its proximal end extends onto the volar surface of the radius. This head lies deep to the pronator teres and flexor carpi radialis, and most of its fibers insert into the tendinous part of head 1.

(4) A narrow, deep head arises from the medial

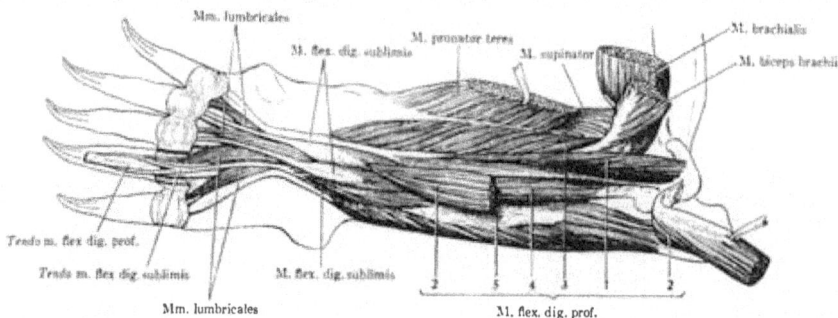

FIG. 97.   Deep muscles of right forearm of *Ailuropoda*, medial view.

of the forearm. Each of the three parts of the sublimis forms a slender terminal tendon beneath the transverse carpal ligament. These are distributed to digits 2, 3, and 4, and are perforated at the metacarpophalangeal joints by the tendons of the profundus. Insertion is into the base of the second phalanx of the digit.

ACTION: Flexes the middle phalanx on the proximal phalanx of digits 2-4.

M. flexor digitorum profundus (figs. 97, 98, 133, 134) is very powerfully developed. It is composed of five heads, and terminates in five strong perforating tendons that are distributed to the digits. Insertion is into the base of the terminal phalanx. The structure of the parts of the muscle is as follows:

(1) The most superficial head arises from the middle part of the medial epicondyle. It lies along the ulnar border of the flexor carpi radialis. Most of the tendon fibers arising from this head are continued into the tendon of digit 1, but it does not form a separate tendon as Wood-Jones (1939a) stated.

(2) A head arises from the lower part of the medial epicondyle, deep to the origins of the palmaris longus and humeral head of the flexor carpi ulnaris. Distally this head attaches to the underlying ulnar head (5), in addition to giving rise to the three heads of the flexor digitorum sublimis.

(3) A head arises from the proximal two-thirds of the volar surface of the radius; the medial border of the origin follows the border of the pronator

border of the condyle of the humerus, just in front of the epicondyle. Its fibers insert on the ulnar head (5).

(5) The ulnar head is by far the largest element of the muscle. It arises from the entire volar surface of the ulna, including the olecranon. The distal three-fourths of its volar surface is covered with a heavy tendinous aponeurosis, and it is chiefly from this aponeurosis that the terminal tendons of the flexor digitorum profundus arise.

Wood-Jones mentions a deep head arising from the olecranon; judging from its position he referred to the head arising from the condyle (4).

ACTION: Flexes all the digits, especially the terminal phalanx on the middle phalanx.

M. pronator quadratus (figs. 96, 133) is an extensive, thick fleshy mass, trapezoidal in outline. The origin is somewhat narrower than the insertion, and is taken from the distal third of the volar surface of the ulna. The muscle fans out somewhat to its insertion, which is made into the distal half of the volar surface of the radius.

ACTION: Pronates the forearm and hand, turning the palm upward.

M. brachioradialis (supinator longus of authors) (figs. 95, 96, 133, 134) is very powerfully developed, with a width of about 50 mm. on the forearm. It arises by two heads, which are separated by a branch of the radial nerve. One head arises from the lateral epicondylar ridge, from a point 60 mm. proximad of the epicondyle up past the middle of the humeral shaft, some of its fibers being joined to adjacent parts of the extensor carpi radialis longus. The other head arises from the deep surface of the triceps lateralis. The two heads promptly fuse, and the resulting common mass inserts into the prominence on the radial side of the distal end of the radius.

ACTION: Flexes the forearm; supinates the forearm and hand, turning the palm downward.

M. extensor carpi radialis longus (figs. 95, 134) arises from the anterior face of the lateral epicondylar ridge. Its ulnar border is inseparable from the adjacent border of the extensor carpi radialis brevis. At about the middle of the forearm the muscle ends in a relatively slender tendon that passes across the carpus, deep to the extensor brevis pollicis, to insert into the radial side of the second metacarpal, just proximad of the center of the bone.

ACTION: Extends the hand and abducts it radialward.

M. extensor carpi radialis brevis (figs. 95, 134) is somewhat more slender than the longus. It is more or less inseparable from the longus laterally, and is even more closely united to the extensor digitorum communis medially, where a tendinous septum is formed. It arises from the distal part of the lateral epicondylar ridge. It remains fleshy somewhat farther distad than the longus, terminating in a tendon that inserts near the base of the third metacarpal, on the radial side of the bone.

ACTION: Extends the hand and adducts it radialward.

M. extensor digitorum communis (figs. 95, 134) is inseparable proximally from the adjacent muscles on either side. It arises from the distal part of the lateral epicondylar ridge. The muscle tapers gradually toward the wrist, becoming very narrow at the proximal border of the dorsal carpal ligament. It terminates in four tendons, which go to the basal phalanges of the second, third, fourth, and fifth digits.

The tendon going to the second digit comes off first, about 20 mm. proximad of the others; the muscle fibers going to this tendon are quite separate from those going to the other three for most of the length of the muscle. The tendon to the third digit comes off independently at the proximal border of the dorsal carpal ligament. The tendon to the fourth and fifth digits is common at first, dividing after ten or twelve millimeters. The tendons go chiefly to the radial sides of the respective digits.

ACTION: Extends digits 2-5.

M. extensor digitorum lateralis (BNA: extensor digiti quinti proprius) (figs. 95, 134) is a rather slender muscle arising from the middle part of the lateral epicondyle and from the condyle itself. At its origin it is more or less inseparable from the adjacent borders of the extensor carpi ulnaris and the extensor digitorum communis. Beneath the dorsal carpal ligament the muscle forms two terminal tendons, which go to the ulnar sides of the basal phalanges of digits 4 and 5.

ACTION: Assists the common extensor in extending digits 4-5.

M. extensor carpi ulnaris (figs. 95, 134) arises by mingled fleshy and tendinous fibers from the distal end of the lateral epicondyle and from the condyle. At its origin its fibers are more or less inseparable from those of the adjacent borders of the anconeus and extensor digitorum lateralis. The flat insertion tendon, which can be separated from the dorsal carpal ligament only with difficulty, attaches to the tubercle on the ulnar side of the base of the fifth metacarpal.

ACTION: Extends the hand and abducts it ulnaward.

M. supinator (figs. 95, 134) arises from the ligaments surrounding the radiohumeral articulation; there is no origin from the lateral condyle of the humerus described by Wood-Jones. Insertion is into the lateral and dorsal surfaces of the radius, from below the head down to the junction of the middle and distal thirds. The proximal two-thirds of the outer surface of the muscle is covered with a heavy tendinous aponeurosis.

ACTION: Supinates the forearm and hand, turning the palm downward.

M. abductor pollicis longus (figs. 95, 96, 98, 134) includes the extensor and long abductor muscles of the thumb in human anatomy. It is a powerful muscle arising from the anterior (radial) half of the dorsal surface of the ulna, from the semilunar notch to the head; from the posterior (ulnar) half of the medial surface of the shaft of the radius, from the bicipital tubercle to a point just distad of the center of the shaft; from the interosseous membrane between these areas; and from the capsule of the elbow joint immediately below the radial collateral ligament. At the distal end of the radius the muscle fibers converge to a powerful compound flat tendon, which passes through the deep notch on the medial (thumb) side of the head of the radius, to insert into the proximal end of the outer surface of the radial sesamoid. The tendon is divisible throughout its length into two elements, and the more lateral of these shows a tendency to subdivide further. There is no attachment to the

Tendo m. flex. carpi rad.

M. flex. carpi rad.

Lig. radiocarp. rol.

Tendo m. abductor poll. longus

Lig. carpi trans. (cut)

Os sesamoid. rad.

M. interosseus 1

M. opponens pollicis

M. abductor poll. brevis

M. flex. poll. brevis

M. flex. carpi uln.
(pars humeralis)

R. prof. rolaris n. uln.

Os pisiforme

M. palmaris brevis (cut)

M. abductor dig. quinti

Mm. adductores digitorum

M. interosseus 4

M. opponens dig. quinti

Tendo com. m. flex. dig. prof.
(reflected)

1

2

3

4

5

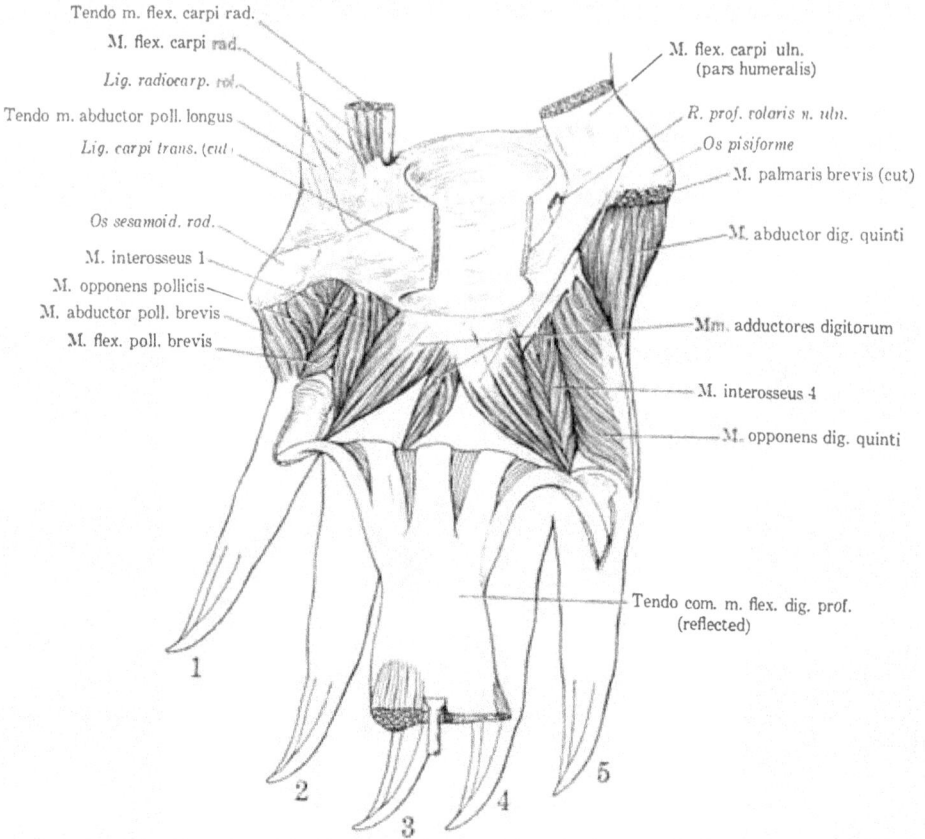

FIG. 98.  Deep muscles of palm of *Ailuropoda*.

pollex, and the "fascial insertion" of the medial slip between the radial sesamoid and the first metacarpal described by Wood-Jones could not be demonstrated.

ACTION: Abducts the radial sesamoid bone.

In a specimen of *Procyon lotor* the terminal tendon of the abductor longus was separated from the scapholunar by the radial sesamoid bone, which was closely bound by fascia to the deep surface of the tendon. The tendon inserted into the radial side of the base of metacarpal 1. In a specimen of *Ursus americanus* and one of *Tremarctos ornatus* the abductor longus terminated in two tendons that passed side by side onto the carpus. The larger of these had the normal insertion into the base of metacarpal 1, whereas the smaller inserted into the radial sesamoid.

M. extensor indicus proprius (figs. 95, 134) is a thin and rather slender muscle arising from

the middle third of the dorsal border of the ulna and extensively from the underlying surface of the abductor pollicis longus. Just before reaching the base of the carpus the muscle forms two terminal tendons, which pass diagonally across the carpus and metacarpus to insert into the base of the first phalanges of digits 1 and 2. The tendon to digit 2 is considerably the larger, and fibrous bands are carried across from it to digit 1.

ACTION: Assists the common extensor in extending digits 1–2.

### D.  MUSCLES OF THE HAND

M. palmaris brevis (figs. 96, 98) does not seem to have been described hitherto in a carnivore. In *Ailuropoda* a small group of muscle fibers arising from the anterior face of the pisiform and inserting partly into the palmar aponeurosis and partly into the skin in front of the outer carpal pad can only represent this muscle. The fibers going to the palmar aponeurosis extend part way across the flexor digiti quinti brevis, while those going to the skin arch laterad. Innervation is by a twig from the palmar division of the deep branch of the ulnar nerve, and the blood supply is by a short twig from the branch of the mediana propria that supplies the outer side of digit 5.

ACTION: Helps to cup the palm of the hand.

**M. abductor pollicis brevis** (fig. 98) is incompletely separable from the opponens and short flexor. It is represented by a group of fibers lying at the distal border of the interspace between the radial sesamoid and the pollex. Origin is from the inner face of the radial sesamoid, and insertion into the radial side of the base of the first phalanx of the pollex.

ACTION: Adducts the radial sesamoid bone.

**M. flexor pollicis brevis** (fig. 98) is a slender muscle incompletely separable from the abductor pollicis brevis. Origin is from the transverse carpal ligament and the scapholunar near the base of the first metacarpal. The muscle inserts into the radial side of the base of the pollex, close to the insertion of the abductor.

ACTION: Flexes and abducts the pollex.

**M. opponens pollicis** (fig. 98) is a large muscle occupying most of the interspace between the radial sesamoid and the pollex. It arises extensively from the inner face of the radial sesamoid, and inserts with the short abductor into the radial side of the first phalanx of the pollex.

ACTION: Adducts the radial sesamoid bone.

In a specimen of *Procyon lotor* the short muscles of the pollex were represented by a superficial and a deep element, which arose from the transverse carpal ligament and the scapholunar (no relation with the radial sesamoid), and inserted into the radial side of the first phalanx. In a specimen of *Ursus americanus* and one of *Tremarctos ornatus* these short muscles of the pollex were represented by a single muscle mass, which arose extensively from the radial sesamoid in addition to the origin from the carpal ligament and scapholunar.

**M. abductor digiti quinti** (figs. 96, 98) is a large muscle arising extensively from the anterior and dorsal surfaces of the pisiform. The fibers converge to a tendon that inserts partly into the underlying surface of the opponens digiti quinti, and partly continues on to the ulnar side of the base of the first phalanx of digit 5.

ACTION: Abducts and flexes the fifth digit.

**M. flexor digiti quinti brevis** (figs. 96, 133) is composed of two heads, one deep to the other, that insert by a common tendon. The superficial head arises exclusively from the connective tissue pad over the pisiform, whereas the deep head arises partly from the inner border of the pisiform and partly from the superficial layer of the transverse carpal ligament. The common tendon gives off a slip to the base of the first phalanx of digit 5, but most of its substance is continued to the base of the second phalanx.

ACTION: Flexes the proximal phalanges of digit 5.

**M. opponens digiti quinti** (figs. 96, 98) is a powerful fleshy muscle arising by two heads. One head takes origin from the tip of the unciform and the adjoining part of the deep layer of the carpal ligament. The other head arises from the anterior surface of the pisiform, deep to the origin of the abductor. Insertion, as Wood-Jones pointed out, is into the sesamoid on the ulnar side of the metacarpophalangeal joint of digit 5.

ACTION: Flexes and adducts the fifth metacarpal.

**Mm. lumbricales** (fig. 97) occupy the usual position between the tendons of the flexor digitorum profundus. Origin is from the wide common tendon of the flexor digitorum profundus, from which four bellies radiate into the intertendinous spaces. Insertions are made by means of flat tendons into the radial sides of the bases of the second phalanges of digits 2 to 5.

ACTION: Flex the basal phalanges of digits 2–5 and draw them toward the thumb.

**Mm. adductores digitorum** (superficial palmar muscles, Wood-Jones) (fig. 98). The most superficial layer of palmar muscles cannot be homologized with the interossei of human anatomy; the belly going to the thumb represents the adductor pollicis of man. Three bellies arise together from the transverse carpal ligament and the fascia covering the underlying carpal bones. The largest belly goes to the radial side of the base of the first phalanx of the fifth digit. Another belly goes to the ulnar side of the first phalanx of the pollex. The middle, and by far the smallest, belly goes to the ulnar side of the second digit. Wood-Jones described a fourth very slender belly to the third digit; this slip was absent in our specimen.

ACTION: Flex the digits; draw digits 1 and 5 toward the midline of the hand.

In a specimen of *Ursus americanus* the arrangement of these muscles was identical with our specimen of *Ailuropoda*.

**Mm. interossei** (fig. 99) are composed of four groups of muscles, made up of ten separate slips. The first group arises from the base of the first metacarpal, and is made up of two slips: these go to the ulnar side of the pollex and the radial side of digit 2, respectively. The second group arises from the third metacarpal, and is made up of three

any importance to its absence in the panda. *Ailuropoda* differs from the bears, and apparently from all other carnivores, in the distinctness of the two heads of the brachialis.

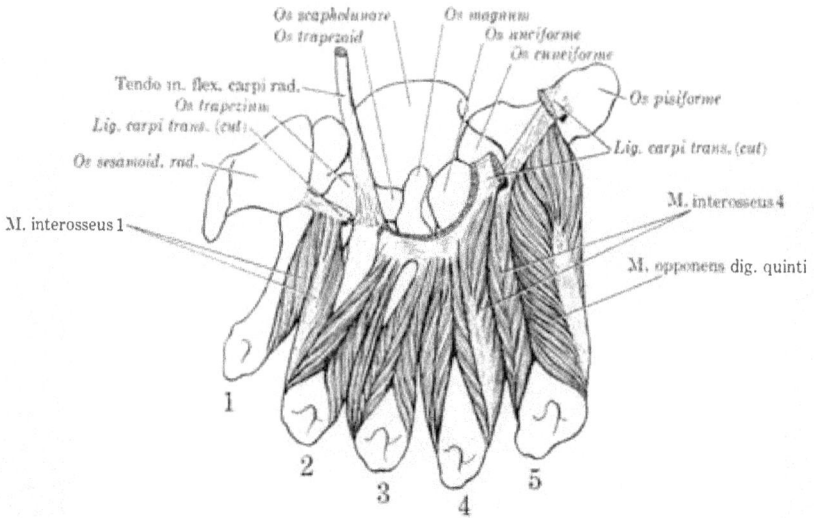

FIG. 99.  Interosseous muscles of manus of *Ailuropoda*.

slips; two of these go to either side of digit 2, while the third, which is very slender, goes to the radial side of digit 3. The third group arises from the fourth metacarpal, and is made up of three heads; two of these go to either side of digit 3, the third going to the ulnar side of digit 4; a few of the fibers are also contributed to the ulnar side of digit 4. The fourth group arises from the fifth metacarpal, and is made up of two heads; one goes to the ulnar side of digit 4, the other to the radial side of digit 5.

ACTION. Flex the phalanges on the metacarpals.

**M. flexor brevis digitorum manus** is absent. This muscle is also absent in bears, but is present in all procyonids. It inserts into the vaginal sheath of digit 5.

E.  REVIEW OF MUSCLES OF THE FORE LIMB

In general the muscles of the fore limb in *Ailuropoda* agree closely with those in *Ursus*. Often correspondence extends down to minor details of muscle structure and attachment sites. In the tabulation of myological characters (p. 197) the panda and the bears disagree in only one point: the short head of the biceps, usually present in *Ursus*, is absent in *Ailuropoda*. Since this head is known to be variable in *Ursus*, I do not attach

There is a generalized increase in the mass of the musculature in the anterior part of the body, particularly in the neck, shoulder, and upper arm. This is evident in a direct comparison of individual muscles with those of *Ursus* and in the heavy surface modeling on the scapula and humerus, and it is indicated in the relative weights of the musculature of the fore and hind limbs (Table 15, p. 195). I can find no functional reason for this heavy musculature. This is the region of the body closest to the head, and furthermore there is a gradient away from the head: the neck and shoulder musculature is most affected, the upper arm less so, and the lower arm and hand least. This strongly suggests a generalized regional effect, centered in the head and decreasing in a gradient away from the head, similar to that seen in the skeleton.

The most distinctive feature of the fore limb in *Ailuropoda* is the enlarged and mobile radial sesamoid bone. The muscles associated with this bone in the panda are the palmaris longus, the opponens pollicis, and the abductor pollicis longus and brevis. Normally in carnivores these muscles insert into the base of the thumb, and the radial sesamoid is a typical sesamoid bone developed in the tendon of the long abductor where it glides over the scapholunar. In bears, however, the radial sesamoid is

TABLE 14.—RELATIVE WEIGHTS OF MUSCLES OF THE SHOULDER AND ARM IN CARNIVORES

| | Ailuropoda* | | Tremarctos | | Ursus americanus** | Canis familiaris** | Leo leo** |
|---|---|---|---|---|---|---|---|
| | Wt. in gms. | % | Wt. in gms. | % | % | % | % |
| Supraspinatus | 122 | 10.8 | 136 | 10.4 | 9.9 | 15.4 | 12.9 |
| Infraspinatus | 119 | 10.5 | 104 | 7.9 | 9.0 | 11.0 | 11.6 |
| Acromiodelt.+Spinodelt. | 85 | 7.5 | 108 | 8.3 | 8.0 | 5.7 | 4.2 |
| Teres major | 72 | 6.4 | 60 | 4.6 | 4.4 | 4.8 | 8.5 |
| Subscapularis+Teres minor | 168 | 14.8 | 188 | 14.4 | 14.5 | 9.4 | 13.1 |
| Biceps | 75 | 6.6 | 110 | 8.4 | 8.3 | 4.8 | 7.1 |
| Coracobrachialis | 16 | 1.4 | 25 | 1.9 | 1.7 | .5 | .2 |
| Brachialis | 52 | 4.6 | 74 | 5.7 | 5.8 | 2.8 | 3.6 |
| Epitrochlearis | 58 | | 56 ⎫ | | | | |
| Triceps longus | 189 | | 237 ⎪ | | | | |
| Triceps lateralis | 95 | 37.4 | 135 ⎬ | 38.6 | 38.3 | 45.7 | 38.7 |
| Triceps medius | 55 | | 57 ⎪ | | | | |
| Anconaeus | 26 | | 19 ⎭ | | | | |
| Totals | 1132 | 100.0 | 1309 | 100.2 | 99.9 | 100.1 | 99.9 |

* Half-grown individual (Su Lin).
** Data from Haughton.

enlarged and the basic panda condition of the muscles already exists: the terminal tendon of the long abductor ends partly in the radial sesamoid (p. 179), and the short muscles (brevis and opponens) attach extensively to the radial sesamoid. In other words, all elements attaching to the radial sesamoid in Ailuropoda already have some attachment to this bone in Ursus, apparently simply as a mechanical result of the enlargement of the sesamoid in bears. The step from the bear condition to the panda condition involves only a further shift of muscle attachments in favor of the sesamoid, and such a shift would probably result automatically from the further enlargement of the sesamoid bone: the size of the bone simply blocks off the tendon of the long abductor from the pollex, and the short muscles from their original attachment sites on the transverse carpal ligament and the scapholunar. Thus, the musculature for operating this remarkable new mechanism functionally a new digit— required no intrinsic change from conditions already present in the panda's closest relatives, the bears. Furthermore, it appears that the whole sequence of events in the musculature follows automatically from simple hypertrophy of the sesamoid bone.

Other subtle differences in the musculature, important from the functional standpoint, are revealed by comparing the relative masses of individual muscles. Such data are available for the shoulder and arm in a series of carnivores (Table 14). These figures reveal that in the panda and the bears the medial rotator of the arm (subscapularis), the abductor of the arm (deltoid), and the flexors of the elbow (biceps, brachialis) are relatively large, whereas in the dog (the horse is very similar) the extensors (supraspinatus, triceps) are dominant. The lion tends to be intermediate between the panda–bear condition and the dog–horse condition. These muscle-mass relations are obviously correlated with the differing mechanical requirements in a limb used for ambulatory walking and prehension versus one used for cursorial running. The morphogenetic mechanisms through which such anatomical differences are expressed, and thus the basis on which natural selection could operate, are unknown. Indeed, in view of Fuld's data on bipedal dogs (p. 148), it is not even certain that differences in muscle-mass relations among related forms are intrinsic to the musculature.

## IV. MUSCLES OF THE HIND LEG

### A. MUSCLES OF THE HIP

1. *Iliopsoas Group*

M. psoas major (fig. 100) lies ventrad of the medial part of the quadratus lumborum. It arises, by successive digitations, from the bodies and transverse processes of all the lumbar vertebrae. Each slip has a double origin: medial fibers arise from the side of the body of the vertebra, and lateral fibers from the transverse process; a part of the quadratus lumborum is embraced between. The muscle is joined posteriorly by the iliacus, and inserts by a wide common tendon with it into the lesser trochanter.

M. iliacus (fig. 100) is a small muscle arising from the ventral face of the ilium. It is more or less inseparable from the psoas major medially, and inserts by a common tendon with it into the anterior border of the lesser trochanter. The fibers of the iliacus insert into the ventral part of the tendon.

M. quadratus lumborum⎽⎽⎽⎽⎽

M. iliocostalis ⎯⎯⎯⎯⎯

M. psoas minor⎽⎽⎽⎽⎽

M. psoas major⎽⎽⎽⎽⎽

M. iliacus⎽⎽⎽⎽

M. iliopsoas⎽⎽⎽⎽⎽                                           ⎽⎽⎽⎽⎽M. obturator externus

\M. quadratus femoris

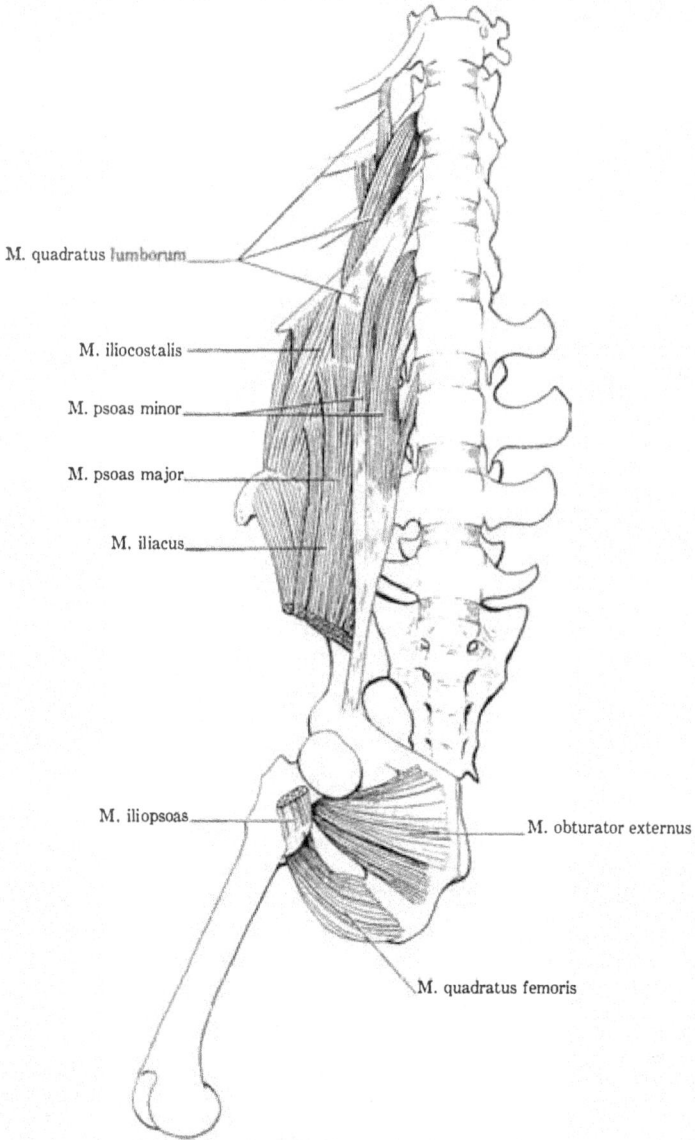

FIG. 100.   Deep muscles of back and hip of *Ailuropoda*, ventral view.

M. psoas minor (fig. 100) lies deep to (ventrad of) the psoas major, from which it is entirely free. It arises from the bodies of the last thoracic and first three lumbar vertebrae, and inserts by a stout flat tendon into the ilium just above the iliopectineal eminence.

ACTION: The iliopsoas flexes the thigh and rotates the femur laterally. When the thigh is fixed, it flexes the pelvis on the thigh.

2. *Gluteal Group*

The gluteal muscles arise chiefly from the ilium, and in *Ailuropoda* they have been affected by the reduction in the area of the wing of the ilium. This reduction in attachment area is not reflected in their mass, which is relatively greater than in any other carnivore examined. As often happens when the area available for muscle attachment is restricted, the muscles of the gluteal group tend to fuse and to extend their areas of origin to fascia. The insertions of these muscles do not differ much from those of *Ursus*.

**M. glutaeus superficialis** (figs. 88, 138) is a broad, thin, fan-shaped sheet completely covering the middle and deep gluteals. It arises, by a wide aponeurosis tightly adherent to the underlying fascia of the middle gluteal, from the iliac crest, the lumbodorsal fascia over the last lumbar vertebra, the entire sacral fascia, the fascia over the first caudal, and, by fleshy fibers, from the anterior border of the ischial tuberosity directly above the attachment of the sacrotuberous ligament. It has no attachment to the transverse processes of the sacrals or caudals, or to the sacrotuberous ligament. In addition, the anteriormost fibers are reflected around the anterior border of the middle gluteal onto the deep surface of the middle gluteal, to insert with these middle gluteal fibers into the fascia covering the dorsal surface of the iliopsoas.

Anteriorly the superficial gluteal borders on the sartorius and tensor fasciae latae, posteriorly on the semimembranosus and biceps. It is not completely separable from the tensor. Its fibers converge rapidly to a stout tendon, which inserts into the prominent scar below the great trochanter. There is a large gluteofemoral bursa beneath the muscle at its insertion.

ACTION: Flexes the thigh and rotates the femur medially.

**M. glutaeus medius** (figs. 88, 138) is the most powerful element of the gluteal complex, although it exceeds the mass of the superficial gluteal much less than in other carnivores. It consists of a single heavy fan-shaped layer, 85 mm. wide, completely hidden beneath the superficial gluteal. It is not completely separable from the underlying deep gluteal. Anterior to the greater sciatic notch, origin is from the lumbodorsal fascia and from the gluteal surface of the ilium; posterior to the notch, origin is from the lateral edge of the crest formed by the fused transverse processes of the sacral vertebrae. Insertion is by mingled muscle and tendon fibers into the dorsal and anterior borders of the great trochanter.

ACTION: Extends and abducts the thigh.

**M. glutaeus profundus** (fig. 138) is the smallest of the gluteal muscles. It lies entirely beneath the middle gluteal, from which it is separated by a large trunk of the superior gluteal nerve; its borders conform rather closely to those of the medius. The profundus consists of a single wide layer, somewhat thinner than the medius. Origin is from almost the entire inferior gluteal line, beginning a short distance behind the anterior superior iliac spine and continuing posteriorly onto the body of the ilium in front of the acetabulum. Insertion is by a wide tendon into the anterior border of the great trochanter, deep to the insertion of the middle gluteal.

ACTION: Abducts the thigh and rotates the femur medially.

**M. tensor fasciae latae** (figs. 88, 137, 138) is not completely separable from the adjacent border of the superficial gluteal. It arises from the lateroventral edge of the ilium, along a line running caudad from the crest. It inserts into the fascia lata in a curved line, convex distally, that begins at the prominence for the insertion of the superficial gluteal and ends at about the middle of the thigh.

ACTION: Tenses the fascia lata and assists the superficial gluteal in flexing the thigh and rotating it medially.

3. *Obturator Group*

**M. gemellus anterior** (figs. 88, 138) is completely free from the obturator internus. It is a small muscle arising from the ischium along the lesser sciatic notch anterior to the ischial spine. The fibers converge to insert into the anterior part of the internal obturator tendon for a distance of 20 mm.

**M. piriformis** (figs. 88, 138) is completely distinct from the middle gluteal, its anterior third being overlapped by the posterior part of the middle gluteal. Origin is from the antero-inferior border of the sciatic notch (as in *Ursus*) and from the lateral edge of the fused transverse processes of the sacral vertebrae. Insertion is made by mingled muscle and tendon fibers into the dorsal (proximal) border of the great trochanter, deep to the insertion of the middle gluteal.

ACTION: Abducts the femur.

**M. obturator internus** (fig. 138) is much smaller than the external obturator, as in the Ursidae. It has the usual origin from the pelvic surfaces of the pubis and ischium where they form the margin of the obturator foramen. The fibers converge to a long flat tendon that passes out over the lesser sciatic notch, to insert into the trochanteric fossa of the femur. There is a large mucous bursa beneath the obturator tendon where it passes over the ischium.

ACTION: Abducts the femur and rotates it laterally.

M. gemellus posterior (fig. 138) is larger than the anterior gemellus, and, like it, is free from the internal obturator. It arises from the ischium immediately in front of the tuberosity and beneath the sacrotuberous ligament. Insertion is narrow and by means of tendon fibers, into the posterior edge of the tendon of the internal obturator. Insertion of the posterior gemellus is distad of the insertion of the anterior gemellus.

ACTION: Abducts the femur and rotates it laterally.

M. quadratus femoris (figs. 88, 100, 138) is a stout quadrilateral muscle arising from the dorsal third of the lateral surface of the ramus of the ischium, directly below the ischial tuberosity. Insertion is by means of a short tendinous aponeurosis into the crescentic inter-trochanteric line.

ACTION: Extends the thigh and rotates the femur laterally.

M. obturator externus (figs. 100, 138) is of the usual triangular form. It arises from the lateral surface of the ascending ramus of the pubis, from the pubis and ischium along the symphysis, from the descending ramus of the ischium caudad of the obturator foramen, and from the external surface of the obturator membrane. The fibers converge strongly to a powerful tendon, which is inserted into the proximal part of the trochanteric fossa.

ACTION: A powerful lateral rotator of the thigh and a weak extensor and adductor.

B. MUSCLES OF THE THIGH

M. semimembranosus (figs. 88, 89, 137, 138, 140) is divided, as in other carnivores, into two subequal parts: an anterior belly that inserts into the femur, and a posterior belly that inserts into the tibia. These arise together from the posterolateral surface of the descending ramus of the ischium immediately below the origin of the biceps and semitendinosus. They promptly divide and run distad, diverging slightly in their course.

The anterior belly lies at first mostly mesad of the posterior belly. It inserts, by fleshy fibers, chiefly into the medial epicondyle of the femur just anterior to the origin of the medial head of the gastrocnemius. The line of origin continues distad onto the tibial collateral ligament. The posterior belly inserts, by mingled fleshy and tendon fibers, into the infraglenoid margin of the median condyle of the tibia.

ACTION: (1) extends the thigh; (2) flexes the leg.

M. semitendinosus (figs. 88, 89, 138) arises from the ischial tuberosity only; there is no extra head from the caudal vertebrae. Origin is by short tendon fibers, above and partly behind the origin of the biceps. Insertion is made in the most part by a short flat tendon, 50 mm. in width, into the anterior crest of the tibia, beneath the insertion of the sartorius. The posterior fibers are continued distad into the fascia of the lower leg.

ACTION: (1) extends the thigh; (2) flexes the leg.

M. sartorius (figs. 88, 89, 137, 139) is a single flat band lying superficially on the median and anterior sides of the thigh. It arises, by mixed fleshy and tendon fibers that are continuous with those of the middle gluteal dorsally, from the anterior superior iliac spine and the inguinal ligament. Insertion is made in a long sinuous line running along the medial border of the patella, across the ligaments of the knee joint, and down along the medial side of the anterior crest of the tibia for about half its length.

ACTION: (1) flexes the thigh; (2) flexes the leg.

M. rectus femoris (figs. 88, 89, 103, 137) is a fusiform muscle wedged in between the vastus lateralis and vastus medialis; it is intimately associated with both these muscles distally. The rectus arises by two short stout tendons that attach close together, one above the other, to a prominent roughened scar on the anterior lip of the acetabulum. Almost the entire deep surface of the muscle is covered with a glistening tendinous aponeurosis, but this does not form a terminal tendon. Insertion is into the proximal border of the patella, partly by fleshy fibers and partly by fibers of the tendinous aponeurosis.

ACTION: Extends the leg and flexes the thigh.

M. vastus lateralis (figs. 88, 102, 103, 138-140) is, as usual, the largest component of the quadriceps extensor group. It is completely inseparable from the vastus intermedius throughout its entire length. Origin is from the posterolateral surface of the great trochanter and the shaft of the femur in a narrow line along the lateral lip of the linea aspera nearly down to the lateral epicondyle. At its distal end it fuses with the rectus femoris and inserts in connection with it into the dorsal and lateral borders of the patella.

ACTION: Extends the leg, assisted by the other muscles of the quadriceps femoris.

M. pectineus (figs. 89, 137) is a wedge-shaped muscle lying between the adductor and the vastus medialis. It may with difficulty be separated into two layers: an anterior ("superficial") and a posterior ("deep"). It is easily separable from the adductor except at its insertion. Origin is by a thin flat tendon from the crest on the anterior border of the ascending ramus of the pubis, from the iliopectineal eminence nearly to the symphysis. The tendon of origin is intimately united, on its superficial surface, with the prepubic tendon (p. 166). Insertion is by a flat tendon, which becomes increasingly heavy distally, into the middle third of the medial lip of the linea aspera. The insertion line terminates inferiorly at the level where it meets the femoral vessels emerging from the hiatus adductorius. The anterior layer is innervated by N. femoralis, the posterior by N. obturatorius.

ACTION: Adducts and flexes the thigh and rotates the femur laterally.

M. gracilis (figs. 89, 137) arises by mingled tendon and fleshy fibers from the entire length of the short symphysis and for some distance up the anterior border of the descending ramus of the pubis anteriorly, and about half way up the posterior edge of the descending ramus of the ischium posteriorly. It is a flat muscle about 70 mm. in width, covering the posteromedial surface of the thigh. It inserts by means of a short tendinous aponeurosis into the medial side of the proximal end of the tibia, immediately behind the insertion of the sartorius. The posterior fibers are continued distad into the fascia of the lower leg.

ACTION: (1) adducts the thigh; (2) flexes the leg.

M. adductor (figs. 88, 89, 102, 137, 138) cannot be separated with any certainty into a magnus, longus, and brevis. As in Ursus (original observation), it is composed of a continuous sheet that is reflected back on itself at its distal (posterior) edge to form a double-layered muscle with a deep pocket separating the two layers; the pocket is open proximally and posteriorly. This is strikingly similar to the structure of the pectoralis major of man as described by Zuckerkandl (1910).

The anterior layer of the adductor arises in a long narrow U-shaped line that descends along the ventral half of the external surface of the acetabular ramus of the pubis, crosses the entire length of the symphysis pelvis, and ascends nearly half way up the descending ramus of the ischium. The posterior layer arises from a relatively small area on the external face of the descending ramus of the ischium, deep to the anterior layer and directly adjoining the area of origin of the external obturator. The anterior layer of the adductor is very wide and thin at its origin, the posterior layer narrow and relatively thick.

The two layers insert side by side into the linea aspera (which is very poorly defined in Ailuropoda and the bears), on the posterolateral side of the

shaft of the femur. Insertion begins proximally just below the level of the third trochanter. The posterior layer is intimately associated with the pectineus at its insertion. Distally, at the distal sixth of the shaft of the femur, both layers leave an opening, the hiatus adductorius, for the passage of the femoral vessels. Distad of the hiatus, insertion is by muscle fibers into the medial side of the posterior surface of the femur, including the medial epicondyle and the adjacent popliteal surface.

ACTION: Adducts and extends the thigh.

M. biceps femoris (figs. 88, 138) is completely differentiated from the glutaeus superficialis and tensor fasciae latae. It is composed of a single head; the small posterior head, which is partly differentiated in Ursus and completely separate proximally in Canis, is indistinguishable in Ailuropoda. The muscle arises, by a short stout tendon, from the lateral part of the ischial tuberosity; no fibers come from the caudal vertebrae or the sacrotuberous ligament. The muscle expands rapidly into a fan-shaped sheet, reaching a width of 185 mm. at its distal end. Near its insertion the muscle terminates abruptly in a continuous wide aponeurosis that passes into the fascia lata proximally and the crural fascia below the knee. Insertion is thus indirectly into the lateral side of the patella, the patellar ligament, and the anterior crest of the tibia. The most distal part of the aponeurotic sheet turns abruptly distad and caudad to the tuber calcis. Insertion of the biceps thus extends from immediately above the knee to the heel, the most distal extension of the biceps insertion known to me for any carnivore.

ACTION: The muscle is chiefly a flexor of the leg; the anteriormost fibers extend the thigh.

M. abductor cruris posterior (abductor cruris caudalis; Ziegler, 1931; Baum and Zietzschmann, 1936). This muscle was present on the left limb only, as a narrow, rope-like tract of fibers. Origin was from the ischial tuberosity immediately beneath the biceps, wedged in between the biceps and the quadratus femoris. The muscle ran distad deep to the biceps and inserted into the posterior surface of the femur a few millimeters above the condyles. Innervation was by a branch of the sciatic nerve.

This muscle is well known in the dog, where it forms a ribbon-like band arising from the sacrotuberous ligament and inserting into the crural fascia. It is described by Shepherd (1883) for Ursus americanus under the name "lesser portion of the adductor," and by Carlsson (1925) for Ursus arctos under the name "caudo-femoralis,"[1] as aris-

[1] Carlsson's "femoro-coccygeus" is the caudofemoralis of Windle and Parsons and the abductor cruris cranialis of Ziegler.

ing from the ischial tuberosity and inserting into the distal part of the femur, as here described for *Ailuropoda*. The muscle is unknown from other carnivores.

**M. tenuissimus** (fig. 88) arises from the fascia over the posterior border of the gluteus superficialis, immediately anterior to the origin of the biceps femoris. The muscle, which is a narrow ribbon only about 12 mm. wide throughout most of its length, lies wholly beneath the posterior border of the biceps femoris. At the distal end of the biceps the tenuissimus is continued into the same fascia as that by which the biceps inserts.

ACTION: Assists the biceps in flexing the leg.

**M. vastus intermedius** lies beneath the vastus lateralis, and the two muscles are inseparable. Extensive origin is taken from the shaft of the femur between the origins of the vastus lateralis and the vastus medialis, from the greater trochanter distad nearly to the patellar surface. Insertion is into the capsule of the knee joint.

**M. vastus medialis** (figs. 89, 139) is triangular in cross section. It arises by a heavy aponeurosis along nearly the entire length of the posteromedial border of the femur. Origin begins on the neck just below the articular capsule and extends along the linea aspera to within a few millimeters of the medial epicondyle. Insertion is into the proximal and medial borders of the patella.

ACTION: Assists the other quadriceps muscles in extending the leg.

## C. MUSCLES OF THE LEG

**M. gastrocnemius** (figs. 101, 138, 140) consists of the usual lateral and medial heads, the edge of the plantaris appearing on the surface between them. The *medial head* is slightly smaller than the lateral. It arises, by mingled tendon and fleshy fibers, from the medial condyle of the femur. At the junction of the middle and lower thirds of the leg it forms a flat tendon that joins the tendon of the lateral head. The *lateral head* is fused inseparably with the plantaris proximally, although a cross section of the two muscles shows a fibrous septum between them; distally, where the gastrocnemius becomes tendinous, they are easily separable. The common origin of the two muscles is from the lateral condyle of the femur. The terminal tendon of the lateral head of the gastrocnemius is smaller than that of the medial head. The two unite and insert into the outer side of the calcaneus. There is no sesamoid in the origin of either head.

ACTION: Extends the foot; flexes the knee.

**M. plantaris** (fig. 101) is inseparable from the lateral head of the gastrocnemius proximally, and arises with it from the lateral condyle of the femur (fig. 102). It forms a stout tendon distally, which twists around that of the gastrocnemius so that it comes to lie externally, and spreads out over the calcaneus. The aponeurosis-like tendon, which attaches to the distal end of the calcaneus on either side, is continuous with the plantar aponeurosis.

ACTION: Assists the gastrocnemius in extending the foot and flexing the knee.

**M. soleus** (figs. 101, 140) is enormously developed, greatly exceeding the combined heads of the gastrocnemius in size. It is a flattened fusiform muscle, 57 mm. in greatest width. Origin is by fleshy fibers from the posterior side of the head of the fibula and the lateral condyle of the tibia, from the distal end of the fibular collateral ligament, and extensively from the intermuscular septum between it and the peroneus brevis. Insertion is into the calcaneus, with considerable attachment also to the deep surface of the common tendon formed by the plantaris and the lateral head of the gastrocnemius.

ACTION: Extends the foot.

**M. popliteus** (figs. 102, 140) is an extensive and rather heavy triangular sheet arising by a powerful flat tendon from the outer side of the lateral condyle of the femur. Insertion is into a long triangular area mesad of the popliteal line on the posteromedial surface of the tibia, for its proximal two thirds.

ACTION: Flexes the leg and rotates it medially.

**M. flexor digitorum longus** (figs. 102, 140) arises almost entirely from the underlying surface of the tibialis posterior; its origin reaches the tibia only behind and below the lateral condyle, where a few of the fibers gain a tendinous attachment. The exposed posterior surfaces of the flexor digitorum longus and the tibialis posterior are covered by a common continuous layer of tendinous fascia where they lie beneath the popliteus. The tendon of the flexor digitorum longus, which is smaller than that of either the flexor hallucis longus or the tibialis posterior, lies in a groove behind the medial malleolus in company with the tendon of the tibialis posterior. It joins that of the flexor hallucis longus from the medial and deep sides to form the conjoined tendon.

ACTION: Flexes the phalanges of all the toes.

**M. flexor hallucis longus** (figs. 102, 140) is the largest of the deep flexor muscles, as is usual in carnivores. Origin is from the posterior surface of the shaft of the fibula throughout nearly its entire length, from the interosseous membrane between

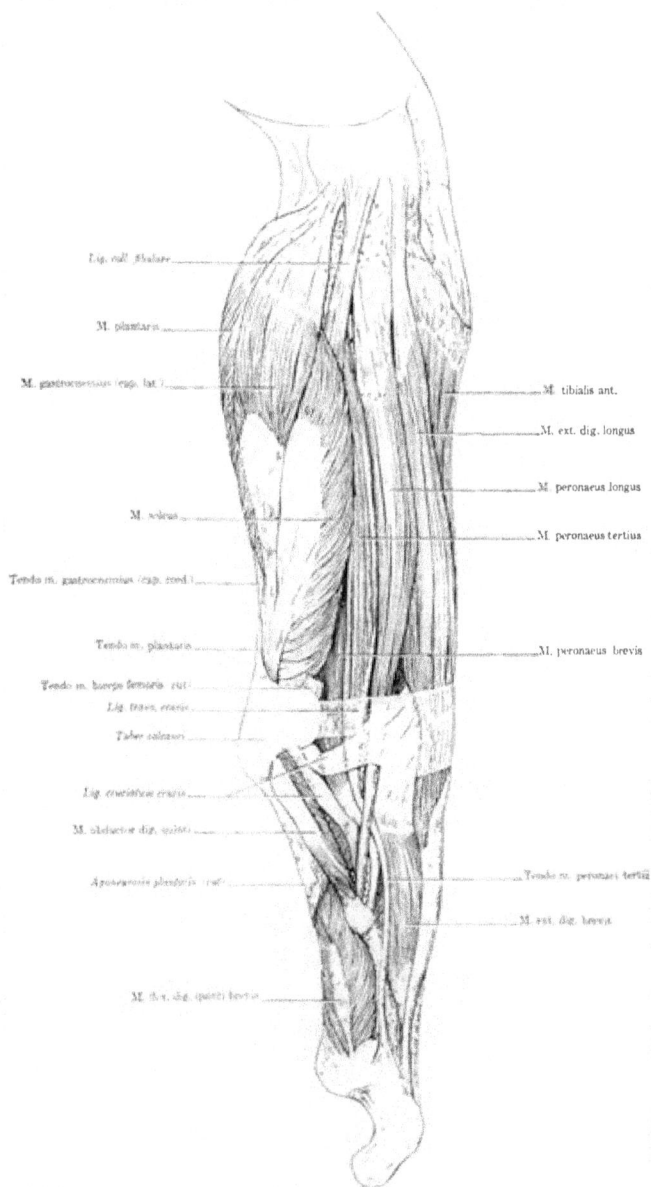

Lig. coll. fibulare

M. plantaris

M. gastrocnemius (cap. lat.)

M. soleus

Tendo m. gastrocnemius (cap. med.)

Tendo m. plantaris

Tendo m. bicepa femoris (st.)

Lig. trans. cruris

Tuber calcanei

Lig. cruciatum cruris

M. abductor dig. quinti

Aponeurosis plantaris (ret.)

M. (b.v. dig. quinti) brevis

M. tibialis ant.

M. ext. dig. longus

M. peronaeus longus

M. peronaeus tertius

M. peronaeus brevis

Tendo m. peronaei tertii

M. ext. dig. brevis

FIG. 101.   Muscles of the right leg of *Ailuropoda*, lateral view.

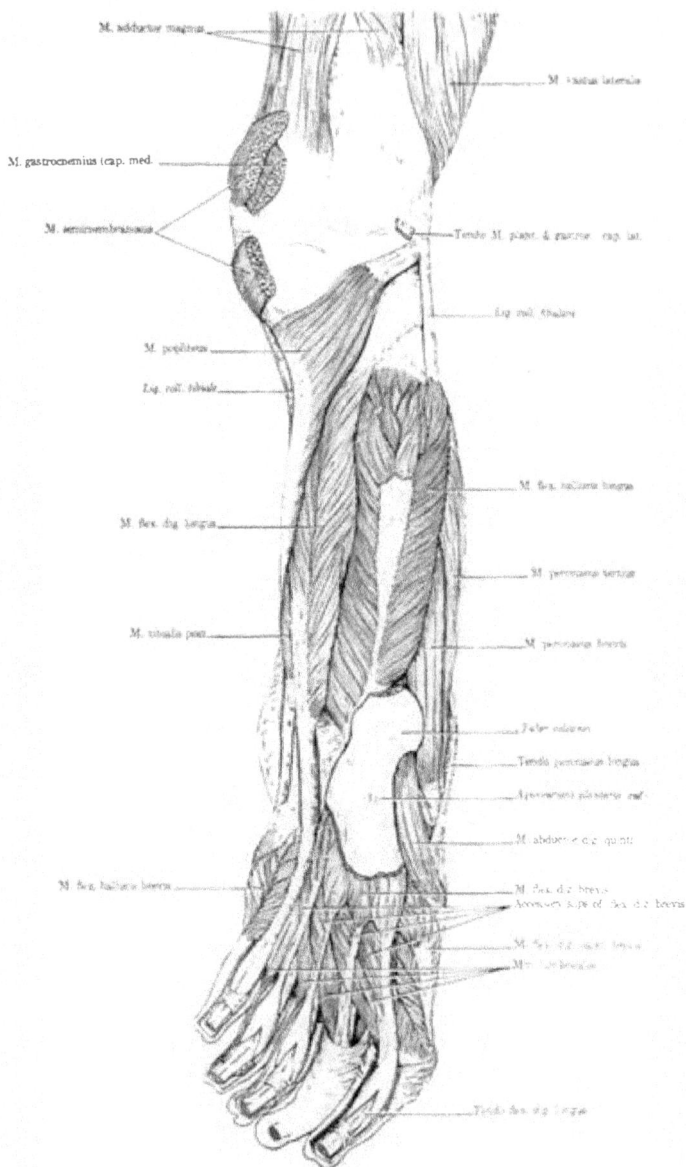

FIG. 102. Muscles of the right leg of *Ailuropoda*, posterior view.

the fibula and tibia, from the adjacent lateral surface of the tibia, and from the septum between the muscle itself and the peroneal muscles. Proximally a very definite group of fibers arises from the fibular collateral ligament. The muscle is bipennate, the tendon beginning at the juncture of the proximal and middle thirds. The tendon, which is very powerful, is joined by that of the flexor digitorum longus. The resulting conjoined tendon breaks up at the proximal end of the metatarsals into five slips, which are distributed to the digits. Each perforates the tendon of the flexor digitorum brevis at the metatarsophalangeal joint, and inserts into the terminal phalanx.

ACTION: Flexes the phalanges of all the toes.

**M. tibialis posterior** (fig. 102) is hidden beneath the popliteus proximally, and partly beneath the flexor digitorum longus distally. Origin, from the posterior surface of the shaft of the tibia lateral to the popliteal line, extends nearly the entire length of the shaft. The stout terminal tendon, after passing through the malleolar groove behind the medial malleolus, passes across the neck of the astragalus to its insertion on the tibial sesamoid.

ACTION: Inverts and extends the foot.

**M. tibialis anterior** (figs. 101, 103, 139) is incompletely separable into two parts; this is true even of the proximal part of the terminal tendon. The separation involves only the superficial fibers, the deeper fibers refusing to separate. Origin is from the anterior surface of the lateral condyle of the tibia and the proximal third of the lateral surface of the shaft of the tibia, with a delicate origin from the proximal half of the fibula. At the distal end of the tibia the muscle forms a powerful flat tendon, which inserts into the outer side of the base of the first metatarsal.

ACTION: Inverts and flexes the foot.

**M. extensor digitorum longus** (figs. 101, 103, 139) arises by a long narrow tendon from a pit on the external condyle of the femur. The muscle expands gradually as it passes distad, reaching a maximum over the distal end of the tibia. The muscle becomes tendinous at the tarsus. The four terminal tendons go to the phalanges of digits 2–5; that to digit 2 is extremely slender and arises as a slip from the tendon to digit 3.

ACTION: Flexes the ankle joint; extends the four lateral toes, with eversion of the foot.

**M. extensor hallucis longus** (figs. 103, 139) is a rather slender muscle arising from the distal half of the medial surface of the fibula; it forms a raphe with the peroneus brevis throughout the length of of its origin. The terminal tendon, which compares with those of the extensor digitorum longus in size,

inserts into the terminal phalanx of the hallux, with considerable fibrous attachment to the basal phalanx. There is no attachment to the tibial sesamoid.

ACTION: Flexes the ankle joint; extends the hallux, with eversion of the foot.

**M. peronaeus longus** (figs. 101 103, 139) arises by mingled fleshy and tendon fibers from a small area on the anterolateral surface of the head of the fibula and an adjacent area on the lateral condyle of the tibia. The muscle becomes tendinous near the distal end of the fibula. The tendon passes over the tendons of the other peroneal muscles, to insert into the base of the fifth metatarsal just posterior to the insertion of the peroneus brevis.

ACTION: Everts and abducts the foot.

**M. peronaeus brevis** (figs. 101, 102, 139, 140) arises from the lateral surface of the shaft of the fibula throughout its distal three fourths. The muscle becomes tendinous after passing through its groove in the lateral malleolus of the fibula. The tendon exceeds those of either of the other two peroneal muscles in size, and inserts into the dorsal surface of the base of the fifth metatarsal.

ACTION: Everts and abducts the foot.

**M. peronaeus tertius** (figs. 101–103, 139, 140) is a very slender muscle lying on top of the much larger peroneus brevis. It reaches the fibula only at its extreme proximal end. The muscle forms its terminal tendon at the distal end of the fibular malleolus, beneath the transverse tarsal ligament. The tendon is somewhat smaller than that of the peroneus brevis, immediately in front of which it lies; it extends to the base of the basal phalanx of digit 5, gradually coming to lie dorsad instead of laterad, and joining the tendon of the extensor digitorum longus.

ACTION: Everts and abducts the foot.

### D. MUSCLES OF THE FOOT

**M. extensor digitorum brevis** (figs. 101, 103) has the usual origin from the coracoid process of the calcaneus. Its structure is complex, but it forms four more or less distinct digitations that go to digits 1–4. That to the lateral side of digit 4 is the most distinct, and is the only one that forms a well-defined tendon. Each of the others bifurcates at the metatarso-phalangeal articulation, to supply adjacent sides of two digits by means of a tendinous expansion. There is some insertion of muscle fibers into the deep surface of the tendons of the extensor digitorum longus, but the tendons of the two muscles remain distinct.

ACTION: Aids the long extensor in extending the toes.

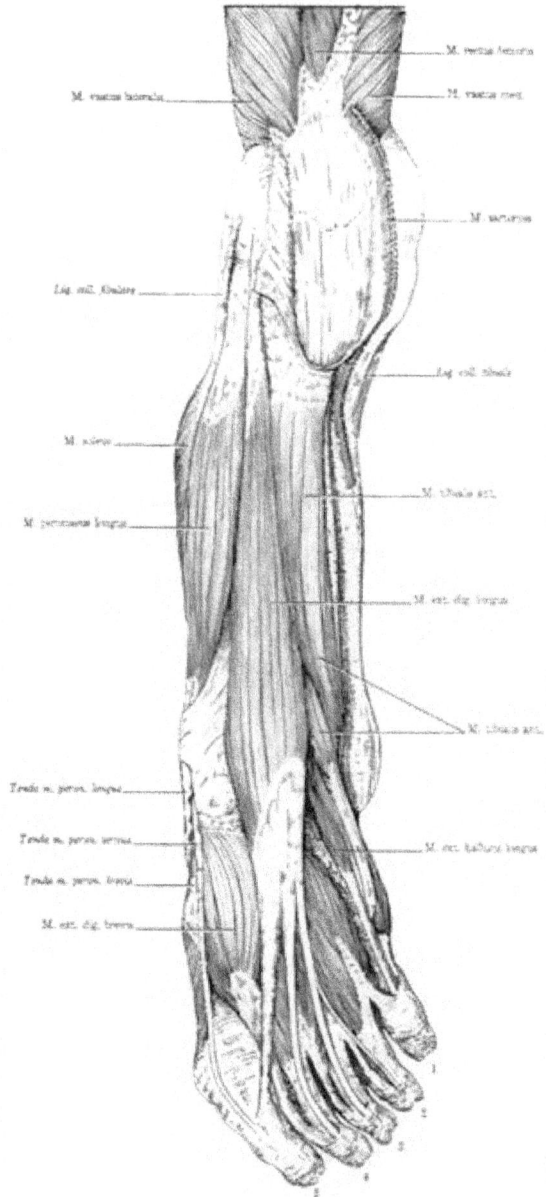

FIG. 103.  Muscles of the right leg of *Ailuropoda*, anterior view.

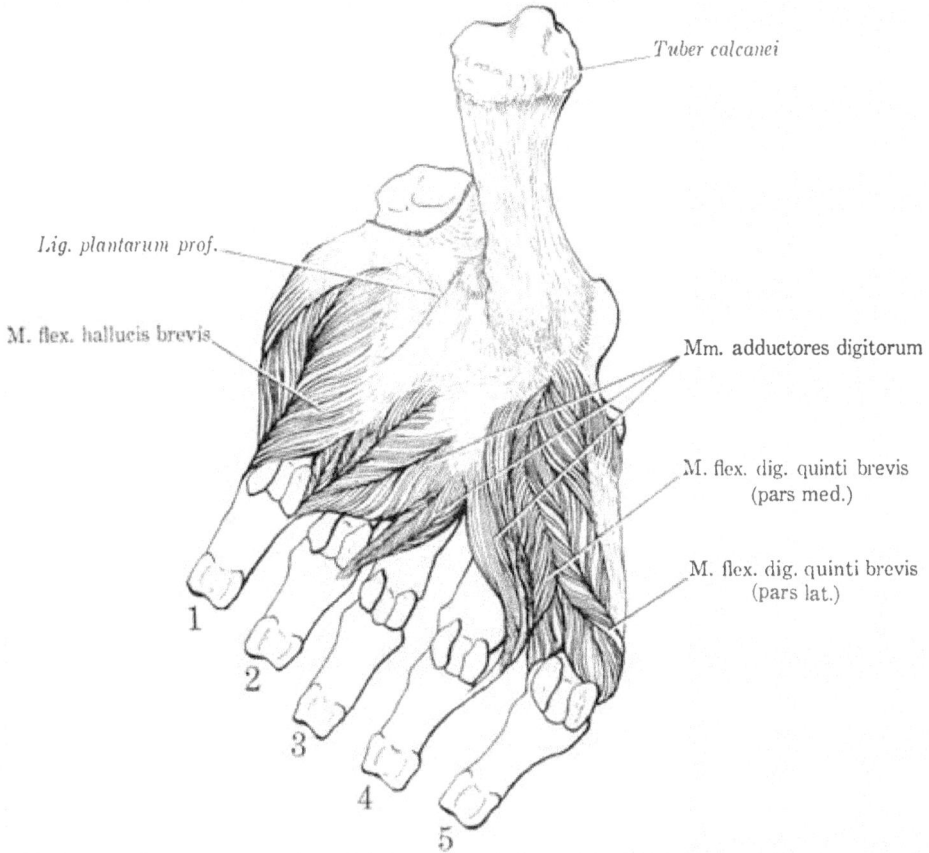

FIG. 104. Muscles of the plantar surface of the right foot of *Ailuropoda*.

**M. flexor hallucis brevis** (figs. 102, 104) is a powerful, complex muscle. It is composed of a very small internal part, and a large bipennate external part. The internal part arises from the plantar ligament in common with the external part, and extends as a very short muscle belly to its insertion on the inner side of the base of the first phalanx. The external part arises from the tibial sesamoid, from the navicular and cuneiform bones, and from the plantar ligament. It inserts into the outer side of the base of the first phalanx of the hallux.

ACTION: Flexes the hallux.

**M. abductor digiti quinti** (figs. 101, 102, 140) is a slender fleshy band of muscle arising from the lateral and ventral sides of the distal end of the calcaneus. Insertion is into the tuberosity of the fifth metatarsal, just proximal to the insertion of the peroneus brevis.

ACTION: Abducts the fifth toe.

**M. flexor digiti quinti brevis** (figs. 102, 104) is a powerful muscle occupying the entire plantar surface of the fifth metatarsal. It is partly separable into a small medial part and a much larger lateral part. The lateral part, in turn, has a bipennate structure. The fibers of the median part arise from a small area on the ventral surface of the cuboid, and this part of the muscle inserts into the medial metatarso-phalangeal sesamoid. The lateral part of the muscle arises from the cuboid, and from the sheath of the peroneus longus along nearly the entire length of the metatarsal. This part inserts into the lateral sesamoid.

ACTION: Flexes the basal phalanx of the fifth toe.

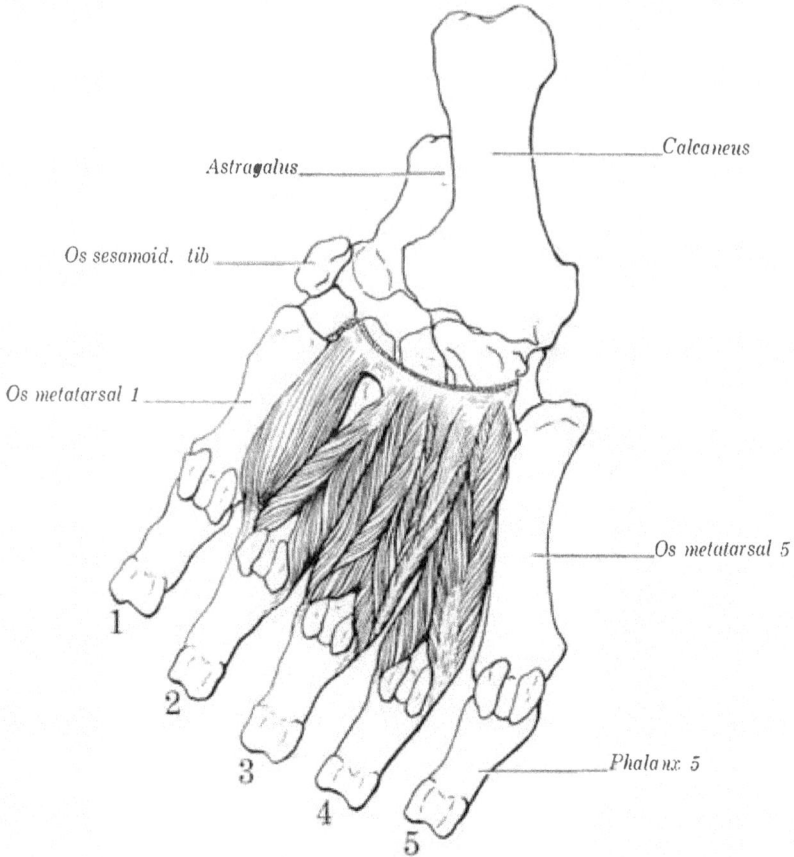

FIG. 105.  Interosseous muscles of right foot of *Ailuropoda*.

**M. flexor digitorum brevis** (figs. 102, 140) ariscs as a continuation of the aponeurosis of the plantaris and from the deep surface of the plantar aponeurosis.  It consists of a fleshy belly that divides into four digitations distally, that going to the fifth toe being the largest.  At the proximal ends of the metatarsals the digitations form slender tendons, which are distributed to digits 2–4.  These tendons are perforated by the tendons of the flexor digitorum longus at the metatarso-phalangeal articulations.  Insertion is into the second phalanx.

Accessory slips, four in number, pass from the superficial surface of the conjoined long flexor tendon to the tendons of the flexor brevis; a few of the most superficial fibers come from the quadratus plantae.  These slips decrease in size from the fifth to the second, and each inserts into the medial side

of the corresponding tendon of the flexor digitorum brevis.

ACTION: Flexes the middle and basal phalanges of digits 2–5.

**M. quadratus plantae** is a wide band arising from the lateral surface of the shaft of the calcaneus, and extending obliquely across the sole to its insertion on the superficial surface of the conjoined long flexor tendon.  The muscle is shot through with tendon fibers, which unite toward the insertion into a central tendon into which the muscle fibers insert in bipennate fashion.

ACTION: Assists the long flexor in flexing the toes.

**Mm. lumbricales** (fig.102), four in number, arise from contiguous sides of the digital slips of the conjoined long flexor tendon.  They insert on the medial sides of the bases of the first phalanges of digits 2–5, that is to the fifth digit being the largest.

ACTION: Flex the basal phalanges of digits 2–5.

**Mm. adductores** (fig. 102) are three bellies on the sole, arising together from the deep plantar ligament and the underlying tarsal bones. The largest and most medial belly is double, and goes to the inner side of the base of the first phalanx of digit 1. The middle belly goes to the lateral side of digit 2. The lateral belly goes to the lateral side of digit 4.

ACTION: Flex the basal phalanges of digits 1, 2, and 4 and draw them toward the midline of the foot.

**Mm. interossei** (fig. 105) are made up of three groups of muscles arising from the plantar ligament and the bases of the metatarsal bones, and inserting into the bases of the proximal phalanges. The first and most medial is a single large independent slip arising between the first and second metatarsals at their bases and going to the medial side of digit 2. The second arises beneath the second metatarsal, slips going to both sides of digit 2 and to the medial side of digit 3. The third arises beneath the fourth metatarsal, and goes to both sides of digits 3 and 4.

ACTION: Flex the phalanges on the metatarsals.

## E. REVIEW OF MUSCLES OF HIND LIMB

The muscles of the hind limb in *Ailuropoda*, like those of the fore limb, agree closely with the corresponding muscles of the bears in gross structure. As in the fore limb, correspondence often extends down to minor details. In the tabulation of myological characters (p. 197), the giant panda and the bears are in complete agreement.

As in the fore limb, comparison of the relative masses of individual muscles reveals subtle differences among representative carnivores (Table 15). These differences are less obviously correlated with functional requirements than was the case in the fore leg, and agreement between *Ailuropoda* and the bears is less close than in the muscles of the fore leg. In the cursorial dog the extensors of the thigh (adductors) and flexors of the leg (biceps) are dominant, whereas in the bears and the giant panda no single muscle stands out, and muscles that adduct, abduct, and rotate are more important than in the dog. As in the fore limb, the lion tends to be intermediate.

The weight relations between fore and hind quarters are significantly different in *Ailuropoda* from those in other arctoid carnivores (Table p. 196; data as in Tables 14 and 15). In the panda the hind quarters are relatively lighter (or the fore

TABLE 15.—RELATIVE WEIGHTS OF MUSCLES OF THE HIP AND THIGH IN CARNIVORES

| | *Ailuropoda*[*] | | *Tremarctos* | | *Ursus americanus*[**] | *Canis familiaris*[**] | *Leo leo*[**] |
|---|---|---|---|---|---|---|---|
| | Wt. in gms. | % | Wt. in gms. | % | % | % | % |
| Iliacus and psoas | 121 | 7.2 | 113 | 4.7 | 4.8 | 4.5 | 10.6 |
| Glutaeus superficialis | 123 | 7.3 | 85 | 3.6 | 4.7 | 1.7 | 1.6 |
| Glutaeus medius | 136 | 8.1 | 158 | 6.6 | 5.9 | 7.3 | 6.6 |
| Glutaeus profundus | 21 | 1.2 | 20 | 1.0 | .4 | .8 | 1.1 |
| Tensor fasciae latae | 21 | 1.2 | 52 | 2.2 | 2.5 | 4.1 | 3.0 |
| Obturator internus | 14 | .8 | 17 | .8 | | | 1.8 |
| Gemellus anterior | 1 | .1 | 2 | .1 | 1.3 | 1.3 | |
| Gemellus posterior | 3 | .2 | 5 | .2 | | | |
| Piriformis | 15 | .9 | 13 | .5 | .9 | .6 | 1.1 |
| Quadratus femoris | 20 | 1.2 | 12 | .5 | .7 | .5 | .7 |
| Obturator externus | 42 | 2.5 | 49 | 2.1 | 8.3 | 1.0 | 1.2 |
| Semimembranosus | 148 | 8.8 | 281 | 11.8 | 4.7 | 4.6 | 12.0 |
| Semitendinosus | 91 | 5.4 | 96 | 4.0 | 4.3 | 6.8 | 4.6 |
| Sartorius | 114 | 6.8 | 149 | 6.3 | 5.1 | 1.9 | 5.4 |
| Rectus femoris | 76 | 4.5 | 174 | 7.3 | 6.3 | 5.0 | 5.0 |
| Vastus lateralis | 157 | 9.3 | 221 | 9.3 | 8.6 | 10.8 | 14.6 |
| Vastus intermedius | | | 50 | 2.1 | .5 | | |
| Vastus medialis | 91 | 5.4 | 57 | 2.4 | 3.3 | 5.8 | |
| Pectineus | 33 | 2.0 | 28 | 1.2 | 1.6 | .6 | .3 |
| Gracilis | 115 | 6.8 | 158 | 6.6 | 6.1 | 4.6 | 4.1 |
| Adductor | 146 | 8.7 | 276 | 11.6 | 14.6 | 22.5 | 13.7 |
| Biceps | 199 | 11.8 | 360 | 15.1 | 15.4 | 16.4 | 12.6 |
| Tenuissimus | | | 6 | .3 | | | |
| Totals | 1687 | 100.2 | 2382 | 100.3 | 100.0 | 100.8 | 100.0 |

[*] Half-grown individual.
[**] Data from Haughton.

RELATIVE WEIGHTS OF MUSCLES OF FORE AND HIND QUARTERS IN CARNIVORES

| | Ailuropoda* | | Tremarctos | | Ursus** | | Canis** | Leo** |
|---|---|---|---|---|---|---|---|---|
| | gms. | $c_i$ | gms. | $c_i$ | gms. | $c_i$ | $c_i$ | $c_i$ |
| Shoulder and arm | 1132 | 40 | 1309 | 35 | 1607 | 36 | 34 | 34 |
| Hip and thigh | 1687 | 60 | 2382 | 65 | 2891 | 64 | 66 | 66 |

* Half-grown individual (Su Lin).
** Data from Haughton.

quarters heavier) and there is no obvious functional reason for this altered relationship, which agrees with the relationships found in the skeleton. It probably reflects a generalized increase in the mass of muscle tissue in the anterior part of the body (p. 182).

## V. DISCUSSION OF MUSCULAR SYSTEM

The data on the muscular system may be conveniently considered under two heads: taxonomic characters, and evidence for the operation of evolutionary mechanisms. It is not intended to imply that these two kinds of data are unrelated to each other.

### TAXONOMIC CHARACTERS

The musculature of the Carnivora fissipeda was reviewed in detail by Windle and Parsons (1897, 1898). The viewpoint of these authors was purely morphological. They summarized the literature, supplemented it with many original dissections, and critically analyzed the resulting mass of data for features that characterize the order Canivora, or that characterize families within the Carnivora. They had data on 55 individuals, representing 25 species, of arctoid carnivores.

The accompanying table (Table 16), expanded from the summary table of Windle and Parsons, summarizes the musculature of the arctoid carnivores from the morphological and taxonomic standpoints. Consideration of the facts in Table 16 yields the following conclusions:

1. The Canidae appear to differ from all other arctoids more than any of the latter do among themselves. But the features peculiar to the Canidae are, apparently without exception, adaptations to cursorial locomotion and therefore do not represent deep-seated primary differences. Practically every one of the canid characters is shared with the likewise highly cursorial Hyaenidae, to which the dogs are only remotely related.

2. The Mustelidae differ among themselves more than do the members of any other family. Nevertheless two features appear to characterize all mustelids: the presence of the deep rhomboid as a distinct muscle,[1] and the presence of an extra head

[1] This is present in Potos, which shares many other anatomical features with the Mustelidae.

of the triceps, arising from the angle of the scapula. Both of these appear to be deep-seated, longstanding features.

3. The Ursidae and Procyonidae resemble each other more than either resembles the Canidae or Mustelidae. For the most part this resemblance is merely the absence in both of specializations such as characterize the dogs and mustelids; in other words, the bears and procyonids share generalized carnivore features.

4. The Ursidae and Procyonidae differ in a number of minor characters. These are not obviously correlated with functional differences, nor is the pattern of the musculature notably more specialized in one family than in the other.

5. Ailuropoda does not differ from the Ursidae in a single myological character (see above for a discussion of the biceps). Indeed, the resemblance is much closer than the table implies. The pattern of the musculature strongly supports the conclusion that the giant panda is closely related to the bears.

### MYOLOGICAL EVOLUTION

Although the pattern of the musculature in the giant panda is practically identical with that of the bears, the musculature differs in other important ways. These differences must be accounted for before we can claim to understand the anatomy of the giant panda. They are:

1. Regional hypertrophy of the musculature.
2. Differences in the relative mass of the individual muscles.
3. Differences in internal muscle structure.
4. Differences in attachment sites

1. Available data show significant size differences between Ailuropoda and the bears in whole regional muscle masses. These regional masses appear to be morphological units rather than functional units: in the head all muscles derived from the mandibular arch are hypertrophied, regardless of function, whereas muscles of other embryonic origin are unaffected, even though they lie in the same general area of the head. Thus in this instance the morphological unit is also a developmental and genetic unit.

The case for the limb musculature is less clear. The ratio between fore quarter weight and hind

## TABLE 16.—MYOLOGICAL CHARACTERS IN THE ARCTOID CARNIVORES

(Modified from Windle and Parsons, 1898)

| | Canidae | URSIDAE Ursus | URSIDAE Ailuropoda | URSIDAE Ailurus* | PROCYONIDAE Bassaricyon† | PROCYONIDAE Bassariscus | PROCYONIDAE Procyon Nasua | PROCYONIDAE Potos | Mustelidae |
|---|---|---|---|---|---|---|---|---|---|
| Omohyoideus | absent | present | present | present | — | present | absent | present | usually present |
| Rhomb. prof. as a distinct muscle | absent | absent | absent | absent | absent? | absent | absent | present | present |
| Biceps | one head | usually two heads | one head | two heads | one head | one head | one head | two heads | one head |
| Coracobrach. longus & brevis. | brevis only | both | both | both | brevis only | brevis only | brevis only | both | both often absent |
| Head of triceps from angle of scapula | absent | absent | absent | absent | absent | absent | absent | absent | present |
| Insertion of pronator teres | above middle of radius | lower end | lower end | lower end | middle | lower end | middle or lower end | lower end | lower end |
| Palmaris longus (ext. or int.) | neither | usually externus only | externus only | both | externus only | both | both present | both present | externus only |
| Two heads of flexor carpi ulnaris | distinct | distinct | distinct | distinct | fused? | fused | usually fused | fused | inconstant |
| Insertion of pronator quadratus | whole length of forearm | lower third | lower third | lower third | — | lower third | variable | lower third | variable |
| Brachioradialis. | absent | present | present | present | present | present | present | present | present |
| Flexor brevis digit. manus. | absent | usually absent | absent | present | — | — | present | present | seldom present |
| Pect. superfic. fused with profundus. | no | yes | yes | no | no | — | no | no | no |
| Caudofemoralis. | absent | absent | absent | present | present | present | present or absent | present | present or absent |
| Abd. cruris caudalis. | to crural fascia | to femur | to femur | absent | absent | absent | absent | absent | absent |
| Gluteus ventralis. | usually present | usually present | present | — | absent? | absent? | usually absent | present | usually present |
| Sartorius | usually double | usually single | single | — | single | double | usually single | single | usually single |
| Semitendinosus (caudal head). | absent | absent | absent | absent | absent | present | present | present | present or absent |
| Soleus. | absent | present | present | present | present | present | present | present | present |
| Flexor brevis digit. pedis. | absent | present | present | present | — | present | present | — | present |
| Tibialis posterior | usually absent | present | present | present | present | present | present | present | present |
| Quadratus plantae. | absent | present | present | present | — | — | present | present | present |

* Data mostly from Carlsson (1925).
† Data mostly from Beddard (1900).

quarter weight in *Ailuropoda* clearly differs from that in other carnivores examined, and this seems to involve the total musculature rather than individual elements. The difference is far less than for the craniomandibular musculature, but is nevertheless considerable. It is impossible, from our data, to determine what, if anything, is involved morphogenetically.

2. It is well known that in the individual a muscle hypertrophies as a result of continuous exercise and atrophies with disuse. It has been shown experimentally that the relative sizes of muscle elements depart significantly from the norm when the forces to which they are habitually subjected are changed (e.g., Fuld, 1901). Therefore observed differences in the relative size of a given muscle, even when consistent in all individuals of a species, may simply reflect the response of that muscle to extrinsic mechanical forces rather than the action of factors intrinsic to the musculature. No morphogenetic mechanism capable of producing selective hypertrophy of individual muscles has so far been demonstrated.

Differences of this kind occur in the musculature of *Ailuropoda* as compared with that of the bears. Involved are both craniomandibular and limb elements. The observed differences are no greater than those distinguishing Fuld's bipedal dogs from his normal controls, and may therefore represent factors extrinsic to the musculature. There is at present no known way of determining whether such differences depend on factors intrinsic or extrinsic to the musculature.

3. Differences in internal muscle structure involve arrangement of fibers, form and extent of tendons and tendinous aponeuroses, length and diameter of fibers, etc. Obviously, profound changes of this kind must have occurred during the phylogeny of vertebrates. The only such difference of any importance observed in the present study was the tendinization of fascial planes in the temporal muscle of *Ailuropoda*. The extent to which such a difference reflects changes in the genetic substrate is unknown.

4. There is considerable variation in the attachment sites of muscles among the carnivores, and these differences usually shift lever advantages in the direction of either speed or power and so are broadly adaptive. Such differences must surely result from the action of selection on genetic systems, but they scarcely exist between *Ailuropoda* and the bears and therefore need not concern us here. The only notable differences in attachment sites between these two groups—failure of the abductor pollicis longus and tibialis posterior to reach the first metapodials—have a purely mechanical cause. The tendons of these muscles already attach partly to the radial and tibial sesamoids, respectively, in bears. Further enlargement of the sesamoids in *Ailuropoda* has simply blocked the tendons off from the metapodials.

## VI. CONCLUSIONS

1. The musculature of *Ailuropoda* is almost identical with that of the Ursidae.

2. Only two significant differences are evident: hypertrophy of the craniomandibular musculature, and failure of the abductor pollicis longus and tibialis posterior to reach their normal attachment sites on the first metapodials.

3. Hypertrophy of the jaw muscles is associated with hypertrophy of *all* muscles derived from the mandibular arch, and extends in a decreasing gradient to the musculature of the neck, shoulders, and upper arm. This condition has a direct, and probably very simple, genetic base.

4. The abductor pollicis longus and tibialis posterior are prevented mechanically from reaching their respective metapodials. The cause for the condition in the panda is therefore extrinsic to the muscular system.

5. Differences in the relative sizes of individual jaw and limb muscles are evident. Some, probably all, are adaptive, but whether the causes for these differences are intrinsic or extrinsic to the muscular system cannot be determined from our data.

# ALIMENTARY SYSTEM

## I. MOUTH

The **hard palate** (fig. 106) is narrow and elongate. Its lateral borders are nearly straight, although there is a slight expansion opposite the fourth premolar and first molar. There are 10 pairs of low palatal ridges, rounded rather than V-shaped in cross section, which meet a faint longitudinal ridge running down the midline. Only the first pair of ridges is transverse; successive pairs are progressively more obliquely displaced, and less and less sharply set off from the surrounding tissue. The last ridge is at the level of the posterior border of the first molar. There is a prominent incisive pad between the incisor teeth and the first pair of palatal ridges. The palate of a second individual (Mei Lan) is similar except that the ridges are even less prominent.

The **soft palate** has a length of 105 mm., ending posteriorly in a square free border, the velum palatinum. Numerous punctures, representing the openings of the palatine glands, are distributed over the anterior part of the soft palate and the extreme posterior part of the hard palate.

The entire palate is unpigmented.

In specimens of *Ursus tibetanus, Tremarctos ornatus, Ailurus fulgens,* and *Procyon lotor* the palatal sculpturing is much more prominent than in *Ailuropoda,* which looks almost degenerate in comparison. The palatal ridges number 8–10, and are V-shaped in cross section and much larger and sharper than in the giant panda. They are also more transversely situated.

## II. SALIVARY GLANDS

The **parotid gland** (figs. 107, 108) is roughly rectangular in form, its height considerably exceeding its width. It is quite extensive, the main part of the gland measuring approximately 90 mm. by 50 mm. The entire gland, with its duct, weighs 57 grams. The gland fills the area between the posterior border of the head posteriorly, a line projected along the upper teeth ventrally, and the posterior border of the masseter muscle anteriorly; dorsally it extends well up onto the ear cartilage.

The dorsal border of the gland is concave, with moderately well-marked pre-meatal and post-meatal processes. The posterior border is nearly straight, but is produced slightly backward at its ventral angle by the underlying internal facial vein. The ventral border is somewhat irregular; it is molded around the submaxillary gland to give a general concave contour. The anterior border is convex.

The gland is much flattened. It is divided into rather small leaf-like lobulations. The parotid duct emerges below the center of the gland, by a dorsal and a ventral root that promptly unite. The substance of the gland is carried forward along the duct on the right side of the head, and small accessory lobules are distributed along the length of the duct on both sides of the head as far as the labial commissure. These lobules open separately into the parotid duct by short ducts of their own. The main parotid duct runs horizontally across the outer face of the masseter, passes internal to the external facial vein at the anterior border of the masseter, to terminate in the cheek near the gum line, opposite the posterior part of the fourth premolar (carnassial).

The **submaxillary gland** (figs. 107, 108) is reniform, with the concavity directed caudad. It measures approximately 50 mm. in height and 35 mm. in width. The entire gland, with its duct, weighs 19 grams. Its surface is nearly smooth, the lobulations being much shallower and more regular than are those of the parotid.

The gland is in contact with the parotid dorsally. Its medial border rests on the sternohyoid muscle. Immediately in front of it is a pair of lymph glands, one on either side of the external facial vein.

The submaxillary duct leaves the deep surface of the gland slightly above its center. It passes forward between the digastric and masseter muscles, then deep to the mylohyoid where it runs along the medial border of the sublingual gland. Beyond the anterior end of this gland it parallels the sublingual duct to the caruncula sublingualis, where the two ducts open side by side. The **sublingual carunculae** are a pair of very prominent papillae, 4 mm. in diameter, situated on the floor of the mouth. They are located 10 mm. anterior to the frenulum of the tongue, and the two carunculae are 9 mm. apart.

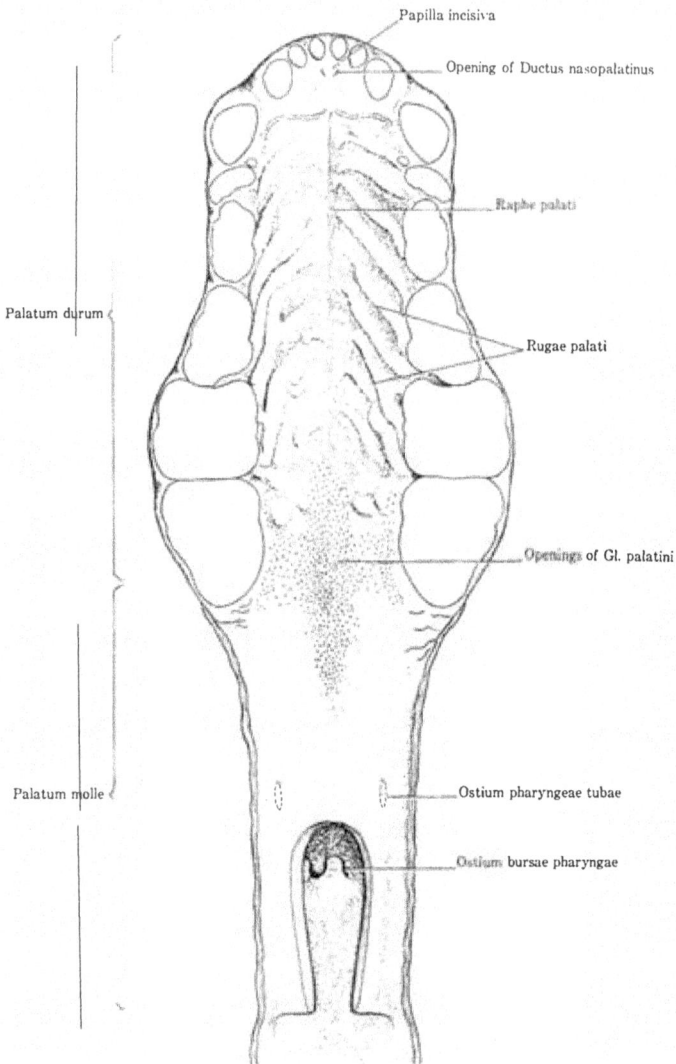

FIG. 106. The hard and soft palates of *Ailuropoda*. A window has been cut in the posterior part of the soft palate to expose the entrances to the pharyngeal bursae.

The **greater sublingual gland** (figs. 107, 108) is elongate and irregular in outline, triangular in cross section posteriorly, and much flattened anteriorly. It is wider posteriorly than anteriorly. An irregular vertical arm is continued up along the submaxillary duct, around the digastric muscle, to the anterior border of the submaxillary gland, with which it is in contact. The main part of the gland (exclusive of the vertical arm) measures 92 mm. in length, with a maximum width of only about 10 mm. It occupies the lateral sublingual space, and is in intimate contact with the mylohyoideus ventrally. It extends from the level of the angular process of the mandible forward to the posterior border of the first lower molar.

The duct may be traced through the substance of the gland, occasionally appearing on its lateral surface. It leaves the gland at its anterior tip,

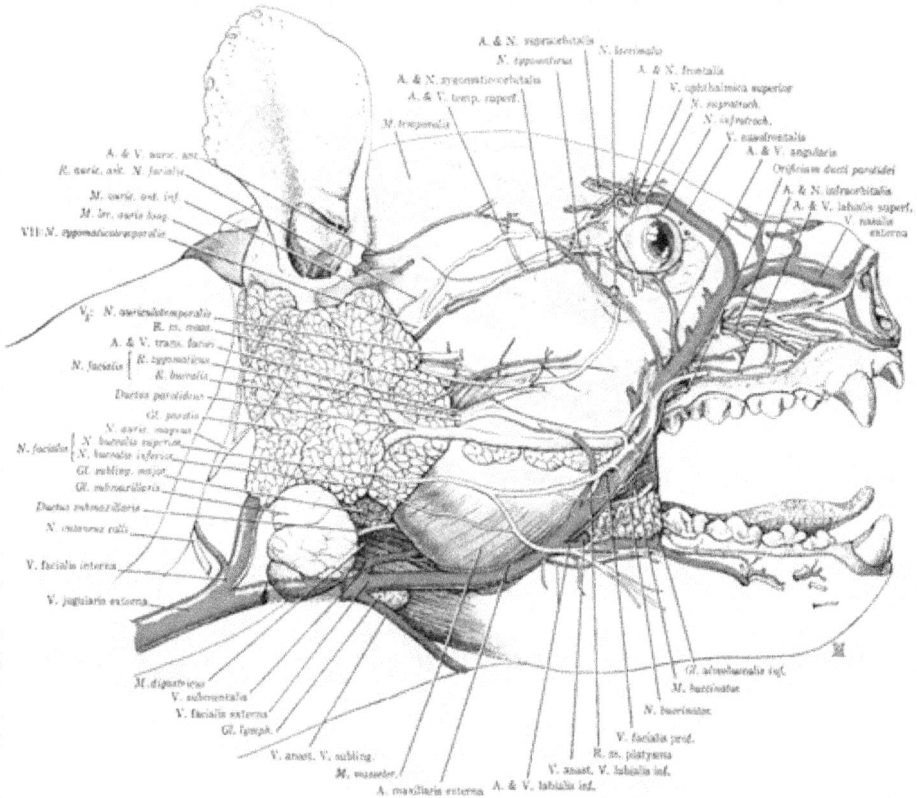

FIG. 107. Superficial dissection of the head of *Ailuropoda*.

and parallels the submaxillary duct to the sublingual caruncle, where it opens.

The **lesser sublingual glands** (fig. 108) are represented by glandular masses situated just deep to the greater sublingual gland, and extending from the posterior border of the greater sublingual gland to the base of the tongue, a distance of 43 mm. Dorsally they are continuous with the palatine glands, and ventrally there is no boundary separating them from the inferior alveobuccal glands.

The **palatine glands** consist of a layer of lobulated glandular tissue under the mucous membrane of the soft palate and the posterior end of the hard palate. Laterally they are continuous with the lesser sublingual glands. Numerous dots, distributed like pin-pricks over the mucous membrane of the soft palate and the posterior part of the hard palate (fig. 106), represent the outlets of these glands.

The **inferior alveobuccal glands** (molar gland) (figs. 107, 108) are well developed. They may be traced on the medial side of the mandible from the symphysis (at the posterior border of the third premolar) back to a point beyond the last molar; the gland mass gradually increases in size posteriorly. Behind the last molar it crosses over to the outside of the mandible, where it is continued forward on the buccinator muscle and deep to the masseter to the labial commissure. Each of the glandular elements opens by an independent duct. There are numerous outlets, hardly visible under a magnifying glass, in the mucous membrane below the teeth on the inner side of the mandible. A double row of 24 or more prominent papilla-like projections, ranging up to a millimeter in diameter, in the mucous membrane of the cheek near the lower molar teeth, mark the outlets of the extra-mandibular part of the gland mass.

The **orbital glands** (fig. 108) form a compact ovate mass of 12-14 independent but closely asso-

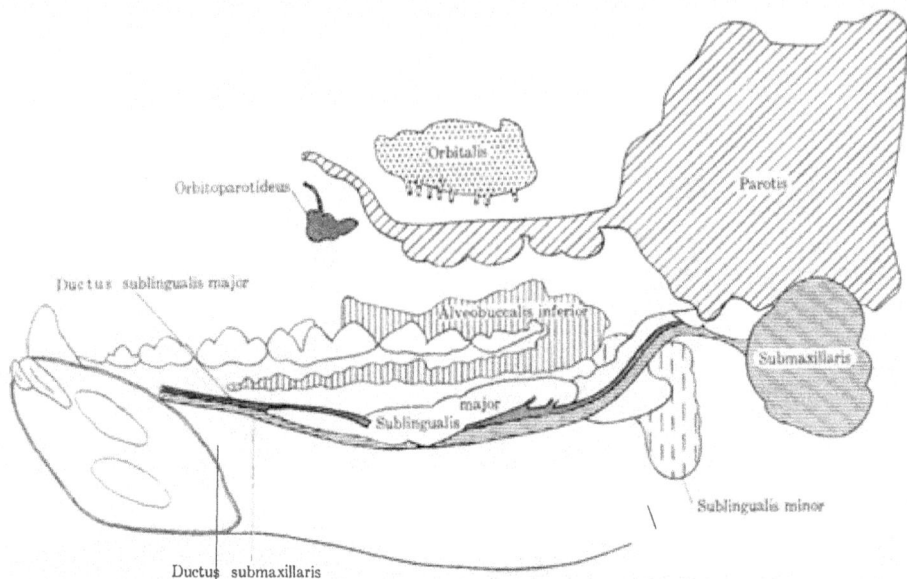

FIG. 108.   Salivary glands of *Ailuropoda*, semi-diagrammatic.

ciated elements situated in the suborbital space immediately above the last upper molar. The much-flattened gland mass lies between the bone and the temporal muscle. It measures 37 mm. in length by about 18 mm. in height. The dozen or more ducts open on low, inconspicuous projections that are scattered over a fold of the oral mucous membrane laterad of the posterior half of the last upper molar.

The **orbitoparotid gland** (fig. 108) is a small structure situated at the inferior corner of the anterior root of the zygoma. It is bounded, as usual, by the anterior border of the masseter posteriorly, the parotid duct dorsally, and the buccinator muscle and oral mucous membrane internally. The gland measures about 10 mm. in diameter. The duct parallels the parotid duct to a point opposite the middle of the second upper molar, where it opens on a minute papilla near the lateral border of the tooth.

Carmalt (1913) described and compared the gross structure of the salivary glands in eight species of fissiped carnivore: *Canis familiaris, Procyon lotor, Ursus tibetanus, Taxidea taxus, Gulo luscus, Mephitis mephitica, Felis domestica,* and *F. leo.* The literature on these glands was reviewed extensively by Fahrenholz (1937). In general the salivary glands are relatively small in carnivores, particularly the serous parotid glands, which may be smaller than the submaxillary gland in predominantly flesh-eat-

ing forms. Carmalt concluded that the form of the salivary glands in carnivores is determined largely by the molding effect of surrounding tissues, and therefore that differences in shape are of no great significance. The parotid gland tends to be large in herbivorous mammals. Among the Carnivora it is large in the bears, immense in *Procyon* (Fahrenholz), "considerably larger than the submaxillary gland" in *Ailurus* (Carlsson, 1925). These are among the most herbivorous of the carnivores. It is small in the Canidae.

*Ailuropoda* resembles other herbivorous carnivores in its large parotid gland. The relative size of this gland (twice the size of the submaxillary) is comparable to the condition in bears, but is far short of the relative size in *Procyon,* in which the parotid is six times the size of the submaxillary.

## III. TONGUE

The tongue (fig. 109) is of moderate length and narrow, and is devoid of pigmentation. It measures 210 mm. from tip to base, and 55 mm. in greatest width. The lateral margins of the oral part are nearly parallel, although the organ tapers slightly toward the tip. There is a prominent frenulum on the inferior surface, situated 75 mm. from the tip. There is a small but distinct median notch at the tip, but no indication of a median furrow on the dorsum. The glosso-epiglottic furrow, on the other hand, is very well marked.

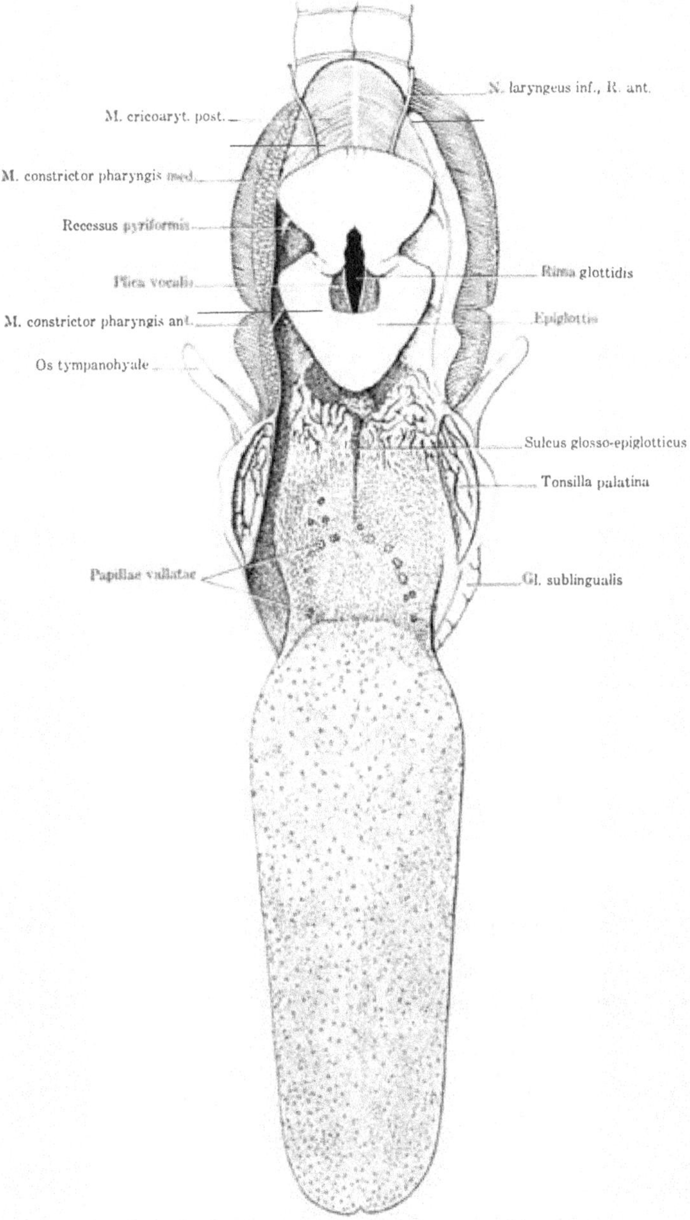

M. cricoaryt. post.

M. constrictor pharyngis med.

Recessus pyriformis

Plica vocalis

M. constrictor pharyngis ant.

Os tympanohyale

N. laryngeus inf., R. ant.

Rima glottidis

Epiglottis

Sulcus glosso-epiglotticus

Tonsilla palatina

Papillae vallatae

Gl. sublingualis

FIG. 109.   Upper surface of tongue of *Ailuropoda*.

Conical papillae cover the entire dorsum from the tip back to the epiglottis. They are quite uniform in size except near the tip, where they are slightly larger, and in the pharyngeal region where they are much larger and sparser. Large conical papillae are also present on the under surface at the tip and for 65 mm. along the lateral margins.

Fungiform papillae are distributed over the entire dorsum of the oral part of the tongue, except for a small area along the midline 30 mm. long and about 5 mm. wide, and situated about 20 mm. back from the tip, where they appear to be absent. They are very conspicuous and are evenly spaced at intervals of 2 to 3 mm., posteriorly showing a tendency to form diagonal rows running from the midline outward and backward. They are not absent over the entire middle of the dorsum, as Raven found in the tongue he examined.

The vallate papillae are arranged in a semicircle, and not in V formation as Raven suggested. There are thirteen papillae; in some cases a small secondary papilla is closely approximated to a larger one and enclosed in the same fossa (these were not counted in arriving at the total). In addition there are three papillae situated irregularly behind the row on the right side, making a total of sixteen. Raven postulated seventeen as the number originally present on the incomplete tongue he examined.

Foliate papillae are absent. Raven identified as foliate papillae two longitudinal slits, asymmetrically placed on the anterior dorsum of the tongue. A single such slit is present on the dorsum near the tongue tip in our specimen. This slit is not glandular and quite evidently represents a mechanical injury.

The lyssa is a small structure, 33 mm. long by about 2 mm. in diameter, situated in the anterior part of the tongue. Its length is thus about 16 per cent of that of the tongue as a whole. The structure, which is oval in cross section, is attached to the mucous membrane at the tip of the tongue anteriorly. Posteriorly it is continued into a thin cord that is lost in the lingual septum.

The gross structure of the tongue in the Carnivora was reviewed by Sonntag (1923), and again by Stadtmüller (1938). Among the Procyonidae and Ursidae, differences appear to involve primarily the number and distribution of the papillae. The fungiform and conical papillae differ little from conditions described here for Ailuropoda. In the procyonids and bears the number of vallate papillae ranges from six to twenty, the larger numbers occurring in the bears. They are more numerous in bears than in any other carnivore. The vallate papillae are arranged in a V, except in certain bears

(Ursus americanus, Helarctos malayanus) in which they are described as forming a semicircle. The Ursidae and Ailuropoda agree in the large number of vallate papillae, and only in these forms do they ever form a semicircle.

According to Stadtmüller the number of vallate papillae in mammals is not correlated either with diet or with degree of development of the sense of taste, but tends to be larger in less primitive forms. Number and arrangement are consistent at or below the family level.

Statements on the foliate papillae are very contradictory. Sonntag found no trace of them in Procyon cancrivora, Nasua narica, Potos, or Ailurus, but observed "some small foliate clefts" in Procyon lotor. Stadtmüller failed to find them in Nasua rufa and Potos. Carlsson says they "stand out prominently" in Ailurus. I could find no trace of foliate papillae in Procyon lotor.

Among the Ursidae, Sonntag observed "small foliate clefts" in Thalarctos and Melursus, and Tuckerman described foliate papillae for Ursus americanus and Helarctos. Stadtmüller, on the contrary, could find no foliate papillae in Ursus tibetanus, Helarctos, and Thalarctos. I failed to find them in Ursus tibetanus.

The lyssa, which is large in the Canidae, is present but small in all ursids and procyonids except Potos, in which it is said to be large.

The tongue appears to differ little among the Procyonidae and Ursidae. The tongue of Ailuropoda most closely resembles that of Ursus.

## IV.  PHARYNX AND ESOPHAGUS

### A.  PHARYNX

The pharynx is relatively capacious. The nasopharynx and pharynx proper together have a total length of about 135 mm., and the width just back of the velum palatinum is about 40 mm. (with the walls flattened out). The pharynx is fusiform in shape, tapering gradually toward the choanae anteriorly and the esophagus posteriorly. The pars nasalis pharyngis is 115 mm. long, thus greatly exceeding the pharyngis propria, which measures only about 20 mm.

A pair of openings, the outlets of the bursae pharyngeae, is situated in the dorsal wall of the nasopharynx (fig. 106). These openings are located 12 mm. anterior to the ventral border of the foramen magnum and 35 mm. anterior to the posterior border of the velum palatinum; they lie immediately in front of the anterior border of the pterygopharyngeal division of the anterior constrictor muscle of the pharynx. They are a pair of crescent-shaped slits, 7 mm. in length, separated by a prominent isthmus 5 mm. in width. The right slit is more prominent and opens into a capacious thin-walled sac, 130 mm. long by 30 mm. in greatest width (flattened out), situated between the esophagus ventrally and the longus colli muscle and centra of the cervical vertebrae dorsally (fig. 110). The bursa, lying in the trough bounded laterally by the prominent longus capitis muscles, extends caudad to the disk between the fifth and sixth cervical vertebrae. The bursa begins with a narrow neck, which expands into an extensive blind sac. A very short septum divides the posterior end of the bursa into right and left halves. The left bursa, into which the left slit opens, is much smaller, measuring only 15 mm. in length.

Proximally the lining of the large right bursa is thrown up into prominent longitudinal ridges, which on the lateral wall are interrupted by two small pocket-like sinuses open anteriorly, and slightly farther caudad by a small oval perforation in the lining of the bursa that opens into a small sinus. An additional pocket-like sinus is present near the extreme posterior end of the bursa.

Killian (1888) failed to find a pharyngeal bursa in the following carnivores: *Canis familiaris*, *Nasua rufa*, *Mephitis mephitica*, *Lutra vulgaris*, *Herpestes griseus*, *Viverra civetta*, *Paradoxurus trivirgatus*, *Felis domestica*. I have examined specimens of *Procyon lotor* and *Ailurus fulgens* and find they have no pharyngeal bursa.

On the other hand, the existence of pharyngeal bursae in bears has long been known (literature reviewed by Killian). These are described by various authors as paired structures, always unequal in size, with relations very similar to those described here for *Ailuropoda*. Such paired bursae have not been described for any other mammal. Pharyngeal bursae have been described for *Ursus arctos*, *U. americanus*, *U. horribilis*, *Melursus ursinus*, and *Helarctos malayanus*. The function of these structures is unknown.

The openings of the auditory tubes are a pair of longitudinal slits in the lateral walls of the nasopharynx at about its posterior third, 15 mm. anterior to the openings of the pharyngeal bursae (fig. 106). They are much less prominent than the latter.

## B. MUSCLES OF THE SOFT PALATE AND

### PHARYNX

**M. levator veli palatini** is a rather narrow band of muscle fibers arising from the petrosal immediately laterad and caudad of the orifice of the auditory tube and from the adjacent lateral wall of the auditory tube. The muscle extends ventrad and caudad, passing internal to the pterygopha-

ryngeus, to insert into the palate. The fibers extend to within a few millimeters of the caudal border of the velum palatinum.

**M. tensor veli palatini** is slightly smaller than the levator. It arises, as a rounded mass of mingled tendon and fleshy fibers, from a groove and ridge in the floor of the middle ear, from the scaphoid fossa of the sphenoid, and from the adjacent lateral wall of the auditory tube. From its origin the muscle passes ventrad and craniad, across the hamular process of the pterygoid. Mesad of the hamular process the muscle becomes tendinous, forming a thin tendinous sheet that runs craniad in the soft palate just inside the pterygoid process. The tendon fibers can be traced craniad nearly to the posterior border of the hard palate.

**M. uvulae** is composed of a pair of narrow bands of muscle extending along the midline of the soft palate and the velum palatinum. Origin is by tendon fibers from the posterior border of the bony palate at the midline, with accessory tendinous slips coming from the soft palate in its anterior quarter. The paired muscle extends caudad to the posterior border of the velum palatinum, where it inserts.

**M. pharyngopalatinus** is a thin layer of fibers lying deep to the constrictor muscles of the pharynx. It is situated at the posterior end of the velum palatinum, where it arises from the aponeurosis of the palate. From this origin the fibers fan out over the lateral and dorsal walls of the pharynx, beneath the middle constrictor and the anterior part of the posterior constrictor.

**M. constrictor pharyngis anterior**, the smallest of the three constrictors, is composed of three elements, which maintain their identity throughout. The most anterior (*Pterygopharyngeus* of human anatomy) is a narrow band of fibers arising from the hamular process of the pterygoid bone. It runs caudad to the neck of the pharyngeal bursa and arches sharply around this structure, its most anterior fibers forming the bulk of the isthmus that separates the ostii bursae. The posterior part of the muscle is overlain by the anterior border of the middle constrictor. All the fibers of the muscle pass to the dorsal midline of the pharynx, where the muscle forms a raphe with its fellow of the opposite side. A posterior muscle (*buccopharyngeus* of human anatomy) lies at first deep to and co-extensive with the pterygopharyngeus. It arises from the medial surface of the pterygoid process and the soft palate mesad of the pterygoid process. As the muscle passes beyond the pterygopharyngeus it splits into subequal parts which arch dorsad, embracing the pharyngopalatinus between them, to their insertion on the dorsal midline of

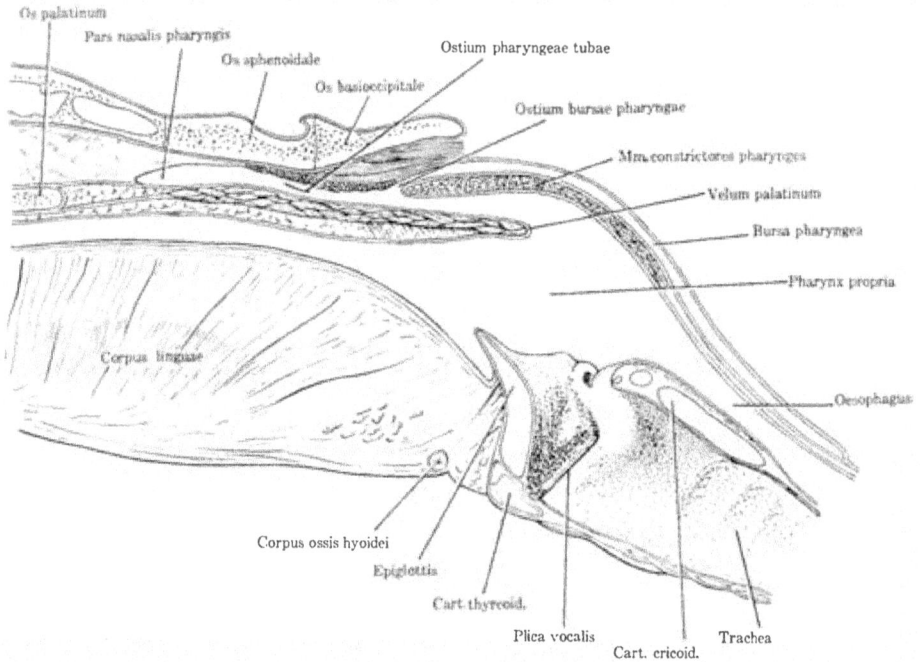

FIG. 110.  Sagittal section through larynx of *Ailuropoda*.

the pharynx.  The *glossopharyngeal* division is a narrow band arising from the side of the root of the tongue at the level of the tonsils.  It runs caudad and slightly dorsad to its insertion, which is into the lateral wall of the pharynx at the level of the thyrohyal arm of the hyoid.  Throughout its length it lies ventrad of the other two parts of the anterior constrictor.

**M. constrictor pharyngis medius** (fig. 85) is composed of a superficial and a deep layer.  The *superficial layer*, which is more or less rectangular in form, arises from the lateral surface of the thyrohyal.  Near its insertion, where it is overlapped by the anterior border of the posterior constrictor, it fuses with the underlying deep layer.  The *deep* layer, which is considerably smaller, arises from the posterior surface of the epihyal.  Both layers insert along the dorsal midline of the pharynx.

**M. constrictor pharyngis posterior** (fig. 85) is the largest and heaviest of the pharyngeal constrictors.  It is partially separable into an anterior superficial part, which partly overlaps a deeper and more caudal posterior part.  The anterior part (*thyreopharyngeus* of human anatomy) arises from the oblique line of the thyroid cartilage be-

tween the superior and inferior thyroid tubercles.  The posterior part (*cricopharyngeus* of human anatomy) arises from a tendinous arch extending from the thyroid cartilage to the dorsolateral border of the cricoid cartilage, and from the entire dorsal surface of the inferior cornu of the thyroid cartilage.  The fibers of the two parts soon become inseparable, and the resulting common mass fans out to its insertion, which is into the median raphe on the dorsal side of the pharynx.

C.  ESOPHAGUS

The esophagus is 35 cm. long and about 20 mm. wide when flattened out dorsoventrally.  As it passes posteriorly from the pharynx, the esophagus gradually moves to the left of the midline.  This deflection is greatest at the level of the third rib, posterior to which it moves back toward the midline, to be deflected to the left again as the diaphragm is approached.  It joins the stomach at the level of the tenth thoracic vertebra, immediately after passing through the diaphragm.  The inner surface of the esophagus is thrown into longitudinal folds which terminate abruptly at the level of the stomach, as Raven (1936) noticed.  Raven describes the smooth epithelium lining the stom-

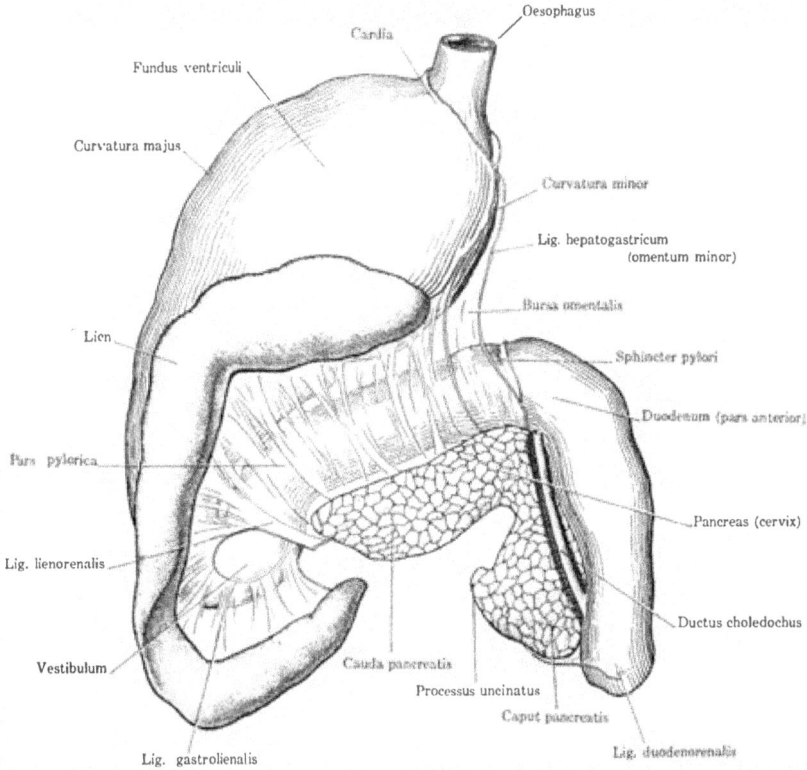

FIG. 111. Stomach, spleen, and pancreas of *Ailuropoda*, dorsal view.

ach as "almost horny"; such a texture is not evident in the specimen at hand.

## V. STOMACH

The stomach, as Raven observed, is elongate and slender (fig. 111). The fundus is only moderately dilated, and the whole cardiac region tapers gradually toward the pylorus. The pylorus is elongate and tubular, with extremely muscular walls. The stomach was empty in the specimen dissected; its length along the greater curvature, from the esophagus to the pyloric sphincter, was 400 mm. This compares with a length of 80 cm. given by Raven for a fully adult individual. There is a very sharp flexure in the stomach near the beginning of the pylorus, so that the pylorus is doubled back against the cardia with its distal end near the esophagus. The strong gastrohepatic ligament holds the stomach in this position.

The lining of the stomach displays rather prominent plicae mucosae throughout. These differ considerably in different regions. In the region

of the fundus they are low and irregular, forming an irregular reticulation. They became much more prominent in the middle region of the stomach, and show a tendency toward a longitudinal arrangement. In the pylorus they take the form of four elevated longitudinal folds. The mucosa is similar over the whole stomach; there is no cornification anywhere. The wall of the pylorus is 8-9 mm. thick. Most of this (about 6 mm.) is accounted for by the tunica muscularis. Raven states that the muscularis was only 2 mm. thick in his specimen.

The stomach is simple in all fissiped carnivores, with a more or less spherical fundus and a cylindrical, thick-walled pylorus (fig 112). The pylorus is characteristically doubled back against the minor curvature. Among the arctoid carnivores there are minor variations in form, but these have no obvious relation to differences in diet. In *Ailuropoda* the stomach is more elongate, particularly the long tubular pylorus, than in any other carnivore examined. In bears ( *Ursus americanus* and

*Canis familiaris*

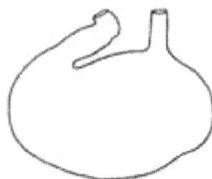

*Ailurus fulgens*

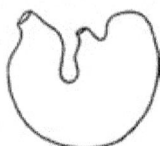

*Bassariscus astutus*

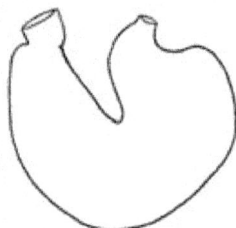

*Procyon lotor*

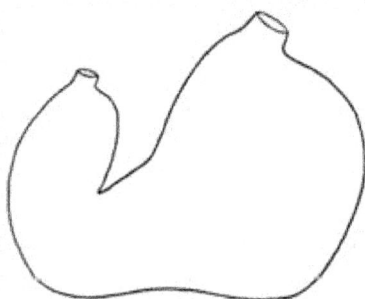

*Helarctos malayanus*

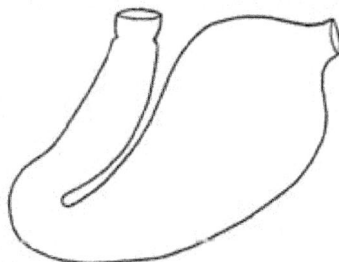

*Ailuropoda melanoleuca*

FIG. 112. Form of the stomach in representative arctoid carnivores, not to scale. (*Canis* from Ellenberger and Baum, *Ailurus* from Flower 1870, others original).

*Helarctos malayanus* examined) the pylorus is rather globular in form. In an adult *Helarctos* the wall of the pylorus is about 6.5 mm. thick, almost as thick as in *Ailuropoda*, but the pyloric region is far shorter than in the panda.

## VI. INTESTINES AND MESENTERY

The intestines of *Ailuropoda* are remarkable for their shortness and the slight differentiation of the various regions. The fixed and preserved intestinal tract, measured with the mesentery still attached, was only 4780 mm. in length from pyloric valve to anus in Su Lin. This is only four times head and body length. In the fully adult individual studied by Raven intestinal length was 5.5 times head and body length. The gut in *Ailuropoda* appears to be as short as in any known carnivore.

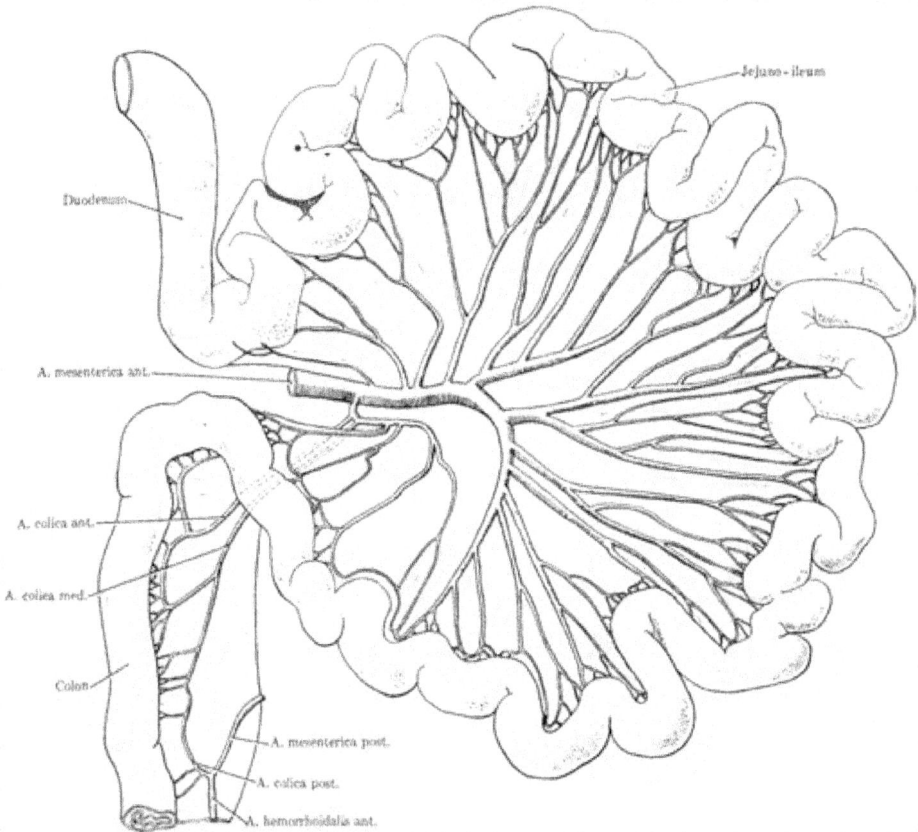

FIG. 113.  Intestinal tract and mesentery of *Ailuropoda*, spread out.  Dorsal view.

The **duodenum** begins a few millimeters to the right of the midline of the body.  It turns caudad rather abruptly at the pyloric sphincter, and runs almost straight back to its juncture with the jejunum.  There is thus scarcely any indication of the U-shaped duodenal loop that characterizes the arctoid carnivores.  The duodenum has a length of only 130 mm. and a diameter of about 25 mm. The duodenorenal ligament is well developed.  Its anterior end is heavier and attaches to the tip of the caudate lobe of the liver.

The heavy wall of the pylorus gives way abruptly to the very much thinner wall of the duodenum at the pyloric sphincter.  Raven describes the mucosa of the duodenum as thrown up into numerous longitudinal folds.  These are not evident in my specimen; the few folds that are present correspond to folds involving the entire wall of the duodenum, and may be considered a post-mortem

effect.  The lumen is lined with close-set villi, each about 2 mm. long, which gives the lining a velvety appearance.

The **jejuno-ileum** is suspended from a short mesentery that is nearly circular in outline (fig. 113).  This part of the intestine is comparatively short, measuring only 3890 mm. in length.  It is not sharply separated from the duodenum.  It is arranged around the circumference of the mesentery in a series of about a dozen U-shaped loops.  The villi lining the jejuno-ileum do not differ in appearance from those lining the duodenum.  There are no Peyer's patches, in which this specimen agrees with the one examined by Raven.

The internal diameter of this part of the intestine varies.  It is about 60 mm. near the duodenum, decreasing gradually to about 20 mm. a meter and a half beyond the duodenum.  The rest of the tract is about 20 mm. in diameter.  The mean internal diameter of the jejuno-ileum is 28.6 mm., based on circumference measurements made at 500 mm. intervals on the opened and flattened-out intestine.

The internal surface area of the entire small intestine, calculated from the measured length of 4020 mm. and a mean internal circumference figure of 90 mm., is 361,800 mm².

There is no **caecum**, and no external indication of the ileo-colic junction. Internally there is no indication of a valve at the juncture between the ileum and colon.

The **colon** (fig. 113) measures 580 mm. in length. The internal diameter is about 31.5 mm., which slightly exceeds the diameter of the lower part of the small intestine. The colon is arranged in a short but well-defined colic loop, which is supplied by a separate branch of the anterior mesenteric artery and vein, and which passes without a sharp boundary into a short straight rectum. The rectum is suspended from a narrow mesocolon, and has approximately the same diameter as the rest of the intestine. It has a length of 180 mm. The lining of the rectum does not differ in appearance from that of the colon.

The internal surface area of the colon–rectum, calculated from the measured length of 760 mm. and a mean internal circumference of 99 mm., is 75,240 mm².

The **mesentery** from which the small intestine is suspended arises from the dorsal midline at the level of the last thoracic vertebra. It is nearly circular in outline, as is characteristic of carnivores,

and is comparatively limited in extent (fig. 113). The anterior mesenteric artery and vein cross it in the form of a short, gently curved arc. The mesenteric vein gives off only four main branches in its course across the mesentery; each of these bifurcates, however, about 15 mm. from its origin. The mesenteric artery gives off seven branches; like the veins, these bifurcate a short distance from their origins. The anterior mesenteric artery and vein each give rise to a well-defined colic branch. The colic vein arises a short distance distad of the origin of the inferior mesenteric vein.

The pattern of the intestinal tract is simple and extremely uniform in the fissiped carnivores (Mitchell, 1905, 1916). Among the Arctoidea, a caecum is present in the Canidae but absent in the Mustelidae, Procyonidae, and Ursidae. A definite colic loop is present in the Ursidae but absent in other arctoids (Mitchell); a bear-like colic loop is present in *Ailuropoda*.

An ileocolic valve is said to be absent in the Procyonidae and Ursidae (Jacobshagen, 1937), but I find a conspicuous sphincter-like ileocolic valve in *Procyon*. No indication of a valve could be found in a specimen of *Ursus americanus*, and there is no valve in *Ailuropoda*.

The relative length of the intestinal tract varies among arctoid carnivores (Table 17). The gut is 4–4.5 times head and body length in most arctoids. It is longer than this in some procyonids (up to 6 times body length in *Potos*, 6–9 times in *Procyon*), but is only 4–4.5 times in *Bassariscus* and *Nasua*.

TABLE 17.—INTESTINAL LENGTH IN ARCTOID CARNIVORES

| | Head and Body Length | Length Small Intestine | Length Colon and Rectum | Total Length Intestine | Intestine Head and Body | Source |
|---|---|---|---|---|---|---|
| Canis lupus...... ............... | 1217 | 4870 | 649 | 5519 | 4.5 | Cuvier |
| | 1000 | .... | ... | 4100 | 4.1 | Landois (1884) |
| Canis familiaris................ | ... | .... | ... | .... | 5–6 | Landois (1884) |
| Bassariscus astutus ........... | [385] | ... | ... | 1525 | 4 | Beddard (1898) |
| Nasua socialis................. | ... | 1875 | 175 | 2050 | 4.5 | Carlsson (1925) |
| Nasua sp..................... | 460 | 1920 | 140 | 2060 | 4.5 | Raven (1936) |
| Potos flavus.................. | ... | 1730 | 250 | 1980 | 4.4 | Carlsson (1925) |
| | 430 | 2340 | 150 | 2490 | 5.8 | Raven (1936) |
| Procyon lotor................. | 594 | .... | ... | 4221 | 7.1 | Cuvier |
| | 490 | 2700 | 200 | 2900 | 5.9 | Raven (1936) |
| | [530] | 4280 | 220 | 4500 | 8.7 | Original |
| Ailurus fulgens............... | 610 | ... | ... | 2641 | 4.3 | Flower (1870) |
| | 425 | 1620 | 180 | 1800 | 4.2 | Carlsson (1925) |
| Thalarctos maritimus.......... | 1244 | .... | ... | 12664 | 10.1 | Cuvier |
| Ursus arctos.................. | 1352 | ... | ... | 10700 | 7.9 | Cuvier |
| Ursus gyas................... | 1720 | .... | ... | 10510 | 6.1 | Original |
| Ursus americanus............. | 900 | 5960 | 160* | 6120 | 6.8 | Raven (1936) |
| | 615 | 4100 | 430 | 4530 | 7.4 | Original |
| Ailuropoda melanoleuca........ | 1460 | 6900 | 1100 | 8000 | 5.5 | Raven (1936) |
| | 1168 | 4020 | 760 | 4780 | 4.1 | Original |

* Evidently an error.

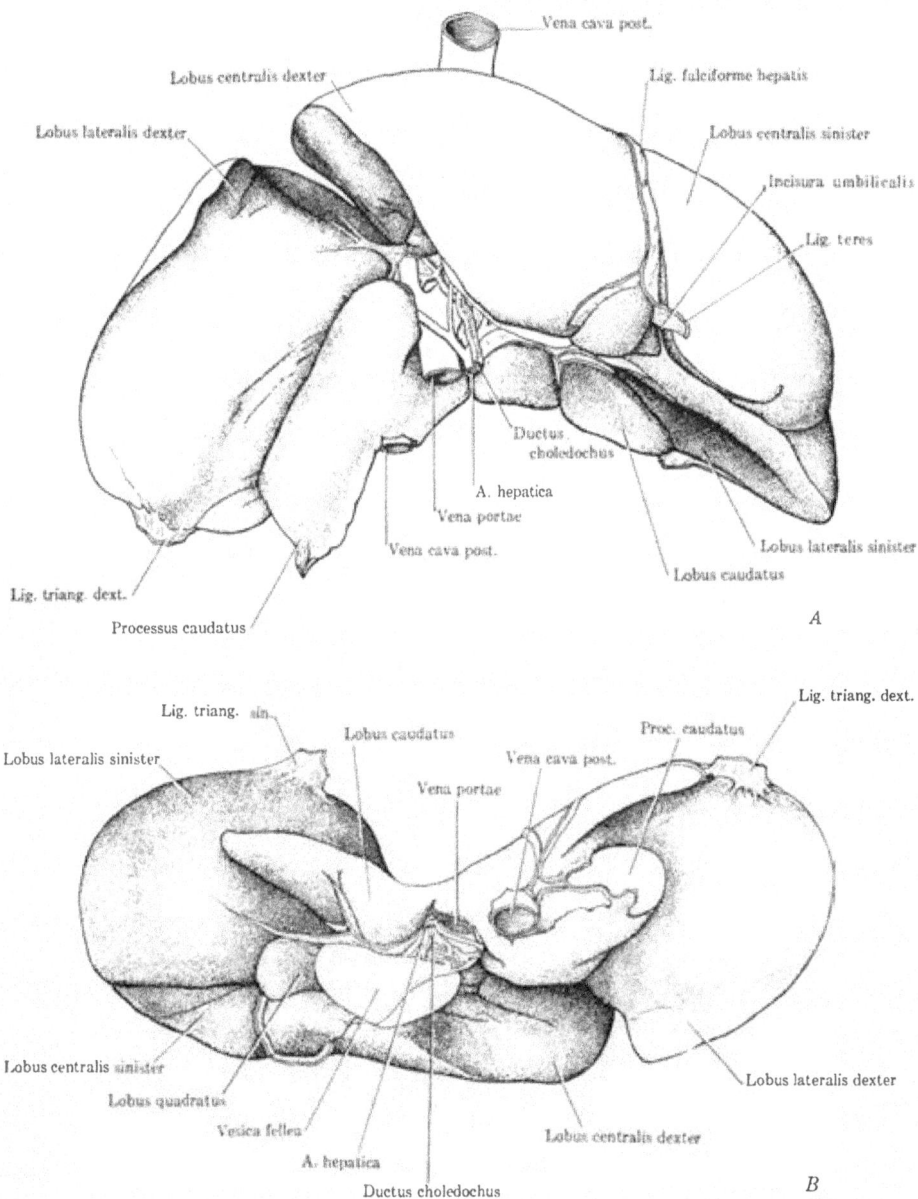

Vena cava post.

Lobus centralis dexter

Lig. falciforme hepatis

Lobus lateralis dexter

Lobus centralis sinister

Incisura umbilicalis

Lig. teres

Ductus choledochus

A. hepatica

Vena portae

Vena cava post.

Lobus lateralis sinister

Lobus caudatus

Lig. triang. dext.

Processus caudatus

A

Lig. triang. sin.

Lobus caudatus

Lig. triang. dext.

Vena cava post.

Proc. caudatus

Lobus lateralis sinister

Vena portae

Lobus centralis sinister

Lobus lateralis dexter

Lobus quadratus

Vesica fellea

Lobus centralis dexter

A. hepatica

Ductus choledochus

B

FIG. 114. Liver of *Ailuropoda*. A, ventral, B, visceral view.

The gut is longest in the bears (6 10, average 7.7 times head and body length). Thus there is a broad correlation with diet, the herbivorous forms tending to have a longer gut (as is general among mammals), but this is by no means a clear-cut correlation in the Carnivora. In no carnivore does gut length approach the proportions (up to 25 times head and body length in artiodactyls) found among mammals that are primarily, rather than secondarily, herbivorous.

The most striking lack of correlation between diet and gut length is in *Ailurus* and *Ailuropoda*. *Ailuropoda* is exclusively herbivorous and *Ailurus* seems to be highly so, and yet gut length in these is among the shortest known for the Carnivora.

## VII.  LIVER AND GALL BLADDER

The liver is small. Fixed *in situ*, it is a dome-shaped organ, very narrow dorsoventrally and with rather sharply arched diaphragmatic and visceral surfaces (fig. 114). It measures 270 mm. in breadth, and weighs 1564 grams. The liver is divided into six distinct lobes, of which the right lateral lobe is the largest. These are not arranged in the echelon formation characteristic of bears and other carnivores. The size relations of the four principal lobes are RL > RC > LC > LL. These relations confirm Raven's findings.

The left lateral lobe is roughly circular in outline when viewed from the visceral surface. It is more or less triangular in cross section. The free margin is devoid of notches, which are often present in other carnivores. A small accessory lobule on the visceral surface near the transverse fissure has been described in both *Ailuropoda* and *Ailurus*. This structure is also present in my specimen, although it is hidden behind the quadrate lobe. A heavy suspensory ligament, the left triangular ligament, attaches to the dorsal margin of the lobe and passes to the corresponding portion of the diaphragm.

The left central lobe is approximately the same size as the left lateral lobe, but it is more flattened and lies mostly anterior to it; only a small triangular section of the central lobe is visible from the visceral surface. Far below the surface of the liver the contact surfaces of these two lobes are joined by a prominent ligament, about 40 mm. in length, that extends laterad from the transverse fissure.

The right central lobe is larger than either of the left lobes, but not so large as the right lateral lobe. When the liver is viewed from the ventral surface, this lobe is trapezoidal in form. There is a shallow fissure along its visceral margin near the falciform ligament, which terminates at a short accessory branch of the falciform ligament, extending diag-

onally across the lower left corner of the lobe. This fissure is continued on the visceral surface of the lobe to a point where the small ligament supporting the fundus of the gall bladder arises. On the diaphragmatic surface of the liver a wide isthmus connects the right central and right lateral lobes.

The quadrate lobe is remarkable for its small size. It is visible only on the visceral surface of the liver, and lies largely in a depression on the visceral surface of the right central lobe. When the gall bladder is inflated it hides much of the quadrate lobe.

The right lateral lobe is the largest lobe in the liver, exceeding the right central lobe slightly in size. Its free margin is rounded and shows a slight notch at the site of the triangular ligament. The right triangular ligament, broader than the left, connects the dorsal border of this lobe with the diaphragm.

The caudate lobe is small but well marked, with a poorly defined papillary process. The basal part of the lobe lies to the left of the portal fissure as a tongue-shaped structure, reaching to approximately the center of the left lateral lobe. The papillary process is separated from the basal part of the caudate lobe by a shallow fissure to the left, from the caudate process by a notch to the right. It is a low, inconspicuous eminence scarcely rising above the level of the caudate lobe.

The caudate process is continuous with the caudate lobe except for the notch separating it from the papillary process. The caudate process is sharply defined but short, extending to the right only to about the middle of the right lateral lobe. It embraces the vena cava as in *Ursus*, but lacks the keel-shaped form characteristic of the bears and other carnivores.

The **gall bladder** is an ovoid sac 55 mm. in length. The gall bladder occupies a prominent fossa, approximately half of which is in the right central lobe and half in the quadrate lobe. It is crossed diagonally by a ligament-like fold of peritoneum. The gall bladder is entirely visible when the liver is viewed from the visceral surface, and when it is distended is partially visible from the ventral side of the liver. It is not visible from the diaphragmatic surface, as it is in most carnivores. The wall of the gall bladder is tough and heavy. Internally the mucosa is thrown up into low, interconnected ridges, which give it a reticulated or honeycomb appearance.

The cystic duct is arranged in a series of S-shaped curves. A small accessory duct emerging from the connective tissue deep to the gall bladder but not traceable to the gall bladder itself, enters the cystic duct 10 mm. before the latter joins the

Ventral       Visceral

*Bassariscus astutus*

*Procyon lotor*

*Ursus americanus*

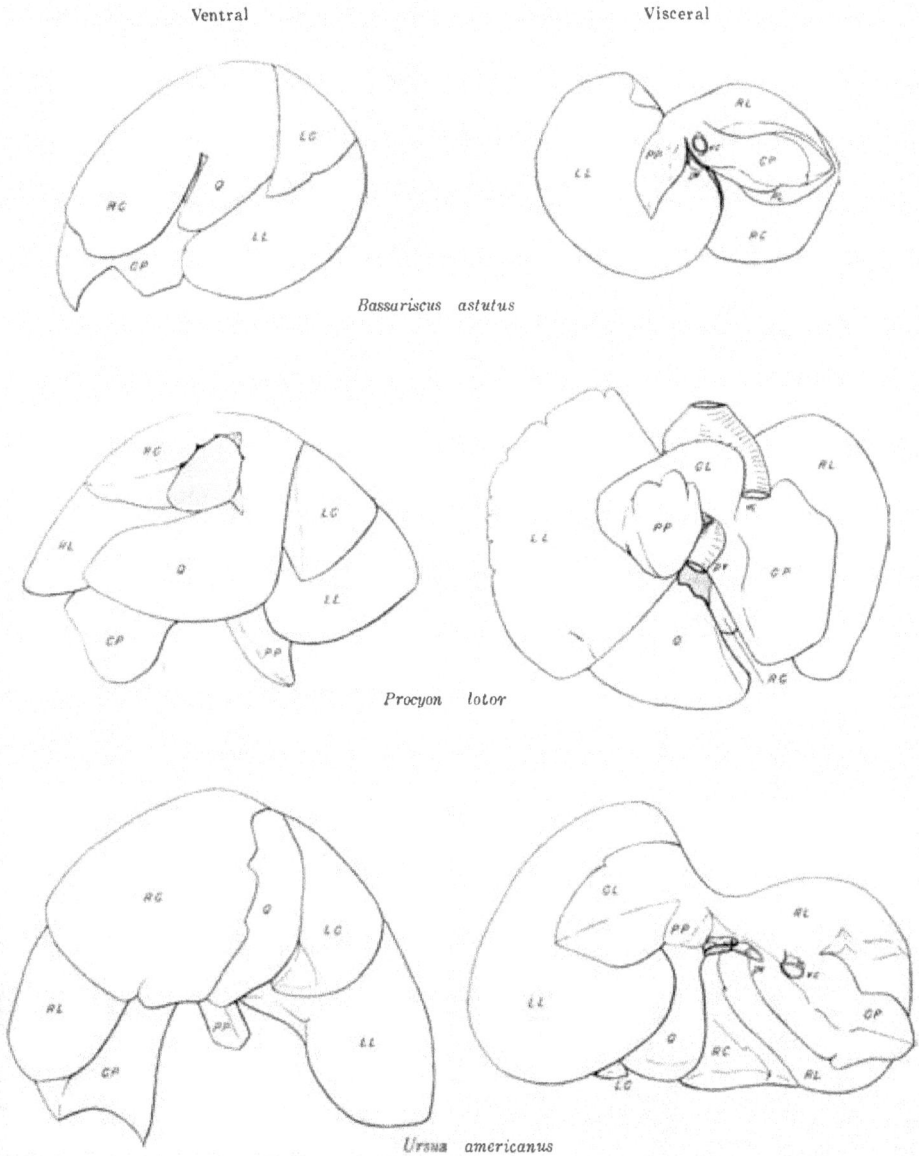

FIG. 115. Livers of representative arctoid carnivores. Not to scale.

hepatic duct. This accessory duct apparently is homologous with the atypical "cyst-hepatic ducts" that have been described in human anatomy. The cystic duct joins the hepatic duct at an acute angle. The collecting branches of the hepatic duct unite to form the hepatic duct proper about 15 mm. from

the juncture of the latter with the cystic duct to form the ductus choledochus.

The **ductus choledochus** is 95 mm. in length. It passes through the vertical arm (caput) of the pancreas to open obliquely into the duodenum, independently of the pancreatic duct, about 115 mm.

from the pylorus, i.e., close to the distal end of the duodenum. The lining of the ductus choledochus is smooth to a point about 15 mm. from its termination, that is, to its entrance into the wall of the duodenum. Then it expands slightly to form an ampulla (ampulla of Vater), whose lining is raised into a series of lamelliform rings (fig. 116). The papilla in the lining of the duodenum at the termination of the ductus choledochus is small but conspicuous.

The comparative anatomy of the liver in mammals was reviewed by Renvall (1903), Meyer (1911), and Siwe (1937), in carnivores by Carlsson (1925). It is evident that the mammalian liver shows consistent and meaningful structural patterns, although there is no agreement as to the causes of these patterns. In all carnivores the liver is divided by deep fissures into four principal lobes, subequal in size: right and left lateral and right and left central. The quadrate lobe is typically large, and lies between the two central lobes. On the visceral surface of the liver there is always a sixth lobe, the caudate lobe, with a well-developed papillary process projecting posteriorly into the omental bursa. A large boat-shaped caudate process extends to the right of the portal fissure. The lobes are typically arranged in echelon in carnivores, with the two central lobes lying most anteriorly and partly overlapping the quadrate and lateral lobes, and the caudate lobe and its appendages lying behind all the others. The caudate may or may not embrace the postcaval vein.

Consistent variations on the basic carnivore pattern have been described (see fig. 115). In the Canidae the accessory lobes are large, the postcaval vein is not embraced by the caudate lobe, and the gall bladder is not visible from the diaphragmatic surface of the liver. In the Procyonidae (two *Procyon lotor*, one *Bassariscus astutus* examined) the accessory lobes are as large as the principal lobes, completely excluding the central

lobes from the visceral surface of the liver. The quadrate is not overlapped by the central lobes on the diaphragmatic surface. Indeed, in the Procyonidae the cystic fissure is no more than a deep notch, leaving the right central and quadrate lobes broadly confluent on the diaphragmatic surface of the liver. The fundus of the gall bladder reaches the diaphragmatic surface. The caudate lobe consists almost entirely of a large papillary process. Renvall's descriptions of the liver of *Procyon lotor* and *Nasua* sp. agree with my observations in all essential respects. Apparently the liver of *Ailurus* is very similar to that of the Procyonidae (Carlsson, 1925, figs. 13-14).

In the Ursidae ( *Ursus americanus* and *Helarctos malayanus* examined) the accessory lobes are relatively small, the postcava is embedded in the caudate lobe, and the gall bladder is not visible from the diaphragmatic surface. Renvall's description and figure of the liver of *Ursus arctos* agree closely with my observations. The liver of *Ailuropoda* resembles in general that of the bears, but the accessory lobes are much reduced. The quadrate lobe is a mere appendage of the right central lobe and is visible only on the visceral surface. The caudate lobe is smaller than in the bears, but still partly embraces the postcava, and the papillary and caudate processes are much reduced. The gall bladder is invisible from the diaphragmatic surface. In both bears and panda the liver is high-domed and much flattened dorsoventrally, although this merely reflects the shape of the cavity into which the liver is molded.

Among vertebrates the liver is larger in carnivores and omnivores than in herbivores (Siwe, 1937; see also Table 18), and is relatively larger in small mammals. Reliable data available to me indicate that the weight of the liver in carnivores is about 3-4 per cent of body weight (Table 18). Unfortunately no reliable figures are available for bears. The relative liver weight in *Ailuropoda* is

TABLE 18.—LIVER WEIGHT IN MAMMALS

| | N | Body weight (gms.) | Liver weight (gms.) | Liver weight Body weight | Source |
|---|---|---|---|---|---|
| *Canis familiaris* ♀ | 4 | 23,710 | 693 | 2.9 | Crile and Quiring (1940) |
| *Canis lupus* ♂ | 1 | 29,940 | 925 | 3.1 | Crile and Quiring (1940) |
| *Potos flavus* ♀ | 1 | 2,620 | 98.6 | 3.8 | Crile and Quiring (1940) |
| *Ailuropoda melanoleuca* ♂ | 1 | 60,000 | 1564 | 2.6 | Original |
| *Felis domestica* ♂ | 52 | 2,822 | 101.5 | 3.6 | Latimer (1942) |
| *Felis domestica* ♀ | 52 | 2,445 | 88.6 | 3.6 | Latimer (1942) |
| *Felis leo* ♂ | 2 | 190,800 | 5725 | 3.0 | Crile and Quiring (1940) |
| *Homo sapiens* ♂ | .. | [60,000] | 1500 | 2.5 | Morris, *Human anatomy* |
| *Equus caballus* ♂ | 5 | 485,310 | 5685 | 1.2 | Crile and Quiring (1940) |
| *Equus caballus* ♀ | 10 | 443,360 | 6176 | 1.4 | Crile and Quiring (1940) |
| *Bos taurus* ♀ | 218 | 413,000 | 5747 | 1.4 | Crile and Quiring (1940) |
| *Sus scrofa* ♂ | 53 | 102,060 | 1488.3 | 1.4 | Crile and Quiring (1940) |
| *Sus scrofa* ♀ | 36 | 102,060 | 1547.3 | 1.5 | Crile and Quiring (1940) |

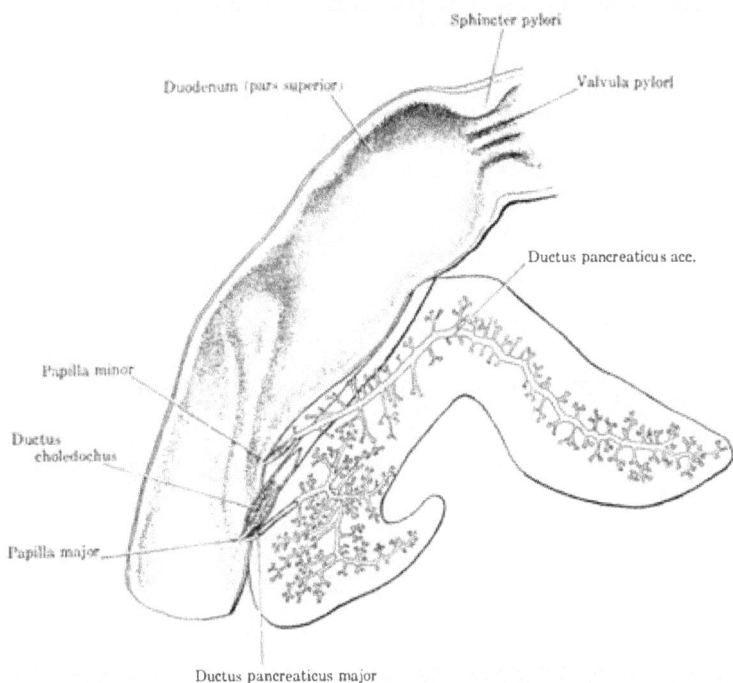

Sphincter pylori

Duodenum (pars superior)

Valvula pylori

Ductus pancreaticus acc.

Papilla minor

Ductus choledochus

Papilla major

Ductus pancreaticus major

Fig. 116.   Pancreatic and common bile ducts of *Ailuropoda*.

slightly less than in any other carnivore in Table 18, but is much greater than in any of the herbivores.

## VIII. PANCREAS AND SPLEEN

The **pancreas** (figs. 111, 116) is a compact, V-shaped structure embracing the stem of the common mesentery and the mesenteric blood vessels between its arms. The lateral edge of the vertical arm (caput pancreaticus) is in intimate contact with the duodenum, while the other (corpus pancreaticus) is related to the greater omentum near the pylorus. The two arms are nearly equal in length, each measuring approximately 85 mm. There is a well-defined processus uncinatus, which is hooked around the anterior mesenteric blood vessels.

The pancreas is drained by two ducts (fig. 116). The more posterior of these appears to be homologous with the main pancreatic duct (Wirsung) because of its position and relation to the ductus choledochus, although it is much less extensive and of smaller caliber than the accessory duct (Santorini). The main duct drains the lower end of the head and the uncinate process. It arises in the uncinate process, turns craniad into the head, and

then caudad at an acute angle, to enter the wall of the duodenum; its course is thus more or less S-shaped. It opens on the papilla major by an independent outlet that is immediately caudad of the outlet of the ductus choledochus. The accessory duct arises in the tail of the pancreas and runs along the corpus and into the anterior end of the head. It opens into the duodenum about 18 mm. craniad of the papilla major. There is no connection between the main and accessory ducts.

No taxonomically significant variation in the gross structure of the pancreas has been demonstrated for the Carnivora. In all it is a compact organ, V-shaped or L-shaped (even circular, Carlsson, 1925). Typically there are two ducts, although one is suppressed in occasional individuals. The main duct opens with the ductus choledochus, the other farther caudad.

The **spleen** (lien) is a long narrow structure, 340 mm. in length and about 40 mm. in width, that lies mostly along the caudal part of the greater curvature of the stomach (fig. 111). It is slightly wider anteriorly than posteriorly. It is also much flattened, its thickness averaging only about 10 mm., so that it has only two surfaces, a gastric and a diaphragmatic. The anterior end of the spleen is bent to the right almost at a right angle, so that it lies dorsad of the fundus of the stomach. The posterior end is also bent to the right to follow the sharp flexure of the stomach at the beginning of the pylorus, which gives the whole spleen the general form of a letter C. The organ is bound rather closely to the stomach throughout its entire length by the gastrolienal ligament, which attaches to the gastric surface at the hilus and does not exceed 30 mm. in width. A narrow lienorenal ligament, attaching to the edge of the spleen near its middle, binds the spleen to the left kidney.

The spleen appears to vary little among the Carnivora. In all forms in which it has been described or in which I have examined it (*Canis, Bassariscus, Procyon, Ursus, Felis*) the spleen is a tongue-shaped organ with an elongate hilus on the gastric surface. It was relatively broader in the procyonids than in the others.

## IX. DISCUSSION OF DIGESTIVE SYSTEM

If the operation of evolutionary mechanisms on the skeleton and musculature is sometimes difficult to interpret, the difficulty is multiplied when we come to the digestive system. The masticatory apparatus usually shows the most exquisite adaptive relations to diet, but the rest of the digestive apparatus may or may not show differences correlated with food habits. A horse, with a simple stomach and intestine only 10 times body length, does as well on a diet of grass as does a cow with its complex stomach and intestine 25 times body length. Yet among mammals there is in fact a broad correlaton between diet and the structure of the digestive system; this correlation is with the mechanical, rather than the chemical, properties of the food (Flower, 1872; Pernkopf, 1937).

Since a higher taxonomic category is usually characterized by a major adaptation, often to a particular diet, we would expect the gut in the vast majority of cases to be no more variable than other taxonomic characters. The fact is that within the family or order the gut tends to remain conservative even in the face of the most extreme changes in diet. No better example of this conservatism could be asked than the herbivorous carnivores. For most features of the digestive system the closest and most consistent correlation is with the taxonomic unit, which exists even where no other correlation can be demonstrated. It is strikingly evident in the liver, where form is tremendously varied but has no conceivable relation to function. All attempts to correlate lobation of the mammalian liver with ramification of the hepatic vessels

or bile ducts, or with posture or other mechanical factors, have failed (Siwe, 1937). Yet lobes and fissures are clearly homologous throughout the Mammalia, and patterns characteristic of orders, families, and genera are evident everywhere (Meyer, 1911).

Variation in the digestive system, then, is not random, even where there is no obvious way that selection can determine form. But it is evident that evolution of the gut involves factors more subtle than the mechanical and architectural requirements that largely determine the evolution of the skeleton and skeletal musculature.

Among the arctoid carnivores, diet ranges from practically exclusively carnivorous in such canids as the coyote, through heavily herbivorous in the bears, to exclusive foliage-eating in the giant panda. These differences in diet are accompanied by corresponding modifications of the masticatory apparatus, but the structure of the remainder of the digestive system is astonishingly uniform throughout this group.

The digestive system of the bears differs from the more generalized carnivore condition in several points, mostly relatively minor and adaptive to a heavily herbivorous diet (but not necessarily one composed of foliage). Such adaptive features are the large parotid gland, the numerous vallate papillae, and the length of the intestine. Other ursid features, not overtly adaptive, are the frequently semicircular arrangement of the vallate papillae, the paired pharyngeal bursae, the small size of the accessory lobes of the liver, the presence of a colic loop in the intestine, the absence of an ileocolic valve, and the globular form of the pyloric region of the stomach.

The digestive system of *Ailuropoda* agrees closely with that of the Ursidae in most of these features. Strikingly different is length of intestine; less extreme are differences in the form of the stomach and liver. The intestine is typically elongate in herbivorous mammals, but there are many exceptions to this rule (Weber, 1928; Jacobshagen, 1937). The exceptions can be only partly explained by large caeca, expanded intestinal diameter, or the tendency for primitive forms to have a short intestine regardless of diet. Secondary *reduction* of intestinal length in connection with secondary herbivory, such as must have taken place in *Ailuropoda* and apparently in *Ailurus*, is something else. A. B. Howell (1925) observed a similar relation in comparing the digestive tract of a nut- and fruit-eating tree squirrel (*Sciurus carolinensis*) with that of a grass-eating ground squirrel (*Citellus beldingi*). The small intestine was nearly twice as long in the *Sciurus* as in the *Citellus*. Howell says "the significance of this discrepancy in length is not understood. It is at variance with what might be expected."

Reduced intestinal length has been shown to be correlated with a herbivorous diet in experimental animals. Haesler (1930) divided a litter of nine pigs into three groups, one of which was raised on an exclusively carnivorous diet, one on an exclusively herbivorous diet, and one on a mixed (normal) diet. At the end of the experiment, in the animals on a herbivorous diet the stomach was largest, the small intestine shortest and with the smallest internal surface area, the caecum largest, and the colon shortest but with the greatest internal surface area (Table 19). In the pigs on a carnivorous diet the stomach was smallest, the small intestine longest but intermediate in surface area, the caecum and colon were smallest. The length differences in Table 19 are far smaller than the differences of hundreds, even thousands, of percentage points in normally herbivorous versus normally carnivorous species of mammals. Wetzel (1928) had earlier had similar results in a less carefully planned experiment on rats.

The data in Table 17 show that the total intestine is relatively about half as long in *Ailuropoda* as in the bears. The difference is due to a shorter small intestine, since relative length of colon is the same in the two groups. In both groups the colon is longer than in any other for which we have data. But whereas colon circumference in our *Ursus americanus* is identical with mean small intestine circumference (27.6 mm.), in *Ailuropoda* the colon circumference (99) exceeds mean small intestine circumference (90) by about 10 per cent. Therefore the relative surface area of the colon is about 10 per cent greater in *Ailuropoda*. Consequently, both in Haesler's experimental animals and in our *Ailuropoda* compared with *Ursus*, length and surface area of small intestine are reduced, and surface area of colon is increased, with an exclusively herbivorous diet. The slight reduction in colon length reported by Haesler was not evident in our carnivore material.

Haesler concluded that the efficient factor determining differences in gut proportions in mammals is the volume of the residue of ingesta that remains insoluble after it has passed through the stomach and small intestine. The more voluminous this is, the larger are the caecum and colon, and vice versa. Where the ingesta is soluble only after being acted upon by bacteria and protozoa in the caecum and/or colon, the small intestine functions largely to transmit the ingesta from stomach to caecum-colon. This is the case in *Ailuropoda* and in Haesler's pigs reared on a herbivorous diet. In

TABLE 19.—PERCENTAGE DIFFERENCES FROM CONTROL ANIMALS IN GUT MEASUREMENTS OF PIGS RAISED ON HERBIVOROUS AND CARNIVOROUS DIETS

(Data from Haesler, 1930)

| Diet | | Length % | Volume % | Internal Surface % |
|---|---|---|---|---|
| Stomach | Herbivorous | ... | + 6.9 | ... |
| | Carnivorous | ... | −10.3 | ... |
| Small Intestine | Herbivorous | −6.2 | −17.6 | −13.6 |
| | Carnivorous | +1.4 | − 8.1 | − 4.0 |
| Caecum | Herbivorous | ... | +50.0 | ... |
| | Carnivorous | ... | −14.3 | ... |
| Colon | Herbivorous | − 2.4 | +35.5 | +17.3 |
| | Carnivorous | −12.4 | −43.0 | −28.0 |
| Total Gut | Herbivorous | −5.3 | + 7.0 | −4.0 |
| | Carnivorous | −1.5 | −19.3 | −9.6 |

such cases the small intestine has little digestive function, and reduced length is advantageous. In ruminants, on the contrary, cellulose solution occurs mainly in the rumen (Dukes, 1935), and the small intestine can therefore function in digestion and absorption, and length is advantageous.

In mammals that habitually ingest large quantities of cellulose, either the stomach is complex or there is a large caecum. *Ailuropoda* has neither, and in this animal the normal ingesta must be practically insoluble until it reaches the colon. With no caecum, and a short and relatively narrow colon, digestion must be remarkably inefficient. Observers have commented on the high proportion of undigested material in the feces of *Ailuropoda* (p. 27).

The stomach of *Ailuropoda* differs from that of *Ursus* chiefly in the extensive development of the pyloric region. In the panda this region is almost gizzard-like. The stomach in Howell's squirrels agreed with conditions in the panda; in the grass-eating *Citellus* the pylorus was more tubular and more muscular than in *Sciurus*. Kneading, mixing, and soaking are prerequisite to cellulose digestion (Dukes, 1935), and in simple stomachs the pylorus is the site of true motor activity (Pernkopf, 1937). Thus the modified pyloric region in *Ailuropoda* appears to perform the kneading function and therefore to be directly adaptive.

The liver is consistently smaller in typically herbivorous than in typically carnivorous mammals, and it appears to be slightly smaller in *Ailuropoda* than in other carnivores. Since protein breakdown and the emulsification, digestion, and absorption of fats are the primary digestive functions of the liver, it is scarcely surprising that this organ is smaller in herbivorous mammals whose diet has a high foliage content. In the Carnivora the accessory lobes appear to be affected first when there is phylogenetic reduction of liver size, and this may explain the much reduced accessory lobes in *Ailuropoda* as compared with the bears and other arctoid carnivores. Since the liver is a passive organ, molded by surrounding organs, we would expect the form of the liver in *Ailuropoda* to reflect the somewhat modified stomach form.

Nothing is known of the morphogenetic mechanisms controlling growth and differentiation of the digestive system. Experiments such as those of Haesler indicate a certain capacity for individual adaptation in the proportions of the gut, but the differences fall far short of those seen in species adapted to extremes of herbivorous or carnivorous diet. Thus selection, operating through genetic mechanisms, must be at least partly responsible for differences in the digestive system such as those seen in *Ailuropoda* as compared with the bears.

## X. CONCLUSIONS

1. The gross morphology of the digestive system of the Ursidae differs in details from that of other arctoid carnivores. Most of these differences represent adaptations to a heavily herbivorous diet, but a few conspicuous differences are not overtly adaptive.

2. The digestive system of *Ailuropoda* agrees closely with that of the Ursidae in nearly all details. It differs in the pyloric region of the stomach, in liver form, and in intestinal proportions.

3. The pylorus is almost gizzard-like in *Ailuropoda*, an adaptation for kneading and mixing the ingesta.

4. The liver is small and the accessory lobes are much reduced. In mammals a small liver is correlated with a herbivorous diet.

5. Length and internal surface area of the small intestine are much reduced in *Ailuropoda* as compared with the bears. The normal ingesta of *Ailuropoda* is probably still insoluble in this part of the gut.

6. Surface area of the colon, the gut region where solubility of fibrous ingesta would be greatest, is greater in *Ailuropoda* than in the bears.

7. Thus all significant differences in gross structure between the gut of *Ailuropoda* and the gut of the Ursidae are directly adaptive to the bulky fibrous diet of the panda.

8. The genetic mechanisms controlling growth and differentiation of the elements of the digestive system are unknown. Consequently nothing is known of the morphogenetic mechanisms whereby adaptive changes in the gut can be effected.

# UROGENITAL SYSTEM

## I. URINARY ORGANS

### A. KIDNEYS

The kidneys are situated with their anterior borders about on a level with the anterior border of the first lumbar vertebra; their long axes converge slightly anteriorly. The anterior border of the right kidney is 15 mm. farther craniad than that of the left. The kidneys weigh 93 and 87 grams, together 180 grams. This represents a ratio to body weight of 1 : 333. The dimensions in millimeters are as follows (measurements in parentheses are from an adult female as given by Raven):

|          | Length    | Width    | Thickness |
|----------|-----------|----------|-----------|
| Right    | 105 (112) | 51 (62)  | 33 (26)   |
| Left     | 100 (108) | 55 (55)  | 31 (25)   |

Each kidney (fig. 135) is composed of several independent lobes or "renculi." The renculi are packed closely together, and the organ as a whole has the usual kidney form. The entire kidney is enclosed in a thin tight-fitting capsule whose walls contain a quantity of fat, and each renculus in turn has an individual capsule of its own. The right kidney is composed of 10 renculi, 5 of which are double, giving a total of 15. The left kidney is made up of 10 renculi, 8 of which are double, for a total of 18. A single layer of the capsular membrane separates the halves of the double renculi. The renculi are arranged around a prominent renal fossa.

The renculi average about 20 mm. in diameter. Each is composed of a heavy cortex, about 6 mm. thick, surrounding a small medulla averaging 7.1 mm. thick. The difference between cortex and medulla is not well marked macroscopically, and the inner and outer zones of the medulla cannot be distinguished. The medulla is composed of from one to three pyramids, each of whose apices forms a very long (4 mm.) and prominent papilla. Many renculi have three papillae. There is a total of 23 papillae in the right kidney. Under a hand lens the numerous foramina papillaris, the terminations of the papillary ducts, can be seen on the papillae.

All the papillae of a single renculus lie together in a common minor calyx. The minor calyces of the several renculi unite, within the renal fossa, into two major calyces, an anterior and a posterior. The two major calyces unite outside the fossa to form the slightly expanded proximal end of the ureter. There is no renal pelvis.

The literature on the structure of the carnivore kidney has been reviewed by Gerhardt (1914), Sperber (1944), and Schiebler (1959). The comparative anatomy of the ursid kidney was described by Guzsal (1960). In all fissiped carnivores, except the Ursidae and Lutrinae, the kidney is simple, with a single papilla or a crest. The simple kidney with a single papilla is the most primitive type of mammalian kidney, and a crest is a slightly modified papilla (Sperber). In the Ursidae (and Lutrinae) the kidney is renculate, the most highly modified kidney type known among the Mammalia. In the Ursidae each kidney is composed of 23–34 renculi, except *Thalarctos*, in which there are twice as many (Table 20). Usually a few renculi are double, in one case even triple. Each renculus has a papilla; when a renculus is double there are two papillae, so the number of papillae is probably an index of the number of units composing the kidney.

Since many of the renculi have three papillae in *Ailuropoda*, the total number of papillae is about the same as in the bears, although the number of renculi is considerably less. From what is known of the ontogeny and comparative anatomy of the mammalian kidney, it is evident that *the multipapillate renculus type of the panda represents a partial consolidation of the unipapillate renculus type of the ursids*, a partial "reversion," so to speak, to the simple kidney type from which the renculate kidney was originally derived.

Among mammals renculate kidneys are associated with large organism size and/or aquatic habits. Factors in addition to organism size must be involved among terrestrial mammals, for the kidneys are simple (although modified in other ways) in as large a mammal as the horse, and among terrestrial carnivores they are renculate in all bears regardless of size, but simple even in the largest of the cats. Dividing the kidney up into renculi reduces nephron length. The factor limiting nephron length is the pressure required to force fluid through

TABLE 20.—NUMBER OF RENCULI COMPOSING KIDNEY IN BEARS

| | Renculi No. | Double renculi No. | Renculi Total | Source |
|---|---|---|---|---|
| *Ursus arctos* | 34 | 0 | 34 | Sperber (1944) |
| *Ursus arctos* | 33 | 3 (1 triple) | 37 | Guzsal (1960) |
| *Ursus americanus* | 28 | 3 | 31 | Guzsal (1960) |
| *Ursus tibetanus* | 22–25 | 1 | 22–26 | Guzsal (1960) |
| *Thalarctos* | 62–65 | several | 65+ | Guzsal (1960) |
| *Melursus* | 23 | 4 | 27 | Gerhardt (1914) |
| *Melursus* | 26–30 | ? | 26–30 | Guzsal (1960) |
| *Helarctos* | 23 | ? | 23 | Original |
| *Ailuropoda* | 10 | 5–8 | 15–18 | Original |

the nephron (Sperber). Relative thickness of cortex and medulla, particularly of the medulla, is reduced in renculate kidneys. Table 21, based on Sperber, gives the absolute and relative dimensions of cortex and medulla in representative arctoid carnivores. Sperber's data show that relative thickness of cortex and medulla (particularly medulla) is greatest in the most primitive kidney types, least in the most highly modified. The figures for carnivores given in Table 21 conform to Sperber's general figures for each kidney type in the Mammalia.

Relative kidney size varies with organism size, the kidneys being relatively larger in small mammals than in large mammals. Beyond this, however, the kidneys are relatively heavier in flesh-eating than in plant-eating mammals (Table 22). In the bears and giant panda the ratio is like that of herbivores rather than like that of other carnivores.

Thus it appears that in *Ailuropoda* the kidney is basically of the ursid type, but that it has begun to revert to a simpler type. The significance of this reversion is not apparent, although there are indications of "fetalization" in other structures in this region—the postcava and external genitalia, for example. It is probably a part of the general dis-

turbance in the lumbosacral region of *Ailuropoda*.

B. URETERS

The right ureter is 195 mm. in length and 4 mm. in diameter; the left is slightly shorter. The ureters are separated by a distance of 95 mm. at their origins, and converge toward the bladder across the psoas muscles. Near the bladder they pass between the external iliac and hypogastric vessels.

The ureters enter the dorsal wall of the bladder at an oblique angle near the neck. The two ureters penetrate the bladder 20 mm. apart.

C. BLADDER

The empty bladder (fig. 118) is an elongate pear-shaped sac, much flattened dorsoventrally. The entire organ lies anterior to the very short symphysis pelvis. The bladder measures 105 mm. in length and 55 mm. in width. The walls are 9 mm. thick.

The lining of the bladder is thrown up into irregular longitudinal folds, except for the area occupied by the trigone. The openings of the ureters appear as a pair of dimple-like depressions, 25 mm. apart. The **trigonum vesicae** is a prominent elongated triangle; the **uvula vesicae** is present as a faint longitudinal elevation along its mid line

TABLE 21.—DIMENSIONS AND PROPORTIONS OF KIDNEYS IN ARCTOID CARNIVORES

| | Kidney size* | Thickness (in mm.) of kidney layers | | Layer thickness × 10 kidney size | | | Source |
|---|---|---|---|---|---|---|---|
| | | Cortex | Medulla | Cortex + medulla | Cortex | Medulla | |
| *Ailuropoda* | 57 | . | . | . | . | . | Raven (1936) |
| | 56 | 6.0 | 7.1 | 2.3 | 1.0 | 1.3 | Original |
| *Ursus arctos* | 65 | 4.0–4.5 | 8.5 | 1.9 | .6 | 1.3 | Sperber (1944) |
| *Helarctos malayanus* | 60 | 5.2 | 6.9 | 2.0 | .9 | 1.1 | Original |
| *Procyon lotor* | 30 | 6.3 | 12.5 | 6.2 | 2.1 | 4.1 | Original |
| | 28 | 5.5 | 10.5 | 5.7 | 1.9 | 3.8 | Sperber (1944) |
| *Nasua narica* | 26 | 5.5 | 10.0 | 6.0 | 2.1 | 3.9 | Sperber (1944) |
| *Canis familiaris* | 40 | 7.0 | 17.0 | 6.0 | 1.7 | 4.3 | Sperber (1944) |
| *Canis lupus* | 51 | 7.0 | 23.0 | 5.9 | 1.4 | 4.5 | Sperber (1944) |

* The cube root of the product of the three dimensions of the kidney.

TABLE 22.—KIDNEY WEIGHTS IN MAMMALS

| | | N | Body weight (gms.) | Kidney weight (gms.) | Kidney weight Body weight | Source |
|---|---|---|---|---|---|---|
| Canis familiaris | | 4 | 23,710 | 152 | .64 | Crile and Quiring (1940) |
| Canis lupus | | 1 | 29,940 | 223 | .74 | Crile and Quiring (1940) |
| Ailuropoda | | 1 | 60,000 | 180 | .30 | Original |
| Ursus horribilis | ♀ | 1 | 142,880 | 548 | .38 | Crile and Quiring (1940) |
| Procyon lotor | ♀ | 1 | 4,536 | 37 | .82 | Crile and Quiring (1940) |
| Felis domestica | ♂ | 52 | 2,822 | 21.1 | .74 | Latimer (1939) |
| | ♀ | 52 | 2,445 | 16.9 | .69 | Latimer (1939) |
| Felis leo | ♂ | 2 | 190,800 | 1610 | .84 | Crile and Quiring (1940) |
| Homo sapiens | ♂ | | | 168 | .59 | Morris, Human Anatomy |
| Equus caballus | ♀ | 10 | 443,360 | 1667 | .38 | Crile and Quiring (1940) |
| | ♂ | 3 | 485,310 | 1972 | .41 | Crile and Quiring (1940) |
| Bos taurus | ♀ | 218 | 413,000 | 983 | .24 | Crile and Quiring (1940) |
| Sus scrofa | ♂ | 53 | 102,060 | 238 | .23 | Crile and Quiring (1940) |
| | ♀ | 36 | 102,060 | 264 | .26 | Crile and Quiring (1940) |

*Ligaments of the Bladder*

The bladder is supported by the usual two sets of ligaments, the "false" ligaments and the "true" ligaments.

The false ligaments are composed of dorsal and ventral elements. A long continuous fold of peritoneum is attached to the dorsum of the bladder. Medially it forms a deep triangular cul-de-sac, roofed over with peritoneum through which the ductus deferentes run. From this fold of peritoneum dorsal and lateral ligaments run to the walls of the pelvic cavity. A single ventral fold of peritoneum runs from the venter of the bladder to the ventral abdominal wall. The **urachus** arises behind the ventral ligament and runs craniad on the belly wall to the umbilicus.

There are three true ligaments from the posterior part of the bladder: the unpaired puboprostatic ligament running from the ventral midline of the neck of the bladder to the pubis, and the pair of lateral ligaments running from the lower part of the bladder to the walls of the pelvis.

## II. MALE REPRODUCTIVE ORGANS

### A. MALE PERINEAL REGION

The perineal region (fig. 117) comprises the anus, the prepuce, and the naked glandular region lying between them. The testes lie immediately caudad of the inguinal canal, which places their caudal borders about on a line with the caudal end of the symphysis pelvis. This means that the caudal end of the testis lies about 35 mm. in front of the penis and 50 mm. laterad of the midline, which places them at a considerable distance from the perineum. In addition, there is no scrotum or other external evidence of the site of the testes in the juvenile individual dissected. At sexual maturity the testicles are very evident.

The **anus** is a transverse aperture, somewhat U-shaped, with the concavity directed ventrally.

It is 30 mm. wide in the contracted condition, and is surrounded by an extensive area of light-colored naked skin. This hairless area is triangular in outline, with the base of the triangle at the root of the tail and the apex continued ventrad to the prepuce. It is granular in texture, the granulations becoming less pronounced ventrally as the prepuce is approached. The dorsal wall of the anus forms a prominent cushion, underlain by fat, which is traversed by deep furrows radiating from the anus. Typical anal glands are absent.

Ventrad of the anus is a narrow vertical median prominence bounded laterally by a deep furrow on each side, which extends from the anus to the dorsal root of the prepuce. It widens slightly toward the anus, into which it is continued, and shows a faint median raphe.

The structure of the external genitalia is remarkable. The penis is entirely withdrawn within a prominent heart-shaped elevation. This elevation, which represents the prepuce, measures about 40 mm. in both transverse and longitudinal diameters. It is sharply constricted off from the surrounding skin by a shallow furrow laterally and a deep excavation dorsally, which gives it a button-like appearance. There is an additional concentric furrow on its surface on either side. Its outer surface is rather well haired, except dorsally, where the naked area is continuous with the naked area of the perineum. An aperture, around which the skin is puckered, occupies the center of the prominence. A faint median raphe extends dorsad from the aperture.

The lining of the prepuce is heavily pigmented and has a puckered, honeycomb appearance. It is reflected to form the covering of the pars intrapraeputialis of the penis. Thus the pars intrapraeputialis appears to be enclosed in a thick-walled pocket, the lining of which would form the outer covering of the body of the penis during erection.

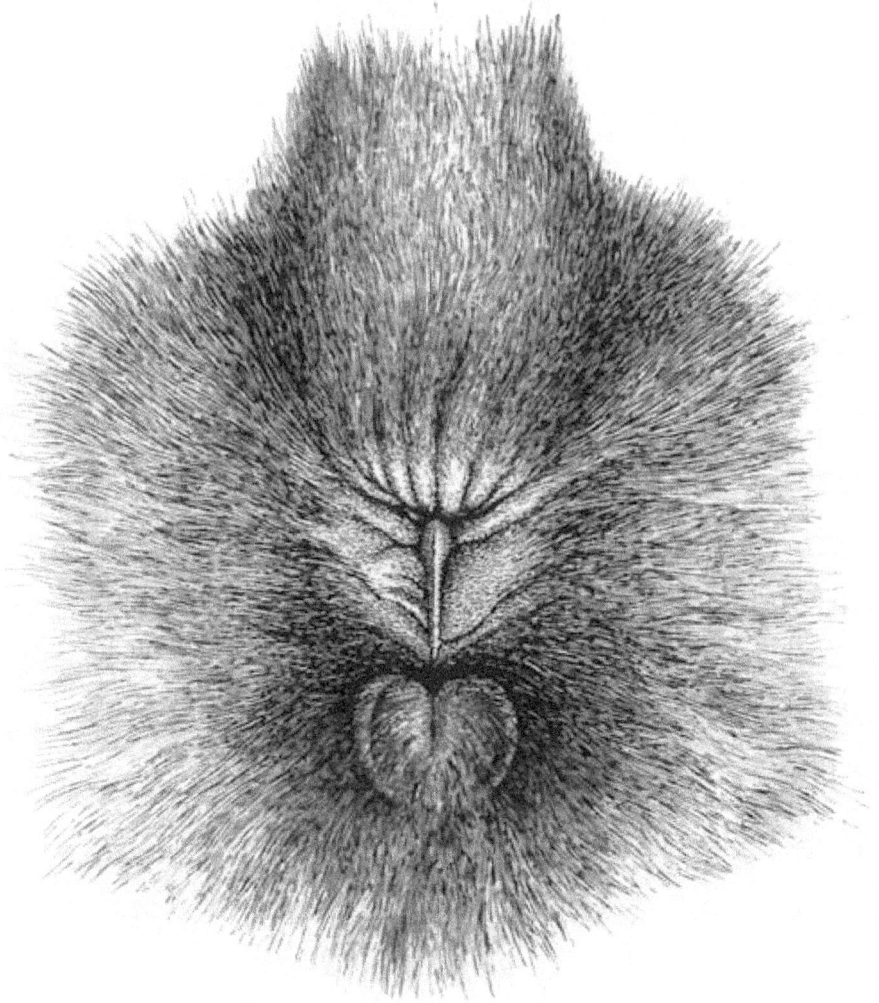

FIG. 117. Perineal region of subadult male *Ailuropoda* (Su Lin).

Dorsally (posteriorly) the lining of the prepuce is attached to the pars intrapraeputialis by a small but conspicuous frenulum.

## B. TESTIS AND ITS APPENDAGES

The testes lie just outside the external inguinal ring, and hence are prepenial in position (fig. 135). The two organs are separated by a distance of 70 mm. There is no true scrotum, and at least in the subadult animal dissected the testes and their wrappings are so embedded in fat that they do not even produce a swelling in the contour of the body.

The testis is an ovate structure, 28 mm. in length, and wider posteriorly than anteriorly. It is considerably flattened dorsoventrally.

The epididymis is relatively large, and is divided into three well-marked regions: caput, corpus, and cauda. The caput is a relatively small expansion occupying the usual position over the anterior end of the testis. The corpus is a flat

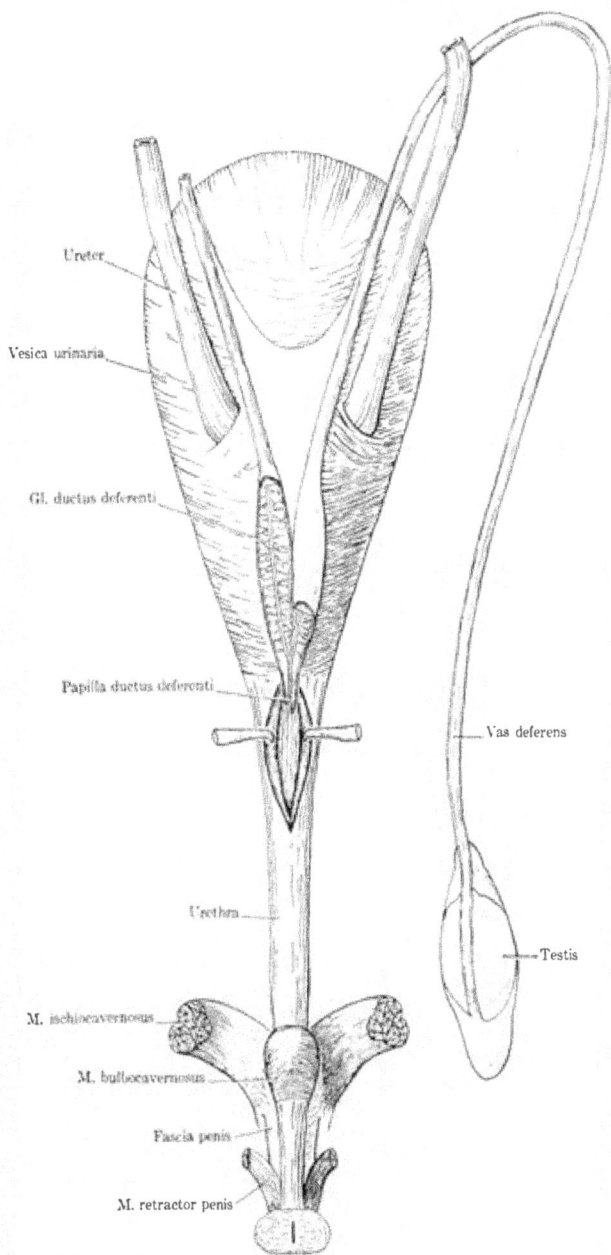

Ureter

Vesica urinaria

Gl. ductus deferenti

Papilla ductus deferenti

Vas deferens

Urethra

Testis

M. ischiocavernosus

M. bulbocavernosus

Fascia penis

M. retractor penis

FIG. 118.  Male reproductive organs of *Ailuropoda*.

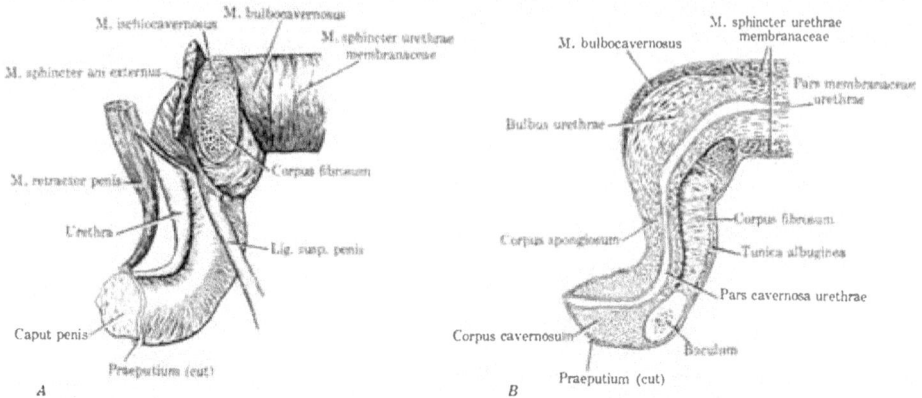

FIG. 119. Penis of *Ailuropoda*. A, lateral aspect, B, longitudinal section.

band, 8 mm. wide, closely applied to the lateral border of the testis. The cauda is by far the largest region of the epididymis. It is a conical caplike structure over the posterior end of the testis.

The **ductus deferens** (fig. 118) is continued from the tail of the epididymis along the medial border of the testis, entering the funiculus spermaticus at the anterior end of the testis. The funicular part of the ductus is about 80 mm. long. At the entrance to the inguinal canal it leaves the spermatic vessels and loops back, ventrad of the terminal vessels of the aorta and the ureter, to the dorsum of the bladder. The last 45 mm. of the ductus, lying on the neck of the bladder, is enlarged and encased in a thick layer of glandular tissue. The ducts from each side, which are considerably enlarged by their glandular investment, approach each other on the neck of the bladder. They unite, 5 mm. before reaching the wall of the urethra, into a common duct, which passes through the wall of the urethra at a very oblique angle. The duct opens into the urethral canal on a small, elongate papilla.

There is no indication of vesicular, prostate, or bulbo-urethral (Cowper's) glands.

The **urethra** is divisible into pars membranacea and pars cavernosa. The pars membranacea is 60 mm. in length, with heavy muscular walls about 4 mm. thick. The lining of the lumen is thrown up into prominent longitudinal ridges at its proximal end. The pars cavernosa is 43 mm. in length. The lining of its lumen is elevated into numerous small longitudinal mucous folds, and the lining of the distal half, except near the external orifice, is irregularly pigmented. There is a prominent longitudinal fold along the dorsal wall of the fossa navicularis.

## C. PENIS

The penis (figs. 118, 119, 135) is remarkable for its small size. It measures only 36 mm. in length (measured from the posterior border of the ischiocavernosus muscle) by 13 mm. in diameter. The corresponding measurements on the penis of a fully adult male (Mei Lan) are 70 mm. by 25 mm. The organ is divided into a button-like pars intrapraeputialis and a cylindrical body. The penis is S-shaped, its tip directed posteriorly. The prepuce was described on page 221.

In addition to its crural attachment to the ischia, the penis is supported by a pair of suspensory ligaments arising from the ischiadic part of the symphysis pelvis. These ligaments attach to the sides of the penis at its base, where the ischiocavernosus, sphincter ani externus, and suspensory ligament have a common attachment. There is also a paired M. retractor penis (p. 172) inserting into the base of the pars intrapraeputialis.

The body or shaft of the penis is composed principally of three cavernous elements, the two corpora fibrosa and the corpus spongiosum. These are enclosed within a common sheath of tough connective tissue, the fascia penis.

The two **corpora fibrosa** (BNA: corpora cavernosa penis) are remarkably small, each scarcely exceeding the corpus spongiosum in size. The corpus fibrosum arises, as the crus penis, from the descending ramus of the ischium, covered by the ischiocavernosus muscle. The two corpora converge to form the body of the penis. Anteriorly they are continued as the baculum, which is lodged in the distal part of the penis but does not extend into the pars intrapraeputialis. Each corpus is enclosed in a tough tunica albuginea, and between the two corpora these are united into a median septum penis.

The corpus fibrosum is composed of dense spongy tissue, divided into two regions differing sharply in structure (fig. 119). The basal part (corresponding to the unossified part of the corpus fibrosum in bears and procyonids) is a firm meshwork with coarse interspaces, resembling the corpus fibrosum of other arctoid carnivores. Between this basal part and the baculum (corresponding to the proximal part of the baculum in bears and procyonids), the meshwork contains an immense number of glistening white fibers, straight and radially arranged. The medial ends of these fibers are deeply embedded in the tunica albuginea. To judge from its position, this part of the corpus fibrosum represents the degenerate proximal part of a formerly much longer baculum.

The corpus spongiosum (BNA: corpus cavernosum urethrae) surrounds the pars cavernosa urethrae, except distally where it is replaced by the corpus cavernosum. It begins proximally as a relatively small bulbus urethrae, which tapers gradually into the corpus. The bulbus is surrounded by a small M. bulbocavernosus.

The pars intrapraeputialis is the hemispherical tip of the penis lying within the preputial cavity. It is broader transversely than dorsoventrally, and is composed of a caput and a collum marked off from the head by a faint constriction. The integument covering the head is continuous with the integument lining the preputial cavity. It is faintly pitted, and is pigmented peripherally, unpigmented centrally. A very small frenulum connects the urethral border of the head with the prepuce. The meatus of the urethra is a vertical slit in the center of the head.

The interior of the pars intrapraeputialis and the distal part of the body of the penis are filled with erectile tissue, the corpus cavernosum. This is exceedingly fine-meshed cavernous tissue, clearly distinguishable from the coarser tissue of the corpus spongiosum.

## D. BACULUM[1]

The baculum is a small, remarkably shaped structure, completely different from that of any other carnivore for which this bone has been described (fig. 120). It is only 24 mm. in length. There is a short, rod-like body from which rounded winglike expansions, deflected downward at an angle of about 45°, arise. These wings occupy more than the distal half of the bone. They are heavy, with slightly irregular rounded edges, and the max-

[1] Description from an adult male (CNHM 31128). The baculum of the specimen dissected was incompletely ossified.

imum width across them is 12 mm. The tip of the bone is a short, rounded, papilla-like projection.

The dorsal border of the baculum forms a rounded keel. It is slightly sinuous in profile, convex over the rodlike base and concave over the winglike processes. The tip is directed slightly downward. The wings form a deep inverted trough for the urethra ventrally.

## III. FEMALE REPRODUCTIVE ORGANS

The female reproductive organs are known only from the description, based on the viscera of an adult individual, given by Raven (1936). The following account is taken from his report (fig. 121).

The ovary is slightly flattened, rounded, and its surface is fissured and pitted, thus having somewhat the appearance on the surface of a highly convoluted brain. It measures 30 mm. in length by 23 mm. in width and 11 mm. in thickness.

The uterine tube is very much contorted but when straightened out measures 95 mm.

The corpus uterus is less than half the length of the cornua and is slightly depressed. The cornua are rounded on the free edge and diminish in thickness toward the broad ligament. The surface of the uterine mucosa is arranged in a mosaic with distinct clefts separating the smooth areas making up its surface. The mucosa has the same appearance over its entire surface from the extremities of the cornua to the cervix. The cervix is strong, with comparatively muscular walls.

The vagina, which has a total length of 85 mm., is narrow, with firm muscular walls. Its mucosa forms a series of closely set, transverse circular folds. Caudally the vagina is bounded ventrally by the tubercle, on the center of which is the urethral opening, laterally and dorsally by the hymen, which is a fold 8 mm. long.

The urogenital sinus, like the vagina and corpus uterus, is flattened so that, though not wide, it is more extensive transversely than dorsoventrally.

Of the specimen under consideration there is preserved only a very little of the skin surrounding the genital and anal openings. It is bare, except for a few hairs. On this skin are the openings of numerous glands, which when squeezed express an oily substance.

Lateral to the dorsal limit of the genital opening on each side is a rather large crypt, which contains the minute openings of many of these glands.

## IV. DISCUSSION OF REPRODUCTIVE ORGANS

The female reproductive organs in the arctoid Carnivora show little variation in gross structure

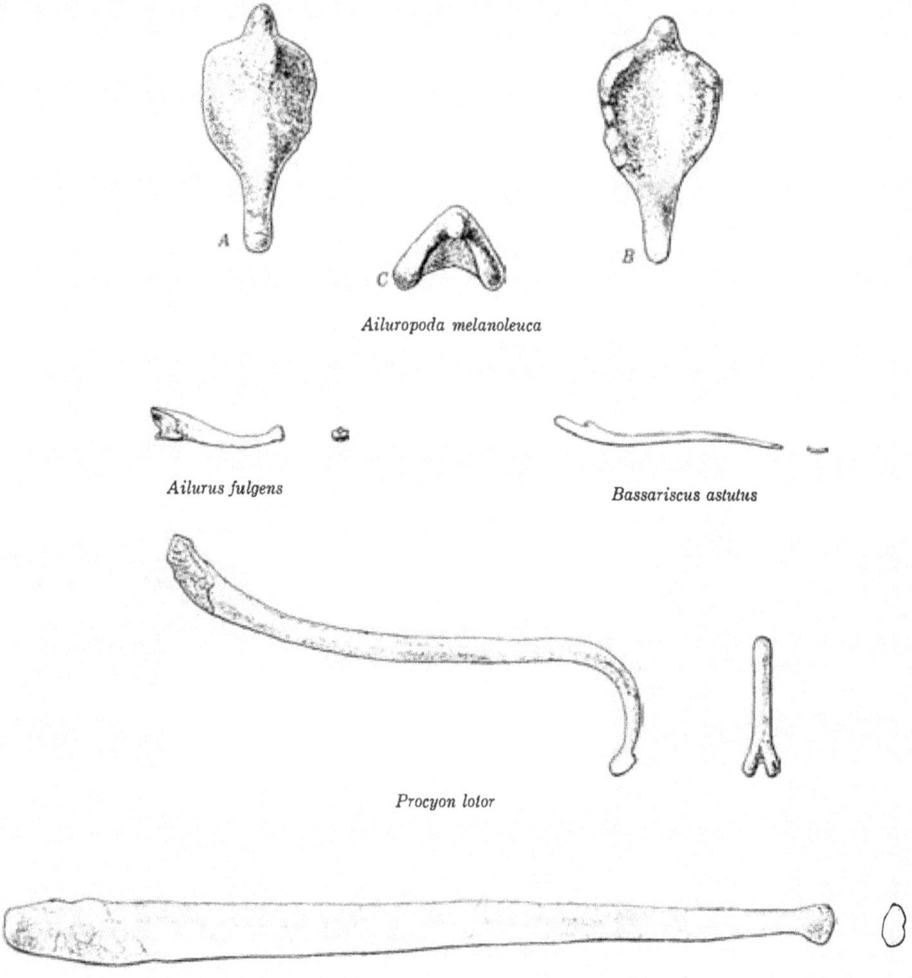

Ailuropoda melanoleuca

Ailurus fulgens

Bassariscus astutus

Procyon lotor

Ursus americanus

FIG. 120. Baculum of *Ailuropoda* and other arctoid carnivores. A, dorsal, B, ventral, C, anterior views. *Ailuropoda* × 2, others × 1 ).

and therefore need not concern us further here. The male organs, on the contrary, show extensive and fundamental differences, both in the accessory sex glands and in the copulatory organ.

The accessory sex glands of the Mammalia were reviewed by Oudemans (1892), who recognized four kinds of glands, and by Disselhorst (1904). Within the Carnivora there are pronounced differences in the degree of development of these several kinds of glands, and these differences are strictly corre-

lated with taxonomic units. No recent or detailed studies exist for the accessory sex glands of the Ursidae or Procyonidae. Owen says: "In the Bear the sperm-ducts are enlarged and in close contact at their terminations, with thick follicular walls" [=glands of ductus deferens]; "beyond this glandular part they retain their width, but contract to open upon the verumontanum. A thin layer of prostatic substance surrounds the beginning of the urethra." He further states that in the Procyonidae and Mustelidae "the prostate is better developed than in the Ursines, especially in the Racoon, in which it is in advance of the neck of the bladder." In *Nasua* sp. "the walls of the vasa defer-

*Ailurus fulgens* differs somewhat from *Procyon* and *Nasua*, and is considerably different from *Ursus* and *Ailuropoda*. In an adult male dissected by me the distal ends of the ductus deferentes

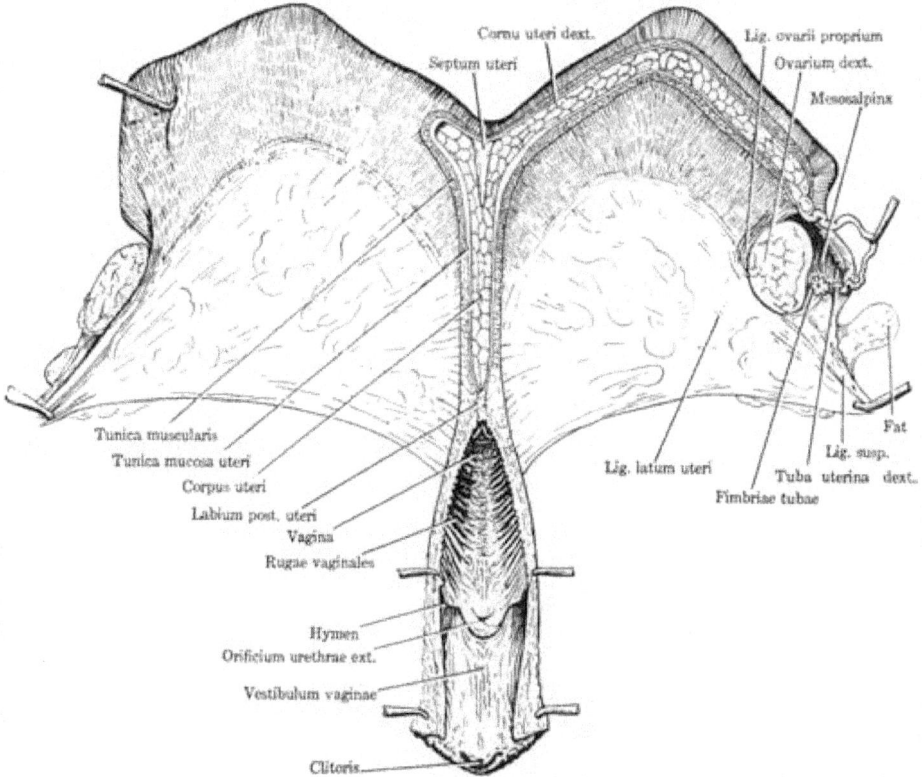

FIG. 121. Female reproductive organs of *Ailuropoda*. Dorsal view, vestibule and vagina opened along mid-dorsal line and spread out. (From Raven, redrawn).

entia are swollen immediately before these vessels enter the urethra, and the prostate has a more sudden projection at its upper end than I have observed in the musteline animals that I have dissected." (Turner, 1849.)

In a specimen of *Procyon lotor* dissected by me the prostate was a large and prominent globular structure surrounding the urethra at the base of the bladder. The distal ends of the ductus deferentes were dilated as in *Ailuropoda*, but these dilations contained no glandular tissue. Instead this portion of the ductus formed an ampulla with thick cavernous walls, somewhat similar to the ampulla of man. Weber (1928) erroneously states that in the Procyonidae the prostate is vestigial and glands of the ductus deferens are present.

were not dilated, there were neither glands of the ductus deferens nor ampullae, and the prostate was present but much smaller and less sharply set off from the urethra than in *Procyon*. This agrees essentially with Flower (1870).

The differences in the male accessory sex glands among the Carnivora, are:

Vesicular glands absent............................all Carnivora
Cowper's glands absent............................Arctoidea
  Prostate large, glands of ductus deferens absent.
    Ampulla ductus deferens small or absent......Canidae
    Ampulla ductus deferens large...........Procyonidae
  Prostate vestigial, glands of ductus deferens present,
    filling ampulla................................Ursidae
Cowper's glands present    }
Prostate present         }..........Aeluroidea
Glands of ductus deferens absent }

This table is based largely on the data compiled by Oudemans.

It is evident that *Ailuropoda* agrees closely with the Ursidae in the structure of the male accessory sex glands, and therefore these structures need not be considered further here. *Ailurus* most closely resembles the Procyonidae, but does not agree fully with any other arctoid carnivore.

For the external genitalia the picture is not so clear. The morphology of the penis was reviewed by Gerhardt (1909, 1933), Pohl (1928), and Slijper (1938). In the arctoid carnivores the penis is characterized by the abdominal position of the prepuce with the shaft long and enclosed in the belly skin (Pocock, 1921), and by the great length of the baculum and sparsity of erectile tissue (Gerhardt, 1933). In the Ursidae and Procyonidae the baculum extends proximally through the entire corpus nearly to the root of the penis, and the corpus fibrosum, which continues proximally from the baculum, is correspondingly short. Except for the intrapreputial part, the bone is clothed only in a thin layer of fascia. The erectile tissue—the corpus cavernosum surrounding the intrepreputial part of the baculum, and the corpus spongiosum surrounding the urethra—is remarkable for its flabbiness, with delicate trabeculae enclosing huge cavities.[1]

The ursid–procyonid–mustelid penis type is a highly specialized derivative of the more primitive vascular type, with the originally vascular corpora fibrosa almost completely replaced by bone. This might be called the "osseous type." As in the likewise highly specialized fibro-elastic type of the artiodactyls, temporary stiffening by engorgement of the corpora fibrosa with blood has been replaced by permanent stiffening through special supporting tissue.

The penis of *Ailuropoda* and *Ailurus* contrasts sharply with the osseous type so characteristic of all other arctoid carnivores. In the two pandas this organ closely resembles the much more primitive penis of the cats and certain viverrids: it is small, posteriorly directed, sub-anal in position, the corpus consisting largely of cavernous tissue, the baculum absolutely and relatively small. *From the ontogenetic standpoint this approaches the fetal condition, and represents a state of arrested development, of "fetalization."*

[1] It is remarkable that there are no descriptions of the penis of any bear or any procyonid. I have dissected this structure in a specimen of *Procyon lotor*, but no bear material was available to me.

Since *Ailuropoda* is an ursid, it must originally have had the highly specialized osseous penis type of the bears. The remarkable structure of the corpus fibrosum strongly supports this conclusion. The antecedents of *Ailurus* are unknown, but certainly they were not ursids, and therefore fetalization of its male external genitalia was independent of the corresponding process in *Ailuropoda*. Fetalization of the genitalia can scarcely be interpreted as adaptive, and if not adaptive it must be associated morphogenetically with some other feature that is adaptive. In *Ailuropoda* there is abundant evidence of disturbance in the whole lumbosacral-pelvic region, apparently associated with strong cephalization of the body axis, and the modified external genitalia may simply reflect this general disturbance. There is no overt indication of such disturbance in *Ailurus*. The only obvious adaptive feature the two pandas have in common is hypertrophy of the masticatory apparatus, and it is difficult (though not impossible) to associate this with fetalization of the male genitalia.

## V.  CONCLUSIONS

1. The kidney of *Ailuropoda* is renculate as in the Ursidae, but the renculi are fewer in number and are multipapillate.

2. The total number of renal papillae is about the same as in bears. This suggests that each renculus in *Ailuropoda* represents a consolidation of several unipapillate renculi of the ursid type.

3. The male reproductive organs of *Ailuropoda* may be divided into two parts:

 (a) The accessory sex glands, which agree closely with the distinctive pattern of the Ursidae.

 (b) The external genitalia, which differ from those of all other arctoid carnivores except *Ailurus*.

4. The Arctoidea (except the Canidae) are characterized by a highly specialized osseous penis, in which erectile tissue has been almost completely replaced by bone, and during erection the organ increases only insignificantly in length and diameter. The penis of the Canidae is unique among mammals.

5. In *Ailuropoda* and *Ailurus* the penis has been arrested at a much more primitive state of development than in other arctoids. The significance of this convergent "fetalization" of the external genitalia in two remotely related forms is unknown. In *Ailuropoda* it may be associated with cephalization of the body axis.

# RESPIRATORY SYSTEM

## I. LARYNX

The **epiglottis** (figs. 109,122) is triangular, with a pointed apex and moderately large rounded wings. The structure is nearly as broad as long. The epiglottis is subpalatal, not retrovelar, in position, the tip lying below and well forward of the posterior margin of the soft palate. A median glossoepiglottic fold connects the epiglottis with the base of the tongue, and a very high and narrow pharyngoepiglottic fold runs laterally and slightly anteriorly from the side of the epiglottis to the wall of the pharynx. The pharyngoepiglottic fold separates a shallow epiglottic depression anteriorly from an extremely deep and roomy pyriform recess posteriorly. The pyriform recess abuts posteriorly against the arytenoid and the arch of the cricoid. Its floor is far below the inferior wall of the esophagus.

### A. CAVITY OF THE LARYNX

The laryngeal cavity is characterized by a very deep vestibulum, the portion of the cavity lying above the vocal folds (fig. 110). The superior laryngeal aperture (fig. 122) is bounded by the epiglottis anteriorly, followed by a short ary-epiglottic fold extending between the epiglottis and the cuneiform cartilage. Behind the cuneiform tubercle the aperture is bounded by the cuneiform and arytenoid cartilages. The outlines of the cuneiform cartilage lying beneath the mucous membrane are clearly visible. The cuneiform tubercle is a conspicuous knob-like elevation formed by the protruding upper end of the cuneiform cartilage. The corniculate tubercle, lying behind the cuneiform tubercle, is a less prominent elevation formed by the corniculate process of the arytenoid.

The ventricular folds lie deep within the cavity of the larynx. Each fold is a heavy, smoothly rounded elevation in the laryngeal wall, broader posteriorly than anteriorly and extending diagonally forward and downward from the cuneiform cartilage to the anterior end of the laryngeal cavity. The vocal lips lie several millimeters below the ventricular folds and are much more prominent. They stand nearer the median line than the ventricular folds. The vocal lip is triangular in cross section. Its thin free border is the vocal fold, or true vocal cord. Between the ventricular and the vocal fold is a shallow recess, the laryngeal ventricle, running the length of the folds and broadly open to the laryngeal cavity. There are no laryngeal sacs. The true cavity of the larynx, the space below the vocal folds, is shallow and scarcely wider than the rima glottidis anteriorly, gradually broadening to the diameter of the larynx posteriorly.

### B. CARTILAGES OF THE LARYNX

#### Figure 123

The laryngeal skeleton is boxy. The margins of the thyroid and cricoid cartilages are only slightly excised, and the thyrohyoid and thyrocricoid membranes correspondingly limited. The result is that almost the entire laryngeal cavity is encased in cartilage.

The **thyroid cartilage** is characterized by broad lamina. The anterior thyroid notch is scarcely indicated, but the posterior thyroid notch is deep, extending more than half way to the anterior margin of the cartilage. The dorsal outline of the cartilage is nearly straight. The anterior and posterior cornua are relatively short and stout, and about equal in length. There is a poorly defined muscular process near the middle of the posterior margin, and from this a faint linea obliqua extends anteriorly and dorsally across the lamina. Above the muscular process, the posterior margin is deeply excavated to form a pit for muscle attachment.

The **cricoid cartilage** is completely divided at the ventral midline, the two halves of the arch separated by an interval of about 2 mm. There is in addition a deep U-shaped notch in the posterior margin at the ventral midline and a shallower notch in the anterior margin. The arch is concave in cross section, and is otherwise practically devoid of surface relief. The lamina is about twice as broad anteroposteriorly as the arch, and is quadrangular in outline, somewhat longer than broad. Its anterior margin has a shallow U-shaped notch at the midline. There is a prominent median keel separating the areas of origin of the two posterior cricoarytenoid muscles. The cricothyroid articulation is at the juncture between arch and lamina.

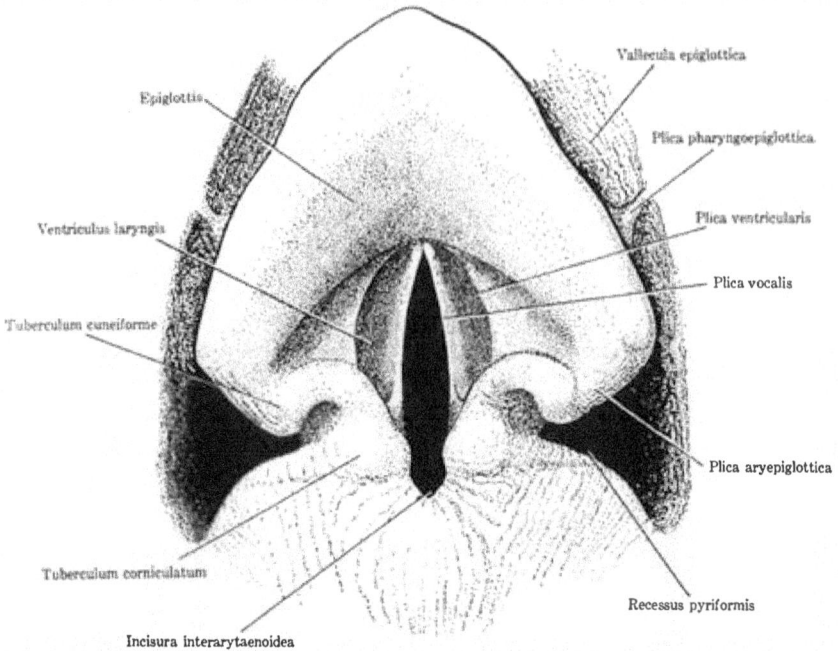

FIG. 122. Laryngeal cavity of *Ailuropoda* from above.

The **arytenoid cartilage** is massive and irregular in form, with well-developed processes. The
median processes of the two arytenoids are in contact at the midline. The apex is short and blunt,
the muscular process moderate in length but very
broad and heavy. The corniculate process is a
very short cylindrical projection on the medial
margin of the cartilage. The vocal process is a
keel-like projection on the ventral surface of the
cartilage.

The cuneiform cartilage is a very large L-shaped
structure attached to the apex of the arytenoid.
A small unpaired interarytenoid cartilage lies immediately anterior to the two median processes of
the arytenoid, and marks the posterior limit of the
interarytenoid notch.

### C. Muscles of the Larynx

**M. aryepiglotticus** (fig. 125) arises from the
interarytenoid cartilage, beneath the oblique arytenoid, and extends almost directly ventrad along
the aryepiglottic fold, lying lateral to the ventricular fold, to insert on the base of the epiglottis.
A few of the posterior fibers insert on the anterolateral margin of the arytenoid cartilage.

**M. cricothyreoideus** (fig. 124) is partially divisible into straight and oblique portions. The
more superficial *pars recta* arises from the medial
ventral border of the arch of the cricoid cartilage,
separated by a small interval from its mate of the
opposite side, and passes straight dorsad to its insertion along the dorsal half of the posterior border
of the thyroid cartilage from the level of the inferior tubercle to the inferior cornu. A few of the
superficial fibers are continuous with some of the
posterior fibers of the thyropharyngeal division of
the posterior constrictor of the pharynx. The
deeper *pars obliqua* arises from the posteroventral
border of the cricoid, and inserts into the posterior
cornu and inner surface of the thyroid cartilage.
A few fibers continue into the cricopharyngeal division of the posterior pharyngeal constrictor.

**M. cricoarytaenoideus posterior** (fig. 125) is
a fan-shaped muscle lying on the dorsal surface of
the lamina of the cricoid cartilage. Origin is from
the middle and posterior thirds of the dorsal surface of the cricoid lamina, where it is separated
from its mate by a median keel on the cricoid lamina. The fibers converge anterolaterally, to insert
on the posterior margin of the muscular process of
the arytenoid cartilage.

**M. cricoarytaenoideus lateralis** arises from
the dorsolateral margin of the cricoid cartilage and
inserts on the anterolateral border of the muscular

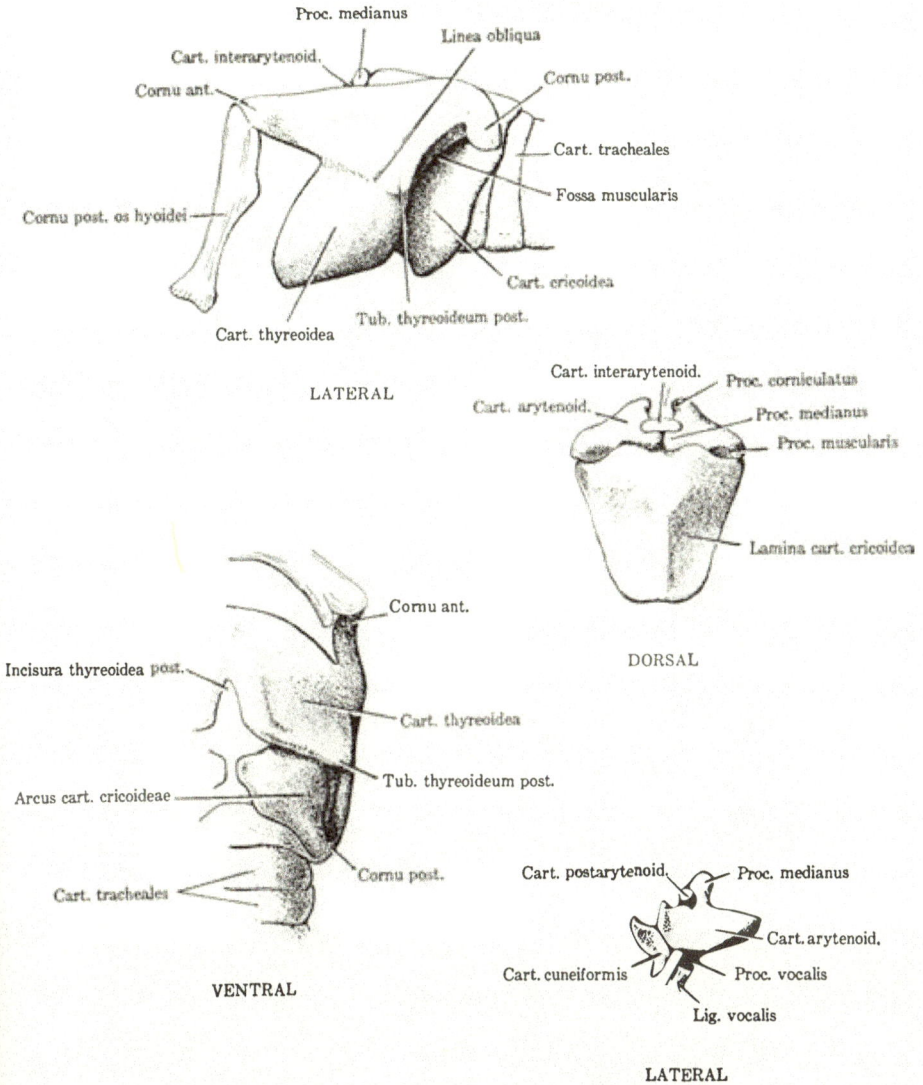

FIG. 123. Laryngeal cartilages of *Ailuropoda*.

process of the arytenoid cartilage. The anterior fibers insert into a narrow raphe shared by the transverse arytenoid.

M. vocalis arises from the thyroid lamina at the ventral midline, and inserts on the muscular process of the arytenoid cartilage. The muscle lies lateral to the vocal ligament.

M. hyoepiglotticus (fig. 125) is a slender paired muscle extending from the ceratohyal to the lin-

gual surface of the epiglottis. The fibers overlap and unite with those of the muscle of the opposite side at the insertion.

M. thyreoarytaenoideus (fig. 125) arises from the midventral border of the thyroid cartilage, passes around the lateral dorsal aspect of the arytenoid cartilage, and inserts on the interarytenoid cartilage. It is not entirely separable from the vocal muscle lying deep to it.

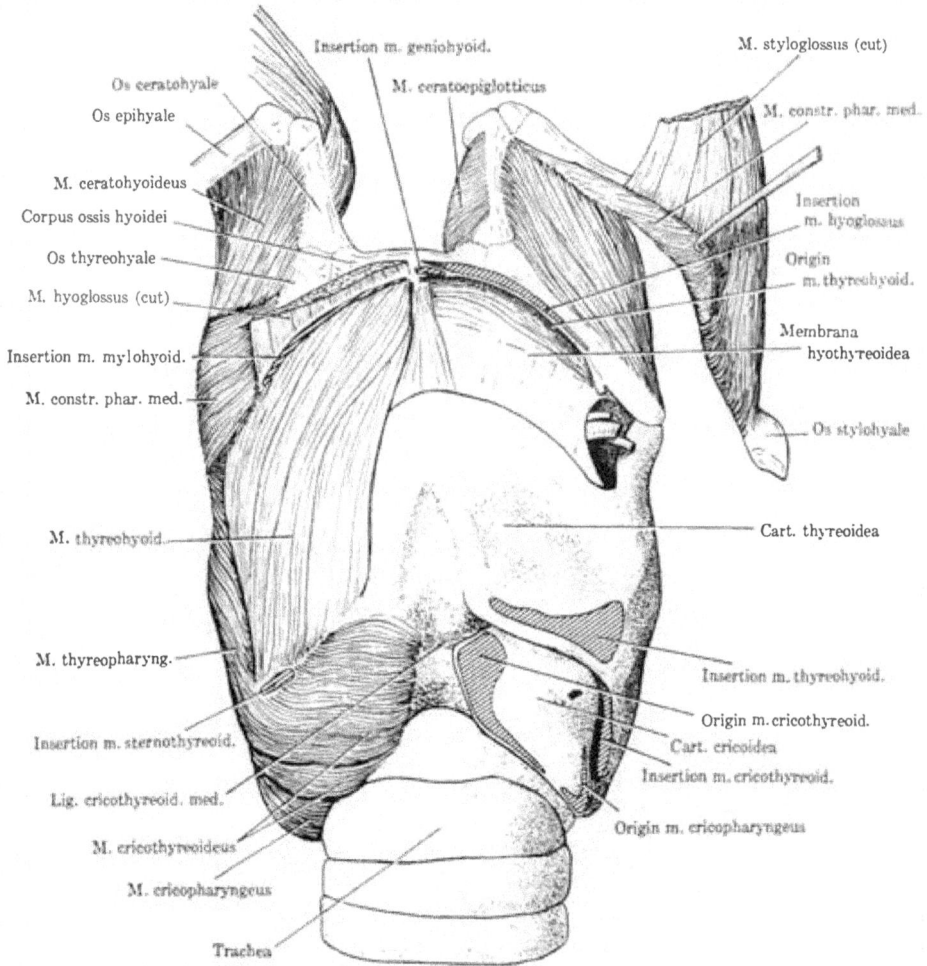

FIG. 124. External laryngeal musculature of *Ailuropoda*, ventral view. Superficial dissection to left, deeper dissection to right.

**M. arytaenoideus obliquus** (fig. 125) is a thin strand of muscle fibers arising from the interarytenoid cartilage at the dorsal midline, crossing the origin of its fellow, and running obliquely anteriorly along the aryepiglottic fold to insert on the epiglottis at the pharyngo-epiglottic fold.

**M. arytaenoideus transversus** (fig. 125) is a well-developed paired muscle arising from the muscular process of the arytenoid cartilage and inserting at the midline on the interarytenoid cartilage. It is overlapped at its insertion by fibers of the oblique arytenoid, aryepiglottic, and external thyroarytenoid muscles.

D. DISCUSSION OF LARYNX

Larynxes of *Canis latrans, Procyon lotor, Nasua narica, Ailurus fulgens, Ursus tibetanus, U. americanus* (juvenile), and *Melursus ursinus* were dissected for comparison with *Ailuropoda* (fig. 126). Among arctoid carnivores, only the larynx of *Canis familiaris* has been well described in the literature. Albrecht (1896) described and compared the mucous membrane folds of the larynx in several arctoids: *Canis, Vulpes, Otocyon, Procyon, Potos, Ursus,* and several mustelids. Göppert (1894) described the cartilage of the epiglottis and the cuneiform cartilage of *Ursus arctos* and several mustelids. Owen

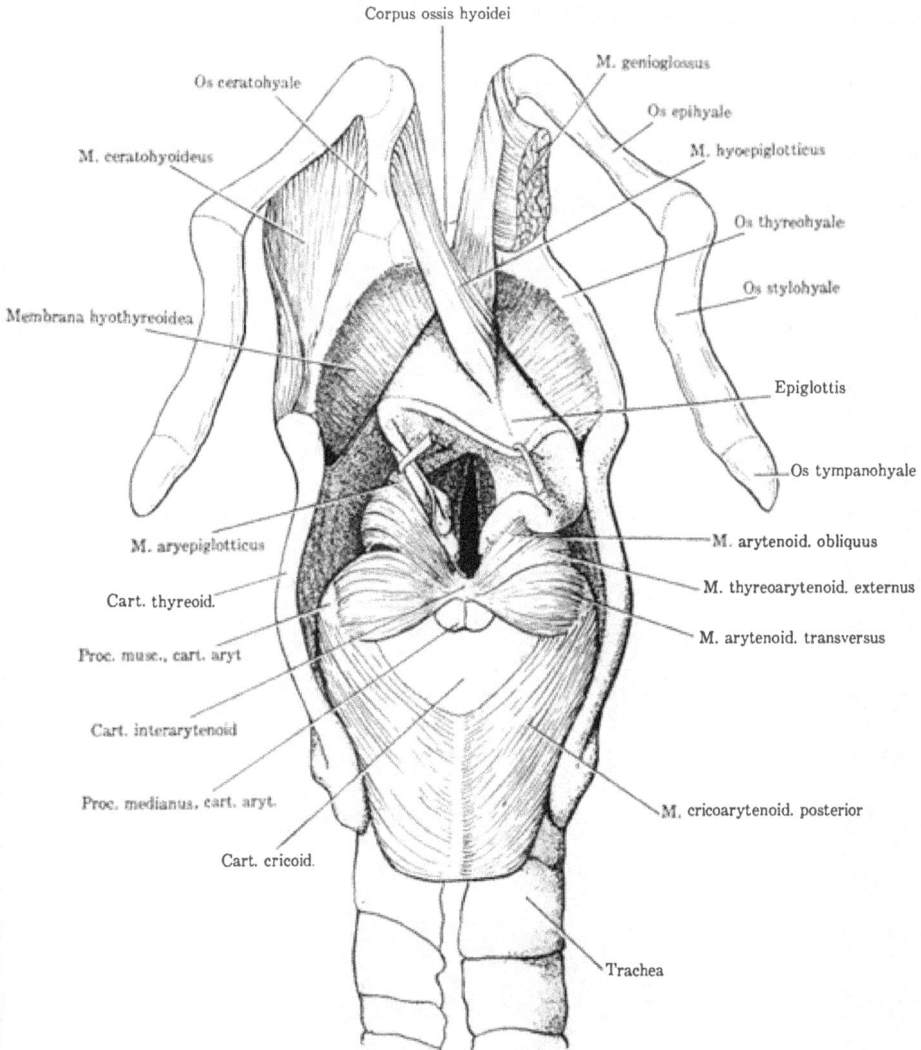

FIG. 125. Intrinsic laryngeal musculature of *Ailuropoda* dorsal view.

(1868) described and figured the laryngeal cartilages of *Ursus*. Fürbringer (1875) studied the intrinsic laryngeal musculature of seventeen species of Carnivora, including *Canis, Procyon, Nasua,* and *Ursus*.

In general, the larynx is most primitive in the Ursidae among the arctoids. This is emphasized by Göppert (1894) for the epiglottal and cuneiform cartilages, and (1937) for the arytenoids. It is confirmed in the present study. The larynx is generally primitive in the Canidae, but with distinct and characteristic specializations. In the Procyonidae the larynx is much reduced, in some respects almost degenerate.

The epiglottis is lanceolate in all arctoids in which it has been examined. In the Canidae the angles of the epiglottis are very sharp and the aryepiglottic folds are narrow and transverse, giving a characteristic triangular shape to the anterior part of the entrance to the larynx. Cuneiform

Canis familiaris

Ailurus fulgens

Nasua narica

Melursus ursinus

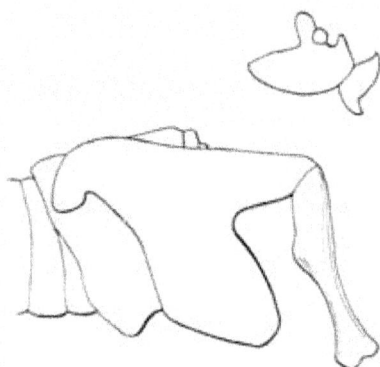

Ailuropoda melanoleuca

FIG. 126. Laryngeal cartilages of representative arctoid carnivores, right lateral view. The arytenoid and cuneiform cartilages are shown separately above the main cartilages.

and corniculate tubercles are present, both pairs lying close to the midline. In the Procyonidae the epiglottis is reduced, especially its lateral wings. The aryepiglottic folds are heavy and run obliquely. A cuneiform tubercle is present, although unsupported by cartilage, but the corniculate tubercle is completely absent. In the Ursidae and *Ailuropoda* the aryepiglottic fold is heavy and runs obliquely, but the line is interrupted at the cuneiform tubercle. Both cuneiform and corniculate tubercles are prominent. The ventricular and vocal folds show little significant variation among the arctoids examined. They are oriented very steeply, and the ventriculus is very deep, in the Canidae.

The thyroid and cricoid cartilages are only slightly excised at their margins in the Ursidae and *Ailuropoda*, and the posterior thyroid notch, while deep, is very narrow, giving a boxy appearance to the laryngeal skeleton. The hyothyroid, cricothyroid, and cricotracheal membranes are correspondingly reduced. The thyroid cornua are moderately long and subequal. There is a sharply defined muscular fossa below the posterior cornu. The posterior thyroid tubercle is large but low. The cricoid arch is intact but deeply incised at the ventral midline (*Melursus*), almost divided (*Ursus malayanus*, Owen), or completely divided (*Ailuropoda* and our specimen of *Ursus americanus*).

In the Canidae the margins of the cartilages are somewhat more excised than in the Ursidae. The posterior thyroid notch is very shallow. The anterior thyroid cornu is normal, but the posterior cornu is extremely short, scarcely differentiated from the thyroid lamina. There is no muscular fossa, and the posterior thyroid tubercle is small. The cricoid arch is intact, and its anterior margin is broadly excised.

In the Procyonidae (including *Ailurus*) the margins of the thyroid lamina are deeply excised, in addition to a very deep posterior thyroid notch. The laryngeal membranes are very extensive. The thyroid cornua are approximately normal. Muscular fossa are absent. The posterior thyroid tubercle is enormous and projecting in *Nasua* and *Ailurus*, absent in *Procyon*. The anterior margin of the cricoid arch is broadly excised (except *Ailurus*), and the posterior margin is reflected in lip-like formation.

The arytenoid is massive and with well-developed processes in the Ursidae and *Ailuropoda*. The median processes of the two arytenoids meet at the midline. The vocal process is large and wing-like. The cuneiform cartilage is large and L-shaped. A rod-like interarytenoid cartilage is lodged between corniculate and median processes.

In the Canidae the arytenoid resembles that of the Ursidae but is less massive. The median process is much reduced. It is notable for the great length of the corniculate process, which extends back as a curved finger-like structure beyond the interarytenoid incisure. The cuneiform is very large and irregular in outline, with a long dorsal process.

In the Procyonidae (including *Ailurus*) the arytenoid is reduced to a triangular flake of cartilage, the apexes of the triangle representing the apex, and the muscular and median processes, respectively. The median processes are well separated at the midline. The corniculate process is entirely absent (*Procyon, Nasua*) or represented by a small elevation (*Ailurus*). The cuneiform cartilage is entirely absent, but the interarytenoid is present as a nodule of cartilage.

There do not appear to be any significant differences in the laryngeal muscles of the Canidae and Ursidae. These muscles were not dissected in the Procyonidae.

### E. SUMMARY OF LARYNX

1. The larynx of the Ursidae is the least specialized among the arctoid carnivores.

2. The larynx of *Ailuropoda* closely resembles that of the Ursidae.

3. In the Canidae the larynx shows numerous characteristic modifications.

4. In the Procyonidae the larynx has undergone degenerative modifications. Thyroid and cricoid are reduced, and the arytenoid and its associated cartilages are degenerate.

5. The functional significance of these differences is unknown.

## II. TRACHEA

The **trachea** (fig. 127) has a length of 270 mm., from the base of the cricoid cartilage to the posterior base of the bifurcation of the bronchi. It is composed of 27 cartilaginous rings, which is the number estimated by Raven (1936). Several pairs of rings are partly united, and this gives them a bifurcated appearance. The diameter of the trachea is 35 mm. (36 mm. in Raven's specimen). The dorsal membranous part of the rings has a maximum width of 6 mm.

The **bronchi** are extremely short, dividing almost immediately into eparterial and hyparterial rami. The base of the bifurcation of the right bronchus is scarcely farther ectad than the border of the trachea, but the left bronchus has a length of 30 mm. before it bifurcates. The right bronchus has a diameter of 41 mm.; that of the left is only 23 mm.

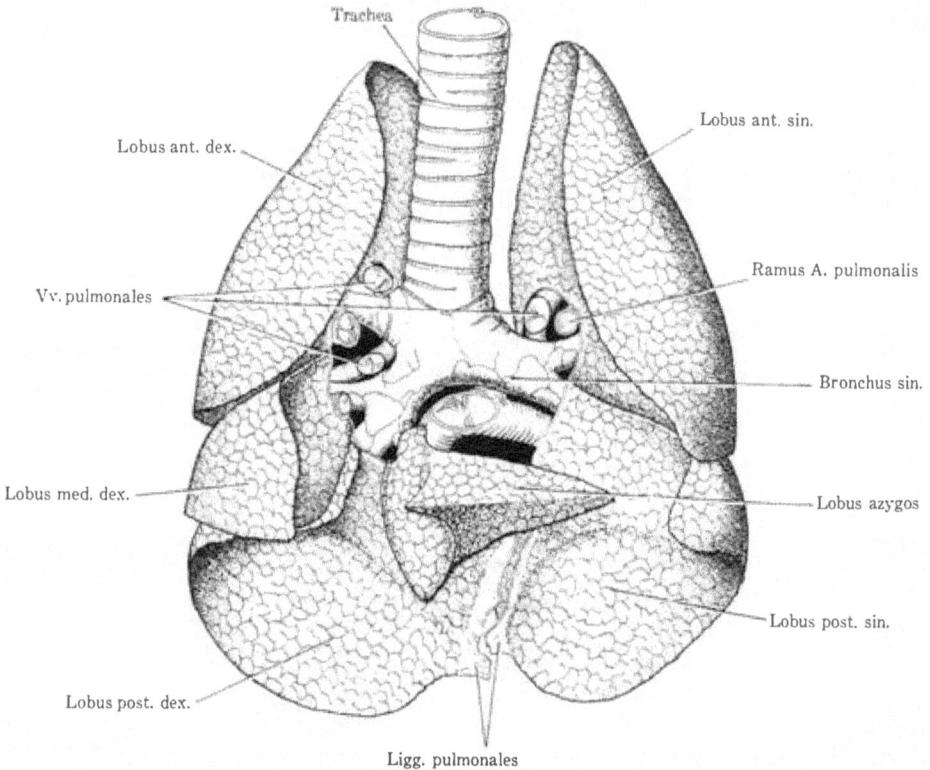

FIG. 127. Trachea, bronchi, and lungs of *Ailuropoda*, ventral view.

## III. LUNGS

The lungs (fig. 127) are elongate wedge-shaped structures. They are made up of completely separate lobes, the lobes of either side being joined only by the bronchi and a small isthmus of the serous coat. The left lung consists of two subequal lobes, both larger than any of the lobes of the right lung. The anterior lobe measures 175 mm. in length, the posterior 165 mm. The anterior and posterior lobes of the right lung are approximately equal in size, each measuring about 135 mm. in length. The very small right median lobe is wedged in between the anterior and posterior lobes. The small pointed azygous lobe lies ventral to the median edge of the right posterior lobe. It is deeply molded by the posterior vena cava, which it embraces from the dorsal side. As in the specimen studied by Raven, the right eparterial bronchus supplies only the anterior lobe. There is a prominent posterior pulmonary liga-

ment at the posterior end of each lung, which attaches to the diaphragm.

### DISCUSSION OF LUNGS

The form of the lungs is molded by the shape of the thoracic cavity, the heart, and the diaphragm. Differences in form attributable to these agents are evident among carnivores, but scarcely seem worth discussing here. The most dramatic character of the lungs among the Carnivora is the difference in the number of lobes. In the Canidae (and all Aeluroidea that have been examined) the left lung is divided into three lobes, whereas in the Procyonidae (including *Ailurus;* Carlsson, 1925), Ursidae, and Mustelidae the left lung is divided into only two lobes (Göppert, 1937). *Ailuropoda* agrees with the second group. The right lung is divided into four lobes (including the azygous) in all fissiped carnivores.

Secondary reduction of lobation appears to be correlated primarily with broadening of the thorax

(Marcus, 1937). No figures are available for the thoracic index in the Procyonidae, Ursidae, and Mustelidae, but it is evident from inspection that the thorax is relatively broader in these than in the dogs, cats, and civets.

## IV. CONCLUSIONS

1. The respiratory system of *Ailuropoda* closely resembles that of the Ursidae.

2. The larynx of the bears and *Ailuropoda* is the most primitive among the arctoid Carnivora. The larynx is specialized, in different directions, in the Canidae and Procyonidae.

3. Lung lobation is similar in the Procyonidae, Ursidae, and Mustelidae. The Canidae and all aeluroid carnivores have one more lobe in the left lung.

# CIRCULATORY SYSTEM

## I. HEART

Two hearts were available for study: the sub-adult heart, fixed *in situ*, of Su Lin, and the fully adult heart, preserved in formalin after removal from the body, of Mei Lan. The description is based largely on the heart of Su Lin; the adult heart was not in suitable condition for detailed study.

The heart, fixed *in situ* in moderate contraction, has the form of a slender cone. The longitudinal diameter greatly exceeds the transverse diameter, and the apex is pointed. The proportions of the heart resemble those in the Ursidae, except that the organ is more slender in *Ailuropoda*. In the Canidae the heart is markedly globular.

The heart of Su Lin (empty, without the pericardium, and with the great vessels cut short) weighs 302 grams, which is 0.5 per cent of total body weight. This heart measures 92 mm. from base to apex (apex=coronary sulcus at the origin of the left longitudinal sulcus),[1] 79 mm. in transverse diameter (greatest distance between the two longitudinal sulci), 77 mm. in sagittal diameter (greatest distance between points intermediate between the two longitudinal sulci), and 252 mm. in circumference (maximum circumference around ventricles). The heart of Mei Lan weighs 530 grams and measures about 115 mm. from base to apex.

In an old male *Tremarctos ornatus*, which died in the Chicago Zoological Park and which weighed 175 pounds at death, the heart formed 0.5 per cent of body weight. Heart weights given by Crile and Quiring (1940) represent 0.8 per cent of total body weight for a fresh specimen of *Ursus horribilis* that weighed 310 pounds, 0.6 per cent for a fresh specimen of *Thalarctos maritimus* that weighed 440 pounds, and 0.4 per cent for another *Thalarctos* that weighed 700 pounds. In the domestic dog the heart forms about 1.1 per cent of adult body weight (Ellenberger and Baum, 1943), in the domestic cat about 0.4 per cent (Latimer, 1942).

## A. EXTERIOR OF THE HEART. (Figure 128.)

The left surface (anterior of human anatomy) of the heart is almost flat, and the right surface is

[1] For heart measurements I have used the method described by Gschwend (1931, Anat. Anz., 72, p. 56).

divided into two planes that meet at an acute angle opposite the left surface. Thus the cross section of the heart is triangular. The auricles are relatively small; the left auricle, much smaller than the right, measures 35 mm. in diameter, the right 52 mm. The auricles are broadly separated from one another by the great vessels. The right auricle lies much higher than the left, almost entirely above the coronary groove. It is wrapped around the base of the aorta. The left auricle lies below the pulmonary artery, mostly below the coronary groove. Its distal two thirds is appressed against the left ventricle.

The longitudinal grooves are well marked. The left is more prominent than the right. The left longitudinal groove begins near the base of the pulmonary artery, beneath the left auricle, and runs diagonally toward the tip of the heart. It crosses over onto the right surface at the incisura cordis, well above the apex of the heart. The position of the incisura cordis is about 20 per cent of the distance between the apex and base of the heart. The right longitudinal groove begins at the root of the posterior vena cava and runs almost straight toward the tip of the heart. Some distance above the tip it unites with the left longitudinal groove. Thus the right ventricle does not reach the tip of the heart, which is formed entirely by the left ventricle. The conus arteriosus is moderately inflated. The right atrium is much inflated and almost globular. The sulcus terminalis appears as a faint groove beginning between the anterior vena cava and the wall of the atrium and running toward the base of the postcava. The left atrium is much smaller than the right. Externally the two atria meet only posteriorly, above the postcava, and here the boundary between them is very indistinct. Anteriorly they are broadly separated by the aorta and pulmonary artery.

## B. INTERIOR OF THE HEART

*Atria*

RIGHT ATRIUM.—The cavity of the distended right atrium is much larger than that of the left, and is much broader than high. The atrium proper measures about 60 mm. in breadth. Except in the auricular region the external wall is thin, only

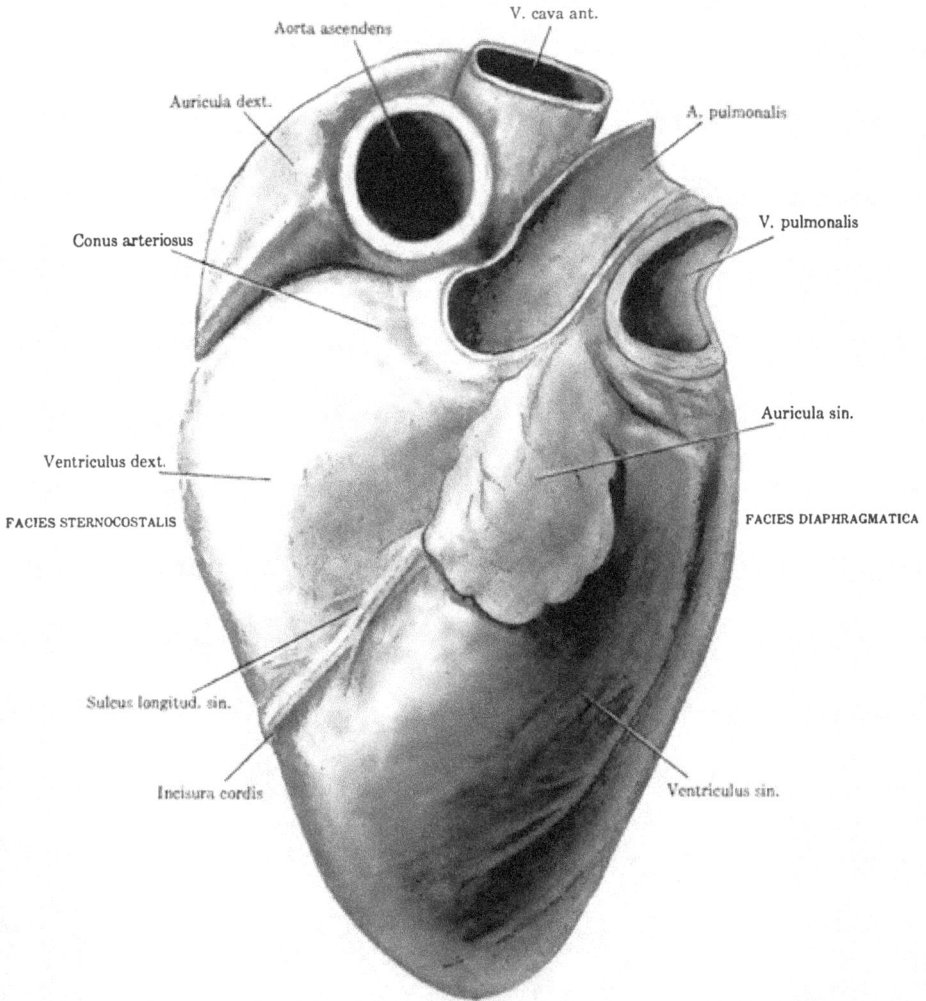

Fig. 128.  Heart of *Ailuropoda* from the left side.

about a millimeter in thickness.  The anterior vena cava enters the atrium from above, the posterior vena cava from behind.  The crista terminalis, corresponding in position to the sulcus terminalis, is a ridge running from the right (anti-septal) side of the anterior caval orifice toward the postcaval orifice.  It is prominent at first, but quickly fades out.  Pectinate muscles are prominently developed in the auricle, and are faintly evident on the external wall of the atrium nearly to the entrance of the postcava.  The septal wall is smooth.

The tuberculum intervenosum is indistinguishable from the crista intervenosa, into which it normally continues.  The tuberculum intervenosum has the form of a conspicuous ridge on the septal wall, running apically and to the right between the orifice of the anterior vena cava and the fossa ovalis.  The fossa ovalis is an inconspicuous shallow and poorly defined depression, only about 7 mm. in diameter, bounded anteriorly by the ridge-like tuberculum intervenosum.  The orifice of the coronary sinus, which is about 7 mm. in diameter, lies

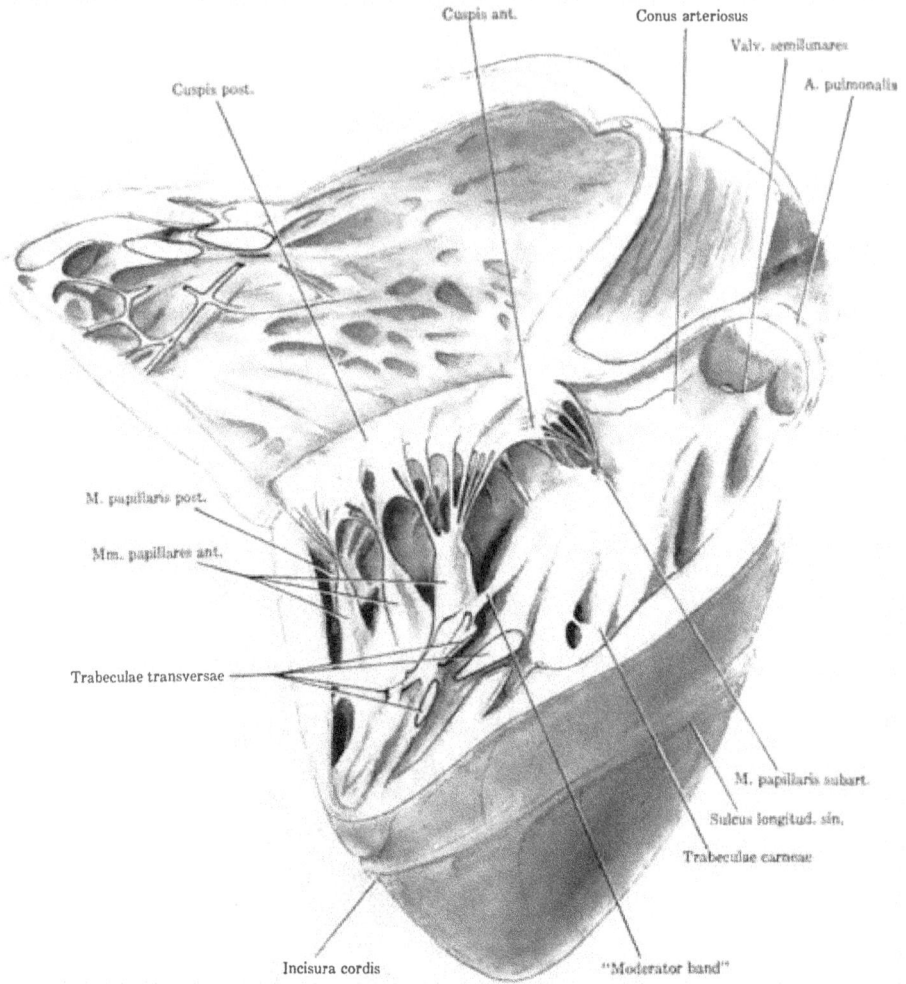

FIG. 129.  Right ventricle of *Ailuropoda*.

directly below (apicalward of) the entrance of the postcava.

LEFT ATRIUM.—The cavity of the atrium proper is ovate, with the long diameter transverse to the long axis of the heart.  The long diameter measures about 40 mm.  The wall is about 6 mm. thick, and thus is much heavier than the wall of the right atrium.  The walls of the auricle are almost paperthin.  The pulmonary veins enter the atrium from above.  The lining of the atrium is completely smooth and practically devoid of relief.  The peripheral part of the auricle contains a meshwork of coarse pectinate muscles, some of them freestanding cylindrical strands.  On the internal wall of the auricle, near its entrance into the atrium, there is a large pillar-like pectinate muscle, 7 mm. in diameter, from which smaller strands pass to the auricular wall.  On the septal wall the site of the foramen ovale is marked by an inconspicuous, very shallow depression.

*Ventricles*

RIGHT VENTRICLE.—The right ventricle (fig. 129) has a triangular cavity, somewhat broader than high, terminating posteriorly in a long funnel-shaped conus arteriosus. The crista supraventricularis is short and extends nearly vertically downward. The ventricular cavity measures about 70 mm. in breadth (measured to base of semilunar valve, and 58 mm. in height (base to apex). The conus accounts for about 37 per cent of the total breadth of the chamber. The external wall has a maximum thickness (near the base of the conus) of about 9 mm.; it is thinnest near the apex. The septal wall is firm, and arches prominently into the cavity. It is smooth and free of trabeculae except near the basal groove. The external wall, on the contrary, is covered with a coarse meshwork of ridges, the trabeculae carneae, except in the conus region. A system of free cord-like trabeculae is present on the external wall. There are four well-developed papillary muscles, situated near the center of the septal wall. There evidently was considerable disturbance of the normal developmental pattern in the right ventricle of Mei Lan, although the arrangement and proportions of structures are generally similar to Su Lin and the Ursidae.

The papillaris subarterialis can scarcely be said to exist. At its customary site, on the septal wall near the beginning of the conus, a single chorda tendinea arises directly from the septum and passes to the cusp of the septal valve. Immediately behind this chorda, but completely separate from it, lies the base of the arteriormost chorda tendinea propria. In the heart of Mei Lan not only the papilla, but also the chorda normally arising therefrom, are completely absent.

Of the four papillary muscles, the first three represent anterior papillary muscles; the fourth, situated most posteriorly in the posterior niche of the ventricle, is the posterior papillary muscle.

The three anterior papillary muscles are situated in a line, the first two close together, the posteriormost one somewhat isolated. All arise from the septum, but the base of each is connected with the external wall by a transverse trabecula. The anteriormost papilla, the largest, is cylindrical, 11 mm. in height by 7.5 mm. in diameter, and terminates in three chordae tendineae that pass to the anterior cusp. The base of this papilla is connected to the external wall by two large plate-like transverse trabeculae, the larger of these 3.5 mm. in diameter. A short but conspicuous ridge-like elevation of the septal wall (representing the moderator band of human anatomy) passes downward and posteriorly to the base of the anteriormost papilla. It fuses with the base of the papilla, where it continues directly into the uppermost of the two plate-like transverse trabeculae. The second papilla stands free of the

septum except at its base. It terminates in a single chorda that subdivides and passes to the anterior and posterior cusps. The base of this papilla is connected to the base of the first papilla and to the external wall by a stout cylindrical transverse trabecula, 1.5 mm. in diameter. The third papilla is slightly smaller than the second, and terminates in a single chorda that passes to the posterior cusp. Its base is connected with the external wall by a short cylindrical transverse trabecula.

A single posterior papillary muscle is situated in the posterior niche of the ventricle. It is stout, but shorter than any of the anterior papillae, and has the shape of a flattened cylinder. It is septal in position, but its base is connected to the external wall by a short stout transverse trabecula. This papilla is two-tipped. A group of 2 3 chordae tendineae arising from each tip ramifies to the posterior and septal cusps.

There are no accessory papillary muscles. A row of 8 direct chordae tendineae arises from the middle part of the septum, the anteriormost lying directly behind (septalward of) the subarterial papilla. These are fairly regularly spaced at intervals of about 7 mm. Each ramifies to the cusp of the septal valve.

Transverse trabeculae.—Ackerknecht (1919) defines these as more or less cylindrical strands that (1) are related to the papillae, and (2) cross the ventricular cavity transversely or obliquely. Thus he distinguishes the transverse trabeculae, which contain a part of the conducting system, from other trabecular structures that often extend across between septum and external wall. Ackerknecht interprets these latter structures as modified trabeculae carneae. In *Ailuropoda* these two trabecular systems are topographically closely related at the base of the anteriormost papilla. Two heavy, flattened-cylindrical transverse trabeculae arise from the base of this papilla and run horizontally to the external wall, where they terminate in the trabecular meshwork situated there. The uppermost of these is continuous at its origin with the moderator band; these two structures together form the "trabecula septomarginalis" of Ackerknecht. Near its origin the upper trabecula gives off a slender trabecular strand that runs independently to the meshwork on the external wall. In addition, the first and second papillae are interconnected at their base by a flattened-cylindrical free trabecula; one slender transverse trabecula arises from the middle of this and a larger transverse trabecula comes from its attachment to the second papilla. Both go to the meshwork on the external wall. Thus four transverse trabeculae, all inserting into the meshwork, arise from the anterior papillae.

From the base of the posterior papilla a short, stout transverse trabecula passes to the external wall in the niche region of the ventricle.

Trabeculae carneae.— The inner surface of the whole external wall is covered with very prominent, coarse trabeculae carneae. These are ridges in high relief, about 3 mm. in diameter, surrounding shallow sinuses. Fleshy trabeculae are least prominent, but still present, on the external wall in the conus region. The general direction of the trabecular ridges is horizontal. The septal wall is smooth and free of trabeculae, except for short, heavy, pillar-like structures in the basal groove.

Two powerful muscular bands, 14 mm. in diameter, arise from the septum near the base of the anteriormost papilla and run horizontally to the external wall, where they insert on the trabecular ridges. These resemble transverse trabeculae, but are not connected either with papillae or with the trabecular meshwork on the external wall, and therefore are interpreted as trabeculae carneae. A similar arrangement, except that the trabeculae were much more slender, was present in one specimen of *Helarctos*.

The trabecular meshwork of cord-like free strands lies on the external wall at the level of the papillae, i.e., at about the middle of the external wall. This system consists of two or three strands, all paralleling the transverse axis of the ventricle, with numerous short thread-like roots arising from the external wall. There are a few interconnections between the main strands. The transverse trabeculae from the papillae insert into this trabecular meshwork.

Tricuspid valve.— The atrioventricular orifice is 42 mm. in length. The anterior and septal (medial) cusps are subequal in size, and the boundary between them is clearly marked. The anterior cusp measures about 40 mm. in breadth. The posterior cusp, much smaller than the other two, is clearly bounded from the septal cusp, less distinctly so from the posterior cusp. No accessory cusps are evident, but the free margin of each primary cusp is deeply notched between the attachments of the chordae tendineae, giving it a scalloped appearance.

The three semilunar valves occupy the usual position at the base of the pulmonary artery. Each forms a deep pocket. In the middle of the free margin of each there is a conspicuous nodulus of Aranti.

LEFT VENTRICLE.—The cavity has the form of an inverted cone, and is smaller than the cavity of the right ventricle. The external wall has a maximum thickness of about 16 mm., and thus is nearly twice as thick as the wall of the right ven-

tricle; it is thinnest at the apex, where it measures about 9 mm. Except in the conus region, the lining is thrown up into prominent longitudinal ridges, much more regular and slightly more prominent than the trabeculae carneae of the right ventricle. There is a simple system of free trabecular strands. Two large and well-formed papillae are present, nearly equal in size, close together on the external wall.

The anterior papillary muscle is pillar-like, about 11 mm. in diameter, and fused to the external wall except at its tip. The tip is truncated, and from it arise two very unequal conical structures from the tips of which the chordae tendineae are given off. The smaller of these conical structures, on the medial side of the papilla tip, terminates in five chordae tendineae that ramify to the external cusp of the bicuspid valve. The larger conical structure is a long cylinder, 10 mm. long, terminating in four chordae that ramify to both valves, but mostly to the septal valve. A single heavy chorda arises from the base of this cylinder and ramifies to the septal valve. This gives a total of ten chordae tendineae. A stout chorda-like strand arises from the septal side of the tip of the papilla and runs upward toward the base of the ventricle, near which it fuses with the septal wall. At several points along its course this strand is united to the meshwork of the fleshy trabecular system.

The posterior papillary muscle is slightly larger than the anterior papilla, and resembles it in form except that the tip of the posterior papilla is more conical. Five chordae tendineae arising from the tip ramify to the cusps of both valves. A sixth chorda, arising partly from the papilla and partly from the external wall, ramifies to both the septal cusp and the external wall. A large transverse trabecula arises by several roots from the septal side of the body of the papilla and runs up toward the septum, to which it attaches near the entrance to the conus.

The system of transverse trabeculae consists, in addition to the strands associated with the papillae, largely of a single strand running freely and more or less horizontally over the septal wall near its middle. Along its course this parent strand is joined by about six smaller lateral roots arising from the septal wall, and at each end by a root from each of the papillary transverse trabeculae. There is also a loose, coarse meshwork of slightly smaller strands in the region between the anterior papilla and the septal wall. Finally, there are a few very short slender trabeculae in the apical region.

TABLE 23.—HEART STRUCTURE OF ARCTOID CARNIVORES

| | Canis* | Bassariscus | Procyon | Ursidae | Ailuropoda |
|---|---|---|---|---|---|
| Form of heart | globular | subglobular | subglobular | conical | conical |
| Right ventricle | | | | | |
| Length of conus | long | very short | very short | short | short |
| Papillaris subart. | well developed | small | slightly larger | small | absent |
| Typical no. of anterior papillae | 1 | 3 | 3 | 3 | 3 |
| Typical no. of posterior papillae | 3 | 0? | 1 | 1 | 1 |
| Transverse trabeculae | moderately stout | slender | absent | slender | heavy |
| Trabecular carneae | well developed | poorly developed | well developed | poorly developed | well developed |
| Free trabeculae on external wall | none | feeble | very feeble | yes | yes |
| Left ventricle | | | | | |
| Apical cones on anterior papillae | no | no | no | yes | yes |
| Trabecular strand on septum | no | yes | no | yes | yes |

* Data largely from Ackerknecht (1919).

The **trabeculae carneae** form a pattern of prominent longitudinal ridges covering all the inner surface of the ventricle except the conus. They tend to converge toward the apex. The ridges vary in width; the broadest are about 5 mm. wide. Adjacent ridges are interconnected in many places by short threadlike strands more or less horizontal in direction.

The **bicuspid valve** is much shorter than the tricuspid, measuring about 20 mm. in length. The cusps are heavier than those of the tricuspid, and the two primary cusps are divided by deep incisions into five accessory cusps.

The aortic ostium is situated in the usual place between the septal valve and the septum, at the base of a funnel-shaped conus arteriosus. The semilunar valves guarding the ostium are typical. There is a nodulus of Aranti in the middle of the free margin of each valve.

## C. DISCUSSION OF HEART

The comparative anatomy of the heart in the Carnivora has been studied by Ackerknecht (1919) and Simič (1938). Ackerknecht's description of the papillary muscles and their adnexa was based on 30 hearts of the domestic dog, one heart of a European fox, and 15 hearts of the domestic cat. He was interested primarily in the range of variation. Simič compared the general structure of the heart in Canis lupus, Vulpes vulpes, Lycaon pictus, Procyon lotor, Meles meles, Zorilla striata, Felis leo, Felis tigris, Felis pardus, and Crocuta crocuta. She listed several characteristic differences between the Arctoidea and Aeluroidea, but did not attempt to characterize heart structure at the family level. It is extraordinary that no one has described the heart of any species of bear.

I have supplemented the data in the literature with dissections of the following hearts:

| | Height in mm. (base—apex) | Weight in gms. |
|---|---|---|
| Bassariscus astutus (♂ ad.) | 26 | 7 |
| Procyon lotor (♂ ad.) | 33 | 19 |
| Procyon lotor (unsexed ad.) | 44 | 42 |
| Helarctos malayanus (♂ ad.) | 94 | 345 |
| Helarctos malayanus (♀ ad.) | 98 | 362 |
| Tremarctos ornatus (♂ ad.) | 113 | 397 |
| Ursus americanus (♂ juv.) | 43 | 35 |
| Ursus americanus (♂ ad.) | 127 | 833 |
| Canis lupus (♂ ad.) | 91 | 265 |
| Felis uncia (♂) | 68 | 132 |

Even from this limited material it is evident that there are characteristic differences among the arctoid carnivores. Some of these are listed in the accompanying table (Table 23). Most relate to the right ventricle; Ackerknecht found that individual variation is also greatest in this ventricle, which is phylogenetically the most recent part of the mammalian heart.

At present there is no sure way of deciding what is primitive and what is specialized in the heart architecture of placental mammals, or indeed whether such terms can be used in comparing heart structure within the Carnivora.[1] I shall therefore avoid such terms here. Whether there is any significant relationship between structural differences and performance of the heart is likewise unknown.

The heart of the Canidae differs from the heart of other arctoid carnivores in practically every feature examined. Some of these differences appear to be fundamental.

[1] Ackerknecht "gained the general impression" that the heart is more primitive in Felis than in Canis, but he does not give the basis for this opinion.

There are consistent differences in heart form among the several families. These reflect the degree of acuteness of the apex, and therefore do not show up in ratios based on measurements of length and diameter of the organ. The globular form of the heart in the Canidae is unlike that of any other known carnivore. The subglobular form in the Procyonidae resembles that of the cats. The position of the incisura cordis seems to be related to the relative sizes of the two ventricles: where it is high the relative height of the right ventricle is less, and vice versa. The incisura is very high in the Canidae. It is near the apex in the Procyonidae, actually almost at the apex in *Bassariscus*. Its position varies among ursid genera; in none is it as high as in canids or as low as in procyonids. In *Ailuropoda* it is as high as in any ursid examined. It appears to be very high in felids.

The conus arteriosus tends to be short in bears, although there is considerable variation among genera. It is longest in *Helarctos*. The conus is longer in *Canis* than in the Ursidae; it is very short in the Procyonidae.

The papillary muscles of the right ventricle are situated on the septum in all arctoid carnivores, whereas in the Aeluroidea the anterior papilla arises from the external wall. The subarterial papilla varies in size and position. In the Canidae and Procyonidae it is well developed (although not as large as in the cats) and situated directly below the supraventricular crest. In the Ursidae and *Ailuropoda* it is small and situated in the conus region. Among the arctoids examined there is a reciprocal relationship between the anterior and posterior papillae: in the Canidae the anterior papilla is typically single and shows little variation in number whereas the posterior is multiple and extremely variable (modal number 3). In the Procyonidae and Ursidae, on the contrary, the anterior papilla is multiple and variable (especially in the Ursidae), and the posterior single and only slightly variable. Among the five bears examined, the number of anterior papillae varied between 2-4 (modal number 3). The number of direct chordae tendineae is also very high in bears (8-15). These conditions suggest that the region of the right ventricle nearest the niche is broadened and least stable in canids, whereas in procyonids and ursids the region toward the conus is broadened and least stable. The anterior and posterior papillae are situated much higher (near the center of the septal wall) in the Procyonidae, Ursidae, and *Ailuropoda* than in the Canidae.

Trabeculae carneae were poorly developed in the right ventricle of all bear hearts examined, whereas they were at least moderately prominent in all pro-

cyonids and are described by Ackerknecht as variable but typically well developed in *Canis*. Typically absent in the Canidae but very characteristic of the Procyonidae, Ursidae, and *Ailuropoda* is a system of free trabecular strands on the external wall. These are restricted to a narrow zone more or less paralleling the transverse axis of the ventricle. Where best developed (*Helarctos*) the strands may form a loose meshwork. The transverse trabeculae of the anterior papillary muscle group insert into this system.

There is much less variation in the left ventricle than in the right. There were two massive papillae, arising from the external wall, in all specimens examined. The posterior papilla is typically slightly the larger. In the Ursidae and *Ailuropoda* one or more small conical structures, from the tips of which groups of chordae arise, sit atop the papillae. These accessory structures are absent in *Canis* and the Procyonidae. A transverse trabecula, at its origin looking like a chorda tendinea, arises from the septal side of the tip of each papilla and runs up to insert near the base of the ventricle in all hearts examined. In *Bassariscus*, the Ursidae, and *Ailuropoda* a free trabecular strand extends more or less horizontally over the septal wall. This strand was usually, but not always, connected with the transverse trabeculae. It was absent in the Canidae and in *Procyon*.

### D. CONCLUSIONS

1. Most differences in heart structure among arctoid carnivores involve the right ventricle. The most characteristic feature of this ventricle is the increased number of cardinal papillary muscles.

2. The structure of the heart in the Canidae differs in several respects from that of the Procyonidae and Ursidae.

(a) The canid heart has a characteristic form.

(b) In the right ventricle the region nearest the conus is stable and the niche region is broadened and variable, whereas in the Procyonidae and Ursidae the reverse is true.

(c) In the right ventricle the cardinal papillae are situated much nearer the basal groove than in the Procyonidae and Ursidae.

3. The structure of the heart in the Ursidae resembles that of the Procyonidae, but differs in several respects.

(a) The ursid heart has a characteristic form.

(b) In the right ventricle the subarterial papilla is situated in the conus region.

(c) In the right ventricle there is a well-developed system of free trabeculae carneae on the external wall.

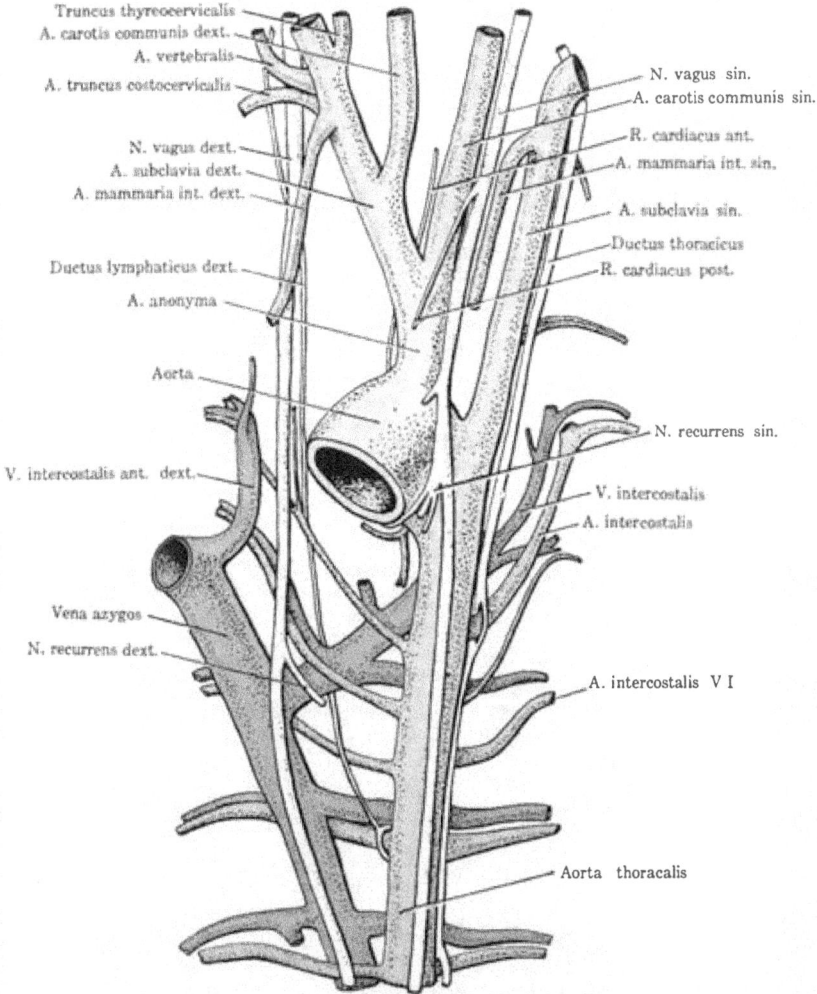

Truncus thyreocervicalis
A. carotis communis dext.
A. vertebralis
A. truncus costocervicalis

N. vagus dext.
A. subclavia dext.
A. mammaria int. dext.

Ductus lymphaticus dext.

A. anonyma

Aorta

V. intercostalis ant. dext.

Vena azygos

N. recurrens dext.

N. vagus sin.
A. carotis communis sin.

R. cardiacus ant.
A. mammaria int. sin.

A. subclavia sin.

Ductus thoracicus
R. cardiacus post.

N. recurrens sin.

V. intercostalis
A. intercostalis

A. intercostalis V I

Aorta thoracalis

Fig. 130. Great vessels of the thorax of *Ailuropoda*.

(d) In the left ventricle the anterior papilla is furnished; with apical cones.

4. The heart of *Ailuropoda* resembles that of the Ursidae in all essential respects.

5. The basis for these differences in heart architecture is unknown.

## II. ARTERIES

### AORTA

The aorta is 45 cm. in length, from the origin of the subclavian artery to the bifurcation that forms the common iliacs. Its diameter at the top of the arch is 26 mm., at the middle of the thorax about 13 mm., and midway between the diaphragm and the terminal bifurcation (below the origin of the renal arteries) about 9 mm. The aorta arises from the left ventricle at the level of the fourth thoracic vertebra, and extends upward and to the left to form the aortic arch. The aorta then runs posteriorly below the vertebral column, lying just to the left of the midline until it emerges from between the crura of the diaphragm, where it moves over to the midline. The vessel terminates at the level of the last lumbar vertebra by breaking up to form the external iliac, hypogastric, and middle sacral arteries.

The arch of the aorta gives rise to two branches in typical carnivore fashion: the innominate and the much smaller left subclavian. These leave the top of the arch in close proximity to one another; they are separated by an interval of less than 5 mm. The smaller visceral branches of the thoracic aorta were not traced. In the abdomen (fig. 135) the celiac artery arises at the level of the fourteenth thoracic vertebra, followed a few millimeters farther posteriorly by the anterior mesenteric. The renal arteries arise at the level of the first lumbar, and the posterior mesenteric at the level of the third lumbar.

INNOMINATE AND COMMON CAROTID ARTERIES

A. anonyma (fig. 130) arises at the level of the fourth rib, and has a length of 30 mm. before the left common carotid is given off. The carotids arise from the innominate independently, the right coming off 20 mm. farther anterior than the left. This is contrary to what Raven (1936) found, and places *Ailuropoda* in Parson's (1902) class A instead of class B.

Each A. carotis communis (figs. 130, 131) passes forward alongside the trachea to the level of the anterior border of the thyroid cartilage. A. thyreoidea ima arises from the common carotid just anterior to the manubrium sterni and passes anteriorly on the ventral surface of the trachea. It supplies the posterior part of the thyroid gland and gives off small branches to the trachea. A. thyreoidea anterior (fig. 131) arises at the level of the third tracheal ring. On the right side of the neck the anterior thyroid arises as a large, very short trunk that promptly breaks up into a number of branches. These supply the anterior end of the thyroid gland, the trachea, the esophagus, and the laryngeal and hyoid musculature. On the left side the anterior thyroid proper supplies only the thyroid gland and the intrinsic laryngeal musculature. A separate branch arising independently from the carotid 20 mm. farther anterior supplies the rest of the laryngeal and hyoid muscles, the trachea, and the esophagus. At the anterior border of the larynx the common carotid divides into the external and internal carotids. As in other carnivores the internal carotid is smaller than the external, but in the panda the internal carotid is relatively large, more than half the diameter of the external carotid, as in bears.

EXTERNAL CAROTID ARTERY

A. carotis externa (fig. 132) curves laterad around the medial and anterior borders of the di-

gastric muscle. The external maxillary is given off at the posterior wall of the mandibular fossa, and beyond this the trunk is continued as the internal maxillary. The internal maxillary immediately curves mesad, so that the entire external carotid trunk describes a pronounced S-curve in the basicranial region. The external carotid gives rise to the following branches:

1. A good-sized branch arises from the lateral wall at the bifurcation into external and internal carotids. It breaks up at once into twigs for the large cervical lymph gland and twigs that supply the anterior end of the sternomastoid muscle and the posterior end of the digastric.

A. pharyngea ascendens[1] (fig. 131) arises as one of the branches of this trunk. It runs anteriorly and mesad to the anterior pharyngeal constrictor muscle, then anteriorly along this muscle. At the posterior border of the levator veli palatini muscle the trunk bifurcates into palatine and pharyngeal branches of subequal caliber. R. palatinus supplies the anterior pharyngeal and palatine musculature, ramifies in the glands of the soft palate, and anastomoses with a descending twig from the internal maxillary and with the ascending and descending palatine arteries. A fine muscle twig, R. m. tensoris tympani, arising from the palatine branch, passes into the middle ear beside the tendon of the tensor veli palatini, which it supplies, and runs to the tensor tympani muscle, where it anastomoses with the other tympanic arteries.

R. pharyngeus runs anteriorly beneath the rectus capitis ventralis, continuing in the medial wall of the eustachian tube to its anterior border, where it divides into a branch to the pharyngeal tonsil and another to the dorsal wall of the nasopharynx. The pharyngeal ramus supplies several minute Rr. eustachii that ramify in the tubal mucosa. A. pharyngeotympanica is given off at the level of the foramen lacerum medium and lies against the eustachian tube in the musculotubarian canal, on its way to the middle ear. Near the tympanic orifice of the eustachian tube the pharyngeotympanic sends a fine anastomotic twig that pierces the wall of the foramen lacerum medium to reach the internal carotid artery. The pharyngeotympanic artery terminates in the tympanic arterial plexus.

2. A branch arises from the bifurcation of the carotids and immediately divides into lateral and medial twigs. The lateral twig accompanies the external branch of the spinal accessory nerve to

[1] This vessel is only partly homologous with the ascending pharyngeal of human anatomy. The posterior meningeal artery comes from the internal carotid in the panda; the inferior tympanic arises from the external carotid.

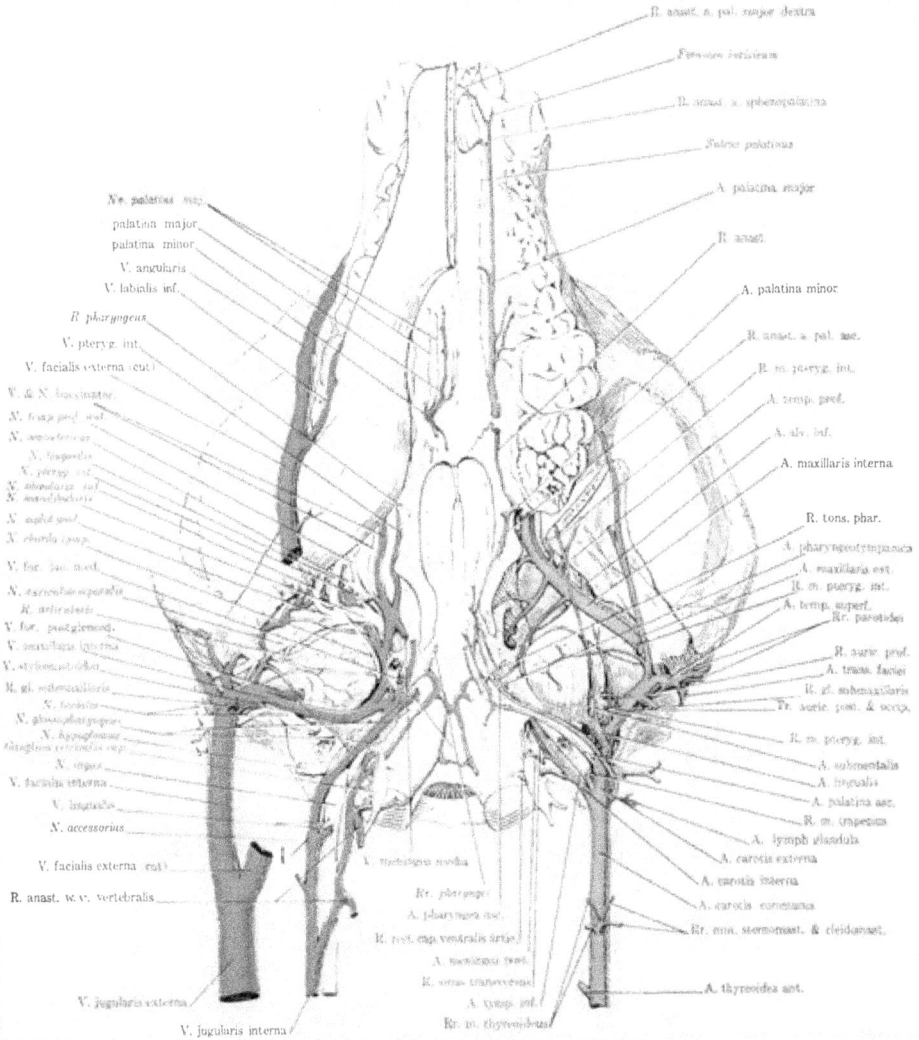

FIG. 131.  Vessels and nerves of the head of *Ailuropoda*, inferior view.

the trapezius.  The medial branch, A. tympanica inferior, runs to the lateral border of the foramen lacerum posterior and accompanies the tympanic branch of the glossopharyngeal nerve in the middle ear.  The inferior tympanic terminates by anastomosing with the other tympanic arteries on the promontorium.

3.  A. palatina ascendens (fig. 131) is a slender vessel arising from the medial wall and running anteriorly and mesad to the pharynx and posterior part of the palate.  It ramifies in the palatine glands and anastomoses with twigs from the ascending pharyngeal and posterior palatine arteries.

4.  A. lingualis (fig. 131) is the largest branch of the external carotid.  It arises from the ventral wall at the level of the hyoid bone, and accompanies the hypoglossal nerve anteriorly and mesad, deep to the mylohyoid muscle, to the lateral border of the hyoglossal muscle.  Here the artery

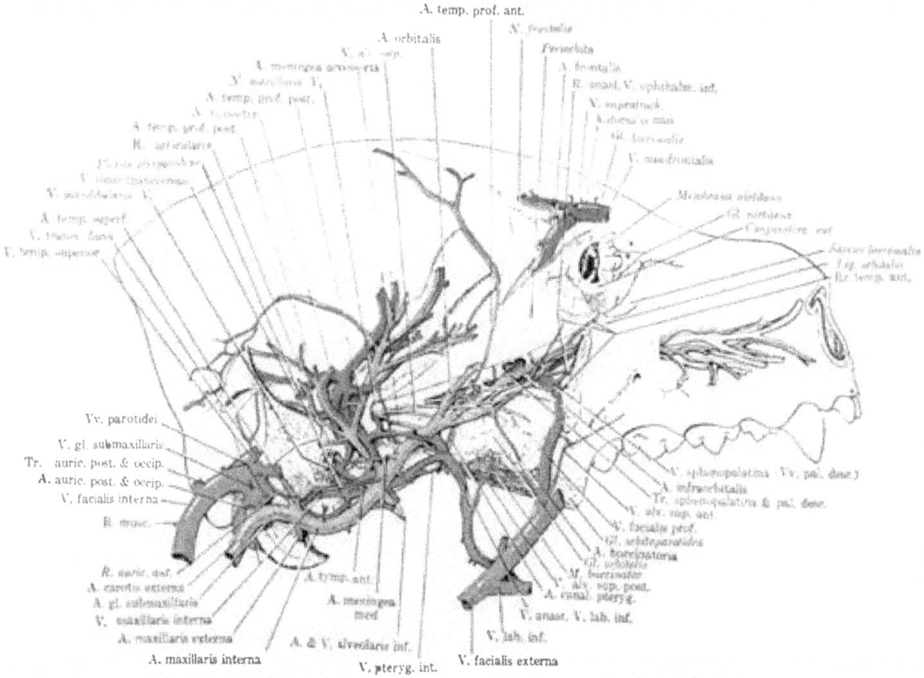

FIG. 132. Deep vessels and nerves of the head of *Ailuropoda*, side view.

gives rise to a good-sized **R. symphyseus**, which accompanies the hypoglossal nerve along the medial border of the styloglossal muscle, then along the lateral border of the genioglossus, to the symphyseal foramen. Numerous twigs from this branch supply the sublingual muscles and the floor of the mouth anterior to the tongue. The main trunk of the lingual runs beneath the lateral border of the hyoglossus, into the body of the tongue, where it ramifies.

Just before passing beneath the mylohyoid, the lingual gives rise to the small **A. submentalis**, which runs forward on the mylohyoideus at its juncture with the digastric.

5. A slender branch arising from the ventral wall just anterior to the lingual runs forward to the pterygoid muscles, which it supplies.

6. **A. auricularis posterior + A. occipitalis** (fig. 132) arise by a common trunk at the anterior border of the mastoid process. The trunk runs laterad beneath the digastric and parotid gland to the posterior border of the base of the pinna. Here the **A. sternocleidomastoidea** is given off to the sternomastoid and cleidomastoid muscles.

**A. stylomastoidea** arises from the posterior side of the auriculo-occipital trunk at its base. It runs mesad over the digastric, dividing into a muscular twig to the digastric and the stylomastoid artery proper. The latter runs beside the facial nerve to the stylomastoid foramen. **A. tympanica posterior** is given off in the facial canal, and accompanies the chorda tympani nerve into the middle ear, where it sends a twig to the malleus and anastomoses with the other tympanic arteries.

**A. occipitalis**, which is considerably smaller than the posterior auricular, appears to arise as a branch of the latter at the boundary between the sternomastoid and cleidomastoid muscles. The occipital gves rise to the following branches: **Rr. musculares**, arising near the base of the artery, supply the adjacent muscles and the atlanto-occipital capsule, and send fine nutrient branches into the back of the skull. **R. occipitalis**, the terminal part of the artery, runs dorsad beneath the splenius. At the ventral border of the rectus capitis posterior major it divides into a superficial and a deep branch. These ramify to the musculature in the occipital region and to the nutrient foramina in the back of the skull, none of the twigs extending beyond the lambdoidal crest. The deep branch also supplies the atlanto-occipital capsule. A slender cutaneous branch runs through to the skin at the back of the head.

A. auricularis is the continuation of the auricular-occipital trunk after the occipital is given off. It divides immediately into muscular and auricular branches. The muscular branch ramifies in the posterior part of the temporal muscle, also giving off a twig that supplies the cartilage of the pinna. A branch, R. mastoideus, arises from the base of the muscular branch and passes to the mastoid foramen, which it enters. The auricular branch then divides into anterior and posterior branches. A. auricularis posterior is distributed over the posterior surface of the pinna and to the musculature of the ear. A. auricularis anterior (fig. 107) passes around the medial side of the pinna to supply structures on its anterior side; a large cutaneous twig from this branch runs across the top of the head toward the midline.

7. A. glandularis is a good-sized vessel arising from the lateral wall of the external carotid opposite and slightly anterior to the preceding trunk. It passes into the submaxillary gland, where it ramifies.

8. A. temporalis superficialis (fig. 132) arises, as a single vessel on the left side of the head and as two independent but closely associated vessels on the right, just behind the angular process of the mandible. Aside from the several small parotid twigs and the small anterior auricular branch, which come off near its base, the superficial temporal may be said to divide, after a short trunk, into two subequal systems: a transverse facial system that ramifies below the zygoma, and a temporal system that ramifies above it.

The superficial temporal gives rise to the following branches: (a) R. auricularis profundus is the first branch given off. It is a small twig that runs to the base of the pinna. (b) Rr. parotidei are small twigs that arise near the base of the artery and pass into the parotid gland. (c) A. transversa facei breaks up into two large branches that ramify over and into the masseter muscle, and a slender transverse facial branch. The transverse facial branch is an extremely delicate twig running across the masseter a short distance below the zygoma; it accompanies the infraorbital branches of the facial nerve, and lies above the parotid duct. Twigs are given off to the masseter, the zygomatic rete, and cutaneous structures over the masseter; the vessel terminates by anastomosing with the superior labial artery. (d) A. zygomaticoorbitalis (fig. 107) arises from the temporal branch of the superficial temporal. It runs across the posterior

end of the zygoma and the lower part of the temporal muscle to the orbit, where it anastomoses with the frontal, supraorbital, and lacrimal arteries. (e) A. temporalis media is the main continuation of the temporal trunk after the zygomatico-orbital branch is given off. It runs up vertically across the posterior part of the zygoma, dividing into anterior and posterior branches as it passes over the upper edge of the zygoma. Both of these branches ramify through the substance of the temporal muscle. (f) R. temporalis superficialis (fig. 107) is a slender twig arising from the zygomatico-orbital artery midway between the eye and the ear. It passes up onto the top of the head just superficial to the temporal aponeurosis, where it ramifies into an extremely delicate rete in the parietal and posterior frontal regions.

At the angular process of the mandible the external carotid gives off the very small external maxillary, beyond which the trunk continues on the medial side of the mandible as the internal maxillary.

A. maxillaris externa (fig. 107), which has none of the cervical branches that arise from it in man, is a slender vessel running across the ventral part of the masseter. Beyond the edge of the digastric it is accompanied by the anterior facial vein. Numerous fine twigs are given off to the masseter, and at the posterior end of the exposed part of the inferior alveobuccal (molar) gland the vessel divides into the superior and inferior labial arteries. A. labialis inferior (fig. 107) runs anteriorly along the inferior border of the molar gland, to which it gives off twigs, anastomosing anteriorly with the mental branch of the inferior alveolar artery. A. labialis superior (fig. 107) is larger than the inferior labial. It passes anteriorly along the superior border of the molar gland, into which it sends twigs, and along the base of the upper lip. Anteriorly it anastomoses with branches of the infraorbital artery. A. angularis is a slender branch arising from the superior labial directly below the eye, and passing up across the anterior root of the zygoma into the orbit.

### The Internal Maxillary Artery

A. maxillaris interna (figs. 131, 132) is so much larger than the external maxillary artery that it appears to be the continuation of the external carotid trunk, with the external maxillary only one of the lesser lateral branches. It arises at the posterior border of the mandible, just above the angular process, and arches forward and upward around the condyle, lying between the external and internal pterygoid muscles. The vessel continues into the space between the coronoid process and the

skull, terminating near the sphenopalatine foramen by dividing into the infraorbital artery and a
trunk for the sphenopalatine and descending palatine arteries. There is no alisphenoid canal.

The internal maxillary gives rise to the following
branches (fig. 132):

1. **A. alveolaris inferior** arises at the inferior
border of the temporal muscle and passes forward
and slightly downward to the mandibular foramen.
The artery lies below the inferior alveolar nerve
as they enter the foramen. The mental branches
emerge from the mandible through the mental foramina, accompanying the corresponding branches
of the nerve.

2. **A. temporalis profunda posterior** comes
off at the neck of the mandible, passing to the temporal fossa between the internal and external pterygoid muscles. Here it divides into posterior and
anterior branches.

The posterior branch gives off a slender **R. articularis** near its base, which passes to the mandibular articulation. Posterior deep temporal vessels
pass back over the root of the zygoma, one of them
entering a nutrient foramen in the temporal bone
at the root of the zygoma, while another anastomoses with a twig of the occipital artery near the
lambdoidal crest. A. masseterica, arising as one
of the branches of the posterior branch, arches
around behind the coronoid process, to enter the
masseter muscle, where it ramifies.

The anterior branch of the posterior deep temporal ramifies in the anterior part of the temporal
fossa, beneath the temporal muscle.

3. **A. tympanica anterior** is a slender vessel
arising at the same level as the deep temporal. It
passes caudad across the external pterygoid muscle, joining the chorda tympani nerve and passing
with it into the petrotympanic fissure. A twig,
given off from the anterior tympanic before it
reaches the fissure, anastomoses with the ascending pharyngeal artery.

4. **A. meningea media** is a small twig, considerably smaller than the accessory meningeal,
arising from the internal maxillary just beyond
the temporalis profunda posterior. In the panda
it is not the main source of the meningeal circulation. It joins the trunk of the mandibular nerve
and passes beside it into the foramen ovale. Within the cranial cavity the vessel anastomoses with
the accessory meningeal.

5. **Rr. pterygoidei**, arising from the internal
maxillary along its course, supply the external and
internal pterygoid muscles. A twig associated
with these goes to the orbital gland.

6. **A. meningea accessoria** is a slender vessel
that enters the orbital fissure, where it lies beside
the maxillary nerve. Within the cranial cavity it
receives the middle meningeal artery, then runs
posteriorly beside the semilunar ganglion to the tip
of the temporal lobe of the brain, where it
breaks up into three branches. These form the
main blood supply to the dura (fig. 143); this was
verified on two specimens. The first branch is distributed over the frontal lobe; the second passes
up in the lateral cerebral fissure, and is distributed
to the adjacent parts of the frontal and temporal
lobes and to the parietal lobe; the third supplies
the dura over the ventral and posterior parts of the
temporal lobe.

7. **A. orbitalis** (ophthalmica of authors) is a
good-sized vessel, only a little smaller than the
deep temporal, arising from the internal maxillary
at the anterior end of the internal pterygoid muscle, about 10 mm. beyond the origin of the posterior deep temporal artery. It passes forward and
upward, lying external to the maxillary nerve, to
pierce the ventral wall of the periorbita at about
its posterior third.

Before entering the orbit, the orbital artery gives
rise to an anterior deep temporal branch, which
passes across the periorbita to the anterior part of
the temporal fossa, where it ramifies. The terminal twigs of this vessel pass out of the temporal
fossa onto the frontal area of the head.

As it pierces the periorbita, the orbital artery
gives rise to a posterior and an anterior branch of
approximately equal size, which arise from opposite sides of the parent trunk. The posterior branch
turns posteriorly, passing beneath the ophthalmic
nerve and through the wall of the superior ophthalmic vein. It passes inside the vein through
the orbital fissure into the cranial cavity. The
anterior branch, A. lacrimalis, accompanies the
lacrimal nerve forward along the lateral rectus
muscle of the eye. At about the middle of the muscle the artery bifurcates into a muscular and a lacrimal ramus. The muscular ramus supplies the
lateral and inferior recti and the inferior oblique,
and supplies an anastomotic twig to one of the
ciliary arteries, while the lacrimal ramus continues
forward to the lacrimal gland.

Immediately after entering the orbit the orbital
artery divides into two equal-sized trunks. The
more superficial trunk, which lies external to the
ocular muscles, supplies structures outside the orbit, terminating as the ethmoidal artery. The
deeper trunk arches around the optic nerve, supplying all the structures within the orbit and anastomosing with the ophthalmic artery.

A. zygomatica arises from the superficial trunk
of the orbital artery as the latter crosses beneath
the ophthalmic nerve. Accompanying the paired
zygomatic nerve along the lateral border of M. rectus superior, it pierces the orbital ligament and
emerges near the posterior corner of the eye. The
terminal twigs of the vessel ramify in the superficial area immediately behind the eye.

After giving off the zygomatic branch, the superficial trunk passes across the proximal parts of the
ocular muscles to the ethmoidal foramen. Just
before entering the foramen it gives rise to A.
frontalis, which pierces the dorsal wall of the
periorbita along with the frontal nerve and the
superior ophthalmic vein (fig. 107); all three structures emerge above the eye, where the artery gives
off a small anterior A. dorsalis nasi, then arches
posteriorly to anastomose with a twig of the zygomatico-orbital artery. Beyond the origin of the
frontal artery the main trunk is continued into the
ethmoidal foramen as R. ethmoidalis, which
unites with the ethmoidal artery below the olfactory bulbs (p. 253).

The deeper trunk of the orbital artery passes
between M. rectus superior and M. retractor oculi,
arches around to the deep side of the optic nerve,
and anastomoses with the ophthalmic artery to
form the minute central retinal artery. A. centralis retinae enters the optic nerve 4 mm. behind
the eyeball, and passes to the eye within the nerve.
Numerous muscular twigs arising from the deeper
trunk of the orbital artery supply M. rectus superior, M. levator palpebrae superior, M. retractor
oculi, M. rectus medialis, and M. rectus inferior.
Two of these twigs terminate by anastomosing
with the muscular ramus of the lacrimal artery.
Aa. ciliares arise from one or more of the muscular twigs and pass forward alongside the optic nerve
to the eye.

8. A. temporalis profunda anterior (fig. 132)
arises from the internal maxillary directly opposite
the origin of the orbital artery. It ramifies in the
most anterior part of the temporal muscle, one or
more of its delicate terminal branches emerging on
the face below the eye and ramifying over the anterior part of the zygoma. A. buccinatoria arises
from the trunk of the anterior deep temporal. It
joins the buccinator nerve and passes with it to the
buccinator muscle.

Beyond the point where the orbital and anterior deep temporal arteries arise, the internal maxillary corresponds to the "third part of the internal
maxillary" of human anatomy. The vessel passes
upward and forward toward the sphenopalatine
foramen, giving rise to the following branches:

9. A. palatina minor (fig. 131) arises at the
posterior border of the alveolar prominence of
the last molar tooth. It immediately arches mesad and ventrad, accompanying the posterior palatine nerve along the anterior border of the internal
pterygoid muscle down to the prominent notch in
the outer border of the vertical pterygoid plate
immediately behind the last molar. After leaving
the notch the vessel bifurcates; an anterior branch
runs forward along the medial border of the last
molar tooth, to anastomose with the major palatine artery; and a posterior branch runs caudad
along the soft palate to anastomose with the major
palatine. Twigs from the posterior branch ramify
to the palatine glands and other structures in the
roof of the pharynx, and a twig from the anastomosis with the major palatine goes to the auditory
tube.

10. A. infraorbitalis (fig. 132), the more lateral of the two terminal branches of the internal
maxillary, accompanies the infraorbital nerve to
the infraorbital foramen. On emerging from the
foramen it ramifies over the lateral side of the nose
(fig. 107). Alveolar branches (Aa. alveolares superiores) from this part of the vessel supply the
premolars, canine, and incisors. A. alveolaris
superior posterior arises from the base of the
infraorbital and pursues a tortuous course back
over the alveolar prominence of the last molar,
giving off numerous twigs that enter the minute
foramina in this region. A. alveolaris superior
media arises a few millimeters farther forward.
It runs forward, ramifying twigs to the area over
the anterior part of the last molar and the next
tooth forward (M$^1$). A. malaris (Bradley) arises
from the infraorbital just before the latter enters
the foramen. It runs out at the anteroventral
corner of the orbit, lying between the periorbita
and the preorbital fat. Branches supply the lower
eyelid and the lacrimal sac, after which the trunk
continues onto the face in front of the eye.

The medial terminal branch of the internal maxillary is a short trunk that divides just before
reaching the closely juxtaposed sphenopalatine foramen and pterygopalatine canal to form the sphenopalatine and descending palatine arteries. A.
sphenopalatina passes into the nose through the
sphenopalatine foramen A. palatina descendens reaches the posterior part of the hard palate
through the pterygopalatine canal. Upon emerging onto the palate through the posterior palatine
foramen, the vessel divides into anterior palatine
and posterior anastomotic branches. A. palatina
anterior (palatina major) considerably exceeds the
posterior anastomotic in caliber. It runs forward

in the mucoperiosteum of the hard palate to the incisive foramen, where it anastomoses with the sphenopalatine artery. The groove for this artery can be seen on the skull, running forward not far from the alveolar border. The posterior, anastomotic branch passes backward along the border of the last molar tooth, to anastomose with the minor palatine artery at the notch in the outer border of the pterygoid plate.

### Internal Carotid Artery

The internal carotid runs forward and mesad from the bifurcation of the common carotid, arching dorsad around the medial border of the origin of the digastric muscle, to enter the foramen lacerum posterior. At the level of the paroccipital process it gives off the posterior meningeal artery. A. meningea posterior sends a minute R. sinus transversus into the foramen lacerum posterior, supplies a twig to the adjacent cranial nerves, and then enters the hypoglossal canal. Within the skull the posterior meningeal ramifies to the dura of the posterior cranial fossa, and anastomoses with the basilar artery.

As it enters the foramen lacerum posterior, the internal carotid is situated anterior to the cranial nerves passing out of the foramen, and laterad of the internal carotid (sympathetic) nerves. Just inside the foramen the artery enters the carotid canal, within which it passes through the middle ear. In the middle ear the carotid canal runs forward and slightly mesad, and is situated below and at first in contact with the petrosal, lying ventrad and slightly mesad of the cochlea (fig. 159). A fine anastomotic twig from the ascending pharyngeal artery joins the internal carotid at the juncture of the foramen lacerum medium with the anteromedial part of the carotid canal. The internal carotid gives off nutrient twigs to the walls of its canal. Emerging from the carotid canal, the artery enters the cavernous sinus. Immediately after entering the sinus it forms a tight knot by arching first posteriorly, then anteriorly upon itself. This is followed in the vicinity of the sella turcica by a tight S-loop, all of which greatly increases the length of the vessel; while the distance traversed within the sinus (from the carotid foramen to the anterior border of the sella) is only 22 mm., the length of the vessel is 68 mm.[1] The internal carotid emerges from the sinus in the vicinity of the tuberculum sellae, and terminates several millimeters anterior to the optic chiasma by dividing into the anterior and middle cerebral arteries.

The internal carotid gives rise to the following branches:

1. A. communicans posterior arises from the internal carotid as soon as it emerges from the sinus. It is a good-sized vessel, exceeding the posterior cerebral in caliber, that runs backward across the base of the brain to join the posterior cerebral. Near its origin, the posterior communicating artery gives rise to the A. chorioidea, which is joined by a twig from the internal carotid before ramifying to the choroid plexus. Farther posteriorly it gives off a good-sized hippocampal twig to the hippocampal gyrus.

2. R. chorioidea, which joins the choroid artery as described above, arises about midway between the origin of the communicans posterior and the terminal bifurcation of the internal carotid.

3. A. ophthalmica is present on the right side only; the origin of the corresponding blood supply on the left side was not traced. The vessel arises from the internal carotid just before its terminal bifurcation, and enters the orbit through the optic foramen. During its course it makes a spiral revolution of 180° around the optic nerve. Situated at first laterad of the nerve, it enters the optic foramen lying dorsad of it, finally emerging from the foramen into the orbit on the medial side of the nerve. In the orbit the vessel terminates by anastomosing with the deep trunk of the orbital artery to form the central retinal artery.[2]

4. A. cerebri media, the larger of the two terminal branches of the internal carotid, arches laterad around the temporal pole into the lateral fissure where it ramifies to the outer surfaces of the frontal, parietal, and occipital lobes. Near its origin the middle cerebral divides into a pair of parallel vessels (these arise separately on the left side), which reunite into a common trunk as they enter the lateral fissure.

5. A. cerebri anterior, the smaller of the terminal vessels, runs toward the midline above the optic nerve. At the midline it unites with its mate from the opposite side to form a common trunk (there is consequently no A. communicans anterior), which immediately arches dorsad into the longitudinal fissure. At the juncture of the two anterior cerebral arteries the large median ethmoidal artery, which equals the common anterior cerebral trunk in caliber, is also given off.

6. A. ethmoidalis interna appears to be somewhat anomalous. The ethmoidal circulation arises from the anterior cerebrals in the form of three vessels: a very large median artery flanked on

---

[1] Tandler (1899) gives the corresponding length of this vessel in a polar bear as 160 mm. (see also p. 257).

[2] Most of the ophthalmic circulation of man has been taken over by the orbital artery in the panda and related animals.

either side by a much smaller artery. The median artery is tied in with the orbital circulation via the ethmoidal foramen, while the lateral arteries run directly to the cribriform plate.

The median ethmoidal artery runs forward in the dura immediately below the longitudinal fissure. Just proximad of the olfactory bulbs it is joined by a large branch that represents the combined ethmoidal rami of the two orbital circulations. The vessel then continues forward, breaking up below and between the olfactory bulbs into numerous terminal branches that pass into the cribriform plate. **A. meningea anterior** arises as a fine twig from the orbital division of the ethmoidal, and ramifies to the dura of the anterior fossa.

The lateral ethmoidal arteries arch toward the midline at the posterior border of the olfactory bulbs, continuing between the bulbs into the cribriform plate.

## THE SUBCLAVIAN ARTERY

The left subclavian arises from the convex side of the arch of the aorta, immediately beyond the origin of the innominate; the bases of these two arteries are almost in contact. The right subclavian begins much farther craniad, as the continuation of the innominate after the right common carotid is given off. Both subclavians have the same relations beyond the origin of the right subclavian (about from the posterior border of the first rib). Beyond the origin of the thyrocervical axis the subclavian is continued as the axillary artery. The subclavian gives off the following branches: (1) the vertebral; (2) the internal mammary; (3) the thyrocervical trunk; and (4) the costocervical trunk.

1. **A. vertebralis** (fig. 130) arises from the dorsal side of the subclavian just anterior to the costocervical trunk, to which it corresponds in size. It passes forward and upward around the M. longus colli, to enter the transverse foramen of the sixth cervical vertebra. Passing craniad through the transverse foramina of succeeding cervical vertebrae from the sixth to the first, it reaches the alar foramen in the atlas greatly reduced in caliber because of the large muscle branches to which it has given rise. Turning mesad through the atlantal foramen, the vessel reaches the spinal canal of the atlas, where it turns forward again and passes into the skull through the foramen magnum, lying immediately above the atlanto-occipital articulation. Within the skull the artery lies at first beside the medulla, then, between the origins of the first spinal and twelfth cranial nerves, it turns toward the midline, terminating on the pyramid about 15 mm. caudad of the pons by uniting with the vertebral

artery of the opposite side to form the unpaired **A. basilaris.** On the left side the basilar also receives an anastomotic twig from the internal carotid; this twig arose outside the skull, entering the cranial cavity through the condylar foramen. The basilar artery runs forward in the ventral median fissure and across the ventral surface of the pons to the anterior border of the pons, where it terminates by dividing into the two superior cerebellar arteries (not into the posterior cerebrals, as it does in man). For a short distance beyond its origin the basilar is composed of two trunks lying side by side, but these soon fuse; this condition is probably an individual anomaly.

The vertebral artery gives rise to the following branches:

(a) **Rr. musculares** arise at the intervertebral spaces, one to each space. These are very large vessels that pass upward between adjacent transverse processes to ramify in the dorsal axial musculature. Near its base each vessel gives off a slender twig **(R. spinalis)** that passes through the intervertebral foramen into the spinal canal.

(b) **A. spinalis posterior**[1] is a threadlike vessel that winds caudad along the side of the medulla to the dorsum of the cord. The paired vessel may be seen lying in the dorsal lateral sulci of the cord in a section through the neck made at the fourth cervical vertebra.

(c) **A. spinalis anterior** is unpaired in the animal dissected, and considerably exceeds the posterior spinal in caliber. It arises from the left vertebral artery at the midline, and runs caudad on the ventral surface of the medulla and cord.

The branches from the basilar artery are:

(d) **A. cerebelli inferior posterior** arises from the basilar (vertebral?) at about the middle of the olive, and (e) **A. cerebelli inferior anterior** at about the posterior third of the pons. These two vessels form a very loose rete on the inferior surface of the cerebellum, to which they send numerous twigs, eventually uniting at the postero-inferior part of the cerebellum to form a common trunk that plunges into the substance of the cerebellum.

(f) **A. auditiva interna** arises as a delicate twig from the anterior inferior cerebellar artery. It accompanies the auditory and facial nerves into the internal acousticomeatus.

(g) **Rr. ad pontem** are given off from the basilar as it crosses the pons.

(h) **A. cerebelli superior,** paired to form the terminal branches of the basilar artery, arises at the anterior border of the pons and runs laterad

[1] No structure corresponding to the R. meningeus of human anatomy could be found.

to the anterior surface of the cerebellum. It is separated from the posterior cerebral artery by the oculomotor nerve, as in man.

Near its origin the superior cerebellar artery receives the posterior communicating branch, which runs caudad from the internal carotid. At this juncture a good-sized middle thalamic twig is given off, on the left side only, to the thalamus; no corresponding structure is present on the right side.

(i) A. cerebri posterior arises from the posterior communicating branch (at about its posterior third), and hence actually belongs to the internal carotid circulation rather than to the vertebral. It is a slender vessel, considerably smaller than the superior cerebellar, that runs laterad, caudad, and dorsad into the notch between the cerebrum and the cerebellum, eventually supplying the posterior part of the cerebrum.

2. A. mammaria interna (fig. 130) takes origin from the ventral wall of the subclavian, immediately opposite the origin of the vertebral artery and costocervical trunk. Extending obliquely ventrad, caudad, and mesad, it meets the internal mammary vein which descends on the opposite side of the vena cava, in the space between the second and third costal cartilages. The artery and vein pass beneath the transverse thoracic muscle side by side, about 10 mm. laterad of the sternum. They pass straight caudad as far as the fifth costal cartilage, then gradually curve toward the midline. The artery is almost in contact with the tip of the xiphoid cartilage.

In each intercostal space the internal mammary artery gives off the usual R. perforans medially and a R. intercostalis laterally. A. thymica arises in the first intercostal space and runs transversely to the thymus. Beyond the last rib cartilage the internal mammary is continued as the anterior epigastric artery.

3. Truncus thyreocervicalis (fig. 130) arises from the medial wall of the subclavian about 15 mm. beyond the origin of the internal mammary artery. It runs forward and outward, ventrad of the brachial plexus and closely applied to the external jugular vein. The thyrocervical trunk gives off three branches. The first and smallest (cervicalis ascendens of Reighard and Jennings) gives off a twig that supplies the sternomastoideus, sternohyoideus, and adjacent muscles; the rest of this branch supplies the posterior cervical lymph gland and a part of the clavotrapezius. The second branch supplies the proximal part of the clavotrapezius and adjacent muscles.

The third branch, A. transversa colli, is the largest and appears to be the direct continuation of the thyrocervical trunk. It passes up around the shoulder to emerge at the scapulohumeral articulation, where it lies between the acromiotrapezius and the supraspinatus. The transverse cervical divides just above the scapulohumeral articulation to form anterior and posterior rami. A third branch, only slightly smaller in size, runs forward into the clavotrapezius.

R. medialis (descendens, BNA) runs dorsocaudad between the rhomboideus and the subscapularis, then turns caudad just before the coracovertebral border of the scapula is reached, passing deep to the rhomboids and levator scapulae. Opposite the infraspinous fossa a branch is sent outward and over the vertebral border of the scapula into the infraspinous fossa, where it anastomoses with the termini of the circumflex scapular and the thoracodorsalis. Other branches supply the rhomboids, the latissimus, the spinotrapezius, the serratus, and the subscapularis. The branch to the latissimus descends along the anterior border of this muscle, sending off short lateral twigs into the muscle, and eventually anastomosing with an ascending branch of the thoracodorsalis. The main trunk of the medial ramus continues beyond the border of the scapula, to anastomose with the sixth intercostal artery.

R. lateralis (ascendens, BNA) passes across the supraspinatus caudad of the occipitoscapularis. Numerous twigs are sent to the occipitoscapularis and spinotrapezius, other twigs entering the supraspinatus fossa to participate in the supraspinatus anastomosis. Near the coracovertebral angle of the scapula it sends a terminal twig down into the supraspinous fossa, which anastomoses with the terminus of the transverse scapular.

Twigs from the lateral ramus pass across M. supraspinatus to the proximal part of M. acromiotrapezius. The most dorsal of these sends a twig down along the scapular spine, which receives twigs from the circumflex scapular, transverse scapular, and external circumflex humeral arteries before it reaches the acromial process of the scapula. This branch is the main source of the Rete acromiale. Other branches from the external circumflex humeral and transverse scapular arteries pass across the neck of the scapula, and form the other roots of the rete.

Since the posterior thyroid artery is absent, the thyrocervical trunk has no relation with the thyroid gland.

4. Truncus costocervicalis dextra (fig. 130) is the first branch given off from the right subclavian. It arises from the dorsal side of the artery, immediately caudad of the origin of the vertebral artery, i.e. at the anterior border of the first rib. Arching upward just outside the pleura, it bifur-

cates near the articulation of the first rib. One branch, A. intercostalis suprema, passes backward just inside the ribs, giving off the usual branches to the intercostal spaces. The other branch, A. cervicalis profunda, immediately passes dorsad between the eighth cervical and first thoracic nerves, then between the necks of the first and second ribs. The vessel emerges on the back of the neck between the longissimus dorsi and multifidus cervicus muscles, where it divides into anterior and posterior branches. The anterior branch ramifies in the biventer cervicis; the posterior branch supplies the longissimus dorsi and multifidus cervicis.

The left costocervical trunk arises from the left vertebral artery. It passes dorsad between the seventh and eighth cervical nerves, giving off a small intercostalis suprema to the first intercostal space. The remainder of the vessel continues dorsad as the cervicalis profunda, passing between the seventh cervical vertebra and the neck of the first rib, beyond which it parallels the course of its fellow on the opposite side.

## AXILLARY ARTERY

A. axillaris (figs. 133, 134) is the distal continuation of the subclavian beyond the origin of the thyrocervical axis. The proximal part of the artery lies between the brachial plexus (dorsad), where it is situated between the seventh cervical and first thoracic nerves, and immediately ventrad of the eighth cervical nerve, and the axillary vein (ventrad). With the foreleg in an extended position the artery curves outward and slightly backward into the leg, where it becomes the brachial artery beyond the origin of the subscapular trunk. The axillary artery gives rise to the following branches: (1) the transverse scapular; (2) the anterior thoracic; (3) the thoracoacromial; (4) the lateral thoracic; (5) the subscapular; (6) the internal humeral circumflex; and (7) the external humeral circumflex.

1. A. transversa scapulae (fig. 133) is the first branch given off by the axillary. It is a good-sized branch arising from the convex side of the curve of the axillary as the latter arches back from the first rib. Running forward, outward and upward, parallel with the transverse cervical artery, it gives off a twig to the anterior division of the superficial pectoral as it passes around the shoulder joint to enter the space between M. suprascapularis and M. infraspinatus. At this point the vessel breaks up into a number of smaller branches. Of these, superficial rami supply the adjacent parts of the supraspinatus and subscapularis, while the largest branch, which appears to be the direct continua-

tion of the transverse scapular, passes through the scapular notch onto the supraspinous fossa of the scapula. Here the larger of two branches ramifies in the supraspinous fossa, eventually anastomosing with the posterior branch of the transverse cervical artery near the vertebral border of the scapula; twigs from this branch pass toward the scapular spine, where they participate in the acromial rete. A smaller branch passes across the neck of the scapula, at the base of the scapular spine, into the infraspinous fossa, where it ramifies and anastomoses with branches of the circumflex humeral scapular artery near the glenoid border and with the descending branch of the transverse cervical artery near the vertebral border. This branch also contributes a twig to the acromial rete.

2. A. thoracalis anterior (fig. 133) is a small vessel arising from the posterior wall of the axillary artery immediately beyond the border of the first rib. It runs caudad across the ventral part of the first intercostal space, which it supplies. It is accompanied by a corresponding vein.

3. A. thoracoacromialis arises from the anterior wall of the axillary immediately beside and internal to the origin of the transverse cervical, which it slightly exceeds in caliber. Passing distad between the anterior and posterior divisions of the pectoral muscle, the thoracoacromialis gives off numerous twigs to both layers of the pectoral musculature, the humeral end of the clavotrapezius and the acromiodelteus.

The main trunk, greatly reduced in caliber, pierces the tendon of the pectoral profundus below the head of the humerus and divides to form ascending and descending rami that run along the pectoral ridge of the humerus. The ascending ramus passes up along the pectoral ridge, pierces the anterior superficial pectoral muscle near the greater tuberosity, and so emerges onto the bicipital groove. The main part of the branch enters a nutrient foramen in the bicipital groove, while a smaller twig continues beneath the tendon of the biceps, where it anastomoses with a branch of the internal humeral circumflex. The descending ramus runs distad along the ridge, to anastomose with a twig from the profunda brachii at the distal border of the tendon of the teres major.

4. A. thoracalis lateralis (fig. 133) arises from the posterior wall of the axillary, 17 mm. distad of the origin of the thoracoacromial artery. It passes caudad, giving off branches to the pectoralis profundus, the panniculus, and the serratus. Intercostal branches to the second to fourth intercostal spaces anastomose with the aortic intercostals. Twigs are also sent to the axillary lymph glands.

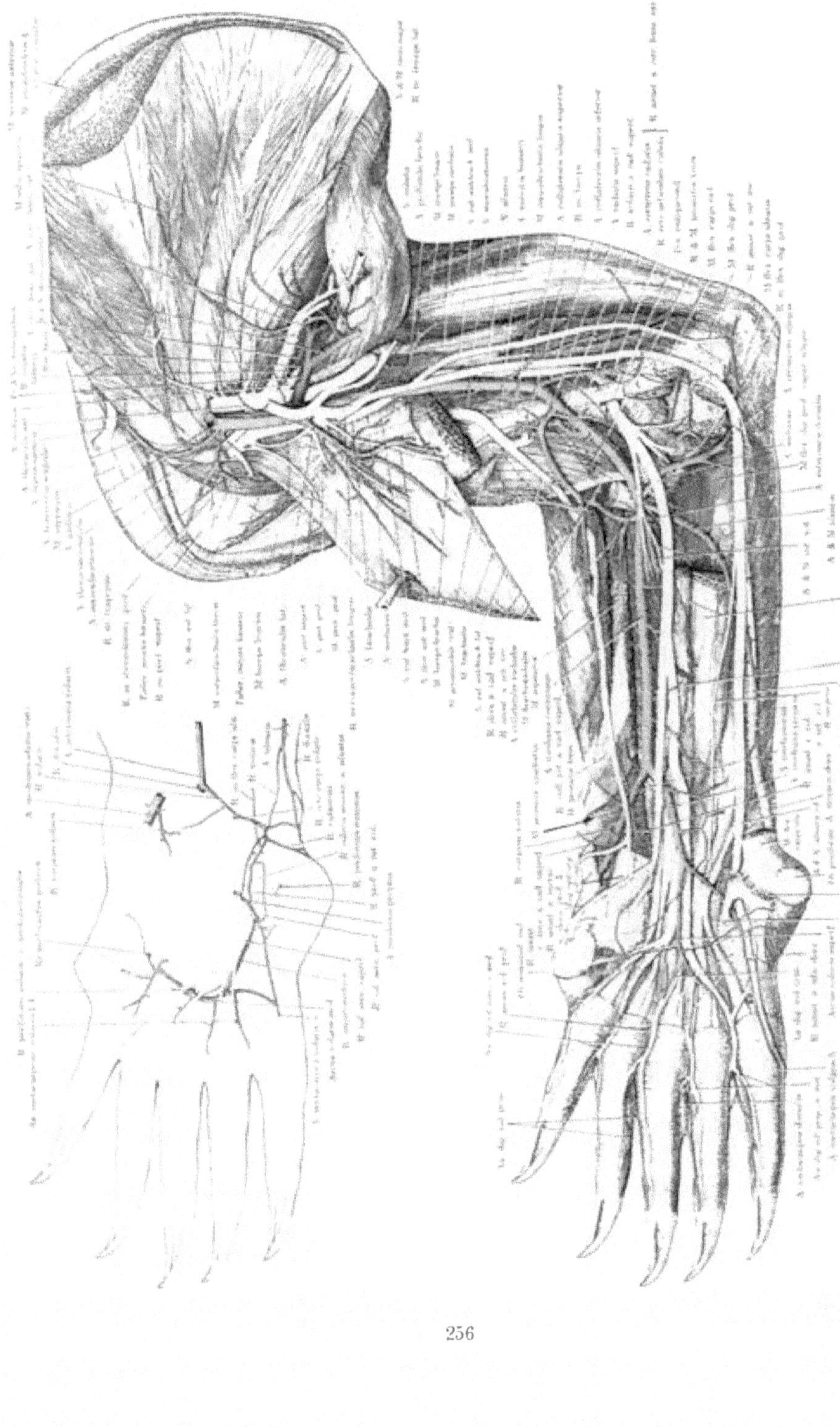

FIG. 133. Arteries and nerves of shoulder and fore leg of *Allavopoda*, medial view.

5. A. subscapularis (fig. 133) takes origin from a trunk that gives rise also to the two circumflex humeral arteries and a large vessel that furnishes the main blood supply to the latissimus, subscapular, and adjacent muscles. This trunk arises from the anterior wall of the axillary about 35 mm. distad of the origin of the thoracoacromial (i.e., opposite the ventral border of the teres minor), and beneath the pectoral musculature. The trunk passes laterally (externally) through the interval between the teres major and the teres minor, emerging at the level of the external surface of the scapula. Here, at the antero-internal border of the triceps longus and 10 mm. beyond its origin from the axillary, the trunk bifurcates to form two branches of approximately equal size: one of these, the subscapular proper, passes caudad beneath the triceps longus; the other, the external humeral circumflex, runs outward in the interval between the triceps longus and the triceps medialis. The small internal humeral circumflex arises from the common trunk about 5 mm. beyond the origin of the trunk from the axillary, at the level of the internal border of the scapula; immediately proximal to it, and from the opposite side of the trunk, arises the large branch supplying the latissimus, subscapularis, teres major and teres minor.

The subscapular artery proper runs along the glenoid border of the scapula for a short distance, then divides to form two terminal branches. The infrascapular branch of the circumflex scapular artery (cf. human anatomy) does not arise from the circumflex scapular, but takes origin independently from the subscapular opposite the scapular notch. The terminal branches of the subscapular are (a) a circumflex scapular, and (b) a slightly smaller dorsal thoracic.

(a) A. circumflexa scapulae (fig. 134) passes into the infraspinous fossa, where the main part of the vessel passes across the fossa parallel to the scapular spine, eventually anastomosing with the descending branch of the transverse cervical and the dorsal thoracic branch of the subscapular near the gleno-vertebral angle of the scapula. A twig from this artery enters the large infraspinous nutrient foramen of the scapula; and a second twig passes toward the spine, where it participates in the acromial rete by anastomosing with a branch of the transverse cervical. Immediately opposite its origin from the subscapular, the circumflex scapular gives off a small anastomotic branch that passes toward the supraglenoid groove, where it anastomoses with the infraspinous branch of the transverse scapular.

(b) A. thoracodorsalis (fig. 134), lying between the teres major and the triceps longus, continues the subscapular artery along the glenoid border of the scapula nearly to the gleno-vertebral angle. Numerous short twigs pass into the triceps longus, and a branch arising at the ventral end of the teres major fossa passes into the latissimus dorsi. The vessel terminates by anastomosing with the circumflex scapular and the descending branch of the transverse cervical near the gleno-vertebral angle.

6. A. circumflexa humeri interna [BNA: anterior] (figs. 133, 134) is a slender vessel that arises from the subscapular trunk just before its terminal bifurcation. The internal circumflex divides a few millimeters beyond its origin (on the left leg these two vessels arise independently side by side). The deeper of the two branches passes along the ventral border of the teres minor, then beneath the coracobrachialis, onto the head of the humerus. Passing up across the lesser tuberosity and beneath the tendon of the biceps, it anastomoses with an ascending branch of the thoracoacromial in the bicipital groove. The more superficial branch of the internal humeral circumflex passes forward external to the coracobrachialis to the proximal end of the biceps, which it supplies; a twig supplies the coracobrachialis.

7. A. circumflexa humeri externa [BNA: posterior] (fig. 133) is a large vessel that arises by bifurcation of the trunk that gives rise to it and the subscapular. The external humeral circumflex passes ectad between the subscapularis and teres major, emerging between the triceps medialis and the triceps lateralis and breaking up into a number of branches beneath the spinodeltoideus. Branches go to both divisions of the deltoid, to the infraspinatus, and to the integument in the shoulder region. Twigs from the deltoid branch enter the acromial rete. A large descending branch supplies the triceps medialis and the triceps longus; this descending branch anastomoses with a branch of the profunda brachii beneath the triceps medialis, then bifurcates. One of the resulting twigs passes to the olecranal rete; the other runs distad with the lateral ramus of the superficial radial nerve, to anastomose with an ascending twig from the dorsal terminal branch of the volar interosseous. There is also an anastomosis with the dorsal interosseous. Nutrient branches enter the foramen in the head of the humerus immediately behind the deltoid ridge.

### BRACHIAL ARTERY

A. brachialis (fig. 133) is the continuation of the axillary beyond the origin of the subscapular trunk. There is no sharp boundary between the brachial and median arteries, but the brachial may be considered as terminating at the level of the

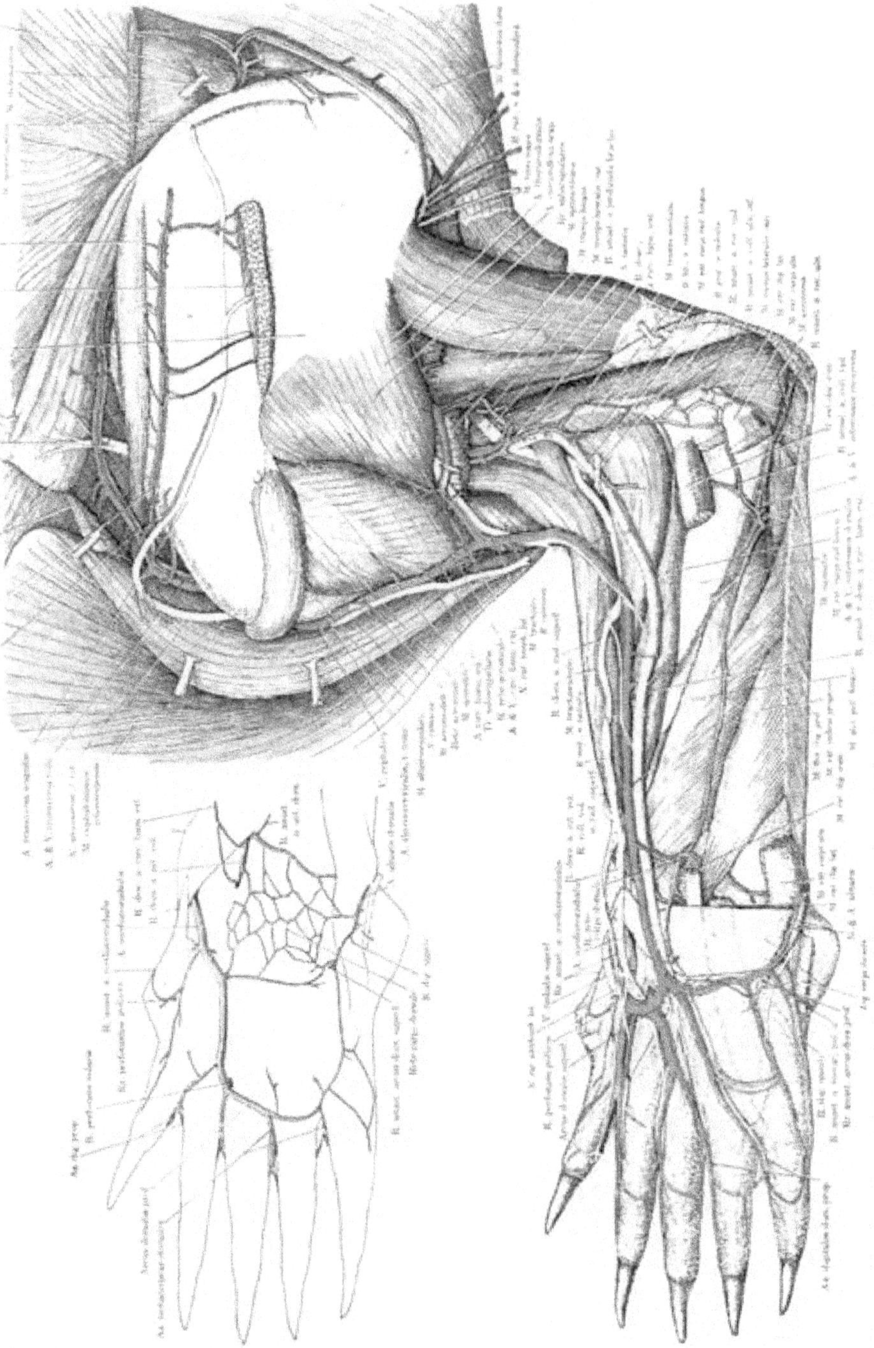

FIG. 134  Arteries and nerves of shoulder and fore leg of *Ailuropoda*, lateral view.

entepicondylar foramen, beyond which the trunk is continued as the median. The brachial artery runs distad along the posterior border of the biceps, and has the following relations with the median nerve: Immediately after passing through the loop of the median nerve, the nerve lies posterior to the artery. Between this point and the elbow the nerve makes a complete spiral revolution around the artery, so that just proximad of the elbow it again occupies a posterior position. The nerve and artery now diverge, the nerve continuing straight distad through the entepicondylar foramen, while the artery follows the crease of the elbow, lying craniad of the nerve. The artery rejoins the nerve below the foramen, and passes distad with it.

The brachial artery gives rise to the following branches in addition to numerous twigs to the flexor musculature of the upper arm: (1) the profunda; (2) the superior ulnar collateral; (3) the inferior ulnar collateral; (4) the superficial radial.

1. **A. profunda brachii** (fig. 133) is a small branch arising from the posterior wall of the brachial artery at the level of the bicipital arch. Immediately beyond its origin the vessel gives off a slender twig that follows the lower border of the tendon of the teres major, thus lying deep to the biceps and brachialis, to the pectoral ridge of the humerus. Here it divides to form ascending and descending rami that run along the pectoral ridge. The ascending ramus anastomoses with the descending ramus of the thoracoacromialis, while the descending ramus passes down along the pectoral ridge to anastomose with a branch of the radial recurrent. A ramus from this twig also supplies the coracobrachialis longus.

The main part of the profunda brachii bifurcates about 5 mm. beyond its origin, one branch entering the medial side of the triceps longus, where it ramifies, while the other enters the medial side of the triceps medialis. A twig from the branch to the triceps medialis accompanies the radial nerve through the space between the triceps medialis and triceps longus to the posterior side of the humerus, where it anastomoses with the descending ramus of the circumflexa humeri externa.

2. **A. collateralis ulnaris superior** (fig. 133) arises, on the right foreleg, from the posterior side of the brachial about 25 mm. proximad of the internal condyle of the humerus. On the left fore leg the two ulnar collateral arteries arise by a short common trunk. The superior collateral crosses the ulnar nerve, lying external to it, then accompanies the nerve downward for a short distance before plunging into the triceps medialis. One branch ramifies in the distal end of the triceps medialis,

while a second passes through this muscle and into the triceps longus, where it ramifies.

3. **A. collateralis ulnaris inferior** arises, on the right leg, about 12 mm. distad of the superior collateral. It accompanies the ulnar nerve, lying distad of it, to the region immediately above the internal condyle. Here the vessel breaks up to form four main branches: (1) A slender branch runs forward, accompanying the median nerve through the entepicondylar foramen. (2) A branch enters the triceps medialis, where it ramifies. (3) The largest branch winds back behind the median epicondyle to the posterior side of the humerus. (4) A slender branch accompanies N. cutaneus antebrachii medianus across the median epicondyle.

4. **A. radialis superficialis** (collateralis radialis superior of veterinary anatomy) (fig. 133) arises from the anterior side of the brachial 10 mm. beyond the origin of the collateralis ulnaris inferior. At its origin it divides into a dorsal branch and a smaller volar branch. The volar branch ramifies extensively to the forearm flexors. The dorsal branch runs across the distal end of the biceps, immediately above the origin of the lacertus fibrosus, dividing into a pair of collateral branches at the anterior border of the biceps; these branches reunite at the carpus after pursuing their separate ways down the fore arm. One of them passes through the brachioradialis to the dorsum of the forearm, where it joins the medial ramus of the superficial radial nerve and accompanies it to the carpus; numerous branches to the brachioradialis considerably reduce the caliber of this vessel. The second collateral branch joins N. cutaneus antebrachii lateralis and V. brachialis superficialis at the crease of the elbow, and runs distad with them in the groove between the pronator teres and brachioradialis. The vessel winds along the distal border of the brachioradialis onto the dorsum of the forearm, where it receives the dorsal collateral branch, then terminates by dividing into subequal terminal twigs. One of these terminal twigs anastomoses with the dorsal branch of the interossea volaris, while the other opens into the anastomotic branch of the medianoradialis, the resulting common trunk forming the radial end of the superficial dorsal arch.

Recurrent twigs to the biceps, with a larger recurrent branch running back in the furrow between the biceps and brachioradialis to ramify to the latter muscle and the distal end of the clavotrapezius, arise from the dorsal branch before it divides into its collateral branches.

The **arcus dorsalis superficialis** is a very delicate double arch with three vessels contributing to its formation. The first arch, which extends across metacarpals 1 and 2, is formed by the common trunk of the radialis superficialis and the anastomotic branch of the medianoradialis radially, and the dorsal branch of the interossea volaris ulnarward. Aa. digitales dorsales communes 1-2 arise from this loop. The second arch extends across metacarpals 3 and 4, and is formed by the dorsal branch of the interossea volaris and the ulnaris dorsalis. It gives rise to digitales dorsales communes 3-4. Each of these digital arteries is joined by a delicate anastomotic branch from the corresponding metacarpea dorsalis at the distal ends of the metacarpal bones.

## MEDIAN ARTERY

A. mediana communis[1] (fig. 133) is the continuation of the brachial beyond the level of the entepicondylar foramen. It passes just medial of the tendon of the biceps onto the forearm. Immediately proximad of the biceps tendon it is joined by N. medianus, which has passed through the entepicondylar foramen. The artery and nerve pass beneath the proximal ends of the flexor carpi radialis and pronator teres, coming to lie in the space between the flexor carpi radialis and the flexor digitorum profundus. The artery lies on the radial side of the nerve. Just proximad of the carpus the artery divides to form two branches of nearly equal size: the median proper and the medianoradial. The first of these passes to the palm, while the other passes around the radial border of the wrist, deep to the tendon of the extensor pollicis brevis, onto the dorsum of the hand.

The common median artery gives off the following branches on the forearm.

1. A. recurrens radialis (Davis, 1941, p. 176) is a small branch arising from the lateral side of the median artery at the level of the entepicondylar foramen. It ascends along the humeromedial border of the brachialis, dividing after about 15 millimeters to form two branches.

One of these branches passes back around the distal end of the insertion tendon of the deltoid, sending twigs to the tendon and to adjacent parts of the brachialis; a twig passes proximad along the medial border of the deltoid tendon, to anastomose with the descending branch of the profunda brachii. Another small twig passes from the main trunk to the distal end of the humerus.

The other branch passes around in front of the distal end of the humerus, beneath the brachialis. Twigs are given off to the distal end of the bra-

chialis. After emerging on the opposite side of the brachialis the vessel breaks up to form numerous terminal twigs, which pass, in contact with the radial nerve, to the extensor carpi radialis longus and brevis.

2. Aa. recurrentes ulnares (fig. 133) are three small branches arising from the medial side of the median artery a few millimeters below the origin of the brachialis anterior. The first of these passes through the pronator teres, emerging on the medial surface of the forearm. In addition to supplying the pronator teres, it sends twigs to the flexor carpi ulnaris, the flexor digitorum profundus, and the palmaris longus. The second branch runs back into the entepicondylar foramen, where it anastomoses with a branch of the collateralis ulnaris inferior. The third branch greatly exceeds the other two in caliber, and arises 20 mm. farther distad. Its origin is adjacent to the origin of the ulnar artery. The vessel forms three main twigs. The smallest passes distad to supply the condylar heads of the flexor digitorum profundus. A second twig passes back to the ulnar articulation, giving off twigs to the proximal ends of the flexor muscles on the ulnar side of the forearm. A third twig passes to the ulnar articulation, giving off twigs to the ulnar head of the flexor digitorum profundus, and terminates in the olecranal region.

3. A. collateralis radialis (fig. 133) arises from the radial side of the median opposite the origin of the ulnar artery. It bifurcates just beyond its origin. One twig supplies M. pronator teres. The other passes around in front of the brachialis, to anastomose with the recurrent interosseous: twigs are given off along its course to the brachialis and the extensor carpi radialis longus.

4. Rr. musculares. Numerous short branches pass from the median artery along its course to contiguous muscles on the flexor side of the forearm.

5. A. ulnaris (fig. 133) is a fair-sized branch, approximately the same diameter as the interossea volaris, that arises from the ulnar side of the median at the level of the insertion of the biceps, i.e., at the proximal fifth of the forearm. It runs to the ulnar side of the forearm, and then toward the carpus, but remains hidden by the flexor musculature throughout its course. It gives off twigs to the flexor muscles situated on the ulnar side of the forearm, and thus its caliber is considerably reduced. Several millimeters before reaching the pisiform, at about the distal quarter of the forearm, it divides into a very slender ulnaris volaris and a larger ulnaris dorsalis. The volaris passes onto the palm, where it anastomoses with the branch of the mediana propria that goes to the outer border of digit 5; the ulnar artery has no

---

[1] I follow the German anatomists in regarding the main artery in the forearm as the median rather than as the radial. Conditions found in lower mammals show that it is erroneous to designate this vessel the radial, as Reighard and Jennings (1935) have done.

connection with the superficial volar arch proper. The ulnaris dorsalis accompanies the dorsal ramus of the ulnar nerve onto the dorsum of the manus just proximad of the pisiform. On the dorsum it anastomoses with the much larger medianoradialis to form the deep dorsal arch, and sends twigs into the dorsal carpal rete; an additional fine twig forms the ulnar half of the delicate superficial dorsal arch with the dorsal branch of the interossea volaris. The branch of the ulnaris dorsalis that goes to the outer side of digit 5 (metacarpea dorsalis 5) gives off an anastomotic loop that passes around the border of the hand to anastomose with metacarpea volaris 5.

6. Aa. interosseae. There is no interossea communis, the volar and dorsal branches arising together, but without the intervention of a common trunk; they come off immediately distad of the ulnaris. A. interossea volaris (fig. 133) slightly exceeds the dorsalis in caliber. It passes distad on the interosseous membrane, accompanied by its vein, to the radiocarpal articulation. Numerous twigs are given off to the deep flexor muscles of the forearm, and nutrient twigs to the ulna and radius. At the radiocarpal articulation it divides into a large dorsal terminal branch and a slender volar terminal branch. The volar terminal branch passes between the heads of the ulna and radius onto the carpus, where it divides; the larger branch passes toward the pisiform, where it anastomoses with the volar branch of the ulnar artery; the smaller branch passes toward the base of the radial sesamoid, to anastomose with a twig from the R. carpeus volaris of the medianoradialis. The dorsal terminal branch perforates the interosseous membrane near the base of the carpus. On the dorsal side of the forearm it first gives off a twig that runs proximad between the extensor digitorum communis and the extensor digitorum lateralis, to anastomose with a descending branch of the interossea dorsalis. The main trunk bifurcates after giving off this twig. The more superficial of the resulting branches runs distad external to the dorsal carpal ligament. At the proximal border of the ligament it gives off a recurrent twig that runs back toward the elbow beside the lateral branch of the superficial radial nerve, to anastomose with a descending branch of the external circumflex humeral. The superficial branch divides on the carpal ligament, one twig passing toward the pollex to anastomose with the anastomotic ramus of the medianoradialis to form the radial half of the superficial dorsal arch, while the other forms the ulnar half of this arch with a twig from the ulnar. The deeper twig of the dorsal terminal branch passes beneath the dorsal carpal ligament, where it enters the dorsal carpal rete.

A. interossea dorsalis (figs. 133, 134) emerges onto the dorsal side of the forearm by perforating M. abductor pollicis longus. It divides immediately into two branches of approximately equal caliber. One of these, A. interossea recurrens, runs back toward the olecranon, giving off twigs to the proximal ends of the extensor muscles of the forearm and continuing into the olecranal rete. The second branch, the main continuation of the dorsal interosseous, runs distad beneath the extensor digitorum. It supplies twigs to the extensor muscles, the largest of these anastomosing with the descending branch of the external circumflex humeral. The vessel terminates by emptying into the dorsal terminal branch of the interossea volaris.

7. A. medianoradialis (figs. 133, 134) arises, as usual in carnivores, from the bifurcation of the common median artery, just proximad of the carpus. The medianoradialis is the larger of the two resulting branches, and passes diagonally radialward with N. cutaneus antibrachii lateralis.

About 25 mm. beyond its origin the medianoradialis gives rise to a branch, R. carpeus volaris (fig. 133), from its medial wall. This branch runs distad beneath the tendons of the flexor muscles and enters the volar carpal rete. A few millimeters farther distad the medianoradialis gives off a long anastomotic ramus that accompanies N. cutaneus antibrachii lateralis around the radial sesamoid, superficial to the tendon of the abductor pollicis longus, to the dorsum, where it receives a delicate anastomotic twig from the brachialis superficialis, then anastomoses with the dorsal branch of the interossea volaris to form a part of the superficial dorsal arch.

Winding up around the base of the radial sesamoid, deep to the tendon of M. abductor pollicis longus, the trunk of the medianoradialis reaches the dorsum manus, where it terminates by anastomosing with the ulnaris dorsalis to form the deep dorsal arch. Upon reaching the dorsum the medianoradialis first gives off (a) a slender perforating twig that passes between the base of the first metacarpal and the radial sesamoid to the vola, where it participates in the formation of the radial end of the deep volar arch. This is followed immediately by (b) a somewhat larger twig that passes distad between the radial sesamoid and digit 1. This twig divides into subequal terminal twigs, one of which supplies the outer border of digit 1, and the other goes to the radial sesamoid. A perforating twig from the latter passes to the vola between the radial sesamoid and the first metacarpal, to participate in the formation of the radial end of the deep volar arch. A second twig passes around the outer border of the radial sesamoid, accompanying the nerve that supplies the radial sesamoid, and empties into the anastomotic loop of the medianoradialis on the vola. At the distal border of the carpus the medianoradialis gives off (c) a twig that passes transversely across the carpometacarpal articulation to anastomose with a corresponding twig from the ulnaris dorsalis. This anastomotic loop gives off several twigs to the dorsal carpal rete.

The **arcus dorsalis profundus** (fig. 134) is formed by the union of the medianoradialis and the ulnaris dorsalis. It lies deep to the extensor tendons of the digits. From it are radiated Aa. **metacarpeae dorsales 1-4**, which run to the corresponding intermetacarpal spaces. The second and third dorsal metacarpals are the largest. Near the middle of the first phalanx each dorsal metacarpal divides into two Aa. **digitales volares propriae**, and at the bifurcation each dorsal metacarpal receives the perforating branches of the corresponding volar common digital.

In addition to the dorsal metacarpal arteries, the deep dorsal arch gives rise to a perforating branch that pierces the interstitium between the second and third metacarpal bones. On the palm it enters the middle of the deep volar arch.

The **arcus volaris profundus** (fig. 133) is slightly smaller in caliber than the superficial volar arch, and is a compound arch with contributory vessels entering it at three points. The main source of the arch is the large perforating branch of the medianoradialis that passes through the second intermetacarpal space. On the vola this vessel divides, one anastomotic loop passing across the base of the first metacarpal to inosculate with a common trunk formed by the union of the two perforating twigs that pass between the radial sesamoid and the first metacarpal. This part of the arch gives rise only to A. **metacarpea volaris 1**. The second and larger anastomotic loop from the perforating branch passes toward the ulnar side of the palm, anastomosing with terminal twigs of the mediana propria to complete the arch. This part of the arch gives rise to Aa. **metacarpeae volares 2–4**. Each volar metacarpal opens into the corresponding common digital artery at the distal end of a metacarpal bone.

8. A. **mediana propria** (fig. 133) accompanies the median nerve to the palm. In the wrist it gives off a large branch to the outer side of digit 5; this branch gives off a transverse anastomotic loop to the parent vessel in the palm; it also receives the terminus of the ulnaris volaris, and beyond the pisiform a slender anastomotic twig from the ulnaris dorsalis. The main trunk of the mediana continues onto the palm, where it curves in a gen-

tle arc (**arcus volaris superficialis**) toward the ulnar side. A branch to the outer side of the pollex, which also supplies a twig to the radial sesamoid, and Aa. **digitales volares communes 1–3** arise from the arch, while the trunk itself is continued as the digitalis volaris communis 4. Each common digital bifurcates at the distal end of the metacarpal bone to form two **Rr. perforantes**, which pass through the interosseous spaces to anastomose with the corresponding dorsal metacarpal artery. The second, third, and fourth common digitals receive the corresponding volar metacarpals from the deep volar arch.

### ABDOMINAL AORTA

*Parietal Rami*

A. **phrenica anterior** (fig. 135) arises from the left ventral wall of the aorta as the latter passes between the medial crura of the diaphragm. Its origin is 12 mm. anterior to the origin of the celiac axis. The vessel divides into right and left branches 25 mm. beyond its origin; the right branch is somewhat smaller than the left (see below under Renal Arteries). A small left posterior phrenic arises from the base of the anterior phrenic. The right posterior phrenic comes from the right renal artery.

### CELIAC ARTERY

A. **coeliaca** (fig. 135) arises from the ventral wall of the aorta immediately after the latter emerges from the diaphragm, i.e., ventrad of the last thoracic vertebra. The celiac artery is a short vessel which passes forward and slightly to the left for about 12 mm., then breaks up to form three branches: the hepatic, the splenic, and the left gastric arteries.

1. A. **hepatica** arises independently from the ventral wall of the celiac artery. It is only slightly smaller than the splenic artery, but much larger than the left gastric. It passes forward alongside the portal vein to the liver, giving off a single large branch (the gastroduodenal). Near the liver the hepatic artery divides into the customary right and left branches, which supply the liver and gall bladder.

A. **gastroduodenalis** is very short, dividing about 5 mm. beyond its origin from the hepatic artery to form two branches of nearly equal size. The larger of these is a short trunk which forks after 9 mm. to form the right gastroepiploic and anterior pancreaticoduodenal arteries. A. **gastroepiploica dextra** runs beneath the duodenum, turns to the left and runs along the pylorus (in the omentum), to anastomose with the left gastroepiploic branch of the splenic near the proximal end of the pylorus. The usual twigs are given off to

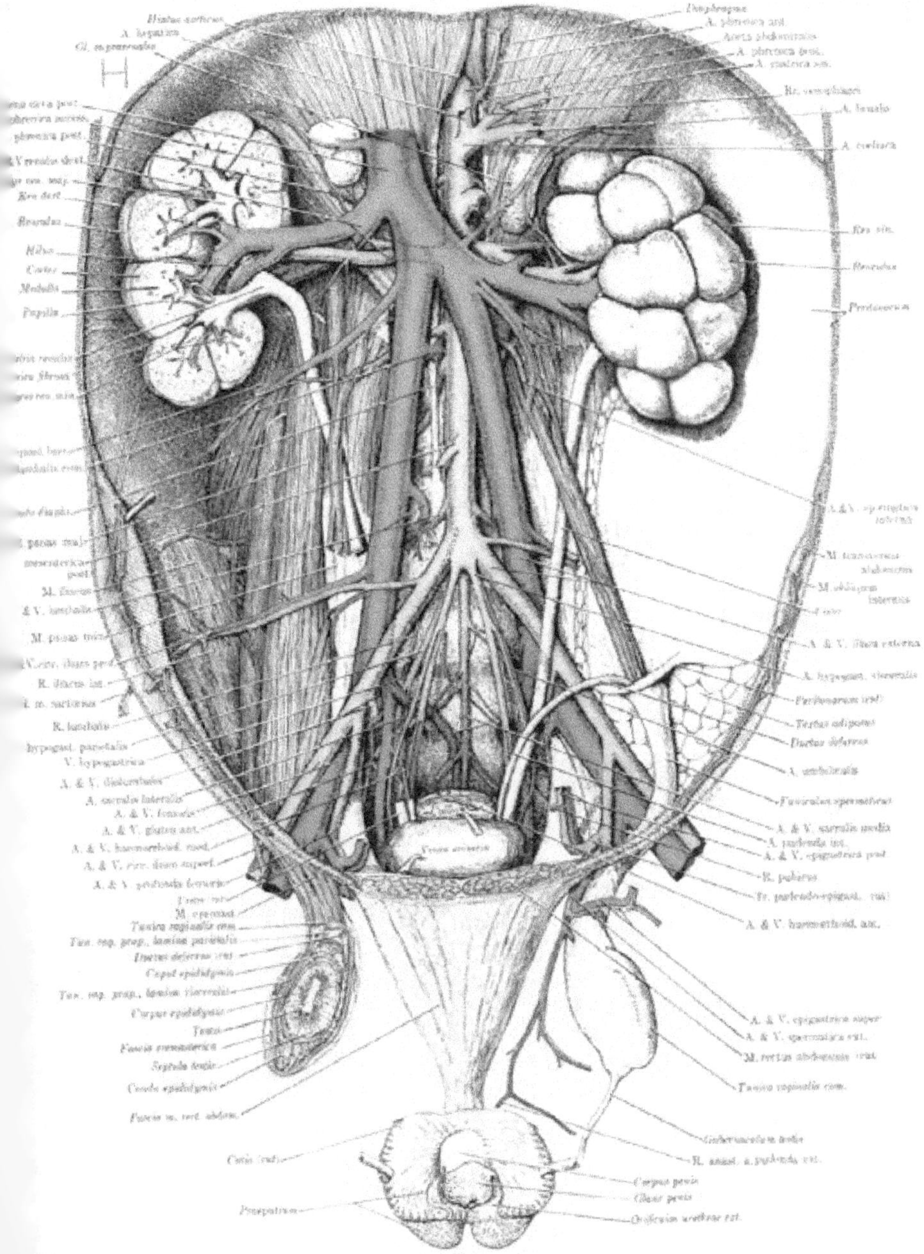

FIG. 135. Vessels and nerves of the abdomen of *Ailuropoda*.

the pylorus and omentum. A. pancreaticoduodenalis anterior runs through the substance of
the head of the pancreas, giving off twigs to the
pancreas and duodenum, and anastomosing with
the posterior pancreaticoduodenal artery near the
caudal end of the duodenum.

The smaller branch of the gastroduodenal artery,
A. gastrica dextra, is more important as a blood
supply to the corpus of the pancreas than to the
stomach. A branch (the right gastric proper) runs
through the lesser omentum, giving off twigs to the
pylorus and eventually anastomosing with the left
gastric in the lesser curvature of the stomach.

2. A. lienalis is the largest branch of the celiac
artery. After giving off the hepatic artery, the
celiac continues for 3 or 4 mm. and then divides
to form the splenic and left gastric arteries. A. lienalis follows the curvature of the gastrolienal ligament. Two pancreatic branches arise from the
proximal end of the artery and supply the cauda
and corpus of the pancreas, also giving off epiploic
twigs to the omentum. Large splenic branches,
which become progressively smaller and shorter
toward the posterior end of the spleen, are given
off from the main trunk of the artery at more or
less regular intervals. In the region of the fundus
of the stomach each splenic branch divides into at
least two twigs near its terminus, one of which goes
to the spleen while the other (the vasa brevia of
human anatomy) passes in the omentum to the
wall of the stomach. Near the posterior end of the
spleen the gastric and splenic twigs are independent, coming off from opposite sides of the main
trunk. The main trunk is continued as the A. gastroepiploica sinistra, which runs in the omentum
along the pylorus to anastomose with the right
gastroepiploic artery.

3. A. gastrica sinistra is the smallest branch
of the celiac artery. It follows the lesser curvature
of the stomach, giving off numerous twigs to the
cardia. A separate anastomotic branch arises high
on the cardia and runs through the lesser omentum
to join the right gastric which runs along the pylorus from the opposite direction. At its base the
left gastric gives rise to two small branches, the
Rr. oesophagi. The more medial of these runs
craniad just to the left of the midline, dividing into
right and left branches at the level of the eso-
phageal opening in the diaphragm. The other
ramus runs craniad, supplying the posterior end
of the esophagus.

ANTERIOR MESENTERIC ARTERY

A. mesenterica anterior arises from the ventral wall of the aorta about 15 mm. caudad of the
celiac artery (fig. 135). It slightly exceeds the

celiac in size. It runs through the mesentery in a
short, sharp arc, giving off the following branches:
(1) the posterior pancreaticoduodenal; (2) the intestinal arteries; and (3) the ileocolic trunk (fig. 113).

1. A. pancreaticoduodenalis posterior arises
from the anterior wall of the anterior mesenteric
about 25 mm. beyond the origin of the latter from
the aorta, i.e., as the anterior mesenteric passes the
edge of the pancreas. Running into the head of
the pancreas, it supplies that region and the posterior end of the duodenum, anastomosing with the
anterior pancreaticoduodenal within the substance
of the pancreas.

2. Aa. intestinales arise from the convex side
of the arch of the anterior mesenteric and radiate
into the mesentery in the usual way. Nine main
branches come off from the arch, and each of these
bifurcates a few millimeters beyond its origin. The
primary loops so formed are further subdivided
down to quinary divisions. Near the intestinal
border of the mesentery the usual inosculations
join the separate branches to one another. The
termination of the arch of the anterior mesenteric
forms a strong anastomosis with a branch of the
ileocolic artery. Twigs from the main branches
before their bifurcation supply the large lymph
gland (pancreas of Asellus) which lies dorsad of
the arch of the anterior mesenteric.

3. The Truncus ileocolicus is the first artery
that arises from the anterior mesenteric; it comes
off several millimeters before the posterior pancreaticoduodenal, and from the opposite side of the
mesenteric artery. The Aa. ileocolicae and col-
icae take origin from this trunk. Two ileocolic
arteries arise from the ileocolic trunk, and the
trunk itself is continued as a third. The latter,
which is the largest ileocolic branch, anastomoses
with the termination of the anterior mesenteric
artery.

The anterior and middle colic arteries arise from
the ileocolic trunk near its origin from the mesenteric artery. A. colica anterior [BNA: colica
dextra] comes off first, followed a millimeter or
two farther distad by the A. colica media. The
anterior colic divides into anterior and posterior
branches near the intestinal wall. The anterior
branch supplies the proximal end of the colon by
means of numerous short intestinal twigs and continues craniad to anastomose with the first branch
of the ileocolic artery; the posterior branch likewise gives off intestinal twigs and continues caudad
to anastomose with the anterior branch of the middle colic. The middle colic divides into anterior
and posterior branches, each of which sends numerous short branches to the colon. The anterior
branch, as noted above, anastomoses with the an-

terior colic; the posterior branch runs caudad and anastomoses with the posterior colic.

### Renal Arteries

Aa. **renales** (fig. 135) arise symmetrically from the lateral walls of the aorta, 20 mm. caudad of the anterior mesenteric, i.e., at the level of the first lumbar vertebra. Each passes almost straight laterad across the crus of the diaphragm to the hilus of the kidney. In the hilus it breaks up into three branches, which in turn ramify to the individual lobules. The renal artery gives off the following branches in addition to the main trunk supplying the kidney:

1. A. **lumboabdominalis** is a large vessel arising from the anterior wall of the renal immediately beyond the origin of the latter from the aorta. The right lumboabdominal passes dorsad of the corresponding vein, whereas the left passes ventrad. On the left side the A. **suprarenalis posterior** arises as the vessel passes the suprarenal body, and runs forward to the posterior end of that organ; on the right side the lumboabdominal gives rise to the right posterior phrenic, and the right posterior suprarenal comes from this. The lumboabdominal runs diagonally backward and outward along the dorsal body wall.

2. A. **suprarenalis anterior** arises on the left side of the body from the anterior wall of the renal beyond the origin of the lumboabdominal. On the right side it is a short lateral branch from the accessory phrenic as the latter vessel passes the suprarenal body.

3. A. **phrenica accessoria.** An accessory phrenic branch arises from the anterior wall of the right renal artery slightly laterad of the middle of the renal. It passes forward and outward, ventrad of the suprarenal body, across the crus of the diaphragm, supplying the dorsal part of the right half of the diaphragm. A similar, but much smaller vessel arising from the left renal does not reach the diaphragm, but loses itself in the fat surrounding the kidney.

### Internal Spermatic Arteries

Aa. **spermatica internae** (fig. 135) arise from the lateral wall of the aorta 20 mm. caudad of the renal artery. The two arteries are given off symmetrically. Each passes diagonally backward and outward to the abdominal inguinal ring, where it is joined by the ductus deferens. At about one-third the distance between its origin and the inguinal ring each spermatic gives rise to a lateral branch that passes to a prominent mass of post-renal fat. Beyond this point the spermatic artery breaks up to form a rete mirabile, which is maintained distad into the epididymus.

### Posterior Mesenteric Artery

A. **mesenterica posterior** (figs. 113, 135) arises from the ventral wall of the aorta at the level of the third lumbar vertebra, 40 mm. behind the origin of the internal spermatics and 45 mm. in front of the posterior end of the aorta. The vessel passes caudad and toward the colon within the mesocolon. Near the colon it gives rise to the small A. **colica posterior,** which passes craniad, giving off numerous twigs to the posterior part of the colon, to anastomose with the middle colic. The main part of the posterior mesenteric is continued caudad as A. **haemorrhoidalis anterior,** which ramifies over the anterior part of the rectum, anastomosing posteriorly with the middle hemorrhoidal.

### Terminal Branches of the Aorta

The aorta terminates abruptly at the level of the posterior border of the fourth lumbar vertebra by breaking up to form two paired vessels and one unpaired vessel. The first and largest of the paired vessels are the external iliacs. The much smaller hypogastrics diverge symmetrically from the midline immediately behind the external iliacs. Thus the continuation of the aorta as a common trunk before the hypogastrics are given off (the so-called hypogastric trunk) is scarcely represented in *Ailuropoda.* Dorsad of the origin of the hypogastrics the much reduced aorta is continued into the tail as the middle sacral artery.

### Hypogastric Artery and Its Branches

Aa. **hypogastricae** arise from the bifurcation of the external iliacs with scarcely an indication of a hypogastric trunk (fig. 136). Each divides almost immediately to form a parietal and a visceral ramus, and these pass caudad, the parietal ramus lying above and a little to the outside of the visceral.

The parietal branch divides at the level of the second sacral foramen into the anterior gluteal artery and the very slender lateral sacral.

1. A. **glutaea anterior** (figs. 136, 138) emerges from the pelvis at the anterior border of M. piriformis (i.e., at the extreme anterior end of the great sciatic foramen), accompanied by the anterior gluteal nerve. It then breaks up into several terminal branches, which ramify to the gluteal muscles and the piriformis. A branch descends toward the trochanteric rete, sending an anastomotic twig to the posterior gluteal artery and participating in the formation of the rete.

2. A. **caudae sacralis lateralis** passes into the tail, where it lies in the groove between the dorsal and ventral sacro-coccygeal muscles.

The visceral branch of the hypogastric gives rise to the following vessels:

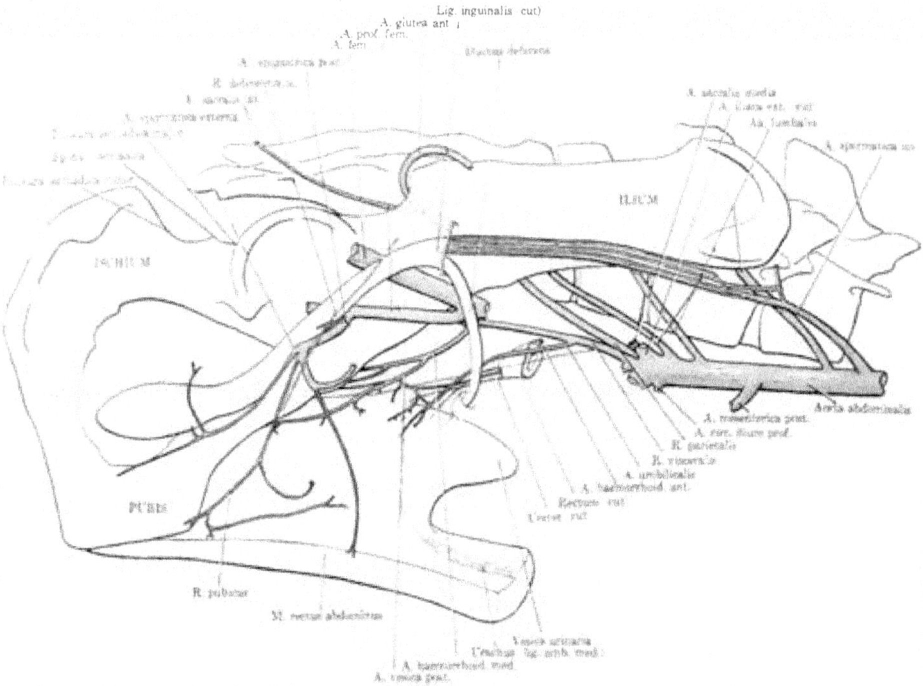

FIG. 136.  Terminal branches of the abdominal aorta in *Ailuropoda*.

1. **A. umbilicalis** (fig. 136) is given off from its lateral wall 20 mm. beyond the origin of the artery itself, and passes back to the bladder. As it nears the bladder the vessel gives off **A. vesicalis anterior**, which ramifies over the anterior part of the bladder. The umbilical artery then ceases to be pervious, and passes around onto the ventral side of the bladder, from where it continues craniad in the lateral umbilical fold as the lateral umbilical ligament.

2. **A. vesicalis posterior** (fig. 136) arises from a trunk common to it and the middle hemor-rhoidal. It passes onto the posterior part of the dorsum of the bladder, where it ramifies. A fine twig runs caudad on the ureter, and a posterior twig anastomoses with a twig from the middle hemorrhoidal.

3. **A. haemorrhoidalis media** (figs. 135, 136) passes caudad and ventrad to the middle part of the rectum, over which it ramifies. Branches go to the urethra, to the ampulla of the ductus deferens, and to the muscles surrounding the rectum. Anteriorly it anastomoses with the anterior hemor-rhoidal, and posteriorly with the posterior hemorrhoidal arteries.

4. **A. glutaea posterior** (fig. 138) is of the same caliber as the internal pudendal, so that the trunk appears to bifurcate to form these two terminal vessels. The posterior gluteal emerges from the pelvis just behind the sciatic nerve, at the posterior border of M. piriformis, and immediately breaks up into terminal branches. These supply the posterior part of the gluteus superficialis, the obturator internus, and the gemelli, and partici-pate in the formation of the trochanteric rete. The branch running to the rete anastomoses with the circumflexa femoris medialis. A posterior branch anastomoses with a terminal branch of the pro-funda at the ischial tuberosity. **A. comitans n. ischiadici** is absent.

5. **A. pudenda interna** is the second of the terminal vessels of the visceral division of the hypo-gastric. It runs caudad beside the rectum, divid-ing near the posterior border of the ischium into the artery of the penis and a trunk for the posterior hemorrhoidal and perineal arteries. (a) **A. peri-naei** bifurcates at its origin. One branch descends vertically, external to M. levator ani and in front of M. sphincter ani externus, to the base of the penis,

giving twigs to the ventral part of the anus and to Mm. ischiocavernosus, bulbocavernosus, and levator penis. The other branch runs caudad, supplying the skin around the dorsal and lateral parts of the anus. (b) A. haemorrhoidalis posterior runs to the anal region, where it ramifies richly in the skin surrounding the anus. A single twig goes to the terminal part of the rectum. (c) A. penis arises from the ventral wall of the internal pudendal 20 mm. before its termination. It descends vertically to the base of the penis, where it breaks up to form three vessels: the artery of the bulb, and the deep and dorsal arteries of the penis. A. bulbi urethrae is a slender branch that runs craniad to ramify over the bulbus urethrae, anastomosing anteriorly with a twig from the middle hemorrhoidal. A. profunda penis is a short branch that enters the crus penis. A. dorsalis penis passes onto the dorsum of the penis, first giving off a delicate twig to the bulbus urethrae; the main trunk runs along the penis to the glans, where it anastomoses with twigs from the external pudendal and with its mate from the opposite side.

EXTERNAL ILIAC ARTERY AND ITS BRANCHES

A. iliaca externa (fig. 135) passes diagonally caudad from the aorta across the ventral surface of M. psoas minor, to the femoral ring. Passing through the ring onto the medial surface of the thigh, it lies in the femoral triangle and takes the name of femoral artery. The external iliac artery lies ventrad of the corresponding vein, and has a length of 100 mm. It gives rise to the following branches: (1) the deep circumflex iliac, (2) the iliolumbar, and (3) the deep femoral.

1. A. circumflexa ilium profunda (fig. 135) arises asymmetrically on the two sides of the body. On the left side it comes off at the very base of the external iliac, while on the right it arises from the external iliac 20 mm. beyond the origin of the latter. The vessel passes deep to the common iliac vein, running laterad and slightly caudad across the dorsal body wall. Twigs from its posterior wall pass into the iliacus and psoas, supplying these muscles and anastomosing with a branch from the iliolumbalis within the muscle tissue. Just before reaching the iliac crest it gives off a branch that pierces the body wall to supply the proximal end of M. sartorius. At the level of the iliac crest the main vessel pierces M. transversus, bifurcating immediately to form anterior and posterior branches that ramify between this muscle and M. obliquus internus. The anterior branch anastomoses with a muscular branch of the lumbar arteries; the posterior branch anastomoses with the superficial circumflex iliac.

2. A. iliolumbalis (fig. 135) arises from the dorsomedial wall just proximad of the deep femoral. It passes dorsad around the external iliac vein and the tendon of the psoas minor, giving off the following branches: (1) A twig arises from its posterior wall 10 mm. beyond its origin and runs back into the pelvic cavity, where it anastomoses with the obturator twig of the profunda femoris. (2) R. lumbalis is a small twig given off from the opposite side and just distad of the preceding. It breaks up in the psoas minor. The main vessel continues as the (3) R. iliacus, which passes laterad across iliopsoas muscles. It gives off several nutrient branches to the body of the ilium and muscular twigs to the iliopsoas muscles. About midway across the psoas major the vessel breaks up to form terminal branches. In addition to muscular branches that supply the gluteus medius and minimus, anastomotic branches run forward to the deep circumflex iliac and the last lumbar.

3. A. profunda femoris[1] (figs. 135 137) arises from the medial wall 40 mm. before the external iliac reaches the femoral ring. It diverges from the external iliac, running almost parallel with the longitudinal axis of the body. It passes through the femoral ring onto the medial side of the thigh, where it lies beneath M. pectineus and in contact with the ventral surface of the ilium just caudad of the iliopectineal eminence. Continuing caudad beneath M. adductor femoris and adductor longus, i.e., across the juncture between the ilium and pubis and across the articular capsule of the hip joint, it reaches the posterior side of the thigh. Here, between the adductor femoris and the quadratus femoris, it breaks up to supply the posterior thigh musculature.

The deep femoral artery gives rise to the following branches:

(a) Truncus pudendo-epigastricus (fig. 135) arises from the ventral wall of the deep femoral at the internal inguinal ring. It divides 10 mm. beyond its origin into the posterior epigastric and external spermatic arteries. A. epigastrica posterior is the larger of the two branches and runs craniad. It gives off a fine twig that supplies the extreme posterior end of M. rectus abdominis, then continues through the suspensory ligament of the bladder to the neck of the bladder. The main trunk of the posterior epigastric gives off a branch to the rectus abdominis, then enters the space be-

[1] The origin of the deep femoral has migrated up inside the inguinal ligament in carnivores, so that in these animals it corresponds to A. obturatoria+A. profunda femoris of human anatomy. The origin of A. circumflexa femoris lateralis has been transferred from the deep femoral (as it is in man) to the femoral. The deep femoral is absent in *Procyon lotor* and some bears (Zuckerkandl, 1907).

tween M. transversus and M. obliquus internus, sending off a fine anastomotic branch to the superficial epigastric; branches ramify over both these muscles and to the rectus. The anterior ends of the vessel anastomose with the superficial and anterior epigastrics. A. spermatica externa runs along the medial border of the spermatic cord to the testis, where it divides. The smaller of the two resulting branches sends twigs into the tissues surrounding the testis and into the skin of the scrotal region, in addition to a twig that enters the prepuce, where it anastomoses with the external pudendal. The other branch of the external spermatic represents A. epigastrica superficialis. It divides in the subcutanea of the inguinal region, the smaller branch running distad on the medial surface of the thigh, while the other runs craniad in the subcutaneous fat over the rectus abdominis, to anastomose with a branch of the posterior epigastric.

(b) R. nutritius is a slender branch arising from its anterior wall just outside the abdominal wall. It passes to the region of the ilium just craniad of the acetabulum.

(c) Rr. musculares pass to the posterior thigh muscles. The first of two large muscular rami arising from the posterior wall of the profunda near its proximal end sends a twig through the obturator foramen. This twig, which apparently represents the obturator artery of human anatomy, gives off pubic, anterior, posterior, and acetabular branches.

(d) A. circumflexa femoris medialis is represented by two branches. A slender branch arising from the medial wall of the profunda at the level of the first muscular ramus apparently represents R. superficialis; it supplies the pectineus and adductor brevis and sends a fine twig to the gracilis. R. profunda arises from the anterior wall of the profunda near the posterior border of the pectineus, passes between the adductor magnus and the obturator externus, and divides into ascending and descending branches on the external surface of the thigh. The ascending branch participates in the trochanteric rete and anastomoses with the posterior gluteal; the descending branch passes down along the posterior border of the vastus lateralis, anastomosing with the ascending perforating branch of the femoral.

(e) One of the terminal branches of the profunda passes ectad between the quadratus femoris and semimembranosus and divides into ascending and descending rami on the external surface of the thigh. The ascending branch breaks up at the ischial tuberosity to form muscular twigs and an anastomotic twig that joins the posterior gluteal; the descending branch runs distad behind the

sciatic nerve, giving off twigs to the posterior thigh musculature.

(f) A. pudenda externa (fig. 137) is a slender twig from the medial terminal branch of the profunda. It runs mesad to the posterior border of the ascending ramus of the pubis, along which it descends to the penis. Entering the ventral wall of the prepuce, it ramifies in the prepuce, anastomosing with its mate from the opposite side and with the pudendal branch of the external spermatic.

## FEMORAL ARTERY

A. femoralis (figs. 136, 137) is the continuation of the external iliac beyond the femoral ring. It lies anterior to the femoral vein, passing first through the femoral triangle, then deep to the adductor femoris and semimembranosus. Finally it emerges into the popliteal space through the interval between the anterior and posterior parts of the adductor longus and magnus (there is no tendinous opening), where it becomes the popliteal artery. It gives rise to the following branches.

(1) A. circumflexa ilium superficialis (fig. 137) arises from the posterior wall of the femoral just beyond the inguinal ligament. It passes back through the femoral ring, then runs craniad on the internal abdominal wall, to anastomose with a descending branch of the deep circumflex iliac. Rr. inguinales arise from the superficial circumflex iliac near its base. They run back toward the inguinal ring, to ramify in the transverse and internal oblique muscles in the inguinal region. The most anterior twig anastomoses with a descending twig of the anterior epigastric.

(2) A. circumflexa femoris lateralis[1] (fig. 137) is by far the largest branch of the femoral. It is a short trunk arising from the anterior wall of the femoral 25 mm. beyond the inguinal ligament. The trunk runs toward the anterior side of the thigh, bifurcating 10 mm. beyond its origin to form two branches of approximately equal size. R. anterior promptly bifurcates again. One resulting branch runs craniad and distad beneath the sartorius and tensor fasciae latae, passing between the branches of the femoral nerve, and giving off twigs to both these muscles. The other branch runs distad in the rectus femoris almost to the knee, giving off numerous twigs to that muscle and a twig to the tensor fasciae latae. R. posterior also bifurcates immediately. One branch passes ectad between the rectus femoris and the vastus medialis to the external surface of the thigh, where it gives off twigs to the gluteal muscles and sends a descending twig down along the boundary between

[1] See note, p. 267.

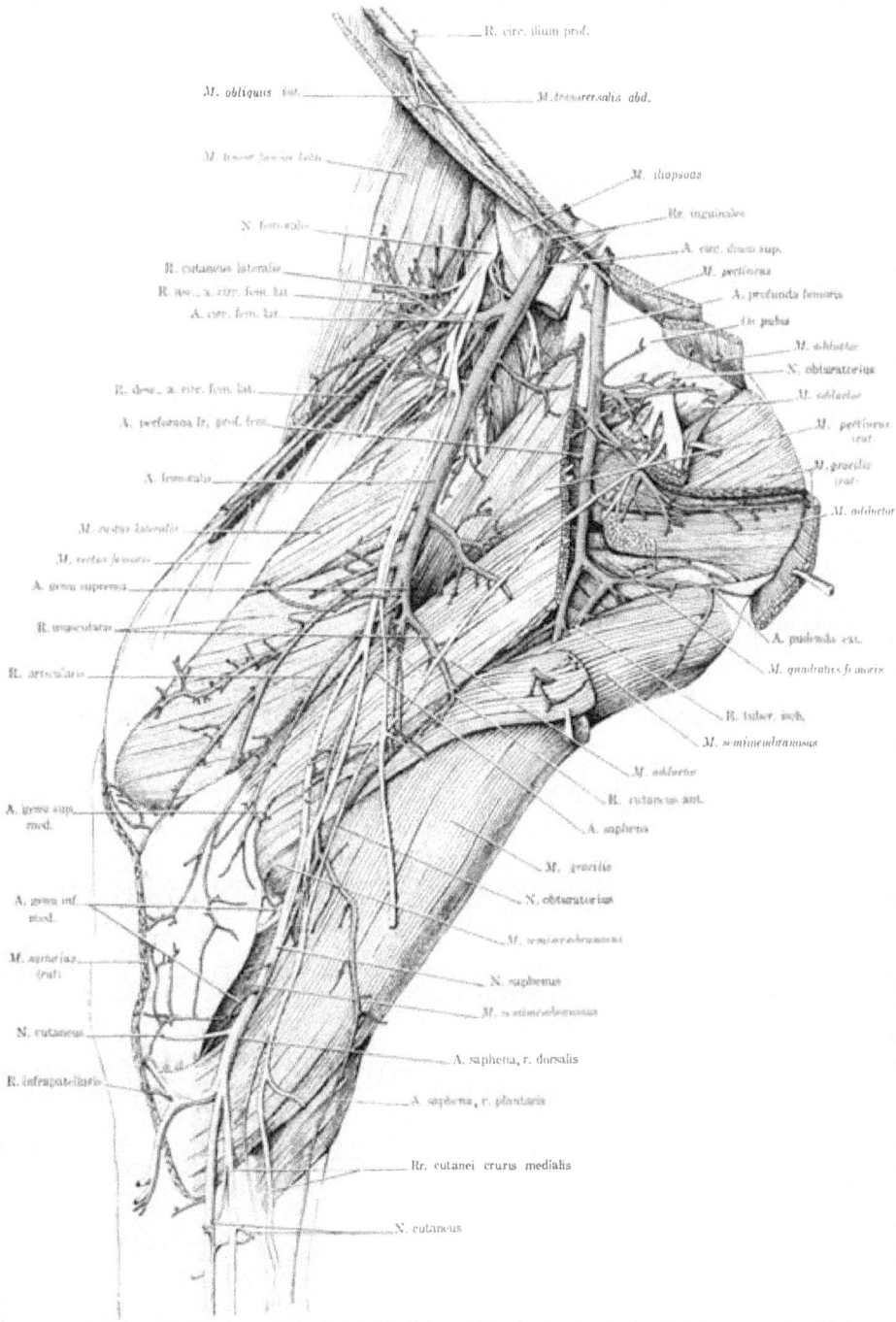

FIG. 137. Vessels and nerves of thigh of *Ailuropoda*, medial view.

the rectus femoris and the vastus lateralis that supplies these muscles; the twig to the vastus lateralis anastomoses with an ascending twig of the superior lateral genicular. The other branch of the posterior ramus runs toward the knee between the rectus femoris and the vastus lateralis, supplying twigs to these muscles and to the vastus intermedius.

(3) **Rr. musculares** arise from both sides of the femoral in its course along the thigh. These supply the sartorius, the gracilis, the rectus, the pectineus, the vastus medialis, the vastus intermedius, and the adductors. A posterior branch arising at about the middle of the thigh and an anterior branch arising a few millimeters farther distad are much larger and more elaborate than the others. The anterior branch sends a twig to the arterial rete at the knee.

(4) **A. genu suprema** (fig. 137) arises from the posteromedial wall of the femoral just before the latter passes beneath the adductor femoris. It breaks up after a few millimeters to form the usual terminal branches. (a) **R. articularis** is the smallest branch. It passes to the articular rete at the knee. (b) **A. saphena** accompanies the saphenous nerve distad. At the level of the medial epicondyle of the femur it divides to form dorsal and plantar branches. The larger dorsal branch accompanies the saphenous nerve to the dorsum of the foot, where it anastomoses with the superficial branch of the anterior tibial artery to form the delicate superficial dorsal arch. From this, the **Arcus dorsalis superficialis**, four fine superficial dorsal metatarsal arteries radiate. These anastomose with the corresponding deep dorsal metatarsal arteries at the metatarso-phalangeal articulations, to form the common digital arteries. The plantar branch passes down the back of the leg in the fascia; below the ventral border of the semimembranosus it lies in the groove for the tibial nerve. At the bifurcation of the tibial nerve, at the distal quarter of the leg, it anastomoses with the superficial branch of the posterior tibial artery. Both the dorsal and plantar branches give off numerous muscular rami to the muscles along their courses. (c) **R. muscularis** is the largest branch of the genu suprema. It passes caudad across the adductor longus, to supply the posterior thigh muscles.

(5) **A. perforans** is a small vessel arising from the femoral just before it reaches the popliteal space. It passes back through M. adductor magnus, along the posterior border of M. vastus lateralis and beneath M. biceps, to the region of the great trochanter. Here it anastomoses with the descending twig of the deep branch of the circumflexa femoris medialis, and participates in the trochanteric rete.

(6) **A. poplitea** (fig. 138) is the continuation of the femoral artery in the popliteal space. It is a very short trunk, dividing near the upper border of the femoral condyles, some distance above the popliteal muscle, into the anterior and posterior tibial arteries.[1] The only branch arising from the popliteal is a muscular ramus to the biceps femoris and tenuissimus.

## ANTERIOR TIBIAL ARTERY

**A. tibialis anterior** (figs. 138, 139) is much the larger of the two tibial arteries. It passes deep to the popliteal muscle, then between the tibia and fibula at the extreme proximal end of the interosseous space, and runs distad on the anterolateral aspect of the leg, lying between the anterior muscles, as far as the ankle. Beyond the tibio-tarsal articulation it continues as the dorsalis pedis artery.

The anterior tibial gives rise to the following branches:

(1) **A. genu superior lateralis** (fig. 138), the larger of the two superior genicular branches, arises from the anterior tibial at its base. It passes laterad above the lateral condyle of the femur. An ascending branch enters the vastus lateralis, within which it anastomoses with a descending branch of the lateral circumflex. A descending branch enters into the deep articular rete.

(2) A very large muscular branch to the biceps and tenuissimus comes off behind and slightly below the superior lateral genicular. A subfascial twig descends across the biceps, to anastomose with the sural artery at the lower border of the biceps.

(3) **A. genu inferior lateralis** (fig. 138) arises 13 mm. beyond the origin of the superior lateral genicular. It runs laterad across the lateral condyle of the femur and the tendon of the lateral head of the gastrocnemius. Only one of the four main branches into which the vessel breaks up passes beneath the fibular collateral ligament; the other three pass superficial to it. Twigs from the vessel participate in the deep articular rete, and a descending twig runs down beneath the peroneus longus, to anastomose with the tibial recurrent artery.

(4) **A. recurrens tibialis** is represented by two small branches arising from the anterior tibial immediately after it has passed through the interosseous space. They run back toward the knee, lying

[1] The term "popliteal" for the distal end of the femoral artery is retained here only for convenience. Because of its division into the tibial arteries in the proximal part of the popliteal space, the popliteal artery gives rise to none of the branches that characterize this artery in man. Many anatomists have attempted to circumvent this difficulty by calling the proximal ends of the anterior and posterior tibials the "deep" and "superficial" popliteals.

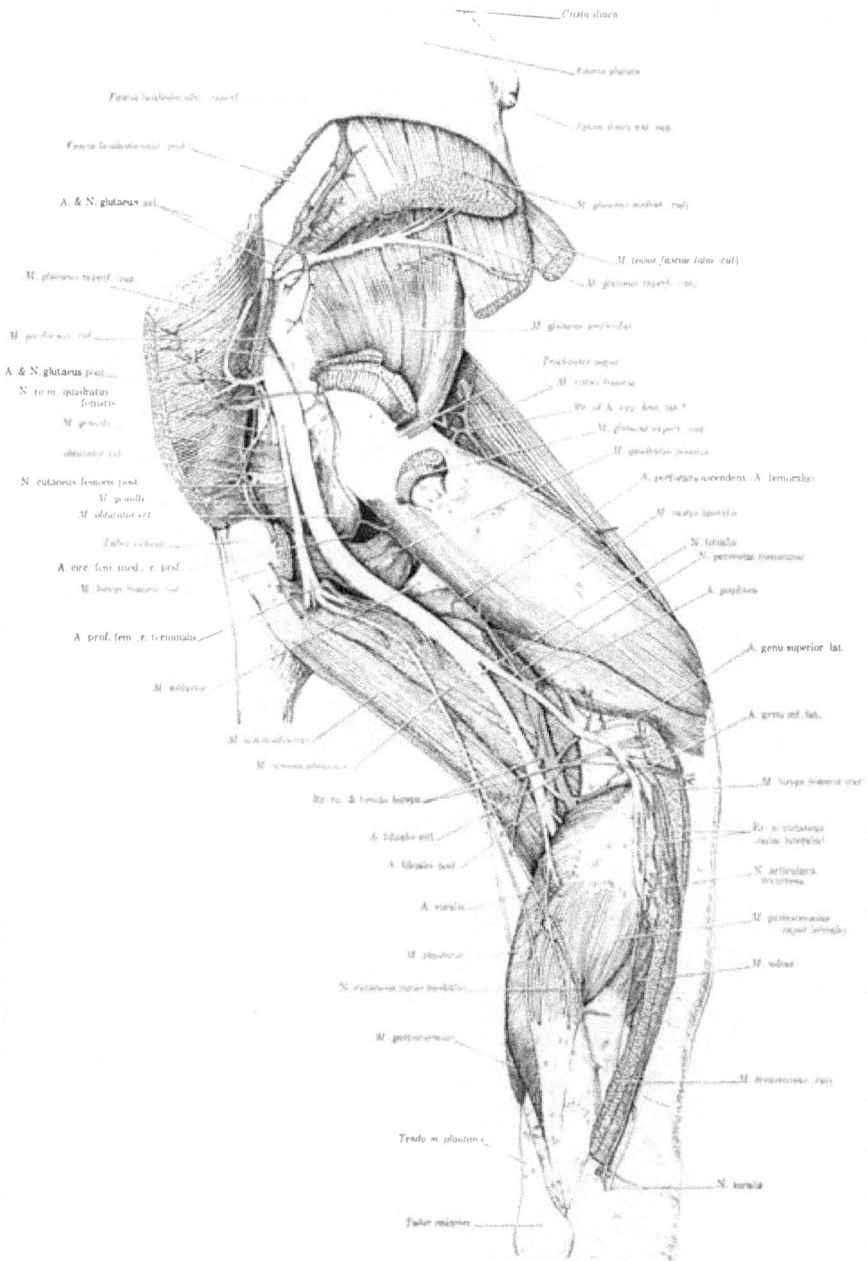

FIG. 138. Vessels and nerves of thigh of *Ailuropoda*, lateral view.

close to the bone beneath the leg muscles, and supply structures in that region. Nutrient twigs to the proximal ends of the tibia and fibula are included.

(5) A. peronaea (fig. 139) is a slender branch, no larger than the several muscle branches with which it is associated, that arises from the anterior tibial at its proximal third. It passes immediately into M. peroneus brevis, running in the substance of this muscle down to the distal third of the leg, and winding around with the muscle to the posterior side of the fibula. Here it joins the perforating branch (8) of the anterior tibial, and the trunk so formed runs distally between the flexor hallucis longus and the peroneus brevis, receiving the sural artery at the tip of the calcaneum, to form the external end of the deep plantar arch.

(6) **Rr. musculares** arise from both sides of the anterior tibial as it passes toward the foot, and supply the surrounding musculature.

(7) **A. tibialis anterior superficialis** (A. n. peronei superficialis, Zuckerkandl) (fig. 139) is an extremely slender vessel arising at about the junction of the middle and lower thirds of the leg. It joins the superficial peroneal nerve and runs with it between the peroneus longus and extensor digitorum longus onto the dorsum of the foot. Here it anastomoses with the dorsal branch of the saphenous artery to form the superficial dorsal arch.

(8) **R. perforans** (fig. 139) is a stout branch coming from the posterior wall of the anterior tibial just above the tibiofibular syndesmosis. It winds around the extensor hallucis longus, perforates the distal end of the interosseous membrane, and is joined by the peroneal artery. The resulting trunk anastomoses with the suralis at the tip of the calcaneum. The perforating ramus represents the perforating section of the primitive interosseous artery.

Just before entering the interosseous membrane the perforating branch gives rise to a short trunk that divides to form the medial and lateral anterior malleolar arteries. **A. malleolaris anterior medialis** (fig. 139) is the larger of the two malleolar arteries. It runs across the medial malleolus, giving off a nutrient twig to the tibia, to the medial malleolar rete. The rete is formed by a twig from the deep plantar branch of the posterior tibial and twigs from the medial tarsal artery, in addition to the malleolar branch. **A. malleolaris anterior lateralis** (fig. 139) runs around the lateral malleolus to the lateral malleolar rete. This rete is formed by interanastomosis between this vessel and twigs from the lateral tarsal artery.

Immediately after passing through the interosseous membrane, the perforating branch gives off a nutrient twig to the distal end of the fibula. One of the terminal twigs of the perforating branch forms the lateral end of the superficial plantar arch by anastomosing with the terminus of the superficial branch of the posterior tibial.

### DORSAL ARTERY OF THE FOOT

**A. dorsalis pedis** (fig. 139) is the direct continuation of the anterior tibial. It divides at the second interosseous space into a branch forming the deep dorsal arch and a much larger perforating branch that joins the lateral tarsal artery to form the deep plantar arch. The dorsalis pedis gives rise to the following branches:

(1) **A. tarsea medialis** (fig. 139), the larger of the two tarsal branches, arises at the same level as the lateral tarsal, at the tibio-tarsal articulation. It ramifies over the medial side of the tarsus, participates in the medial malleolar rete, and sends a twig around onto the sole to anastomose with a twig from the first deep plantar metatarsal artery. The main trunk of the artery runs around the medial border of the tarsus, to anastomose with the deep branch of the posterior tibial artery.

(2) **A. tarsea lateralis** (fig. 139) runs across the tarsus to its lateral side, where it ramifies. It participates in the lateral malleolar rete and the dorsal pedal rete, anastomoses with a descending branch of the sural artery, with the arcuate artery to form the deep dorsal arch, and forms the lateral end of the plantar arch. A twig arising from the lateral tarsal near its base runs into the tarsus between the astragalus and the calcaneum, ramifying as a nutrient artery of the tarsus.

(3) **A. metatarsea dorsalis 1** arises from the dorsalis pedis just proximad of the tarso-metatarsal articulation. At the base of the first metatarsal it breaks up into a perforating branch that passes through the first intermetatarsal space to join the first deep plantar metatarsal artery; a branch that supplies adjacent sides of the first and second digits; and a branch that supplies the outside of the first digit with one twig, and sends another around the first metatarsal to the deep plantar arch, and gives off an anastomotic twig to the medial tarsal artery.

(4) **A. arcuata** (fig. 139) is the dorsal terminal branch of the dorsalis pedis. It arches laterad from the second interosseous space, forming the deep dorsal arch by anastomosing with a descending branch from the lateral tarsal artery. **Aa. metatarseae dorsales profundae 2-5** are radiated from this arch. Each receives its corresponding superficial dorsal metatarsal near the middle of

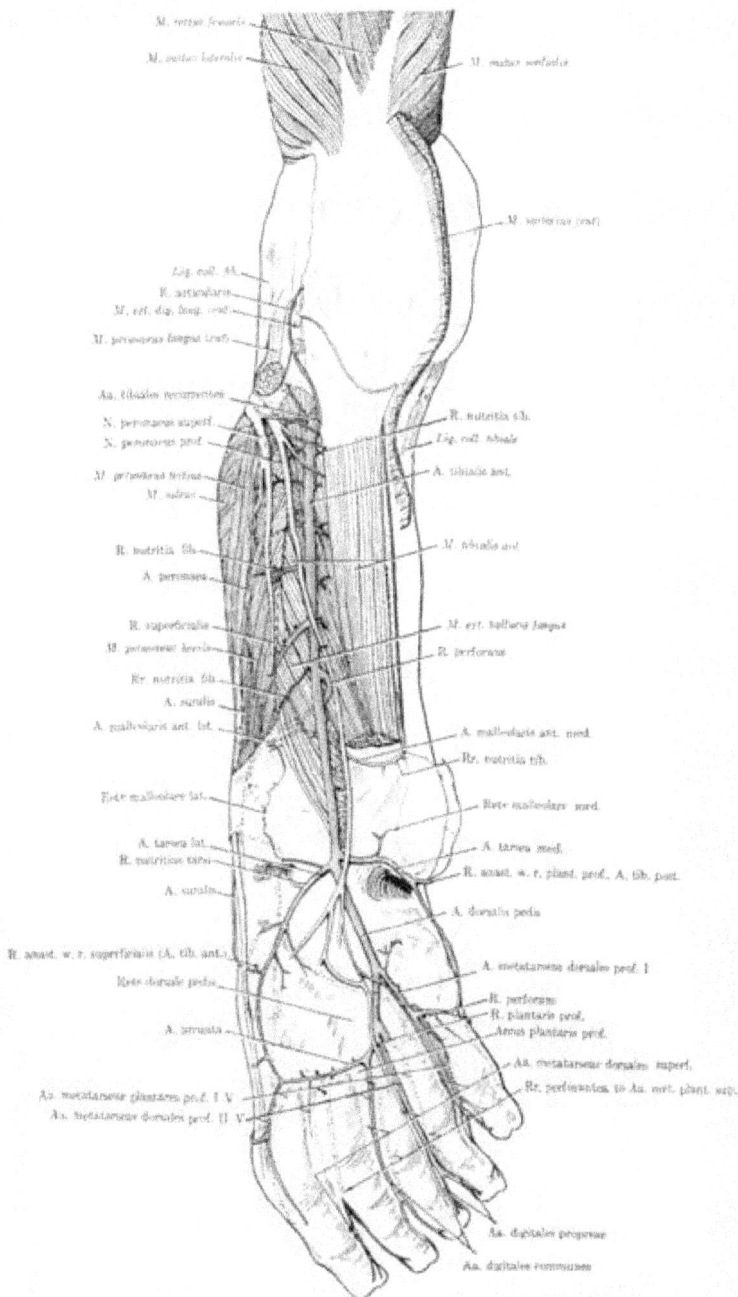

FIG. 139. Arteries and nerves of lower hind leg of *Ailuropoda*, anterior view.

the metatarsus, and the anterior perforating branch from the plantar metatarsal at the metatarso-phalangeal articulation. The resulting dorsal digitals divide immediately into digitales propriae.

5) R. plantaris profundus (fig. 139) is the plantar terminal branch of the dorsalis pedis. It perforates the second intermetatarsal space to reach the planta, where it joins a branch of the lateral tarsal artery to form the deep plantar arch. This, the Arcus plantaris profundus (fig. 139), arches across the bases of the metatarsals, radiating the deep plantar metatarsal arteries. Each A. metatarsea plantaris profundus receives its corresponding superficial plantar metatarsal near the head of the metatarsal bone, and each resulting common vessel gives off an anterior perforating branch at the metatarso-phalangeal articulation, beyond which it continues distad as the plantar digital artery. The anterior perforating branches join the dorsal digital arteries at the metatarso-phalangeal articulations.

### POSTERIOR TIBIAL ARTERY

A. tibialis posterior (fig. 140), the smaller of the two tibial arteries, accompanies the tibial nerve superficial to the popliteal muscle. At the lower-most quarter of the leg it divides into superficial and deep plantar branches. The superficial plantar branch forms the superficial plantar arch, while the deep plantar branch terminates in the tarsus.

The posterior tibial gives rise to the following branches:

(1) A. genu superior medialis (fig. 140) runs medially just above the medial head of the gastro-cnemius and beneath the femoral head of the semi-membranosus. It emerges on the medial side of the thigh between the femoral head of the semi-membranosus and the adductor longus, and anastomoses with the articular branch of the genu suprema and with the dorsal branch of the saphena.

(2) A. genu inferior medialis (fig. 140) runs medially beneath the medial head of the gastro-cnemius and between the two heads of the semi-membranosus. On the medial side of the knee it anastomoses with the superior medial genicular and the dorsal branch of the saphena.

(3) A. genu media (fig. 140) arises from the posterior tibial beside the origin of the superior medial genicular. It passes directly into the knee joint.

(4) A. suralis (fig. 140) is the largest branch given off by the posterior tibial in the popliteal space. It runs distad over the gastrocnemius and plantar muscles, in which it exhausts itself. A slender cutaneous branch runs subfascially with N. cutaneus surae medialis, perforating the fascia

at the distal border of the biceps, where it receives the descending branch of the large muscular ramus of the anterior tibial. The sural terminates by anastomosing with the much larger perforating branch of the anterior tibial at the distal end of the fibula.

(5) Rr. musculares arise from the posterior tibial in its course along the leg, and pass to the muscles of this region. The largest of these are two vessels arising opposite one another at the lower border of the popliteal muscle. The *medial* of these two branches follows the lower border of M. popliteus, giving off twigs to that muscle, the flexor digitorum longus, and the posterior tibial. It terminates at the distal quarter of the tibia as a tibial nutrient branch. The *lateral* of the muscular branches passes into the soleus, where it ramifies.

(6) R. plantaris superficialis (fig. 140), the larger of the two terminal branches of the posterior tibial, receives the plantar branch of the saphena near its origin, and then continues across the sole with the medial plantar branch of the tibial nerve, to terminate as the superficial plantar arch. The first of the superficial plantar metatarsals arising from this arch supplies the outer side of digit 1, and the remaining four anastomose with the corresponding deep plantar metatarsals at the metatarso-phalangeal joints.

(7) R. plantaris profundus (fig. 140) gives off a slender anastomotic branch at the tibio-tarsal articulation that passes around the medial border of the ankle to anastomose with the descending branch of the medial tarsal artery. The plantaris profundus itself terminates as a nutrient artery of the ankle joint.

### INTEROSSEOUS ARTERY

A. interossea, the third primary branch of the popliteal artery, is greatly modified and represented only in part in *Ailuropoda* (fig. 142). The most proximal part of this vessel, which typically arises from the popliteal and runs distally through the popliteal space, is missing. The middle section is represented by the peroneal artery, which here is a branch of the anterior tibial that anastomoses distally with the perforating branch of the anterior tibial. The perforating section of the interosseous is represented by the perforating branch of the anterior tibial, and the distal section, which typically continues into the dorsal pedal artery, is represented by the distal part of the anterior tibial.

### DISCUSSION OF ARTERIES

During ontogenetic development the anlagen of the systemic vessels first appear as elaborate capil-

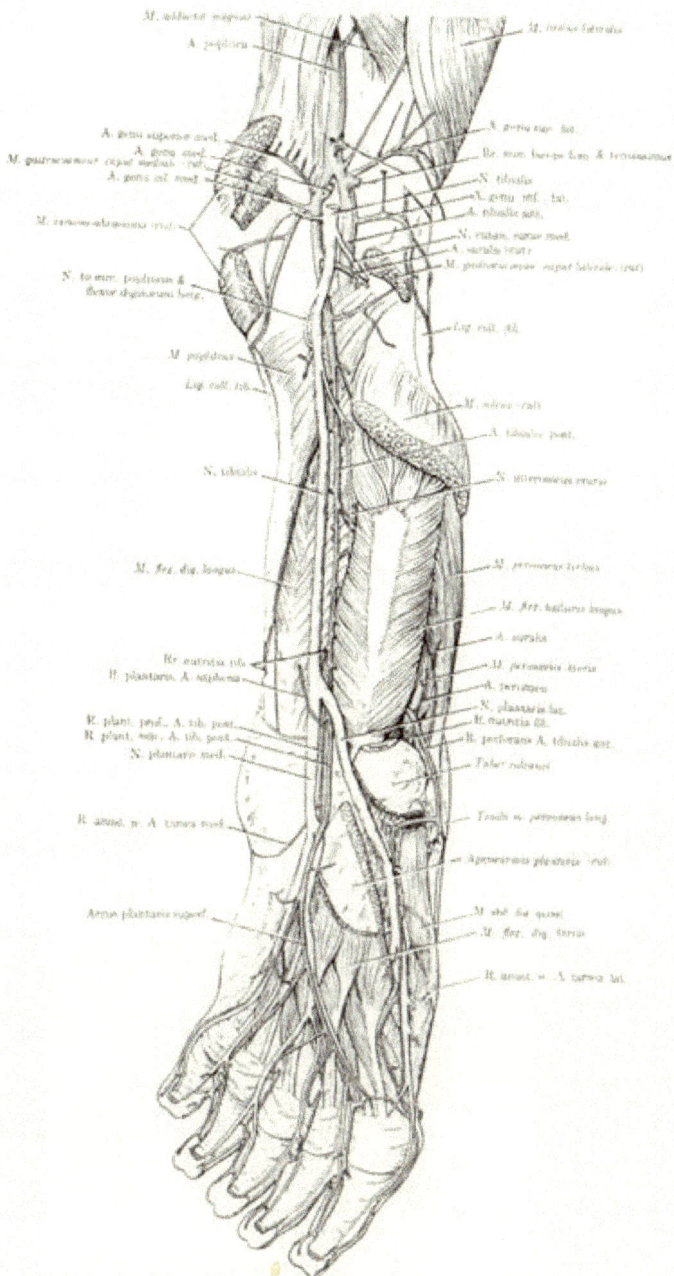

FIG. 140. Arteries and nerves of lower hind leg of *Ailuropoda*, posterior view.

lary networks, the patterns formed by these networks becoming increasingly irregular away from the heart. The arteries and veins arise by enlargement and differentiation of pathways through the networks (Copenhaver, 1955). The only function of the vessels is to transport fluids to and from the tissues, and obviously this can be accomplished via an almost infinite variety of potential vessel patterns. Individual variations in patterns occur, but the choice among the multiple potential pathways through the primary network is not random; the vessels form definite patterns that are faithfully replicated in individual after individual. Definite vessel patterns also tend strongly to be characteristic for taxa of mammals. Several factors are known to contribute to determining the particular pathways that are followed, but the relative roles of these factors are poorly understood. Experimental studies (e.g., Clark, 1918, Am. Jour. Anat., 23, p. 37; Clark et al., 1931, Anat. Rec., 50, p. 129), and comparative studies of adult vessel patterns, both show that heredity somehow plays an important part, although it is not clear to what extent vessel patterns reflect genetic factors acting directly on the forming vessels (intrinsic factors) and to what extent genetic factors acting on surrounding tissues (extrinsic factors) are involved. The studies of Sawin and Nace (1948) and Sawin and Edmonds (1949) indicate that extrinsic factors (genetic factors at second hand, so to speak) are almost wholly responsible. Chemical and mechanical factors associated with blood flow also play a part after circulation is established (Copenhaver, 1955).

Comparative studies show that basic patterns can be identified throughout the systemic circulation in the Carnivora (Davis, 1941; Story, 1951), and somewhat more broadly throughout the Mammalia (Tandler, 1899; Zuckerkandl, 1907; Hafferl, 1933). Variations in a particular basic pattern occur in several different ways: (1) the site at which a vessel arises from a parent trunk may shift proximally or distally; (2) the relative calibers of collateral vessels or vessel systems may vary reciprocally; (3) embryonic trunks may drop out in whole or in part, their terminal ramifications having been captured by another vessel; and (4) the calibers of vessels vary with the physiological demands of the tissues they supply.

Within the Carnivora, at least, the basic patterns vary in characteristic ways among the several families, subfamilies, and genera. Patterns that are "primitive" in the sense that they resemble those found in the most primitive placentals tend to occur in those carnivores that display generally primitive morphological features. Specialized vessel patterns are found in more advanced

carnivores. A hierarchy of patterns, increasingly refined from ordinal down to generic level, is evident in all parts of the carnivore arterial system wherever adequate samples have been studied. Thus the arteries appear to supply trustworthy data, which may be used to support data from other sources, on inter-relationships among the Carnivora.

On the other hand, the circulatory system is perhaps unique among the organ systems in being a passive distribution system. We can scarcely imagine vessel pattern as a factor limiting adaptive radiation within the Mammalia, nor can we visualize natural selection acting directly on blood vessels as it does on bones, muscles, nerve tissue, etc. Thus vessel patterns are of no help in understanding the evolution of functional mechanisms. At best they may reflect function; they can scarcely direct or channel function. Within the Mammalia the circulatory system is useful to the comparative anatomist only as one of several sources of data from which relationships may be inferred.

I have not tried to compare in detail all parts of the circulatory system of *Ailuropoda* with other carnivores. In general, only those parts for which comparative data already exist will be considered.

### Branches of Aortic Arch

The manner in which the carotids and subclavians arise from the arch in mammals may be grouped into five types (Hafferl, 1933). All terrestrial carnivores fall into his type II, in which both common carotids and the right subclavian arise from a common trunk, the left subclavian arising independently. Parsons (1902) found that two further subtypes of branching are represented among terrestrial carnivores: type A, in which the two carotids arise from the innominate independently, and type B, in which there is a short common carotid trunk after the right subclavian is given off. Raven (1936) added several observations to those tabulated by Parsons. I have added 11 observations on arctoids, making a total of 33 individual arctoid carnivores for which data are available (Table 24).

All of the 14 canids so far examined represent type A. The Procyonidae and Ursidae are more variable but are predominantly type B, except *Procyon lotor*, which appears to favor type A. Of the two specimens of *Ailuropoda* that have been checked, one represents type A and the other type B.

It has been commonly assumed that the type of arch pattern in mammals depends on mechanical factors, such as are reflected in body build, rather than genetic factors. This opinion was confirmed by Sawin and Edmonds (1949), who concluded from extensive breeding experiments on rabbits that there is "little indication of dominance and segregation characteristic of mendelian inheritance," and that variations in the aortic arch pattern are determined by hereditary differences in regional growth centers in which the vessels are located.

TABLE 24.—BRANCHES OF AORTIC ARCH IN ARCTOID CARNIVORES

|  | Type A | Type B |
|---|---|---|
| Canis familiaris | 4/4 |  |
| Canis lupus | 3/3 |  |
| Canis latrans | 1/1 |  |
| Lycaon pictus | 2/2 |  |
| Vulpes fulva | 1/1 |  |
| Vulpes vulpes | 3/3 |  |
| Procyon lotor | 3/4 | 1/4 |
| Nasua sp. | 1/3 | 2/3 |
| Potos flavus |  | 1/1 |
| Ailurus fulgens |  | 1/1 |
| Ailuropoda melanoleuca | 1/2 | 1/2 |
| Helarctos malayanus |  | 1/1 |
| Ursus americanus |  | 3/3 |
| Ursus gyas | 1/4 | 3/4 |

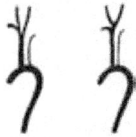

*Carotid Circulation*

The pattern of the carotid circulation in the Carnivora has been reviewed by Tandler (1899), Davis and Story (1943), and Story (1951). Tandler showed that any pattern of carotid circulation found among mammals can easily be derived from a single basic type (fig. 141, A). In this basic pattern the common carotid terminates in three main trunks, which apparently are always laid down during ontogeny: the external carotid, which primarily supplies extra-cranial structures except the upper jaw and primary sense organs; the internal carotid, which supplies the brain, eyeball, and ear; and the stapedial, which is the primary vessel for the upper jaw, the adnexa of the eye, and the nose. These three trunks are interconnected by anastomotic vessels, through which one trunk can capture the terminal branches of another. The proximal part of a trunk disappears after its terminal part has been captured. The carotid pattern of any mammal can easily be derived by dropping out sections of this basic pattern.

In adult Carnivora the stapedial artery has disappeared, its terminal branches having been taken over by the external carotid (fig. 141, B). In the Aeluroidea the external carotid tends to take over the internal carotid circulation as well; in the domestic cat the internal carotid is completely suppressed, and of the three primary trunks only the external carotid remains. Among the Arctoidea there are minor variations of the basic arctoid pattern (Story, 1951), but these are almost wholly associated with differences in head proportions, muscular development, and sense organs. In general, *Ailuropoda* shares more characters with the Ursidae than with the Procyonidae or Canidae (Story, 1951).

A striking example of the close agreement between *Ailuropoda* and the Ursidae is the elongation and looped arrangement of the subdural part of the internal carotid. In all other carnivores the carotid passes straight through the sinus cavernosus, but in a specimen of *Thalarctos* described by Tandler the vessel immediately arched caudad in the sinus, forming a long U-shaped loop twisted around its own long axis, along the medial border of the petrosal. I found an identical situation in a specimen of *Ursus americanus*, in which the subdural part of the carotid measured 60 mm. while the linear distance traversed by this part of the vessel was only 12 mm., a ratio of 1 : 5. Exactly the same condition was present in *Ailuropoda* (p. 252), except that the posterior prolongation was not as extensive, with a ratio of only 1 : 3.

*Branches of the Abdominal Aorta*

This part of the circulatory system has received little detailed comparative study, probably because few significant variations have been found among mammals (Hafferl, 1933). In the dog and cat there are no common iliacs; there is a common hypogastric trunk, but it is very short. The pattern in *Ailuropoda* differs little from that in the domestic dog and cat, and resembles even more closely the pattern in a specimen of *Ursus americanus* dissected by me. The only notable difference between *Ailuropoda* and other carnivores is that the iliolumbalis arises from the external iliac trunk instead of from the hypogastric trunk. This general agreement is somewhat unexpected in view of the shortening of the lumbar region and indications of other profound disturbances in the posterior part of the axial skeleton in *Ailuropoda*. Sawin and Nace (1948) concluded that variations in the posterior aortic region in inbred races of rabbits resulted from the interaction of regional growth centers, which were genetically different in each race. In other words, as in the branches of the aortic arch, variations were determined by extrinsic factors.

*Arteries of the Fore Limb*

These vessels have been reviewed most recently by Zuckerkandl (1907) and Hafferl (1933) for mammals in general, and by Davis (1941) for the Carni-

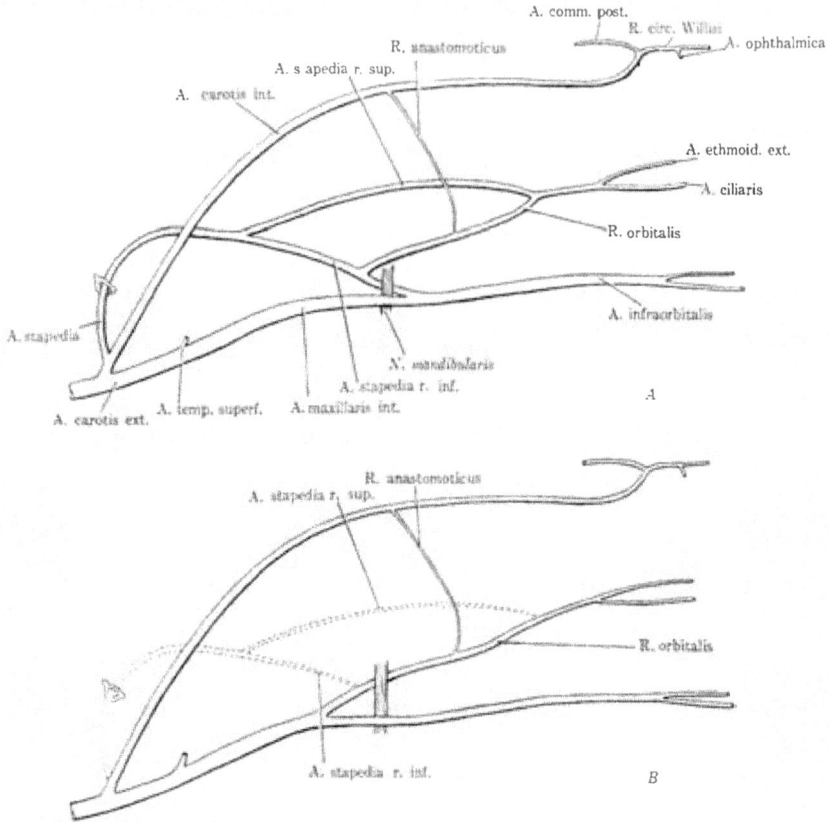

FIG. 141. Basic pattern of the carotid circulation in mammals (A), and in arctoid carnivores (B). Embryonic vessels that have disappeared are indicated by broken lines. Note particularly the anastomotic ramus, through which the external carotid captures the internal carotid circulation in cats.

vora. The primary artery of the forearm, both phylogenetically and ontogenetically, is the interossea, which primitively is the direct continuation of the brachial artery. Two collateral deep vessels, the median and ulnar arteries, provide alternative pathways. Three types, based on which of these vessels is dominant, may be recognized: the interossea type, the mediana type, and the ulnaris type. Most arctoid carnivores belong to the mediana type, although in some (Canidae, Procyon, Ailurus) the median and interosseous arteries are subequal in caliber.

The pattern of the arteries of the fore limb is generally primitive in the Carnivora, and distinctive patterns tend to be associated with the various taxa. Among the arctoid carnivores the pattern in the Canidae is very primitive and uniform within the family. The Procyonidae and Ursidae (in-

cluding Ailuropoda) have a common pattern, which is more specialized than in any other group of carnivores; Procyon is somewhat aberrant. These arctoids are unique in that the brachial artery does not pass through the entepicondylar foramen (although the median nerve does). The bifurcation of the common median artery into subequal mediana propria and medianoradial arteries tends to be shifted distally toward the carpus; in the bears and panda it is near the carpus. The Procyonidae and Ursidae also share other less conspicuous features in the arterial pattern of the fore limb. The bears and panda agree with each other particularly closely.

*Arteries of the Hind Limb*

Comparative studies of these vessels in the Mammalia were made by Bluntschli (1906) and Zucker-

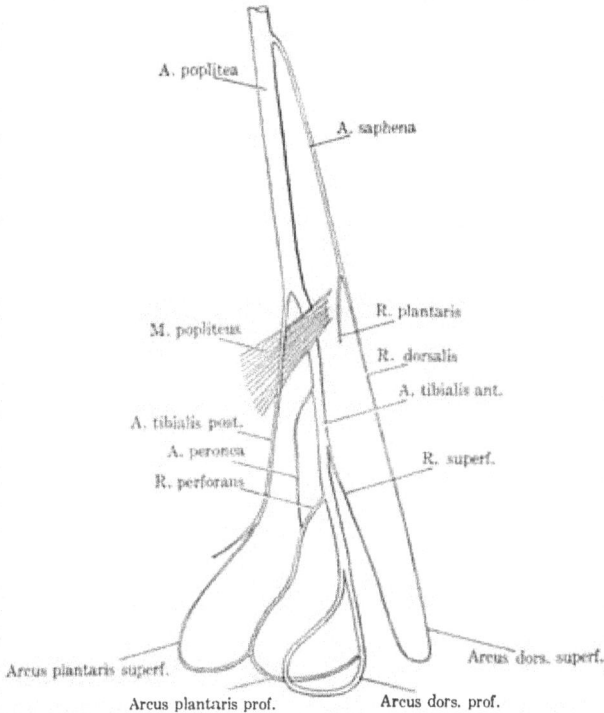

FIG. 142. Diagram of chief arteries of the hind leg in the Carnivora. The remains of the primitive interossea is represented by the peroneal, the perforating branch of the anterior tibial, and that part of the anterior tibial distal to the perforating branch.

kandl (1907). Our knowledge of the patterns in the Carnivora is much less satisfactory than for the fore limb, although Zuckerkandl's material included 18 carnivores, and valid generalizations as to patterns within the order are not yet possible.

In the thigh region the deep femoral is often absent in bears. Zuckerkandl refers specifically to its absence in one (*Helarctos*) of three bears dissected by him; in the second case (*Melursus*) he describes a profunda, but in the third (*Thalarctos*) he does not state whether the profunda was present or absent. It was absent in a specimen of *Ursus americanus* dissected by me. It was also absent in one specimen each of *Procyon*, *Mustela*, *Viverra*, and *Lutra* dissected by Zuckerkandl. Absence of the profunda is otherwise unknown as a normal condition in placental mammals.

The primary vessel of the lower leg and foot is the interossea, which is laid down in the embryos of all mammals that have been studied (Bluntschli, 1906). Three collateral vessels that develop later —the saphena, tibialis anterior, and tibialis posterior—provide alternative pathways to the lower

leg and foot. Each of these four vessels may be enlarged or reduced to produce a variety of patterns. Bluntschli called three of these the interossea type, the saphena type, and the [anterior] tibial type. The fourth could be called the posterior tibial type. In all Carnivora so far examined, the anterior tibial is the main trunk of the lower leg and foot (fig. 142). The saphena and posterior tibial persist as relatively minor vessels, and the interossea is partly suppressed, partly represented by the threadlike peroneal, and distally has been captured by the anterior tibial.

In my specimen of *Ursus americanus* the saphena was nearly as large as the anterior tibial, making this specimen intermediate between the saphena and anterior tibial types.

The arteries of the hind limb in *Ailuropoda* do not differ in any important respect from the carnivore pattern as now known.

CONCLUSIONS

1. Arterial patterns are elements of a passive distribution system, and therefore reflect function

rather than directing function. Vessel pattern cannot be a factor that limits or channels adaptive radiation, and therefore is not directly subject to natural selection.

2. Vessel patterns are not themselves inherited. Differences are apparently produced almost exclusively by differences in mechanical forces in the vessel environment during ontogeny, and these are hereditary. Therefore vessel patterns have a certain taxonomic value.

3. Vessel patterns characteristic of taxa are evident throughout the arterial system in the Carnivora.

4. Where comparative data are available, arterial patterns in *Ailuropoda* resemble those of the Ursidae more closely than those of any other family or genus of Carnivora.

## III. VEINS

### Vena Cava Anterior and Its Tributaries

The anterior vena cava has an external diameter of 20 mm., and a length of 90 mm. before it bifurcates to form the innominates. It receives the following tributaries: (1) the azygos; (2) the internal mammaries; (3) the costocervical axis; and (4) the innominates.

1. V. azygos enters the dorsal side of the vena cava at a point about midway between the right auricle and the junction of the innominate veins, i.e., at the level of the fifth thoracic vertebra. At its origin the azygos lies well to the right of the midline, but it gradually moves mesad until at the level of the ninth thoracic vertebra it lies along the midline. Immediately after its origin it gives off a branch from its left wall that runs cephalad to the second and third intercostal spaces. Bilateral branches begin at the level of the sixth vertebra, a large left branch supplying the fourth right intercostal space and the third, fourth, and fifth left intercostal spaces; the corresponding right branch supplies the sixth right intercostal space. Successive intercostal branches are more or less symmetrically arranged back to the diaphragm, where the azygos terminates by bifurcating into branches that supply the fourteenth intercostal spaces.

2. Vv. mammariae internae enter the ventral wall of the vena cava independently, just caudad of the origin of the innominates. The right internal mammary enters about 15 mm. directly behind the left. Extending obliquely ventrad, caudad, and mesad, each joins the artery of the same name and passes with it beneath the transverse thoracic muscle, where it supplies the ventral intercostal spaces.

3. **Truncus costocervicalis** enters the right dorsolateral wall of the anterior vena cava at about the same level as the right internal mammary vein. The costocervical trunk runs craniad and slightly laterad, dividing to form three branches: (1) V. intercostalis I arises opposite the first intercostal space, which it supplies; (2) **V. vertebralis** and (3) **V. cervicalis profunda** arise opposite the first rib by bifurcation of the trunk. The vertebral vein joins the artery of the same name, and together they pass into the transverse foramen of the sixth cervical vertebra. The deep cervical vein slightly exceeds the vertebral vein in caliber. It runs craniad with the deep cervical artery.

4. **Vv. anonymae** arise by bifurcation of the anterior vena cava at the level of the posterior border of the first rib. Each innominate is very short, breaking up to form the axillary and jugulars immediately in front of the rib. **V. jugularis anterior** is an unpaired vessel arising from the medial wall of the left innominate, about midway in the course of the latter. Running craniad along the ventral midline of the trachea, the anterior jugular gives off the V. thyreoidea posterior at the level of the hyoid. Here it bifurcates, each branch running laterad and craniad to anastomose with the lingual vein.

### Internal Jugular Vein

V. jugularis interna arises from the medial wall of the innominate, thus from the convex side of the curve of the latter vein as it arches around the first rib. The left internal jugular arises somewhat farther distad than the right, probably because of the origin of the anterior jugular from the left innominate. Each internal jugular runs craniad beside the corresponding common carotid artery, the vein lying toward the outside. The diameter of the internal jugular is 4 mm. V. thyreoidea anterior dextra arises at the level of the artery of the same name. A smaller branch opening independently into the internal jugular immediately caudad of the anterior thyroid apparently corresponds to the occasional V. thyreoidea media of human anatomy. V. thyreoidea anterior sinistra opens into the left jugular 25 mm. caudad of the corresponding artery.

At the level of the cricoid cartilage the internal jugular receives the large R. anastomotica, which lies mesad of the vagus nerve. The anastomotic branch gives off two large vessels to the vertebral vein, as well as smaller twigs to the pharyngeal plexus. Much diminished in caliber, the anastomotic ramus enters the foramen lacerum posterior where it empties into the inferior petrosal sinus.

The internal jugular accompanies the carotid artery as far craniad as the origin of the digastric muscle, where the vein and artery diverge. As the vein approaches this point it crosses over the artery, passing ventrad of it. The internal jugular continues anteriorly beside the glossopharyngeal nerve to the base of the postglenoid process, where it receives numerous pharyngeal branches from the pharyngeal plexus and terminates by uniting with the medial branch of the internal facial vein. The pharyngeal plexus is a network of veins draining the walls of the pharynx, from the level of the foramen magnum to the posterior nares. One of the pharyngeal rami communicates with the sinus cavernosus through the foramen lacerum medium.

### Venous Sinuses of the Dura Mater

The combined veins of the vertebral canal pass through the foramen magnum into a deep exoccipital groove that opens at the hypoglossal canal into the sigmoid groove for the transverse sinus. The sinus transversus extends from the opening of the superior petrosal sinus, laterally, to the posterior lacerated foramen, medially. The sinus petrosus superior is entirely surrounded by bone, beginning at the posterosuperior angle of the petrosal bone and running along its superolateral margin. The superior petrosal sinus is large posteriorly, where it drains into the lateral branch of the internal branch of the internal facial vein through the postglenoid foramen. Anterior to this foramen the superior petrosal sinus is a narrow canal opening from the sinus cavernosus at the lateral wall of the foramen ovale. The sinus petrosus inferior is the direct continuation of the transverse sinus from the foramen lacerum posterior to the dorsum sellae, where it becomes the cavernous sinus. The sinus cavernosus fills the sella turcica and opens anteriorly into the ophthalmic vein.

### External Jugular Vein

V. jugularis externa (figs. 107, 131), with a diameter of 9 mm., is considerably larger than the internal jugular. The external jugular enters the innominate vein between the internal jugular and axillary veins, and runs forward immediately laterad of the sternomastoid muscle, dividing at the posterior border of the submaxillary gland to form the external and internal facial veins. Only one branch, the thyrocervical trunk,[1] is received in the cervical region.

[1] This designation is used for this trunk because the branches that it receives are practically identical with the branches of the thyrocervical artery. This condition is quite different from the usual arrangement in man, the domestic cat, etc.

The transverse scapular arises from the jugular on the right side of the body (cf. p. 283), but this does not seem to be the normal condition.

V. thyreocervicalis is a large vessel entering the external wall of the external jugular about 50 mm. craniad of the origin of the latter. It curves away from the jugular to join the thyrocervical artery, which it accompanies toward the scapulo-humeral articulation. The vein receives the following tributaries: (1) The large V. transversa colli enters the thyrocervical 40 mm. beyond the origin of the latter. It joins the corresponding artery, accompanying it around the shoulder joint to the lateral shoulder region. About 10 mm. farther distad the thyrocervical bifurcates to form two branches of approximately equal size: (2) a large muscular ramus that accompanies the corresponding artery to the proximal part of the clavotrapezius and adjacent muscles, and (3) the cephalic vein (p. 284).

### Internal Facial Vein

V. facialis interna (posterior) (figs. 107, 131, 132) arches dorsad and craniad to the base of the ear, in front of which it terminates by entering the postglenoid foramen, to be continued within the skull as the transverse sinus. V. sternocleidomastoidea arises from the internal facial near its base; it accompanies the artery of the same name. V. auricularis and V. occipitalis arise by a common trunk, as was the case with the corresponding arteries; the ramifications of both veins agree closely with those of the arteries, except that the main auricular veins do not come from this trunk. The occipital vein gives off the large Vv. mastoideae, which communicate with the sinus transversus.

V. temporalis superficialis (fig. 132) is a powerful vein given off over the base of the ear cartilage. It gives off a stout branch at its base that runs across the root of the zygoma to anastomose with the transverse facial; twigs from this branch go to the masseter and to the postglenoid rete. V. transversa facei arises higher. It receives the anastomotic branch described above, then joins a masseteric branch of the artery of the same name and runs anteriorly with it. V. auricularis anterior (fig. 107), the larger of the two accompanying veins of the anterior auricular artery, arises opposite and a little above the transverse facial. It joins the corresponding artery, and passes with it onto the front of the ear. V. auricularis posterior comes off at the upper third of the root of the zygoma. It gives off twigs to the base of the pinna, receives an anastomotic twig from the occipital-auricular trunk, gives off a slender accompanying branch of the anterior auricular artery, and then joins the posterior auricular artery at the level of the dorsal border of the zygoma. Its further ramifications agree with those of the corresponding artery. Beyond the origin of the posterior auricular, the temporal trunk is continued as V. temporalis media. The ramifications of this vein agree with those of the artery of the same name.

Immediately beyond the origin of the superficial temporal the internal facial vein arches sharply mesad around the mastoid process. Twigs are given off in this region to the parotid and submaxillary glands. In front of the mastoid process arises the small V. stylomastoidea, which passes into the stylomastoid foramen. Opposite this a slender vessel arises and passes across the medial part of the mandibular condyle, laterad of the postglenoid process, to join the pterygoid rete farther anteriorly. Twigs arising from this vessel near its base form a delicate postglenoid rete on the postglenoid process.

The internal facial appears to bifurcate in front of the mastoid process to form two vessels of approximately equal size. One of these, which may be regarded as the continuation of the internal facial trunk, soon enters the postglenoid foramen. The postglenoid foramen leads into a bony canal that passes dorsad in front of the auditory meatus, to open into the cerebellar cavity of the skull. Beyond this canal the vein continues as the transverse sinus.

The other terminal branch of the internal facial is V. maxillaris interna (figs. 131, 132). This vessel arches around the base of the postglenoid process, to be joined by the terminus of the internal jugular at the medial border of that process. The resulting common trunk passes forward between the medial border of the postglenoid process and M. levator veli palatini, to break up into the pterygoid plexus at the posterior border of the temporal fossa.

The **Plexus pterygoideus** gives rise to the following branches:

1. *Vv. alveolaris inferior* (paired accompanying veins).

2. *V. temporalis profunda posterior.*

3. *V. masseterica.*

4. *V. tympanica anterior.*

5. *V. foramina ovalis* (accompanies A. meningea accessoria).

6. *Vv. pterygoidei.*

7. *V. meningea media.*

These vessels, with the exceptions noted, accompany the corresponding arteries.

Anteriorly the pterygoid plexus drains into a powerful anastomotic branch, which passes along the ventral border of the buccinator muscle to empty into the inferior labial vein near the juncture of the latter with the external facial. Numerous small Vv. buccinatoria and a large V. alveolaris superior posterior empty into the anastomotic branch in its course along the muscle.

EXTERNAL FACIAL VEIN

V. facialis externa (anterior) (figs. 107, 131, 132) follows the anterior border of the masseter forward and upward to a point in front of the anterior root of the zygoma. Continuing upward in front of this root of the zygoma, it divides in front of the orbit into the external nasal and nasofrontal veins. The external facial receives the following tributaries along its course:

1. A transverse communicating branch passes from the external facial near the posterior end of the digastric, to the sublingual branch of the anterior jugular. A twig from this communicating branch passes forward between the mylohyoid and hyoglossus, to anastomose with the lingual vein.

2. V. submentalis enters the external facial directly opposite the preceding branch. It receives a twig from the submaxillary gland, then passes across the digastric and between the digastric and masseter to the superficial surface of the mylohyoid. Here it joins the submental artery, and the further course of the two vessels agrees closely.

3. V. labialis inferior (figs. 107, 131) is received at the posterior end of the exposed part of the inferior alveobuccal gland. The vein passes forward with the artery on the mandible, the ramifications of the two vessels agreeing.

4. A muscular twig from the platysma enters the external facial a few millimeters farther distad.

5. V. facialis profunda (figs. 107, 132) enters the deep surface of the external facial at the dorsal border of the inferior alveobuccal gland. It lies directly beneath the external facial as far as the lower border of the zygoma, then passes behind the anterior root of the zygoma to the common outlet of the sphenopalatine foramen and pterygopalatine canal. Just before reaching the foramina the trunk divides into a V. sphenopalatina and a pair of small Vv. palatina descendens. These vessels enter the foramina with the corresponding arteries.

V. alveolaris superior anterior enters the deep facial at its base, and numerous smaller alveolar twigs from the minute foramina below the orbit open into the deep facial along its course. There are also muscle twigs from the temporal muscle. Below the orbit the deep facial gives off a large communicating branch, which pierces the ventral wall of the periorbita to anastomose with the inferior ophthalmic; a twig from this branch passes out of the ventral side of the orbit, to anastomose with the angular vein on the face.

Just beyond the deep facial, the external facial receives a common trunk formed by (6) a muscular branch from the masseter and (7) V. labialis superior (fig. 107).

8. A communicating branch arising in front of the anterior root of the zygoma arches upward and backward across the temporal muscle, to anastomose with the anterior auricular vein.

9. V. angularis (fig. 107), which enters the external facial just above the foregoing, follows the angular artery.

10. Several nutrient twigs from the jugal enter below and in front of the orbit.

11. V. nasofrontalis (fig. 107), the more posterior of the two terminal vessels, arches around to the dorsal side of the orbit. Just above the orbit it receives V. frontalis, which follows the corresponding artery. The nasofrontal then anastomoses with the superior ophthalmic vein, which it meets immediately above the eye but outside the periorbita.

12. V. nasalis externa (fig. 107), the anterior of the terminal vessels, passes forward on the side of the nose. Several communicating branches pass up over the bridge of the nose, to anastomose with corresponding vessels from the opposite side. At the nasal aperture the trunk of the external nasal vein bifurcates, a dorsal and a ventral branch anastomosing with corresponding vessels from the opposite side to encircle the nasal cartilages immediately in front of the premaxillary and nasal bones.

### Ophthalmic Vein

V. ophthalmica arises from the sinus cavernosus, from which it passes into the orbit through the orbital fissure. The vessel runs forward in the orbit, to be perforated by the orbital artery at about the posterior third of the orbit. At this point the ophthalmic breaks up into its terminal branches.

1. V. ophthalmica superior, by far the largest of the terminal branches, accompanies the frontal artery through the dorsal wall of the periorbita. V. ethmoidalis, which accompanies the corresponding artery through the ethmoidal foramen, enters the vessel near the posterior end of the orbit. As it passes anteriorly the superior ophthalmic receives a muscle twig that perforates the periorbita independently. Directly above the eye, and just before passing out of the orbit, it receives a vein that emerges from the frontal sinus through a small foramen in the dorsomedial wall of the or-

bit. Upon emerging from the orbit the superior ophthalmic becomes the nasofrontal vein, and this communicates openly with the external facial vein.

2. V. centralis retinae is a thread-like vessel that comes off immediately below the superior ophthalmic. It joins the deep branch of the orbital artery and follows it (and the central retinal artery in which the orbital artery terminates) into the optic nerve and thence into the eye ball.

3. V. lacrimalis follows the corresponding artery to the lacrimal gland, where it anastomoses with a twig from the angular vein.

4. Vv. musculares, two in number, supply the ocular muscles.

5. V. ophthalmica inferior, the most ventral branch of the ophthalmic, runs toward the eye between M. rectus inferior and the periorbita. It terminates by anastomosing with the communicating branch of the deep facial vein immediately below the eye.

### Axillary Vein

V. axillaria is the largest and most posterior of the triad of branches in which the innominate terminates.[1] The left axillary (14 mm. in diameter) is considerably larger than the right (11 mm.). The axillary arches around the anterior border of the first rib, becoming the brachial vein beyond the point where it receives the subscapular trunk. It has a length of about 70 mm. The axillary receives the following tributaries: (1) A small branch enters the anterior wall of the axillary 20 mm. beyond the origin of the external jugular. It breaks up into a number of branches that drain the longus colli and the anterior end of the scalenus; the largest branch passes ectad beside the axillary artery, to anastomose with a branch from the internal circumflex humeral. (2) V. thoracoacromialis enters immediately distad of the preceding vein. It accompanies the corresponding artery. (3) A muscular ramus, nearly as large as the thoracoacromialis and entering immediately behind and ventrad of it, drains the anterior parts of the superficial and deep pectoral muscles. (4) V. transversa scapulae on the right side of the body enters the external wall of the external jugular 45 mm. beyond the origin of the latter. On the left side it empties into the axillary a few mm. distad of the thoracoacromialis. The vein accompanies the corresponding artery into the space between M. suprascapularis and M. infraspinatus; its branches correspond

---

[1] The arrangement of the vessels in this region, particularly the origin of the transverse cervical and transverse scapular veins from the external jugular, makes it impossible to distinguish a definitive subclavian vein.

closely with those of the artery. (5) **V. thoracalis anterior** enters the posterior wall of the axillary slightly distad of the preceding branches. It accompanies the corresponding artery. (6) **V. thoracalis lateralis** enters the posterior wall of the axillary immediately before the latter divides to form the subscapular and brachial veins. It accompanies the corresponding artery to the deep pectoral and panniculus muscles, but does not receive the intercostal branches. About 70 mm. beyond its origin the axillary vein of the left fore leg bifurcates to form two branches of nearly equal size: (7) **V. subscapularis**, into which both circumflex humerals empty, and (8) **V. brachialis**. On the right leg the subscapular enters the axillary at the same level as it does on the left leg, but does not receive the circumflex humerals and consequently is much smaller. The circumflex humerals of this leg empty into a common trunk 20 mm. in length, which enters the axillary independently immediately distad of the subscapular.

The subscapular vein accompanies the subscapular artery, receiving branches that with a few exceptions conform closely to the branches of the artery. The large arterial ramus to the latissimus and subscapular muscles is accompanied by two veins whose ramifications do not correspond exactly with those of the artery. The more proximal of the two veins receives the intercostal branches (which in the arterial system come from the lateral thoracic) and the branch draining the latissimus; the distal branch drains the subscapular, teres major, and teres minor.

The two circumflex humerals, whose ramifications conform closely with those of the corresponding arteries, enter the subscapular vein independently. **V. circumflexa humeri interna** is composed of a pair of collateral vessels (a single vessel on the right leg) that enter the anterior wall of the subscapular 15 mm. beyond the origin of the latter vein. The two collateral trunks embrace the subscapular artery between them, immediately beyond which they are connected by a transverse communicating anastomosis. **V. circumflexa humeri externa** accompanies the corresponding artery through the septum between the long and lateral heads of the triceps onto the lateral side of the shoulder. It then runs along the ventral borders of the spinodeltoid and acromiodeltoid to the cephalic vein, into which it opens.

### BRACHIAL VEIN AND ITS TRIBUTARIES

V. brachialis is the continuation of the axillary beyond the origin of the subscapular trunk. It lies mesad and slightly caudad of the corresponding artery, to which its course and branchings conform

very closely as far as the elbow. Here, anterior to and slightly proximad of the entepicondylar foramen, the brachial bifurcates to form two vessels of approximately equal size: the superficial brachial and a trunk from which the ulnar and interosseous veins arise. This trunk receives **Vv. collateralis radialis, recurrens radialis, and recurrens ulnaris** before its bifurcation.

**V. brachialis superficialis** accompanies its artery distad on the forearm, receiving a large communicating branch from the cephalic in the lower third of the forearm, to the radiocarpal articulation. Here it divides into volar and dorsal branches. The volar branch forms an arch with the ulnar vein which conforms closely to the superficial arterial arch. The dorsal branch passes around the base of the radial sesamoid onto the dorsum, where it forms an anastomotic arch with the cephalic; the digital veins from digits 1, 2, and 3 open into this arch, and a perforating branch pierces the interstitium between the second and third metacarpals to form the deep volar arch with a branch from the ulnar.

**Vv. ulnaris, interosseus dorsalis, and interosseus volaris** arise together at the level of the corresponding arteries, accompanying them distad and conforming closely to their ramifications.

### CEPHALIC VEIN

V. cephalica (fig. 134) arises as one of the terminal branches of the thyrocervical vein. Passing around in front of the head of the humerus, beneath M. clavotrapezius, it emerges on the lateral side of the shoulder. Here it receives the external circumflex humeral, and then runs distad over the biceps and brachioradialis to the hollow of the elbow. Joining the lateral ramus of the superficial branch of the radial nerve on the flexor side of the forearm, it runs distad with it to the carpus. Here it divides into radial and ulnar branches. The radial branch forms an arch with the anterior brachial on the radial side of the dorsum, while the ulnar branch forms a similar arch with a branch of the ulnar vein on the ulnar side of the dorsum. The dorsal digital veins open into the resulting compound arch, the veins from the first, second, third, and radial side of the fourth into the radial arch, and the veins from the ulnar side of the fourth and from the fifth digits into the ulnar arch. There is a slender accessory vein from the ulnar side of the fifth digit.

### VENA CAVA POSTERIOR AND ITS TRIBUTARIES

The **vena cava posterior** (fig. 135) is double up to the level of the renal veins; the undivided anterior part of the postcava is only 55 mm. long.[1] The undivided part receives the following tributaries:

1. **Vv. phrenicae posterior** enter the vena cava on either side, just anterior to the renal veins. Thus the right is considerably farther forward than the left. Each posterior phrenic receives a short V. suprarenalis as it passes across the suprarenal gland.

2. Each **V. renalis** enters by a short trunk common to it and the lumboabdominal. The right is 25 mm. farther anterior than the left. As it approaches the kidney, the renal first receives a branch from the posterior part of the kidney, then two branches from the middle and anterior parts of the kidney, respectively.

3. **V. lumboabdominalis** joins the renal posteriorly on the right side and anteriorly on the left. Each joins its corresponding artery, which it follows closely.

### HYPOGASTRIC VEINS

**V. hypogastrica** (fig. 135) unites with the external iliac to form the common iliac. The junction takes place slightly anterior to the junction of the corresponding arteries. As usual, the vein differs from the artery in not having separate parietal and visceral divisions. The vein lies lateral to, and between, the parietal and visceral rami of the artery.

**V. sacralis media** enters the right hypogastric immediately before the latter enters the common iliac. From here the middle sacral runs diagonally caudad and mesad to the midline, where it joins the middle sacral artery and runs with it into the tail.

**V. glutaea anterior**, one of the two main tributaries of the hypogastric, enters its medial wall 20 mm. before its termination. Beyond this point the hypogastric continues posteriorly as a common trunk formed by the union of the middle and posterior hemorrhoidal, posterior gluteal, perineal, and penial veins. The courses of these veins correspond with those of the arteries of the same names.

[1] Raven found a similar condition in his specimen of *Ailuropoda*, so a double postcava may be normal for this species. Among the bears, the postcava divides at the normal level in a specimen of *Ursus americanus* figured by Raven, and in a specimen of *Ursus americanus* dissected by me. Raven described and figured a double postcava for *Ailurus fulgens*; this vessel was normal, but the precava was double in a specimen of *Ailurus* described by Sonntag (1921), and the postcava divides normally, at the same level as the abdominal aorta, in a specimen of *Ailurus* dissected by me. According to Beddard (1909) a double postcava occurs frequently in the Mustelidae. McClure and Huntington (1929) showed that the occurrence of a double postcava in placental mammals represents the persistence of parts of the embryonic system of cardinal veins. In view of other indications of disturbance in the lumbosacral region in *Ailuropoda*, the occurrence of a double postcava is interesting.

### PORTAL SYSTEM

The portal vein arises in the porta of the liver by the union of short right and left branches coming from the liver substance. Running caudad across the caudal lobe, it gives off (1) the splenic vein dorsad of the cervix of the pancreas, and immediately posterior to this (2) the pyloric vein. **V. coronaria ventriculi** is absent, the pyloric vein supplying the parts normally supplied by it. A few millimeters caudad of the pyloric vein the portal vein divides to form (3) the large anterior mesenteric vein and (4) the smaller posterior mesenteric vein. The total length of the portal vein is about 60 mm.

1. **V. lienalis** conforms closely to the artery of the same name, following the curvature of the gastrolienal ligament and radiating branches to the spleen which correspond to the splenic branches of the splenic artery.

2. **V. pylorica** is slightly smaller than the splenic vein, and arises from the portal vein just caudad of it. The pyloric vein immediately curves sharply cephalad, passes ventrad of the splenic vein, and accompanies the right gastric artery around the lesser curvature of the stomach. Branches are given off to the pancreas, to the duodenum, to the stomach along the whole lesser curvature, and to the esophagus.

3. **V. mesenterica anterior** may be described as the posterior continuation of the portal vein. It arises near the anterior mesenteric artery, and its course and branchings follow the arrangement of that artery very closely. The termination of the vein anastomoses with the termination of the ileocolic vein in the region of the ileum.

4. **V. mesenterica posterior** arises from the portal vein caudad of the origin of the pyloric vein. It promptly breaks up into a number of veins that supply the ileocolic region. The anterior and middle colic veins come off by a very short common trunk near the origin of the posterior mesenteric; the vein then continues as the ileocolic vein, dividing farther distad to form two main branches.

**Vv. colica anterior** and **media** conform closely to the arteries of the same names. The anterior colic vein divides into anterior and posterior branches near the intestine. The anterior branch anastomoses with the posterior branch of the ileocolic, giving off short twigs to the colon; the posterior branch anastomoses with a small anastomotic branch given off by the middle colic. The middle colic supplies the entire posterior half of the colon.

## COMMON ILIAC VEINS

The common iliac veins (V. iliaca communis, fig. 135 run craniad as far as the middle of the kidneys before they unite to form the posterior vena cava. The confluence of the common iliacs takes place slightly to the right of the midline, and ventrad of the aorta, at the level of the first lumbar vertebra. The common iliacs receive the following tributaries: (1) Vv. spermatica internae enter symmetrically, 20 mm. anterior to the origin of the internal spermatic arteries, at the confluence of the common iliacs. Each accompanies its corresponding artery to the testis, with a branch coming from the posterior renal fat. (2) Vv. lumbales consist of two vessels entering the mediodorsal wall of the right common iliac. The first of these is a large vessel entering 20 mm. behind the confluence of the two common iliacs. Branches are distributed from this trunk to the first three lumbar vertebrae. The second lumbar vein enters the common iliac at the junction of the third and fourth lumbar vertebrae; it is distributed to the fourth and fifth lumbars. (3) V. circumflex ilium profunda enters the lateral wall of each common iliac at the level of the corresponding artery. Its branches are the same as those of the artery. At the level of the articulation between the first and second sacral vertebrae the common iliac divides to form the hypogastric and external iliac veins.

## EXTERNAL ILIAC VEIN

V. iliaca externa fig. 135) is much the larger of the two roots of the common iliac. Running across the ilium in front of the iliopectineal eminence, it passes through the femoral ring posterior to the corresponding artery, and becomes the femoral vein. The external iliac receives the following branches: (1) V. iliolumbalis enters the medial wall at the level of the corresponding artery, whose branches it follows. 2) V. epigastrica posterior enters its medial wall at the iliopectineal eminence, i.e., at the level of the corresponding artery. The course of the vein agrees closely with that of the artery, branching to form V. spermatica externa and the posterior epigastric proper. 3) V. profunda femoris enters the external iliac at the femoral ring. It joins the deep femoral artery, and the course of the two vessels is similar. The main trunk of the vein consists of an anastomotic branch with the popliteal vein.

V. femoralis lies posterior to the femoral artery in the upper part of the thigh, but just below the middle of the thigh it becomes superficial to mesad of the artery. It receives two branches, V. circumflexa femoris lateralis and V. muscularis posterior. which agree closely with the cor-

responding arteries. At almost exactly the middle of the thigh the femoral vein divides to form the great saphenous and popliteal veins. The popliteal considerably exceeds the great saphenous in caliber.

V. saphena magna runs distad with the corresponding artery and the saphenous nerve. In the thigh its branchings correspond closely with those of A. genu suprema, in addition to a large muscle branch that runs forward to the knee. Between the distal ends of the heads of the semimembranosus it receives a slender branch that accompanies the plantar branch of the saphenous artery to near the distal end of the tibia, where it anastomoses with the tibialis posterior. Just beyond the distal end of the tibia the saphena magna receives an anastomotic branch, chiefly from the tibialis posterior, that runs around the tibial border of the tarsus. At the distal end of the tarsus it receives a smaller anastomotic branch from the tibialis anterior. The dorsal venous arch is formed chiefly by the saphena magna, supplemented by two small terminal twigs of the saphena parva and the superficial branch of the anterior tibial. Five dorsal metatarsal veins arise from the arch, and accompany the corresponding arteries to the toes.

V. poplitea accompanies the popliteal artery into the popliteal space, where it breaks up into a number of terminal branches. As the vein enters the popliteal space it receives a perforating branch that corresponds to the perforating branch of the femoral artery. The popliteal vein receives the following tributaries in the popliteal space, in addition to various muscle branches:

1. An anastomotic branch with the profunda femoris, which does not accompany an artery, runs proximad between the heads of the semimembranosus.

2. A genicular trunk is formed by veins whose ramifications agree with those of the genicular arteries.

3. V. saphena parva enters the posterior wall of the popliteal at about the center of the popliteal space. It runs distad on the back of the leg beneath the biceps, lying successively across the lateral head of the gastrocnemius and the soleus. At the distal end of the fibula it receives a strong anastomotic branch from the tibialis posterior. then continues along the lateral border of the tarsus and foot.

A twig arising from the saphena parva at the distal end of the fibula passes onto the tarsus, where it is joined by the distal end of the superficial anterior tibial vein; the resulting common trunk joins the much larger saphena magna to form the superficial dorsal arch. At the tarsometatarsal articulation the saphena parva gives off a branch that passes across the dorsum of the foot to the space between digits 4 and 5, where it is joined by a branch from the superficial arch to form the digital vein to the outer side of digit 5.

The saphena parva continues along the lateral border of the foot, anastomosing at the metatarsophalangeal articulation with the vein that supplies the outer side of digit 5.

4. V. suralis enters the popliteal where that vessel bifurcates into the anterior and posterior tibial veins. In addition to muscle branches to the plantaris and both heads of the gastrocnemius, it receives an anastomotic twig arising from the saphena parva near the distal end of the soleus.

5. V. tibialis anterior is slightly larger than the posterior tibial vein. It accompanies the artery of the same name through the proximal end of the interosseous space and distad along the anterolateral aspect of the leg, its branches corresponding closely to those of the artery. At the middle of the leg it divides into a larger lateral and a smaller medial branch, which flank the artery.

V. tibialis anterior superficialis arises from the lateral branch at the lower third of the leg and accompanies the superficial branch of the anterior tibial artery onto the dorsum of the foot. Here it joins a branch from the saphena parva, the resulting common trunk forming one end of the superficial dorsal arch.

The *medial* accompanying vein gives off V. tarsea medialis at the tibio-tarsal articulation, an anastomotic branch to the saphena magna in the proximal part of the tarsus, and an anastomotic branch with the lateral accompanying vein in the proximal metatarsal region, and terminates by opening into the second superficial dorsal metatarsal vein.

The *lateral* accompanying vein gives off the large V. tarsea lateralis at the tibio-tarsal articulation. The lateral tarsal supplies a nutrient vein to the tarsus. At the second inter-metatarsal space the lateral accompanying vein gives rise to two perforating branches that pass through to the deep

plantar arch. The deep dorsal arch is composed of two parallel vessels that flank the corresponding artery. The more distal of these, in which the lateral accompanying vein terminates, gives off Vv. metatarseae dorsales profundae 3 5, which enter the corresponding superficial veins near the heads of the metatarsals.

6. V. tibialis posterior accompanies the posterior tibial artery along the back of the leg. Near the distal end of the tibia it gives off a strong anastomotic branch, which passes across the leg deep to the tendon of Achilles and M. soleus, to the saphena parva. The tibialis posterior is continued beyond the anastomotic branch, considerably reduced in caliber, to the tibio-tarsal articulation. Here it divides into a superficial branch that runs around the medial side of the tarsus to anastomose with the saphena magna, and a deep branch that anastomoses with the nutrient branch of the proximal part of the tarsus.

A powerful trunk arises from the transverse anastomotic branch that passes between the saphena parva and the posterior tibial. This trunk runs distad beneath the shaft of the calcaneum, breaking up at the posterior border of the astragalus into a leash of three vessels that form both plantar arches. The *medial* of the three supplies the medial side of digit 1. The *middle* one forms the arch proper by anastomosing with a twig from the saphena parva. Branches to the lateral side of digit 1, to adjacent sides of digits 2, 3, and 4, and to the medial side of digit 5 arise from the arch; each is joined by the corresponding deep plantar metatarsal vein. The *lateral* branch runs to the lateral side of the tarsus, where it receives the terminal branches of the lateral tarsal vein. At the middle of the tarsus the vessel divides into medial and lateral branches. The medial branch arches across the sole, giving off an anastomotic branch to the saphena magna and terminating by entering the perforating branch of the anterior tibial. The lateral branch runs down the lateral border of the ankle, then arches across the sole to form the proximal of the two deep plantar arches. It terminates by entering the perforating branch of the anterior tibial vein.

# DUCTLESS GLANDS

## I. HYPOPHYSIS

The hypophysis (fig. 144) is a flattened pear-shaped structure situated posterior and slightly ventral to the optic chiasma. It is connected to the floor of the third ventricle by a short infundibulum. The hypophysis lies almost horizontally in the sella, which in *Ailuropoda* is deep, with prominent anterior and posterior processes. The hypophysis measures 10.5 mm. in length, about 9 mm. in transverse diameter (measured after bisection), and 5.5 mm. in vertical diameter. The organ was not weighed.

In sagittal section the hypophysis is seen to be composed of a smaller anterior lobe lying anteriorly and ventrally, and a larger neural lobe lying posteriorly and dorsally. The pars intermedia could not be differentiated macroscopically from the pars posterior. A dark-colored pars tuberalis embraces the infundibular stalk as far forward as the optic chiasma. As in the Ursidae, a well-developed recessus hypophysis extends from the bottom of the third ventricle through the infundibular stalk and into the posterior lobe nearly to its posterior end. Below the recessus hypophysis a hypophyseal cleft separates the anterior lobe from the posterior lobe, as it does in the bears; there is no cleft above the recessus.

In an adult female *Ursus americanus* the hypophysis is similar in size and topography to that of *Ailuropoda* but is less broadened and flattened. In this bear it measures 12.2 mm. in length, 6.6 mm. in transverse diameter, and 6.5 mm. in vertical diameter.

The hypophysis of *Thalarctos* and *Ursus arctos* were described by Hanström (1947), and that of *Ailurus fulgens* by Oboussier (1955). The topography of the hypophysis in *Ailuropoda* closely resembles that of the bears and lesser panda (especially the bears) and differs considerably from that of the Canidae. Except for a very brief description of the hypophysis of *Potos* by Oboussier, the structure of this organ in the Procyonidae is unknown.

## II. THYROID

The thyroid is composed of the customary pair of lateral lobes that lie on either side of the trachea, and are connected by a narrow isthmus. The lobes are somewhat asymmetrically situated in the specimen dissected, the left being more posterior than the right. This condition is reflected in the direction of the isthmus, which runs diagonally instead of transversely.

Each lobe has a length of about 55 mm. and a width of about 20 mm. The right lobe extends from the cricoid cartilage back to the sixth tracheal ring; the left from the second tracheal ring to the tenth. The isthmus crosses the seventh tracheal ring.

The thyroid is supplied by anterior and posterior vessels, which come from the thyrocervical trunks and the internal jugular veins.

## III. PARATHYROID BODIES

The parathyroids appear as a pair of small oval whitish structures on the dorsal surface of the thyroid gland. They are symmetrically placed, one being located on each lateral lobe about 20 mm. from its anterior tip. Each body measures about 12 mm. in length and 4 mm. in width. The left body is partly buried in the substance of the thyroid, while the right lies wholly on the surface.

## IV. THYMUS

The thymus is an elongate bilobed gland, pale chocolate brown in color. It is rather well developed, with a length of 117 mm. The gland lies wholly within the mediastinum, its anterior end reaching only slightly beyond the middle of the first costal cartilage. The left lobe considerably exceeds the right in size. Both lobes lie to the left of the left innominate vein, and are crossed ventrally by the left mammary artery and vein.

A quantity of fat at either end of the thymus indicates that regression of this structure was well under way.

The thymus is supplied by branches from the mammary vessels.

# NERVOUS SYSTEM

## I. BRAIN

The brain of the adult female giant panda Pan Dee was described briefly by Mettler and Goss (1946). The description given here is based on the brain of the subadult male Su Lin. It was embalmed *in situ* and later removed by sectioning the skull. The brain was undamaged.

The brain of Su Lin weighed 238 grams, minus the dura but including the pia mater and arachnoid. This gives a ratio to body weight of 1 : 252. It measured 115 mm. in total length and 85 mm. in breadth. The brain of the adult male Mei Lan weighed 277 grams, giving a ratio to body weight of about 1 : 496. This brain was partly decomposed and not suitable for study.

In dorsal view the brain is almost circular in outline, but is somewhat acuminate anteriorly. The olfactory bulbs project prominently beyond the cerebrum. Posteriorly the cerebrum covers a little less than half of the cerebellum. In lateral view the brain is almost flat inferiorly. The superior outline is arched, acuminate anteriorly and truncated at the posterior margin of the cerebellum. An endocranial cast of an adult skull (fig. 143) is much depressed in the frontal region, giving the brain an almost triangular outline in profile view. This reflects the degree of expansion of the dorsal sinus system in the skull of this individual.

### RHOMBENCEPHALON

#### Medulla oblongata

This region is short and broad, and conical in form, tapering posteriorly. The distance from the rear margin of the pons to the decussation of the pyramids is 12.5 mm. The pyramids stand out prominently, and the median ventral fissure is correspondingly deep. The olive region is broad and flat. Cranial nerves IX XII arise at the usual sites. The roots of the glossopharyngeal, vagus, and accessorius cannot be separated from one another. The corpus trapezoides, lying immediately behind the pons, is not clearly defined. From it arise the facial and auditory nerves (VII and VIII). The abducens (VI) arises in the angle between the lateral border of the pyramid and the posterior border of the corpus trapezoides.

#### Pons

The pons is a flattened eminence, 27 mm. in transverse diameter. It is broadest at its posterior margin and therefore somewhat trapezoidal in outline. The basilar sulcus is very shallow. The root of the trigeminal nerve (V) arises from the posterolateral angle of the pons.

#### Cerebellum

The cerebellum is spindle-shaped in dorsal view, almost circular in sagittal section. It measures 59 mm. in breadth by 36 mm. in length, and weighs about 35 grams, about 15 per cent of total brain weight. On a mid-sagittal section (fig. 146) the cortex is extensive and richly foliated, the medulla correspondingly small. The central gray substance is small and stellate, the limbs of the arbor vitae slender. A narrow, deep fastigium extends nearly vertically from the roof of the fourth ventricle to the central gray substance. Directly opposite the fastigium the primary fissure divides the cerebellum into anterior and posterior parts. The anterior part is slightly the larger. The relations of the remaining lobes and fissures are shown in the illustration.

In dorsal view the anterior lobe is broad, with a U-shaped posterior boundary marked by the primary fissure. The lunate lobule (simplex of Bolk, 1906, and Haller, 1934) is narrow and crescent-shaped, embracing the anterior lobe from behind. The posterior boundary is easily distinguished because the folia of the lunate are continuous across the paramedian sulcus, whereas those of the median lobe are not. The limbs of the lunate lobule exclude the ansiform lobule from contact with the anterior lobe, except at the extreme anterior end of the cerebellum. The unpaired lobulus medianus posterior of Bolk (1906), separated from the paired lateral lobes by the paramedian sulcus, is divided by transverse fissures into a short median lobe (tuber vermis), a longer pyramis, a uvula, and a nodulus. The tuber vermis is straight as in other arctoids.

The ansiform lobule is large and very similar to that of the Ursidae, composed of two crura separated by a deep and slightly S-shaped intercrural sulcus. It hides the paraflocculus almost completely in dorsal view. The pteroid area (crus I

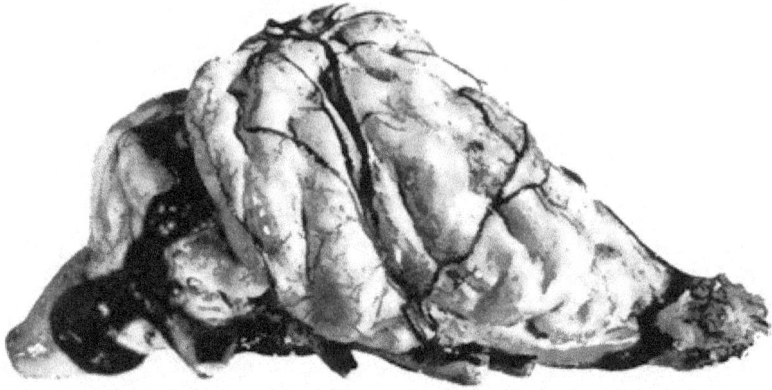

FIG. 143.   Endocranial cast of adult female *Ailuropoda* (CNHM 36758).   Lateral view (× 1).

of the ansiform lobule) is broad and triangular, and continues without interruption into crus II. Crus II is worm-like, with regular transverse folia, and is faintly S-shaped.   Bolk describes a secondary, ventrally concave loop (the "ansula") in crus II in *Ursus arctos*, *Thalarctos maritimus*, and *Felis leo*, and I found this loop well developed in two specimens of *Ursus americanus*.   It is absent in the brain of *Ailuropoda*.   Medially crus II continues without interruption into the paramedian lobule, which descends vertically on the posterior

surface of the cerebellum, lying between the pyramis and the medial end of the paraflocculus.

The paraflocculus closely resembles that of the Ursidae.   It is a large U-shaped lobe composed of regular transverse folia, giving it a worm-like appearance.   The larger superior limb abuts against the inferior end of the paramedian lobule, the smaller and shorter inferior limb terminates against the flocculus.   The petrosal lobule, at the convexity of the U, does not protrude beyond the remainder of the paraflocculus.   The flocculus is a

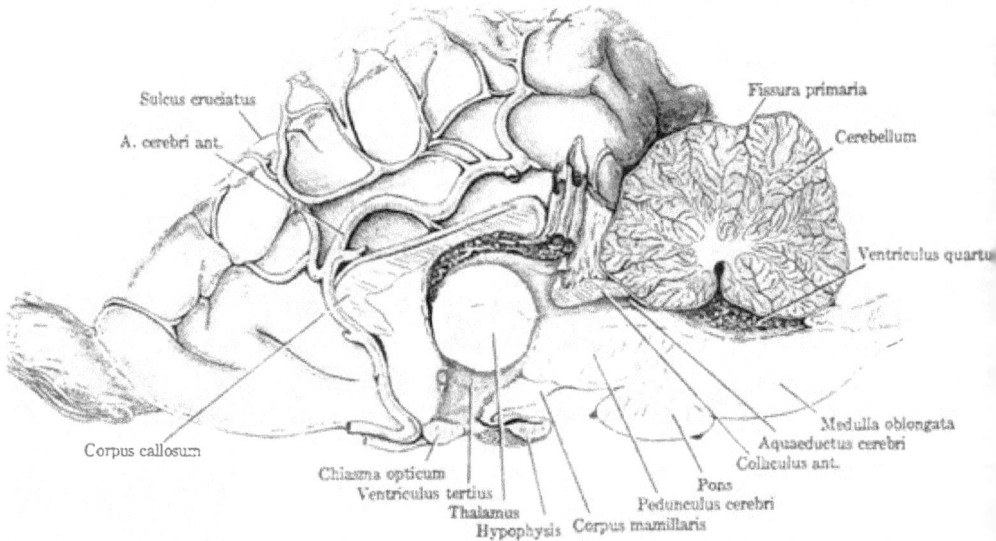

FIG. 144.   Brain of *Ailuropoda*, mid-sagittal section (× 1).

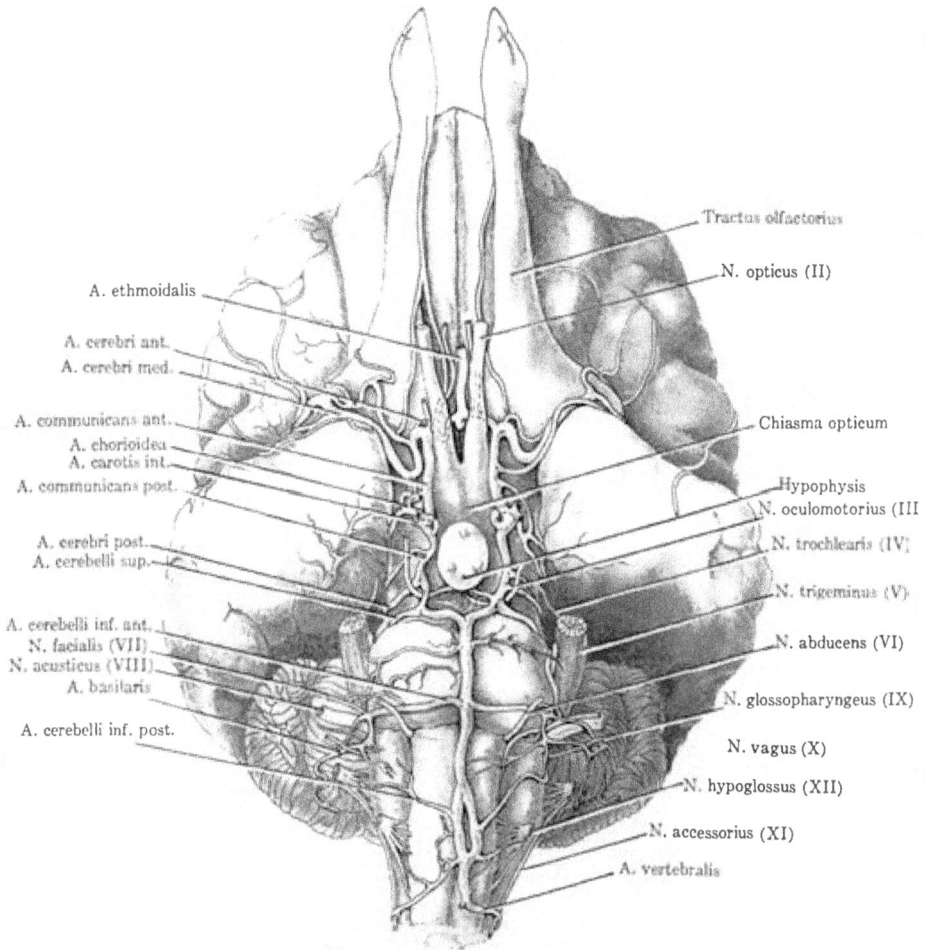

Tractus olfactorius

N. opticus (II)

A. ethmoidalis

A. cerebri ant.
A. cerebri med.

A. communicans ant.
A. chorioidea
A. carotis int.
A. communicans post.

Chiasma opticum

Hypophysis
N. oculomotorius (III

A. cerebri post.
A. cerebelli sup.

N. trochlearis (IV)

N. trigeminus (V)

A. cerebelli inf. ant.
N. facialis (VII)
N. acusticus (VIII)
A. basilaris

N. abducens (VI)

N. glossopharyngeus (IX)

A. cerebelli inf. post.

N. vagus (X)

N. hypoglossus (XII)

N. accessorius (XI)

A. vertebralis

FIG. 145.   Brain of *Ailuropoda*, inferior view (× 1).

small lamella wedged in between the inferior limb of the paraflocculus and the cerebellar peduncle.

*Fourth ventricle*

On sagittal section this appears as a roomy chamber, narrowing rather abruptly anteriorly and posteriorly. Its floor is distinctly concave.

MIDBRAIN AND THALAMUS

These structures were studied only on a midsagittal section through the brain (fig. 144).

*Midbrain*

The aquaeductus cerebri (sylvii) is of almost uniform diameter in sagittal section, only a little larger

posteriorly than anteriorly. It lies only slightly above the level of the fourth ventricle. The corpora quadrigemina (colliculi anteriores and posteriores) roof over the anterior part of the aqueduct. Each anterior quadrigeminate body is a low rounded hillock, much broader than long. The posterior body, on the contrary, scarcely forms an elevation.

The optic tract emerges from beneath the pyriform lobe of the cerebrum, closely applied to the cerebral peduncle. In front of the tuber cinereum the optic tract leaves the optic chiasma, from which the optic nerves (II) arise. Mettler and Goss commented on the small diameter of the optic

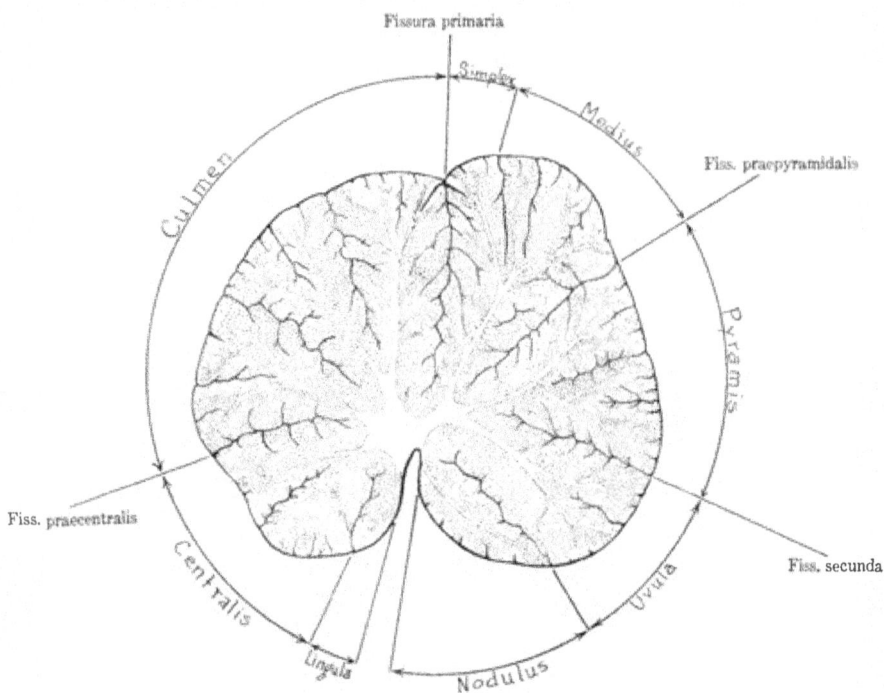

FIG. 146. Cerebellum of *Ailuropoda*, mid-sagittal section.

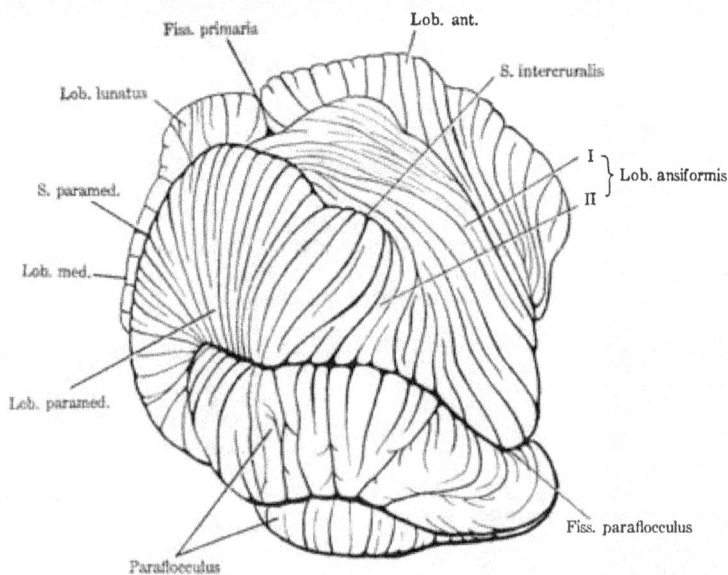

FIG. 147. Cerebellum of *Ailuropoda*, lateral view.

292

nerves, but I find them relatively no smaller than in a specimen of *Ursus americanus*.

A sagittal section through the cerebral peduncles at the interpeduncular fossa is nearly rectangular in outline. In inferior view the peduncles appear as broad tracts emerging from beneath the optic tracts and converging to disappear into the pons. The mammillary bodies form a low rounded eminence, scarcely subdivided into a paired structure, lying in the angle between the limbs of the cerebral peduncles. The oculomotor nerve (III) arises as usual from the interpeduncular fossa.

### Thalamus

In mid-sagittal section the thalamus is circular, surrounded by a rather narrow third ventricle.

### CEREBRUM

In mid-sagittal section the corpus callosum appears as the usual U-shaped structure, 31 mm. in length, with a nearly straight body, a sharply bent knee, and a slightly arched splenium. A deep sulcus corporis callosi separates it from the cerebral convolutions lying directly above it.

### Gyri and sulci

These were mapped by Mettler and Goss on the brain of the panda Pan Dee. The configuration in our specimen differs from theirs only in unimportant details. The nomenclature used here is largely that of Papez (1929).

As in carnivores in general, the pattern of gyri and sulci in *Ailuropoda* is characterized by a concentric series of vertical arches (the arcuate convolutions) arranged around a central sylvian fissure, with vertical furrows predominating over horizontal on the whole cerebral cortex. There is a deep sylvian fossa, with the sylvian fissure and sylvian gyri (first arcuate convolution) hidden from view within the fossa, as in the Ursidae (Holl, 1899; Smith, W. K., 1933a), *Procyon* (Papez, 1929), and Mustelidae (Holl, 1899). The lips of the sylvian fossa are formed by the second arcuate convolution, composed of the anterior and posterior ectosylvian gyri. The anterior ectosylvian gyrus is more slender and lies slightly deeper than the posterior. The third arcuate convolution is composed of the anterior and posterior suprasylvian gyri.

The coronal sulcus is conspicuous, sinuous, and oriented at an angle of about 45° to the basal plane of the brain. It is continuous dorsally with the lateral sulcus, as in the Ursidae. The inferior temporal gyrus is represented by the inferior loop connecting the posterior ectosylvian and posterior suprasylvian gyri, and is continuous with both of these gyri. The temporal lobe of the cortex, represented by the sylvian, posterior ectosylvian, poste-

rior suprasylvian, and inferior temporal gyri (Papez, 1929), is only moderately developed as compared with that of the dog or cat, resembling that of the bears.

The coronal gyrus is very large and bifid inferiorly (this cleft was absent in the brain of Pan Dee). In *Ursus* and other arctoids the inferior end of the coronal gyrus extends forward beneath the posterior sigmoid gyrus to meet the inferior end of the anterior sigmoid gyrus. In *Ailuropoda*, however, the coronal gyrus is separated from the anterior sigmoid gyrus by the downward expansion of the posterior sigmoid gyrus.

The postcruciate gyrus is continuous anteriorly with the posterior sigmoid gyrus. It is well developed and subdivided by short shallow furrows, and is considerably more extensive than the corresponding gyrus in our specimen of *Ursus americanus* (fig. 149). The postcruciate gyrus, together with the coronal gyrus, represents somatic afferent area I.

The ansate sulcus, separating the postcruciate from the posterior sigmoid area, is a short sagittal furrow unconnected with any other furrow. In bears the ansate may be similarly isolated (Haller, 1934, fig. 195), or it may be connected with the lateral sulcus (fig. 148).

The sigmoid gyri, surrounding the cruciate sulcus, are extensive. The posterior sigmoid gyrus (motor area I) is much expanded ventrally. The inferior, expanded part of this gyrus corresponds to the facial-masticatory motor area in *Ursus* (Smith, W. K., 1933b). The cruciate sulcus, separating the frontal from the sigmoidal area, extends only a short distance onto the medial surface of the hemisphere, and is not connected with any other sulcus.

Anteriorly there is a well-developed frontal area. It is divided into three well-marked frontal gyri: a superior, separated from the posterior sigmoid by the cruciate sulcus, a middle frontal, and an inferior frontal (proreal). The superior frontal gyrus, the "ursine lozenge," is about as well developed as in the bears. The short sagittally directed proreal sulcus extends forward from the presylvian sulcus, separating the middle and inferior frontal gyri.

The lateral gyrus is broad, and is subdivided into two parts by a parietal sulcus, as in *Ursus*. The lateral sulcus is continuous with the postlateral sulcus, which separates the posterior suprasylvian gyrus from the ectolateral gyrus. The postlateral sulcus terminates at about the level of the lower third of the cerebrum, on both sides of the brain; in the brain of Pan Dee it continued down into the temporal pole, as in *Ursus*. In the brain of Su Lin the ectolateral gyrus is interrupted by a short

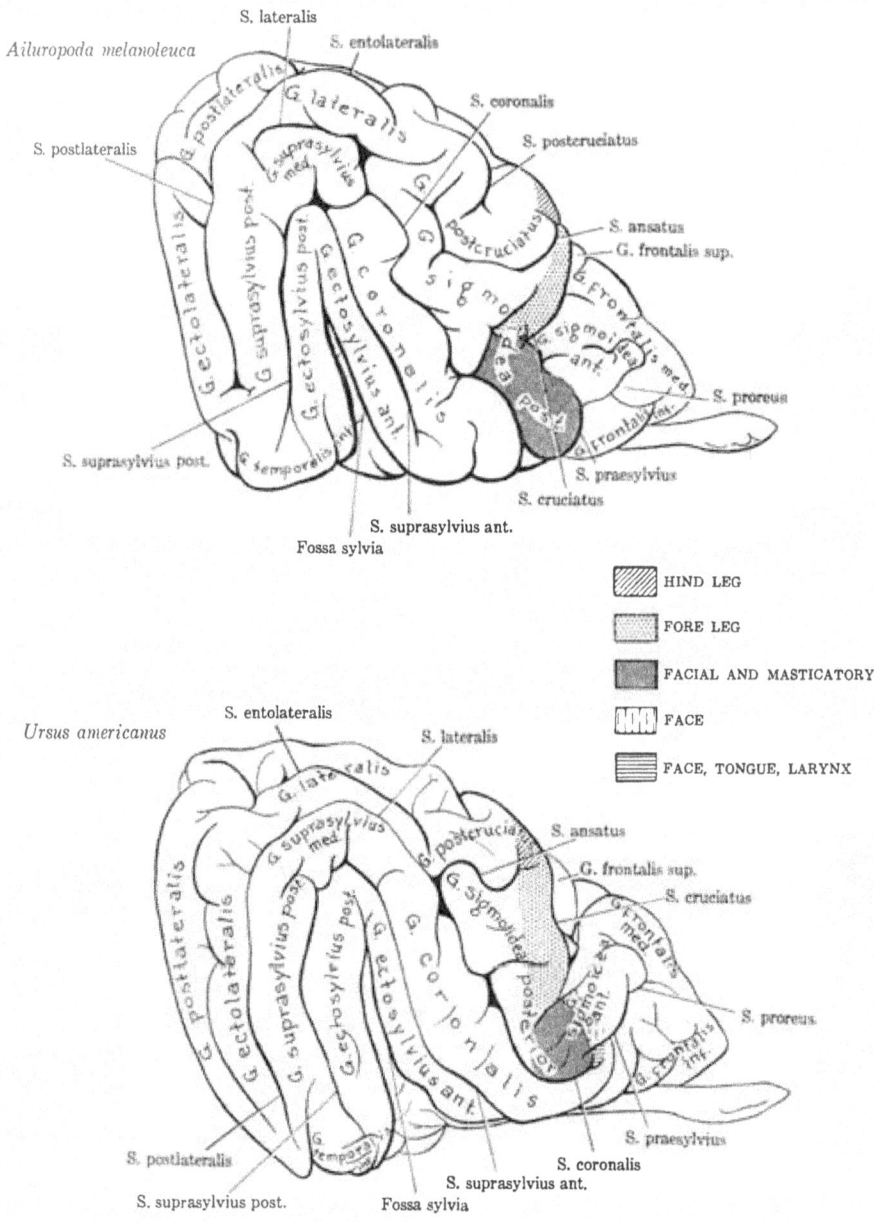

FIG. 148. Right cerebral hemisphere of *Ailuropoda* and *Ursus* to show patterns of gyri and sulci. Lateral view. Motor area I in *Ursus* mapped from Smith (1933b). Note particularly the expanded masticatory motor area in *Ailuropoda*.

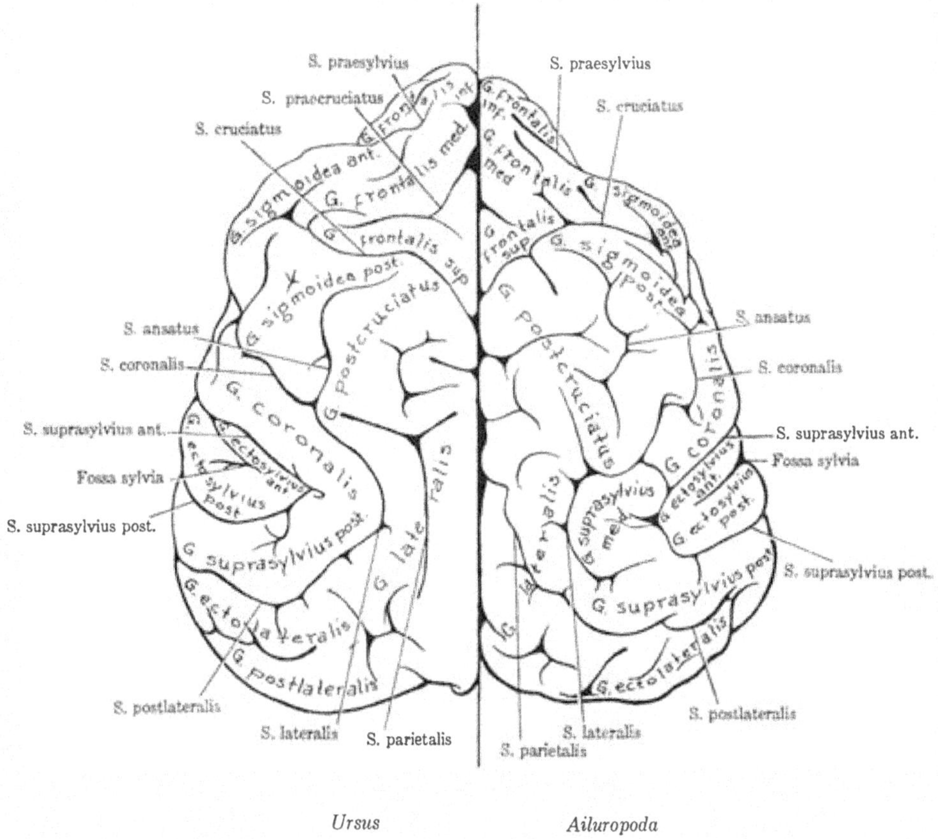

*Ursus*                              *Ailuropoda*

Fig. 149. Right cerebral hemisphere of *Ailuropoda* and left cerebral hemisphere of *Ursus americanus* to show patterns of gyri and sulci. Dorsal view.

transverse furrow in the temporal region; this secondary furrow is only indicated by a notch in the brain of Pan Dee, and is completely absent in *Ursus*.

On the medial surface of the cerebrum (fig. 150) the cortex is divided by a deep and nearly continuous furrow, paralleling the corpus callosum, into a dorsal and a ventral system of gyri. The furrow begins posteriorly with a very deep and nearly vertical calcarine sulcus, which above terminates abruptly in a short transverse furrow. Behind the calcarine sulcus lies the broad lingual gyrus, cleft by a postcalcarine sulcus and behind this by a paracalcarine sulcus, both of which parallel the calcarine sulcus. A short intercalary sulcus connects anteriorly with a long cingular sulcus, from which three short lateral furrows go off at right angles. Anteriorly, the cruciate sulcus is continued into a

U-shaped rostral sulcus. The genual sulcus is a short diagonal fissure behind the rostral sulcus. The system of sulci on the medial surface of the rostral region is much simpler than in *Ursus* (see also Smith, W. K., 1933a, fig. 6).

The inferior end of the calcarine sulcus is continuous with a well-developed sulcus on the inferior surface of the brain, running laterad behind the rhinal fissure. According to Elliot Smith (1902) this sulcus is fully developed only in bears (see also Smith, W. F., 1933a, fig. 8), and was called by him the "ursine sulcus." It is as well developed in *Ailuropoda* as in the bears.

The parasplenial gyrus is remarkably broad. It is bounded inferiorly by the corpus callosum, posteriorly by the calcarine sulcus, and superiorly by the intercalary and cingular sulci. Anteriorly it continues without interruption into the cingular

*Ailuropoda melanoleuca*

S. verticalis

S. cingularis    S. intercalaris

S. suprasplenialis

S. cruciatus

G suprasplenialis

med

G parietalis med

G parasplenialis

S. postcalcarinus

sup

G parietalis

G frontalis

G cingularis

Corpus callosum

S. paracalcarinus

G lingualis

Thalamus

S. calcarinus

G rectus

S. rostralis

S. ursinus

S. genualis

*Ursus americanus*

S. intercalaris

S. verticalis

S. cingularis    S. suprasplenialis

S. cruciatus

G suprasplenialis

G parietalis med

S. genualis

G parasplenialis

S. calcarinus

S. rostralis

G frontalis sup

G cingularis

Corpus callosum

S. paracalcarinus

G lingualis

G subcallosa

Thalamus

G rectus

S. ursinus

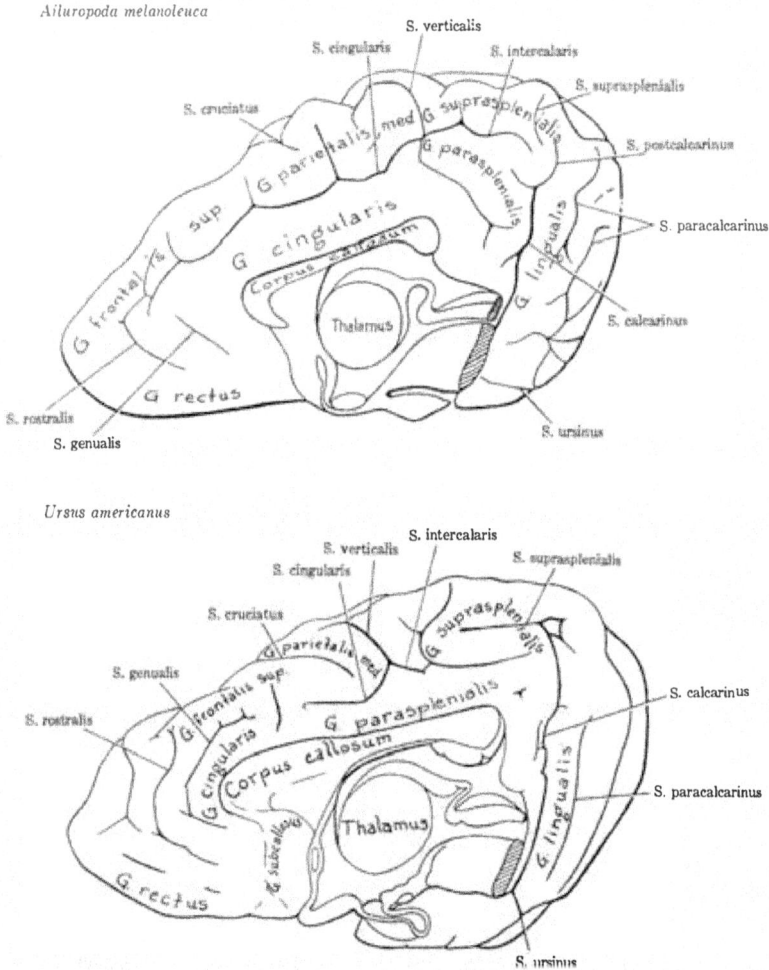

FIG. 150.  Medial surface of right cerebral hemisphere of *Ailuropoda* and *Ursus* to show patterns of gyri and sulci.

gyrus, which is also notably broad. The straight and subcallosal gyri are poorly marked. The suprasplenial gyrus bears a short, nearly vertical suprasplenial sulcus instead of the longitudinal one usually present in carnivores. The middle parietal gyrus is much longer than in *Ursus*. Because of the short distance that the cruciate sulcus extends onto the medial surface of the hemisphere, the middle parietal gyrus is continuous with the superior frontal gyrus.

CENTRAL OLFACTORY STRUCTURES

The olfactory brain of *Ailuropoda* is much reduced compared with the corresponding structures

in a brain of *Ursus americanus*. The bulbs are relatively smaller, and the olfactory stalks slender.

The olfactory bulbs are ovate structures, about 16 mm. in length, lying anterior to the cerebrum. The olfactory tracts are prominent but slender. Each divides posteriorly into lateral and medial parts. The lateral olfactory tract is much the larger. It is a rope-like structure that diverges from the midline as it runs posteriorly; it terminates in the pyriform lobe. The medial olfactory tract is a short flat band that separates from the lateral tract and runs posteriorly and medially to the olfactory tubercle. The olfactory tubercle is a low eminence, perforated by numerous holes for blood vessels, lying just anterior and medial to the tip of the pyriform lobe. Between the olfactory tubercle and the optic tract is a rather broad diagonal band of Broca, the lateral end of which disappears beneath the pyriform lobe.

## DISCUSSION OF BRAIN

Comparative studies of the brain in the Carnivora have dealt almost entirely with the pattern of the gyri and sulci in the cerebral cortex. The morphology of these structures was compared by Krueg (1880), Mivart (1885b), Holl (1889), Klatt (1928), Papez (1929) and Haller (1934). Motor areas in the cortex of *Ursus* were mapped by W. K. Smith (1933b), and both motor and sensory areas in *Procyon* by Welker and Seidenstein (1959) and in *Canis* most recently by Pinto Hamuy, Bromiley and Woolsey (1956).

The brain of *Procyon* has been figured by Klatt, Papez, and Welker and Seidenstein, that of *Nasua* by Klatt, and of *Ailurus* by Flower (1870) and Klatt. Bear brains have been figured by Mivart, Papez, W. K. Smith (1933a), Haller, and others. I had the following arctoid brains available for comparison: *Bassariscus astutus* (1), *Procyon lotor* (3), *Nasua narica* (1), *Ailurus fulgens* (1), *Ursus americanus* (2).

The question of whether the sulci demarcate physiological subdivisions of the cortex or are mere artifacts resulting from expansion of the cortex is of considerable importance, since it is unlikely that the brains of more than a few species will ever be studied experimentally in the living state. This question has been much disputed (Haller, 1934). The work of Welker and Seidenstein indicates that at least in the Carnivora the sulci do delimit true physiological subdivisions, the correspondence in *Procyon* extending down to such small anatomical units as the individual digits. They found a faithful relation maintained despite individual variations in the location and orientation of the sulci.

Of similar interest is the question of whether there is a correlation between degree of receptor specialization and degree of cortical elaboration. Such a correlation has been found for every example of a highly specialized function that has been checked experimentally (reviewed by Welker and Seidenstein, 1959), and we may therefore assume with some confidence that similar correlations exist in animals where experimental verification is impossible.

The pattern of gyri and sulci is remarkably uniform in all canids (Mivart, 1885b; Klatt, 1928), and more primitive than that of the Procyonidae and Ursidae. The Procyonidae and Ursidae, in

turn, have a common pattern. The pattern in *Ailurus* is more primitive than in *Procyon* and *Nasua*, but definitely represents the procyonid-ursid type (Klatt).

In the procyonids and bears the sigmoidal (motor I) and coronal and postcruciate (somatic afferent) areas of the cortex are greatly expanded, and elaboration of these areas is associated with a corresponding elaboration of the motor and sensory functions (Smith, W. K., 1933b; Welker and Seidenstein, 1959). The morphological result of this expansion is that (1) the superior end of the sylvian fossa tends to be crowded posteriorly, (2) the sylvian gyri (first arcuate convolution) are crowded into the sylvian fossa, where they are hidden from view, and (3) the postcruciate area is considerably divided up by secondary fissures, especially in the Procyonidae. On the medial surface of the hemisphere the cruciate sulcus fails to meet the cingular sulcus, at least in *Procyon*, *Ailurus*, and the Ursidae. These two sulci meet in all canids.

The bears and procyonids differ in a few important respects, and in several minor details summarized briefly by Mettler and Goss. The frontal area of the cortex is relatively larger in bears, and the superior frontal gyrus appears on the surface as a well-developed "ursine lozenge," a structure that is rudimentary in procyonids and absent in other carnivores. The procyonid brain is notable for the great expansion of the postcruciate area (the central part of somatic afferent area I). As a result of this expansion the continuity of the coronal-lateral sulcus is broadly interrupted, whereas in the Ursidae these two sulci are continuous as in other arctoids. Welker and Seidenstein (1959) have shown that this expanded part of somatic afferent area I is devoted to the hand in *Procyon*. In the bears the lateral gyrus is divided longitudinally by a parietal sulcus (often indicated in dogs), whereas in procyonids this gyrus is narrower and lacks the parietal sulcus.

Gross differences in the cerebral cortex between the Canidae on the one hand, and the Procyonidae and Ursidae on the other, are attributable almost entirely to expansion of three areas in the procyonid-bear brain. These are (1) the postcruciate-coronal area, (2) the sigmoidal area, and (3) the frontal area. These cannot be attributed to differences in brain size, since the procyonids are considerably smaller than large dogs. Experimental studies have shown, on the contrary, that elaboration of the first two of these areas is associated with elaboration of manual and prehensile functions in procyonids and bears.

In *Ailuropoda* the pattern of gyri and sulci agrees closely with that of the Ursidae. Mettler and Goss state that the arrangement in *Ailuropoda* "is so similar to what is seen in the bears that one is forced to rely on small variations from the ursine pattern to detect any differences in the brain." The brain of Su Lin differs in minor details from the brain of Pan Dee as described and figured by Mettler and Goss, but confirms the close similarity in gross brain structure between the giant panda and the bears. The cortex of *Ailuropoda* differs in two points that seem to be of importance: (1) The postcruciate area is considerably larger than in *Ursus*. A similar, though even more extensive elaboration of this area is associated with elaboration of sensory functions of the hand in *Procyon* (Welker and Seidenstein). It is reasonable to assume a similar correlation in *Ailuropoda*. (2) The inferior end of the posterior sigmoid gyrus is considerably larger than in *Ursus*. This is the facial-masticatory motor area in *Ursus* (Smith, W. K., 1933b), and its elaboration in *Ailuropoda* is associated with elaboration of the masticatory function. The motor area for the fore limb does not appear to be any larger than in *Ursus*.

*Thus the two elements of major adaptive specialization in* Ailuropoda *(the hand and the masticatory apparatus) are both associated with elaboration of the corresponding areas of the cerebral cortex.*

The gross structure of the cerebellum offers little of interest within the Carnivora. Eight carnivores, including three arctoids (*Canis familiaris*, *Ursus arctos*, *Thalarctos maritimus*) were included in the material used by Bolk (1906). In general, the cerebellum is better developed in bears than in *Canis*. This is particularly evident in crus II of the ansiform lobule, in which a secondary loop (the ansula) is present in bears. The ansula is absent in *Ailuropoda* and the Procyonidae.

Among the Carnivora, the cerebellum is largest in the Ursidae (15.8–16.3 per cent of total brain weight in three individuals), smallest in the Canidae (average 9.5 per cent in 16 domestic dogs) (Putnam, 1928). No values are available for any procyonid. My figure for *Ailuropoda* (15 per cent) is very similar to that for the bears.

CONCLUSIONS

1. Gross differences in brain structure among arctoid carnivores involve chiefly the cerebral cortex.

2. In the Canidae the cerebral cortex is less specialized than in the Procyonidae and Ursidae.

3. In the Procyonidae and Ursidae the cerebral cortex has been modified by expansion of three areas: the sigmoidal, coronal and postcruciate, and frontal. The first two are associated with enhanced prehensile and tactile functions of the fore limb in raccoons and bears.

4. In gross structure the brain of *Ailuropoda* agrees closely with the brain of the Ursidae in all respects.

5. The postcruciate gyrus (somatic afferent area for the fore limb) and the inferior end of the posterior sigmoid gyrus (masticatory motor area) are larger in *Ailuropoda* than in *Ursus*.

II. CRANIAL NERVES

*N. Opticus* (II) (fig. 151)

The optic nerve emerges from the optic foramen, to pursue a faintly S-shaped course to the eye ball. It has a diameter of about 2.5 mm., and its length from the optic foramen to the back of the eye ball is 50 mm.

*N. Oculomotorius* (III) (fig. 151)

The oculomotor nerve is the most medial of the nerves passing out of the orbital fissure. Just before reaching the base of the rectus superior muscle it divides into superior and inferior branches. The smaller superior branch passes along the lateral border of the rectus superior, supplying that muscle and giving off a fine twig to the levator palpebrae superioris.

The inferior branch passes forward between the rectus superior and the retractor oculi, then beneath the optic nerve. At about the middle of the optic nerve it gives off a branch to the rectus medialis, a branch to the rectus inferior, then the *Radix brevis ganglii ciliaris*, and is itself continued as a branch to the oblique inferior.

*N. Trochlearis* (IV) (fig. 151)

The trochlear nerve is the most dorsal of the nerves passing out of the orbital fissure. It passes forward above the rectus superior and levator palpebrae superior to the dorsal border of the superior oblique. The nerve enters the latter muscle at about its middle.

*N. Trigeminus* (V)

N. Ophthalmicus (Trigeminus 1)

The ophthalmic nerve emerges from the skull through the orbital fissure, situated within the ophthalmic vein. It emerges from the vein at the posterior third of the orbit, where the vein breaks up into its terminal branches. The ophthalmic nerve has only two main branches, the frontal and the nasociliary.[1] The nerve separates into these branches at the semilunar ganglion.

1. N. frontalis (fig. 152) is slightly smaller than the nasociliary. It accompanies the frontal artery and superior orbital vein over the dorsal surface of

---

[1] The lacrimal branch of the human ophthalmic forms a part of the maxillary nerve in carnivores (see p. 30).

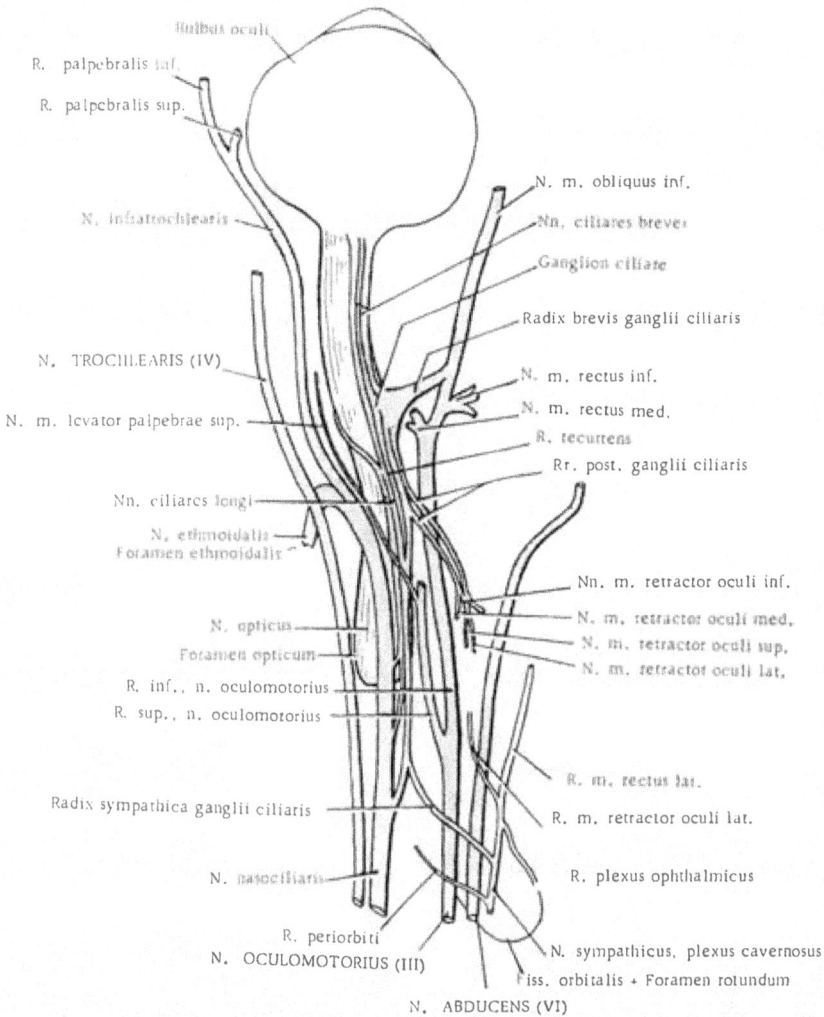

FIG. 151. Nerves of right orbit of *Ailuropoda*, dorsal view (semi-diagrammatic). The frontal, lacrimal, and zygomatic nerves have been removed.

M. obliquus superior, all three structures piercing the dorsal wall of the periorbita at about the middle of the orbit and passing together into the supraorbital space.

**Rr. periorbiti**, the first branches of the frontal, are a pair of delicate twigs arising from the frontal as it emerges from the orbital fissure. They pass to the dorsal wall of the periorbita. At their bases the periorbital branches receive a sympathetic twig from the plexus cavernosus.

The frontal nerve breaks up into three subequal terminal branches as it pierces the periorbita. **N. supratrochlearis**, the first to come off and the most laterally situated, passes forward above the pulley of the superior oblique muscle, emerging onto the forehead immediately above the eye. **N. supraorbitalis** runs immediately in front of the postorbital ligament, continuing onto the forehead above and behind the eye. **R. frontalis**, the most medial of the terminal branches, runs

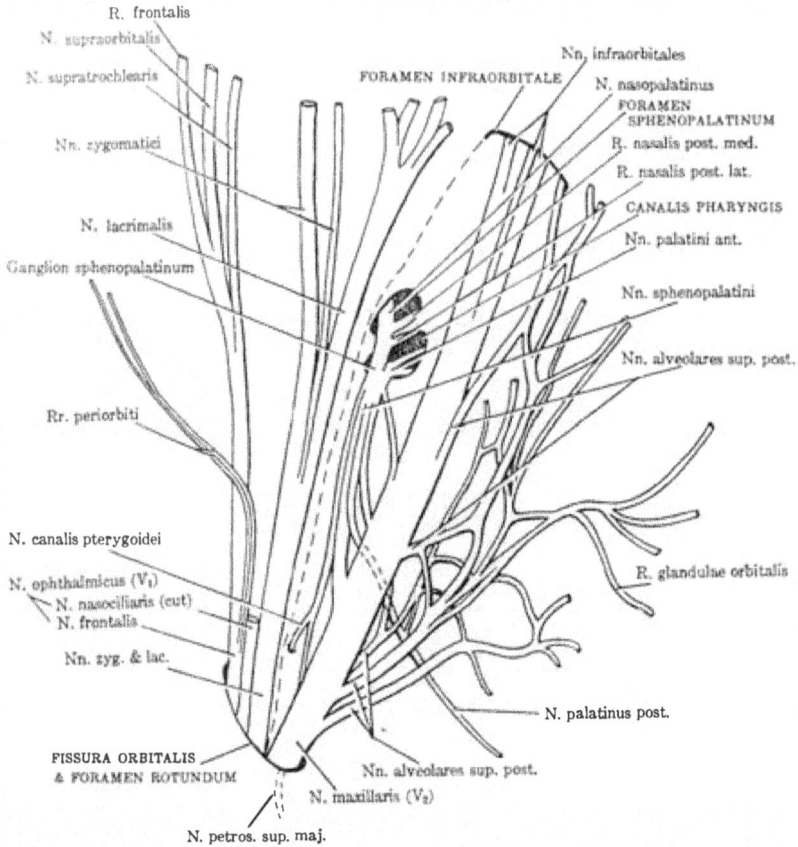

FIG. 152. Maxillary nerve (V₂) and frontal branch of ophthalmic of *Ailuropoda*. Dorsal view.

onto the forehead beside the supraorbital nerve, passing into the frontal area above the eye.

2. **N. nasociliaris** runs forward, at first lying on the retractor muscles of the eye, then passing between the superior rectus and the optic nerve. The nasociliary terminates, after crossing over the optic nerve, by dividing into the infratrochlear and ethmoidal nerves. The nasociliary nerve gives rise to the following branches:

(a) **Nn. ciliares longi,** two in number, come off before the nasociliary reaches the level of the optic foramen. These arise by three roots, with a fourth root **(Radix sympathicus ganglii ciliaris)** coming from the plexus cavernosus. Beyond the optic foramen the two nerves separate. One passes to the medial side of the optic nerve, while the other remains on its lateral side, joining the short ciliary nerves at the level of the ciliary

ganglion and continuing forward with them. As it approaches the ciliary ganglion, the lateral long ciliary nerve gives off the **Radix longa ganglii ciliaris.**

(b) **N. infratrochlearis,** the smaller of the two terminal branches, passes forward under the pulley of the obliquus superior muscle. It divides into superior and inferior palpebral branches directly beneath the pulley.

(c) **N. ethmoidalis** arches back around the base of the obliquus superior, to enter the ethmoidal foramen.

**Ganglion ciliare** is a small, triangular, much flattened body situated on the lateral side of the optic nerve about 20 mm. behind its entrance into the eye ball. *Roots:* (a) The short root is a short, heavy branch derived from the branch of the oculomotor supplying the obliquus inferior. (b) The long root arises from the more lateral of the two long ciliary nerves. (c) The sympathetic root, which comes from the plexus cavernosus, accompanies the long ciliary nerve and is macroscopically inseparable from it through most of its course. *Branches:* (a) Several **Nn. ciliares breves** leave the anterior end of the ganglion and accompany the long ciliary nerve to the eye ball. (b) Two branches leaving the posterior end of the ganglion supply the retractor oculi. (c) A slender recurrent branch passes on the optic nerve back to the optic foramen.

### N. maxillaris (Trigeminus 2)

The maxillary nerve (fig. 152) emerges from the skull through the combined orbital fissure and foramen rotundum. The maxillary nerve lies in the lateral part of the foramen, and is separated from the ophthalmic nerve by the periorbita. It passes anteriorly along the inferior border of the periorbita, giving off numerous branches in the suborbital space, and terminating near the infraorbital foramen by breaking up into several infraorbital nerves.

The branches of the maxillary nerve are:

1. **N. meningeus medius** can be seen as a delicate twig running along the posterior border of the anterior branch of the middle meningeal artery. It arises from the common trunk of the lacrimal and zygomatic nerves just before that trunk enters the orbital fissure.

2. The trunk for the lacrimal and zygomatic nerves arises from the maxillary inside the skull. The common trunk of the two nerves passes forward inside the periorbita, dividing into lacrimal and zygomatic components at the posterior third of the orbit. **N. lacrimalis**, the most ventral component, passes forward to the lacrimal gland. Twigs from this nerve leave the orbit at the outer angle of the eye, passing across the zygoma to anastomose with the zygomatic branch of the facial nerve. **Nn. zygomatici**, two in number, leave the orbit by piercing the orbital ligament. They anastomose with temporal branches of the facial nerve in the temporal region.

3. **Nn. alveolares superiores posteriores** arise by five roots from the lateral side of the maxillary nerve as it lies in the suborbital space. These roots unite to form a loose plexus that extends nearly from the orbital fissure to the infraorbital foramen, and twigs arising from this plexus ramify to the minute foramina in the alveolar prominence; thus they supply the molar teeth exclusively. The most anterior twig passes into the infraorbital foramen.

4. **Nn. sphenopalatini** arise by four roots from the medial side of the maxillary nerve in the posterior half of the orbit. These roots unite just before they enter the sphenopalatine ganglion. The **ganglion sphenopalatinum** is situated just outside the opening of the pharyngeal canal, and is quite inconspicuous. The following branches arise from it: (a) **N. palatinus posterior** is a slender twig arising from the posterior end of the ganglion. It passes backward, joining the A. canalis pterygoidei and accompanying it through the notch in the outer border of the vertical pterygoid plate to the soft palate. (b) **N. canalis pterygoidei** also arises from the posterior end of the ganglion. It enters a small foramen situated directly below the optic foramen, through which it passes to the roof of the pharynx. (c) **Nn. palatini anteriores** arise from the anterior end of the ganglion. They enter the pterygopalatine canal, emerging onto the hard palate through both the greater and the lesser palatine foramina. (d) **N. nasopalatinus**, the largest nerve arising from the ganglion, immediately joins the sphenopalatine artery and passes with it into the sphenopalatine foramen.

5. **Nn. infraorbitales**, to the number of three, are the terminal branches of the maxillary nerve. They accompany the infraorbital artery through the infraorbital foramen, five main branches emerging to ramify over the side of the face. **Rr. alveolares superiores anteriores** from these branches pass, without the intervention of a plexus, into the minute foramina situated just above the gum line; thus they supply the premolar, canine, and incisor teeth.

### N. mandibularis (Trigeminus 3)

The mandibular nerve (fig. 153) is smaller than the maxillary division of the trigeminus. It emerges from the skull through the foramen ovale as a large trunk, accompanied on its medial side by the much smaller masticator nerve.

The **ganglion oticum** is situated on the posterior (lateral) surface of the nerve.

Four nerves arise from the mandibular proximal to the otic ganglion, before the nerve divides into anterior and posterior parts:

1. **N. spinosus** comes off at the mouth of the foramen. It is a slender recurrent twig that passes back through the foramen ovale.

2. **N. buccinatorius** also arises at the mouth of the foramen. It passes forward between the heads of the external pterygoid muscle, across (external to) the inferior alveobuccal gland, which it supplies, and on into the cheek. It communicates with terminal twigs of the buccal branch of the facial nerve on the cheek.

3. **N. pterygoideus internus** is a twig arising from the ventral side of the mandibular at the

mouth of the foramen. It runs forward across the posterior end of the ventral head of the external pterygoid muscle into the internal pterygoid muscle.

4. **N. pterygoideus externus** arises at the angle between the two divisions of the mandibular. It accompanies the buccinator nerve to the external pterygoid muscle, which it supplies.

The posterior division of the mandibular passes laterad between the external pterygoid muscle and the medial end of the mandibular condyle. Just beyond the medial end of the condyle it breaks up into its terminal branches. Near this point it gives off a slender root that passes back to the otic ganglion.

The branches arising from the posterior division are:

5. **N. lingualis**, the first of the terminal branches, passes forward and downward between the external and internal pterygoid muscles. It is joined, at an acute angle, by the chorda tympani at the posterior border of the internal pterygoid. At the anterior border of the internal pterygoid the lingual nerve lies between that muscle and the mylohyoid. It then passes between the mylohyoid and the sublingual gland, which it supplies, into the tongue. Here, immediately after crossing ventrad of the duct of the submaxillary gland, it breaks up into its several terminal branches. **N. sublingualis**, the most dorsal of these terminal branches, runs forward to supply the sublingual gland and the mucous membrane on the ventral side of the tongue.

6. **N. alveolaris inferior** accompanies the inferior alveolar artery forward between the internal pterygoid muscle and the lower part of the deep temporal muscle. The nerve lies above the artery as they pass together into the mandibular foramen. The terminal branches emerge from the mandible through the mental foramina.

7. **N. mylohyoideus** arises beside the inferior alveolar nerve. It accompanies the inferior alveolar as far as the anterior border of the internal pterygoid muscle, then separates from the nerve to arch around the muscle and pass into the mylohyoid. Twigs arising from the nerve just before it enters the mylohyoid supply the digastric.

8. **N. auriculotemporalis**, the largest branch of the mandibular nerve, arises from the mandibular by a single root, with several delicate twigs coming from the otic ganglion. There is no relation with the middle meningeal artery, which enters the orbital fissure and hence is associated with the maxillary division of the trigeminus. The auriculotemporal nerve passes laterad between the internal pterygoid muscle and the condyle of the

mandible, then across the neck of the mandibular condyle, lying first ventrad, then mesad of the internal maxillary artery. It breaks up into its terminal branches near the lateral end of the condyle.

The auriculotemporal gives off the following branches: (a) **R. articularis**, a slender branch arising near its base, passes to the medial end of the mandibular articulation. (b) **N. meatus auditorii externi** runs dorsad to the base of the auditory meatus. (c) **Rr. parotidei** are represented by several fine twigs that pass into the substance of the parotid gland. (d) **R. auricularis anterior**, a single large branch arising just distad of the nerve to the external auditory meatus, passes up along the anterior side of the pinna. (e) **Rr. temporales superficiales**, the final terminal branches of the auriculotemporal, pass forward and upward onto the lower part of the anterior temporal region. A stout communicating branch arising from the common trunk of the superficial temporal anastomoses with the zygomaticotemporal branch of the facial nerve, and some of the twigs of the superficial temporal terminate by anastomosing with the zygomatic ramus of the zygomaticotemporal branch.

9. The anterior division of the mandibular, **N. masticatorius** (fig. 153), runs laterad above (deep to) the dorsal head of the external pterygoid muscle, giving off a stout root to the otic ganglion along the way. As it lies above the muscle it divides into anterior and posterior branches. The anterior branch, **N. temporalis profundus anterior**, ramifies in the deep temporal muscle, mesad of the coronoid process of the mandible. The posterior branch passes into the temporal muscle behind the coronoid process, where it divides into the posterior deep temporal and masseteric nerves. **N. temporalis profundus posterior** ramifies in the temporal musculature posterior to the coronoid process. **N. massetericus** arches around behind the coronoid process into the masseteric muscle, where it ramifies.

**N. abducens** (VI) is the most ventral of the nerves passing out of the orbital fissure. It passes forward on the retractor oculi, then perforates the inferior division of the retractor oculi to reach the medial surface of the rectus lateralis, in which it terminates.

*N. facialis* (VII)

The facial nerve (fig. 153) enters the internal auditory meatus in company with the auditory nerve and the internal auditory artery, and leaves the skull through the stylomastoid foramen, in company with the auricular branch of the vagus. These two nerves pass laterad and ventrad together, situated in a conspicuous groove, beneath

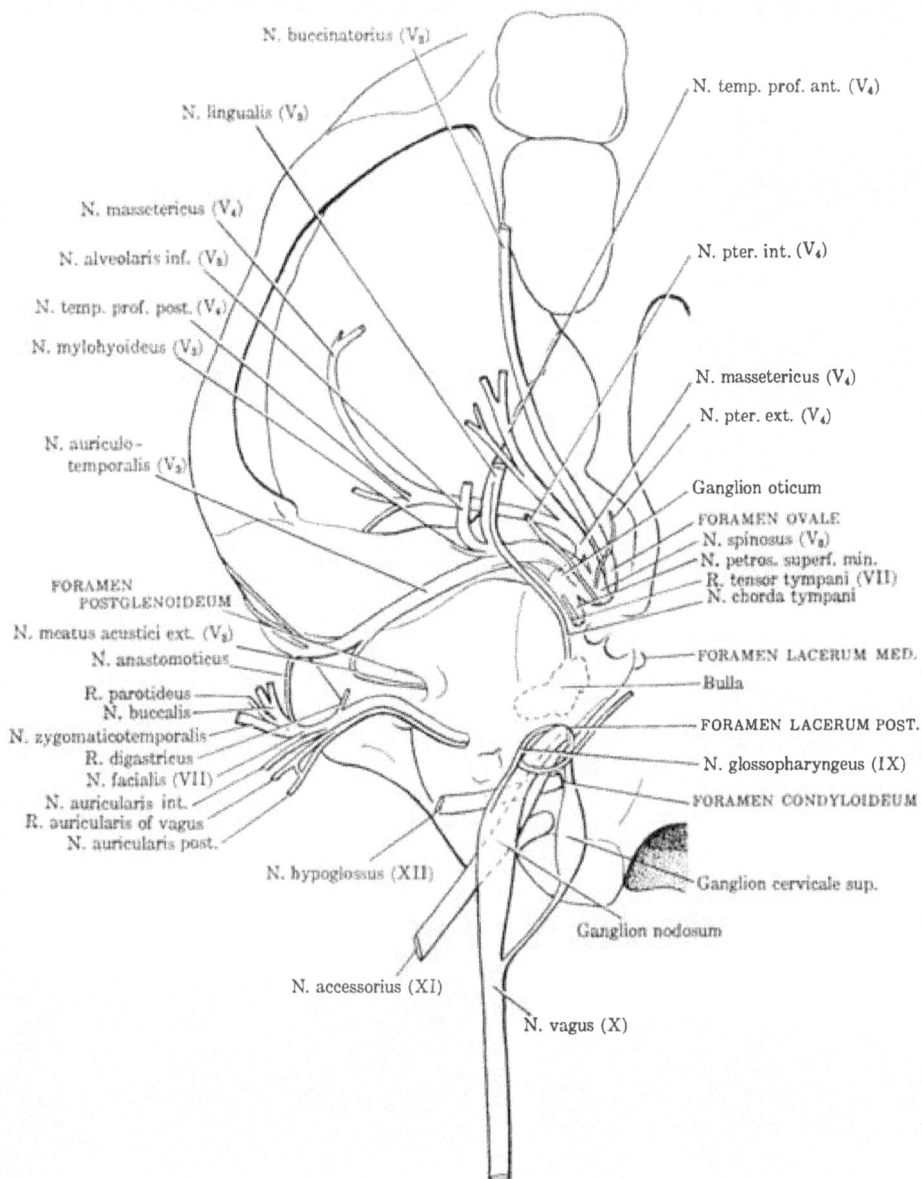

N. buccinatorius (V₂)

N. temp. prof. ant. (V₄)

N. lingualis (V₃)

N. massetericus (V₄)

N. alveolaris inf. (V₃)

N. temp. prof. post. (V₄)

N. mylohyoideus (V₃)

N. pter. int. (V₄)

N. massetericus (V₄)

N. pter. ext. (V₄)

N. auriculo-
temporalis (V₃)

Ganglion oticum

FORAMEN OVALE
N. spinosus (V₂)
N. petros. superf. min.
R. tensor tympani (VII)
N. chorda tympani

FORAMEN
POSTGLENOIDEUM

N. meatus acustici ext. (V₃)

N. anastomoticus

FORAMEN LACERUM MED.

Bulla

R. parotideus
N. buccalis
N. zygomaticotemporalis
R. digastricus
N. facialis (VII)
N. auricularis int.
R. auricularis of vagus
N. auricularis post.

FORAMEN LACERUM POST.

N. glossopharyngeus (IX)

FORAMEN CONDYLOIDEUM

N. hypoglossus (XII)

Ganglion cervicale sup.

Ganglion nodosum

N. accessorius (XI)

N. vagus (X)

Fig. 153. Posterior cranial nerves of *Ailuropoda*, ventral view.

303

the external auditory meatus and the cartilaginous meatus, and between the mastoid process and the postglenoid process. The collateral branches are given off in this region. At the external border of the mastoid process the facial divides into its terminal branches. The collateral branches of the facial nerve are as follows:

1. **N. auricularis posterior** arises at the stylomastoid foramen. At first accompanied by the auricular branch of the vagus, it passes up between the posterior border of the pinna and the insertion of the sternocleidomastoid, to break up into several branches that ramify over the posterior surface of the pinna and supply the auricular muscles. One of these branches **(R. occipitalis)** pierces the sternocleidomastoid and splenius, accompanied by the occipital branch of the posterior auricular artery, to pass along the occipital crest toward the dorsal midline.

2. **N. auricularis internus** is somewhat smaller than the posterior auricular. It arises farther distad, and passes through the substance of the parotid gland to the posterior side of the cartilaginous meatus, which it enters.

3. **R. digastricus**, which is slightly more slender than the internal auricular, is a short branch arising from the opposite side of the facial. It passes back to the posterior end of the digastric, which it supplies.

4. **R. anastomoticus** is a short anastomotic loop that passes across to the auriculotemporal branch of the mandibular. It arises from the facial just before that nerve breaks up into its terminal divisions.

The facial divides into its two main terminal divisions (the zygomaticotemporal and the buccal) opposite the external border of the mastoid process. These ramify beneath and through the parotid gland, while a third slender branch, the parotid, terminates in the parotid gland. The ramifications of the terminal branches are as follows:

5. **N. zygomaticotemporalis** (fig. 107) is slightly larger than the buccal nerve. It passes anteriorly beneath the parotid gland, breaking up after a short distance into its three main divisions, whose several branches emerge from beneath the parotid and ramify over the side of the head. (a) **R. temporalis** breaks up into a number of twigs that ramify, interanastomosing among themselves, over the temporal region. One fine twig **(R. auricularis anterior)** passes toward the anterior side of the ear. The other twigs terminate in the vicinity of the eye, where they anastomose with the nerves of that region. (b) **R. zygomaticus** passes across the zygoma toward the eye, re-

ceiving several slender anastomotic twigs from the auriculotemporal (V3). It terminates by anastomosing with the lacrimal nerve (V2) near the outer angle of the eye. (c) **R. buccalis** (bucco-labialis of authors) accompanies the parotid duct to the corner of the mouth. Here it receives a stout communicating branch from the adjacent superior buccal nerve, then continues into the upper lip.

6. **N. buccalis** (fig. 107) divides into superior and inferior branches, which pass across the masseter to the upper and lower lip, respectively. These two nerves interanastomose along their course.

7. **N. intermedius.** The **chorda tympani** emerges from the skull through the petrotympanic fissure, and runs downward and forward along the medial border of the postglenoid process. Passing between the external and internal pterygoid muscles with the mandibular nerve, it joins the lingual near the origin of the latter.

### N. Glossopharyngeus (IX) (fig. 153)

The glossopharyngeal nerve emerges from the skull through the foramen lacerum posterior in close association with, and laterad of, the vagus. Just beyond the foramen it gives off a branch that runs beside the vagus to the nodose ganglion. Immediately beyond this, two short branches (**Rr. pharyngei**) run back to join the pharyngeal branch of the vagus. The nerve then runs ventrad across the pharynx, gives off an **R. muscularis** to the pharyngeal muscles and slender **Rr. tonsillares** to the tonsil. Passing just mesad of the hyoid, it enters the dorsum of the tongue at the level of the hyoid.

### N. Vagus (X) (fig. 153)

The vagus nerve emerges from the foramen lacerum posterior in company with the glossopharyngeal and spinal accessory nerves. It passes caudad with these nerves and the hypoglossal nerve, forming the prominent ganglion nodosum just caudad of the posterior border of the skull. Beyond this the vagus receives the sympathetic trunk from the anterior cervical ganglion, and the resulting vagosympathetic trunk continues through the neck to divide once more into its component elements at the anterior border of the first rib.

In the basicranial region the vagus receives communications from the glossopharyngeal, spinal accessory, and hypoglossal nerves. Immediately in front of the ganglion nodosum a communicating branch passes between it and the anterior cervical ganglion of the sympathetic, and immediately behind this ganglion there is a communicating branch with the first cervical nerve.

The vagus gives rise to the following branches in the basicranial region: **R. auricularis** accompanies the facial nerve through the stylomastoid foramen, the auricular lying deep to the facial, and winds with it around the anterior side of the mastoid process and up the back of the pinna. Between the mastoid process and the base of the pinna the auricular branch divides into two branches, one of which communicates with the posterior auricular branch of the facial nerve, while the other branch enters a special opening in the medial surface of the cartilage of the pinna. **R. pharyngeus** arises by two roots, which come from the vagus at either end of the nodose ganglion; in addition, the anterior root receives several twigs from the hypoglossal, and the posterior root a twig from the anterior cervical ganglion of the sympathetic. **R. oesophageus** is a slender twig arising from the posterior root of the pharyngeal ramus. **N. laryngeus anterior** arises from the postero-internal side of the nodose ganglion.

At the anterior border of the first rib the sympathetic cord splits off from the vago-sympathetic trunk, and the vagus continues into the thorax. Cardiac and pulmonary branches are given off in the thorax. The left **N. recurrens** arises at the level of the aortic arch and loops around the concavity of the arch.

The two vagi converge in the thorax, uniting into a common trunk at the level of the eleventh thoracic vertebra. The resulting trunk continues caudad between the aorta and the esophagus.

### N. Accessorius (XI) (fig. 153)

The spinal accessory nerve leaves the skull through the foramen lacerum posterior, in company with the glossopharyngeal and vagus nerves. The spinal accessory divides into its internal and external branches immediately after it has passed out of the foramen.

**R. internus** (accessory), which is considerably smaller than the external branch, is a short trunk that joins the trunk of the vagus anterior to the nodose ganglion.

**R. externus** (spinal) winds around behind M. digastricus, lying dorsad of the common carotid artery and the internal jugular vein, to the inner surface of M. sternomastoideus. Passing caudad beneath M. clavotrapezius, into which it sends branches, the nerve continues caudad beneath the acromiotrapezius and spinotrapezius, in which it terminates. While still beneath M. sternomastoideus the nerve gives rise to a branch, which is joined by a root from the second cervical nerve, that passes into the sternomastoid. At nearly the same level the spinal accessory receives a short communicating branch from the second cervical nerve.

### N. Hypoglossus (XII)

After emerging from the skull through the anterior condyloid foramen (fig. 153), the hypoglossal nerve passes dorsad of the vagus, common carotid artery, and internal jugular vein, to the inner border of the origin of M. digastricus. The **R. descendens** arises from its posterior border at this point. It passes caudad with the great vessels of the neck, receiving a communication from the posterior root of the pharyngeal branch of the vagus and giving off twigs to the throat muscles. A twig coming off at the same level apparently represents one end of the Ansa hypoglossi, which communicates with the first cervical nerve.

At the origin of the digastric the hypoglossal arches ventrad, craniad, and mesad, to join the lingual artery and pass with it beneath the mylohyoideus and along the medial border of the styloglossus. The nerve at first lies mesad of the lingual artery, then crosses ventrad of it to lie laterad of the symphyseal branch of the artery, the main trunk of the artery having passed beneath M. hyoglossus. At about the middle of the tongue, as it lies between the styloglossal and genioglossal muscles, the terminal branches of the hypoglossal communicate with the terminal branches of the lingual nerve.

### III. CERVICAL PLEXUS

The ventral divisions of the first four cervical nerves form the roots of the cervical plexus (fig. 154). The first cervical nerve participates in the plexus only by means of a slender communicating ramus with $C_2$, and only a small anterior part of $C_4$ enters into the plexus. Thus the plexus is made up chiefly of $C_2$ and $C_3$.

**N. cervicalis I**, after emerging from the perforating foramen in the base of the transverse process of the atlas, gives rise to the following branches: (1) A slender posterior communicating branch that passes back to the root of $C_2$. (2) A small anterior communicating branch, arising opposite to and slightly distad of the preceding branch, which passes forward to the ganglion nodosum of the vagus nerve. After passing ventrad of N. accessorius, the first cervical bifurcates to form two large branches. The more anterior of these (3) gives off a communicating branch to N. hypoglossus; the remainder of the nerve supplies the sternomastoideus. The posterior branch (4) passes caudad to supply the thyroid musculature.

**N. cervicalis II** gives rise to the following branches from its anterior side: (1) A small communicating branch with the root of $C_1$. (2) A slightly larger branch that joins a small branch from the spinal accessory to supply the sternomastoid muscle. (3) A communicating branch with the main part of the spinal accessory. Immediately distad of (3) the bulk of the nerve is joined by part of $C_3$, passes through M. sternomastoideus, and bifurcates to form N. cutaneus colli and N. auricularis magnus.

N. cervicalis III divides to form a large anterior branch and a small posterior branch. Most of the anterior branch forms a communicating branch with $C_2$; from the posterior side of this communicating branch a small twig passes into M. atlantoscapularis, where it forms an ansa with a corresponding branch from $C_4$ within the substance of the muscle. The posterior branch supplies M. rectus capitis.

N. cervicalis IV participates in the cervical plexus only through a small anterior branch that runs forward into M. atlantoscapularis, forming the second root of the ansa described above.

## IV. NERVES OF THE FORE LIMB

### BRACHIAL PLEXUS

The brachial plexus (fig. 154) is composed of the ventral branches of the fourth to eighth cervical and the first thoracic nerves. The axillary artery is immediately ventrad of the plexus proximally, where it lies between $C_7$ and $Th_1$, ventrad of $C_8$. Farther distally the artery passes between the roots of the lateral anterior thoracic nerve and dorsal to the lateral component of the median nerve.

Nn. cervicales IV and V enter the plexus only insofar as a small branch from each unites to form the origin of the phrenic nerve. Most of $C_4$ has no relation with the plexus, but forms two nerves; the smaller anterior one communicates with a branch from $C_3$, while the posterior one supplies the trapezius. The bulk of $C_5$ forms the lateral cutaneous brachial nerve, which follows the cephalic vein, supplying the integument of the anterolateral surface of the upper arm. $C_4$ and $C_5$ are united by a small communicating branch. N. dorsalis scapulae arises from the fifth cervical.

N. cervicalis VI gives rise to short slender anterior and posterior branches proximally, which join the phrenic nerve. Immediately distal to the phrenic branches it divides to form three main branches of approximately equal size: (1) An anteroventral branch, which gives off a slender ramus to M. pectoralis superficialis anterior, then continues as N. suprascapularis. (2) A mediodorsal branch, which runs caudad to participate in the formation of the dorsal cord. Two Nn. subscapulares arise from the anterior border of this branch. They are distributed exclusively to the subscapular muscle. (3) A short stout communicating branch that runs straight caudad to connect with the seventh cervical nerve.

N. cervicalis VII gives rise proximally to a short diagonal communicating branch with the eighth cervical; one of the roots of the thoracic nerve takes origin from this communicating branch. Farther distad $C_7$ gives rise successively to: (1) a dorsal branch, which forms one of the roots of the dorsal cord, (2) an anterior communicating branch with $C_6$, arising slightly distad of the preceding branch, (3) the small N. thoracalis anterior lateralis, which arises ventrally, immediately distad of the preceding two. A part of this branch is continued across to the posterior side of $C_8$, forming the delicate ansa pectoralis. About 20 mm. farther distad the nerve gives off (4) a stout posterior branch, the ansa mediana, which usually interconnects the musculocutaneous and median nerves but here connects to the posterior cord rather than to the median nerve. Beyond the ansa mediana the trunk continues as (5) N. musculocutaneus.

N. cervicalis VIII gives rise proximally to a communicating branch with $C_7$. The second root of the long thoracic nerve arises from the opposite (posterior) side. Farther distad $C_8$ divides into dorsal and ventral branches of approximately equal size. The dorsal branch forms one of the roots of the dorsal cord, the ventral branch one of the roots of the posterior cord. A twig arising from the posterior border of the dorsal branch gives off branches to the deep pectoral muscle, then continues as N. thoracalis media. From this site also arises the posterior limb of the slender ansa pectoralis, whose anterior limb comes from the base of the lateral anterior thoracic nerve ($C_7$).

N. thoracalis I runs distally to join in the formation of the posterior cord. At its base it is joined by a stout communicating branch from the second thoracic nerve.

The three fasciculi (cords) of the brachial plexus thus have the following composition and relations:

*Fasciculus anterior* is formed chiefly of $C_7$, although it receives some of its substance from $C_6$. Distally it continues as the musculocutaneous nerve.

*Fasciculus posterior* is formed chiefly by roots from $C_8$ and $Th_1$. It also receives a root (the ansa mediana) from the anterior fascicle. The posterior cord gives rise to the median and ulnar nerves.

*Fasciculus dorsalis* is formed by roots from $C_6$, $C_7$, and $C_8$, and gives rise to the axillary and radial nerves.

N. phrenicus arises chiefly from the fifth cervical, with additional slender roots coming from the fourth and sixth. It is also connected with the posterior cervical ganglion of the sympathetic.

N. com. N. hypoglossus

N. com.
ganglion
of
N. vagus

N. to sternomastoid.

N. to sternomastoid.
N. cutaneus colli
N. auricularis magnus

C₁

N. accessorius (XI) to M. trapezius

N. to rectus capitis

C₂

C₃

Nn. to atlantoscap.

C₄

N. to trapezius

N. cut. brach. lat.

C₅

N. to pect. alpha

N. dors. scapulae

N. suprascapularis

N. subscap. upper
N. subscap.
FASCICULUS ANT.
N. musculocutaneus
Ansa pectoralis
Ansa mediana
N. axillaris

C₆

FASCICULUS DORS.
N. radialis

N. medianus

C₇

C₈

N. cut. brach.med.

N. ulnaris

Tb₁

N. cut. antebr. med.
BICIPITAL ARCH
N. cut. brach. med.

R. com.
N. th. 2

N. thor. ant. lat.
Nn. to pect. prof.
FASCICULUS POST.
N. thor. ant. med.

N. to panniculus

N. to teres major

N. phrenicus    N. intercostalis I

N. subscap.

N. thoracodorsalis

N. intercostobrachialis
(Intercostal II)

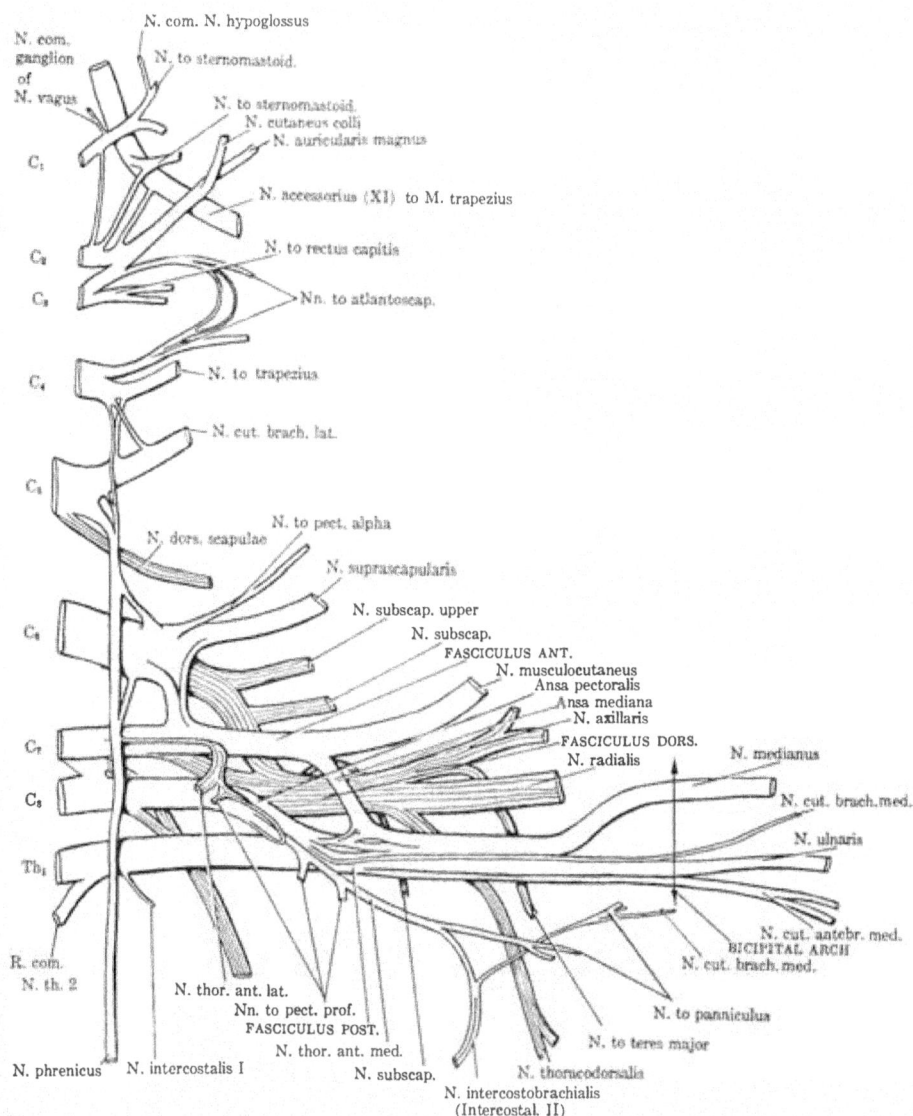

Fig. 154. Left cervical and brachial plexuses of *Ailuropoda*.

## Discussion of Brachial Plexus

The brachial plexus of *Ailuropoda* was described and figured by Harris (1939). His specimen differed from ours, and from all other Carnivora, in that C₅ contributed a large branch. The larger part of this branch went to the dorsal cord, a smaller twig to the anterior cord. It also was the main source of the suprascapular nerve, which arose by two roots: a large one from C₅ and a smaller one from C₆. According to Thomas (1930) this is the primitive condition found in marsupials and insectivores. Otherwise Harris's specimen agreed closely with mine.

The mammalian brachial plexus has been reviewed by Thomas (1930) and Harris (1939). Harris

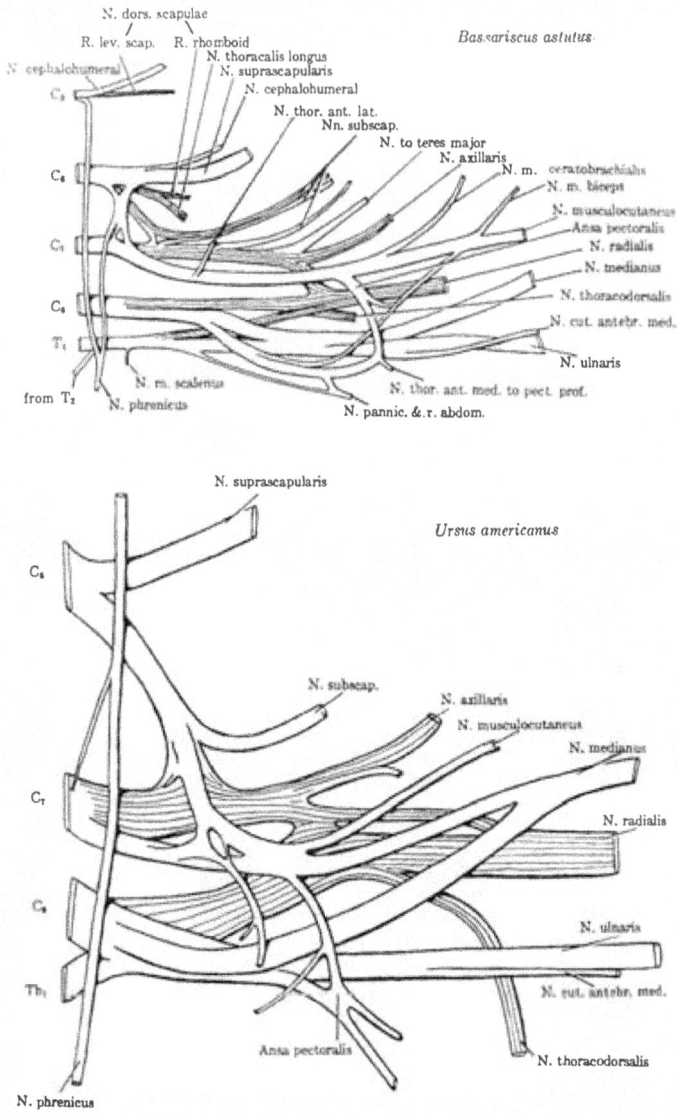

FIG. 155. Brachial plexus of *Bassariscus astutus* and *Ursus americanus* to illustrate the non-ursid and ursid types of arctoid plexus.

apparently was unaware of Thomas's study. The material dissected by Thomas included 7 arctoid carnivores, that of Harris 5, but neither author gives individual descriptions and therefore their work was of little use to me. I have dissected the brachial plexus of the following arctoid carnivores: *Nyctereutes procyonoides, Vulpes fulva, Bassaris-*

*cus astutus, Procyon lotor, Potos flavus, Ailurus fulgens* (2), *Ursus americanus.*

There seem to be few consistent differences among the Arctoidea, although minor individual variations are numerous. The plexus is slightly more prefixed in the Ursidae and *Ailuropoda* than in other arctoids (fig. 155). This is evident in the origin of several of the nerves: the subscapular comes from $C_6$ instead of $C_7$; the median comes from $C_7$-$Th_1$, whereas in *Bassariscus, Ailurus*, and the canids it comes from $C_8$ $T_1$, or even from $Th_1$ alone (*Vulpes*); the dorsal cord has a large root from $C_6$ that is lacking in other arctoids. The ansa mediana, which interconnects the median and musculocutaneous, is very heavy in prefixed plexuses; it is absent in *Bassariscus* and the Canidae. A slender ansa mediana was present in a specimen of the insectivore *Echinosorex*, and appears in the several insectivores figured by Thomas.

*Procyon* and *Nasua* tend to be intermediate between the Ursidae and other arctoids in most respects. *Ailurus* is more primitive than *Procyon* and *Nasua*.

The brachial plexus of *Ailuropoda* agrees with that of *Ursus* in all essential respects.

### PERIPHERAL NERVES OF THE FORE LIMB

**N. axillaris** arises from the dorsal cord. It accompanies the external humeral circumflex artery through the interval between the triceps longus and triceps medialis to the external side of the leg (fig. 133). The main trunk is distributed to the deltoids, a branch passing across the surgical neck of the humerus, beneath the acromiodeltoideus, to supply the distal end of the clavotrapezius. **N. cutaneus brachii lateralis** (fig. 134) arises from the axillary after it reaches the external side of the leg, and accompanies the cephalic vein across the biceps to the curve of the elbow, where it gives off a cutaneous twig to the volar side of the forearm, then continues onto the dorsum of the forearm to terminate by anastomosing with the lateral branch of the superficial radial nerve.

**N. musculocutaneus** (fig. 133) is the main continuation of the anterior cord. It runs toward the shoulder joint, passing between the coracobrachialis longus and brevis, and innervating both divisions of this muscle. The nerve bifurcates immediately after emerging from beneath the coracobrachialis longus. One of the branches so formed continues anteriorly, accompanying the bicipital branch of the internal humeral circumflex artery into the proximal end of the biceps. The other branch runs distad between the biceps and the coracobrachialis longus, accompanying the delicate descending ramus of the profunda artery. Near the bend of the elbow the nerve runs deep to the biceps and, at the end of the insertion of the deltoid, breaks up to form three branches. The smallest of these innervates the brachialis; a second runs around the anterior side of the humerus to join a branch from the radial nerve; the third is continued onto the forearm as the lateral antibrachial cutaneous. **N.**

**cutaneus antibrachii lateralis** (fig. 133) emerges between the biceps and brachialis, joins the superficial brachial artery and vein, and accompanies them distally. Near the carpus it gives off a short anastomotic twig to the dorsal cutaneous branch of the median nerve, and the resulting branch accompanies the continuation of N. cutaneus antibrachii lateralis up over the base of the radial sesamoid onto the dorsum of the manus.

**N. cutaneus brachii medialis** arises from the loop between the medial anterior thoracic and intercostobrachial nerves. Passing laterad, it bifurcates to form two branches that pass through the panniculus muscle to the medial side of the upper arm. The more anterior of these branches supplies the integument on the posteromedial side of the upper arm as far distad as the humeral condyle, while the posterior branch winds around to the posterior side of the upper arm, to supply the integument over the olecranon.

**N. cutaneus antibrachii medialis** appears to be represented by two separate nerves. The more anterior of these arises from the posterior cord between the origins of the median and ulnar nerves. It is closely applied to the anterior side of the ulnar nerve as far as the bicipital arch, then runs toward the surface, passing anteriorly over the brachial artery, to supply the integument on the distal anteromedial part of the upper arm and continuing on to the flexor side of the fore arm. The posterior branch arises from the posterior cord behind the ulnar nerve. It bifurcates just distad of the bicipital arch, both of the resulting rami running side by side just superficial to the brachial vein. The more anterior ramus runs across the humeral epicondyle onto the flexor side of the fore arm, while the posterior ramus supplies the integument over the medial side of the olecranon.

**N. medianus** (fig. 133) arises from the posterior cord. It winds around the axillary and brachial arteries (see p. 259), and runs through the entepicondylar foramen to reach the fore arm. Since the brachial artery detours around the foramen, the artery and nerve diverge a short distance above the foramen; immediately below the foramen they come together again. At this point the nerve gives rise to a short branch that supplies the pronator teres. A second, much larger branch arises a few millimeters farther distad, passes ulnaward beneath the pronator teres and flexor carpi radialis, and supplies the flexor carpi ulnaris, the flexor digitorum sublimis, and the flexor digitorum profundus.

On the forearm the nerve passes deep to the pronator teres and flexor carpi radialis at the level of the bicipital tendon, emerging on the ulnar side of the pronator teres, and passing distad between it and the flexor digitorum profundus. The median artery lies deep to the nerve for slightly more than half the length of the forearm; then the two diverge, the nerve passing somewhat ulnaward over the tendon of the flexor digitorum sublimis, while the artery continues straight distad. N. interosseus volaris arises immediately beyond the entepicondylar foramen.

Near the middle of the forearm the median nerve gives off a large cutaneous branch which receives an anastomotic twig from the lateral antibrachial cutaneous nerve and then accompanies the main continuation of that nerve up around the base of the radial sesamoid onto the dorsum manus.

The main trunk of the median nerve divides at the carpus into a large branch that goes to the radial sesamoid and to both sides of the pollex and the radial side of digit 2, and a second branch that continues onto the palm. The palmar branch closely follows the volar arch of the median artery, radiating digital nerves to the ulnar side of digit 2, to both sides of 3 and 4, and to the radial side of digit 5. The last receives an anastomotic twig from the volar branch of the ulnar nerve. Slightly distad of the middle of the forearm the median nerve gives off a large branch, which passes to the volar and external sides of the radial sesamoid.

N. ulnaris (figs. 133, 134) arises from the posterior cord; it is made up chiefly of fibers from the first thoracic nerve. It lies between the brachial artery and brachial vein as far as the bicipital arch, then passes deep to the vein, to emerge posterior to it near the elbow joint. Running around behind the humeral epicondyle, it reaches the forearm where it lies at first between the humeral and ulnar heads of M. flexor carpi ulnaris. Just beyond the elbow joint the ulnar nerve divides into dorsal and volar rami. R. dorsalis manus runs up behind the pisiform, beneath M. flexor carpi ulnaris, onto the back of the hand, where it supplies the outside of digit 5 and sends an anastomotic twig to the most lateral of the superficial branches of the radial nerve. R. volaris manus runs distad on the fore arm, giving off a long branch to the carpal pad near its origin, and perforating the transverse carpal ligament near the inner border of the pisiform. It continues onto the palm, where it supplies the outer side of digit 5 and sends an anastomotic twig to the volar branch of the median nerve.

N. radialis (fig. 134) is the main continuation of the dorsal cord. A branch arising from its posterior side at the level of the top of the teres major tendon supplies the triceps longus; a ramus from this branch goes to the epitrochlearis. The nerve then enters the triceps medialis and lateralis. Winding around the shaft of the humerus in the musculospiral groove, giving off a branch to the anconeus, it divides into a superficial and a deep branch near the origin of the median epicondylar ridge. About 10 mm. before its bifurcation it gives off a branch to the brachialis.

The *superficial branch* of the radial nerve is represented by the usual lateral and medial rami. These arise independently (on both legs), however, their origins from the radial being separated by an interval of 40 mm. The *lateral ramus* arises first, at the proximal end of the ectepicondylar crest, and comes to the surface between the lateral head of the triceps and the brachioradialis just above the elbow joint. It runs distad near the border of the brachioradialis, breaking up at the carpus into twigs that supply both sides of digits 3 and 4 and the inner side of 5. The outermost twig gives off an anastomotic ramus to the dorsal branch of the ulnar nerve. The *medial ramus* takes origin at the humeroradial articulation, and comes to the surface between the brachioradialis and the extensor carpi radialis longus. It passes distad on the radial side of the cephalic vein, breaking up at the carpus into twigs that supply both sides of digit 2. The outermost twig receives an anastomotic twig from N. cutaneus antibrachii lateralis.

The *deep branch* of the radial nerve runs diagonally ulnaward and distad beneath M. supinator. At the ulnar border of the supinator it breaks up into branches that supply the extensor muscles of the fore arm. One branch, N. interosseus dorsalis, accompanies the dorsal interosseous artery distad to the carpus.

## V. THORACIC NERVES

The ventral primary divisions of the thoracic nerves have the general mammalian arrangement, all but the first two and the last being of the simple typical form. Each passes laterad in the intercostal space along the posterior border of a rib, giving off a large lateral cutaneous branch that pierces the intercostal musculature, while the much smaller ventral branch continues toward the sternum.

N. thoracalis 1 considerably exceeds the other thoracic nerves in caliber. It is joined to the second thoracic nerve by a stout branch. The main mass of the nerve joins the brachial plexus, and hence is distributed chiefly to the foreleg. A slender branch (N. intercostalis) continues in the intercostal space between the first and second ribs. It does not give off a lateral cutaneous branch.

N. thoracalis 2 is more slender than the first, but larger than the succeeding thoracic nerves. After giving off a stout communicating branch to the first thoracic, it enters the space between the external and internal intercostals where it divides into anterior and lateral branches. The lateral branch, after piercing the external intercostal and scalenus muscles, anastomoses with N. thoracalis anterior medialis and N. cutaneus brachii medialis.

N. thoracalis 14 (the last thoracic nerve) gives off a stout communicating branch with the first lumbar nerve just beyond its exit from the intervertebral foramen. The nerve passes laterad between the quadratus lumborum and the kidney. At the lateral border of the quadratus lumborum, just before entering the abdominal wall, it divides into a ventral and a lateral branch. The ventral branch continues ventrad between the transversus and the internal oblique. The lateral branch pierces the internal oblique near the anterior end of the ilium.

## VI. NERVES OF THE HIND LIMB

The lumbosacral plexus (fig. 156) is composed of the ventral branches of the last thoracic, the four lumbar, and the five sacral nerves. The root of each nerve is connected with the root of the succeeding nerve by a communicating loop, and a communicating branch is given off to the corresponding ganglion of the sympathetic trunk.

N. iliohypogastricus arises chiefly from the first lumbar nerve, but also receives a strong root from the last thoracic. On the right side division into anterior and posterior branches takes place immediately, while on the left there is a common trunk for some distance. The anterior branch passes through the quadratus lumborum (on the left side the common trunk goes through the psoas minor instead) to the space between the transversalis and internal oblique. Here the anterior branch communicates with the last intercostal nerve, and the posterior branch with the ilioinguinalis.

N. ilioinguinalis arises from the first lumbar nerve. After giving off twigs to the psoas muscles, it passes caudad to the inguinal canal. Just before reaching the canal it pierces the transversus abdominis and divides into anterior and posterior branches between this muscle and the internal oblique. The anterior branch communicates with the iliohypogastric and external spermatic nerves. The posterior branch accompanies the spermatic cord to the pudendal region.

N. spermaticus externus is a slender branch from the second lumbar. It runs across the ventral surfaces of the psoas muscles, dividing beneath the psoas minor into two. The external spermatic supplies the spermatic cord, the abdominal muscles, and cutaneous structures in and around the genitalia.

N. cutaneus femoris lateralis is represented by two independent branches on the right side, and by a single trunk on the left. The nerve is the main continuation of the second lumbar nerve. It pierces the abdominal wall at the junction of the sartorius and the internal oblique, and ramifies on the anterior and lateral surfaces of the thigh.

N. femoralis (fig. 137) is the continuation of the third lumbar nerve, supplemented by roots from the second and fourth. It passes between M. iliacus and M. psoas major, emerging from beneath the psoas at the level of the inguinal ligament. It immediately breaks up into terminal branches, which pass between the branches of A. circumflexa femoris lateralis and scatter to their destinations; only the anterior cutaneous and saphenous nerves accompany the femoral artery along the thigh.

The femoral nerve forms five main branches. Four of these are muscular rami, while the fifth gives origin to both the anterior cutaneous and the saphenous. The two most anterior branches supply M. sartorius from its inner side. The third and largest branch passes between M. rectus femoris and M. vastus medialis, supplying these muscles and M. vastus intermedius. The fourth branch divides 20 mm. beyond the lateral circumflex femoral artery to form the anterior cutaneous and saphenous nerves. R. cutaneus anterior diverges from the saphenous near the point where the femoral artery runs beneath M. adductor femoris; it continues distad, supplying the skin over the lower medial surface of the thigh. N. saphenus, after the femoral artery leaves the surface, accompanies the saphenous artery to the lower leg. At the level of the medial epicondyle of the femur it gives off a slender branch that joins a branch from the obturator nerve to form the roots of the posterior R. cutaneus cruris medialis. R. infrapatellaris arises from the saphenous at the level of the patella, and joins the patellar plexus. At the distal end of the tibia the saphenous receives an anastomotic branch from the medial crural cutaneous nerve, then continues onto the dorsum of the foot to supply adjacent sides of digits 1 and 2. The fifth and most medial branch of the femoral nerve passes back, deep to the femoral artery, to supply the anterior layer of M. pectineus.

N. obturatorius arises mainly from the fourth lumbar nerve, with a smaller common root from L 2 3. It emerges from the pelvis at the anterior corner of the obturator foramen, so that it comes to lie immediately in front of M. adductor longus. Passing between the adductor brevis and the adductor longus, the nerve breaks up at once to form four branches of very unequal size. The most anterior is a slender twig supplying the pectineus. The next twig, also slender, goes to the adductor brevis. The third is a larger branch that goes to the deeper layers of the adductor longus. The fourth and most posterior is a large branch that passes through the adductor to the inner surface of the gracilis, which muscle it supplies. A long branch arises from the ramus to the gracilis, passes along the medial side of the thigh to the level of the knee, and forms one of the roots of the posterior R. cutaneus cruris medialis.

**N. glutaeus anterior** (fig. 138) receives fibers from the fourth lumbar and first sacral nerves (these unite to form the so-called Truncus lumbosacralis), and from the second sacral. It emerges from the pelvis through the extreme anterior end of the great sciatic foramen, accompanied by the anterior gluteal vessels. The point where these emerge coincides with the boundary between the piriformis and the gluteus medius, and the nerve lies ventrad and slightly caudad of the vessels. The nerve gives off a branch to the piriformis, then passes between the gluteus medius and the gluteus minimus, through the anterior part of the gluteus superficialis, which it also supplies, to the tensor fasciae latae, in which it terminates. A separate branch to the piriformis comes off at the posterior side of the base of the anterior gluteal.

**N. glutaeus posterior** (fig. 138) arises, almost as a medial branch of the sciatic, from a loop formed by the lumbosacral trunk and second sacral nerve with a trunk from the third and fourth sacral nerves. This loop may conveniently be referred to as the sciatic loop. An independent branch to the quadratus femoris arises from the loop beside the origin of the posterior gluteal. The posterior gluteal nerve passes out of the pelvis lying on the dorsal surface of the sciatic nerve. Beneath the piriformis it divides into branches that supply the gluteus superficialis and gluteus medius.

**N. ischiadicus** (fig. 138) is the main branch arising from the loop described above. It emerges from the sciatic foramen immediately anterior to M. gemellus anterior and deep to M. piriformis. Running caudad across the gemelli and the tendon of the obturator internus, it passes down the thigh and terminates at the junction of the middle and distal thirds of the thigh by dividing into the common peroneal and tibial nerves.

**N. cutaneus femoris posterior** (fig. 138) arises from the posterior side of the sciatic near its base. At the level of the ventral border of the ischial tuberosity it gives off muscular rami to the posterior thigh muscles, then continues distad in the groove between the biceps femoris and the semitendinosus.

**N. peronaeus communis** (fig. 138) is much smaller than the tibial nerve. It crosses the proximal ends of the lateral head of the gastrocnemius and the soleus, and the fibular collateral ligament, under cover of the biceps femoris, finally entering the space between the peroneus longus and peroneus brevis. In the popliteal space the common peroneal gives off muscular twigs to the biceps femoris; a superficial branch of N. cutaneus surae lateralis that pierces the fascia at about the middle of the leg; and a deeper branch of N. cutaneus surae lateralis that pierces the fascia at the lowest fifth of the leg. The latter anastomoses with a branch of N. cutaneus surae medialis to form N. suralis. The sural nerve receives a branch from the intermediate dorsal cutaneus nerve, and is then distributed to the lateral side of the foot.

The common peroneal breaks up at the junction of the upper and middle thirds of the leg into three terminal branches: a muscular branch, the superficial peroneal, and the deep peroneal.

1. **R. muscularis** runs anteriorly beneath the peroneus longus and the extensor digitorum longus to the tibialis anterior, which it supplies. This branch corresponds to the recurrent articular branch of human anatomy, but here it fails to supply the knee joint.

2. **N. peronaeus superficialis** runs distad between the long and short peroneal muscles, then crosses beneath the peroneus longus and pierces the fascia at the distal quarter of the leg. Over the fibular malleolus it breaks up into terminal branches. **N. cutaneus dorsalis medialis** ramifies to the lateral side of digit 2, both sides of digits 3 and 4, and the inner side of digit 5. The twig to digit 5 is joined by a twig from the intermediate dorsal cutaneus nerve. **N. cutaneus dorsalis intermedius** bifurcates into the branch that joins the twig of the medial dorsal cutaneus to the inner side of digit 5, and a branch that joins the sural nerve to supply the outer side of digit 5.

3. **N. peronaeus profundus** runs beneath the extensor digitorum longus, then winds back, from medial to lateral, beneath the extensor hallucis brevis. As it emerges from beneath this muscle it joins the dorsalis pedis artery, and passes with it onto the dorsum of the foot. At the tarsus the nerve breaks up into three branches. The most lateral and largest of these supplies the extensor brevis. The middle branch ramifies through the extensor brevis, then emerges to join the medial branch. The medial branch radiates twigs that supply adjacent sides of digits 2 and 3 and of digits 1 and 2.

**N. tibialis** (fig. 138), the second of the two terminal branches of the sciatic, considerably ex-

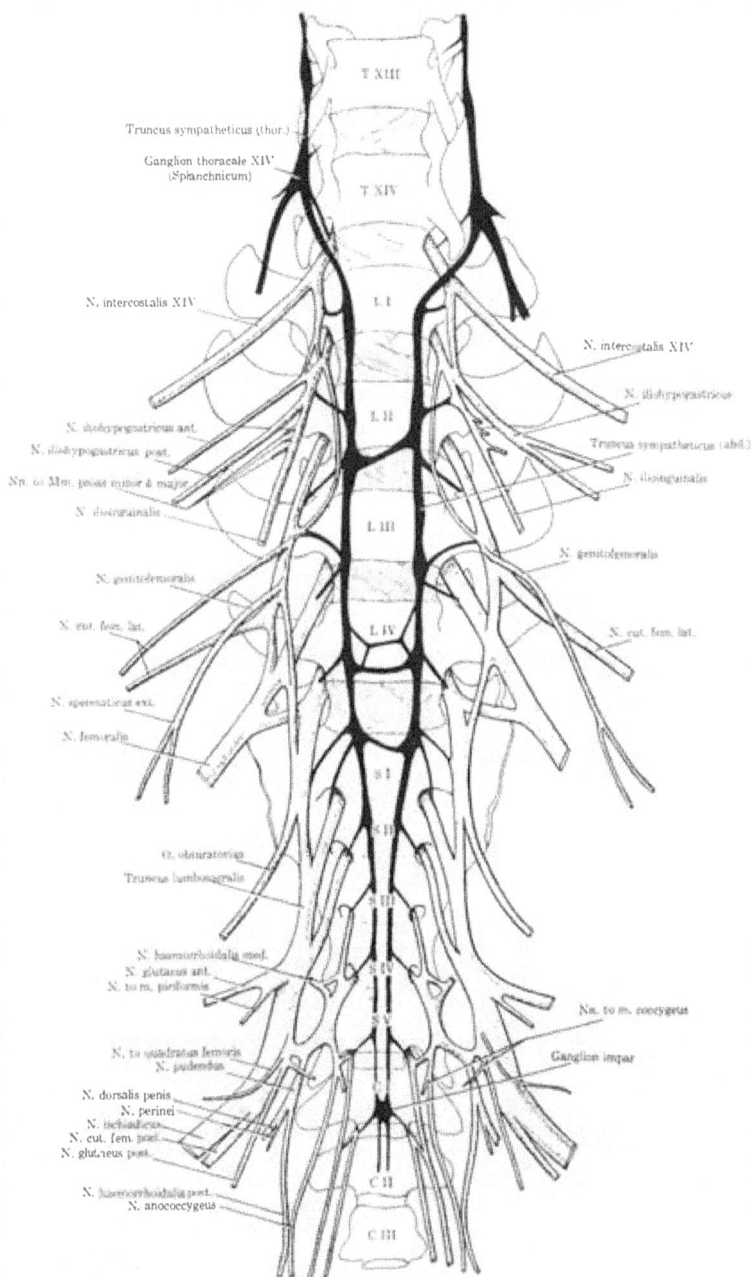

FIG. 156. Lumbosacral plexus of *Ailuropoda*, ventral view.

313

ceeds the common peroneal in size. It runs across the popliteal space and disappears beneath the medial head of the gastrocnemius, under which it continues toward the planta. The following branches

eral plantar nerve. **N. plantaris medialis** is slightly larger than the lateral nerve. At the distal end of the tibia it divides into medial and lateral branches. The medial branch accompanies

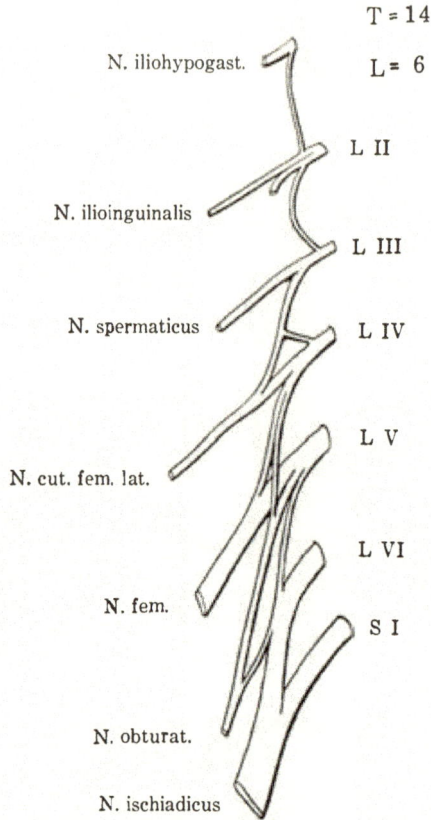

FIG. 157. Lumbosacral plexus of *Ursus americanus*, ventral view.

are given off in the popliteal space: (1) **Rr. musculares** supply both heads of the gastrocnemius, the plantaris, soleus, and popliteus. (2) **N. cutaneus surae medialis** runs obliquely laterad and distad across the lateral head of the gastrocnemius, perforating the fascia at the lowest fifth of the leg and anastomosing immediately with the lateral sural cutaneous nerve to form N. suralis. (3) **N. interosseus cruris** arises at the distal end of the popliteal space, and runs distad in the space between the flexor hallucis longus and the flexor digitorum longus.

The tibial nerve divides at the lowest quarter of the leg into the medial plantar nerve and the lat-

the superficial plantar arch of the posterior tibial artery across the sole, radiating nerves to the digits. These supply the inner side of digit 2, both sides of digits 3 and 4, and the inner side of digit 5. The lateral branch supplies both sides of digit 1, and the outer side of digit 2. **N. plantaris lateralis** runs diagonally across the sole, deep to the conjoined tendon of the digital flexors, to the base of metatarsus 5. Here it divides into two branches. The more medial of these supplies the muscles of the sole, in addition sending a twig to the lateral side of digit 4. The lateral branch supplies the lateral border of digit 5, in addition sending a twig to its abductor muscle.

TABLE 25.—COMPOSITION OF LUMBOSACRAL PLEXUS IN CARNIVORES[1]

| | Canis familiaris[2] | Ursus americanus | Ailuropoda melanoleuca | Felis domestica[3] |
|---|---|---|---|---|
| No. thoracolumbar vertebrae.. | 13+7 | 14+6 | 14+4 | 13+7 |
| No. sacral vertebrae | 3 | 5 | 5 | 3 |
| Lumbar plexus roots | L3-L6 | L3-L6 | L2-L4 | L4-L7 |
| Iliohypogastricus | L1-2 | L1 | Th14-L1 | L1-2 |
| Ilioinguinalis | L3 | L2 | L1 | L3 |
| Spermaticus ext. | L3-L4 | L3 | L2 | L4 |
| Cutan. fem. lat. | L3-L4 | L4 | L2 | L4-L5 |
| Femoralis | L4-L5-L6 | L4-L5-L6 | L2-L3-L4 | L5-L6 |
| Obturatorius | L4-L5-L6 | L4-L5-L6 | L2-L3-L4 | L6-L7 |
| Ischiadicus | L6-L7-S1 | L5-L6-S1 | L4-S1-4 | L6-L7-S1 |

[1] Main roots indicated in boldface.
[2] Data from Havelka (1928) and Ellenberger and Baum (1943).
[3] Data from Reighard and Jennings (1935).

N. haemorrhoidalis media arises from the third and fourth sacral nerves. It passes to the rectum. The posterior hemorrhoidal arises from the pudendal nerve (see below).

N. pudendus arises from the posterior part of the sciatic loop, and hence contains fibers from the third and fourth sacral nerves. It divides almost at once into the dorsal nerve of the penis, the perineal, and the posterior hemorrhoidal nerves; the first two form a short common trunk.

The first pair of Nn. coccygei arises from the posterior part of the sciatic loop and the fifth sacral nerve; each promptly divides into two branches. The more lateral branch, which apparently corresponds to N. anococcygeus of human anatomy, supplies the skin above the anus with one branch, a second branch continuing into the tail. The medial branch supplies M. coccygeus.

DISCUSSION OF LUMBOSACRAL PLEXUS

Apparently the lumbosacral plexus of the Carnivora has been described only for the domestic dog (Havelka, 1928; Ellenberger and Baum, 1943) and the domestic cat (Reighard and Jennings, 1935). I have dissected this plexus in a specimen of Ursus americanus (fig. 157).

The composition of the plexus in these four carnivores is compared in Table 25. In the cat the lumbar plexus is postfixed by about one spinal nerve as compared with the dog, but the sacral plexus arises from the same spinal nerves in both. Since Ursus typically has one more thoracic than Canis, the first lumbar is the fifteenth thoracolumbar instead of the fourteenth as in Canis, and therefore in the bear the whole plexus apparently is shifted caudally one segment on the spinal cord. Otherwise the lumbosacral plexus of Canis and Ursus appears to differ only in minor details, in spite of the shorter lumbar region in Ursus, and probably represents the typical pattern of the Arctoidea. The origin of the lumbosacral trunk is

more postfixed onto the sacrum in Ursus, but this merely means that sacralization of the last (7th) lumbar in Ursus has not affected the ventral branches of the spinal nerves. The plexus pattern in the dog, bear, and cat is very similar to that of the domestic ungulates (Ellenberger and Baum, 1943).

In Ailuropoda the plexus differs in fundamental ways that cannot be explained by mere shifting of the area of sacralization. The whole plexus is shifted anteriorly about two spinal nerves as compared with Ursus. In addition, the lumbar plexus is compressed; its roots embrace only three spinal nerves, whereas in Ursus and Canis they embrace five. On the contrary, the sciatic plexus is expanded, embracing five spinal nerves instead of three as in the others, and in general is a much looser and more complex network. The origin of the peripheral nerves from the lumbosacral plexus closely resembles the pattern in the other arctoids; thus differences are limited to those parts of the nerve complex lying close to the vertebral column.

We have detected an area of disturbance in the lumbosacral region of Ailuropoda affecting the bones (p. 85), the muscles (p. 196), the blood vessels (p. 285), and the genitalia (p. 228). It now appears that the nerve pattern in this area is likewise atypical. Thus the patterns of all tissues in this region, regardless of function and regardless of their varying times of differentiation during ontogeny, show unmistakable signs of morphogenetic disturbance. These manifestations undoubtedly have a common underlying cause, acting early in ontogeny. We have been unable to find any adaptive significance in the new patterns, and therefore interpret it as due to a general disturbance of morphological homeostasis in the lumbosacral region.

VII. SYMPATHETIC SYSTEM

A complete dissection of the sympathetic system was not attempted. Only the cords and the structures intimately related to them are included in the following description.

### SYMPATHETIC TRUNKS

Ganglion cervicale anterior is a fusiform structure, 12 mm. in length, lying just laterad of M. rectus anticus ventralis at the level of the occipital condyle. It is pierced by a branch of the internal carotid artery that supplies M. rectus anticus ventralis. In addition to communicating branches with the posterior cranial and cervical nerves, it gives off a multiple (3 strands) internal carotid nerve from its anterior end, and from its posterior end a stout communicating branch that joins the vagus immediately caudad of the nodose ganglion.

N. caroticus internus accompanies the internal carotid artery into the sinus cavernosus, where it forms the plexus cavernosus. A branch from this plexus passes into the orbit closely applied to the abducens nerve, and ramifies to the periorbita and the rectus lateralis and retractor oculi muscles, in addition to supplying the sympathetic root of the ciliary ganglion. A twig also goes to the ophthalmic plexus.

The vago-sympathetic trunk runs caudad in the neck to the anterior border of the first rib. Here the sympathetic splits off from the vagus, dividing almost at once into a median cardiac branch and a lateral branch that communicates with the posterior cervical ganglion. There is no middle cervical ganglion.

Ganglion cervicale posterior is an irregular flattened structure, 15 mm. in length, pierced by the phrenic nerve. It communicates anteriorly and laterally with the sixth, seventh, and eighth cervical nerves, medially with the trunk of the sympathetic that splits off from the vagus, and posteriorly, by a stout branch, with the first thoracic ganglion.

### THORACIC AND ABDOMINAL REGIONS

The thoracic gangliated cords lie ventrad of the heads of the ribs from the first to the fourteenth, on either side of the bodies of the vertebrae. There are 14 thoracic ganglia, the number thus corresponding with the number of intercostal nerves. Ganglion thoracale 1 is considerably larger than those that follow. It is an irregular-shaped structure with communicating branches to the posterior cervical ganglion and the first intercostal nerve. Posteriorly it continues into the thoracic cord. The first thoracic and posterior cervical ganglia are united in addition by the Plexus vertebralis, through which the vertebral artery passes.

The remaining thoracic ganglia, back to the fourteenth, are small swellings in the thoracic cord. Ganglion thoracale 14 (Ganglion splanchnicum) is large and irregular in form. N. splanchnicus and the abdominal sympathetic cord arise from it posteriorly.

The abdominal gangliated cord (fig. 156), after leaving the last thoracic ganglion, arches toward the midline so that the abdominal cords lie beneath the bodies of the vertebrae. The two cords are united at several places by communicating branches that pass transversely across the ventral surfaces of the vertebrae.

At the sacrum the two cords move even closer together. They pass side by side to the Ganglion impar, which lies beneath the first caudal vertebra. Beyond this a pair of slender cords continues distad into the tail.

### VIII.  CONCLUSIONS

1.  The gross structure of the brain in *Ailuropoda* agrees closely with that of the Ursidae.

2.  Two areas of the cerebral cortex are more extensive in *Ailuropoda* than in *Ursus*. These are (a) the portion of somatic sensory area I that is devoted to the hand, and (b) the portion of motor area I that is devoted to mastication.

3.  The brachial plexus of *Ailuropoda* agrees closely with that of *Ursus* in all essential respects.

4.  The lumbosacral plexus of *Ailuropoda* differs in important respects from that of *Ursus*. This is interpreted as due to the general disturbance of morphological homeostasis in the lumbosacral region.

# SPECIAL SENSE ORGANS

Of the special sense organs only the eye and the middle ear were studied in detail. The gross structure of the tongue was described on page 202, and the bony supporting structure of the olfactory organ on page 54.

## I. EYE

The eye ball is nearly spherical. The optic nerve leaves the eye ball slightly below and lateral to the posterior pole.

The eye is surrounded by the usual incomplete bony ring, which is completed posteriorly by a stout orbital ligament. The orbital ring is nearly circular in outline, measuring 40 mm. in anteroposterior diameter by 37 mm. in dorsoventral diameter. A prominent and well-marked cushion of fat, situated outside the periorbita, occupies the anteroinferior corner of the orbit.

The periorbita is a heavy, opaque capsule of connective tissue that surrounds all the orbital structures behind the orbital ring; medially it is continuous with the periosteum of the skull. On the skull its limits are marked by the superior and inferior orbital crests. It has the usual elongate conical form. The periorbita contains two sheets of muscle fibers that extend nearly its entire length. These sheets, one dorsal and the other ventral, run obliquely into a narrow muscle-free longitudinal band at the center of the outer wall of the periorbita.

The trochlea occupies the usual position directly above the eye ball. It is an elongate cartilaginous tunnel, 6 mm. in length, through which the tendon of the superior oblique muscle passes. Attachment is to the periorbita, which at this point is firmly united to the underlying bone by heavy tendon fibers. The most medial fibers of the levator palpebrae superioris arise from the anterior part of the surface of the trochlea.

Of the eye lids only the nictitating membrane could be examined, the true lids having been removed with the skin. The **nictitating membrane** (palpebra tertius) is a very prominent fold of conjunctivum that projects from the medial border of the eye over the medial part of the eye ball. Its free border is nearly square, with a slight concavity at the center and rounded corners. This border is heavily pigmented on both its outer and inner surfaces. The membrane is supported by a broad central strip of cartilage, the nictitating cartilage, which begins medially with a rounded tip, then extends along the eye ball in a gentle arc concave dorsally, and terminates by expanding slightly in the free border of the membrane. The width of the cartilage is rather uniform, about 4 mm. Above and below the medial end of the cartilage are the ovate, lobulated **Harderian glands.**

### LACRIMAL APPARATUS

The **lacrimal gland** is situated on the lateroventral surface of the eye ball, the bulk of the gland lying directly beneath the postorbital ligament. It is a thick, moderately elongated body, 15 mm. in length by 10 mm. in greatest width, placed below the levator palpebrae superioris and behind (outside) the tendinous expansion of that muscle.

The lacrimal papillae and lacrimal ducts were destroyed when the animal was skinned. The two lacrimal ducts open independently into the lacrimal sac; the openings are 3 mm. apart. The superior opening is considerably smaller than the inferior one.

The **lacrimal sac** is an inconspicuous, vertically elongated sac, 25 mm. in length. The superior lacrimal duct opens at its upper tip, so that there is no fornix.

### MUSCLES OF THE ORBIT

There are eight orbital muscles, seven of which are ocular while the eighth (levator palpebrae superioris) has no attachment to the eye ball. All are enclosed within the periorbita.

**Mm. recti,** four in number, arise around the optic foramen. The origins of the four muscles are continuous with one another, except for a space between the rectus superior and the rectus lateralis through which the retractor is continued to its origin farther posteriorly. The rectus muscles together form a cone that encloses the retractor, and the external surface of each lies against the periorbita, except for the rectus superior which is separated from the periorbita by the levator palpebrae superioris. Insertion is by means of flat tendons into the sclera in front of the equator.

317

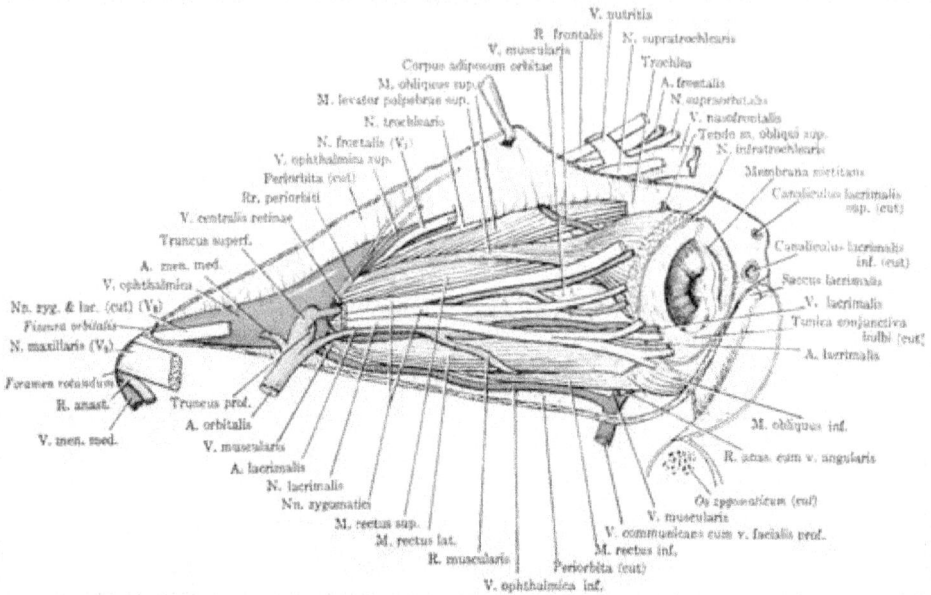

FIG. 158. Right orbit of *Ailuropoda*, lateral view.

The rectus medialis is the largest, then the lateralis, the inferior, and finally the superior, which is the smallest of the four. The lateral border of the inferior is united to the ventral border of the lateralis by a prominent tendinous intersection for nearly the posterior half of these two muscles. Adjacent borders of the inferior and medialis, and of the medialis and superior, are united by similar but slightly shorter tendinous intersections. Thus the cone formed by the recti is completely closed in its posterior part, except for the space between the superior and lateralis through which the retractor passes.

M, levator palpebrae superioris is a narrow band of muscle, expanding suddenly at its insertion, that lies dorsad of the rectus superior and immediately beneath the periorbita. Origin is taken from the ridge running forward and upward from the dorsal border of the optic foramen, the levator arising anterior to the rectus superior. Insertion is into the upper eye lid. A small independent group of short medial fibers arises from the surface of the trochlea and passes forward and outward to join the main mass of the muscle near its insertion.

M. obliquus superior arises directly anterior to the levator palpebrae superioris. The muscle forms a round tendon at the posterior border of the trochlea. This tendon, as usual, passes through the trochlea, then turns abruptly at a right angle, to insert on the sclera in front of the equator on the dorsal surface of the eye ball.

M. obliquus inferior occupies the usual position below the eye ball. Origin is within the lacrimal fossa, and the muscle crosses the end of the rectus inferior to reach its insertion at the ventral edge of the rectus lateralis.

M. retractor oculi is enclosed within the cone formed by the four rectus muscles. The muscle arises far behind the optic foramen, just anterior to the orbital fissure, and passes between the superior and lateral recti to gain the interior of the orbit. Before passing inside the recti the muscle divides into superior and inferior parts, and within the recti each of these divides again, the superior forming the superior and medial divisions and the inferior forming the inferior and lateral divisions. The four resulting heads surround the optic nerve, and insert on the sclera between and slightly behind the heads of the recti. The inferior head of the retractor is perforated by the abducens nerve.

The retractor muscle is supplied by branches from the ciliary ganglion.

## II. MIDDLE EAR

The bony part of the middle ear was described by Segall (1943). My description of the skeletal elements is largely from the same specimen used

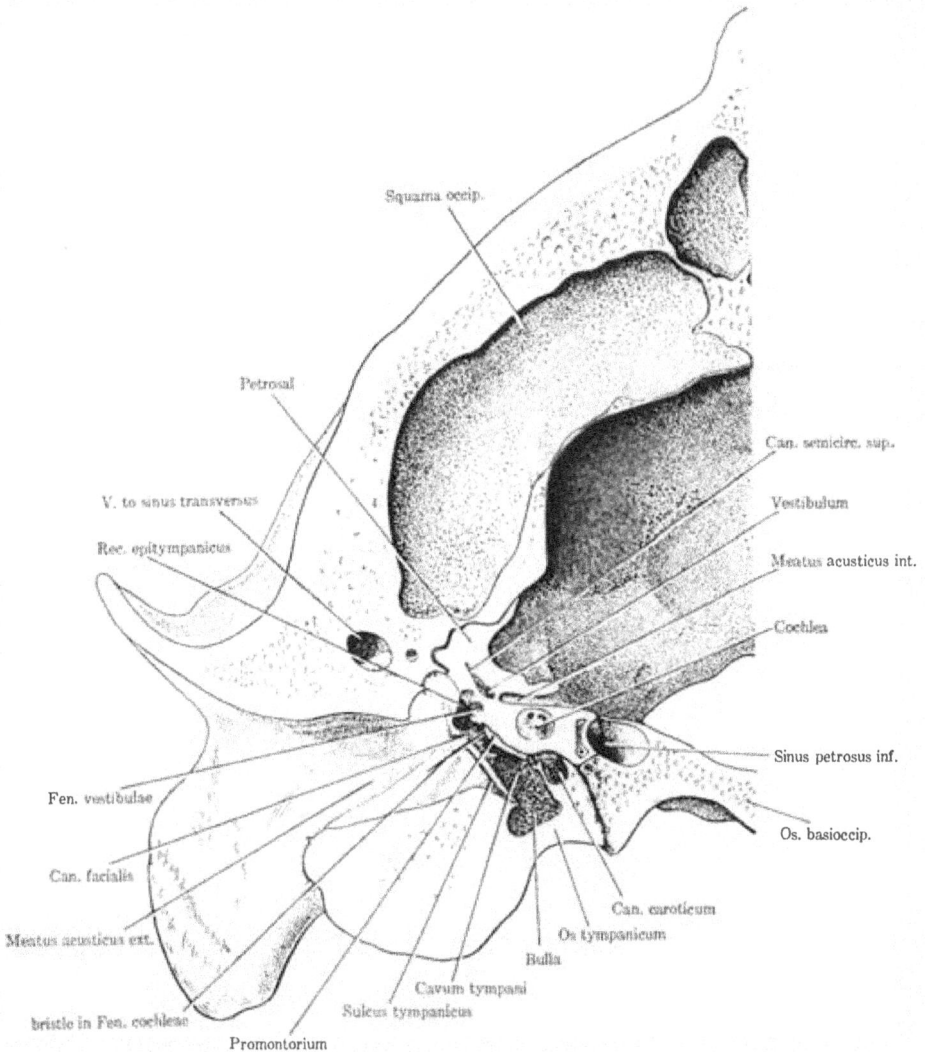

FIG. 159. Frontal section through right auditory region of *Ailuropoda*, posterior view.

by him, an adult female skull sectioned frontally through the middle and internal ear (fig. 159).

The whole basioccipital region is greatly shortened in *Ailuropoda*, and the auditory region looks as if it were strongly compressed between the postglenoid process anteriorly and the mastoid and paroccipital processes posteriorly. Even the external acoustic meatus and canal are elliptical in cross section, much higher than broad, as if compressed anteroposteriorly. The medial end of the

enormous postglenoid process lies directly beneath the tympanic cavity, whereas in *Ursus* this process is entirely anterior and lateral to the cavity.

The external acoustic canal is about the same relative length as in *Ursus*, measuring about 22 mm. It is transverse and slopes only very slightly downward and outward. The tympanic forms its floor and the lowest part of the anterior and posterior walls. The greater part of the canal is formed by the squamosal. Externally there is no indication of a bulla: the inferior surface of the tympanic is flat and only slightly below the level of the basi-occipital. In ventral view the tympanic is triangular in *Ursus*: in *Ailuropoda* the anterior half of the triangle is missing and the external acoustic canal and foramina at the anterior margin of the tympanic are shifted far posteriorly. The long axis of the tympanic forms an angle of about 45° with the long axis of the skull.

At the anterior margin of the tympanic the petro-tympanic fissure for the chorda tympani lies most laterally (fig. 18). Medial to this is the large musculotubular foramen, incompletely divided by a ridge into a medial semicanalis tubae auditivae and a lateral semicanalis m. tensoris tympani. The musculotubular foramen is variable, even from side to side in the same individual. The foramen lacerum posterior is situated behind the middle of the medial margin of the tympanic. The carotid foramen lies anteriorly within the posterior lacerated foramen. Lateral to the lacerated foramen, between the posterior margin of the tympanic and the paroccipital process, is a deep pit, the hyoid fossa, in which the hyoid articulates with the skull. There are two small vascular canals in the antero-medial part of this fossa. Anterolateral to the hyoid fossa, and separated from it by a thin wall, is the stylomastoid foramen, which is continued laterally into a trough-like groove. The stylomastoid foramen transmits the facial nerve, the auricular branch of the vagus, and the stylomastoid artery. In the posterior wall of the postglenoid process, near the external acoustic meatus, is the large postglenoid foramen, which transmits the dorsal facial vein.

## TYMPANIC MEMBRANE

The tympanic ring, to which the tympanic membrane is attached, forms an angle of about 35° with the sagittal plane of the skull. It is considerably more vertical in position than in a specimen of *Ursus americanus*. The ring consists of a shallow sulcus, in which the tympanic membrane is attached, surrounded by a sharp tympanic ridge. The ring is incomplete superiorly, terminating in the anterior and posterior tympanic spines, which bound a tympanic notch 6.5 mm. wide.

The pars tensa of the tympanic membrane is thin, almost transparent, and nearly circular in outline. Its vertical diameter is about 10.5 mm., its horizontal diameter about 11 mm. To judge from the tympanic ring, the membrane was considerably smaller in a specimen of *Ursus americanus*. From the external aspect the membrane is slightly concave. The apex of the resulting cone corresponds to the sharp bend in the distal third

of the manubrium of the malleus, and not to the apex of the manubrium, and is nearly central in position. The lateral process of the malleus produces a slight projection, the prominentia malleo-laris, in the membrane. From it an anterior and a posterior malleolar fold radiate to the corresponding spines at the extremities of the tympanic sulcus. These two folds embrace a superior triangular area, the flaccid portion of the tympanic membrane. The flaccid membrane continues laterally, separating an air space (the suprameatal fossa) from the auditory canal proper. The suprameatal fossa communicates medially with the tympanic cavity through a minute space posterior to the neck of the malleus, bounded by the neck of the malleus, the long arm of the incus, and the chorda tympani.

## TYMPANIC CAVITY

The tympanic cavity is remarkable for the small size of the bulla, but otherwise resembles that of *Ursus americanus*. It is an irregular chamber, much higher than broad, lying in an oblique position. The vertical axis lies at about 45° to the horizontal plane, and the longitudinal axis forms an angle of about 25° with the long axis of the skull. The cavity measures 17 mm. in anteroposterior diameter, 18 mm. in vertical diameter (including the epitympanic recess), and 9 mm. in greatest transverse diameter.

The roof is formed medially by the periotic, laterally by the squamosal. Anteriorly the roof continues over a low transverse ridge into the epitympanic recess; there is no epitympanic sinus. The facial nerve is visible medial and posterior to the epitympanic recess; it leaves the tympanic cavity opposite the oval window, through a foramen in the floor of the epitympanic recess.

The floor and anterior and posterior walls are formed by the tympanic. The bulla is a relatively very small and uninflated hypotympanic recess, 6.5 mm. in transverse diameter, in the floor of the cavity. Anteriorly the cavity continues into the large musculotubular canal, which transmits the auditory tube medially and the tensor tympani muscle laterally. The petrotympanic (Glaserian) fissure, through which the chorda tympani leaves the tympanic cavity, is a minute opening in the anterior wall of the cavity, just below the epitympanic recess and lateral to the musculotubular canal. The chorda tympani enters the cavity through the iter chorda tympani posterior, a small opening in the posterolateral wall between the epitympanic recess and the annulus tympanicus. At its distal end this canal opens into the stylomastoid canal, within which the chorda tympani arises from the facial nerve.

The periotic forms the greater part of the medial wall of the tympanic cavity. There is a slit-like cavity containing a small amount of cancellous tissue in the part of this bone adjoining the inferior petrosal sinus. A similar, but much broader cavity filled with cancellous tissue is present in *Ursus*. A much larger cancellated cavity in the dorsolateral part of the periotic of *Ursus* is completely absent in *Ailuropoda*. The promontorium protrudes into the tympanic cavity as a rounded elevation, separated from the tympanic membrane by a remarkably short distance. Directly above the promontorium, at the bottom of a shallow depression, is the vestibular (oval) window, which is closed by the base of the stapes. The pyramidal eminence, around which the tensor tympani rides, is a conspicuous circular process behind and slightly below the vestibular window. The cochlear (round) window is situated posterior to the promontorium.

The carotid canal, which transmits the internal carotid artery, runs anteriorly in the tympanic bone, just below the periotic and separated from the tympanic cavity by a thin wall. Anteriorly it opens directly into the cavernous sinus at the anterior margin of the petrosal; it does not first emerge to the outside through a foramen lacerum medium as it does in bears.

### Auditory Ossicles

The malleus was described by Segall (1943), who states that it is very similar to the mallei of *Ailurus* and the Ursidae. The incus and stapes closely resemble the corresponding bones in other carnivores.

#### Ligaments of the Ossicles

The posterior malleolar fold extends posteriorly from the superior margin of the tympanic membrane, the posterior surface of the malleus, and the posterior tympanic spine. It encloses the chorda tympani and its cartilaginous support. The anterior malleolar ligament runs from the anterior tympanic spine and the roof of the epitympanic recess to the anterior process and free border of the lamina of the malleus. It is enclosed by the anterior malleolar fold, which continues around the chorda tympani. The superior malleolar ligament is very short and joins the head of the malleus to the roof of the epitympanic recess. The lateral malleolar ligament is absent; the flaccid membrane supports the malleus laterally.

#### Muscles of the Ossicles

The *M. tensor tympani* is an oval-shaped muscle 7 mm. long and 3 mm. wide. The tendinous fibers of origin begin within the bony auditory canal, arising from the bony septum of the musculotubular canal and the anterolateral wall of the canal. The body of the tensor tympani lies in a deep fossa in the medial wall of the tympanic cavity. The terminal tendon runs ventrolaterally to insert on the muscular process of the malleus. The *M. stapedius* arises from the spout-like lateral process of the promontorium and inserts on the ventral crus of the stapes.

### Auditory Tube

The auditory (Eustachian) tube extends from the tympanic orifice in the anterior wall of the tympanic cavity to the pharyngeal orifice near the middle of the lateral border of the pharyngeal tonsil, at the level of the dorsum sellae. The lateral wall of the tube is membranous; the medial wall is thicker and contains cartilage in its anterior two thirds. The cartilage is 12 mm. long, tapering to a tip just inside the osseous portion. The cartilage produces a swelling, the torus tubarius, in the pharyngeal mucosa lateral to the pharyngeal tonsil. The pharyngeal orifice is a slit-like opening 7 mm. in length.

### Discussion of the Middle Ear

The auditory region of the arctoid Carnivora was studied by Segall (1943), who expanded the earlier work of Van Kampen (1905). Segall concluded that this region is similar in procyonids and bears, differing in several diagnostic features from the auditory region of the Canidae. In the structure of the auditory region the Canidae form a very compact group.

Superficially the middle ear of *Ailuropoda* looks quite different from that of the Ursidae. The tympanic bone is much smaller and very differently shaped, the anterior carotid foramen is internal instead of external, there is no foramen lacerum medium, and the bulla is reduced to a very small hypotympanic recess. The whole tympanic cavity is more oblique in position. All these, and other less conspicuous differences, can be attributed to strong anteroposterior compression of the middle ear in *Ailuropoda*, which appears to be near the limit that is compatible with normal functioning. Compression of the auditory region, in turn, is a consequence of the posterior shift of the root of the zygomatic arch and the enormous size of the postglenoid process, and thus is directly related to masticatory requirements.

# COMPARATIVE ANATOMY AND EVOLUTION: AN EVALUATION
## OF THE TEST PROBLEM

The main purpose of this study was to test the extent to which the methods of comparative anatomy can be used to explain, in terms of causal mechanisms, the kind of morphological differences with which the anatomist (and taxonomist) customarily deals. The data from each section have been reviewed at the end of each section, and conclusions presented. Here the general problem will be reviewed.

There are two parts to the problem: (1) What is the closest known relative of *Ailuropoda*, and how closely does it represent the structural ancestry of *Ailuropoda*, and (2) to what extent can we infer the morphogenetic mechanisms through which the specialized characters of *Ailuropoda* were produced by natural selection?

## I. THE RELATIONSHIPS OF AILUROPODA

Every morphological feature examined indicates that the giant panda is nothing more than a highly specialized bear. Therefore, *Ailuropoda* can either be placed in the family Ursidae, or—if its differences from the Ursidae are deemed sufficiently great—in a monotypic family of its own. *Ailuropoda* differs from the Ursidae far less than either does from any other group of carnivores, and this similarity is best expressed by including *Ailuropoda* in the Ursidae. The bears have not usually been divided into subfamilies, so the "true" bears may conveniently be placed in a subfamily Ursinae, and the giant panda in a subfamily Ailuropodinae, within the family Ursidae.

*Ailurus* resembles *Ailuropoda* in several features involving the masticatory apparatus and the fore foot, the two extremely specialized structures in both genera. Some students (e.g., Gregory, 1936) associated *Ailuropoda* with *Ailurus*, and therefore with the Procyonidae, on the basis of these resemblances. There is also a resemblance in the male external genitalia, a structure that is curiously aberrant in these two genera. In all other morphological respects *Ailurus* obviously has nothing to do with *Ailuropoda* or the Ursinae. The similarities between *Ailurus* and *Ailuropoda* that Gregory and others have emphasized are convergences resulting from similar functional requirements;

they are not similarities resulting from common ancestry. The proper allocation of *Ailurus* is somewhat uncertain. Except for the specialized conditions mentioned above, its morphology resembles that of the Procyonidae more closely than that of any other family, but these resemblances may represent common primitive features. I am not sure that *Ailurus* belongs with the Procyonidae, which is where all modern authors place it, but in the absence of clear evidence to the contrary it seems best to leave it there.

Modern paleontologists regard the Canidae as the central stock of the arctoid carnivores. The Canidae diverged early into four or more lines that evolved into or were ancestral to the several groups of arctoid carnivores. The bears arose from one of these, the amphicynodontine dogs (otherwise now extinct), about the middle of the Miocene. This makes them the youngest of all carnivore families. The Procyonidae arose much earlier, apparently, but not certainly, from the true "canine" dog stock. The amphicynodontine and canine lines have been independent since the Eocene, so if the canine origin of the procyonids is borne out the bears and procyonids are only rather remotely related.

Paleontologists are fond of referring to the modern Canidae as remarkably primitive, as virtually early Tertiary fissipeds, and thus as representing the structural conditions from which all procyonids and ursids were derived. This is true of the skull, and particularly of the dentition, but, as we have seen throughout this work, almost every detail of the postcranial anatomy of modern dogs differs from all other carnivores. These differences do not represent retention of primitive features, and are often difficult to interpret as adaptive. In the aggregate they set the modern dogs sharply apart from all other arctoid carnivores. It is these features that led such anatomists as Mivart and Flower to place the dogs apart in a separate suborder. In many ways the Procyonidae and Ursidae, and even the Mustelidae, resemble each other more closely than they do the dogs. We must conclude that, except in the masticatory apparatus, the morphology of the procyonids and bears is generally more primitive than that of the dogs. Sim-

ilarities between procyonids and bears are then
due partly to convergence (in the masticatory apparatus), and partly to retention of common primitive characters.

Except for the allocation of *Ailuropoda*, these
questions are not very relevant to the objectives
of the present study. For our purposes we need
only know that *Ailuropoda* is indeed a bear, and
therefore that its morphology is in fact a remodeling of the morphology of the Ursidae. Of this
there can be no reasonable doubt. We do not know
how similar to *Ursus* was the presumed ancestor
of *Ailuropoda*. The living bears form a compact
group centered around *Ursus*, and we have assumed that the morphology of *Ursus* represents
the structural ancestry of *Ailuropoda*.

The bears are already considerably modified for
a herbivorous diet, and to a considerable extent
the morphology of *Ailuropoda* is an extension, so
to speak, of the adaptive modifications already
present in the bears. We are not concerned with
the origin of the ursid characters in *Ailuropoda*,
however adaptive to its way of life they may be,
but only with the morphological differences between *Ursus* and *Ailuropoda*.

## II. MORPHOGENETIC MECHANISMS IN THE EVOLUTION OF AILUROPODA

Two factors are primarily responsible for adaptive modifications in the morphology of mammals:
locomotion, and food and feeding. These two factors operated in a most remarkable—almost unique
—way on *Ailuropoda*. Together they hold the
key to the evolution of this animal from its ursine
ancestors.

In mammals the major forces impinging on locomotion are escape from enemies, pursuit of prey
and wandering in search of food or water. We have
seen (p. 22) that in the case of *Ailuropoda* each
of these forces is reduced practically to zero, that
selection pressures for locomotor efficiency are relaxed almost to the vanishing point. This means
that severe impairment of locomotor efficiency
could be tolerated, provided such impairment was
genetically linked with some other character that
conferred even slight advantage. Moreover, the
necessity for breaking down or circumventing such
"pleiotropic" linkages in order to permit restora-
tion of locomotor efficiency would be minimal.
Thus in *Ailuropoda* pleiotropic relations that in
other mammals are masked by the necessity for
maintaining a high level of over-all efficiency may
still be evident. As will be seen below, there is
abundant evidence that such pleiotropic relations
are present in unmasked form in *Ailuropoda*. They

will be extremely helpful in inferring the epigenetic
basis for the adaptive features.

### ADAPTIVE DIFFERENCES

The masticatory apparatus has undergone enormous adaptive modification in *Ailuropoda*. Almost
every structure in the head differs in some way
from its counterpart in the bears. Most of these
are readjustments of the head morphology to a few
major adaptive changes and require the postulation
of no intrinsic mechanism other than the ability
of the tissues to respond to extrinsic forces during
ontogeny. Ignoring minor polishing effects, only
four major adaptive changes seem to be required
to derive the head morphology of *Ailuropoda* from
that of the Ursidae. These are:

(1) Increased cheek tooth size. Reasons were
given above (p. 130) for postulating a very simple
mechanism, perhaps involving a single change, for
this transformation. The cheek tooth battery almost surely represents a morphogenetic unit in
*Ailuropoda*, as in other mammals, and has re-
sponded as a unit to selection. The effect of evolutionary allometry, which requires no genetic
mechanism not already present in the bears, is seen
in the surface sculpturing of the cheek teeth.

(2) Increased mass of bone tissue in the skull.
This is associated with a generalized increase in
bone tissue in the whole axial region, and a disturbance of pattern in the axial region, concentrated in the lumbosacral region. These latter
conditions are non-adaptive, even inadaptive. The
fact that an area, rather than a functional unit, is
involved strongly suggests that a simple one-factor
mechanism is responsible. Klatt and Oboussier
(1951) describe a similar situation in bulldogs, and
interpret it as due to a genetically controlled alteration in growth gradient affecting all tissues in the
head region.

(3) Elevation of the mandibular articulation
above the level of the toothrow. This mechanically advantageous condition occurs generally in
herbivorous mammals and is obviously adaptive.
Its morphogenetic basis is unknown.

(4) Increase in the total mass of the masticatory
musculature. This is most pronounced in the masticatory musculature, but extends, apparently in a
sharply descending gradient, into the musculature
of the shoulder and upper arm. Only a simple
epigenetic mechanism would be likely to produce
so non-selective (although generally adaptive) a
condition. Indeed, the studies of Klatt (1950) and
Klatt and Oboussier (1951) on dogs show that a
comparable increase in masticatory musculature,
and likewise extending onto the forequarters, has

taken place in the bulldog type as part of a general increase in the mass of all tissues of the head. Thus no genetic mechanism peculiar to the musculature need be postulated.

Superimposed on this generalized increase there is a selective increase in the mass of those components of the jaw musculature that produce horizontal movements of the jaw. These movements are mechanically advantageous in a herbivorous carnivore. Such localized differences in the composition of a muscle complex presumably reflect the action of selection on factors controlling localized muscle differentiation. The studies of Schumacher (1961b) on the human masseter in edentulous individuals and in cases of pronounced bite anomalies show, however, that profound adaptive changes in the architecture of this muscle may take place during the life of the individual, and thus represent physiological adaptations entirely independent of the genetic system. The effectiveness of the temporal muscle, the most important jaw flexor, is enhanced by increased pennation, and this may involve the action of selection on unknown factors controlling the differentiation of the internal architecture of this muscle. Adaptive alteration in skeletal muscles was obviously one of the most important elements in the adaptive radiation of mammals, and it is a serious handicap that we know practically nothing of the morphogenetic mechanisms controlling muscle differentiation and growth.

Thus it seems likely that an astonishingly simple system, consisting of fewer than half a dozen genetic factors, is involved in the highly modified masticatory apparatus of *Ailuropoda*. The basic elements of this complex—enlarged cheek teeth, enlarged jaw musculature, and increased bone thickness in the skull—seem to require postulation of no more than one, or at most two, factors each. The mechanism involved in the further refinements described under (3) and (4) above cannot be deduced and therefore are of unknown complexity.

The gross structure of the remainder of the alimentary tract shows numerous differences from the Ursidae. For the most part these are more subtle than differences in the masticatory apparatus, although the very short small intestine in *Ailuropoda* is as striking as any of the masticatory differences. All gross differences between the gut of *Ailuropoda* and that of the Ursidae are in the direction of modifications found in other mammals that ingest large quantities of fibrous plant material, and therefore we have regarded them as adaptive. Similar changes induced by feeding controlled diets to experimental animals are always similar to, but less extreme than, those seen in *Ailuropoda*.

We must therefore assume that the conditions in *Ailuropoda* have a genetic basis of some kind, but nothing is known of the morphogenetic mechanisms controlling such manifestations.

The second obviously adaptive structure in *Ailuropoda* is the manual grasping mechanism. This structure is already partly developed in the Ursidae. We have concluded (again ignoring minor polishing effects) that simple hypertrophy of the radial sesamoid was all that was required to produce this mechanism from conditions already existing in bears. No new morphogenetic mechanism need be postulated for the muscles operating the sesamoid (p. 183), the ligaments (p. 139), or the diarthrodial joint (p. 140). The homeotic effect seen in the sympathetic enlargement of the tibial sesamoid in *Ailuropoda* strongly suggests that a very simple mechanism, perhaps involving a single factor, lies behind the hypertrophy of the radial sesamoid. The fact that some hypertrophy of both radial and tibial sesamoids is present in the bears indicates that the epigenetic mechanism was already present in the ancestors of *Ailuropoda*.

Finally, the elaboration of areas of the cerebral cortex that are associated with both of the preceding structures (p. 298) certainly reflects the action of natural selection. Other changes in the cortex, too subtle to be detected, would have to form a part of the over-all adaptation. These include such important elements as the recognition of bamboo as food, behavior appropriate to utilizing it as food, etc. The nature of the morphogenetic mechanisms controlling differentiation of the brain is unknown, and consequently we cannot even guess at the complexity of the mechanisms that lie behind morphological differences between the brain of *Ailuropoda* and that of the ursines.

## NON-ADAPTIVE AND INADAPTIVE DIFFERENCES

In addition to these overtly adaptive conditions there is another group of differences between *Ailuropoda* and the ursines to which no adaptive significance can be assigned. Some of these, such as reduction in the number of thoracolumbar vertebrae (a homeotic effect), and the form of the pelvis, exceed the range of normal variation in the whole of the Carnivora. It is difficult, perhaps impossible, to prove conclusively that a particular departure from an anatomical norm is not adaptive in some obscure way. I spent a great deal of time and effort trying to find a plausible functional explanation for the peculiarities in limb proportions, vertebral column, and pelvis and sacrum seen in *Ailuropoda*, and finally concluded that the probability that these are directly adaptive is so small that some other explanation must be sought.

Grüneberg (1952) says of the laboratory mouse that "all genes which have been studied with any care have manifold or 'pleiotropic' effects." It is reasonable to assume that this would likewise be true of the genes responsible for the morphological differences that distinguish taxa in nature, although in most cases such effects would be masked. No other explanation seems reasonable for many of the inadaptive conditions in *Ailuropoda*, and we may therefore look for evidence of such pleiotropic effects. Stockard (1941) emphasized that in crosses between dogs of different breeds "modified structural responses are sometimes localized or limited to certain narrow regions, while other parts of the animal conform to the usual or normal pattern," and that "extreme structural disharmonies . . . are frequently found to occur in hybrids." Stockard emphasized the role of endocrine disturbances in producing the conditions he found. To explain the localization of the effects he pointed out that comparable growth stages of various tissues and regions of the body are reached at different times during ontogeny. In more modern language, they are "competent" at different times. He suggested that such endocrine disturbances were temporary, and affected those tissues that happened to be competent at the time of the disturbance. In hereditary conditions it is the timing of the disturbance that is genetically determined.

Klatt (1939, 1948, 1950) and Klatt and Oboussier (1951) made detailed metrical studies of the extreme morphological types represented by the bulldog and greyhound types of dog to determine what anatomical features are affected, and the direction and extent to which they are altered. These purely morphological studies were supplemented with breeding experiments, including backcrosses between the two types. Certain characteristics of the bulldog type parallel those we have found in *Ailuropoda*: overdevelopment of the anterior half of the body, with strongest development of the head; shortening of the vertebral column, with disturbances in the morphology of the vertebrae. In the head, the relative weights of the skull and the craniomandibular musculature were increased to almost exactly the same degree, indicating that a common morphogenetic mechanism is responsible for the enlargement of both. The brain was only slightly heavier in bulldogs. In other respects the bulldog type contrasts strongly with *Ailuropoda*. The relative weight of the eye balls and hypophysis is increased in bulldogs. The face is greatly shortened, the legs are shortened in a gradient running distally, and the skin is much thicker. Klatt dismisses the usual interpretation of the bulldog type as merely chondrodystrophic. He regards

the striking and permeating morphological differences between the bulldog and greyhound type as probably due to a few genetically controlled differences in growth gradients acting during early ontogeny. The studies of Klatt and Stockard emphasize the role that simple genetic mechanisms, acting on ontogenetic processes, may play in producing conditions comparable to (and even similar to) those seen in *Ailuropoda*.

Some of the conditions in *Ailuropoda* are most plausibly explained as representing portions of morphogenetic fields in which the morphogenetic unit does not coincide with the functional unit. Selection on any element in the morphogenetic field would then affect the field as a whole, and intense selection could result in random non-adaptive alterations in parts of the field not involved in the adaptive change. No other explanation is reasonable for the broadening of the vertebrae (including the caudals) and proximal parts of the ribs in *Ailuropoda*. The skull and axial skeleton form a topographic unit in the developing embryo, and in *Ailuropoda* the boundaries of the affected area can be drawn with considerable precision (p. 87).

Other conditions represent gradients of generalized alteration centered in an area of intense adaptive modification. Such a situation is evident in the general increase in quantity of compacta in the skeleton of *Ailuropoda*. The entire skeleton is affected, but in a gradient of decreasing intensity centered in the skull (p. 122). The condition is adaptive only in the skull. This more generalized effect is distinct from, and so to speak superimposed on, the morphogenetic field effect discussed above.

There is an area of intense morphological disturbance in the lumbosacral region of *Ailuropoda*. Here it is not only a single tissue (bone) that is affected. Many structures in this area, regardless of their ontogenetic origin, are modified in non-adaptive ways. Such alterations are evident in the skeleton, external genitalia, circulatory system, and lumbosacral plexus. At least the male genitalia and postcaval vein are modified in the direction of fetalization, which suggests interruption or slowing down of ontogenetic development. The sharp localization of the affected region again points to a simple morphogenetic mechanism as causal agent. The variety of tissues and organ systems involved makes it likely that the effect manifests itself relatively early in ontogeny.

This area of profound disturbance lies in the axial region. It is most plausibly explained as a pleiotropic effect associated with the adaptive modification of the skull and/or masticatory musculature. Atypical genitalia occur in two other

carnivores in which the masticatory apparatus is
hypertrophied: the lesser panda (*Ailurus*), and the
spotted hyena (*Crocuta*). In neither of these have
I been able to detect any indication of disturbance
in other structures in the lumbosacral region.

There is indication, not statistically verifiable
from our small samples, of evolutionary allometry
in limb proportions in *Ailuropoda* and the bears
(p. 39). Although if present it would affect the
morphology of *Ailuropoda*, such changes would not
result from selection for bone length and would
require no genetic mechanism not already present
in the bear ancestry of the panda.

Thus it appears that most of the differences between *Ailuropoda* and the bears can be attributed
to a few simple morphogenetic mechanisms. The
action of most of these mechanisms can be identified with reasonable certainty. It is true that corresponding effects have not been discovered in
laboratory mammals, such as the mouse, whose
genetics have been studied intensively, although
many gene effects of corresponding magnitude are
known (Grüneberg, 1952). The gene effects we
have postulated as having been selected for in
*Ailuropoda* all involve intensification of differentiation or growth of tissues, whereas the gene effects known in laboratory and domestic animals
practically always interfere with normal ontogenetic processes and result in deficiencies.[1] Grüneberg even refers to the gene effects in the laboratory mouse in general as "pathological." There
certainly is no *a priori* reason why interference
with normal ontogenetic processes cannot take the
form of speeding them up or prolonging the period
of differentiation or growth.

The various morphogenetic effects we have identified in *Ailuropoda* may be summarized as follows:

1. Generalized effect on a single tissue.
   (a) Gradient: skeleton, musculature.
   (b) Morphogenetic field: dentition, axial
       skeleton.
2. Localized pleiotropic effect on all tissues of a
region: lumbosacral region.
3. Homeotic effect: vertebral column, radial
and tibial sesamoids.
4. Evolutionary allometry: tooth crown pattern, limb proportions(?).[2]

This is not presented as a complete catalog of
the genetic history of *Ailuropoda*. As we have

[1] Notable exceptions are muscular hypertrophy in cattle
(Kidwell *et al.*, 1952), and gigantism.

[2] These are practically identical with the factors listed by
Rensch (1960, p. 129) as "providing a sufficient explanation
of animal transformation even at the level of systemic alterations." I had not seen Rensch's work at the time these
words were written.

seen, there are several important adaptive features
for which we are completely unable to get at the
genetic background. Unquestionably there has been
much refinement of the gross adaptive changes, involving natural selection and genetic mechanisms,
and this is a part of the hidden evolutionary history of *Ailuropoda*. It is not, however, very relevant to our major thesis.

What is important is that there is, I believe,
clear evidence that the major, decisive, adaptive
modifications characterizing *Ailuropoda* can be
traced to a very small number of epigenetic mechanisms. I do not intend to imply that each of
these modifications arose in one step, nor do I regard the question of how quickly or slowly the
definitive condition was achieved as particularly
important in the present context. It is important
that natural selection was able to operate through
this small number of epigenetic mechanisms to
produce, from a given ancestral condition, an integrated and highly adapted organism, at least
generically distinct from its contemporaries. This
relatively simple situation makes it possible in a
favorable case, such as is presented by *Ailuropoda*,
to infer causes from effects, and thus to explain in
terms of causal mechanisms the kind of structural
differences with which the comparative anatomist
deals.

## CONCLUSIONS

1. Structural differences among mammals are
determined largely by the mechanical demands of
support, locomotion, and feeding.

2. In the giant panda, selection pressure for locomotor efficiency is reduced almost to zero, whereas selection pressure for efficiency in handling food
is intense. In terrestrial mammals the demands of
support are a function of organism weight, and
would be the same in *Ailuropoda* as in a bear of
comparable size.

3. The aggregate of many anatomical features
shows that the giant panda is a highly specialized
bear.

4. Structural differences between *Ailuropoda*
and the bears fall into two categories: (a) overtly
adaptive modifications in the feeding and digestive
mechanisms, including central nervous structures;
and (b) non-adaptive differences found throughout
the body.

5. The adaptive modifications in the mechanisms for food manipulation (manus) and primary
food treatment (masticatory apparatus) involve
only regional hypertrophy of tissues and the consequential effects thereof.

6. Such hypertrophies result from changes in growth gradients acting in early ontogeny. Regional specificity results from the timing of such changes. The underlying genetic mechanisms are relatively simple.

7. The non-adaptive modifications are pleiotropic effects that are linked genetically to the adaptive modifications. In most mammals such non-adaptive modifications are eliminated to produce a condition of functional homeostasis. They have been retained in *Ailuropoda* because selection pressure for over-all efficiency is below the critical threshold.

8. Very few genetic mechanisms perhaps no more than half a dozen were involved in the primary adaptive shift from *Ursus* to *Ailuropoda*. The action of most of these mechanisms can be identified with reasonable certainty.

9. Therefore it appears possible, using the methods of comparative anatomy, at least in favorable cases to explain structural differences in terms of causal mechanisms.

# REFERENCES

ACKERKNECHT, EBERHARD
  1919. Die Papillarmuskeln des Herzens. Untersuchungen an Karnivorherzen. Arch. Anat. Physiol. (anat. 1918, pp. 63–136, 12 figs., pls. 4–5.

ALBRECHT, HEINRICH
  1896. Beitrag zur vergleichenden Anatomie des Säugethierkehlkopfes. Sitzungsber. K. Akad. Wiss. Wien (Math.-Naturw.), 105 (3), pp. 227–322, 1 fig., 7 pls.

ALIX, E.
  1878. Sur les poches pharyngiennes de l'ours jongleur (Ursus labiatus). Bull. Soc. Philom. Paris, (7) 1, pp. 47–48.

ANTHONY, R.
  1903. De l'action morphogenique des muscles crotaphytes sur le crâne et le cerveau des carnassiers et des primates. C. R. Acad. Sci. Paris, 137, pp. 881–883.

ANTHONY, R., and ILIESCO, G. M.
  1926. Étude sur les cavités nasales des carnassiers. Proc. Zool. Soc. London, 1926, pp. 989–1013, 9 figs.

BARDENFLETH, K. S.
  1913. On the systematic position of Aeluropus melanoleucus. Mindeskr. Japetus Steenstrup, art. 17, 15 pp., 3 figs., 1 pl.

BAUM, HERMANN, and ZIETZSCHMANN, OTTO
  1936. Handbuch der Anatomie des Hundes. Ed. 2 (revised of ELLENBERGER-BAUM, Anatomie des Hundes. 1, Skelett- und Muskelsystem. 242 pp., 180 figs. Berlin, Parey.

BEDDARD, F. E.
  1895. On certain points in the anatomy of the cunning bassarisc, Bassariscus astutus. Proc. Zool. Soc. London, 1898, pp. 129–131.
  1900. On the anatomy of Bassaricyon alleni. Proc. Zool. Soc. London, 1900. pp. 661–675.
  1902. Mammalia. Cambridge Nat. Hist., v. 10. 605 pp. London, Macmillan.
  1909. On some points in the structure of Galidea elegans, and on the postcaval veins in the carnivores. Proc. Zool. Soc. London, 1909, pp. 477–496, 9 figs.

BIEGERT, J.
  1957. Der Formwandel des Primatenschädels und seine Beziehungen zur ontogenetischen Entwicklung und den phylogenetischen Spezialisationen der Kopforgane. Morph. Jahrb., 98, pp. 77–199, 15 figs.

BLUNTSCHLI, HANS
  1906. Die Arteria femoralis und ihre Äste bei den niederen catarrhinen Affen. Eine vergleichend-anatomische Untersuchung. Morph. Jahrb., 36, pp. 276–461, 85 figs.

BÖKER, HANS
  1935. Einfuhrung in die vergleichende biologische Anatomie der Wirbeltiere. I. 228 pp., 225 figs. Jena, Fischer.

BOLK, LOUIS
  1906. Das Cerebellum der Säugetiere. Eine vergleichend anatomische Untersuchung. 337 pp., 183 figs., 3 pls. Jena, Fischer.

BRADLEY, O. C.
  1948. Topographical anatomy of the dog. Ed. 5, revised by T. GRAHAME. 319 pp., 128 figs. Edinburgh, Oliver & Boyd.

BRAUS, HERMANN
  1929. Anatomie des Menschen (ed. 2, 1. Berlin, Springer.

BROCKLEHURST, H. C.
  1936. The giant panda. Jour. Soc. Pres. Fauna Empire, 28, pp. 21–23, 1 fig.

BROOM, ROBERT, and ROBINSON, J. T.
  1949. Photographs of some recently discovered specimens of Australopithecinae. Yearbook Phys. Anthrop., 5, pp. 55–59.

BUTLER, P. M.
  1939. Studies of the mammalian dentition.—Differentiation of the post-canine dentition. Proc. Zool. Soc. London, 109 (B), pp. 1–36, 28 figs.
  1946. The evolution of carnassial dentitions in the Mammalia. Proc. Zool. Soc. London, 116, pp. 198–220, 13 figs.

CARLSSON, ALBERTINA
  1925. Ueber Ailurus fulgens. Acta Zool., 6, pp. 269–305, 3 pls.

CARMALT, CHURCHILL
  1913. The anatomy of the salivary glands in the Carnivora. Stud. Cancer & Allied Subj., 4, pp. 155–190, 4 figs., 7 pls.

CARTER, T. D.
  1937. The giant panda. Bull. N. Y. Zool. Soc., 40, pp. 6–14.

[Chjan, Kh.-Yu and Liu, L.
  1959. [Anatomy of the digestive system of Ailuropoda melanoleuca.] In Chinese, Russian summary. Acta Zool. Sinica, 11, pp. 443–449, 6 figs. (not seen).

COBB, W. M.
  1943. The cranio-facial union and the maxillary tuber in mammals. Amer. Jour. Anat., 72, pp. 32–105.

COLBERT, E. H.
  1938. The panda: a study in emigration. Nat. Hist., 42, pp. 33–39.

COLTON, H. S.
  1929. How bipedal habit affects the bones of the hind legs of the albino rat. Jour. Exp. Zool., 53, pp. 1–11, 5 figs.

COPENHAVER, W. M.
  1955. Heart, blood vessels, blood, and entodermal derivatives. In Analysis of development (ed. by WILLIER, WEISS, and HAMBURGER. 735 pp. Philadelphia, Saunders.

COTTAM, CLARENCE, NELSON, A. L., and CLARKE, T. E.
  1939. Notes on early winter food habits of the black bear in George Washington National Forest. Jour. Mam., 20, pp. 310–314.

CRARY, D. D., and SAWIN, P. B.
  1952. A second recessive achondroplasia in the domestic rabbit. Jour. Hered., 43, pp. 255–269, 6 figs.

CRILE, GEORGE, and QUIRING, D. P.
  1940. A record of the body weight and certain organ and gland weights of 3690 animals. Ohio Jour. Sci., 40, pp. 219–259.

DAVID, ARMAND
1869. Extrait d'une lettre du même, datée de la Principaute Thibetaine (independente) de Mou-pin, le 21 Mars 1869. Nouv. Arch. Mus. Hist. Nat. Paris, Bull., 5, pp. 12–13.
1871. Rapport adressé a Mm. les professeurs-administrateurs du Mus. d'Hist. Naturelle. Nouv. Arch. Mus. Hist. Nat. Paris, Bull., 7, pp. 75 100.

DAVIS, D. D.
1941. The arteries of the forearm in carnivores. Field Mus. Nat. Hist., Zool. Ser., 27, pp. 137-227, 34 figs.
1949. The shoulder architecture of bears and other carnivores. Fieldiana, Zoology, 31, pp. 285-305, 8 figs.
1955. Masticatory apparatus in the spectacled bear *Tremarctos ornatus*. Fieldiana, Zoology, 37, pp. 25-46, 8 figs.
1958. Tarsal ligaments of the spectacled bear. Fieldiana, Zoology, 39, pp. 91 105, 7 figs.

DAVIS, D. D., and STORY, H. E.
1943. The carotid circulation in the domestic cat. Field Mus. Nat. Hist., Zool. Ser., 28, pp. 1-47, 9 figs.

DISSELHORST, RUDOLF
1904. Die männlichen Geschlechtsorgane der Monotremen und einiger Marsupialen. Denkschr. Med.-Naturw. Ges. Jena, 6 (2), pp. 119-150, 34 figs., 7 pls.

DOLGO-SABUROFF, B.
1929. Ueber Ursprung und Insertion der Skelettmuskels. Anat. Anz., 68, pp. 80-87, 2 figs.
1935. Ueber einige Eigentümlichkeiten der Knochenstruktur an den Anheftstellen der Sehnen. Morph. Jahrb., 75, pp. 393-411, 11 figs.

DUKES, H. H.
1935. The physiology of domestic animals. ed. 3. 643 pp. Ithaca, Comstock.

EDGAR, J. H.
1929. The haunts of the giant panda. Jour. W. China Border Res. Soc., 3. p. 27.

EISLER, PAUL
1912. Die Muskeln des Stammes. *In* BARDELEBEN, Handbuch der Anatomie des Menschen. 2, Abt. 2, Teil 1, 705 pp. Jena, Fischer.

ELFTMAN, H. O.
1929. Functional adaptations of the pelvis in marsupials. Bull. Amer. Mus. Nat. Hist., 58, pp. 189-232, 12 figs., 5 pls.

ELLENBERGER, WILHELM, and BAUM, HERMANN
1943. Handbuch der vergleichenden Anatomie der Haustiere (ed. 18). 1155 pp., 1669 figs. Berlin, Springer.

ENGELMANN, C. H.
1938. Ueber die Grosssäuger Szetchwans, Sikongs, und Osttibets. Z. Säug., 13 (sonderheft), pp. 1-76, 36 pls.

FAHRENHOLZ, CURT
1937. Drüsen der Mundhöhle. *In* BOLK, GÖPPERT, KALLIUS, and LUBOSCH, Handbuch der vergleichenden Anatomie der Wirbeltiere, 3, pp. 115-210. Berlin, Urban & Schwarzenberg.

FAUSSEK, V.
1906. Biologische Untersuchungen in Transkaspien. Russ. Geogr. Obshch., 27 (2), pp. 1 192, 4 pls. [Warning coloration in *Ailuropoda*.]

FLOWER, W. H.
1869. On the value of the characters of the base of the cranium in the classification of the order Carnivora. Proc. Zool. Soc. London, 1869, pp. 4-37, 15 figs.
1870. On the anatomy of *Aelurus fulgens* Fr. Cuv. Proc. Zool. Soc. London, 1870, pp. 752-769, 10 figs.
1872. Lectures on the comparative anatomy of the organs of digestion of the Mammalia. Med. Times & Gazette, 1872 (1), pp. 215 ff.; (2), pp. 1 ff., 40 figs.
1885. An introduction to the osteology of the Mammalia (ed. 3). 382 pp. London, Macmillan.

FULD, ERNST
1901. Ueber Veränderungen der Hinterbeinknochen von Hunden in folge Mangels der Vorderbeine. Arch. Entwm. Org., 11, pp. 1 64, 1 fig., 4 pls.

FÜRBRINGER, MAX
1875. Beitrag zur Kentniss der Kehlkopfmuskulatur. 119 pp. Jena, Dufft.

GADOW, H. F.
1933. The evolution of the vertebral column. 356 pp. Cambridge Univ. Press.

GERHARDT, ULRICH
1909. Ueber das Vorkommen eines Penis- und Clitorisknochens bei Hylobatiden. Anat. Anz., 35, pp. 353-358, 6 figs.
1914. Das Urogenitalsystem der Säugetieren. *In* BRONN, Klassen und Ordnungen des Tierreichs. 6, Abt. 5, Mammalia, Buch 2, 48 pp., 3 pls.
1933. Kloake und Begattungsorgane. *In* Handbuch der vergleichenden Anatomie der Wirbeltiere (ed. by BOLK, GÖPPERT, KALLIUS, and LUBOSCH). 6, pp. 267-350. Berlin, Urban & Schwarzenberg.

GERVAIS, PAUL
1870. Mémoire sur les formes cérébrales propres aus carnivores vivants et fossiles. Nouv. Arch. Mus. Hist. Nat. Paris, (1) 6, pp. 103-162, 7 pls.
1875. De l'*Ursus melanoleucus* de l'abbe Armand David. Gervais Jour. Zool., 4, pp. 79-87, 2 pls.

GOLDSCHMIDT, RICHARD
1940. The material basis of evolution. 436 pp. New Haven, Yale Univ.

GÖPPERT, ERNST
1894. Ueber die Herkunft des Wrisberg'schen Knorpels. Ein Beitrag zur vergleichenden Anatomie des Säugethierkehlkopfes. Morph. Jahrb., 21, pp. 68-151, 13 figs., 2 pls.
1937. Kehlkopf und Trachea. *In* Handbuch der vergleichenden Anatomie der Wirbeltiere (ed. by BOLK, GÖPPERT, KALLIUS, and LUBOSCH). 3, pp. 797-866.

GREGORY, W. K.
1936. On the phylogenetic relationships of the giant panda (*Ailuropoda*) to other arctoid Carnivora. Amer. Mus. Nov., 878, pp. 1-29, 22 figs.

GRÜNBERG, KARL
1948. Genes and pathological development in mammals. Symposia Soc. Exper. Biol., 2, pp. 155-176.
1952. The genetics of the mouse (ed. 2). Biblio. Gen., 15, 650 pp., 96 figs., 16 pls.

GSCHWEND, THEODOR
1931. Das Herz des Wildschweines. Anat. Anz., 72, pp. 49-89, 8 figs.

GUZSAL, E.
1960. Vergleichende anatomische Untersuchungen an Bärennieren. Act. Vet. Hungar., 10, pp. 401-410.

HAAS, FRITZ
1911. Der tibetanische Bär. Ber. Senckenberg Naturf. Ges., 42, pp. 259-261, 1 fig.

HAAS, GERHARD
1963. Beitrag zum Verhalten des Bambusbaren (*Ailuropus melanoleucus*). Zool. Garten, 27, pp. 225-233, 12 figs.

HAESLER, KURT
1930. Der Einfluss verschiedener Ernährung auf die Grössenverhältnisse des Magen-darmkanals bei Säugetieren. Z. Züchtung (B), 17, pp. 339-412, 4 figs.

HAFFERL, ANTON
1933. Das Arteriensystem. *In* Handbuch der vergleichenden Anatomie der Wirbeltiere (ed. by BOLK, GÖPPERT, KALLIUS, and LUBOSCH). 6, pp. 563-684.

HAINES, R. W.
1932. The laws of muscle and tendon growth. Jour. Anat. (London), 66, pp. 578-585, 11 figs.

HALLER VON HALLERSTEIN, V.
1934. Zerebrospinales Nervensystem. I. Äussere Gliederung des Zentralnervensystems. In Handbuch der vergleichenden Anatomie der Wirbeltiere (ed. by BOLK, GÖPPERT, KALLIUS, and LUBOSCH). 2, pp. 1-318.

HANSTRÖM, BERTIL
1947. A comparative study of the hypophysis in the polar bear and some Swedish Carnivora. K. Sven. Vet.-Akad. Handl., 24 (7), pp. 1-46, 30 figs.

HARKNESS, RUTH
1938a. The lady and the panda. 288 pp. New York, Carrick & Evans.
1938b. The baby giant panda. 126 pp. New York, Carrick & Evans.

HARRIS, WILFRED
1939. Morphology of the brachial plexus. 117 pp. London, Oxford Univ.

HAUGHTON, SAMUEL
1864. Notes on animal mechanics. No. IV. On the muscular anatomy of the lion. Proc. R. Irish Acad., 9, pp. 85-93.
1866a. Notes on animal mechanics. No. XII. On the muscular anatomy of the Irish terrier, as compared with that of the Australian dingo. Proc. R. Irish Acad., 9, pp. 504-507.
1866b. Notes on animal mechanics. No. XIV. On the muscles of the Virginian bear. Proc. R. Irish Acad., 9, pp. 508-511.

HAVELKA, F.
1928. Plexus lumbo-sacralis u psa [Plexus lumbosacralis of the dog]. In Czech, German summary. Biol. Spisy Vysoké Skoly Zverolélarské, 7 (4), pp. 1-40, 4 figs.

HILDEBRAND, MILTON
1952. An analysis of body proportions in the Canidae. Amer. Jour. Anat., 90, pp. 217-256, 15 figs.

HOLL, M.
1899. Ueber die Insel des Carnivorgehirns. Arch. Anat., 1899, pp. 217-266, 3 pls.

HOROWITZ, S. L., and SHAPIRO, H. H.
1955. Modification of the skull and jaw architecture following removal of the masseter muscle in the rat. Amer. Jour. Phys. Anthrop., 13, pp. 301-308, 6 figs.

HOWELL, A. B.
1925. On the alimentary tracts of squirrels with diverse food habits. Jour. Wash. Acad. Sci., 15, pp. 145-150, 2 figs.
1926. Anatomy of the wood rat. 225 pp. Baltimore, Williams & Wilkins.
1944. Speed in animals. 270 pp. Univ. of Chicago Press.

HOWELL, J. A.
1917. An experimental study of the effect of stress and strain on bone development. Anat. Rec., 13, pp. 233-252, 7 figs.

HUXLEY, J. S.
1932. Problems of relative growth. 276 pp. London, Methuen.

JACOBI, ARNOLD
1923a. Zoologische Ergebnisse der Walter Stötznerschen Expedition nach Szetschwan, Osttibet und Tschili auf Grund der Sammlungen Dr. Hugo Weigolds. II. Mammalia. Abh. Ber. Mus. Tierk Völkerk. Dresden, 16 (1), pp. 1-55.
1923b. Weitere Bemerkungen Dr. Weigolds zu den gesammelten Säugetieren. Abh. Ber. Mus. Tierk. Völkerk. Dresden, 16 (2), pp. 71-76.

JACOBSHAGEN, E.
1937. Mittel- und Enddarm. In Handbuch der vergleichenden Anatomie der Wirbeltiere (ed. by BOLK, GÖPPERT, KALLIUS, and LUBOSCH). 3, pp. 563-724.

KIDD, WALTER
1901. Note on the arrangement of the hair on the nasal region of Aeluropus melanoleucus. Proc. Zool. Soc. London, 1904, p. 373.
1920. Initiative in evolution. 262 pp. London, Witherby.

KIDWELL, J. F., VERNON, E. H., CROWN, R. M., and SINGLETARY, C. B.
1952. Muscular hypertrophy in cattle. Jour. Hered., 43, pp. 63-68, 4 figs.

KILLIAN, GUSTAV
1888. Ueber die Bursa und Tonsilla pharyngea. Eine entwicklungsgeschichtliche und vergleichend-anatomische Studie. Morph. Jahrb., 14, pp. 618-711, 43 figs., 2 pls.

KLATT, BERTHOLD
1912. Ueber die Veränderung der Schädelkapazität in der Domestikation. Sitzungsber. Ges. Naturf. Fr. Berlin, 1912, pp. 153-179, 9 figs.
1928. Vergleichende Untersuchungen am Caniden und Procyoniden. Zool. Jahrb. (allg.), 45, pp. 217-292, 8 figs.
1939. Erbliche Missbildungen der Wirbelsäule beim Hund. Zool. Anz., 128, pp. 225-235, 9 figs.
1941-43. Kreuzungen an extremen Rassentypen des Hundes (Bulldogge-Windhundkreuzungen). I-IV. Z. Menschl. Vererb. Konstl., 25-28.
1948. Messend anatomische Untersuchungen an gegensätzlichen Wuchsformtypen. Arch. Anat. Entwm. Org.
1950. Craniologisch-physiognomische Studien an Hunden. Mitt. Hamburg. Zool. Mus., 50, pp. 9-129, 50 figs.

KLATT, BERTHOLD, and OBOUSSIER, H.
1951. Weitere Untersuchungen zur Frage der quantitativen Verschiedenheiten gegensätzlichen Wuchsformtypen beim Hund. Zool. Anz., 146, pp. 223-240.

KLEINSCHMIDT, ADOLF
1948. Funktionell-morphologische Beobachtungen am Becken der Säuger unter besonderer Berücksichtigung der Primaten. Verh. Deutschen Zool. Kiel, 1948, pp. 95-103, 7 figs.

KRUEG, I.
1880. Ueber die Furchen an der Grosshirnrinde der zonoplacentalen Säugetiere. Z. Wiss. Zool., 33.

KÜHNE, KONRAD
1936. Die Zwillingswirbelsäule. Z. Morph. Anthrop., 35, pp. 1-376, 121 figs.

LACROIX, PIERRE
1051. The organization of bones. 235 pp. Philadelphia, Blakiston.

LANDAUER, C. A.
1962. A factor analysis of the facial skeleton. Human Biol., 34, pp. 239-253.

LANDOIS, H.
1884. Ueber ein anatomisches Unterscheidungsmerkmal zwischen Haushund und Wolf. Morph. Jhb., 9, pp. 163-165.

LANKESTER, E. R.
1901. On the affinities of Aeluropus melanoleucus, A. Milne-Edwards. Trans. Linn. Soc. London, (2) 8, pp. 163-171, 2 figs., 3 pls.

LATIMER, H. B.
1939. The prenatal growth of the cat: VIII. The weight of the kidneys, bladder, gonads and uterus, with weights of the adult organs. Growth, 3, pp. 89-108.
1942. The prenatal growth of the cat: XII. The weight of the heart in the fetal and in the adult cat. Growth, 6, pp. 341-349, 1 fig.

LEBEDINSKY, N. G.
1938. Ueber die funktionelle Bedeutung der verschiedenen Höhe des Ramus ascendens mandibulae bezw. des Unterkiefergelenkes bei Säugetieren. Vierteljahrschr. Naturf. Ges. Zürich (suppl.), 83, pp. 217–224, 6 figs.

LEONE, C. A., and WIENS, A. L.
1956. Comparative serology of carnivores. Jour. Mam., 37, pp. 11–23.

LIPS, RUDOLF
1930. Modificationen in Zusammenhang von Funktion und Gelenkflächen-äusbildung am Carpalsegment arctoider Carnivoren. Z. Säug., 5, pp. 105–240, 126 figs., 5 pls.

LUMER, HYMAN
1940. Evolutionary allometry in the skeleton of the domestic dog. Amer. Nat., 74, pp. 439–467.

LYDEKKER, RICHARD
1901. Detailed description of the skull and limb-bones [of Ailuropus melanoleucus]. Trans. Linn. Soc. London (2) 8, pp. 166–171, 2 figs.

MCCLURE, C. F. W., and HUNTINGTON, G. S.
1929. The mammalian vena cava posterior. Amer. Anat. Mem., 15, pp. 1–149, 46 pls.

MCCLURE, F. A.
1943. Bamboo as panda food. Jour. Mam., 24, pp. 267–268.

MCGREW, P. O.
1938. Dental morphology of the Procyonidae with a description of Cynarctoides, gen. nov. Field Mus. Nat. Hist., Geol. Ser., 6, pp. 323–339, 10 figs.

MARCUS, H.
1937. Lungen. In Handbuch der vergleichenden Anatomie der Wirbeltiere (ed. by BOLK, GÖPPERT, KALLIUS, and LUBOSCH). 3, pp. 909–988. Berlin, Urban & Schwarzenberg.

MATTHEW, W. D.
1937. Paleocene faunas of the San Juan Basin, New Mexico. Trans. Amer. Phil. Soc., 30, 510 pp., 85 figs., 65 pls.

MATTHEW, W. D., and GRANGER, WALTER
1923. New fossil mammals from the Pliocene of Szechuan, China. Bull. Amer. Mus. Nat. Hist., 48, pp. 563–598, 27 figs.

MAYNARD SMITH, J., and SAVAGE, J. G.
1956. Some locomotory adaptations in mammals. Jour. Linn. Soc. London (zool.), 42, pp. 603–622, 14 figs.

METTLER, F. A., and GOSS, L. J.
1946. The brain of the giant panda (Ailuropoda melanoleuca). Jour. Comp. Neur., 84, pp. 1–9, 5 figs.

MEYER, FERDINAND
1911. Terminologie und Morphologie der Säugetierleber, nebst Bemerkungen über die Homologie ihrer Lappen. 144 pp., 2 pls. Hannover, Schaper.

MIJSBERG, W. A.
1920. Die Anatomie der Verbindungen der Beckenknochen bei der Säugetieren, in Bezug auf die statischen Einflüsse, denen das Becken ausgesetzt ist. Anat. Hefte, 58, pp. 453–615, 32 figs.

MILNE-EDWARDS, ALPHONSE
1870a. Note sur quelques mammifères du Thibet oriental. Ann. Sci. Nat., Zool., ser. 5, art. 10, 1 p.
1870b. Note sur quelques mammifères du Thibet oriental. C. R. Acad. Sci. Paris, 70, pp. 341–342.

MILNE-EDWARDS, H., and MILNE-EDWARDS, A.
1868–74. Recherches pour servir à l'histoire naturelle des mammifères. 2 vols. Paris.

MITCHELL, P. C.
1905. On the intestinal tract of mammals. Trans. Zool. Soc. London, 17, pp. 437–536, 50 figs.

MITCHELL, P. C.
1916. Further observations on the intestinal tract of mammals. Proc. Zool. Soc. London, 1916, pp. 183–251, 30 figs.

MIVART, ST. GEORGE
1885a. On the anatomy, classification, and distribution of the Arctoidea. Proc. Zool. Soc. London, 1885, pp. 340–404.
1885b. Notes on the cerebral convolutions of the Carnivora. Jour. Linn. Soc. London (zool.), 19, pp. 1–25, 11 figs.

MORRISON-SCOTT, T. C. S.
1939. The giant panda. Finding the solution to a zoological puzzle. Field, Feb. 11, 1959.

MOSS, M. L.
1958. Rotations of the cranial components in the growing rat and their experimental alteration. Acta Anat., 32, pp. 65–86, 8 figs.

MURRAY, P. D. F.
1936. Bones: a study of the development and structure of the vertebrate skeleton. 203 pp. Cambridge Univ. Press.

MUYBRIDGE, EADWEARD
1957. Animals in motion (ed. by L. S. Brown). 74 pp., 183 pls. New York, Dover.

NAUCK, E. T.
1938. Extremitätenskelett der Tetrapoden. In Handbuch der vergleichenden Anatomie der Wirbeltiere (ed. by BOLK, GÖPPERT, KALLIUS, and LUBOSCH). 5, pp. 71–248. Berlin, Urban & Schwarzenberg.

NEUBAUER, GABRIELLE
1925. Experimentelle Untersuchungen über dei Beeinflussung der Schädelform. Z. Morph. Anthrop., 23, pp. 411–442, 16 figs., 3 pls.

OBOUSSIER, H.
1955. Zur Kenntnis der Hypophysis des Panda (Ailurus fulgens F. Cuv.). Zool. Anz., 154, pp. 1–8, 3 figs.

OSBORN, H. F.
1929. The titanotheres of ancient Wyoming, Dakota, and Nebraska, 1. U. S. Geol. Surv. Monogr., 55, 701 pp.

OSGOOD, W. H.
1932. Mammals of the Kelley-Roosevelts and Delacour Asiatic Expeditions. Field Mus. Nat. Hist., Zool. Ser., 18, pp. 193–339, 2 figs., 3 pls.

OUDEMANS, J. T.
1892. Die accessorischen Geschlechtsdrüsen der Säugethiere. Natk. V. Holland. Maatschap. Wetenschap., (3) 5, pp. 1–96, 16 pls.

OWEN, RICHARD
1868. On the anatomy of vertebrates. 3, Mammals. 915 pp. London, Longmans, Green.

PAPEZ, J. W.
1929. Comparative neurology. 518 pp. New York, Crowell.

PARSONS, F. G.
1900. The joints of mammals compared with those of man. Jour. Anat. (London), 34, pp. 41–68, 14 figs., pp. 301–323, 10 figs.
1902. On the arrangement of the branches of the mammalian aortic arch. Jour. Anat. (London), 36, pp. 389–399, 12 figs.

PAULLI, SIMON
1900. Ueber die Pneumaticität des Schädels bei den Säugethieren. III. Morph. Jahrb., 28, pp. 483–564, 36 figs., 3 pls.

PEN, HUNG-SHOU
1943. Some notes on the giant panda. Bull. Fan Mem. Inst. Biol. (n.s.), 1, pp. 64–71.

PERNKOPF, EDWARD
1937. Die Vergleichung der verscheidenen Formtypen des Vorderdarmes der Kranioten. *In* Handbuch der vergleichenden Anatomie der Wirbeltiere (ed. by BOLK, GÖPPERT, KALLIUS, and LUBOSCH). 3, pp. 477-562.

PFUHL, WILHELM
1936. Die gefiederten Muskeln, ihre Form und ihre Wirkungsweise. Z. Anat. Entwg., 106, pp. 749-769, 15 figs.

PINTO HAMUY, T., BROMILEY, R. B., and WOOLSEY, C. N.
1956. Somatic afferent areas I and II of the dog's cerebral cortex. Jour. Neurophysiol., 19, pp. 485-499.

POCOCK, R. I.
1921. The external characters and classification of the Procyonidae. Proc. Zool. Soc. London, 1921, pp. 389-422, 3 figs.
1929. Some external characters of the giant panda (*Ailuropoda melanoleuca*). Proc. Zool. Soc. London, 1929, pp. 975-981, 3 figs.
1939. The prehensile paw of the giant panda. Nature, 143, pp. 206, 381.

POGOGEFF, I. A., and MURRAY, M. R.
1946. Form and behavior of adult mammalian skeletal muscle in vitro. Anat. Rec., 95, pp. 321-329, 3 pls.

POHL, LOTHAR
1928. Zur Morphologie der männlichen Kopulationsorgane der Säugetiere. Z. Anat. Entwg., 86, pp. 71-119, 8 figs., 3 pls.

POHLE, J.
1934. Karies beim Bambusbären. Z. Säug., 9, pp. 436-437, 2 figs.

PUTNAM, I. K.
1928. The proportion of cerebellar to total brain weight in mammals. P. K. Akad. Wetenschap. Amsterdam, 31, pp. 155-168.

RAVEN, H. C.
1936. Notes on the anatomy of the viscera of the giant panda (*Ailuropoda melanoleuca*). Amer. Mus. Nov., 877, pp. 1-23, 15 figs.

REIGHARD, JACOB, and JENNINGS, H. S.
1935. Anatomy of the cat (ed. 3). 486 pp. New York, Holt.

REINHART, ALOYS
1929. Ueber die Form der Scapula bei Säugetieren. Z. Tierzücht. Züchtungsbiol., 16, pp. 233-289, 36 figs.

RENSCH, BERNHARD
1960. Evolution above the species level. 419 pp. Columbia Univ. Press.

RENVALL, THORSTEN
1900. Däggdjurslefvern, dess form och flikar, speciellt hos gnagarne [The mammalian liver, its form and lobation, especially in the rodents]. Abo, Aktiebolaget Polytypos' Boktryckeri, 192 pp. (In Swedish.)

REYNOLDS, EDWARD
1931. The evolution of the human pelvis in relation to the mechanics of the erect posture. Pap. Peabody Mus., 11, pp. 255-334, 10 figs., 3 pls.

RODE, KARL
1935. Untersuchungen über das Gebiss der Bären. Monog. Geol. Pal., (2) 7, pp. 1-162, 25 figs., 8 pls.

ROOSEVELT, THEODORE, and ROOSEVELT, KERMIT
1929. Trailing the giant panda. 278 pp. New York, Scribner's.

SAGE, DEAN
1935a. Hunting the giant panda. China Jour., 22, pp. 35-40.
1935b. In quest of the giant panda. Nat. Hist., 35, pp. 309-320.

SAWIN, P. B.
1945. Morphological studies of the rabbit. 1. Regional specificity of hereditary factors affecting homoeotic variations in the axial skeleton. Jour. Exp. Zool., 100, pp. 301-329, 3 figs.
1946. Morphogenetic studies of the rabbit. III. Skeletal variations resulting from the interaction of gene determined growth forces. Anat. Rec., 96, pp. 183-200, 3 figs.

SAWIN, P. B., and EDMONDS, H. W.
1949. Morphogenetic studies of the rabbit. VII. Aortic arch variation in relation to regionally specific growth differences. Anat. Rec., 105: pp. 377-397, 2 figs.

SAWIN, P. B., and HULL, I. B.
1946. Morphogenetic studies of the rabbit. II. Evidence of regionally specific hereditary factors influencing the extent of the lumbar region. Jour. Morph., 78, pp. 1-26, 6 figs.

SAWIN, P. B., and NACE, M. A. G.
1948. Morphogenetic studies of the rabbit. V. Inheritance pattern of an asymmetrical vascular pattern. Jour. Morph., 82, pp. 331-354, 6 figs.

SCHAEFFER, BOBB
1947. Notes on the origin and function of the artiodactyl tarsus. Amer. Mus. Nov., 1356, pp. 1-24, 9 figs.

SCHÄFER, ERNST
1938. Der Bambusbär (*Ailuropus melanoleucus* A. M.-Edw.). Zool. Gart., 10, pp. 21-31, 9 figs.

SCHIEBLER, T. H.
1959. Morphologie der Nieren und ihre Ableitungswege. Handbuch Zool., 8 (21), pp. 1-84, 44 figs.

SCHMID, F.
1873. Ueber die gegenseitige Stellung der Gelenk- und Knochenaxen der vorderen und hinteren Extremität bei Wirbelthieren. Arch. Anthrop., 6, pp. 181-199, 15 figs.

SCHNEIDER, K. M.
1939. Einiges vom grossen und kleinen Panda. Zool. Gart., 11, pp. 203-232, 64 figs.
1952. Vom Bambusbären. Natur und Volk, 82, pp. 275-283, 5 figs.

SCHULTZ, A. H., and STRAUS, W. L., JR.
1945. The numbers of vertebrae in primates. Proc. Amer. Phil. Soc., 89, pp. 601-626, 4 figs.

SCHUMACHER, G. H.
1961a. Funktionelle Morphologie der Kaumuskulatur. 262 pp. Jena, G. Fischer.
1961b. Funktionsbedingter Strukturwandel des M. masseter. Morph. Jahrb., 102, pp. 150-169, 12 figs.

SCOTT, J. H.
1957. Muscle growth and function in relation to skeletal morphology. Amer. Jour. Phys. Anthrop., 15, pp. 197-234, 9 figs.

SEGALL, WALTER
1943. The auditory region of the arctoid carnivores. Field Mus. Nat. Hist., Zool. Ser., 29, pp. 33-59, 4 figs.

SHELDON, W. G.
1937. Notes on the giant panda. Jour. Mam., 18, pp. 13-19.

SHEPHERD, F. J.
1883. Short notes on the myology of the American black bear (*Ursus americanus*). Jour. Anat. (London), 18, pp. 103-117.

SICHER, HARRY
1944. Masticatory apparatus in the giant panda and the bears. Field Mus. Nat. Hist., Zool. Ser., 29, pp. 61-73, 5 figs.

SIMIĆ, VLADETA
1938. Zur Anatomie des Carnivorherzens. Morph. Jahrb., 82, pp. 499-536, 12 figs.

SIMPSON, G. G.
1945. The principles of classification and a classification of mammals. Bull. Amer. Mus. Nat. Hist., 85, pp. 1–350.

SIMPSON, G. G., and ROE, ANNE
1939. Quantitative zoology. 414 pp. New York, McGraw-Hill.

SIVERS, WOLFGANG VON
1931. Die Struktur der Hand- und Fusswurzel des Höhlenbären von Mixnitz. Palaeobiologica, 4, pp. 257–304, 15 figs., 6 pls.

SIWE, S. A.
1937. Die Leber. In Handbuch der vergleichenden Anatomie der Wirbeltiere (ed. by BOLK, GÖPPERT, KALLIUS, and LUBOSCH). 3, pp. 725–774.

SLIJPER, E. J.
1938. Vergleichend anatomische Untersuchungen über den Penis der Säugetiere. Acta Ned. Morph., 1, pp. 375–418, 22 figs.
1946. Comparative biologic-anatomical investigations on the vertebral column and spinal musculature of mammals. Verh. K. Ned. Akad. Wet., (2) 42, no. 5, pp. 1–128, 125 figs.

SMITH, G. E.
1902. Descriptive and illustrated catalogue of the physiological series of comparative anatomy contained in the museum of the Royal College of Surgeons of England (ed. 2). 2, D. Nervous system—brain: Reptilia, Mammalia. pp. 110–125, 138–486, 224 figs. London.

SMITH, W. K.
1933a. Cerebral hemispheres of the American black bear (Ursus americanus). Arch. Neur. Psychiat., 30, pp. 1–13, 8 figs.
1933b. Motor cortex of the bear (Ursus americanus). Arch. Neur. Psychiat., 30, pp. 14–39, 10 figs.

SMITH-WOODWARD, A.
1915. On the skull of an extinct mammal related to Aeluropus found in Burma. Proc. Zool. Soc. London, 1915, pp. 425–428.

SONNTAG, C. F.
1921. On some abnormalities in the Carnivora. Proc. Zool. Soc. London, 1921, pp. 587–590, 2 figs.
1923. The comparative anatomy of the tongues of the Mammalia, VIII. Carnivora. Proc. Zool. Soc. London, 1923, pp. 129–153, 11 figs.

SOWERBY, A. DE C.
1932. The pandas or cat-bears. China Jour., 17, pp. 296–299, 7 figs.
1933. The pandas or cat bears and the true bears. China Jour., 19, pp. 257–259, 8 pls.
1934. Hunting the giant panda. China Jour., 21, pp. 30–32, 2 figs.
1936a. Big game animals of the Chinese–Tibetan borderland. China Jour., 25, pp. 285–296, 11 pls.
1936b. A baby panda comes to town. China Jour., 25, pp. 335–339.
1937a. The giant panda's diet. China Jour., 26, pp. 209–210.
1937b. Mammals of China, Mongolia, eastern Tibet and Manchuria requiring protection. China Jour., 27, pp. 248–258.

SPERBER, IVAR
1944. Studies on the mammalian kidney. Zool. Bid. Uppsala, 22, pp. 249–431, 29 figs., 3 pls.

STADTMÜLLER, F.
1938. Zunge Mundhöhlenboden. In Handbuch der vergleichenden Anatomie der Wirbeltiere (ed. by BOLK, GÖPPERT, KALLIUS, and LUBOSCH). 5: pp. 955–1010, 49 figs.

STARCK, DIETRICH
1935. Kaumuskulatur und Kiefergelenk der Ursiden. Morph. Jahrb., 76, pp. 104–147, 19 figs.
1953. Morphologische Untersuchungen am Kopf der Säugetiere, besonders der Prosimier. Ein Beitrag zum Problem des Formwandels des Säugershcüdels. Z. Wiss. Zool., 157, pp. 169–219.

STOCKARD, C. R.
1941. The genetic and endocrinic basis for differences in form and behavior (as elucidated by studies of contrasted pure-line dog breeds and their hybrids.) Amer. Anat. Mem., 19, 775 pp., 113 pls.

STÖCKER, LUDWIG
1957. Trigeminusmuskulatur und Kiefergelenk von Elephas maximus L. Morph. Jahrb., 98, pp. 35–76, 15 figs.

STORY, H. E.
1951. The carotid circulation in the Procyonidae. Fieldiana: Zool., 32, pp. 477–557, 17 figs.

STROMER VON REICHENBACH, ERNST
1902. Die Wirbel der Land-Raubtiere, ihre Morphologie und systematische Bedeutung. Zoologica (Stuttgart), 15 (36), 276 pp., 5 pls.

TANDLER, JULIUS
1899. Zur vergleichenden Anatomie der Kopfarterien bei den Mammalia. Denkschr. K. Akad. Wiss. Wien (Math.-Naturw. Cl.), 67, pp. 677–784, 17 figs., 8 pls.

TAYLOR, ALFRED
1935. Skeletal changes associated with increasing body size. Jour. Morph., 57, pp. 253–274, 2 figs.

THOMAS, L.
1930. Le plexus brachial chez les mammifères. Bull. Soc. Hist. Nat. Toulouse, 60, pp. 1–216, 83 figs.

TORNIER, GUSTAV
1888. Die Phylogenese des terminalen Segments der Säugethier-Hintergliedmassen. Morph. Jahrb., 14, pp. 223–328, 2 pls.

TURNER, H. N.
1849. Notes on the dissection of the Paradoxurus typus, and of Dipus aegyptius. Proc. Zool. Soc. London, 1849, pp. 24–28.

VAN KAMPEN, P. N.
1905. Die Tympanelgegend des Säugetierschädels. Morph. Jahrb., 34, pp. 321–722, 96 figs.

WADDINGTON, C. H.
1953. The evolution of adaptations. Endeavour, 12, pp. 134–139.

WASHBURN, S. L.
1946a. The effect of facial paralysis on the growth of the skull of rat and rabbit. Anat. Rec., 94, pp. 163–168, 2 figs.
1946b. The effect of removal of the zygomatic arch in the rat. Jour. Mam., 27, pp. 169–172, 4 figs
1947. The relation of the temporal muscle to the form of the skull. Anat. Rec., 99, pp. 239–248, 3 figs.

WATERMAN, H. C.
1929. Studies on the evolution of the pelvis of man and other primates. Bull. Amer. Mus. Nat. Hist., 58, pp. 585–642, 10 figs., 1 pl.

WEBER, MAX
1927–28. Die Säugetiere (ed. 2). 1, 444 pp.; 2, 898 pp. Jena, Fischer.

WEIDENREICH, FRANZ
1913. Ueber das Hüftbein und das Becken der Primaten und ihre Umformung durch den aufrechten Gang. Anat. Anz., 44, pp. 497–513, 3 figs.
1922. Ueber die Beziehungen zwischen Muskelapparat und Knochen und den Charakter des Knochengewebes. Anat. Anz., 55 (Egänz), pp. 28–51.

WEIDENREICH, FRANZ
1926. Wie kommen funktionelle Anpassungen der Aus-
senformer des Knochenskelettes zustande? Paleo.
Zeitschr., 7, pp. 34–44.
1940. The external tubercle of the human tuber calcanei.
Amer. Jour. Phys. Anthrop., 26, pp. 473–486.
1911. The brain and its role in the phylogenetic transformation of the human skull. Trans. Amer. Phil.
Soc., 31, pp. 321–442, 56 figs.

WELKER, W. I., and SEIDENSTEIN, SIDNEY
1959. Somatic sensory representation in the cerebral
cortex of the raccoon (Procyon lotor). Jour. Comp.
Neur., 111, pp. 469–501, 12 figs.

WETZEL, GEORG
1928. Der Magen-Darmschlauch der Ratte bei pflanz-
lichen und tierischen Nahrung. Arch. Entwm., 114.

WILSON, E. H.
1913. A naturalist in western China. 2 vols., 251, 229 pp.
London, Methuen.

WINDLE, B. C. A., and PARSONS, F. G.
1897. On the myology of the terrestrial Carnivora.—
Part I. Muscles of the head, neck, and fore-limb. Proc.
Zool. Soc. London, 1897, pp. 370–409, 11 figs.
1898. The myology of the terrestrial Carnivora.—Part
II. Proc. Zool. Soc. London, 1898, pp. 152–186, 6 figs.

WINGE, HERLUF
1895–96. Jordfundne og nulevende rovdyr (Carnivora)
fra Lagoa Santa, etc. E. Museo Lundii, 2, part 2.

WOLFFSON, D. M.
1950. Scapula shape and muscle function, with special
reference to the vertebral border. Amer. Jour. Phys.
Anthrop., 8, pp. 331–338, 1 pl.

WOOD-JONES, F.
1939a. The forearm and manus of the giant panda,
Ailuropoda melanoleuca, M.-Edw. with an account of
the mechanism of its grasp. Proc. Zool. Soc. London,
109 (B), pp. 113–129, 15 figs., 1 pl.
1939b. The "thumb" of the giant panda. Nature, 143,
pp. 157, 246.

WORTHMANN, FRITZ
1922. Zur Mechanik des Kiefergelenks. Anat. Anz., 55,
pp. 305–316, 6 figs.

WYSS, T.
1948. Die Kraftfelder in festen Körpen. Vierteljahrschr.
Naturf. Ges. Zürich, 93, pp. 151–186, 47 figs.

ZIEGLER, HERMANN
1931. Die Innervationsverhältnisse der Beckenmuskeln
bei Haustieren im Vergleich mit denjenigen beim Menschen. Morph. Jahrb., 68, pp. 1–45, 4 figs., 1 pl.

ZIMMERMANN, A.
1933. Zur vergleichenden Anatomie des Kniegelenkes.
Morph. Jahrb., 71, pp. 589–598, 4 figs.

ZUCKERKANDL, EMIL
1907. Zur Anatomie und Morphologie der Extremitäten-
arterien. Sitzungsber. K. Akad. Wien, (3) 116, pp. 459–
730, 14 figs., 6 pls.
1910. Zur Anatomie und Morphologie der Musculi pec-
torales. Sitzungsber. K. Akad. Wien, (3) 119, pp. 469–
558, 3 pls.

# INDEX

Abdominal tendon, 166
Adaptive differences, 323
Allometry, 39
Angular process, 61
Ankle joint, 141
Ansa hypoglossi, 305
  mediana, 306
  pectoralis, 306
Antebrachiocarpal joint, 137
Anterior palatine foramen, median, 51
Anus, 221
Aorta, 245
Aortic arch, 276
Aponeurosis palmaris, 177
Artery(ies)
  alveolares superiores, 251
    inferior, 250
  angularis, 249
  anonyma, 246
  arcuata, 272
  auditiva interna, 253
  auricularis anterior, 249
    posterior 248
  axillaris, 255
  basilaris, 253
  brachialis, 257
  buccinatoria, 251
  bulbi urethrae, 267
  carotis communis, 246
    externa, 246
    interna, 252
  caudae sacralis lateralis, 265
  centralis retinae, 251
  cerebelli inferior, 253
    superior, 253
  cerebri anterior, 252
    media, 252
    posterior, 254
  cervicalis profunda, 255
  chorioidea, 252
  ciliares, 251
  circumflexa femoris lateralis, 268
    medialis, 268
  circumflexa humeri externa, 257
    interna, 257
  circumflexa ilium profunda, 267
    superficialis, 268
  circumflexa scapulae, 257
  coeliaca, 262
  colica anterior, 264
    media, 264
    posterior, 265
  collateralis radialis, 260
  collateralis ulnaris inferior, 259
    superior, 259

Artery(ies)
  comitans n. ischiadici, 266
  communicans anterior, 252
    posterior, 252
  costocervicalis dextra, 254
  digitales dorsales communes, 260
    volares communes, 262
  dorsalis nasi, 251
  dorsalis pedis, 272
  dorsalis penis, 267
  epigastrica posterior, 267
    superficialis, 268
  ethmoidalis interna, 252
  femoralis, 268
  frontalis, 251
  gastrica dextra, 264
    sinistra, 264
  gastroduodenalis, 262
  gastroepiploica dextra, 262
    sinistra, 264
  genu inferior lateralis, 270
    medialis, 274
  genu media, 274
  genu superior lateralis, 270
    medialis, 274
  genu suprema, 270
  glutaea anterior, 265
    posterior, 266
  haemorrhoidalis anterior, 265
    media, 266
    posterior, 267
  hepatica, 262
  hypogastricae, 265
  ileocolicae, 265
  iliaca externa, 267
  iliolumbalis, 267
  infraorbitalis, 251
  intercostalis suprema, 255
  interossea (manus) dorsalis, 261
    recurrens, 261
    volaris, 261
  interossea (pes), 274
  intestinales, 264
  labialis inferior, 249
    superior, 249
  lacrimalis, 250
  lienalis, 264
  lingualis, 247
  lumboabdominalis, 265
  malaris, 251
  malleolaris anterior, 272
  mammaria interna, 254
  masseterica, 250
  maxillaris externa, 249
    interna, 249
  mediana communis, 260
  mediana propria, 262

Artery(ies)
  medianoradialis, 261
  meningea accessoria, 250
    anterior, 253
    media, 250
    posterior, 252
  mesenterica anterior, 264
    posterior, 265
  metacarpeae dorsales, 262
    volares, 262
  metatarsea dorsalis I, 272
  metatarseae dorsales profundae, 272
  metatarseae plantaris profundus, 274
  occipitalis, 248
  ophthalmica, 252
  orbitalis, 250
  palatina anterior, 251
    ascendens, 247
    descendens, 251
    minor, 251
  pancreaticoduodenalis anterior, 264
    posterior, 264
  penis, 267
  perforans, 270
  perinaei, 266
  peronaea, 272
  pharyngea ascendens, 246
  pharyngeotympanica, 246
  phrenica accessoria, 265
    anterior, 262
  poplitea, 270
  profunda brachii, 259
  profunda femoris, 267
  profunda penis, 267
  pudenda externa, 268
    interna, 266
  radialis superficialis, 259
  recurrens, radialis, 260
  recurrens tibialis, 270
  recurrentes ulnares, 260
  renales, 265
  saphena, 270
  spermatica externa, 268
    interna, 265
  sphenopalatina, 251
  spinalis anterior, 253
    posterior, 253
  sternocleidomastoidea, 248
  stylomastoidea, 248
  subclavia, 253
  submentalis, 248
  subscapularis, 257
  suprarenalis, 265
  suralis, 274

335